VALUING ENVIRONMENTAL PREFERENCES

D1522457

For my mother and father—a strange gift I know, but sent with love and thanks

Ian

For Renee with love
Ken

VALUING ENVIRONMENTAL PREFERENCES

Theory and Practice of the Contingent Valuation Method in the US, EU, and Developing Countries

Edited by

IAN J. BATEMAN and KENNETH G. WILLIS

OXFORD

UNIVERSITY PRESS

OXFORD
UNIVERSITY PRESS

Great Clarendon Street, Oxford OX2 6DP

Oxford University Press is a department of the University of Oxford.
It furthers the University's objective of excellence in research, scholarship,
and education by publishing worldwide in

Oxford New York

Athens Auckland Bangkok Bogotá Buenos Aires Cape Town
Chennai Dar es Salaam Delhi Florence Hong Kong Istanbul Karachi
Kolkata Kuala Lumpur Madrid Melbourne Mexico City Mumbai Nairobi
Paris São Paulo Shanghai Singapore Taipei Tokyo Toronto Warsaw
with associated companies in Berlin Ibadan

Oxford is a registered trade mark of Oxford University Press
in the UK and in certain other countries

Published in the United States
by Oxford University Press Inc., New York

© The Contributors 1999

The moral rights of the author have been asserted
Database right Oxford University Press (maker)

First published 1999
Published New as paperback 2001

All rights reserved. No part of this publication may be reproduced,
stored in a retrieval system, or transmitted, in any form or by any means,
without the prior permission in writing of Oxford University Press,
or as expressly permitted by law, or under terms agreed with the appropriate
reprographics rights organization. Enquiries concerning reproduction
outside the scope of the above should be sent to the Rights Department,
Oxford University Press, at the address above

You must not circulate this book in any other binding or cover
and you must impose this same condition on any acquirer

British Library Cataloguing in Publication Data
Data available

Library of Congress Cataloging in Publication Data
Valuing environmental preferences: theory and practice of the
contingent valuation method in the US, EU, and developing
countries / edited by Ian J. Bateman and Kenneth G. Willis.
p. cm.
Includes bibliographical references and index.
1. Environmental economics.   2. Contingent valuation.   3. Public
goods.   I. Bateman, Ian.   II. Willis, K. G. (Kenneth George)
HC79.E5V2615   1999
333.7—dc21   98–46711
ISBN 0–19–828853–0
ISBN 0–19–924891–5 (pbk)

1 3 5 7 9 10 8 6 4 2

Typeset by Pure Tech India Ltd, Pondicherry
http://www.puretech.com
Printed in Great Britain
on acid-free paper by
Bookcraft (Bath, Ltd)
Midsomer Norton, Somerset

FOREWORD

BY KENNETH J. ARROW

Under well-known conditions, the market is known to produce a Pareto efficient outcome. These conditions are the absence of increasing returns to scale and the absence of externalities, including as one extreme case public goods for which there is no rivalry in use. When these conditions prevail, there is no particular need for policy, no public works, if Pareto efficiency were the only criterion. Of course, there are other criteria, distributive in nature: mitigation of the income inequality that might result from the free market, equal treatment of equals, and the like.

For the present volume, the important point is the presence of externalities. There are many kinds of externalities, but those of concern here arise from the effect of human activity on the environment of other humans (and, in some views, on other living beings). They are part of the class of externalities arising from the physical fact that certain resources are fluids; they are sometimes referred to as *fugitive resources*. Water and air are the obvious examples. Because they move so readily, they cannot easily be made property. The problems do not only arise in what are usually thought of as environmental problems. Since water flows underground, drawing well water depletes the water available to nearby users. (This same issue comes up in drilling for oil.) Since above-ground water moves in streams, upstream use can deprive downstream users of water. The attempts of achieving equity and control have led to a body of water law quite at variance with usual concepts of property, which, as economists have repeatedly demontrated, has resulted in gross inefficiencies in the allocation of water use, especially in arid regions such as some parts of California.

The specific set of problems we call environmental have usually to do with the use of air and water as dumping ground for wastes. Wastes would not be a problem if property rights were well-defined; those creating waste as a by-product of production would have to pay for its disposition. But since property rights are absent for fugitive resources, the market will fail to balance benefits and costs. More specifically, the fugitive resources will be taken by individual users as free goods and therefore used to excess relative to a social optimum.

Ever since Jules Dupuit's 1844 study of the criteria for public works, such as bridges and highways, economists have urged the simulation of market criteria when the market itself does not function. This procedure has come to be known as benefit–cost analysis. While there are distinct logical problems with the procedure, these are undoubtedly secondary compared with the problems of empirical implementation. In any application, there is always some need for data beyond that supplied by the market. When, as in Dupuit's applications, the issue is solely one of increasing returns, the main issue is that of determining a demand curve, from which the consumers' surplus is derived. The market will directly provide only the demand at one point, but of course by comparison of different observed situations (over time or over space) demand curves may derived; that is what econometrics is all about after all.

When externalities are involved instead of or in addition to increasing returns the market provides even less information. The benefits from cleaning up a stream by better sewage treatment are not being sold and could not be sold, since there is no way of excluding downstream beneficiaries for nonpayment. How does one measure the marginal benefit at a given level, let alone a whole demand curve. If the beneficiaries are firms, e.g. fisheries, then one might try to measure the benefits by objective technological analysis of increased output or decreased costs, for example, the value of the fishery net of expenses. But suppose that the benefits inhere to consumers and are essentially questions of tastes, the absence of throat irritation due to the various components of smog or prevention of a decrease of visibility in the areas of the Southwest United States which have unusually clear atmospheres. Then the market provides no signals at all.

It is to meet this issue that the technique of contingent valuation was developed. To find the values not manifest in the market, one can ask individuals what values they would place on the good. Somewhat similar techniques are employed by industry to find out if it would be worthwhile to develop a new product; a survey is taken among potential customers, asking if they would buy a product with given specifications and price. An obvious rejoinder is that a hypothetical question does not elicit as accurate a response as a real choice in the market.

A further extension of the use of contingent valuation has probably been mostly responsible for fuelling the controversy about its validity. In the United States, there is legal liability for environmental damages, especially oil spills. To the extent that these damages are externalities, governmental bodies are allowed to collect them on behalf of a diffuse public. Contingent valuation has been used to evaluate these externalities, and there is therefore a large pecuniary stake in the accuracy of this method.

What has raised the stakes in both public decision-making and legal liability has been the increase in the scope of the externalities. John Krutilla and Burton Weisbrod in the 1960s introduced the ideas of *existence value* and *option value*. These are not values derived from the active use of the fugitive resource. Rather they are what courts have called *passive use*. An individual is interpreted to receive satisfaction from the fact that an unspoiled wilderness exists, though he or she may never visit it. The evidence that these are genuine values comes from contingent valuations, which consistently show positive willingness to pay to preserve amenities outside the respondent's probable visiting range. Thus, the average United States household expressed a willingness to pay $37 to preserve Prince William Sound in Alaska from a repetition of the *Exxon Valdez* oil spill, although in all probability most of them had never heard of that place before the spill took place. It is the passive-use valuation that has contributed the most to the magnitude of the issue of the validity of contingent valuation.

The following essays represent the most extensive examination of contingent valuation to date. By now, a considerable body of contingent valuations exist. Disturbing paradoxes appear in some of the responses. Some, particularly psychologists, have argued from these data (and others) that not merely is the meaning of contingent valuations obscure but that the whole economic analysis of preference is ill-founded. The specific techniques of contingent valuation are also examined, including the statistical problems associated with the analysis of the responses. Finally, case studies and the relation of contingent valuation to the governmental framework are analyzed.

These essays will undoubtedly determine the standards of the field and influence its future acceptability for years to come. They repay careful study.

ACKNOWLEDGEMENTS

We are grateful to Philip Cooper, Stavros Georgiou, Andreas Graham, and Nikki DeCoteau for assistance in the checking of manuscripts and in particular to Frances Randell, who wrestled all the chapters into a consistent format. We are also grateful to staff at Oxford University Press for their support throughout this project. Most of all we would like to thank the contributors for the prodigious effort which went into the writing of this book—many thanks to you all.

I.J.B.
K.G.W.

CONTENTS

CONTRIBUTORS

VIRGINIA ABIAD
Virginia Abiad is a consultant who lives in Quezon City, Philippines; she holds a Doctor of Business Administration degree. Her major field of expertise is the financial, economic, and policy analysis of projects. She has extensive experience in designing and conducting field surveys in a variety of fields, including water supply, sanitation, electric power, agriculture, rural finance, and marketing. She has consulted for numerous public, private, and international agencies, and has had fellowships to study in the Philippines, Japan, and the United States. For thirteen years she was Professor of Economics at the University of the Philippines.

WIKTOR ADAMOWICZ
Wiktor Adamowicz is a Professor in the Department of Rural Economy, and an adjunct professor in the Department of Economics, University of Alberta, Edmonton, Alberta. He received his Ph.D. from the University of Minnesota in 1988. His thesis research examined the consistency of non-market valuation methods with rational-choice axioms embodied in economic theory. Since then, he has focused on designing, testing, and applying non-market valuation techniques. He has authored over 100 articles, reports, and conference papers on environmental valuation, incorporation of non-market goods into economic analysis, land-use planning, and cost–benefit analysis. His main research areas include the use of discrete choice models for modelling recreation-site choice and the use of stated-preference methods for valuing environmental amenities. He has been a visiting professor at the University of Newcastle and an invited lecturer at Portland State University, Oregon. He is on the editorial board of the *Journal of Agricultural and Resource Economics* and was the editor of the *Canadian Journal of Agricultural Economics*.

IAN BATEMAN
Ian Bateman is Reader in Environmental Economics at the School of Environmental Sciences, University of East Anglia and Senior Research Fellow at the Centre for Social and Economic Research on the Global Environment (CSERGE), Universty of East Anglia and University College London. He holds the B.Soc.Sci. in Economics from the University of Birmingham, the M.Sc. (with Distinction) in Agricultural Economics from the University of Manchester and a Ph.D. in Economics from the University of Nottingham. His research interests include the development of methods for the evaluation of preferences for non-market goods (including

environmental and health risk issues) and the application of such methods through the medium of Geographical Information Systems. He is co-author with R. Kerry Turner and David Pearce of *Environmental Economics* (Hemel Hempsterd and Baltimore, Harvester Wheatsheaf / Johns Hopkins, 1994). Ian lives in a small village outside Norwich with his wife and their burgeoning family (three children at last count). Together with Norwich City FC they have almost made him forget a once passionate interest in football.

JOHN BERGSTROM

John Bergstrom, Ph.D. (Texas A&M University), is an Associate professor of Natural Resource and Environmental Economics, Department of Agricultural and Applied Economics, University of Georgia, Athens. His research and teaching programmes focus on applied welfare economics, natural resource and environmental valuation, experimental economics, and applications of economics to natural resource planning and environmental policy at the federal, state, and local levels. He has published numerous professional journal articles related to contingent valuation theory and applications. He is a member of the Association of Environmental and Resource Economists, the American Economic Association, and the American Agricultural Economics Association.

FRANÇOIS BONNIEUX

François Bonnieux holds Ph.D. in both Statistics and Economics and is currently Research Leader at the National Institute for Agronomical Research (INRA) in Rennes, and consultant to the EU and OECD. He specializes in non-market valuation and has participated in a research programme for the French Ministry of the Environment on the potential benefits of an improvement in the quality of inland water. He was also called as an expert in the Amoco Cadiz case. He is currently involved in programmes examining the provision of public goods by agriculture, with a special emphasis on countryside valuation, and works on the integration of non-market goods in cost–benefit analysis.

KEVIN BOYLE

Kevin Boyle is Libra Professor of Envrionmental Economics at the Department of Resource and Policy, University of Maine. He is one of the leaders in the development and refinement of contingent valuation. His research focuses on potential biases in contingent valuation and on extending the limits of the application of this methodology. He chooses applications that have important public policy implications, including the protection of scenic beauty, valuing endangered species, groundwater contamination, etc. Recently he has begun work investigating the usefulness of conjoint analysis for valuing non-market goods and services, and hedonic valuation of surface-water quality. He is an Associate Editor for the Journal of Environmental Economics and Management.

PETER BOXALL

Peter Boxall has M.Sc.'s in Ecology from the University of Calgary and Resource Economics from the University of Alberta. He is currently completing his Ph.D. at the latter institution. Much of his early research focused on non-market valuation of fish and wildlife resource use, where he used discrete-choice travel-cost analysis to examine lottery rationed hunting, recreational fishing, and wildlife viewing. Peter is currently the leader of a non-timber valuation research programme at the Canadian Forest Service in Edmonton. The major focus of the programme is non-market valuation, and a primary focus has been the development of new valuation methodologies such as the stated-preference application described in this book. Peter is also conducting research on the effect of forest fires on recreation values, and the non-use values of wildlife species threatened by industrial forest use.

RICHARD CARSON

Richard T. Carson is Professor of Economics at the University of California, San Diego, Senior Fellow at the San Diego Super Computer Center, and Research Director for International Environmental Policy at the University of California's Institute for Global Conflict and Cooperation. He is co-author with Robert Mitchell of *Using Surveys to Value Public Goods: The Contingent Valuation Method* (Washington, DC: Resources for the Future, 1989). He served as a principal investigator on the State of Alaska's economic damage assessment for the Exxon Valdez oil spill and has conducted contingent valuation studies on a range of topics.

KYEONGAE CHOE

KyeongAe Choe is a director of Infrastructure Development and Environmental Analysis (I.D.E.A.) Associates in Finland. Previously, she was working as an environmental economist in the Centre for International Development at the Research Triangle Institute. She has Ph.D. and Master's degrees in Economics and Planning from the university of North Carolina at Chapel Hill. Since 1989, she has worked for the World Bank and other international agencies on the application of the contingent valuation method for estimating demand for infrastructure development in the context of developing countries. Her research focuses on the use of both market and non-market valuation techniques for measuring environmental benefits as well as public investment cost–benefit analyses. Recently, she has begun work investigating the usefulness of contingent valuation method for prioritizing municipal investment projects. She has worked in West Africa, India, Vietnam, Central Asia, and transcaucasian regions such as Kazahkstan and Georgia.

NICK FLORES

Nicholas E. Flores is an assistant professor at the Department of Economics, University of Colorado, Boulder. His research is centred around the theory of public goods, with a special emphasis on how that theory applies to environmental goods. Contemporary topics which are of particular interest to him include the interrelatedness of public goods and its effect on their values; the theoretical consistency of altruism in cost–benefit analyses; and the adequacy of national economic accounts in reflecting social welfare when revised to include environmental values.

COLIN GREEN

Colin Green is a reader in Environmental Economics at the School of Geography and Environmental Management, Middlesex University. He has been working in contingent valuation for the last Fifteen years and has undertaken studies for the Office of Water Services, the Department of the Environment, the National Rivers Authority, the Ministry of Agriculture, Fisheries and Food, and the Department of Transport amongst others.

W. MICHAEL HANEMANN

Michael Hanemann is a Professor in the Department of Agricultural & Resource Economics at the University of California, Berkeley. He was educated in England, where he obtained a BA in PPE at Oxford and an M.Sc in Economics at the London School of Economics, and in the USA, where he obtained a Ph.D in economics at Harvard University. Since his dissertation, he has specialized in the economic analysis of individual behaviour, with particular application to issues in environmental and natural resource economics and policy. He has played a leading role in the development of both the revealed preference (travel demand) and the stated preference (contingent valuation) approaches to the valuation of environmental and other non-market resources. He has worked on Mono Lake (with John Loomis), the Colorado River, and the Exxon Valdez oil spill (with Richard Carson), and many other environmental issues. His research interests also include welfare economics, risk regulation, water pricing and allocation, and irreversibility in natural resource systems.

NICK HANLEY

Nick Hanley is Professor of Natural Resource Economics at the Institute of Ecology and Resource Management, University of Edinburgh, Scotland. His main research interests are environmental valuation, the economics of pollution control, and the impact of agriculture on the countryside. He has extensive consultancy experience with governmental and international organizations, such as the UK Department of the Environment and the OECD. With Clive Spash, he is co-author of *Cost Benefit Analysis and the Environment* (Aldershot: Edward Elgar, 1994).

BARBARA KANNINEN

Barbara Kanninen is an assistant professor at the Hubert H. Humphrey Institute of Public Affairs at the University of Minnesota. She has been a Gilbert White Visiting Fellow at Resources for the Future and a visiting senior economist at the National Oceanic and Atmospheric Administration. She earned her Ph.D. in 1991 from the Department of Agricultural and Resource Economics at the University of California, Berkeley. Her current research interests concern the statistical, issues raised by transportation demand modelling and contingent valuation.

IAN LANGFORD

Ian Langford completed his Ph.D. in Environmental Epidemiology in 1992, and has since worked on a number of projects linked to applied and spatial statistics, epidemiology, environmental economics, and risk assessment. He is currently a senior research fellow of the Centre for Social and Economic Research on the Global Environment, University of East Anglia, Norwich, and University College, London. He has published widely on the theory and applications of multi-level modelling in various fields, and is an ESRC Visiting Fellow working on multi-level modelling with Professor Harvey Goldstein at the Institute of Education, London. His interests include cricket, writing songs, and having a good time at conferences.

DONALD LAURIA

Donald T. Lauria is Professor of Water Resources Engineering at the University of North Carolina at Chapel Hill. His major field of interest is community water supply and sanitation in developing countries. He has co-directed several contingent valuation studies during the past decade in Africa, Asia, and Latin America. His current research is on the use of contingent valuation findings for selecting improved levels of water and sanitation service using mathematical optimization models. During his thirty-year career at the University of North Carolina, he has worked in forty different countries, undertaking projects for such agencies as the World Bank, the Inter American Development Bank, US AID, UNDP, and WHO. He has numerous publications and reports, mostly in the engineering literature.

JOHN LOOMIS

Dr John Loomis is a professor in the Department of Agricultural and Resource Economics at Colorado State University. Previously he was a professor at the University of California, Davis. Prior to joining UC-Davis, he was employed as an economist with the Bureau of Land Management and US Fish and Wildlife Service for seven years. He has recently written a book entitled *Integrated Public Lands Management* that evaluates the planning of National Forests, Parks, Wildlife Refuges, and BLM lands.

He has published over sixty journal articles on the valuation of wildlife, wetlands, wilderness, rivers, and fisheries. He uses travel-cost and contingent valuation methods to value not only recreation users' willingness to pay but the general public's willingness to pay to preserve natural environments. The case studies have involved the preservation of Mono Lake in California, the Northern Spotted Owl, and wetlands in California.

JORDAN LOUVIERE

Jordan J. Louviere is Professor and Chair, Department of Marketing, Faculty of Economics, Sydney University, Australia. He received his Ph.D. in Quantitative Geography and Transportation Planning, with a minor in Mathematical Psychology, from the University of Iowa in 1973. Since that time, he has authored or co-authored more than 100 scholarly journal articles, chapters in books and volumes, monographs, and the like dealing with theory, methods, and applications of models of consumer decision-making and choice behaviour. He has served on the faculties of Florida State University, the University of Wyoming, the University of Iowa, the Australian Graduate School of Management, the University of Alberta, and the University of Utah. He is currently the Foundation Chair of the newly formed Department of Marketing in the Faculty of Economics at Sydney University. Jordan serves on the editorial boards of the *Journal of Marketing Research, Journal of Consumer Research, Journal of Retailing*, and *International Journal of Retailing and Consumer Services*, and is a former member of the editorial board of *Transportation Research*. He has served as a consultant on hundreds of major projects in Australia, Canada, Europe, New Zealand, and the US.

JOHN McKEAN

John R. McKean is emeritus professor at Colorado State University. He previously taught at the universities of Alberta, Washington, and Idaho. He received a Ph.D. in Economics from the University of Washington, Seattle in 1967. His current work includes research on the economics of drought, funded by the National Science Foundation, and university contracts with the US Fish and Wildlife Service and US Biological Service. He is also interested in non-market benefits measurement, economic impact analysis, and computable general equilibrium models applied to ecosystems. His publications include 58 refereed journal articles in *Economic Systems Research, Geoforum, Journal of Financial and Quantitative Analysis, Journal of Business, Journal of Economic Theory, Journal of Forecasting, Journal of Soil and Water Conservation, Journal of Economic Issues, Kyklos, Land Economics, Society and Natural Resources, Water Resources Research, Western Journal of Agricultural Economics*, and others; 8 chapters in books; and 167 university or government reports. He is completing manuscripts for reference books on econometrics and regional economics.

ROBERT CAMERON MITCHELL

Robert Cameron Mitchell is a professor of Geography at Clark University in Worcester, Massachusetts. He received his Ph.D. in Sociology from Northwestern University. Before coming to Clark he was a senior fellow at Resources for the Future in Washington, DC. He has an extensive background in survey research and for the past fifteen years his research has focused on environmental perceptions and valuation in the United States. He is co-author, with Richard Carson, of *Using Surveys to Value Public Goods: The Contingent Valuation Method* (Washington, DC: Resources for the Future, 1989).

ALISTAIR MUNRO

Alistair Munro, an economics lecturer in the School of Economic and Social Studies at the University of East Anglia, graduated with a BA in Mathematics and Economics from the University of Warwick and has an M.Phil. and a D.Phil. from the University of Oxford. His main research interests lie in welfare economics and environmental economics. Currently, as well as researching the effects of economic behaviour on biological evolution, he is part of two research teams: one investigating biases in the contingent valuation method and one modelling the impact of tradable permits on pollution in the Forth Estuary.

WILLIAM PARKE

William R. Parke is an Associate Professor of Economics at the University of North Carolina, Chapel Hill. Since graduating from Yale University, he has published a variety of Monte Carlo simulation studies of econometric estimation and forecasting procedures.

PIERRE RAINELLI

Pierre Rainelli holds a Ph.D. in Economics and is a *directeur de recherche* at the National Institute for Agronomical Research (INRA) in Rennes, where he is in charge of an environmental economics research team. His main areas of interest include the control of agricultural pollution and the role of economic incentives in reducing agricultural nitrate emissions and in improving animal diet. He also participates in programmes on environmental agreements and is currently involved in consultancy work for the EU, OECD, and the French Ministry of the Environment. He was called as an expert in the Amoco Cadiz case.

ROBERT SUGDEN

Robert Sugden is Professor of Economics at the University of East Anglia. His research interests include welfare economics, social choice theory, choice under uncertainty, experimental economics, and the exploration of issues at the interface of philosophy and economics. He is currently the director of a project which investigates potential biases in the contingent valuation method and looks for ways of correcting for these.

JOFFRE SWAIT

Joffre Swait is currently at the Marketing Department, College of Business Administration, University of Florida, Gainsville. He received his Ph.D. from the Massachusetts Institute of Technology in 1984, where he specialized in modelling discrete-choice behaviour, with emphasis on transportation demand analysis. Subsequently, his interests widened to include applications in logistics and, more recently, marketing. He has published in major journals his research work in discrete-choice modelling, consumer heterogeneity, choice-set formation, fusion of different data types, and so forth. His current major research efforts are in consumer heterogeneity, choice-data fusion and brand-equity measurement using choice models. Before taking up his present position, he gained extensive consulting experience in North and South America, where he has studied consumer behaviour modelling in such diverse areas as transportation, telecommunications, packaged goods, financial services, computer hardware, tourism, and so forth.

SYLVIA TUNSTALL

Sylvia Tunstall is a sociologist and a social survey specialist at the Flood Hazard Research Centre, Middlesex University. Contingent valuation studies in which she has been involved include assessments of traffic nuisance, river restoration, river-water quality improvements, alleviation of low flows in rivers, and improvements in water and sewerage services.

CYNTHIA TURINGAN

Cynthia Turingan is an Associate Professor in the School of Urban and Regional Planning at the University of the Philippines. Her major field of interest is regional development planning. She has worked on a variety of projects, including social and environmental impact analysis, regional growth, resettlement evaluation, rural transport, land-use planning, and pollution abatement. In addition to her professorial work, she has held positions in the private and public sectors in the Philippines and has performed numerous consulting assignments for Filipino and international agencies.

R. KERRY TURNER

R. Kerry Turner is Professor of Environmental Sciences at the University of East Anglia and Director of the Centre for Social and Economic Research on the Global Environment (CSERGE), University of East Anglia and University College London. He has specialized in environmental resource management and economics research since the mid-1970s and has a particular interest in the applied and policy – relevant aspects of environmental economics. He has served on and provided consultancy to a number of national and international environmental protection and management committees, bodies, and regulatory agencies. He has also published widely on a range of environmental economics and policy topics.

RICHARD WALSH

Richard G. Walsh teaches recreation economics at Colorado State University and is author of a textbook on the subject. He was educated at the University of Wisconsin, where his Ph.D. dissertation dealt with development of recreation resources in the Lake States. He is best known for his work comparing the benefits and costs of recreation and environmental quality programmes in the Rocky Mountains. He completed empirical studies of the option, existence, and bequest values to the general population from preservation of air and water quality, wilderness areas, natural rivers, fish and wildlife, forest quality, and developed recreation facilities. He has studied the effects of water quality, water level, forest quality, and congestion on demand for recreation. He measured the potential benefits of reduced crowding during peak days of recreation use of rivers, lakes, trails, campgrounds, and ski areas. His latest work is a statistical forecast of the demand for fishing and hunting into the 21st century. These studies emphasize the importance of economics in managing recreation, wildlife, and related environmental resources for the future. He is author or co-author of four books and over 100 scientific papers and reports. He was awarded the American Agricultural Economics Association prize for outstanding published research. His biography is listed in Marquis's *Who's Who in America* and *Who's Who in the World*.

DALE WHITTINGTON

Dr Whittington is a Professor of Environmental Sciences and Engineering, and City and Regional Planning, at the University of North Carolina at Chapel Hill. His recent research focuses on the use of environmental valuation techniques in the public policy arena. Since 1986 he has worked for the World Bank and other international agencies on the development and application of the contingent valuation method and other valuation techniques for estimating household demand for improved water and sanitation services in developing countries. He is a co-author of the recent OECD publication, *Project and Policy Appraisal: Integrating Economics and the Environment*; *Water Management Models in Practice: A Case Study of the Aswan High Dam (The Netherlands: Elsevier, 1983)*; and a textbook on public policy analysis, *Expert Advice for Policy Choice*. In 1992–3 he directed a project funded by the US Environmental Protection Agency and the Texas Water Commission to develop improved methods to determine an economic value of the Galveston Bay estuary system.

MICHAEL WILLIAMS

Michael Williams is a principal at Intelligent Marketing Systems (IMS) Inc., Edmonton, Alberta. IMS is a marketing research firm which focuses its research on understanding and predicting customer/consumer behaviour and decision-making processes. IMS has clients in business and government sectors in North America, Australia, and Europe. He is responsible for the management and development of IMS business direction, operations, and research technologies. He is also the designer of IMS software, including CONSURV, NteLOGIT, and Decision Support Systems, distributed worldwide. He obtained his MBA from the University of Alberta, 1990 and draws upon his skills in Computing Science (B.Sc., 1985) to make IMS among the leaders in market research techniques and technology.

KENNETH G. WILLIS

Kenneth G. Willis is Professor of Environmental Economics at Newcastle University, where he received his Ph.D. in Migration and Labour Mobility. After early work in this area and on regional economic development issues, his research concentrated on valuing the benefits of environmental protection. He has completed empirical studies of the use and passive-use values of green belts, nature conservation, forest quality and recreation, various agri-environmental policies, enhancing river flows, flood protection, the opportunity costs of biodiversity priorities and targets, decision-making in environmental protection cases, and experts' judgement of environmental benefits. His main research areas include hedonic price models and the accuracy of contingent values in cost–benefit analysis. He has authored or co-authored a number of books and over 100 papers and reports, and has worked in West Africa, India, Iran, and Malaysia.

1

Introduction and Overview

IAN J. BATEMAN
KENNETH G. WILLIS

1.1. BACKGROUND

In a world with unlimited environmental resources, in which environments were pure public goods, it would be unnecessary to have methods to determine the best allocation of resources amongst competing alternative uses. But resources are limited and indeed many natural environmental resources are decreasing. It is therefore desirable to assess the benefits of protecting and enhancing environmental resources compared with the opportunity costs or benefits forgone of alternative uses. Contingent valuation (CV) evolved as a method to quantify the benefits of non-marketed environmental goods and attributes so that they could be entered directly into cost–benefit calculations. CV was seen both as an alternative method of valuation to travel-cost (TC) and hedonic pricing (HP) models and as being able to quantify some types of benefits, such as non-use or passive-use benefits, which lie outside the scope of TC and HP studies.

Hanemann (1992) traces the empirical roots of CV back to 1958 and a US National Park Service-funded study of outdoor recreation in the Delaware River Basin area (marking the start of an ongoing institutional involvement with the CV method which is reflected in the contents of this volume). The method was used only sporadically during the 1960s and exclusively in the US (Loomis, in Chapter 18, considers in detail the development of CV in the US). However, the 1970s saw a gradual but sustained growth in applications such that, by the end of the decade, the CV method was given official recognition by the US Water Resources Council as a recommended valuation technique. The decade also witnessed the first European applications of the technique (Bohm, 1972; Dahlberg, 1974).

The 1980s saw an explosion in the number of CV studies undertaken in the US, the establishment of a more substantial European literature, and the first developing world applications (e.g. the study by Whittington *et al.* (1990) conducted in 1986). With this increase in applications came an intensification in the degree of academic debate. Areas of interest included how the results of CV studies could differ depending on the framing of the issue, payment vehicle, elicitation method, etc., as well as investigation of divergence in results across the CV, TC, and HP methods where they were applied to common goods. This heightening of the academic debate was reflected in the publication of two milestone books concentrating solely upon the CV method. Cummings *et al.* (1986) provided a high-quality 'state of the art' assessment of the technique with commentary from a range of interested parties representing a variety of opinions. This debate was taken further by Mitchell and Carson (1989), who both set the method within the context of economic theory and considered a plethora of empirical, social survey, and psychological issues. The decade also witnessed a further incorporation of CV into the institutional decision-making process, largely stimulated by the acceptance of the method under the Comprehensive Environmental Response, Compensation and Liability Act (CERCLA) 1980 in the USA, as a technique to measure the extent of natural resource damages from the spillage of hazardous substances. CERCLA assessments were open to court scrutiny and this provided a further impetus for refinement to the accuracy and reliability of the CV method. The 1989 case, *Ohio v. US Department of the Interior* (DOI), stating that both use and non-use values should be taken into consideration in DOI decisions (District of Columbia, 1989), gave a further fillip to the use of CV to measure natural resource damages. Such institutional acceptance was not wholly confined to the US, as evidenced by the UK Treasury's acceptance, in 1987, of a cost–benefit study of coastal defences in which recreational benefits were assessed via the CV method (Turner *et al.*, 1992).

This heady combination of academic interest and institutional endorsement meant that the CV method entered the 1990s as the dominant technique for the valuation of non-market environmental costs and benefits. Indeed the decade started confidently both in empirical and theoretical terms. Empirically, the review by Navrud (1992) showed that CV was being extensively used in Europe while increasingly examples from developing countries were beginning to appear in the literature (e.g. Whittington *et al.*, 1992). Theoretically, the apparent problem of large divergence between CV estimates of individuals' willingness to pay (WTP) and willingness to accept (WTA) compensation for the same good (seen by some as evidence of Kahneman and Tversky's (1979) Prospect Theory) was interpreted as a virtue by Hanemann (1991), who built upon earlier work by Randall and Stoll (1980) to argue that such results reflected the underlying income and substitution elasticites of public goods and as such CV was producing correct welfare measures.

Institutional endorsement of the CV method also continued apace, with further funding of US studies by the Environmental Protection Agency, and a further court ruling favouring the assessment of non-use values (State of Utah, 1992). In the UK the Department of the Environment approved the CV method as one which 'may be applied extensively since it can be used to derive values for almost any environmental change' (Department of the

Environment, 1991: 58). In only slightly more cautious mood the European Union began to assess the potential of the technique for the valuation of landscape change (see Bonnieux and Rainelli, Chapter 17).

With all the portents so favourable it seemed (as one eminent commentator stated at the time) that the debate had progressed beyond whether or not the CV method was valid, to consideration of more minor refinements of technique. All that was required now, it seemed, was a sufficiently high-profile case study to establish the technique firmly in the minds of decision-makers. Such raised awareness was soon to be achieved, although perhaps not in the way in which CV *aficionados* would have preferred.

On the night of 24 March 1989, the oil tanker Exxon Valdez ran aground in Prince William Sound, Alaska, releasing some 11 million gallons of crude oil. Over the next six months this, the largest oil spill in US waters to date, resulted in the death of 36,000 sea-birds, 1,000 sea otters, and over 150 bald eagles (Maki, 1991). Following CERCLA guide-lines and the lead of the US courts, the State of Alaska quickly moved to commission some of the most eminent researchers in the field to undertake an extensive and thorough CV assessment of the non-use damages caused by this disaster. Shortly thereafter, and concerned about the size of damage assessment which might result from such a study, the Exxon Company commissioned a number of equally eminent economists to investigate the validity of the CV technique with respect to problems such as the embedding issue (where values for a good are conditional upon the circumstances of its presentation) suggested in a then-unpublished but widely circulated paper by Kahneman and Knetsch (1990).

The Exxon Company had good reason to quail at the prospect of having to pay non-use value compensation for a disaster of such colossal magnitude, a magnitude reflected in the report to the State of Alaska, which valued these damages at some $2.8 billion (based on median WTP values of $31 per household; Carson *et al.*, 1992). However, Exxon's riposte showed a masterly command of publicity as the research they funded resulted in a high-profile symposium (Cambridge Economics, 1992) and book (Hausman, 1993), both of which were highly critical of CV, particularly where applied to the assessment of non-use values. The extent to which this influenced the final out-of-court settlement of about $1.1 billion for non-use damages is uncertain, particularly given controversy regarding whether Exxon's $2.5 billion clean-up programme represented response or restoration (use-value losses were additional to these passive-use values, and were estimated to be some $30 million for lost recreational fishing and $100 million for lost commercial fishing, amongst other lost use values).

The Exxon Valdez episode marked the consolidation of a division in the academic perception of the CV technique which is reflected in the debates of Cummings *et al.* (1986) and which Boyle and Bergstrom (Chapter 7) trace back as far as Scott (1965). Two distinct camps of academic commentators were now drawn up, both highly eminent, both having strong theoretical and methodological arguments, but both disagreeing fundamentally about the basic validity of the CV technique. The degree of disagreement soon spilled over into journal articles, with the publication of Kahneman and Knetsch's (1992a) embedding article receiving an immediate rebuff from Smith (1992), which in turn raised an equally swift reply (Kahneman and Knetsch, 1992b). However, institutional involvement and the use of CV in official damage assessments meant that this debate was of more than academic interest. As a consequence the National Oceanic and Atmospheric Administration (NOAA) commissioned a prestigious 'Blue-Ribbon Panel' of economists and survey specialists, co-chaired by Nobel laureates Kenneth Arrow and Robert Solow, to investigate the CV method. After carefully considering a wide range of issues, the panel's resultant report (Arrow et al., 1993) gave the method a qualified bill of health but only if studies were conducted to a rigorous set of guide-lines which were explicitly spelt out.

The current edition of the CV bibliography prepared by Carson et al., (1995) contains over 2,000 studies and papers. However, very few of these studies conform to the guide-lines set down by Arrow et al. (1993). It seems that the applied literature will have to be re-evaluated and perhaps even rerun along such more rigorous lines if we are to have confidence in the results obtained. In the meantime controversy over the CV method continues to be as heated as ever, as shown by the contrary opinions expressed in recent papers such as those of Diamond and Hausman (1994), Hanemann (1994), and Portney (1994).

And so we arrive at the present day. The importance of the CV technique remains undimmed, supported, protagonists would argue, by the endorsement (albeit qualified) of the NOAA panel. Institutional acceptance, already high in the US, continues to expand in Europe and elsewhere, buoyed up by a continued and rising tide of applications. However, as indicated this does not mean that the arguments over the CV method have ended. Detractors still echo Scott's claim that hypothetical questions yield hypothetical answers, giving numbers which, according to Diamond and Hausman, may often be worse than having no numbers at all. On the protagonists' side the argument often states that many observed problems are the consequence of poor or inadequate design or execution. We also detect a growing middle ground of alternative views which side-step the debate regarding the absolute validity of CV estimates, preferring to use the method as an interesting experimental tool by which the processes underlying individual decision-making may be investigated. Yet others view CV estimates as being of relative validity, providing additional information to the decision-making process.

This volume has therefore been written at a time of widespread and heated (one might even say acrimonious) debate. To reflect this we have invited specially written submissions from commentators on both sides of that debate (as well as some of those others who see it as an interesting experimental tool regardless of the question of absolute validity of estimates). We have been delighted with the results of this exercise and hope that it provides a valuable input to this most important debate.

1.2. THE STRUCTURE OF THIS BOOK

In planning this book we wished to embrace all aspects of the current debate: theoretical; methodological; empirical; and institutional. Accordingly we identified the topics within each of these general headings which seemed most pertinent and invited those commentators whom we felt most appropriate to contribute. We were overwhelmed with the response received to such invitations (only one of the authors invited to submit declined to do so) and feel that the assembled list of contributors contains some of the most exciting authors currently writing in the CV arena.

Part I of this volume (Chapters 2 to 6) considers the conceptual theoretical context and underpinnings of CV. In many respects this is where the most fundamental disagreements of the CV debate originate and this is reflected in the varied views expressed. Part II (Chapters 7 to 13) explores detailed questions on the methodological application of CV. The success of any particular CV study depends crucially upon the ability of the methods used accurately to reflect the underlying preferences of individual respondents. Given the complexity of such a task, a detailed investigation of methodology is clearly justified. Part III (Chapters 14 to 16) extends this investigation by looking at some special topics in CV through case studies. Finally, Part IV (Chapters 17 and 18) considers the institutional dimension of CV use in both the US and the European Union (EU), within which CV is adopted as a practical tool to inform choices in the public sector about resource allocation in the environment field.

Although this volume covers a wide range of topics, it is not a manual of how to apply the CV method. Such books are already in circulation and we saw no reason to replicate what has already been done extremely well. Rather it attempts to present the state of the art in CV. It points readers in the right direction, and helps them to avoid many of the pitfalls in CV of which novices, and some experts, may be unaware. No consensus is presented about which aspects of technique should be adopted and which discarded, nor on how CV analysis should be undertaken. We see the current debate surrounding CV as a potential source of strength rather than weakness. If the method can survive the present severe scrutiny then it should be enhanced by such a process. We hope that the contributions presented in the following chapters will contribute positively to that debate, and we devote the remainder of this chapter to an overview of those contributions.

1.3. CONTEXT AND CONTENT OF SPECIFIC CHAPTERS

The use of CV to estimate WTP, and hence the utility of specific goods, is firmly rooted in economic theory. However, concern is expressed by some philosophers and environmentalists about the ability of the method to value environmental goods, since individuals have no experience in purchasing them, nor of modifying their choices in light of what they experience from their purchases, nor of learning about their preferences for and characteristics of environmental goods. There may be problems of (1) cognition: difficulties of observing, understanding a particular environmental system, and weighing up the attributes of the good; (2) incongruity: individuals being unable to accept that price can capture all the relevant information about a good and its value; and (3) composition: the inability of individuals to accept that an environmental good or service can be 'commodified' in order to be priced separately from its intrinsic contribution to the whole. Part I opens with 'The Place of Economic Values in Environmental Valuation' (Chapter 2), in which Kerry Turner explores some aspects of the environmental values debate in the wider context of sustainable economic development. Turner points out that the adoption of a systems perspective and the recognition of ecosystem primary value serves to emphasize the 'strong-sustainability' approach to policy and the need for safe minimum standards. A healthy ecosystem is seen as being valuable beyond those beliefs which are computed simply in terms of human preferences. But what is not argued is that all environmental assets have unmeasured value and therefore all assets should be protected. Whilst CV is not seen as applicable to questions of systems value, it is seen as providing valuation opportunities in the context of both individual use and non-use environmental values.

Other disciplines have also expressed concerns over the application of CV. Psychologists have criticized the simple tenets of utility theory in terms of individual perceptions and decisions, the divergence between WTA and WTP measures of environmental values, embedding, preference reversals, and so on. In Chapter 3 Michael Hanemann responds to some of these challenges to economic theory by reviewing the theory of the utility model, and relating it to Kahneman and Tversky's (1979) model of loss aversion, as well as discussing the importance of substitution effects in valuation, and what embedding means in economic theory.

Apart from one or two exceptional situations, CV is the only technique capable of measuring passive-use or non-use values, and it is such applications which have led to the most strident criticisms of the method. Since passive-use values, and public goods, are not traded in the market-place, CV estimates their value by setting up a hypothetical market in which respondents bid for quantities of these goods. Estimates of the WTP value for these environmental goods are usually in terms of motives: option, bequest, and pure existence values *per se*. It is argued that the general public have no experience of such purchases in the market-place, have not learned by experience the cost to them of making the wrong decision, and are therefore unlikely to provide an accurate estimate of the value of such goods. However, in Chapter 4 Richard Carson, Nicholas Flores, and Robert Mitchell point out that researchers are usually ignorant of consumers' motives in any economic decision, market or non-market. Instead, they argue that errors in measuring passive-use values can be avoided by careful CV design in terms of commodity definition, resource familiarity, and substitute availability, thus ensuring the respondent clearly understands the nature of the good being offered and can therefore make an informed decision. The payment and provision aspects of a good are recognized as affecting values in both hypothetical and actual markets.

With prior chapters being generally supportive of the CV method, Robert Sugden sounds a first cautionary note in chapters where he considers the special problems which arise when valuing public as opposed to private goods. In Chapter 5, as part of a wide-ranging review of the literature, Sugden argues that conventional expectations regarding incentive compatibility may be insufficient to explain the complex preferences underpinning CV responses regarding public goods. This argument is extended in the following chapter, where Sugden examines 'Alternatives to the Neo-Classical Theory of Choice'. From a starting-point of standard Hicksian theory the chapter moves on to consider an array of alternative explanations of commonly observed CV biases. Particular attention is paid to the possibility of response-mode effects (say where CV scenarios are moved from being simply commodity–money trades to being commodity–commodity exchanges) and to the implications of Tversky and Kahneman's (1991) theory of reference-dependent preferences. Such a theory, Sugden suggests, may well explain the apparently excessive divergence between WTP and WTA. Conversely, CV may well provide a useful testbed for examining such controversial and fundamentally challenging theories.

Part II, on methodology, also opens in somewhat critical vein. Kevin Boyle was a prominent contributor to the Exxon symposium and has since written lucidly on problems related to embedding. His chapter with John Bergstrom (Chapter 7) reflects a cautious view of CV in its title 'Doubt, Doubts, and Doubters'. However, the subtitle, 'The Genesis of a New Research Agenda?', more accurately sums up the spirit of the chapter as Boyle and Bergstrom argue, against those who have dismissed CV out of hand, in favour of a move to a structured (rather than the present random) programme of research into the CV method. Such a programme, they argue, should be characterized not by the presumptions of innocence or guilt which dominate the present arguments, but by a spirit of empirical impartiality (perhaps tinged with a healthy dose of scepticism), in which evidence leads to conclusions and not vice versa.

The work of psychologists has long been recognized as being of key importance to the optimal design and interpretation of CV studies. Psychology sees people as more fallible and complex than neo-classical economics usually assumes. Moreover, psychologists also model how beliefs and preferences are formed and learnt, and how information is acquired. Thus psychological models bring an enhanced dynamic perspective to the environmental valuation procedure. In Chapter 8 Colin Green and Sylvia Tunstall show how the development of psychological considerations might improve CV studies. They illustrate the need to define the good precisely in assessing values, and use the Fishbein–Ajzen model to investigate how cognitive beliefs, attitudes, social norms, behavioural intentions, etc. can be incorporated within both the design of a CV model and the design of the interview schedule.

Conflicting viewpoints about the accuracy and reliability of respondents' judgements about the value of the environment can arise because values are contingent upon the repertory of strategies which the study or interviewer brings to the valuation task. The implications of differences in subjects' and experimenters' assumptions about which strategies are appropriate in experimental studies need to be examined, as does the impact of differences between the motivating aspects of experimental and applied settings upon study results and their transferability. One issue which cuts across these concerns is the problem of the amount of information on which a decision should be based. In Chapter 9 Alistair Munro and Nick Hanley consider the evidence regarding information effects and link this to the issue of uncertainty to develop a model of the optimum level of information provision. In so doing they tackle the thorny problem of how much information is enough and conclude that calls for decisions to be based upon full information are both infeasible and inconsistent with market decision-making. Munro and Hanley also provide a bridge between the philosophical tone of preceding chapters and the applied, statistical nature of the remaining chapters of Part II.

A large body of the CV literature focuses upon issues of bias such as framing effects, starting-point and anchoring, information effects, payment vehicle, elicitation methods, and rules of choice. In comparison to these, the issue of sampling design has received relatively little attention. Following the criteria set down by Mitchell and Carson (1989), a proportional or stratified random sample is often adopted without much thought to the spatial distribution of sampling points. The sample size in most CV studies is constrained by budget considerations; but effective sampling design requires a balance between the research issue, research costs, time, and the desired level of precision of the results. Consideration of survey cost, or the absence of a defined sampling frame, may concentrate a survey within certain geographical areas without consideration of the implications of such a strategy. In Chapter 10, KyeongAe Choe, William Parke, and Dale Whittington analyse the efficiency gains and losses from varying the number of sampling units (at either stage) in a two-stage stratified random sample, using Monte Carlo simulation. Their results suggest that increasing the number of geographic areas at the first stage of sampling whilst maintaining a specified sample size for the second stage will generate small marginal gains in statistical efficiency, whilst increasing the sample size at the second stage generates a predictable rate of gain in statistical efficiency irrespective of the number of geographic areas selected in the first stage.

The statistical theme is continued in Chapter 11, where Michael Hanemann and Barbara Kanninen address an impressive range of issues to produce what may well become a standard work concerning the statistical issue raised in dichotomous-choice CV research. The chapter opens with a consideration of the dual statistical and economic requirements of an adequate analytical model. Here topics include the integration of CV analyses with random utility models; the consideration of positive and negative preferences as well as states of indifference; and problems in common approaches to estimating welfare measures from CV data. The discussion then moves on to consider the problems of statistical estimation and design. Here Hanemann and Kanninen highlight fundamental concerns regarding the restrictions and suitability of certain commonly used statistical models and propose a number of alternatives which satisfy the criteria of optimal design. The chapter concludes with a suite of additional topics, ranging from a detailed consideration of non-response bias to an analysis of the strengths and weaknesses of using double-bounded elicitation methods.

From the broad spectrum of topics considered in the previous chapter, Ian Langford and Ian Bateman focus down upon a specific issue in Chapter 12, the separation of individual-level from response-level effects within CV surveys. However, the approach adopted for this investigation has considerably wider implications for the design and analysis of CV studies. Langford and Bateman use a multi-level modelling (MLM) approach to focus specifically upon the hierarchy of effects which are at play in any social survey. The MLM approach concentrates upon the variance in the model and divides it into variance due to individuals' personal characteristics (income, activities, etc.) and variance due to the bid amount asked of those individuals. The approach used is highly flexible and can be applied to a variety of CV-study designs, some of which are considered subsequently in Chapter 15.

Stated-preference (SP) techniques are similar in principle to a dichotomous-choice CV model: respondents state a preference for a good with a particular bundle of characteristics compared to the same good in which one or more characteristics have changed, along with price. Both techniques therefore use hypothetical markets; however, SP studies focus attention upon the separate parts of the bundle of characteristics which constitutes a specific good. SP models have been used most frequently in the field of transport planning, where they have determined values for time, convenience, comfort, etc. SP models, however, have only recently been applied to valuing environmental goods and services. In Chapter 13 Vic Adamowicz and colleagues compare the advantages and disadvantages of both SP and CV models within the context of valuing outdoor recreation. This chapter also provides an empirical link into Part III, wherein selected applications issues are considered.

While a number of chapters focus upon the problems associated with the notion of non-use or passive-use values, this does not mean that controversies regarding the longer-established concept of option value have been resolved. Dick Walsh and John McKean open Part III (Chapter 14) by reviewing the history of environmental option values, and formulating a more comprehensive model and welfare measure of option price as the sum of a payment for the indirect use of a resource, plus the payment for direct on-site use in an *ex ante* framework. Option as an access right is an essential part of a site visit, as is some indirect (anticipatory) use value generated during the process of thinking about and planning the trip. But the latter indirect-use values can exist without site visits for resource-related activities such as obtaining information from reading and watching television. Experimental economic techniques are applied to investigate the size and magnitude of option and anticipatory values for American wilderness, and the interaction between a possible site visit and an actual visit. Increasing the number of options available was found to shift the demand curve to the right for indirect use per site, whilst anticipatory values appear to increase at a decreasing rate holding sites visited constant. Future growth in the option price of recreation experience may result from increases in the value of indirect relative to direct use. It is clearly necessary to take option price into consideration in environmental valuation, otherwise too few resources may be devoted to environmental and resource protection.

Another long-standing debate in CV applications concerns the design of the WTP question and the effects of changing that design. Economists have for some time recognized drawbacks in the use of simple open-ended questions, and the bulk of recent studies have adopted variants of the dichotomous-choice approach. However, critics have argued that this merely exchanges one set of obvious biases for another suite of more subtle problems. In Chapter 15 Ian Bateman, Ian Langford, and Jon Rasbash review theoretical arguments concerning different elicitation methods and present an empirical test of a variety of these techniques. Approaches considered range from simple open-ended questions to complex, triple-bounded dichotomous-choice designs. While the impact of switching elicitation technique is shown to be substantial, the authors note that there are a variety of conflicting ways in which these findings may be interpreted and conclude that this remains an unresolved issue within the debate surrounding the validity of CV estimates.

The CV method has recently proved its worth in developing countries, where factors such as market distortions complicate shadow pricing exercises and the limited availability of housing market data prohibits the use of HP models of environmental attributes. Part III concludes with Chapter 16 by Donald Lauria, Dale Whittington, and colleagues, who describe one of the largest and most complicated CV surveys undertaken to date in a developing country. This study, which was funded by the World Bank, examines the crucial issue of household demand for improved sanitation services. The widespread lack of financial resources in developing countries constrains government subsidy and investment solutions to sanitation problems, and means beneficiaries have to pay a large proportion of the cost if sanitation services are to be provided. It is crucial, therefore, in the decision to provide improved sanitation services and for the financial profitability of the project that accurate and reliable information on household demand for sanitation services is obtained, namely how many households would respond if offered the opportunity to purchase improved sanitation services at a given price. International agencies often simply assume that households will be willing to pay some flat-rate amount proportion of annual income for water supply projects or for sanitation services. However, the study presented shows that such simple percentage-based measures are poor estimators of household WTP, in this case resulting in significant overestimates of benefit values. Whilst this study reveals a much lower WTP than previously assumed, casting doubt upon the viability of some infrastructure decisions, this does not mean that the households studied will never have piped water and sewerage treatment. Rather it is a question of investment timing as income levels increase and the demand for such services grows. The study also reveals the crucial importance of giving people time to think in responding to CV surveys and shows that this factor can have a significant impact upon WTP estimates.

Part IV concludes this volume with an appraisal of the institutional frameworks within which CV is applied. In Chapter 17 François Bonnieux and Pierre Rainelli consider the gradual but increasing application of CV within the decision-making processes of the European Union (EU). The last two decades have seen increasing public concern over increasing levels of pollution, loss of natural habitat, and environmental degradation in the EU, which have been translated into legislative action in many fields. Such legislation has often been driven by a BATNEEC approach (Best Available Technology Not Entailing Excessive Costs), so as to maintain competitiveness and financial efficiency, without any quantification of the benefits from environmental improvements. A considerable number of CV studies have been undertaken in the EU, of which a small number have influenced decisions and policies in individual member states. But there is a notable absence of guidance regarding the use of valuation techniques within decision-making at a EU level. However, the authors argue that ongoing efforts to reform the EU's Common Agricultural Policy, as well as new initiatives such as the recent Environmental Impact Assessment Directive, seem likely to result in a rise in the use of cost–benefit analysis, which may well increase the application of monetary appraisal techniques such as CV.

The EU experience is in stark contrast to the use of CV by Federal and State governments in the USA. This volume concludes with Chapter 18, in which John Loomis provides a review of the emergence of CV in the early 1960s, through its widespread adoption by the US Water Resources Council and US Army Corps of Engineers in the 1980s, to its central role in the estimation of natural resource damages in the CERCLA Act of 1980 and the Oil Pollution Act of 1990. As discussed in our opening comments, although subject to sustained attack by psychologists before and by other economists during the Exxon Valdez case, the NOAA Blue-Ribbon Panel concluded that carefully designed and implemented CV studies do convey useful information for judicial and administrative decisions regarding passive-use and existence values. As Loomis points out, not only did the recommendations of Arrow and others on the NOAA Panel raise the standards which CV must meet for policy and damage assessment purposes, but they also defined a detailed research agenda for the coming years. The debate regarding CV is therefore far from resolved.

REFERENCES

Arrow, K. J., Solow, R., Portney, P. R., Leamer, E. E., Radner, R., and Schuman, E. H. (1993), Report of the NOAA panel on contingent valuation, *Federal Register*, 58: 4602–14.

Bohm, P. (1972), 'Estimating Demand for Public Goods: An Experiment', *European Economic Review*, 3: 111–30.

Cambridge Economics, Inc. (1992), *Contingent Valuation: A Critical Assessment*, proceedings of a symposium held in Washington, 2–3 April 1992, Cambridge Economics, Inc., Cambridge, Mass.

Carson, R. T., Mitchell, R. C., Hanemann, W. M., Kopp, R. J., Presser, S., and Rudd, P. A. (1992), *A Contingent Valuation Study of Lost Passive Use Values Resulting from the Exxon Valdez Oil Spill*, Report to the Attorney General of the State of Alaska, Natural Resource Damage Assessment Inc., San Diego.

——Wright, J. L., Carson, N. J., Alberini, A., and Flores, N. E. (1995), *A Bibliography of Contingent Valuation Studies and Papers*, Natural Resource Damage Assessment Inc., San Diego.

Cummings, R. G., Brookshire, D. S., and Schulze, W. D. (eds.) (1986), *Valuing Public Goods: An Assessment of the Contingent Valuation Method*, Rowman and Allenheld, Totowa, NJ.

Dahlberg, A. (1974), *Geografisk rorlighet: sociala och ekonomiska effekter* (Geographic mobility: social and economic effects), Department of Economics, University of Umeå, Sweden (in Swedish).

Department of the Environment (1991), *Policy Appraisal and the Environment*, HMSO, London.

Diamond, P. A., and Hausman, J. A. (1994), 'Contingent Valuation: Is Some Number Better than No Number?' *Journal of Economic Perspectives*, 8(4): 45–64.

District of Columbia (1989), *Ohio* v. *Department of the Interior*, D.C. Cir., 880 F.2d 432.

Hanemann, W. M. (1991), 'Willingness to Pay and Willingness to Accept: How Much Can They Differ?' *American Economic Review*, 81: 635–47

——(1992), Preface, in S. Navrud (ed.), *Pricing the European Environment*, Scandinavian University Press, Oslo.

——(1994), 'Valuing the Environment through Contingent Valuation', *Journal of Economic Perspectives*, 8(4): 19–43.

Hausman, J. A. (1993), *Contingent Valuation: A Critical Assessment*, Elsevier Science Publishers, BV, Amsterdam.

Kahneman, D., and Knetsch, J. L. (1990), 'Valuing Public Goods: the Purchase of Moral Satisfaction', unpublished manuscript, University of California, Berkeley.

——and——(1992a), 'Valuing Public Goods: the Purchase of Moral Satisfaction', *Journal of Environmental Economics and Management*, 22: 57–70.

——and——(1992b), 'Contingent Valuation and the Value of Public Goods: Reply', *Journal of Environmental Economics and Management*, 22: 90–4.

——and Tversky, A. (1979), 'Prospect Theory: an Analysis of Decisions under Risk', *Econometrica*, 47: 263–91

Maki, A. W. (1991), 'The Exxon Oil Spill: Initial Environmental Impact Assessment', *Environmental Science and Technology*, 25: 24–9.

Mitchell, R. C., and Carson, R. T. (1989), *Using Surveys to Value Public Goods: The Contingent Valuation Method*, Resources for the Future, Washington.

Navrud, S. (ed.) (1992), *Pricing the European Environment*, Scandinavian University Press, Oslo.

Portney, P. R. (1994), 'The Contingent Valuation Debate: Why Economists Should Care', *Journal of Economic Perspectives*, 8(4): 3–17.

Randall, A., and Stoll, J. R. (1980), 'Consumer's Surplus in Commodity Space', *American Economic Review*, 70: 449–55

Scott, A. (1965), 'The Valuation of Game Resources: Some Theoretical Aspects', *Canadian Fisheries Report*, 4, Department of Fisheries of Canada, Ottawa, Ontario.

Smith, V. K. (1992), 'Arbitrary Values, Good Causes and Premature Verdicts', *Journal of Environmental Economics and Management*, 22: 71–89.

State of Utah (1992), *State of Utah* v. *Kennecott Corporation*, Memorandum Decision and Order, No. CIV 86–0902G, United States District Court, Utah.

Turner, R. K. Bateman, I. J., and Brooke J. S. (1992), 'Valuing the Benefits of Coastal Defence: a Case Study of the Aldeburgh Sea Defence Scheme', in A. Coker and C. Richards (eds.), *Valuing the Environment: Economic Approaches to Environmental Evaluation*, Belhaven Press, London, pp. 77–100.

Tversky, A., and Kahneman, D. (1991), 'Loss Aversion in Riskless Choice: a Reference Dependent Model', *Quarterly Journal of Economics*, 106: 1039–61.

Whittington, D., Briscoe, J., Mu, X., and Barron, W. (1990), 'Estimating the Willingness to Pay for Water Services in Developing Countries: a Case Study of the

Use of Contingent Valuation Surveys in Southern Haiti', *Economic Development and Cultural Change*, 38: 293–311.

Whittington, D., Lauria, D., Wright, A., Choe, K., Hughes, J. A., and Venkateswarlu, S. (1992), *Household Demand for Improved Sanitation Services: A Case Study of Kumasi, Chana*, Water and Sanitation Report 3, UNDP Water and Sanitation Program, World Bank, Washington.

PART I

Theory

2

The Place of Economic Values in Environmental Valuation

R. KERRY TURNER

2.1. INTRODUCTION

While the scale and severity of environmental problems continue to grow (it is now commonplace to refer to these environmental pressures and damage costs as part of the 'global environmental change' process) the deployment of scarce resources to mitigate these negative trends via environmental conservation highlights a fundamental valuation question. How much environmental conservation should there be, and therefore what is nature's value? Conventional economics couches its answer in terms of human individual preferences for particular things (including the environment) and the argument that something is of instrumental value to the extent that some individual is willing to pay for the satisfaction of a preference. Underlying this approach is the axiomatic assumption that individuals almost always make choices (express their preferences) which benefit (directly or indirectly) themselves or enhance their welfare. Utilizing a cost–benefit approach, economists then argue that nature conservation benefits should be valued and compared with the relevant costs. Conservation measures should only be adopted if it can be demonstrated that they generate net economic benefits.

Some environmentalists (including a minority of economists), on the other hand, either claim that nature has non-anthropocentric intrinsic value and non-human species possess moral interests or rights, or that while all values are anthropocentric and usually (but not always) instrumental the economic approach to environmental valuation is only a partial approach. These environmentalist positions lead to the advocacy of environmental sustainability standards or constraints, which to some extent obviate the need for the valuation of specific components of the environment. Taking the polar case, some ecocentrists seem to be arguing that all environmental resources should be conserved regardless of the costs of such a strategy, i.e. that environmental assets are infinitely valuable and the environmental standards are absolute (Hargrove, 1992).

In this chapter we first examine various aspects of the environmental values debate in the wider context of the sustainable economic development strategy and goal. We then set out an expanded values classification in order to define the limits of the conventional environmental economics concept of total economic value (use plus non-use values). Particular attention is paid to the definition and measurement of bequest and existence values, as well as to some recent findings in the newly emerging 'ecological economics' literature which have implications for resource systems valuation (Perrings *et al.*, 1995). We conclude with some environmental conservation policy implications.

2.2. SUSTAINABLE ECONOMIC DEVELOPMENT

Figure 2.1 portrays the sustainability debate in terms of four overlapping sustainability positions (world-views) which encompass both technocentric (left-hand side) and ecocentric (right-hand side) views (Turner, 1993). Broadly speaking, technocentrists are optimistic about the extent of current and future substitution possibilities between different forms of capital (including environmental resources) and therefore believe that the economic growth process will probably not be overly constrained by either absolute or relative resource scarcities. They also assume that individual utility functions are smooth, signifying extensive substitution between human wants. Eco-centrists, on the other hand, believe that 'limits' to growth are already, or will shortly become, binding. They point out that the waste assimilation capacity provided by the environment is showing signs of 'stress', as are other of the regulatory systems, e.g. climate control and nutrient cycling. This type of environmental 'resource' is not substitutable and must therefore be protected by environmental standards and regulations. Social limits to growth may also be significant. Ecocentrists tend to refer to human needs, rather than wants, and emphasize the lack of substitution between different needs. Finally, they are not satisfied with utilitarian ethics and wish to see this constrained or replaced by equity-based rules, or other ethical rules which recognize the interests and rights of non-human nature.

Weak sustainability requires the maintenance of the total capital stock—composed of K_m (manufactured or reproducible capital); K_h (human capital, or the stock of knowledge and skills); K_n (natural capital: exhaustible and renewable resources, together with environmental structures, functions, and services)—through time with the implicit assumption of infinite substitution possibilities between all forms of capital. The Hartwick Rule (Hartwick, 1978) is also used to buttress the weak-sustainability position by regulating the intergenerational capital bequests. The rule lays down that the rent obtained from the exploitation of the natural capital stock by the current generation should be reinvested as reproducible capital which forms the future generations' inheritance. This inheritance transfer should be at a sufficient level to guarantee non-declining real consumption (well-being) through time.

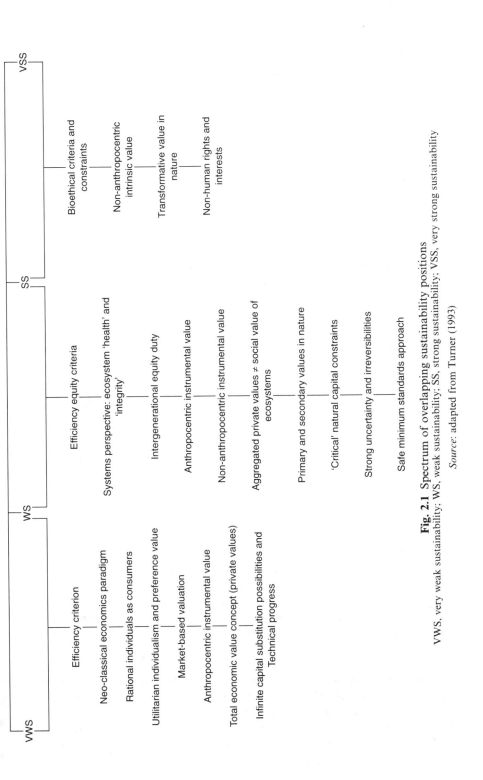

Fig. 2.1 Spectrum of overlapping sustainability positions

VWS, very weak sustainability; WS, weak sustainability; SS, strong sustainability; VSS, very strong sustainability

Source: adapted from Turner (1993)

The implicit capital substitutability assumption underpins the further argument that extensive scope exists over time for the decoupling of economic activity and environmental impact. The decoupling process is mediated by technical progress and innovation. While total decoupling is not possible, and with the important exception of cumulative pollution, society's use of resources can be made more efficient over time (i.e. the amount of resources used per unit of GNP goes down faster than GNP goes up and the aggregate environmental impact falls). From the weak-sustainability perspective a key requirement will therefore be increased efficiency in research and development, i.e. new knowledge properly embodied in people, technology, and institutions.

From the strong-sustainability perspective some elements of the natural capital stock cannot be replaced (except on a very limited basis) by man-made capital and therefore there is a concern to avoid irreversible losses of environmental assets. Some of the functions and services of ecosystems in combination with the abiotic environment are essential to human survival; they are life-support services (e.g. biogeochemical cycles) and cannot be replaced. Other multi-functional ecological assets are at least essential to human well-being if not to eventual human survival (e.g. landscape, space, and relative peace and quiet). We might therefore designate those ecological assets which are essential in either sense as being 'critical natural capital' (Pearce *et al.*, 1990). Supporters of the 'deep ecology' very strong sustainability position argue for a particular type of non-substitutability based on an ethical rejection of the trade-off between man-made and natural capital. The strong-sustainability rule therefore requires that we at least protect critical natural capital and ensure that it is part of the capital bequest.

2.3. INSTRUMENTAL AND INTRINSIC VALUE IN NATURE

The term 'valuing the environment' means different things to different people depending on which of the world-views in Figure 2.1 they find acceptable. Economists have generally settled for a taxonomy of total environmental value, interpreted as 'total economic value' (TEV), which distinguishes between use values and a remainder, termed non-use value. TEV has, however, been the subject of much debate among environmental economists and others, and also provides the fuzzy boundary with alternative concepts of environmental value.

Put simply, non-use value covers situations in which individuals who do not make use, or intend to make use, of any given environmental asset or attribute would nevertheless feel a 'loss' if such things were to disappear. They may just wish to see various environmental entities conserved 'in their own right' (termed existence value); or conservation may be supported on the basis of retaining options and opportunities for one's children, grandchildren, and future generations beyond (termed bequest value). But on closer inspection the non-use category does not have well-defined boundaries. This is because the existence-value component can be defined in a variety of ways to include a range of possible motivations, some of which are 'outside' the scope of conventional utilitarian economic thought.

It turns out that the TEV taxonomy can itself be encompassed, in principle, by a more general valuation typology, containing four separate forms of value in relation to environmental resources (see Table 2.1). The four categories of value are distinguished in terms of their anthropocentric or

Table 2.1   A General Value Typology

---

1. *Anthropocentric Instrumental Value*

This is equivalent to

'total economic value' = use + non-use value. The non-use category is bounded by the existence value concept, which has itself been the subject of much debate. Existence value may therefore encompass some or all of the following motivations:

  i. intragenerational altruism: resource conservation to ensure availability for others; vicarious use value linked to self-interested altruism and the 'warm glow' effect of purchased moral satisfaction;
 ii. intergenerational altruism (bequest motivation and value): resource conservation to ensure availability for future generations;
iii. stewardship motivation: human responsibilities for resource conservation on behalf of all nature; this motivation may be based on the belief that non-human resources have rights and/or interests and as far as possible should be left undisturbed.

If existence value is defined to include stewardship then it will overlap with the next value category outlined below.

2. *Anthropocentric Intrinsic Value*

This value category is linked to stewardship in a subjectivist sense of the term 'value'. It is culturally dependent. The value attribution is to entities which have a 'sake' or 'goods of their own', and instrumentally use other parts of nature for their own intrinsic ends. It remains an anthropocentrically related concept because it is still a human valuer that is ascribing intrinsic value to non-human nature.

3. *Non-Anthropocentric Instrumental Value*

In this value category entities are assumed to have sakes or goods of their own independent of human interests. It also encompasses the good of collective entities, e.g. ecosystems, in a way that is *not* irreducible to that of its members.

But this category may not demand moral considerability as far as humans are concerned.

4. *Non-Anthropocentric Intrinsic Values*

This value category is viewed in an objective value sense, i.e. 'inherent worth' in nature, the value that an object possesses independently of the valuation of valuers. It is a meta-ethical claim, and usually involves the search for strong rules or trump cards with which to constrain anthropocentric instrumental values and policy.

Source: adapted from Hargrove (1992).

non-anthropocentric basis and by their instrumental or intrinsic characteristic. Existence value (as variously defined in the literature) seems to overlap the anthropocentric instrumental value and anthropocentric intrinsic value categories. As one crosses this philosophical boundary the conventional economic notions of utility and welfare cease to always retain their 'accepted' relationship, i.e. if welfare is increased, utility increases. We take a closer look at existence value and 'pure' altruistic motivations in Section 2.4.2. For now, we merely emphasize the finding that total environmental value (TV) is not necessarily equivalent to TEV; much depends on the specific world-view one adopts prior to the valuation exercise. Figure 2.1 summarizes some of the main valuation concepts and assumptions, as well as policy principles that characterize the different world-views within environmentalism.

The typology distinguishes between two types of instrumental value and two types of intrinsic value in nature. Both forms of instrumental value (i.e. of use to humans—categories 1 and 3 in Table 2.1) are not in themselves controversial, but a substantial debate has been in progress for some time over the meaning and significance of intrinsic value in nature (Turner and Pearce, 1993; Pearce, 1994; Turner et al., 1994). Instrumental values are relative and usually linked to individuals and their preferences or needs (category 1 in Table 2.1). The economic message is therefore that if more biodiversity conservation, for example, is chosen, then the opportunity to satisfy other preferences or needs is foreclosed. So all resource-allocation policy decisions incur opportunity costs (i.e. forgone alternative options). Thus the instrumental value of biodiversity is not absolute; it is relative and as such can be balanced (in a cost–benefit assessment) against other 'good' things or 'worthy' causes that individuals may want to use or support.

Some environmental philosophers (bioethicists) have usually interpreted intrinsic value as 'inherent worth' (category 4 in Table 2.1) and as such completely separate from the human–environment valuation relationship. According to this position non-human biota, and perhaps even non-sentient things, have moral interests or rights to existence. An extreme version of bioethics would make environmental rights absolute and therefore not open to trade-offs, on the basis of a 'deep ecology' meta-ethical principle (Rolston, 1988).

It is not, however, necessary to ascribe absolute value to environmental conservation/preservation in order to provide more safeguards against biodiversity and other environmental loss than currently exist. Such extra safeguards could be justified in terms of 'Q-altruism' motivations (value category 2 in Table 2.1) (Randall, 1991; Randall and Stoll, 1991). Here moral principles recognizing the 'interests' of non-human species and their supporting habitats could be used to buttress a case for extra, but not unlimited, sacrifices incurred to better safeguard biodiversity. The values expressed are still anthropocentric but relate to intrinsic qualities in nature.

Existence value therefore derives from individuals who feel a benefit from just knowing that a particular species, habitat, or ecosystem does exist and will continue to exist somewhere on the planet. According to some analysts, the economic literature which seeks to appropriately define and measure existence value as part of a comprehensive valuation framework has arrived at a consensus view that both use value and non-use value can be distinguished formally using standard welfare measures from neo-classical economic theory (Larson, 1993). Other analysis highlight the differences that have emerged in the literature (Lant, 1994). It seems to us that if there is such a consensus it is only in a restricted context. We take a closer look at existence value motivations in a later section.

A number of writers also seem to agree that existence value can only be measured by survey methods (such as contingent valuation). Since existence values involve neither personal consumption of derived products nor *in situ* contact, economists have used a special structure of preferences to model existence value. They have assumed either so-called 'weak separability' or 'strong separability' between the non-market good that is the subject of existence value and market goods. When preferences take these forms, the non-market good cannot be identified via conventional market demand theory and analysis. Existence value of the non-market good cannot therefore be measured by indirect observation of individuals' behaviour, and the only option is direct questioning via surveys.

Larson (1993) has questioned some of this consensus thinking and in particular argues that in a number of real-world choice situations neither 'weak' nor 'strong' separability assumptions are very realistic. Instead it is likely in a number of situations that changes in the level of the public good will give rise to existence value that is traceable in principle from observed changes in behaviour (spending money and/or time in reading about or protesting in some way about the environmental change, e.g. species or habitat loss or degradation). It remains to be seen whether valuation techniques other than contingent valuation can adequately capture aspects of existence value. Some economists and many non-economists also question whether in practice contingent valuation methods can yield reliable measures of existence value. The methods are both expensive and demanding on researchers if acceptable reliability and validity testing protocols are to be met.

Bequest motivations underpinned by an intergenerational equity concern would add further support to biodiversity conservation enhancement—see Figure 2.1. From the strong-sustainability position, both existence and bequest value could be better conserved by the adoption of the principle of a safe minimum standard—a sufficient area of habitat to be conserved to ensure the continued provision of ecological functions and services at the ecosystem 'landscape' level—unless the social costs of doing so are 'unacceptably' high (Bishop, 1978; Perrings and Pearce, 1994). A further principle, the precautionary principle, would, if adopted, ensure the recognition of bequest motivations and value. In essence, this principle lays down that the opportunity set for future generations can only be assured if the level of, for example, biodiversity they inherit is no less than that available to present generations. So some sort of 'inheritance' is passed, 'intact', across time. This bequest will take the form of a stock of human, physical, and natural capital (Pearce *et al.*, 1989).

To recap, we have argued that the motivations behind non-use value are some combination of: individuals' perceived benefits; altruism towards friends, relatives, or others who may be users (vicarious use value); altruism towards future generations of users (bequest value); and altruism toward non-human nature in general (existence value) (see Table 2.1). But several questions remain to be fully answered, including what precisely is meant by altruistic motives and behaviour and which values are instrumental and which could be intrinsic. We do not yet have anything like a full picture of the mutually exclusive set of motivations underlying individual preferences for environmental goods.

The largely philosophical debate over the need for and composition of an adequate environmental ethic has become rather sterile. This is the case because the discussion has focused on instrumental value (category 1 in Table 2.1) versus non-anthropocentric intrinsic value (category 4 in Table 2.1) in nature, i.e. relative versus absolute valuations. In the real world of pragmatic policy-making the instrumental–intrinsic distinction is only usefully maintained if it is interpreted solely in an anthropocentric (human-centred) way, i.e. discussion of value categories 1 and 2. Thus a case for environmental conservation should be supported not only on the grounds of the significant amount of human instrumental value that is at stake, but also because this allows society to set things aside (Pearce *et al.*, 1990; Turner, 1993) and exempt them from use. According to Hargrove (1992) this would reflect 'our desire as individuals, as a society, and as a historically evolved culture to value some things noninstrumentally and to set them aside and protect them from exploitation'.

It is also the case that when we consider the value of whole environmental systems, the conventional economic valuation may not be sufficient. What we need to assess and conserve is the structural and functional value of 'healthy' evolving ecosystems, despite the formidable uncertainties surrounding likely thresholds for system change. The fundamental life-support services provided by a 'healthy' ecosystem have a 'prior' value in the sense that the continued existence of this system 'integrity' determines the flow of all the instrumental and intrinsic values (actual and potential) connected to components of the system (see Figure 2.1). A rough approximation of the significance of this 'primary' ecosystem value may be indirectly gained by deployment of 'damage avoidance', 'substitute service', or 'replacement cost' methods (Turner and Pearce, 1993; Gren *et al.*, 1994). We take a more detailed look at the primary value idea in a Section 2.5.

2.4. VALUES AND MOTIVATIONS

2.4.1. Bequest values and motivation

While individual motivations are not generally explicitly addressed in conventional economic analysis, they are a particular point of focus in the sustainability debate. This is especially the case when bequest and existence values are under examination and the provision of the underlying environmental public goods cannot be adequately explained by the neo-classical theory of self-interest. What seems clear to some strong-sustainability supporters is that the model of human behaviour that supports conventional economics is too simplistic and needs refinement through observations of actual behaviour. There is a need for more interdisciplinary and transdisciplinary experimental work (both in the laboratory and in the 'field') in order to gain a better understanding of the 'cognitive black box of behaviour' (Shogren and Nowell, 1992).

From the conventional economics perspective ('weak-sustainability' positions in Figure 2.1) pervasive market failure connected to the provision of environmental goods and services is a recognized problem. Corrective action should take the form of 'proper' resource pricing. Efficiency prices are therefore seen as an essential element in the sustainable development process. This valuation theory is based on the familiar assumption that households maximize utility subject to an income constraint while choosing a bundle of market and non-market goods, and that willingness to pay (WTP) is a function of prices, income, and household tastes and conditioning variables such as household size, environmental attitudes, etc. The anchor points for weak sustainability therefore are: utilitarian philosophy, individualism (consumer sovereignty), and instrumental anthropocentrism.

Utilitarianism and its practical counterpart cost-benefit analysis have, however, some possible ethical drawbacks. Efficiency prices are conditional upon the prevailing distribution of income and wealth in society (intragenerational equity concern). If this distribution is not considered appropriate then efficiency prices can be questioned as allocation guide-lines. Supporters of the weak sustainability position tend to side-step the equity issue. As far as equity over generational time is concerned, their faith in the power of technical change and its induced substitution possibilities allows weak-sustainability advocates to claim that future generations will almost certainly be better off than the present generation.

Supporters of strong-sustainability positions are more reticent about capital substitution and emphasize the uncertainty and irreversibility characteristics of much environmental degradation and loss processes. They argue, for example, that the utility and welfare impacts of biodiversity loss and consequent ecological degradation are not distributed equally. They put

equity and actual compensation overtly at the core of the sustainable development strategy. In the intragenerational context their main concern is that
the poorest individuals and countries often face the largest relative losses
from biodiversity depletion and ecosystem degradation. Many low- and
lower-middle-income developing countries display a high degree of resource
dependency (both in their domestic economic activities and their export
trade) (Barbier, 1994). For most low-income economies a sustainable development path requires careful management of the natural resource base so
that natural capital is not overdepreciated and future economic progress
inhibited. A further worrying trend in developing economies is the concentration of the poorest groups in 'ecologically fragile' zones—areas where
environmental damage threatens economic welfare (Barbier *et al.*, 1994). It is
clear that the economic livelihoods and welfare of the poorest income groups
in low-potential areas are at greater risk from increasing environmental
degradation and biodiversity loss. Because the underprinning ecosystems
in these areas are relatively less resilient and stable, then the problems of
threshold effects, ecosystem collapse, and scarce resources may be particularly severe for these poor households.

But it is equally clear that any change in biodiversity and/or pollution
loadings that affect ecological functioning and resilience also has implications for future generations. The conversion and modification of ecosystems
by the current generation may actually mean 'less' biodiversity and waste
assimilation capacity available for future generations. It is even conceivable
that the actions of the present generation in this context are pushing future
generations inevitably towards the 'minimum' or 'threshold' level of biodiversity necessary to maintain welfare and even existence. The current
generation may be making future generations unavoidably worse off by
reducing their economic opportunities set. The world may be experiencing
greater ecological scarcity, with one of the implications being that future
generations will face a significantly increased cost burden in order to maintain ecosystem function and service provision.

The equity questions and considerations raised by the biodiversity
loss and pollution problems point to fundamental ethical motivations
(altruistic behaviour and bequest motivations and value) and concerns
over sustainable economic development. According to the Brundtland
Report, 'Humanity has the ability to make developments sustainable—to
ensure that it meets the needs of the present without compromising the
ability of future generations to meet their own needs' (WCED, 1987). If
the desirability of the goal of sustainable development is accepted then
society must develop economically and socially in such a way that it minimizes the effects of its activities, whose costs are borne by the poorest
members of the present generation and by future generations. In cases
where the activities and significant effects are unavoidable, the poor today
and future generations must be compensated for any costs they incur. The

central rationale for sustainable development is therefore to increase peo-ple's standard of living (broadly defined) and, in particular, the well-being of the least advantaged people in societies, while at the same time avoiding uncompensated future costs (Pearce *et al.*, 1989; Daly and Cobb, 1989; Turner, 1993).

The mechanism by which the current generation can ensure that the future is compensated, and is not therefore worse off, is through the transfer of capital bequests. Capital (including natural biodiversity and other capital) provides the opportunity and capability to generate well-being through the creation of material goods and environmental goods and services that give human life its meaning. More specifically, if intergenerational equity is accepted as an objective (and therefore bequest motivations and value are taken to exist and be important) the present generation is required to ensure that the health, diversity, resilience, and productivity of natural systems is maintained or enhanced for the benefit of future generations.

The intergenerational equity goal can be achieved by strategies aimed at fostering an efficient, diversified, and ecologically sustainable economy; by maintaining natural capital stocks, and in particular 'critical' natural capital that is non-substitutable and therefore whose loss is irreversible (i.e. a 'constant capital' rule); by adopting safe minimum standards and the pre-cautionary principle which suggests 'risk-averse' behaviour in the face of uncertainty and lack of full scientific knowledge; and finally by adopting policies that enhance ecological, social, and economic diversity so that the next generation is left with an equivalent resource endowment (allowing for some trading between different forms of capital) and opportunities for social and economic activity (Young, 1992, 1993).

For many commentators traditional ethical reasoning is faced with a number of challenges in the context of the sustainable development debate. Very strong sustainability thinking takes a systems perspective, which demands an approach that privileges the requirements of the system above those of the individual. This will involve ethical judgements about the role and rights of present individual humans as against the system's survival and therefore the welfare of future generations. We have also already argued that the poverty focus of sustainability highlights the issue of intragenerational fairness and equity.

So 'concern for others' is an important issue in the debater. Given that individuals are, to a greater or lesser extent, self-interested and greedy, sustainability analysts explore the extent to which such behaviour could be modified and how to achieve the modification (Turner, 1988; Pearce, 1992). Some argue that a stewardship ethic (weak anthropocentrism; Norton, 1987) is sufficient for sustainability, i.e. people should be less greedy because other people (including the world's poor and future generations) matter and greed imposes costs on these other people. Bioethicists would argue that people should also be less greedy because other living things matter and greed imposes costs on these other non-human species and things. This would be stewardship on behalf of the planet itself (Gaianism) in various forms up to 'deep ecology' (Naess, 1973).

The ethical argument at the core of the intergenerational equity proposition is that future generations have a right to expect an inheritance (capital bequest) sufficient to allow them the capacity to generate for themselves a level of well-being no less than that enjoyed by the current generation. The requirement is therefore for an intergenerational social contract that guarantees the future the same 'opportunities' that were open to the past. Philosophers have put forward two ethical positions which can be seen as supportive of the constant capital rule. The first is known as the 'Lockean standard' view, after the philosopher John Locke. This lays down that each generation should leave 'enough and as good for others'. A more modern view, known as the 'justice as opportunity' view, holds that the present generation does not have a right to deplete the economic and other opportunities afforded by the resource base. Since the resource base cannot literally be passed on 'intact', what is proposed is that future generations are owed compensation for any reduction (caused by the current generation) in their access to easily extracted and conveniently located natural resources. If justice is to prevail, the future's loss of productive potential must be compensated for (Page, 1982; Pasek, 1992).

Bequest value may be particularly significant for populations local to an ecosystem or natural environment who currently enjoy many of its benefits. Such individuals tend to want to see their way of life or intimate association with the ecosystem ('a sense of place') passed on to their heirs and future generations in general.

2.4.2   Existence value and motivations

There is a growing body of evidence to suggest that some of the basic conventional economic axioms are systematically violated by humans in controlled conditions and in their everyday life—in particular, the transitivity axiom (the preference reversal phenomenon) (Lichtenstein and Slovic, 1971; Grether and Plott, 1979). This phenomenon is usually interpreted as evidence of non-transitivity of preferences (Loomes and Sugden, 1983). Loomes *et al.* (1989) have argued that regret theory can explain such reversals, but they have also been explained as the result of: differences between individuals' responses to choice and valuation problems (Slovic and Lichtenstein, 1983); the devices used by experimenters to elicit valuations; and the 'random lottery selection' incentives system (Holt, 1986; Karni and Safra, 1987; Segal, 1988) Nevertheless, recent experimental work, controlling for experimental design shortcomings, has confirmed the existence of systematic violations of transitivity. Further, the pattern of violation was found to be consistent with regret theory (Loomes *et al.*, 1991).

Other analysis suggests that utility is assigned to gains or losses relative to a reference point, not states of wealth; that there is loss aversion and that choices and values are systematically influenced by alternative means of framing one and the some problem (Kahneman and Tversky, 1979). These are important complications for non-market economic valuation research to confront. The type of environmental resource involved and the actual valuation context are also very significant factors in any valuation exercise. Thus the reference operating condition 'familiarity with the good' needs considerable formal clarification in the light of evidence that suggests individuals engage in 'incomplete optimization' and are subject to 'preference learning'. Thus it may well be that individuals find it difficult to predict their future tastes; they rely on past experiences but in a very imperfect and selective way, and thereby violate the economic rationality paradigm.

Existence and, to a lesser extent, bequest values are likely to play an increasingly important role in environmental management decisions (such as biodiversity conservation and ambient environmental quality improvements). Therefore better data on human motivations and the interpretation of contingent valuation questions is urgently required. Without a proper theory of motivations contingent valuation value estimates may mislead policy-makers (Stevens *et al.*, 1991). Kahneman and Knetsch (1992*a, b*), for example, argue that some apparently altruistic motivations involved in contributing to public goods involve improvements in an individual's welfare and therefore altruism is really the purchase of moral satisfaction, the 'warm glow effect', and deep down is a self-regarding motivation—'enlightened self-interest' (Andreoni, 1990). In these cases, contingent valuation bids will not, they argue, reflect the inherent economic value of the environmental public good (for a critical review of the Kahneman and Knetsch position, see Harrison, 1992).

Evidence is also lacking over the behaviour of existence values for environmental assets over time (temporal stability) (Loomis, 1989; Reiling *et al.*, 1990). Currently it would seem that such values are relatively stable over periods of a few years but longer-term evidence is not available (Stevens *et al.*, 1994).

Andreoni (1990) has shown that, in the public goods context, individual WTP could be related both to the amount contributed towards the provision of the public good and to the degree of social approval an individual perceives to be associated with making such a contribution (probably relative to some average contribution). Part of the individual motivation is therefore a 'warm glow' effect connected to the act of giving. Some individuals may be wholly motivated by warm glow, others entirely by the value of the public goods, and some may derive utility from both sources ('impure altruism'). Thus value estimates derived from contingent valuation surveys will not necessarily indicate economic surplus value derived from the public good under test.

The notion of social approval can be extended into a concept of the 'social interest' and the holding by an individual of social preferences separate from self-interested private preferences. Margolis (1982), for example, posits two separate concerns—self-interest and social or group interest—that underline human motivation. The origin of social interest may be explained by theories of reciprocal altruism, or mutual coercion, or by sociobiological factors (Sen, 1977; Elster, 1989; and Wilson, 1987, respectively). In the Margolis model individuals allocate income between social and private preferences so as to be seen to be doing their 'fair share' for the provision of collective social welfare. The contingent valuation WTP estimate may be more a personal judgement about socially acceptable fair shares than the inherent economic value of the environmental resource in question.

The Margolis analysis strains the bounds of enlightened self-interest, i.e. even though individuals make trade-offs between social and private interests, their behaviour may still be motivated by ethical preferences for justice and fairness. Nevertheless, it still seems that 'pure altruism' is not captured, and existence value interpreted as anthropocentric intrinsic value of nature seems to require such a motive. This value component does not make the agent better off (in economic welfare terms) and requires a moral 'commitment' (Sen, 1977) which is not in any way related to self-interest.

Commitment can be defined in terms of a person choosing an act that he believes will yield a lower level of personal welfare to him than an alternative that is also available to him. The person does not directly desire to reduce their own welfare, but adherence to one's moral commitments will be as important as personal economic welfare-maximization and may conflict with it. Thus the human valuer recognizes an intrinsic 'moral resource' value in non-human nature and is prepared to give up scarce resources to conserve such nature even though no use or *in situ* contact is contemplated. They are also unlikely to accept compensation for the loss of environmental resources, especially if the resources have the characteristics of uniqueness and non-substitutability. Thus some zero bids in contingent valuation surveys are protest bids related to ethical commitments, or a related refusal to link nature conservation and money expenditure (Stevens *et al.*, 1991). Some individuals may therefore exhibit lexicographic preferences (violating the axiom of utility function continuity) when faced with the loss of some environmental resource such as, for example, a particular species of animal.

Sagoff (1988) has sought to make a clear distinction between the individual's role as a consumer and as a citizen. As a citizen the individual only and separately considers the benefits or disbenefits of a policy, project, or course of action to the society (usually national, but in some contexts increasingly on a global basis) as a whole. The citizen is guided in his or her deliberations by 'ethical rationality', which is underpinned by sentiment and by historical, cultural, ideological, and other motivations and values. Most environmental valuation contexts are relevant to the citizen part of the 'dual self' and not to the consumer. Aggregate WTP is therefore an inappropriate measure of 'environmental worth' and economics plays no significant role in the political process of environmental standards setting and commitment.

But Sagoff seems to push the case, based on intuition and constructed examples, too far. Public budgets are always limited and social opportunity costs relating to allocation decisions are always present. Therefore the citizen's deliberation process will include economic considerations alongside others. Once environmental standards have been set, of course, social opportunity costs valuations are required. More fundamentally, is it really the case that the consumer/citizen distinction is absolutely clear-cut? Some experimental evidence indicates that even in the context of market transactions some individuals refuse to trade or accept rewards if they perceive the operating conditions are 'unfair'.

Stevens *et al.* (1994) have recently tested a decomposed WTP function related to the public's WTP for bald eagles in the USA. They used the following function: They used the following function:

$$WTP = f(D, GC, FS, EQ, RV, X)$$

where D = duty; GC = good cause; FS = fair share; EQ = general environmental quality; RV = resource value and X = vector of socio-economic characteristics.

Test results indicate that WTP does include a payment for joint products such as fairness and not just inherent resource value. They conclude that fair-share payment might be interpreted as a lower bound of resource value but payment for a 'good cause' (i.e. environmental quality in general) provides little indication of resource value. They also note that decomposition of WTP will still not provide a satisfactory measure of Hicksian surplus value if embedding is a pervasive characteristic of the CV process.

The distinction between the individual as a citizen and as a consumer is not an either/or issue, but is more properly interpreted to mean that humans play a multidimensional role. As citizens, individuals are influenced by held values, attitudes; and beliefs about public-type goods and their provision. In this context, property rights (actual and/or perceived), social choices; and moral concerns can all be involved in a conflict situation (e.g. nature conservation versus development). Contingent valuation studies deployed in order to help policy-makers resolve or mitigate the conflict would tend to be constrained by bias problems and 'protest' bidding by significant numbers of survey respondents. Some future research effort may therefore be usefully reorientated towards the design and testing of referendum-type surveys (Common *et al.* 1993).

In a dichotomous-choice referendum format, the survey would operate like a sophisticated opinion poll. Bid values could be selected to reflect different estimates of the actual opportunity costs of conserving some environmental asset. Individual respondents would be asked to vote on these actual costs at stake, or in terms of a reallocation of public expenditure. This approach would not provide willingness-to-pay estimates in terms of consumer surplus value and would not therefore provide data directly commensurate with standard cost–benefit analysis. However, it would provide policy-relevant allocative choice information which could complement other analysis results (Blamey, 1995).

2.5. ECOSYSTEM VALUATION: JOINTLY DETERMINED ECONOMIC AND ENVIRONMENTAL SYSTEMS

The economic valuation literature indicates that the economic production function approach is a fruitful way to elicit direct and indirect use values of environmental systems. Indirect (revealed-preference) methods fit into this approach and have been used to estimate recreation/family use values. Direct (stated-preference) methods such as contingent valuation have proved to be more controversial but the balance of evidence, in the context of use values, does seem to be favourable for a fairly extensive range of environmental goods (Farber and Costanza, 1989; Turner, 1991; Barbier, 1993, 1994). The estimation of non-use values is, as we have shown, much more complex. Limited pioneering work with conjoint analysis (contingent ranking and/or contingent choice) offers the prospect of more progress in non-use valuation. The contingent-choice format is likely to be more acceptable to economists than the ranking procedure (Adamowicz *et al.*, 1994; see also Chapter 13).

Recent advances in the development of ecological economic models and theory all seem to stress the importance of the overall system, as opposed to individual components of that system. This points to another dimension of total environmental value, the value of the system itself. The economy and the environment are now jointly determined systems linked in a process of coevolution, with the scale of economic activity exerting significant environmental pressure. The dynamics of the jointly determined system are characterized by discontinuous change around poorly understood critical threshold values. But under the stress and shock of change the joint systems exhibit resilience, i.e. the ability of the system to maintain its self-organization while suffering stress and shock. This resilience capacity is however related more to overall system configuration and stability properties than it is to the stability of individual resources.

The adoption of a systems perspective serves to re-emphasize the obvious but fundamental point that economic systems are underpinned by ecological systems and not vice versa. There is a dynamic interdependency between economy and ecosystem. The properties of biophysical systems are part of the set of constraints which bound economic activity. The constraints set has its own internal dynamics which react to economic activity exploiting environmental assets (extraction, harvesting, waste disposal, non-consumptive users). Feedbacks then occur which influence economic and social relationships. The evolution of the economy and the evolution of the constraints set are interdependent; 'coevolution' is thus a crucial concept (Common and Perrings, 1992).

Norton and Ulanowicz (1992) advocate a hierarchical approach to natural systems (which assumes that smaller subsystems change according to a faster dynamic than do larger encompassing systems) as a way of conceptualizing problems of scale in determining biodiversity policy. For them, the goal of sustaining biological diversity over multiple human generations can only be achieved if biodiversity policy is operated at the landscape level. The value of individual species, then, is mainly in their contribution to a larger dynamic, and significant financial expenditure may not always be justified to save ecologically marginal species. A central aim of policy should be to protect as many species as possible, but not all.

Ecosystem health (stability and resilience or creativity), interpreted in terms of an intuitive guide, is useful in that it helps focus attention on the larger systems in nature and away from the special interests of individuals and groups (ibid.). The full range of public and private instrumental and non-instrumental values all depend on protection of the processes that support the health of larger-scale ecological systems. Thus when a wetland, for example, is disturbed or degraded, we need to look at the impacts of the disturbance on the larger level of the landscape. A successful policy will encourage a patchy landscape.

The 'integrity' of an ecosystem is more than its capacity to maintain autonomous functioning (its health); it also relates to the retention of 'total diversity', i.e. the species and interrelationships that have survived over time at the landscape level (Norton, 1992). A number of ecological services and functions can be valued in economic terms, while others cannot because of uncertainty and complexity conditions. Taking wetlands as our example, these systems provide a wide array of functions, services, and goods of significant value to society—storm and pollution buffering function, flood alleviation, recreation and aesthetic services, etc. We can therefore conceive of 'valuing' a wetland as essentially valuing the characteristics of a system, and we can capture these values in our TEV framework. But since it is the case that the component parts of a system are contingent on the existence and contributed proper functioning of the whole, then putting an aggregate value on wetlands and other ecosystems is quite a complicated matter.

Private economic values may not capture the full contribution of component species and processes to the aggregate life-support functions provided by ecosystems (Gren et al., 1994). Furthermore, some ecologists argue that some of the underlying structure and functions of ecological systems which are prior to the ecological production functions cannot be taken into account in terms of economic values. Total Economic Value will therefore underestimate the true value of ecosystems. The prior value of the ecosystem structure has been called 'primary value' and consists of the system characteristics upon which all ecological functions depend (Turner and Pearce, 1993). Their value arises in the sense that they produce functions which have value (secondary value). The secondary functions and values depend on the continued 'health', existence, operation, and maintenance of the ecosystem as a whole. The primary value notion is related to the fact that the system holds everything together (and is thus also referred to as a 'glue' value) and as such has, in principle, economic value. Thus the Total Value of the ecosystem exceeds the sum of the values of the individual functions (ibid.). It can also be argued that a healthy ecosystem contains an ecological redundancy capacity and there is thus an 'insurance' value in maintaining the system at some 'critical' size in order to combat stress and shocks over time.

To summarize, the social value of an ecosystem may not be equivalent to the aggregate private total economic value of that same system's components, because of the following factors:

1. The full complexity and coverage of the underpinning 'life-support' functions of healthy evolving ecosystems is currently not precisely known in scientific terms. A number of indirect use values within systems therefore remain to be discovered and valued (quasi-option value; i.e. the conditional expected value of information).
2. Because the range of secondary values (use and non-use) that can be instrumentally derived from an ecosystem is contingent on the prior existence of such a healthy and evolving system, there is in a philosophical sense a 'prior value' that could be ascribed to the system itself. Such a value would, however, not be measurable in conventional economic terms and is non-commensurate with the economic (secondary) values of the system.
3. The continued functioning of a healthy ecosystem is more than the sum of its individual components. There is a sense in which the operating system yields or possesses 'glue' value, i.e. value related to the structure and functioning properties of the system which hold everything together.
4. A healthy ecosystem also contains a redundancy reserve, a pool of latent keystone species/processes which are required for system maintenance in the face of stress and shock.

We now are in a position to bring together all the elements in the total environmental value framework. These are laid out in Figure 2.2, with TEV as a part of TV and non-anthropocentric intrinsic value as a completely separate notion not commensurate with the other components.

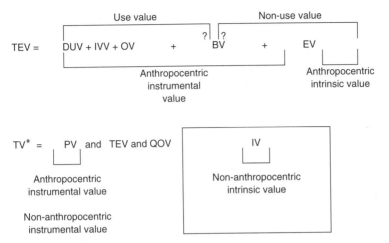

Fig. 2.2 Total environmental value and total economic value

TV, total environmental value; TEV, total economic value; DUV, direct use value; IUV, indirect use value; OV, option value (including bequest value); QOV, quasi option value; EV, existence value; PV, primary value; IV, intrinsic value; BV, bequest value.

* The separate components of TV are not additive: they are different dimensions of value.

2.6. CONCLUSIONS

The adoption of a systems perspective and the recognition of ecosystem primary value serves to emphasize the strong-sustainability approach to policy and the need for sustainability constraints (e.g. safe minimum standards). Estimation of the total value of wetlands, forests, etc. will involve complex problems to do with system boundaries, scale, thresholds, and value component aggregation. Given the inevitable uncertainties involved, a precautionary (risk-averse) approach based on maximum ecosystem conservation is a high priority. So in this sense the primary value concept (in terms of value dimensions 1, 3, and 4 in the list above) is directly relevant to the conservation versus development policy debate. The 'prior value' dimension (factor 2 in the list above) of primary value is however only of philosophical interest and is not amenable to quantification. Nevertheless, a 'healthy' ecosystem is seen as being valuable beyond those benefits that can be computed simply in terms of consumptive preferences. Self-organizing systems maintain a degree of stable functioning across time. They provide a sufficiently slowly changing context to which human individuals and cultures can adapt their practices. Ethically it could be argued that sustainability could be interpreted as requiring that no generation has a right to destabilize the self-organizing systems that provide the context for all human activity and therefore possess 'primary' value (Costanza *et al.*, 1992).

What is not being argued is that all environmental assets have significant unmeasured value and therefore all assets should be protected. Rather it is the ongoing 'healthy' system that possesses primary value and this requires biodiversity conservation at the landscape scale.

There is still, however, the thorny problem of actually deciding, on a rational basis, the 'scale' from which to manage environmental public goods. The 'scale' choice problem is in fact a public policy decision and as such is underdetermined by the mere provision of scientific information. Available scientific information contains inaccuracies and uncertainties such that it is not possible to specify minimum viable populations and minimum habitat sizes for the survival of species (Hohl and Tisdell, 1993). Biodiversity and other environmental conservation decisions, for a considerable time to come, will have to be based on ethical considerations. It has been concluded that 'society may choose to adopt the safe minimum standard not because it results from a rigorous model of social choice, but simply because individuals in the society feel that the safe minimum standard is the "right thing to do"' (Bishop and Ready, 1994). But let us not forget the significant instrumental value that biodiversity and other environmental resources possess. A suitably comprehensive and long-term view of instrumental value— one that protects ecosystems' services by protecting the health and integrity of systems over the long run—is probably sufficient to realize the case for more environmental conservation and will carry with it aesthetic and intrinsic moral values as well (Turner, 1988; Costanza *et al.*, 1992). Adoption of the safe minimum standard and the precautionary principle also shifts the burden of justification to those who would destroy biodiversity and other environmental assets because of their development activities.

Contingent valuation methods are not applicable to questions of system value but they do provide valuation opportunities in the context of both individual use and non-use environmental values. For non-use values they provide the only potential monetary valuation option, but as we have seen may require further design changes and testing before they can play even an heuristic role in cost–benefit policy analysis and decision-making.

At least three alternative debating positions can now be distinguished, as the contingent valuation literature and research has passed through several phases since the early 1960s (Mitchell and Carson, 1989). A growing number of strong-sustainability adherents favour some combination of the latter two positions outlined below:

- The majority of contingent valuation practitioners believe that the method shows great promise and is capable of yielding both use and non-use values across an extensive range of environmental contexts. The reliability and validity testing protocol (Arrow *et al.*, 1993) adopted in response to earlier criticisms of contingent valuation is now thought to be sufficient to show that the results are not random answers. Therefore some forms of contingent valuation can provide theoretically consistent and plausible measures of preference values for some types of environmental resources (Smith, 1993). This class of contingent valuation-relevant environmental resources, however, remains unbounded and an open research question. The next stage in the evolution of the method should be one in which a 'valuation protocol' is developed in order to get a standardized set of definitions of environmental 'commodities'. According to Smith (1993) the definitional structure must be consistent with people's environmental perceptions, compatible with ecological constraints and interrelationships, and responsive to policy-makers' requirements for valuation data. Non-use values will be much more difficult to estimate and the empirical record so far is much more restricted. There is also a link between use and non-use values in the sense that use values may depend on the level of services attributed to non-use values. Aggregation of values ('defining the extent of the market') is also not a straightforward matter in the non-use value context.

- Some critics of contingent valuation hold that the method has largely failed to yield any plausible non-use environmental values. They stress that 'embedding or mental account' bias problems and citizen preference revelation problems are common and interrelated (Common et al., 1993). If, as some practitioners have suggested (Mitchell and Carson, 1989), contingent valuation estimates of the values relating to 'unfamiliar' environmental resource contexts ought to be compared to referenda results, this still does not get the method 'off the hook', because while contingent valuation might outperform referenda, the resulting value estimates cannot then qualify as legitimate 'economic' data for incorporation into standard cost-benefit analysis. Contingent valuation should therefore be restricted to use value estimation. Referendum-type contingent valuation surveys, contingent ranking or contingent choice models ('conjoint analysis') might, however, play a useful role in the revelation of citizen or social preference values (Adamowicz et al., 1994; see also Chapter 13). This data would then form one component in a multi-criteria assessment approach seeking to determine relative social values.

- Other critics of contingent valuation argue that the method is only applicable in a severely restricted range of contexts, i.e. ones in which individuals can directly perceive the environmental resource or change in a resource's status (Bowers, 1993). It has no further role to play in estimating citizen evaluations and non-use values. To argue that contingent valuation does have such a role is to make a 'category mistake' (Sagoff, 1988). All economic valuation methods also, according to these critics, fail to capture non-anthropocentric and intrinsic value, and probably even anthropocentric intrinsic value in nature.

REFERENCES

Adamowicz, W., Louviere, J., and Williams, M. (1994), 'Combining revealed and stated preference methods for valuing environmental amenities', *Journal of Environmental Economics and Management*, 26: 271–92.

Andreoni, J. (1990), 'Impure Altruism and Donations to Public Goods: a Theory of Warm Glow Giving', *Economic Journal*, 100: 464–77.

Arrow, K., Solow, R., Portney, P. R., Leamer, E. E., Radner, R., and Schuman, W. (1993), Report of the NOAA Panel on Contingent Valuation, Resources for the Future, Washington.

Barbier, E. B. (ed.) (1993), *Economics and Ecology: New Frontiers and Sustainable Development*, Chapman and Hall, London.

——(1994), 'Natural Capital and the Economics of Environment and Development', in A. M. Jansson, M. Hammer, and R. A. Costanza (eds.), *Investing in Natural Capital: the Ecological Economics Approach to Sustainability*, Island Press, New York.

——Burgess, J. C., and Folke, C. (1994), *Paradise Lost? The Ecological Economics of Biodiversity*, Earthscan, London.

Bishop, R. C. (1978), 'Endangered Species and Uncertainty: the Economics of a Safe Minimum Standard', *American Journal of Agricultural Economics*, 57: 10–18.

——and Ready, R. C. (1994), 'Endangered Species and the Safe Minimum Standard', *American Journal of Agricultural Economics*, 73: 309–12.

Blamey, R. K. (1995), *Citizens, Consumers, and Contingent Valuation*, Ph.D. thesis, Australian National University, Canberra.

Bowers, J. (1993), 'A Conspectus on Valuing the Environment', *Journal of Environmental Planning and Management*, 36: 91–100.

Common, M., and Perrings, C. (1992), 'Towards an Ecological Economics of Sustainability', *Ecological Economics*, 6: 7–34.

——Blamey, R. K., and Norton, T. W. (1993), 'Sustainability and Environmental Valuation', *Environmental Values*, 2: 299–334.

Costanza, R., Norton, B. G., and Haskell, B. D. (eds.) (1992), *Ecosystem Health: New Goals for Environmental Management*, Island Press, Washington.

Daly, H., and Cobb, J. B. (1989), *For the Common Good*, Beacon Press, Boston.

Elster, J. (1989), 'Social Norms and Economic Theory', *Journal of Economic Perspectives*, 3: 99–117.

Farber, S., and Costanza, R. (1989), 'The Economic Value of Wetland Systems', *Journal of Environmental Management*, 24: 41–55.

Gren, I-M., Folke, C., Turner, R. K., and Bateman, I. (1994), 'Primary and Secondary Values of Wetland Ecosystems', *Environmental and Resources Economics*, 4: 55–74.

Grether, D. M., and Plott, C. R. (1979), 'Economic Theory of Choice and the Preference Reversal Phenomenon', *American Economic Review*, 69: 623–38.

Hargrove, C. (1992), 'Weak Anthropocentric Intrinsic Value', *The Monist*, 75: 183–207.

Harrison, G. (1992), 'Valuing Public Goods with the Contingent Valuation Method: a Critique of Kahneman and Knetsch', *Journal of Environmental Economics and Management*, 23: 248–57.

Hartwick, J. (1978), 'Substitution among Exhaustible Resources and Intergenerational Equity', *Review of Economic Studies*, 45: 347–54.

Hohl, A., and Tisdell, C. A. (1993), 'How Useful are Environmental Safety Standards in Economics? The Example of Safe Minimum Standards for Protection of Species', *Biodiversity and Conservation*, 2: 168–81.

Holt, C. A. (1986), 'Preference Reversals and the Independence Axiom', *American Economic Review*, 76: 508–15.

Kahneman, D., and Knetsch, J. L. (1992*a*), 'Valuing Public Goods: the Purchase of Moral Satisfaction', *Journal of Environmental Economics and Management*, 22: 57–70.

—— and —— (1992*b*), 'Contingent Valuation and the Value of Public Goods: Reply', *Journal of Environmental Economics and Management*, 22: 90–4.

—— and Tversky, A. (1979), 'Prospect Theory: an Analysis of Decisions under Risk', *Econometrica*, 47: 263–91.

Karni, E., and Safra, Z. (1987), ' "Preference Reversal" and the Observability of Preferences by Experimental Methods', *Econometrica*, 55: 675–85.

Lant, C. L. (1994), 'The Role of Property Rights in Economic Research on US Wetlands Policy', *Ecological Economics*, 11: 27–34.

Larson, ?? (1993), 'On Measuring Existence Value', *Land Economics*, 69: 377–88.

Lichtenstein, S., and Slovic, P. (1971), 'Reversals of Preferences between Bids and Choices in Gambling Decisions', *Journal of Experimental Psychology*, 89: 46–55.

Loomes, G., and Sugden, R. (1983), 'A Rationale for Preference Reversal', *American Economic Review*, 73: 428–32.

—— Starmer, C., and Sugden, R. (1989), 'Preference Reversal: Information Processing Effect or Rational Nontransitive Choice', *Economic Journal*, 99: 140–51.

—— —— and —— (1991), 'Observing Violations of Transitivity by Experimental Methods', *Econometrica*, 59: 425–39.

Loomis, J. B. (1989), 'Reliability of Contingent Valuations', *American Journal of Agricultural Economics*, 71: 76–84.

Margolis, H. (1982), *Selfishness, Altruism and Rationality: a Theory of Social Choice*, Cambridge University Press, Cambridge.

Mitchell, R. C., and Carson, R. (1989), *Using Surveys to Value Public Goods: the Contingent Valuation Method*, Resources for the Future, Washington.

Naess, A. (1973), 'The Shallow and the Deep, Long Range Ecology Movement: a Summary', *Inquiry*, 16: 95–100.

Norton, B. G. (1987), *Why Preserve Natural Variety?* Princeton University Press, Princeton, NJ.

—— (1992), 'Sustainability, Human Welfare and Ecosystem Health', *Environmental Values*, 1: 97–111.

—— and Ulanowicz, R. E. (1992), 'Scale and Biodiversity Policy: a Hierarchical Approach', *Ambio*, 21: 246–9.

Page, T. (1982), 'Intergenerational Justice as Opportunity', in D. Maclean and P. Brown (eds.), *Energy and the Future*, Rowman and Littlefield, Totowa, NT.

Pasek, J. (1992), 'Philosophical Aspects of Intergenerational Justice', in H. Giersch (ed.), *Economic Progress and Environmental Concerns*, Springer-Verlag, Berlin.

Pearce, D. W. (1992), 'Green Economics', *Environmental Values*, 1: 3–13.

——(1994), 'Commentary', *Environment and Planning* A, 26: 1329–38.

Pearce, D. W., Markandya, A., and Barbier, B. E. (1989), *Blueprint for a Green Economy*, Earthscan, London.

Pearce, D. W., Barbier, B. E., and Markandya, A. (1990), *Sustainable Development*, Earthscan, London.

Perrings, C., and Pearce, D. W. (1994), 'Threshold Effects and Incentives for the Conservation of Biology', *Environmental and Resource Economics*, 4: 13–28.

——Turner, R. K., and Folke, C. (1995), 'Ecological Economics: The Study of Interdependent Economic and Ecological Systems', EEEM Working Paper 9501, University of York.

Randall, A. (1991), 'The Value of Biodiversity', *Ambio*, 20: 64–8.

——and Stoll, J. R. (1991), 'Nonuse Value in a Total Valuation Framework', in R. D. Rowe *et al.*, *Contingent Valuation of Natural Resource Damage due to the Nestucca Oil Spill*, Final Report, Department of Wildlife, State of Washington, British Columbia Ministry of Environment, and Environment, Canada.

Reiling, S. D., Boyle, K. J., Phillips, M., and Anderson, M. (1990), 'Temporal Reliability of Contingent Values', *Land Economics*, 60: 128–34.

Rolston, H. (1988), *Environmental Ethics*, Temple University Press, Philadelphia.

Sagoff, M. (1988), 'Some Problems with Environmental Economics', *Environmental Ethics*, 10: 55–74.

Segal, U. (1988), 'Does the Preference Reversal Phenomenon Necessarily Contradict the Independence Axiom?' *American Economic Review*, 78: 233–6.

Sen, A. K. (1977), 'Rational Fools: a Critique of the Behaviour Foundations of Economic Theory', *Philosophy and Public Affairs*, 16: 317–44.

Shogren, J. F., and Nowell, C. (1992), 'Economics and Ecology a Comparison of Experimental Methodologies and Philosophies', *Ecological Economics*, 5: 101–26.

Slovic, P., and Lichtenstein, S. (1983), 'Preference Reversals: a Broader Perspective', *American Economic Review*, 73: 596–605.

Smith, V. K. (1993), 'Non-market Valuation of Environmental Resources: an Interpretative Appraisal', *Land Economics*, 69: 1–26.

Stevens, T. H., Echeverria, J., Glass, R. J., Hager, T., and More, A. M. (1994*a*), 'Measuring the Existence Value of Wildlife: What Do CVM Estimates Really Show?' *Land Economics*, 67: 390–400.

——More, T. A., and Glass, R. J. (1994*b*), 'Interpretation and Temporal Stability of CV Bids for Wildlife Existence: a Panel Study', *Land Economics*, 70: 355–63.

Turner, R. K. (1988), 'Wetland Conservation: Economics and Ethics', in D. Collard *et al.* (eds.), *Economics, Growth and Sustainable Environments*, Macmillan, London.

——(1993), 'Sustainability: Principles and Practice', in R. K. Turner (ed.), *Sustainable Environmental Economics and Management*, Belhaven Press, London.

——(1991), 'Economics and Wetland Management', *Ambio*, 20: 59–63.

——and Pearce, D. W. (1993), 'Sustainable Economic Development: Economic and Ethical Principles', in E. B. Barbier (ed.), *Economics and Ecology*, Chapman and Hall, London.

——Pearce, D. W., and Bateman, I. J. (1994), *Environmental Economics: An Elementary Introduction*, Harvester Wheatsheaf, Hemel Hempstead.

Wilson, E. O. (1987), *On Human Nature*, Harvard University Press, Cambridge, Mass.

WCED (World Commission on Environment and Development), (1987), *Our Common Future*, Oxford University Press, Oxford.

Young, M. D. (1992), *Sustainable Investment and Resources*, Parthenon Publishing, Carnforth, Lancs., and Unesco, Paris.

——(1993), *Some Practical Implications of Inter-Generational Equity, the Precautionary Principle, Maintenance of Natural Capital and the Discount Rate*, CSIRO Working Document 93/5, Canberra.

3

The Economic Theory of WTP and WTA

W. MICHAEL HANEMANN

3.1. INTRODUCTION

Contingent valuation is an empirical approach to measuring economic concepts. As such, it is an exercise in the application of economic theory. Therefore, at the outset it may be useful to review the economic theory of what is being measured in a contingent valuation survey, namely individuals' willingness to pay (WTP) or willingness to accept (WTA) for changes in some environmental amenity.

Before embarking on this theoretical investigation, however, it is important to emphasize its empirical underpinning. Economic theory does not tell us what people care about, or how they care. As Simon (1986) puts it, 'neoclassical economics provides no theoretical basis for specifying the shape and content of the utility function'. These are empirical matters, and they are likely to vary from one individual to another. In the notation used below, where the item being valued is denoted q, economic theory does not tell us how much a person likes q, or why. It does not tell us, either, about the units in which a person effectively perceives q; these may be entirely different from the units in which the item is measured by the researcher. Thus, economic theory cannot tell us whether the individual sees 3 units of q, say, as any different from 4, or whether he considers a change from 3 units to 12 a large change or a small one.[1] Therefore, while economic theory can show the implications of particular assumptions about the utility function, whether people actually have those preferences is an empirical question.

My aim here is to examine the properties of the welfare measures under alternative preference structures for q and to identify the observable implications for measured WTA and WTP, whether measured through indirect methods based on revealed preference or direct methods such as contingent valuation.[2]

---

[1] Just as, in the consumer context, economic theory does not tells us whether an individual considers 3 grains of sugar, say, any different from 4 grains, or 12 as substantially more than 3.

[2] In Hanemann (1982) I examined the observable implications of alternative preference structures for q with respect to ordinary and compensated demand functions for market

The basic economic model of individual utility is set out in Section 3.2. Section 3.3 reviews how WTP or WTA vary with the magnitude of the perceived change in the item being valued. Section 3.4 and 3.5 deal with how WTP and WTA vary with the individual's income. Section 3.6 deals with the economic theory of the disparity between WTP and WTA. Section 3.7 considers a related phenomenon, the disparity between values for gains and losses. Section 3.8 reviews some other explanations of the gain/loss disparity that have appeared in the literature, including prospect theory and the concept of loss aversion, and Section 3.9 reviews explanations based on models of individual behaviour under uncertainty, including uncertainty about one's preferences or what the item might be worth. Section 3.10 touches on substitution and complementarity among alternative q's, and how this affects WTP and WTA. The conclusions are summarized in Section 3.11.

3.2. THE UTILITY MODEL

The theoretical model that provides the setting for this analysis was first articulated by Mäler (1974) and runs as follows. An individual has preferences for various conventional market commodities whose consumption is denoted by the vector x, as well as for non-market environmental amenities denoted by q. Depending on the context these may be a single amenity, in which case q is a scalar, or several amenities, in which case q is a vector. The individual takes q as given—in effect it is a public good to her. By contrast, she can freely vary her consumption of the private market goods, x.[3] Her preferences are represented by a utility function $u(x,q)$ which is continuous and non-decreasing in its arguments, and strictly quasi-concave in x.[4] However, I do not necessarily assume that her utility is quasi-concave in q. If it *is* quasi-concave, I show below that this implies certain properties for WTP and WTA. But, there is no compelling reason why quasi-concavity should apply; as indicated above, how the individual feels towards q is an empirical question.[5]

goods. Some of the issues considered here are also discussed in Ch. 4, by Carson, Flores, and Mitchell.

[3] This model can also be considered a variant of Lancaster's (1966) model of consumer demand with product characteristics if the elements of y are interpreted not as levels of public good supply but, rather, as attributes of the x's. The key thing is that the consumer takes the q's as exogenous. In Hanemann (1982) I called this the Generalized Lancaster Model, and I contrasted it with another approach to modelling consumer demand for quality, the Houthakker–Theil model, which provides the theoretical foundation for the hedonic pricing literature.

[4] Thus, the elements of q are viewed as goods rather than bads. But, because I do not assume that preferences are strongly monotonic in q, I leave open the possibility that the individual is indifferent to q.

[5] Of course, the same applies to preferences for the x's. We typically assume that utility is quasi-concave in x, but this is mainly for analytical convenience since it rules out corner solutions in which purchases are concentrated on just a few market commodities. Whether or

The individual faces a budget constraint based on her (disposable) income y and the prices of the market commodities, p. Given the budget constraint, she chooses her consumption by solving

$$\max_{x} u(x,q) \qquad \text{subject to } \Sigma p_i x_i \leqslant y \qquad (3.1)$$

taking q as given. This yields a set of ordinary demand functions, $x_i = h^i(p,q,y)$, $i = 1,\cdots,N$ and an indirect utility function, $v(p,q,y) \equiv u[h(p,q,y),q]$, which have the conventional properties with respect to (p, y). By the envelope theorem, the indirect utility function is non-decreasing in $q : v_q(p,q,y) = u_q \geqslant 0$.[6] The dual to the utility maximization in (3.1) is an expenditure minimization:

$$\min_{x} \Sigma p_i x_i \qquad \text{subject to } u(x,q) \geqslant u. \qquad (3.2)$$

This yields a set of compensated demand functions, $x_i = g^i(p,q,u)$, $i = 1,\cdots,N$, and an expenditure function, $m(p,q,u) \equiv \Sigma p_i g^i(p,q,u)$, which have the conventional properties with respect to (p,u). I will make frequent use of the identities $u \equiv v[p,q,m(p,q,u)]$ and $y \equiv m[p,q,v(p,q,y)]$, which reflect the fact that $y = m(p,q,u)$ is the inverse of $u = v(p,q,y)$, and vice versa. It follows from this that

$$m_q(p,q,u) = -\frac{v_q(p,q,y)}{v_y(p,q,y)} \qquad (3.3a)$$

$$m_u(p,q,u) = \frac{1}{v_y(p,q,y)}. \qquad (3.3b)$$

Hence,

$$v_q(p,q,y) = -\frac{m_q(p,q,u)}{m_u(p,q,u)}. \qquad (3.3c)$$

From (3.3a), the expenditure function is non-increasing in $q : m_q \leqslant 0$. The second derivative with respect to q depends on what is assumed about the curvature of the utility function:

LEMMA 3.1. If $u(x,q)$ is quasi-concave in (x,q), then $m(p,q,u)$ is convex in q, which is equivalent to $v(p,q,y)$ being quasi-concave in (q,y).

This chapter deals with welfare measures for changes in q. These welfare measures were first proposed by Mäler (1971, 1974) as an extension of the standard theory of welfare measurement for price changes that had been

not this is realistic is an empirical question. With the q's, since the individual does not select them herself, there is less cause to assume quasi-concavity for them.

[6] Where the meaning is unambiguous, I use subscripts to denote first and second derivatives. Thus, v_q is the first derivative of $v(p,q,y)$ with respect to q. This will be a scalar or vector depending on whether q is treated as a scalar or vector.

formulated by Hicks (1943). Suppose that q changes from q^0 to q^1. Accordingly, the individual's utility changes from $u^0 \equiv u(p, q^0, y)$ to $u^1 \equiv v(p, q^1, y)$. (I am assuming no change in p or y.) By analogy with the Hicksian measures for price changes, Mäler proposed the compensating and equivalent variation measures, C and E, defined respectively by

$$v(p, q^1, y - C) = v(p, q^0, y) \tag{3.4a}$$

and

$$v(p, q^1, y) = v(p, q^0, y + E). \tag{3.4b}$$

These measures are the focus of this chapter. Observe that

$$\text{sign}(C) = \text{sign}(E) = \text{sign}(u^1 - u^0).$$

If $\Delta u \equiv u^1 - u^0 \geqslant 0$, so that the change is regarded as an improvement, C measures the individual's maximum willingness to pay (WTP) to secure the change, while E measures her minimum willingness to accept (WTA) to forgo it. Conversely, if $\Delta u \leqslant 0$, so that the change in q makes things worse, then $-E$ measures the individual's WTP to avoid the change, while $-C$ measures her WTA to tolerate it.[7] In either case, WTA − WTP = $E − C$. I refer to this below as the WTP/WTA Disparity.

Given the duality between the indirect utility function and the expenditure function, equivalent definitions of C and E in terms of the latter are

$$C \equiv C(q^0, q^1, p, y) = m(p, q^0, u^0) - m(p, q^1, u^0) \tag{3.5a}$$

and

$$E \equiv E(q^0, q^1, p, y) = m(p, q^0, u^1) - m(p, q^1, u^1). \tag{3.5b}$$

In terms of Hurwicz and Uzawa's (1971) *income compensation function*,

$$I(p^a, q^a; p^b, q^b, y) \equiv m[p^a, q^a, v(p^b, q^b, y)], \tag{3.6}$$

which measures the minimum income required to attain a utility level corresponding to $v(p^b, q^b, y)$ when facing prices p^a and environmental quality q^a, the equivalent definitions are

$$C = y - I(p, q^1; p, q^0, y) \tag{3.6a}$$

and

$$E = I(p, q^0; p, q^1, y) - y. \tag{3.6b}$$

The income compensation function will be used in several parts of the analysis below. For fixed (p^a, q^a), $I(p^a, q^a; p^b, q^b, y)$ is an ordinal

---

[7] I adopt the convention that, while C and E can be positive or negative, WTP and WTA are always defined so as to be non-negative.

transformation of $v(p^b, q^b, y)$ and therefore can itself serve as a demand-generating, indirect utility function.[8]

One can re-write (3.4b) in a manner that highlights the linkage between C and E. Let $y' \equiv y + E$; then,

$$v(p, q^1, y - C) = v(p, q^0, y) \qquad (3.4a)$$

and

$$v(p, q^1, y' - E) = v(p, q^0, y'). \qquad (3.4b')$$

Hence, E can be thought of as being like C if C was calculated from an income base of y':

$$E(q^0, q^1, p, y) = C[q^0, q^1, p, y + E(q^0, q^1, p, y)]. \qquad (3.7a)$$

Similarly, let $y'' \equiv y - C$; then, instead of (3.4a) one has

$$v(p, q^1, y'') = v(p, q^0, y'' + C) \qquad (3.4a')$$

and

$$v(p, q^1, y) = v(p, q^0, y + E). \qquad (3.4b)$$

Thus, C is like E if E was calculated from an income base of y'':

$$C(q^0, q^1, p, y) = E[q^0, q^1, p, y - C(q^0, q^1, p, y)]. \qquad (3.7b)$$

Equations (3.7a) and (3.7b) constitute a linked pair of functional equations which were first noted by Cook and Graham (1977). Another duality between C and E follows immediately from (3.5a,b)

$$C(q^0, q^1; p, y) = -E(q^1, q^0; p, y) \qquad (3.8a)$$

and

$$E(q^0, q^1; p, y) = -C(q^1, q^0; p, y). \qquad (3.8b)$$

This result can be quite useful in practice since, if one can recover the $C(\cdot)$ function from responses to WTP questions in a contingent valuation survey, by interchanging q^0 and q^1 in this function it becomes possible to infer the respondents' WTA values even though they were asked no questions about their WTA. Suppose, for example, that the indirect utility function takes the form

$$u = v(p, q, y) = T[\alpha(p, q) + \beta(p) \ln y, p], \qquad (3.9)$$

where $\alpha(\cdot)$ is some increasing function of q. Given an increase from q^0 to q^1, the compensating variation for this change is[9]

---

[8] The usefulness of the income compensation function for analysing C and E was emphasized by McConnell (1990).

[9] A random utility version of this model appears in Ch. 11.

$$C(q^0, q^1, p, y) = \text{WTP} = y\left[1 - e^{\{[\alpha(p,q^0) - \alpha(p,q^1)]/\beta(p)\}}\right]; \qquad (3.9a)$$

from (8b), the equivalent variation for the same change is

$$E(q^0, q^1, p, y) = \text{WTA} = y\left[e^{\{[\alpha(p,q^1) - \alpha(p,q^0)]/\beta(\dot{p})\}} - 1\right]. \qquad (3.9b)$$

Using the responses to a contingent valuation question on WTP, it may be possible via (3.9a) to obtain estimates of $[\alpha(p, q^1) - \alpha(p, q^0)]$ and $\beta(p)$. These can be inserted into (3.9b) to form an estimate of WTA. Loomis *et al.* (1990) apply this approach to discrete-response CV data on people's WTP to protect wetlands in the San Joaquin Valley of California. In that particular case, using the model in (3.9) they find that the implied estimate of WTA is about 15–20 per cent larger than the estimated WTP.

I have used the notation $C \equiv C(q^0, q^1, p, y)$ and $E = E(q^0, q^1, p, y)$ in order to emphasize the dependence of C and E on (i) the starting value of q, (ii) the terminal value of q, and (iii) the value of (p, y) at which the change in q occurs. In the following sections I investigate aspects of these relationships.

3.3   THE ELASTICITY WITH RESPECT TO q

In this section, I examine how C and E vary with q^1 and q^0 which, for now, I treat as vectors. From (3.5a), if $m(p, q^1, u^0)$ is convex in q^1, then C is concave in q^1. Invoking Lemma 3.1, if $u(x, q)$ is quasi-concave in (x, q), it follows that C is concave in q^1. With regard to q^0, the situation is a little different, and one obtains the property of quasi-convexity rather than convexity. From (3.6a), C depends on q^0 via the monotone increasing transformation $m[p, q^1, v(p, q^0, y)]$. This income compensation function inherits the quasi-concavity of $v(\cdot)$ in q^0; the minus sign turns C into a *quasi-convex* function of q^0. A similar analysis applies to E viewed as a function of q^0 and q^1. Moreover, C and E have similar properties with respect to $\Delta \equiv q^1 - q^0$:

PROPOSITION 3.1. If $u(x, q)$ is quasi-concave in (x, q), then
   C is concave in q^1 and Δ,
   C is quasi-convex in q^0,
   E is quasi-concave in q^1 and Δ,
   and E is convex in q^0.

The distinction between concavity and quasi-concavity is significant because the former, but not the latter, provides a link to the elasticity of WTP or WTA with respect to q. A continuous, non-negative function $f(x)$ defined over $x \geq 0$, for which $f(0) = 0$, is said to be *star-shaped* if $f(\lambda x)/\lambda$ is increasing in $\lambda, 0 < \lambda \leq 1$. When x is a scalar, this implies that the elasticity of $f(x)$ with respect to x exceeds unity. If $f(x)$ is convex, non-negative, and satisfies $f(0) = 0$, then $f(x)$ is star-shaped (Pecaric *et al.* 1992).[10] Similarly, if $f(x)$ defined over $x \geq 0$ is concave, non-negative, and satisfies $f(0) = 0$, then $f(x)$ is what is sometimes called *lower star-shaped*; i.e. $f(\lambda x)/\lambda$ is decreasing in $\lambda, 0 < \lambda \leq 1$, which, for scalar x, implies that the elasticity of $f(x)$ with respect to x is less than unity. Observe that $C = 0$ when $\Delta = 0$. Hence, the following:

PROPOSITION 3.2.   If $u(x,q)$ is quasi-concave in (x,q), the elasticity of C with respect to each element of Δ is less than unity.

Otherwise, however, it is not possible to say much in general about how C or E varies with the magnitude of the change in q.

   So far I have considered the dependence of C or E on q^1 or q^0 taken separately. However, one might wonder whether there are utility models in which C or E depends just on the difference $(q^1 - q^0)$, independently of q^1 or q^0. For this to be true, one requires that $\partial C / \partial q^1 \equiv -\partial C / \partial q^0$, and similarly for E. Implicit differentiation of (3.4a,b) shows that this condition is satisfied for C if $v_q(p, q^1, y - C) \equiv v_q(p, q^0, y)$. This, in turn, implies an indirect utility function of the form

$$v(p, q, y) = T[\phi(p, y) + \psi(p) \cdot q, p], \qquad (3.10)$$

in which case one obtains

$$C = y - \phi^{-1}[\phi(p, y) - \psi(p)(q^1 - q^0), p] \qquad (3.10a)$$

and

$$E = \phi^{-1}[\phi(p, y) + \psi(p)(q^1 - q^0), p] - y, \qquad (3.10b)$$

where ϕ^{-1} denotes the inverse of $\psi(p, y)$ with respect to y. If the utility function does not conform to (3.10), then C and E depend on q^1 and q^0 separately.

   These results on how C and E vary with q also carry over to other utility models with a similar formal structure, including models of choice under uncertainty. By way of illustration, let $V(x,z)$ be any function of two or more variables, where x is a scalar while z can be a scalar or a vector. I assume that $V(\cdot)$ is increasing in x; it can be increasing or decreasing in z. Let $x = M(u, z)$ be the inverse of $u = V(x, z)$. The equivalent of Lemma 3.1 is:

LEMMA 3.2. $M(u,z)$ is convex (concave) in z if and only if $V(x,z)$ is quasi-concave (quasi-convex) in (x,z).

I use x as the numeraire for valuing changes in z. Suppose that z changes from z^0 to z^1, while x remains constant; the value of this change measured in terms of x is given by $C^z = C^z(x, z^0, z^1)$ and $E^z = E^z(x, z^0, z^1)$, where

---

[10] This does not hold for a function that is quasi-convex and satisfies $f(0) = 0$.

$$V(x - C^z, z^1) = V(x, z^0) \tag{3.11a}$$

and

$$V(x, z^1) = V(x + E^z, z^0). \tag{3.11b}$$

Clearly, sign $(C^z) = \text{sign}(E^z) = \text{sign}(u^1 - u^0)$; the sign depends on the direction of change in z as well as whether V is increasing or decreasing in z. $C^z > 0$ is the WTP for an improving change, while $E^z > 0$ is the WTA; when $C^z < 0$, $-E^z$ is the WTP to avoid the change, while $-E^z$ is the WTA to endure it. In either case, $E^z - C^z$ measures WTA $-$ WTP. The equivalent of Propositions 3.1 and 3.2 is:

PROPOSITION 3.3.   (i) If $V(x,z)$ is quasi-concave in (z,x), then C^z is concave in z^1 and quasi-convex in z^0, while E^z is quasi-concave in z^1 and convex in z^0. If $V(x,z)$ is increasing in z, then C^z is concave in $\Delta \equiv z^1 - z^0$ and the elasticity of C^z with respect to each element of Δ is less than unity. If $V(x,z)$ is decreasing in z, then E^z is convex in $\Delta \equiv z^0 - z^1$ and the elasticity of E^z with respect to each element of Δ exceeds unity.

(ii) If $V(x,z)$ is quasi-convex in (z,x), then C^z is convex in z^1 and quasi-concave in z^0, while E^z is quasi-convex in z^1 and concave in z^0. If $V(x,z)$ is increasing in z, then C^z is convex in $\Delta \equiv z^1 - z^0$ and the elasticity of C^z with respect to each element of Δ exceeds unity. If $V(x,z)$ is decreasing in z, then E^z is concave in $\Delta \equiv z^0 - z^1$ and the elasticity of E^z with respect to each element of Δ is less than unity.

If $V(\cdot)$ is viewed as a direct utility function, C^z and E^z in (3.11a,b) measure compensating and equivalent surplus; if $V(\cdot)$ is an indirect utility function, they measure compensating and equivalent variation. When $V(\cdot) = v(p,q,y)$ is viewed as a function of y and q, Proposition 3.3 yields the results reported in Propositions 3.1 and 3.2. When $v(p,q,y)$ is viewed as a function of (p,y) it yields results about traditional welfare measures for price changes. Let C^p and E^p denote the compensating and equivalent variation when prices change from p^0 to p^1 while q and y stay unchanged; these satisfy

$$v(p^1, q, y - C^p) = v(p^0, q, y) \tag{3.12a}$$

and

$$v(p^1, q, y) = v(p^0, q, y + E^p). \tag{3.12b}$$

When $u(x, q)$ is quasi-concave in x, $v(p,q,y)$ is quasi-convex in (p,y) and decreasing in p; hence, the results in part (ii) of Proposition 3.3 apply to C^p and E^p, with y taking the role of x and p that of z. For example, the elasticity of E^p with respect to each element of $\Delta^p \equiv p^0 - p^1$ is less than unity.[11]

---

[11] Note that this says nothing about the elasticity of *demand for* the x's with respect to p, which should not be confused with the elasticity of E^p with respect to Δ^p.

3.4. AN ALTERNATIVE CHARACTERIZATION OF THE WELFARE MEASURES

Before proceeding further, it is convenient to introduce an approach to characterizing C and E that provides an alternative to (3.4a,b) and (3.5a,b). This approach produces useful results when q is a scalar. Therefore, in this section and Sections 3.5 and 3.6, I assume that q is a scalar rather than a vector.[12] The approach is based on a counterfactual situation where the individual *could* by her own action change the level of q. Suppose that she could purchase q in some market at a price of π. This market is purely imaginary, since q is actually a public good, but it permits us to contemplate what the individual's demand curve for q would look like if it could be observed. Instead of (3.1) she would now solve

$$\max_{x,q} u(x,q) \qquad \text{subject to} \sum p_i x_i + \pi q \leqslant y. \qquad (3.13a)$$

Denote the resulting ordinary demand functions by $x_i = \hat{h}^i(p,\pi,y)$, $i = 1,\ldots,N$, and $q = \hat{h}^q(p,\pi,y)$. In this particular context, it *does* matter what one assumes about the curvature of $u(x,q)$ with respect to q. If one assumes that utility is quasi-concave in (x,q), then $\hat{h}^q(\cdot)$ has the standard properties of an ordinary demand function. If one assumes otherwise, then $\hat{h}^q(\cdot)$ may lack the standard properties of a demand function; for example, if utility is quasi-convex in q, there is a corner solution to (3.13a) rather than an interior solution. In this section, I will assume that $u(x,q)$ is jointly quasi-concave in (x,q). The indirect utility function corresponding to (3.13a) is $\hat{v}(p,\pi,y) \equiv u\left[\hat{h}(p,\pi,y), \hat{h}^q(p,\pi,y)\right]$. The dual to (3.13a) is a minimization problem:

$$\min_{x,q} \sum p_i x_i + \pi q \qquad \text{subject to} \ u(x,q) \geqslant u. \qquad (13.3b)$$

This generates a set of compensated demand functions, $x_i = \hat{g}^i(p,\pi,u)$, $i = 1,\ldots,N$, and $q = \hat{g}^q(p,\pi,u)$, and an expenditure function $\hat{m}(p,\pi,u) \equiv \sum p_i \hat{g}^i(p,\pi,u) + \pi \hat{g}^q(p,\pi,u)$. By virtue of the assumed quasiconcavity of $u(x,q)$, these functions have the standard properties with respect to (p,π,u). In the analysis that follows, it will be useful to map between the indirect utility and expenditure functions $v(p,q,y)$ and $m(p,q,u)$ and their notional counterparts $\hat{v}(p,\pi,y)$ and $\hat{m}(p,\pi,u)$. The optimization problem in (3.1) is linked to that in (3.13a) by the following relationship:

$$v(p,q,y) \equiv \hat{v}[p, \hat{\pi}(p,q,y), y + \hat{\pi}(p,q,y) \cdot q], \qquad (3.14a)$$

$$\hat{v}(p,\pi,y) = \max_q v(p,q,y - \pi q). \qquad (3.14b)$$

---

[12] The analysis in these sections also applies when q is a vector but only one element changes. If q is a vector and several elements change, the analysis applies to each element that changes taken by itself.

Similarly, the optimization in (3.2) is related to its notional counterpart in (3.13b) as follows:

$$m(p,q,u) \equiv \hat{m}[p, \hat{\pi}(p,q,u), u] - \hat{\pi}(p,q,u) \cdot q, \qquad (3.14c)$$

$$\hat{m}(p, \pi, u) = \min_q \pi q + m(p,q,u). \qquad (3.14d)$$

For any given values of q, p, and u, the equation $q = \hat{g}^q(p, \pi, u)$ may be inverted to obtain $\pi = \hat{\pi}(p,q,u)$, the *inverse* compensated demand function for q : $\hat{\pi}(\cdot)$ is the price that would induce the individual to purchase q units of the environmental amenity, given that she wished to attain a utility level of u and could buy private goods at prices p. Similarly, one can invert the notional ordinary demand function $\hat{h}^q(\cdot)$ to obtain the Marshallian analog of $\hat{\pi}(p,q,u)$. In this case, one needs to supplement the individual's income so that she can afford to buy both q and the x's. Hence, for given (p,q,y) one solves the equation $q = \hat{h}^q(p,q,y + \pi q)$ for $\pi = \hat{\pi}(p,q,y)$. This is the price that would induce the individual to purchase q units of the environmental amenity in the notional market if her income were appropriately supplemented so that she would also choose to purchase the quantity of the x's that she did actually buy in the real market with prices p and income y. The two inverse demand functions are related by the identities

$$\hat{\pi}(p,q,y) \equiv \hat{\pi}[p,q,v(p,q,y)] \qquad (3.15a)$$

$$\hat{\pi}(p,q,u) \equiv \hat{\pi}[p,q,m(p,q,u)]. \qquad (3.15b)$$

Since $\hat{m}_\pi(p, \pi, u) = \hat{g}^q(p, \pi, u)$, differentiation of (3.14c) yields

$$-\hat{\pi}(p,q,u) = m_q(p,q,u). \qquad (3.16)$$

Thus, $\hat{\pi}(\cdot)$ can be thought of as the individual's marginal WTP or WTA for an incremental unit of q—i.e. her shadow price for q. Mäler (1974), who first used $\hat{\pi}(p,q,u)$ to characterize the welfare measures C and E, called $\hat{\pi}(p,q,y)$ the individual's 'demand price' for q and $\hat{\pi}(p,q,u)$ her 'compensated demand price'. By analogy with private market goods, he proposed classifying q on the basis of how demand price varies with income, classifying q as normal if $\partial \hat{\pi}(p,q,y)/\partial y > 0$ and inferior if $\partial \hat{\pi}(p,q,y)/\partial y < 0$. Using (3.15a) and (3.16) one obtains

$$\hat{\pi}_y(p,q,y) = \hat{\pi}_u(p,q,u) \cdot v_y(p,q,y) = -m_{qu}(p,q,u) \cdot v_y(p,q,y).$$

Since $v_y > 0$, it follows that

$$\text{sign}\,[\hat{\pi}_y(p,q,y)] = \text{sign}\,[\hat{\pi}_u(p,q,u)] = -\text{sign}\,[m_{qu}(p,q,u)].$$

Hence, q is normal iff $\hat{\pi}_u > 0$ or $m_{qu} < 0$, and inferior iff $\hat{\pi}_u < 0$ or $m_{qu} > 0$. Finally, combining equation (3.16) with equations (3.5a) and (3.5b) yields the alternative characterization of C and E

$$C = C(q^0, q^1; p; y) = \int_{q^0}^{q^1} \hat{\pi}(p, q, u^0)dq, \qquad (3.17a)$$

$$E = E(q^0, q^1; p; y) = \int_{q^0}^{q^1} \hat{\pi}(p, q, u^1)dq. \qquad (3.17b)$$

3.5. THE INCOME ELASTICITY OF WTP AND WTA

Differentiation of (3.17a) yields

$$\frac{\partial C}{\partial y} = v_y(p, q^0, y) \int_{q^0}^{q^1} \hat{\pi}_u(p, q, u^0)dq, \qquad (3.18a)$$

and similarly for $\partial E/\partial y$. It follows from (3.16) and (3.18a) that the sign of m_{qu} (i.e. whether q is normal or inferior) determines how C and E vary with income. Assume that $q^1 \geqslant q^0$, so that $C \geqslant 0$ and $E \geqslant 0$; then

$$\text{sign}\left(\frac{\partial C}{\partial y}\right) = \text{sign}\left(\frac{\partial E}{\partial y}\right) = -\text{sign}(m_{qu}(p, q, u)).^{13} \qquad (3.18b)$$

Moreover, it follows from (3.18a) that $\partial C/\partial y = \partial E/\partial y = 0$ whenever $m_{qu} = 0$. For that to happen, the expenditure and indirect utility functions must have the form

$$m(p, q, u) = \phi(p, u) - \psi(p, q), \qquad (3.19a)$$

and

$$v(p, q, y) = T[y + \psi(p, q), p], \qquad (3.19b)$$

in which case

$$C = E = \psi(p, q^1) - \psi(p, q^0). \qquad (3.19c)$$

There has been some discussion in the literature about the likely magnitude of the income elasticities of C and E, $\eta_C \equiv (\partial C/\partial y)(y/C)$ and $\eta_E \equiv (\partial E/\partial y)(y/E)$. However, *several different* income elasticities are sometimes discussed indiscriminately. In particular, it is necessary to distinguish η_C and η_E from two other income elasticities: (1) the income elasticity of the *demand function* for q, $\eta_q \equiv [\partial \hat{h}^q(p, \pi, y)/\partial y](y/q)$; and (2) the income elasticity of the *demand price* for q, $\eta_\pi \equiv [\partial \hat{\pi}(p, q, y)/\partial y](y/\pi)$, which is sometimes called the 'price flexibility of income'. The latter has received attention following the work of Randall and Stoll (1980), who used it to place bounds on E, C, and $E - C$. There has been some tendency to interpret estimates of η_C from contingent valuation surveys as conveying information about the magnitude of either η_q or η_π. For example, Brookshire *et al.* (1980: 484) take

---

[13] When $q^1 \leqslant q^0$, this changes to: sign $(\partial C/\partial y) = \text{sign}(\partial E/\partial y) = \text{sign}(m_{qu})$.

the coefficient in a regression of ln WTP on ln y (i.e. η_C) and use it as an estimate of η_π. McFadden and Leonard (1993: 185) argue that an empirical finding of $\eta_C < 1$ in a contingent valuation survey is prima facie evidence of the unreliability of the survey because, in their view, environmental protection is a luxury good and it should have an income elasticity of demand (i.e. η_q) that exceeds unity.[14]

To be sure, circumstances *do* exist where $\eta_C = \eta_\pi = \eta_q$. When the utility function corresponds to equation (3.19b), application of (3.15a,b) yields $\pi = \hat{\pi}(p,q,y) = \psi_q(p,q)$ and $q = \hat{h}^q(p,q,y+\pi q) = \psi_q^{-1}(\pi,p)$. Conversely, the no-income-effect forms of $\hat{\pi}(p,q,y)$ and $\hat{h}^q(p,q,y)$ imply $m_{qu} = 0$. Hence,

PROPOSITION 3.4. The following are equivalent: $\eta_C \equiv 0$; $\eta_E \equiv 0$; $\eta_\pi \equiv 0$; $\eta_q \equiv 0$; the indirect utility function has the form given in (3.19b).

However, when η_C and η_E are *non*-zero, in general they are different from η_q and η_π. The relationships among these elasticities can be quite complex, as I now show.

Comparing η_C and η_π, application of the Mean Value Theorem to (3.17a) yields $C = \hat{\pi}(p,\tilde{q},u^0)\cdot(q^1-q^0)$ for some $\tilde{q}\in[q^0,q^1]$. Similarly, application of the Mean Value Theorem to (3.18a) yields $\partial C/\partial y = v_y(p,q^0,y)\cdot\hat{\pi}(p,\bar{q},u^0)\cdot(q^1-q^0)$ for some $\bar{q}\in[q^0,q^1]$. Combining these two expressions and manipulating yields

$$\eta_C = \eta_\pi \cdot \left[\frac{m_u(p,\bar{q},u^0)}{m_u(p,q^0,u^0)}\right] \cdot \left[\frac{\hat{\pi}(p,\bar{q},u^0)}{\hat{\pi}(p,\tilde{q},u^0)}\right], \tag{3.20}$$

where η_c is evaluated at (q^0,q^1,p,y) and η_π is evaluated at $(p,\bar{q},\bar{y})$, with $\bar{y} \equiv m(p,\bar{q},u^0) < y$. The first term in square brackets on the right-hand side of (3.20) is less than unity when $m_{uq} < 0$ (i.e. when q is a normal good) and greater than unity when q is an inferior good. If $u(x,q)$ is quasi-concave in q, the second term in square brackets on the right-hand side of (3.20) is less than unity when $\tilde{q} < \bar{q}$ and greater than unity when $\tilde{q} > \bar{q}$, but in general there is no way to determine which of these inequalities applies. Therefore, in general there is no way to pin down whether η_C is greater or less than η_π.

More definite results can be obtained in some specific cases. For example, Hanemann (1991) identifies the class of utility models for which η_π is a non-unitary constant (i.e. independent of p, q, y):

$$u = v(p,q,y) = T\left([y^{1-\eta_\pi} + (1-\eta_\pi)G(p,q)]^{\frac{1}{1-\eta_\pi}},p\right), \tag{3.21a}$$

where $G(\cdot)$ is increasing in q, and η_π is some constant $\neq 1$. This implies

$$C/y = 1 - \left[1 - (1-\eta_\pi)y^{(\eta_\pi-1)}\Delta\right]^{\frac{1}{1-\eta_\pi}} \tag{3.21b}$$

---

[14] Kriström and Riera (1996) offer a sceptical review of the empirical evidence supporting this claim.

and

$$E/y = \left[1 + (1 - \eta_\pi)y^{(\eta_\pi - 1)}\Delta\right]^{\frac{1}{1 - \eta_\pi}} - 1 \qquad (3.21c)$$

where $\Delta \equiv G(p, q^1) - G(p, q^0)$. Differentiation yields

$$\eta_C = \frac{1 - (1 - c)^{\eta_\pi}}{c}, \qquad (3.21d)$$

$$\eta_E = \frac{(1 + e)^{\eta_\pi} - 1}{e}, \qquad (3.21e)$$

where $c \equiv C/y$ and $e \equiv E/y$. Observe that, while η_π is constant with the utility function (3.21a), in general η_C and η_E vary with (p, q^0, q^1, y) through their dependence on c and e. Observe also that, consistent with Proposition 3.4, $\eta_\pi \equiv 0$ implies $\eta_C \equiv \eta_E \equiv 0$. Equation (3.21d) implies that $\eta_C > \eta_\pi$ when $\eta_\pi < 1$, and $\eta_C < \eta_\pi$ when $\eta_\pi > 1$; for small c, it implies that $\eta_C \approx \eta_\pi$.[15] For example, when $c = 0.001$, $\eta_\pi = 0.05$ implies $\eta_C = 0.050024$, $\eta_\pi = 0.5$ implies $\eta_C = 0.500125$, $\eta_\pi = 1.5$ implies $\eta_C = 1.499625$, and $\eta_\pi = 5$ implies $\eta_C = 4.99001$. When $c = 0.1$, the values that correspond to $\eta_\pi = 0.05$, 0.5, 1.5, and 5 are $\eta_C = 0.052542$, 0.513167, 1.46185, and 4.0951.

Equations (3.21d,e) suggest that, when η_π is a constant equal to unity, η_C and η_E are also equal to unity. This is in fact true. The analogue of (3.21a) for the case where $\eta_\pi \equiv 1$ can be shown to be

$$u = v(p, q, y) = T(G(p, q) + \ln y, p) \qquad (3.22a)$$

where $G(\cdot)$ is increasing in q. This implies

$$C/y = 1 - e^{-\Delta}, \qquad (3.22b)$$

$$E/y = e^\Delta - 1, \qquad (3.22c)$$

where, as before, $\Delta \equiv G(p, q^1) - G(p, q^0)$. It follows from (3.22b,c) that $\eta_\pi \equiv 1$ implies $\eta_C \equiv \eta_E \equiv 1$. The converse is also true. Implicitly differentiating (3.4a) yields

$$\eta_C \equiv \frac{\partial C}{\partial y} \cdot \frac{y}{c} = \frac{v_y(p, q^1, y - C) - v_y(p, q^0, y)}{v_y(p, q^1, y - C)} \cdot \frac{y}{C}. \qquad (3.23)$$

Differentiating (3.4b) yields a similar equation for η_E. Equating the right-hand side of (3.23) to unity and solving the resulting partial differential equation yields (3.22a). Hence,

PROPOSITION 3.5.   The following are equivalent: $\eta_C \equiv 1$; $\eta_E \equiv 1$; $\eta_\pi \equiv 1$; the indirect utility function has the form given in (3.22a).

---

[15] Analogous results hold for η_E and η_π.

In general, however, when $\eta_\pi \neq 0$ or 1, η_π and η_C or η_E are *distinct* quantities, though equations (3.20) and (3.21d,e) suggest that they are likely to be close in value. Therefore, this appears to vindicate Brookshire et al.'s intuition that information about η_C (or η_E) is a useful guide to the magnitude of η_π.

When it comes to η_q, the situation is different. This appears to be more sharply distinct from η_C (or η_E) than η_π. The difference can be seen in several ways. The demand function $q = \hat{h}^q(p, \pi, y)$ is obtained as the solution to the maximization in (3.14b). The resulting first-order condition can be written

$$\pi = v_q(p, q, y - \pi q)/v_y(p, q, y - \pi q). \tag{3.24a}$$

Implicitly differentiating this yields the income elasticity of demand

$$\eta_q \equiv \frac{\partial \hat{h}^q}{\partial y} \cdot \frac{y}{q} = \left(\frac{\pi v_{yy} - v_{qy}}{v_{qq} - 2\pi v_{yq} + \pi^2 v_{yy}} \right) \cdot \frac{y}{q}, \tag{3.24b}$$

where all the derivatives v_{yq}, v_{yq}, etc. are evaluated at $(p, q, y - \pi q)$. Comparing (3.24b) with (3.23) should convince the reader that, while both η_q and η_C depend on v_{yq} and v_{yy}, they do so in different ways, involving quite different formulas. For a comparison, think of the conventional compensating and equivalent variation measures for price changes, C^p and E^p in (3.12a,b). The income elasticity of C^p or E^p is not the same as the income elasticity of demand for x's; one pertains to variation in the ordinary demand curve while the other pertains to variation in the area under the compensated demand curve. It is not surprising that these are different numbers.[16]

Another indication of the difference between η_q and η_C or η_E comes from a result about η_π developed in Hanemann (1991). I show there that

$$\eta_\pi = \eta_q/\sigma, \tag{3.25}$$

where σ is the Allen–Uzawa elasticity of substitution between q and the x's as a group. When one or more of the x's is a perfect substitute for q, $\sigma = \infty$; when there is *no* substitution between any of the x's and q, $\sigma = 0$. Therefore, η_π and η_q could be orders of magnitude apart. To the extent that η_C and η_E are likely to be close in value to η_π, (3.25) implies that they, too, could be orders of magnitude different from η_q.

If the income elasticity of demand η_q is constant, but not equal to 0 or 1, it follows from Willig (1976b) that, the indirect utility function $\hat{v}(p, \pi, y)$ takes the form

$$u = \hat{v}(p, \pi, y) = T\left([y^{1-\eta_q} + \psi(\pi, p)]^{\frac{1}{1-\eta_q}}, p \right). \tag{3.26}$$

---

[16] The same holds for the distinction between the elasticity of E^p with respect to Δ^p and the elasticity of demand for the x's with respect to p, mentioned in footnote 11. Quasi-concave preferences for x imply that the former is less than unity, while placing no constraint on the magnitude of the latter.

One can map from this to $v(p,q,y)$ using (3.14a), but in general no closed-form results are available. Nevertheless, the following observation can shed some light on the dissimilarities in utility implications of constant η_q versus constant η_C. If η_C is a non-unitary constant, integration of (3.23) yields the following formula for the income compensation function

$$m[p, q^1, v(p, q^0, y)] = y + K(p, q^0, q^1)y^\eta, \tag{3.27a}$$

where $\eta_C = \eta_E = \eta \neq 1$ and $K(p, q^0, q^1) \lessgtr 0$ as $q^0 \lessgtr q^1$. One can deduce the ordinary demand function $\hat{h}^q(p, \pi, y)$ that would correspond to this by noting that

$$\{\partial m[p, q^1, v(p, q^0, y)]/\partial q^0\}/\{\partial m[p, q^1, v(p, q^0, y)]/\partial y\} = v_q(p, q^0, y)/v_y(p, q^0, y)$$

and then using (3.24a). Thus, the ordinary demand function for q that is implied by (3.27a) is obtained by solving

$$\pi = \frac{(y - \pi q^0)^{\eta_C} \partial K(p, q^0)/\partial q^0}{1 + \eta_C(y - \pi q^0)^{\eta_C^{-1}} K(p, q^0)} \tag{3.27b}$$

for q^0 as a function of (p, π, y), where q^1 has been suppressed as an argument in $K(\cdot)$. Implicitly differentiating (3.27b) yields the demand elasticity η_q that corresponds to (3.27a). In general this is not a constant, independent of (p, π, y). This establishes that a constant elasticity of WTP, η_C, is generally not associated with a constant elasticity of demand, η_q.

There is an exception when $\eta_q \equiv 1$. From (3.25), this implies that $\eta_\pi = 1/\sigma$. When $\sigma \equiv 1$, this yields $\eta_\pi \equiv 1$, and the utility function takes the form

$$u = v(p, q, y) = T[\ln y + K(p) \cdot \ln q, p]. \tag{3.28}$$

Since $\eta_q \equiv 1$, in this case one has $\eta_q \equiv \eta_\pi \equiv \eta_C \equiv \eta_E \equiv 1$, by virtue of Proposition 3.5. With (3.28), therefore, not only is a constant η_C associated with a constant η_q, but they also take the same value. However, (3.19b) and (3.28) are the *only* cases where that occurs. When $\eta_q \equiv 1$ but σ is a constant other than unity, the utility function can be shown to take the form

$$u = v(p, q, y) = T\left([y^{(\sigma-1)/\sigma} + K(p) \cdot q^{(\sigma-1)/\sigma}]^{\frac{\sigma}{\sigma-1}}, p\right). \tag{3.29a}$$

Here, one has $\eta_q \equiv 1$ and $\eta_\pi \equiv 1/\sigma$, which makes it a special case of the constant-η_π utility model (3.21a). From (3.21d,e), one has

$$\eta_C = \frac{1 - (1 - c)^{\frac{1}{\sigma}}}{c}, \tag{3.29b}$$

$$\eta_E = \frac{(1 + e)^{\frac{1}{\sigma}} - 1}{e}, \tag{3.29c}$$

where $c \equiv C/y$ and $e \equiv E/y$. Therefore, while η_C and η_E are not constant, they both take values close to η_π, so that $\eta_C \approx \eta_E \approx 1/\sigma$. In this case, since $\eta_q \equiv 1$ while σ can have any value (except unity) between zero and infinity, η_C and η_q can be an order of magnitude apart.

This analysis reinforces what is suggested by the comparison of (3.23) with (3.24b): in general, information about the numerical magnitude of η_q alone, without specific information about the form of the utility function, provides little guidance regarding the likely magnitude of η_C, and vice versa. Therefore, McFadden and Leonard's approach of assessing the reliability of a contingent valuation survey on the basis of whether or not the estimate of η_C corresponds with their intuition about the magnitude of η_q seems somewhat questionable.

3.6. THE DISPARITY BETWEEN WTP AND WTA

To put things into perspective, it is useful to start by summarizing what is known about the relationship between WTP and WTA for changes in income or prices. If there is a pure change in income—i.e. (p,q) stay unchanged while income changes from y^0 to $y^1 = y^0 + \Delta y$—the resulting compensating and equivalent variation welfare measures defined by analogy with (3.4a,b) are *the same*: the maximum WTP for this change and the minimum WTA both equal Δy. But when the change involves either p or q, the compensating and equivalent variation measures are generally different. For price changes, the difference between the compensating and equivalent variation—C^p and E^p in (3.12a,b)—depends simply on an income effect. Willig (1976a) showed operationally how to bound this difference using information on the value of the income elasticity of demand for the commodities whose prices change. Randall and Stoll (1980) extended Willig's analysis to welfare measures for changes in q; they found that, with appropriate modifications, Willig's formulas carry over to C and E as defined in (3.4a,b), and they showed that one can bound $(E - C) = (\text{WTA} - \text{WTP})$ using information on the value of η_π over the interval $[q^0, q^1]$. Hanemann (1991) used (3.25) to show that the elasticity η_π actually involves not only an income effect but also a substitution effect. In this section, I elaborate on these results and extend them. I will refer to the difference in welfare measures, $(E - C)$, as the *WTP/WTA disparity*.

Using C^p and E^p, suppose for simplicity that only the price of good 1 changes; the WTP/WTA disparity for this price change is

$$E^p - C^p = \int_{p_1^0}^{p_1^1} [m_{p_1}(p, q, u^0) - m_{p_1}(p, q, u^1)] dp_1, \qquad (3.30a)$$

which implies

$$\text{sign}(E^p - C^p) = \text{sign}\big(m_{p_1 u}(p, q, u)\big). \tag{3.30b}$$

Moreover,

$$\frac{\partial C^p}{\partial y} = v_y(p^0, q, y) \int_{p_1^1}^{p_1^0} m_{p_1 u}(p, q, u^0) dp_1. \tag{3.31}$$

Assume that $p_1^1 \leqslant p_1^0$, so that $u^1 \geqslant u^0$, $C^p \geqslant 0$, and $E^p \geqslant 0$; it follows from (3.31) that

$$\text{sign}\left(\frac{\partial C^p}{\partial y}\right) = \text{sign}\left(\frac{\partial E^p}{\partial y}\right) = \text{sign}\big(m_{p_1 u}(p, q, u)\big) \tag{3.32}$$

and

$$E^p \gtrless C^p \Leftrightarrow \partial C^p / \partial y \gtrless 0 \Leftrightarrow \partial E^p / \partial y \gtrless 0.^{17} \tag{3.33}$$

For price changes, the second cross-partial derivative $m_{p_1 u}$ is the key to determining the sign and magnitude of the WTP/WTA disparity. Observe that

$$m_{p_1 u}(p, q, u) = g_u^1(p, q, u) = h_y^1(p, q, m(p, q, u)) \cdot m_u(p, q, u). \tag{3.34}$$

Since $m_u > 0$, the term $m_{p_1 u}$ reflects the income effect associated with good 1:

$$\text{sign}\big(m_{p_1 u}(p, q, u)\big) = \text{sign}\big(h_y^1(p, q, y)\big).$$

Hence the result that, for a price change, the WTP/WTA disparity depends simply on the income effect associated with the commodity involved. This also carries over to multiple price changes: WTA > WTP if all the goods whose prices change are normal goods, and WTA < WTP if they all are inferior goods.

Mäler (1974) established an analogous result for a change in q, viz., WTA > WTP if q is normal in Mäler's sense, and WTA < WTP if q is inferior. He obtained this by rearranging (3.5a,b) into the form

$$E - C = \int_{q^0}^{q^1} [m_q(p, q, u^0) - m_q(p, q, u^1)] dq, \tag{3.35a}$$

which implies

$$\text{sign}(E - C) = -\text{sign}\big(m_{qu}(p, q, u)\big). \tag{3.35b}$$

Combining this with (3.18b) yields the result that, when $q^1 \geqslant q^0$,[18]

---

[17] When $p_1^1 \geqslant p_1^0$, one has: sign $(\partial C^p / \partial y) = -\text{sign}(m_{p_1 u}) = -\text{sign}(E^p - C^p)$, and similarly with $\partial E^p / \partial y$.

[18] When $q^1 \leqslant q^0$, one has: $\text{sign}(\partial C / \partial y) = \text{sign}(\partial E / \partial y) = -\text{sign}(E - C)$.

$$E \gtrless C \Leftrightarrow \partial C/\partial y \gtrless 0 \Leftrightarrow \partial E/\partial y \gtrless 0. \qquad (3.3b)$$

Not only is (3.36) analogous to the result for a price change, (3.33), but also both are examples of a general result on the WTP/WTA disparity that was first noticed by Cook and Graham (1977). Given $C^z = C^z(x, z^0, z^1)$ and $E^z = E^z(x, z^0, z^1)$ as defined in (3.11a,b), and assuming now that z is a scalar, one has:

PROPOSITION 3.6   (WTP/WTA disparity):
1. If C^z and E^z are non-negative,

$$E^z \gtrless C^z \Leftrightarrow \partial C^z/\partial x \lessgtr 0 \Leftrightarrow \partial E^z/\partial x \lessgtr 0.$$

2. If C^z and E^z are non-positive,

$$E^z \gtrless C^z \Leftrightarrow \partial C^z/\partial x \lessgtr 0 \Leftrightarrow \partial E^z/\partial x \lessgtr 0.$$

3. If V is non-decreasing in both x and z,

$$\text{sign}(E^z - C^z) = -\text{sign}(M_{zu}(u, z)) = \text{sign}(V_x V_{xz} - V_z V_{xx}).$$

4. If V is non-decreasing in x but non-increasing in z,

$$\text{sign}(E^z - C^z) = \text{sign}(M_{zu}(u, z)) = \text{sign}(V_z V_{xx} - V_x V_{xz}).$$

5. $E^z \equiv C^z \Leftrightarrow u = V[x + \phi(z)]$ for some function $\phi(\cdot)$.

PROOF. Cook and Graham (1977) established (1) and (2) by using the representation in (3.4a′) and (3.4b′) to obtain

$$E^z(x, z^0, z^1) = C^z[x + E^z(x, z^0, z^1), z^0, z^1], \qquad (3.37a)$$
$$C^z(x, z^0, z^1) = E^z[x - C^z(x, z^0, z^1), z^0, z^1]. \qquad (3.37b)$$

Hence,

$$E^z - C^z = C^z[x + E^z(x, z^0, z^1), z^0, z^1] - C^z(x, z^0, z^1)$$
$$= E^z(x, z^0, z^1) - E^z[x - C^z(x, z^0, z^1), z^0, z^1], \qquad (3.37c)$$

from which (1) and (2) follow directly. With regard to (3) and (4), by proceeding along the lines leading up to (3.35a), one obtains

$$E^z - C^z = \int_{z^1}^{z^0} [M_z(u^1, z) - M_z(u^0, z)] dz,$$

from which the first sign equalities in (3) and (4) follow directly. For the second, implicitly differentiate $u = V(x, z)$ to obtain

$$M_{zu} = \frac{\partial^2 x}{\partial z \partial u} = \frac{1}{V_x^3}(V_z V_{xx} - V_x V_{zx}), \qquad (3.38)$$

and note that $V_x \geqslant 0$. Point (5) follows from the observation that $M_{zu} = 0 \Leftrightarrow x = M(u, z) = \gamma(u) + \phi(z)$.   QED

Proposition 3.6 provides a general characterization of the WTP/WTA disparity. When $V(\cdot) = v(p, q, y)$ is viewed as a function of y and q, Proposition 3.6 yields (3.19a, b, c) and (3.36); when $v(p, q, y)$ is viewed as a function of y and p_1, it yields (3.33). It requires no substantive restriction on $V(\cdot)$ other than differentiability. In particular, it does not require quasi-concavity. Loehman (1991) and Ebert (1993) invoke quasi-concavity in their analysis of the WTP/WTA disparity, but this is unnecessary.[19] Loehman also introduces assumptions equivalent to $V_{xx} \leqslant 0$ and $V_{zx} \geqslant 0$, but, as Ebert points out, the signs of these derivatives are not invariant with respect to a monotone transformation of $V(\cdot)$. The lack of invariance does not apply to the derivatives in parts (3) and (4) of Proposition 3.6. Let $\tilde{V}(x, z) \equiv T[V(x, z)]$ be a monotone transformation, with $T'(\cdot) \geqslant 0$, and let $\tilde{M}(u, z)$ denote the inverse of $u = \tilde{V}(x, z)$. Implicit differentiation yields $\tilde{M}_{zu} = \{V_z V_{xx} - V_x V_{xz}\}/V_x^3 T' = M_{zu}/T'$. Thus, the sign of M_{zu} is invariant with respect to a monotone transformation of utility, and likewise that of $\{V_z V_{xx} - V_x V_{zx}\}$.

In the case of C and E, on the basis of (3.36) one might be inclined to conclude that the WTP/WTA disparity depends simply on an income effect, corresponding to the difference in the base income at which they are evaluated. This is how Cook and Graham characterize the situation—C and E 'differ by only a wealth effect' (1977: 147)—and many other commentators have expressed a similar view (e.g. Diamond *et al.* 1993: 65). While correct, it is misleading, since the 'wealth effect' in (3.36) is *not* the same as what is called the 'income effect' in consumer demand theory. In the case of C^p and E^p, it *is* true that the WTP/WTA disparity depends on the income effect associated with the cross-partial derivative $m_{p_1 u}$, as indicated in (3.34). In the case of C and E, the WTP/WTA disparity depends on the cross-partial derivative m_{qu}. But there is a crucial difference between these two derivatives. Using (3.16) and implicitly differentiating $q = \hat{g}^q(p, \pi, u)$ yields

$$m_{qu}(p, q, u) = \frac{\hat{g}_u^q(p, \pi, u)}{\hat{g}_\pi^q(p, \pi, u)}. \tag{3.39}$$

The numerator in (3.39) represents what would be called the 'income effect' if q were a marketed commodity, based on the derivative of its demand function with respect to income, since

$$\hat{g}_u^q(p, \pi, u) = \hat{h}_y^q(p, \pi, \hat{m}(p, \pi, u)) \cdot \hat{m}_u(p, \pi, u), \tag{3.40}$$

which is analogous to (3.34). But, comparing (3.39) with (3.34), there is an extra component in m_{qu} that does not arise in $m_{p_1 u}$: the denominator in (3.39) is the own-price derivative of the compensated demand function for q. In

---

[19] V quasi-concave in (x, z) is equivalent to $\{V_x^2 V_{zz} - 2V_x V_z V_{xz} + V_z^2 V_{xx}\} \leqslant 0$. This is neither necessary nor sufficient to fix the sign of $\{V_x V_{zx} - V_z V_{xx}\}$. Figures 3.5 and 3.6 below provide a graphical illustration that quasi-concavity is not required to sign $(E^z - C^z)$.

Hanemann (1991) I show that, when converted to elasticity form, this involves the Allen–Uzawa elasticity of substitution between q and the x's as a group, σ, weighted by the budget share of the x's:

$$\hat{g}_\pi^q \cdot (\pi/q) = -\sigma(1 - \alpha), \qquad (3.41)$$

where $\alpha \equiv \pi q/(y + \pi q)$. Hence, the denominator in (3.39) represents what would be called the 'substitution effect' if q were a marketed commodity; it reflects the curvature of the indifference curves between q and the x's as a group. This, in turn, reflects the convexity of the expenditure function in q, since implicitly differentiating $q = \hat{g}^q(p, \pi, u)$ and using (3.16) yields

$$\hat{g}_\pi^q(p, \pi, u) = -\frac{1}{m_{qq}(p, q, u)}. \qquad (3.42)$$

Thus, even if there is only a small income effect, and even if α (the budget share of q) is small, there can still be a substantial disparity between WTP and WTA if the elasticity of substitution, σ, is sufficiently low.

To summarize, there is a strong similarity between the formal results on WTP and WTA for price changes and changes in q: how WTP or WTA varies with income is linked to the direction of the WTP/WTA disparity, both being determined by a cross-partial derivative of the expenditure function. But, this should not obscure the fundamental difference in the structure of the derivatives.[20] The derivative involved in price changes, $m_{p_i u}$, reflects an income effect; the derivative involved in changes in q, m_{qu}, reflects not only an income effect but also a substitution effect.[21] Moreover, the substitution effect is likely to be more influential than the income effect in determining the magnitude of m_{qu}, and therefore the size of the WTP/WTA disparity. The Engel aggregation condition requires that the income elasticities of demand for the x's and q, weighted by their budget shares, sum to unity; this tends to limit the possible size of the income effect associated with q. By contrast, the substitution effect can vary all the way from zero to infinity. Hence, the denominator in (3.39), more than the numerator, is likely to influence the value of the ratio.[22]

A graphical illustration of these points may be helpful. Figure 3.1 illustrates the WTP/WTA disparity for the case where q is a scalar and the x's are represented by a composite commodity with a price of unity. The initial utility is $u^0 = u(y, q^0) = v(1, q^0, y)$. When q rises from q^0 to q^1, utility increases to $u^1 = u(y, q^1) = v(1, q^1, y)$. The indifference curves exhibit a diminishing marginal rate of substitution between x and q, consistent with

[20] This parallels the difference between η_C, the income elasticity of WTP, and η_q, the income elasticity of demand, discussed in S. 3.5.

[21] The same holds for M_{zu} if $V(x, z)$ is treated as a direct utility function, with z taking the role of q. It can be shown that M_{zu} is the ratio of terms representing an income effect for z and a substitution effect between z and x.

[22] Hanemann (1991) presents some numerical examples that support this conclusion.

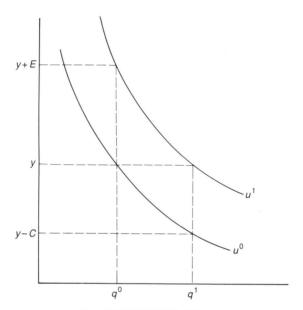

Fig. 3.1 WTP/WTA disparity

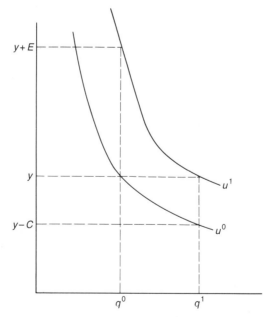

Fig. 3.2 WTP/WTA disparity: low elasticity of substitution

$u(x, q)$ being quasi-concave in (x, q). The monetary measures of the utility change, C and E, are indicated on the vertical axis. The situation depicted is one where $E > C$. It can be seen from the diagram that two factors account for the WTP/WTA disparity. One is the *curvature* of the indifference curves, which corresponds to the substitution effect in the denominator of (3.39). When these are *more highly* curved, as in Fig. 3.2, which corresponds to a *lower* Allen–Uzawa elasticity of substitution between q and x, the WTP/WTA disparity *widens*. The second factor is the *spacing* of the indifference curves, which determines the income effect in the numerator of (3.39). In Fig. 3.1, the indifference curves for u^0 and u^1 are *parallel* displacements, which corresponds to a unitary income elasticity η_q. The WTP/WTA disparity *widens* if indifference curves are spaced as in Fig. 3.3, where the marginal rate of substitution between q and x *rises* along any ray from the origin, implying an income elasticity $\eta_q > 1$. Conversely, if the indifference curves are spaced as in Fig. 3.4, where the marginal rate of substitution *falls* along any ray from the origin, implying a negative η_q (q is an inferior good), the WTP/WTA disparity changes direction: $E < C$.

Figures 3.5 and 3.6 show what happens when the indifference curves are *concave*, i.e. $v(q, y)$ is quasi-convex in (q, y). In that case, as noted earlier, the demand function $\hat{g}^q(p, \pi, u)$ is not well-behaved, since the minimization

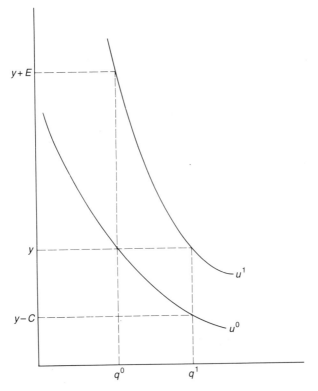

Fig. 3.3 WTP/WTA disparity: income elasticity exceeds unity

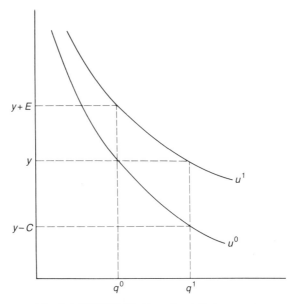

Fig. 3.4 WTP/WTA disparity: inferior good

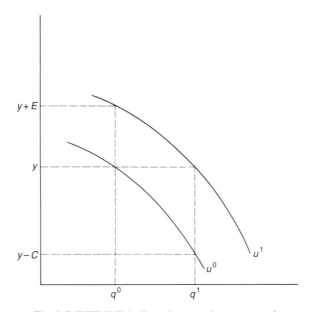

Fig. 3.5 WTP/WTA disparity: quasi-convex preferences

problem in (3.14d) yields a corner solution for q. The important point is that, when $v(q, y)$ is quasi-convex in (q, y), the cross-partial derivative m_{qu} still

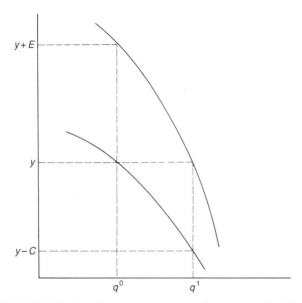

Fig. 3.6 WTP/WTA disparity: quasi-convex preferences and inferior good

involves the combination of an income effect and a substitution effect, but the substitution effect is now positive rather than negative, which *reverses* the sign of m_{qu} for a given spacing of the indifference curves.[23] Hence, when $v(q, y)$ is quasi-convex in (q, y) and the indifference curves are parallel displacements, as in Fig. 3.5, one now has $m_{qu} > 0$, compared with $m_{qu} < 0$ for $u(x, q)$ quasi-concave in (x, q) (cf. Fig. 3.1), and the WTP/WTA disparity changes direction: $E < C$. Figure 3.6 depicts the case where $v(q, y)$ is quasi-convex in (q, y) but the indifference curves are spaced as in Fig. 3.4; the spacing of the indifference curves offsets their curvature, the net effect is $m_{qu} < 0$, and the standard WTP/WTA disparity obtains.

If the indifference curves were parallel straight lines, unlike those shown in Figs. 3.1–6, there would be *no* WTP/WTA disparity.[24] As noted above, this is equivalent to a utility model with the form of (3.19b). This form implies perfect substitution (linear indifference curves) in the *indirect* utility function between y and $\psi(p, q)$. That may or may not involve perfect substitution in the *direct* utility function between q and the x's. Examples where it does are

$$u = u(x_1 + \psi(q), x_2, \ldots, x_N) \qquad (3.43a)$$

---

[23] One now has $\hat{g}_\pi^q \gtrless 0$, which reverses the sign of m_{qu} in (3.39).
[24] When there is *no* WTP/WTA disparity for q, Cook and Graham (1977) call q a 'replaceable' commodity; when $E \neq C$ they call q an 'irreplaceable' commodity. In some ways this seems an unfortunate choice of terminology; it would be odd to call a marketed commodity 'irreplaceable' whenever $E^p \neq C^p$.

and

$$u = u(x_1 + \psi_1(q), \ldots, x_N + \psi_N(q)). \qquad (3.43b)$$

In (3.43a), x_1 is a perfect substitute for q; in (3.43b), *every* x_i is a perfect substitute for q. In both cases, the denominator in (3.39) is infinite, corresponding to $\sigma = \infty$ in (3.41); at the same time, the numerator is zero.[25] By contrast, the utility model

$$u = T[\psi(p,q) + y\phi(p), p] = K\left[\phi(p) \cdot \left(y + \frac{\psi(p,q)}{\phi(p)}\right), p\right] \qquad (3.44)$$

generates $m_{qu} = 0$ without imposing perfect substitution between q and any of the x's. In this case, the numerator in (3.39) is zero, but the denominator is finite. Thus, perfect substitution between y and some function of q is both necessary and sufficient for the absence of a WTP/WTA disparity, while perfect substitution between the x's and q is sufficient but not necessary.

3.7. THE DISPARITY BETWEEN GAINS AND LOSSES

Over the past fifteen years, considerable evidence has accumulated regarding the presence of a pattern of behaviour in judgement and choice involving phenomena known variously as *loss aversion*, the *endowment effect*, or *status quo bias*.[26] The essence of these phenomena is that individuals weigh losses more heavily than comparable gains. The evidence comes from experiments in which researchers have elicited values for changes in an item like q. However, the changes are different from those considered so far. Up to now, I have compared the WTP for some particular change in q to the WTA for the same change in q. By contrast, many of the empirical experiments compare the WTP for an *increase* in q with the WTA for a comparable *decrease* in q. As I now show, this is a somewhat different matter.

Let $\Delta \geqslant 0$. I now use notation that distinguishes between a gain in q, where $q^1 \equiv q^0 + \Delta$, and a loss in q, where $q^1 \equiv q^0 - \Delta$. Since the absolute change is the same, these are *symmetric* changes in q.[27] In the case of a gain, utility changes from $u^0 \equiv v(p, q^0, y)$ to $u^+ \equiv v(p, q^0 + \Delta, y)$, while in the case of a loss it changes from u^0 to $u^- \equiv v(p, q^0 - \Delta, y)$. Setting $q^1 = q^0 + \Delta$ in (3.4a, b) or (3.5a, b) yields welfare measures that I denote C^+ and E^+, where

---

[25] This can be seen by manipulating the indirect utility functions which are, respectively,

$$u = T[y + \psi(q)p_1, p] \text{ and} \qquad (3.43c)$$
$$u = T[y + \sum \Psi_i(q)p_i, p]. \qquad (3.43d)$$

[26] References include Thaler (1980), Knetsch and Sinden (1984), Samuelson and Zeckhauser (1988), Knetsch (1989), and Kahneman *et al.* (1990).

[27] For much of the analysis in this section, q need not be a scalar: q^0, q^1, and Δ can all be vectors.

$C^+ \geq 0$ and $E^+ \geq 0$; setting $q^1 = q^0 - \Delta$ yields welfare measures that I denote C^- and E^-, where $C^- \leq 0$ and $E^- \leq 0$. Their relationship to WTP and WTA is: $WTP^+ = C^+$; $WTA^+ = E^+$; $WTP^- = -E^-$; and $WTA^- = -C^-$.

The discussion in Section 3.6 focused on the WTP/WTA disparity, $[WTA^+ - WTP^+]$ or $[WTA^- - WTP^-]$. By contrast, what I will call the 'gain/loss disparity' focuses on an individual's valuation of a gain versus a loss as measured by the difference between her WTA to suffer the loss and her WTP to secure the gain, $[WTA^- - WTP^+]$.

From (3.5a,b),

$$WTA^- - WTP^+ = -C^- - C^+ = m(p, q^0 - \Delta, u^0) + m(p, q^0 + \Delta, u^0) \\ - 2m(p, q^0, u^0).$$

Hence, $WTA^- \gtreqless WTP^+$ according to whether

$$\frac{m(p, q^0 - \Delta, u^0) + m(p, q^0 + \Delta, u^0)}{2} \gtreqless m(p, q^0, u^0). \qquad (3.45)$$

Observe that $q^0 = [(q^0 - \Delta) + (q^0 + \Delta)]/2$. Since (3.45) must hold for *all* Δ, it is equivalent to requiring Jensen's inequality. Combining this with Lemma 3.1 yields the following:[28]

PROPOSITION 3.7. A necessary and sufficient condition for the gain/loss disparity to occur (i.e. $WTA^- \geq WTP^+$) is that $m(p, q, u^0)$ is a convex function of q or, equivalently, that $v(p, q, y)$ is quasi-concave in (p, y). A necessary and sufficient condition for the disparity to run in the opposite direction $(WTA^- \leq WTP^+)$ is that $m(p, q, u^0)$ is a concave function of q.

Thus, while quasi-concavity is not required for the WTP/WTA disparity, as noted in the discussion of Proposition 3.6, it is essential to the gain/loss disparity. In terms of the utility model $V(x, z)$ used there, if one defines separate WTP and WTA measures for a symmetric increase and decrease in z, a parallel development yields (using the obvious notation):

PROPOSITION 3.8. The following are equivalent:
1. $WTA_z^- \geq (\leq) WTP_z^+$
2. $M(u, z)$ is convex (concave) in z; and
3. $V(x, z)$ is quasi-concave (quasi-convex) in (x, z).

When q is a scalar, the condition for the gain/loss disparity to occur takes the form

$$WTA^- \gtreqless WTP^+ \text{ as } m_{qq} \gtreqless 0. \qquad (3.46)$$

While the WTP/WTA disparity for q depends on m_{qu}, the gain/loss disparity depends on m_{qq}. Thus, whereas the WTP/WTA disparity involves

[28] Part of this result was also obtained by Loehman (1991) and Ebert (1993).

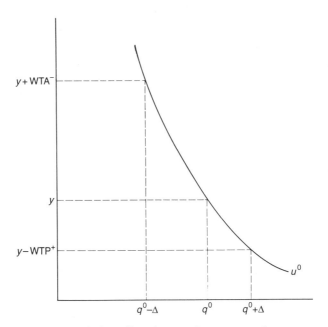

Fig. 3.7 Gain/loss disparity: quasi-concave preferences

both income and substitution effects, from (3.42) the gain/loss disparity hinges entirely on the substitution effect. This is illustrated in Figure 3.7, which depicts a situation where $u(x, q)$ is quasi-concave in $(x,\ q)$, leading to convex indifference curves. The monetary measures of utility change, WTA$^-$ and WTP$^+$, are indicated on the vertical axis. The gain/loss disparity involves a single indifference curve, so that the spacing of indifference curves (i.e. the income effect) is of no consequence. The curvature of the indifference curve is the key: the disparity arises because of the convexity of the indifference curve corresponding to u^0. Figure 3.8 shows what happens when the indifference curves are concave, corresponding to a quasi-convex $v(q,\ y)$. In that case, the gain/loss disparity runs in the opposite direction. Hence, the sign and magnitude of the disparity are determined by the curvature of the indifference curve corresponding to u^0.

When q is a scalar, it follows from (3.45) and (3.46) that there is *no* gain/ loss disparity if and only if $m_{qq} = 0$, which is equivalent to an expenditure function of the form

$$m(p,q,u) = \phi(p,u) - \psi(p,u)q, \qquad (3.47)$$

where $\psi(p, u) > 0$. The utility model in (3.47) somewhat resembles those in (3.10) and (3.19a), but it is not exactly the same as either. The model in (3.47) is a special case of (3.10) since it generates

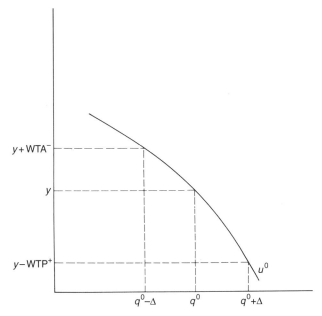

Fig. 3.8 Gain/loss disparity: quasi-convex preferences

$$C^+ = -C^- = \psi(p, u^0)\Delta, \tag{3.47a}$$

$$E^+ = -E^- = \psi(p, u^+)\Delta, \tag{3.47b}$$

but (3.10) does not necessarily imply (3.47). While (3.47) characterizes utility functions where $m_{qq} = 0$, (3.19a, b) characterize those where $m_{qu} = 0$. Neither implies nor is implied by the other. Thus, (3.47) yields $[E^+ - C^+] = [\psi(p, u^+) - \psi(p, u^0)]\Delta$, which can be positive or negative depending on whether $\psi(p, u)$ is increasing or decreasing in u. Hence, there can be a positive or negative WTP/WTA disparity combined with *no* gain loss disparity. Conversely, (3.19b) implies $[\text{WTA}^+ - \text{WTP}^+] = [\text{WTA}^- - \text{WTP}^-] = 0$, but it also implies that

$$[\text{WTA}^- - \text{WTP}^+] = 2\psi(p, q^0) - \psi(p, q^0 - \Delta) - \psi(p, q^0 + \Delta) \gtrless 0,$$

depending on whether $\psi(p, q)$ is concave or convex in q. Thus, with (3.19a,b), while there is no WTP/WTA disparity, there can be a positive or negative gain/loss disparity.

If $\psi(p, u)$ in (3.47) is independent of u, this yields a model that is consistent with both $m_{qq} = 0$ and $m_{qu} = 0$—i.e. it also is nested within (3.9a, b). That model is

$$u = T[y + \psi(p)q, p], \tag{3.48a}$$

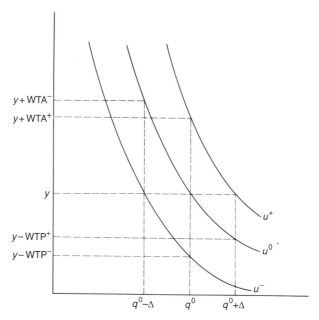

Fig. 3.9 Gain/loss disparity exceeds WTP/WTA disparity

and it generates

$$C^+ = E^+ = C^- = E^- = \psi(p)\Delta, \qquad (3.48b)$$

so that there is both no WTP/WTA disparity and no gain/loss disparity.

An implication is that the gain/loss disparity can be larger or smaller than the WTP/WTA disparity, depending on the form of the utility function. For example, Fig. 3.9 depicts a situation where the gain/loss disparity exceeds the WTP/WTA disparity, while Fig. 3.10 depicts the reverse, both involving preferences that are quasi-concave in (x, q). What is required in order to rank order the two disparities? By definition, the gain/loss disparity $[\text{WTA}^- - \text{WTP}^+]$ exceeds the WTP/WTA disparity $[\text{WTA}^+ - \text{WTP}^+]$ when $\text{WTA}^- > \text{WTA}^+$, i.e. when

$$-C^- E^+ = m(p, q^0 - \Delta, u^0) - m(p, q^0, u^+) > 0. \qquad (3.49a)$$

Similarly, the gain/loss disparity exceeds the WTP/WTA disparity $[\text{WTA}^- - \text{WTP}^-]$ when $\text{WTP}^- > \text{WTP}^+$, i.e. when

$$E^- \quad C^+ = m(p, q^0 + \Delta, u^0) - m(p, q^0, u^-) > 0. \qquad (3.49b)$$

The following proposition identifies circumstances in which those inequalities obtain:[29]

---

[29] This extends a result mentioned in footnote 25 of Hanemann (1991).

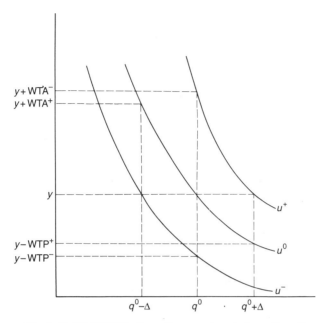

Fig. 3.10 WTP/WTA disparity exceeds gain/loss disparity

PROPOSITION 3.9. A sufficient condition for the gain/loss disparity to exceed the WTP/WTA disparity is that the utility function has the form

$$u = T[\phi(p, y) + \psi(p, q), p], \tag{3.50}$$

where $\psi(p, q)$ is a concave function of q, or

$$u = T[\phi(p, y) \cdot \psi(p, q), p], \tag{3.51}$$

where $\psi(p, q)$ is a log-concave function of q.[30] If $\psi(p, q)$ is a convex function of q in (3.50), or a log-convex function in (3.51), the WTP/WTA disparity exceeds the gain/loss disparity.

PROOF. The expenditure function corresponding to (3.50) takes the form

$$y = K[\zeta(p, u) - \psi(p, q), p], \tag{3.50a}$$

where $\zeta(p, u)$ is the inverse of $T[\cdot, p]$ with respect to its first argument, and $K[\cdot, p]$ is the inverse of $\phi(p, y)$ with respect to y. Applying (3.49a)—a similar argument can be made using (3.49b)—one finds that, with (3.50), $-C^- - E^+ > (<)0$ when

$$K[\zeta(p, u^0) - \psi(p, q^0 - \Delta), p] > (<)K[\zeta(p, u^+) - \psi(p, q^0), p]$$

---

[30] A function $f(x)$ is said to be *log-concave* if $\ln f(x)$ is a concave function of x, and similarly with log-convex.

or, equivalently, when

$$\zeta(p,u^0) - \psi(p,q^0-\Delta) > (<)\zeta(p,u^+) - \psi(p,q^0)$$

or

$$\psi(p,q^0) - \psi(p,q^0-\Delta) > (<)\zeta(p,u^+) - \zeta(p,u^0). \qquad (3.52)$$

Now, since $u^0 = T[\phi(p,y) + \psi(p,q^0), p]$, it follows that

$$\zeta(p,u^0) = \phi(p,y) + \psi(p,q^0); \qquad (3.53a)$$

and, since $u^+ = T[\phi(p,y) + \psi(p,q^0+\Delta), p]$, it follows that

$$\zeta(p,u^+) = \phi(p,y) + \psi(p,q^0+\Delta). \qquad (3.53b)$$

Combining (3.53a) and (3.53b) yields

$$\zeta(p,u^+) - \zeta(p,u^0) = \psi(p,q^0+\Delta) - \psi(p,q^0). \qquad (3.54)$$

Substituting (3.54) into (3.52), $-C^- - E^+ > (<)\,0$ when

$$\psi(p,q^0) - \psi(p,q^0-\Delta) > (<) \quad \psi(p,q^0+\Delta) - \psi(p,q^0)$$

or

$$\psi(p,q^0) > (<)[\psi(p,q^0+\Delta) + \psi(p,q^0-\Delta)]/2. \qquad (3.55)$$

Since (3.55) must hold for *all* Δ, as in (3.45) it is equivalent to requiring Jensen's inequality: iff $\psi(p,q)$ is a concave function of q, then $\psi(p,q^0) >$ the right-hand side of (3.55); iff it is a convex function of q, $\psi(p,q^0) <$ the right-hand side of (3.55). In the case of the utility model (3.51), the expenditure function takes the form

$$y = K[\zeta(p,u)/\psi(p,q), p]. \qquad (3.51a)$$

The condition for $-C^- - E^+ > (<)0$ is that

$$\psi(p,q^0)/\psi(p,q^0-\Delta) > (<)\ \zeta(p,u^+)/\zeta(p,u^0)$$

or, equivalently, that

$$\psi(p,q^0)^2 > (<)\psi(p,q^0+\Delta) \cdot \psi(p,q^0-\Delta),$$

from which the result follows directly.   QED

It should be noted that, if $\psi(p,q)$ is a concave function of q in (3.50) or a log-concave function in (3.51), those indirect utility functions are quasi-concave in q. However, the converse is *not* true: a utility function can be quasi-concave in q without taking the form in (3.50) or (3.51). Figure 3.10 illustrates such a case. Utility models to which Proposition 3.9 applies include (3.28) and (3.29a), provided that $\sigma \geqslant 1$. Proposition 3.9 also applies to the constant-η_π utility models, (3.21a) and (3.22a), since they have the structure of (3.50). In these models if $G(p, q)$ is concave in q, the gain/loss disparity exceeds the WTP/WTA disparity. To the extent that quasi-concave utility models possessing the structure of Proposition 3.9 are common in real life, this suggests that efforts at empirical measurement will detect a larger gain/loss disparity than WTP/WTA disparity. Moreover, it follows from (3.55) that the difference between the two disparities is greater (smaller) when $\psi(p, q)$ is more (less) concave in q. Finally, the results in Proposition 3.9 also carry over to the welfare measures C^z and E^z in (3.11a, b), where z can now be a vector:

PROPOSITION 3.10. A sufficient condition for the gain/loss disparity to exceed the WTP/WTA disparity with the utility model $V(x, z)$ is that it have the form

$$u = V[\phi(x) + \psi(q)] \tag{3.58a}$$

where $\psi(\cdot)$ is a concave function of q, or

$$u = V[\phi(x) \cdot \psi(q)] \tag{3.58b}$$

where $\psi(\cdot)$ is a log-concave function of q. If $\psi(q)$ is a convex function in (3.58a), or a log-convex function in (3.58b), the WTP/WTA disparity exceeds the gain/loss disparity.

3.8. LOSS AVERSION AND OTHER EXPLANATIONS OF DIVERGENCE BETWEEN WTP AND WTA

I have emphasized the role of substitution and income effects in accounting for divergences between WTP and WTA for changes in q. Many instances of a divergence between elicited WTP and WTA values have been reported in the literature. However, the reader may wonder whether my analysis provides the only—or, indeed, the most plausible—explanation of the observed divergences. It certainly is not the only explanation. At least four other explanations have been proposed by other researchers: transaction costs; loss aversion or the endowment effect associated with Tversky and Kahneman's (1991) reference dependence model; models that invoke economic responses to uncertainty in valuation; and respondent satisficing and other survey-related phenomena.

I start with the survey-related explanations. Most of the existing evidence for what I have called the WTP/WTA disparity comes from contingent valuation surveys that use an *open-ended* question format, as opposed to a *closed-ended* format. In my experience, the open-ended format is generally less reliable and is vulnerable to several factors that can exaggerate the disparity between WTP and WTA. There is substantial evidence that respondents find it much harder to answer an open-ended than closed-ended valuation question, regardless of whether it involves market versus non-market goods, or use versus non-use values. If one presents people with a specific cost for an item, as in the closed-ended format, they can usually say quite readily whether or not they would be willing to pay (or accept) this amount. But, asking them to identify their *maximum* WTP, or *minimum* WTA, is typically an onerous request that requires much cognitive effort. In order to bracket one's WTP accurately, one must have experienced—or be able to imagine—not only buying the good but also *refusing to buy* it because the price is too high. When survey respondents face a difficult task, they often seek to simplify it or evade it, using a variety of what Krosnick (1991) has called *satisficing* strategies. For example, they may offer a response that does not fully supply the requested information but is good enough; or they may answer a *different* question that they find easier. In an open-ended contingent valuation survey, respondents may feel satisfied offering *an* amount that they are willing to pay, just not their maximum WTP, or *an* amount they are willing to accept, just not their minimum WTA.[31] Thus, they systematically understate WTP and overstate WTA. There is also considerable evidence that respondents often reply to an open-ended WTP question by saying instead what they think the item could *cost*, as long as this is an amount they are willing to pay. In ordinary life, there is a social norm against overpaying; you shouldn't pay more for something than it really costs. Respondents apply this in CV surveys, too. A similar norm can arise with WTA surveys: you shouldn't sell something for less than a buyer will pay. Therefore, respondents may answer an open-ended WTA question by saying instead what they think a buyer is likely to offer, as long as this is an amount they are willing to accept. Thus open-ended WTP questions may elicit the truncated WTP distribution, truncated from above; and open-ended WTA questions may elicit the truncated WTA distribution, truncated from below. In both cases, the truncation exaggerates the disparity between WTP and WTA.

Turning to economic explanations, transaction costs were suggested by Randall and Stoll (1980) and Brookshire *et al.* (1980) as an explanation of the WTP/WTA disparity. Transaction costs and search costs are perhaps even more relevant for the gain/loss disparity. If you own an item and lose it, it may take you some time to find the perfect replacement; these costs of search and other transaction costs are avoided if you don't lose the item. But, if you never had the item in the first place, you would expect to have to search for it and incur transactions costs anyway. Thus, these costs drive a wedge between what you are prepared to pay for a gain and what you have to be compensated to accept a loss.

---

[31] Along these lines, Magat *et al.* (1988) observe that 'the cognitive search process that many consumers use for determining their reservation price probably starts by finding an acceptable price for the product and then approaching the maximum willingness to pay *from below*' (italics added).

Loss aversion and the endowment effect are associated with Tversky and Kahneman's (1991) reference dependence model. This extends to riskless choice Kahneman and Tversky's (1979) prospect theory model of choice under uncertainty. In both models, choice outcomes are evaluated using a utility function that has three essential characteristics. The first is *reference dependence*: people have *relative* rather than absolute preferences for items, and they judge a situation not in terms of absolute levels of attributes but rather relative to some reference level. This can be the *status quo*, the pre-existing level of the item, or it can be a *norm* or an *expectation* regarding the item's level. Whatever it is, the reference point serves as a benchmark for valuation: everything else is either a gain in some dimension (an improvement over the reference point in that dimension) or a loss (a decrease relative to the reference point). Figure 3.11(*a*) illustrates this for the two-dimensional case, where $\bar{y}$ is the reference level of y and $\bar{q}$ the reference level of q. Given the reference point, Tversky and Kahneman's second postulate is *loss aversion*: losses are weighed more heavily ('loom larger') than corresponding gains. This is represented by the indifference curve in Fig. 3.11(*a*), which is *steeper* in the upper-left quadrant than in the lower-right quadrant. The asymmetry creates a kink (discontinuity in the slope) at the status quo point. Their third postulate is *diminishing sensitivity*: the marginal value of both gains and losses *decreases* with distance from the reference point, in that the slope of the indifference curve through a point is flatter the further it is located from the reference point, as shown in Fig. 3.11(*a*). Alternatively, they postulate *constant* sensitivity, which holds that the slope of the indifference curve is the same for all points located on the same side of the reference point, as depicted in Fig. 3.11(*b*). Tversky and Kahneman show that preferences implied by these three postulates can explain many observed behavioural phenomena in both real markets and economic experiments, including the endowment effect (Thaler 1980), status quo bias (Samuelson and Zeckhauser 1988), and other behavioural asymmetries involving gains versus losses.

The notion of reference dependence can readily be incorporated into a standard utility model. Let $(\bar{x}, \bar{q})$ denote the reference point that the individual applies when assessing outcomes involving different levels of (x, q). Then, her utility function takes the form $u = u(x, q; \bar{x}, \bar{q})$. In terms of the conventional, neo-classical utility model, $\bar{x}$ and $\bar{q}$ are additional parameters in the utility function. These affect the demand functions and the indirect utility and expenditure functions, which now take the form $x_i = h^i(p, q, y; \bar{x}, \bar{q})$, $x_i = g^i(p, q, u; \bar{x}, \bar{q})$, $v(p, q, y; \bar{x}, \bar{q})$, and $m(p, q, y; \bar{x}, \bar{q})$. These functions have the standard properties with regard to (p, q, y) and (p, q, u), except that, if the indifference curves are kinked at $(\bar{x}, \bar{q})$, the demand functions will be discontinuous at that point.[32] But, while $u(x, q; \bar{x}, \bar{q})$ may be more realistic than

---

[32] Empirical examples of reference-dependent demand models include Putler (1992) and Hardie *et al.* (1993).

W. MICHAEL HANEMANN

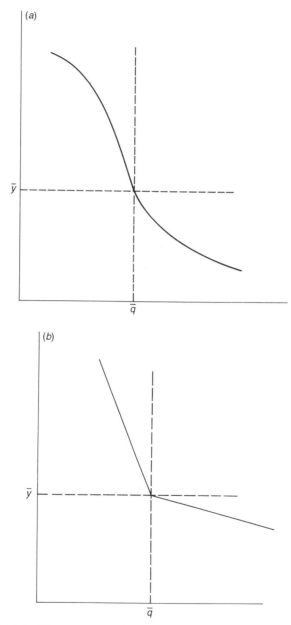

Fig. 3.11 Indifference curve with reference dependence loss aversion and (a) diminishing sensitivity and (b) constant sensitivity

the standard model, $u(x, q)$, it can be viewed as a particular case of the standard model with a more specific structure.

By way of illustration, Tversky and Kahneman (1991) discuss a particular form of reference dependence they call *additive constant loss aversion* which, for bivariate preferences, takes the form $V(x_1, x_2) = u_1(x_1) + u_2(x_2)$ where, for $i = 1, 2$,

$$u_i(x_i) = \begin{cases} \phi_i(x_i) - \phi_i(\bar{x}_i) & \text{if } x_i \geqslant \bar{x}_i, \\ [\phi_i(x_i) - \phi_i(\bar{x}_i)]/\lambda_i & \text{if } x_i \geqslant \bar{x}_i, \end{cases}$$

for some constants $\lambda_i > 0$. A particular example, considered by Hanemann (1987) and used by Tversky and Kahneman to illustrate additive constant loss aversion, is where the ϕ_i's are *linear*. Letting $V(\cdot, \cdot)$ be an indirect utility function, the linear additive constant loss aversion model is

$$u = v(q, y) = T[\alpha(q - \bar{q}) + \beta(y - \bar{y})] \tag{3.59a}$$

where $T' \geqslant 0$ and

$$
\begin{array}{llll}
\alpha = \alpha_1 & \text{if } q \geqslant \bar{q} & \text{and} & \alpha = \alpha_0 & \text{if } q < \bar{q} \\
\beta = \beta_1 & \text{if } y \geqslant \bar{y} & \text{and} & \beta = \beta_0 & \text{if } y < \bar{y}
\end{array}
\tag{3.59b}
$$

with $0 < \alpha_1 < \alpha_0$ and $0 < \beta_1 < \beta_0$. The resulting indifference map is depicted in Fig. 3.12, which corresponds to Tversky and Kahneman's Figure V. With this model, given a change in q from $q^0 = \bar{q}$ to either $q^+ = \bar{q} + \Delta$ or $q^- = \bar{q} - \Delta$, while $y = \bar{y}$, one finds that

$$\text{WTP}^+ = \alpha_1\Delta/\beta_0, \quad \text{WTA}^+ = \alpha_1\Delta/\beta_1, \quad \text{WTP}^- = \alpha_0\Delta/\beta_0, \text{ and}$$
$$\text{WTA}^- = \alpha_0\Delta/\beta_1.$$

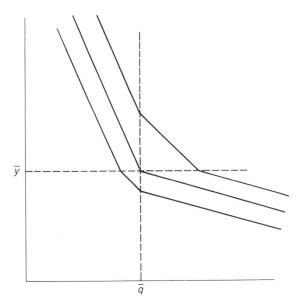

Fig. 3.12 Indifference curves for the linear additive constant loss aversion model

The assumptions on α and β imply

$$\alpha_0/\beta_1 > \alpha_1/\beta_1 > \alpha_1/\beta_0 \quad \text{and} \quad \alpha_0/\beta_1 > \alpha_0/\beta_0 > \alpha_1/\beta_0.$$

Because of these inequalities, as Tversky and Kahneman observe, the model exhibits the gain/loss disparity [WTA$^-$ > WTP$^+$]. As noted by Hanemann (1987), it also exhibits the WTP/WTA disparity [WTA$^+$ > WTP$^+$, WTA$^-$ > WTP$^-$], and this is smaller than the gain/loss disparity [WTA$^-$ > WTA$^+$].

Propositions 3.6, 3.7, and 3.9 predict these results and show that they are certainly not limited to the linear additive constant loss aversion model. For the WTP/WTA disparity, inversion of $v(q, y)$ in (3.59a) and differentiation yields

$$m_u(q, u) = \begin{cases} \zeta'(u)/\beta_1 & \text{if } \zeta(u) - \alpha(q - \bar{q}) \geqslant 0, \\ \zeta'(u)/\beta_0 & \text{if } \zeta(u) - \alpha(q - \bar{q}) < 0, \end{cases}$$

where $\alpha > 0$ is as specified in (3.59b), $\zeta(\cdot) \equiv T^{-1}(\cdot)$, and $\zeta' \geqslant 0$. Since $\beta_0 > \beta_1$, m_u falls as q increases, implying that $m_{qu} < 0$; the WTP/WTA disparity then follows from part (3) of Proposition 3.6. With regard to the gain/loss disparity, it can be shown that the function $\psi(q) \equiv \alpha(q - \bar{q})$ is a *concave* function of q when α is specified as in (3.59b). The monotone transformation $T(\cdot)$ in (3.59a) makes $v(q, y)$ a quasi-concave function of q, and the result follows immediately from Proposition 3.7. Moreover, since $\psi(q)$ is concave, $v(q, y)$ meets the sufficient condition, (3.50), in Proposition 3.9 for the gain/loss disparity to exceed the WTP/WTA disparity.

Considering loss aversion generally, reference dependence *per se* is not required in order to generate the gain/loss disparity. From Proposition 3.7, the essential requirement is convex indifference curves—i.e. less than perfect substitution in the indirect utility function between y and some function of q. Tversky and Kahneman's first and second postulates create this convexity through the kink at the reference point, as Figs. 3.11(a) and (b) show. But one does not need either a kink or a reference point in order to obtain convex indifference curves. All that one needs is the assumption of a quasi-concave utility function. Given that, one obtains a gain/loss disparity at each point along an indifference curve. In short, while reference-dependent preferences represent a separate explanation of the gain/loss disparity, they can also be subsumed under my explanation based on quasi-concavity and a disparity inversely proportion to the magnitude of the substitution effect.[33]

3.9. WTP AND WTA IN THE FACE OF UNCERTAINTY

The economic literature on choice under uncertainty and related literatures on bargaining and auctions have generated a variety of results that, in fact,

---

[33] I have no doubt that reference-dependent preferences occur, perhaps even frequently. However, I believe that the concept of reference dependence becomes most interesting when combined with models for the formation and change of the reference point. In a dynamic context, the concept has considerable bite; in a static context, it adds relatively little.

imply some form of disparity between WTP and WTA. In the context of univariate preferences for an uncertain income, Pratt (1964) showed that the buying price (i.e. WTP) equals the selling price (i.e. WTA) for a lottery if preferences are risk-neutral, but that they diverge if preferences are risk-averse or risk-prone. In single-offer bargaining with asymmetric information, it is optimal for the buyer to make an offer that is somewhat lower than his signal of the item's worth and for the seller to make an offer that is somewhat higher than his signal (Samuelson 1983). Similarly, it is optimal for bidders in first-price sealed-bid auctions to bid less than their private estimate of what the item is worth (Harris and Raviv 1981).

However, it is only recently that researchers have formally connected these results to the literature on WTP and WTA. Kolstad and Guzman (1995) develop the analogy between a subject's articulation of WTP or WTA in a contingent valuation survey and an agent's forming a bid in a sealed-bid auction. They consider double-sided auctions where some bidders are sellers and others are buyers. In their model, the divergence between expressed WTP and WTA arises from bidders' uncertainty about their value for the item. They show that, if the bidder is a buyer unsure of her value and information acquisition is costly, her bid to buy the item will be shaved downwards relative to her true WTP. Similarly, if the bidder is a seller, her asking price for the item will be shaved upwards relative to her true WTA. They also show that, as the cost of information acquisition decreases, the gap between buyer's bid price and seller's asking price shrinks.

Sileo (1995) develops a different type of model involving individuals who possess only imperfect access to their true preferences. Unlike conventional models of preference uncertainty (including that of Kolstad and Guzman), which assume cardinal utility, this uses ordinal preferences. True preferences are given by a conventional, ordinal utility function as in (3.1), but individuals base decisions on their perceptions, which are related to true preferences via a 'sensation of preference' function. Given a choice between two consumption bundles, if the sensation of preference is high, the individual can easily tell that one bundle is the better choice; if the sensation of preference is low, the choice is perceived to be far less transparent. Imperfect access to true preferences is reflected in a requirement that the sensation of preference exceed some threshold before the individual is aware of a particular preference. To assess changes in welfare, Sileo uses a maximin criterion derived from Bewley's (1986) *inertia assumption*, which holds that the individual is willing to accept a change 'only if it leads to a sure improvement'. Given this preference structure, Sileo models trade by an individual endowed with a consumption bundle and shows that the result is status quo bias, in that the individual requires more compensation to give up a good than she is willing to pay to acquire the same good.

Various other researchers have made arguments along similar lines to the effect that survey responses are likely to understate true WTP because of either strategic behaviour or risk aversion in the face of preference uncertainty. Magat *et al.* (1988), for example, suggest an analogy with real markets where people choose to understate their true valuation because they see it as a bargaining situation. Hoehn and Randall (1987) distinguish between value formation (which may be affected by uncertainty, time constraints, or incomplete optimization) and value statement (which may be affected by strategic behaviour). Although the models vary, they have this in common: they do not necessarily imply any disparity between WTP and WTA *in the individual's true preferences*. They predict a disparity in the individual's *overt behaviour* reflecting her reaction to the situation she faces—a downward bias in her expressed WTP relative to her true WTP, or an upward bias in her expressed WTA relative to her true WTA. In this regard, they resemble the survey-related explanations for a disparity between WTP and WTA mentioned earlier.

The key feature underlying all these explanations is a fundamental *asymmetry* in the consequences of providing too high a response versus too low a response. The asymmetry stems from the fact that true WTP or WTA are upper or lower bounds on value. The point can be illustrated most simply as follows. Assume an open-ended elicitation format. Suppose the individual is a buyer. Denote her true WTP by v, and let b be the price she states she is willing to pay. Her pay-off in the event that she obtains the item is $h(v - b)$, where $h' \geqslant 0$, and $h(x) \geqslant (\leqslant)0$ as $x \geqslant (\leqslant)0$. Because v is her maximum willingness to pay, she is unambiguously worse off having the item and paying any $b > v$ than not having it at all and getting $h(0) = 0$. However, b may also affect whether or not she gets the item. Let $\theta(b)$ represent the probability of her obtaining the item, where $\theta \geqslant 0$ and $\theta' \geqslant 0$. The objective function guiding her response is $W = h(v - b) \cdot \theta(b)$; this can be thought of as her expected utility.[34] She selects the response by maximizing W with respect to b. Assuming an interior solution, the first-order condition is

$$h'(v - b) \cdot \theta(b) = h(v - b) \cdot \theta'(b) \tag{3.60a}$$

which is solved for $b^* = b(v)$. Given that $h' \geqslant 0, \theta \geqslant 0$, and $\theta' \geqslant 0$, it follows from (3.60a) that, at the optimum, $h(v - b^*) \geqslant 0$, which implies that $b^* \leqslant v$. Hence, it is optimal for her expressed WTP to understate her true WTP. Conversely, if she is buyer and a is her asking price, while v is her true WTA, her pay-off is $h(a - v)$, where $h(\cdot)$ has the same properties as above. Since v is her minimum willingness to accept, at any $a \leqslant v$ she is worse off selling the item than keeping it and receiving $h(0) = 0$. Her choice of a may affect whether or not the item is sold; let $\phi(a)$ be an indicator or the probability that a sale occurs, with $\phi \geqslant 0$ and $\phi' \leqslant 0$. The asking price is determined by maximizing $W = h(a - v) \cdot \phi(a)$. Assuming an interior solution, the first-order condition is

---

[34] In the case of Sileo's model, $\theta(b)$ would be a binary indicator for whether or not she buys the item, rather than a probability. Still, his model implies the asymmetry in $h(\cdot)$.

$$h'(a - v) \cdot \phi(a) = -h(a - v) \cdot \phi'(a), \qquad (3.60b)$$

which is solved for $a^* = a(v)$. By the same line of argument as before it follows that $h(a^* - v) \geqslant 0$, which implies that $a^* \geqslant v$. Hence, it is optimal for expressed WTA to overstate true WTA.

But, while models with this structure—whether based on preference uncertainty/ignorance, strategic behaviour, or satisficing by survey respondents—imply a divergence between expressed and true WTP or WTA, they do not address the relationship between true WTP and true WTA. They are thus not inconsistent with a transactions cost explanation of the divergence between true WTP and WTA, or my explanation in sections 3.6 and 3.7 based on income and substitution effects.[35]

Moreover, it can be shown that choice under uncertainty with risk aversion generates divergences between true WTP and true WTA that parallel the WTP/WTA and gain/loss disparities in Sections 3.6 and 3.7 and can be explained using the same framework, modified for the distinctive features associated with risk. I present two examples here, deferring a more extensive discussion of valuation under uncertainty until another occasion.

The first example involves univariate preferences for an uncertain income stream. Consider an individual with an uncertain income, x, and a cardinal utility-of-income function, $u(x)$. Let $E\{x\} \equiv \mu$, and write income as $x = \mu + \epsilon$, where $E\{\epsilon\} = 0$. I assume that $\mu \geqslant 0$. The value to the individual of her uncertain income is measured by the certainty equivalent, x^*; this is her selling price, in the sense that she would be willing to exchange the risky income x for a certain income of x^*. If she is risk-averse, $x^* < \mu$. Her *risk premium* is $\pi = \pi(\mu) \equiv \mu - x^*$, where

$$E\{u(x)\} = u(\mu - \pi). \qquad (3.61a)$$

Conversely, $\gamma = \gamma(\mu)$ defined by

$$E\{u(x + \gamma)\} = u(\mu) \qquad (3.61b)$$

is the premium she would require to accept the risky income x instead of enjoying a certain income of μ. For a risk-neutral individual with utility

$$u(x) = a + bx, \qquad (3.62)$$

$\pi = \gamma = 0$. Pratt (1964) introduced the coefficient of absolute risk aversion, $r(x) \equiv -u''(x)/u'(x)$, and showed that, apart from risk neutrality, the only utility function with constant risk aversion is the exponential

$$u(x) = -\exp(-\lambda x) \qquad (3.63)$$

---

[35] Since Sileo's model uses an underlying utility model like (3.1), it is certainly consistent with my explanation.

for some $\lambda \geqslant 0$, where $r(x) = \lambda$. Pratt showed that π is independent of μ if and only if r is constant, as in (3.62) and (3.63). Moreover, when r is constant, $\pi = \gamma$ (LaValle 1978). Pratt also showed that π decreases with μ if and only if there is decreasing risk aversion (i.e. $r'(x) \leqslant 0$).

Despite the difference in setting, these results can all be shown to follow from Proposition 3.6. In the terms used there, the change is from a situation of no risk (i.e. a certain income of μ), analogous to z^0, to one of an uncertain income stream, x, analogous to z^1. For a risk-averse individual, the change lowers her utility. From (3.61a), she is willing to pay a premium of π to get rid of the risk; π measures her WTP to avoid risk. Similarly, from (3.61b), γ measures her WTA to put up with risk. The equivalence can be made more transparent, and the results can be broadened, using the framework introduced by Rothschild and Stiglitz (1970) for ordering distribution functions. Let $F(\epsilon, s)$ be the c.d.f. of ϵ, where $s \geqslant 0$ is a shift parameter. An increase in s signifies a mean-preserving increase in the spread of the distribution. By convention, there is no uncertainty (the distribution is a mass point) when $s = 0$. Denote expected utility by

$$V(\mu, s) \equiv E\{u(x)\} = E\{u(\mu + \epsilon)\} = \int u(\mu + \epsilon)F_\epsilon(\epsilon, s)d\epsilon \qquad (3.64)$$

$V(\mu, s)$ is increasing in μ; for a risk-averse individual, it is decreasing in s. Thus, it is isomorphic to $V(x, z)$ in Proposition 3.6. In terms of V, π and γ satisfy

$$V(\mu, s) = V(\mu - \pi, 0), \qquad (3.61a')$$

$$V(\mu + \gamma, s) = V(\mu, 0). \qquad (3.61b')$$

Hence, π is equivalent to $-E^z$ and γ is equivalent to $-C^z$.

Assuming $\pi \geqslant 0$ and $\gamma \geqslant 0$, Proposition 3.6 then implies that

$$\pi = \gamma \Leftrightarrow \partial \pi(\mu)/\partial \mu = 0 \Leftrightarrow \{V_\mu V_{\mu s} - V_s V_{\mu \mu}\} = 0, \qquad (3.65)$$

$$\pi > (<)\gamma \Leftrightarrow \partial \pi(\mu)/\partial \mu < (>) \quad 0 \Leftrightarrow \{V_\mu V_{\mu s} - V_s V_{\mu \mu}\} > (<)0. \qquad (3.66)$$

The term in braces can be signed from the assumptions on risk preferences. In the case of risk neutrality, (3.62), one finds from (3.64) that $V_{\mu \mu} = V_{\mu s} = 0$. In the case of exponential utility, (3.63), by differentiating (3.64) one finds that $V_{\mu s} = -\lambda V_s$ and $V_{\mu \mu} = -\lambda V_\mu$, which ensures that $\{V_\mu V_{\mu s} - V_s V_{\mu \mu}\} = 0$. Thus, Pratt's results on constant risk aversion follow from (3.65). With respect to (3.66), decreasing risk aversion implies that

$$u''(x)^2 < u'''(x) \cdot u'(x).\text{[36]} \qquad (3.67)$$

---

[36] The assumption of decreasing risk aversion implies that, in Mäler's terminology, the avoidance of risk is an inferior good. Whether that is plausible is an empirical question.

Assume that ϵ has a finite support $[\epsilon_L, \epsilon^U]$. Differentiation of (3.64) and integration by parts yields

$$
\begin{aligned}
V_s V_{\mu\mu} &= \int_{\epsilon_L}^{\epsilon^U} u''(\mu + \epsilon) \left[\int_{\epsilon_L}^{\epsilon} F_s(t,s)dt \right] d\epsilon \cdot \int_{\epsilon_L}^{\epsilon^U} u''(\mu + \epsilon) F_\epsilon(\epsilon,s) d\epsilon \\
&\leqslant (\epsilon^U - \epsilon_L) \int_{\epsilon_L}^{\epsilon^U} u''(\mu + \epsilon)^2 \left[\int_{\epsilon_L}^{\epsilon} F_s(t,s)dt \right] F_\epsilon(\epsilon,s) d\epsilon \\
&< (\epsilon^U - \epsilon_L) \int_{\epsilon_L}^{\epsilon^U} u'''(\mu + \epsilon) u'(\mu + \epsilon) \left[\int_{\epsilon_L}^{\epsilon} F_s(t,s)dt \right] F_\epsilon(\epsilon,s) d\epsilon \\
&\leqslant \int_{\epsilon_L}^{\epsilon^U} u'(\mu + \epsilon) F_\epsilon(\epsilon,s) d\epsilon \cdot \int_{\epsilon_L}^{\epsilon^U} u'''(\mu + \epsilon) \left[\int_{\epsilon_L}^{\epsilon} F_s(t,s)dt \right] d\epsilon \\
&= V_\mu V_{\mu s}
\end{aligned}
\tag{3.68}
$$

where the second inequality follows from (3.67), while the first and third use a result on the product of integrals in Apostol (1957: 245).[37] Thus, not only does (3.66) imply Pratt's result on decreasing risk aversion, but it also generalizes it from paying for complete certainty to paying to avoid a mean-preserving increase in risk.

The second example uses the utility function in (3.1) defined over both market goods, x, and the non-market q, and applies it to a setting of uncertainty. In my example, the uncertainty involves the level of q rather than the prices of market goods, p. Therefore, it is convenient to suppress the prices and simply write the indirect utility function as $v(q,y)$. Since one can think of this as implying a separate univariate utility-of-income function, $u(y)$, for each level of q, it is an instance of *state-dependent preferences*, where each possible level of q defines a separate state. To keep things simple, I consider two possible states, the status quo condition, q^0, and a worse condition, $q^1 < q^0$. With the status quo, utility is $u^0 = v(q^0, y)$; but with probability θ it will change to $u^1 = v(q^1, y)$. This formulation is widely used in the literature on health risks and insurance, with q denoting health status.[38] Two key assumptions in that literature are that 'one's overall utility is greater when in good health than in ill health' (Viscusi and Evans 1990)

$$
v(q^0, y) > v(q^1, y)
\tag{3.69}
$$

and that ill-health may affect—and, in particular, reduce—one's marginal utility of income, thereby making it optimal to have less than full income insurance:

$$
v_y(q^0, y) \geqslant v_y(q^1, y).
\tag{3.70}
$$

---

[37] Under decreasing risk aversion, $u'(x)$ is decreasing in x, while $u''(x)$ is increasing; I assume that $u'''(x)$ is increasing in x.

[38] Early examples include Zeckhauser (1970), Arrow (1974), and Cook and Graham (1977).

Since $u(x, q)$ is increasing in q, (3.69) is necessarily satisfied. Assuming maximization of expected utility, the compensating variation, $C^{q\theta} = C^{q\theta}(y, q^0, q^1, \theta)$, and equivalent variation, $E^{q\theta} = E^{q\theta}(y, q^0, q^1, \theta)$, are defined by

$$\theta \cdot v(q^1, y - C^{q\theta}) + (1 - \theta) \cdot v(q^0, y - C^{q\theta}) = v(q^0, y) \qquad (3.71a)$$

and

$$\theta \cdot v(q^1, y) + (1 - \theta) \cdot v(q^0, y) = v(q^0, y + E^{q\theta}). \qquad (3.71b)$$

Given (3.69), $C^{q\theta}$ and $E^{q\theta}$ are both non-positive; $-E^{q\theta}$ measures the individual's WTP to avoid the risk of a reduction in q, while $-C^{q\theta}$ measures her WTA to endure this risk.

Although there is an obvious resemblance between (3.71a,b) and (3.4a,b), there are some important differences between $C^{q\theta}$ or $E^{q\theta}$ and the welfare measures C or E. A striking example is the following. Evans and Viscusi (1991) find empirically that, for certain minor health effects, 'utility in an unhealthy state is tantamount to drop in income', which implies an indirect utility function of the form

$$u = v[y + \psi(q)] \qquad (3.72)$$

for some increasing function $\psi(\cdot)$.[39] The resulting welfare formulas are

$$\theta \cdot v[y - C^{q\theta} + \psi(q^1)] + (1 - \theta) \cdot v[y - C^{q\theta} + \psi(q^0)] = v[y + \psi(q^0)], \quad (3.72a)$$

$$\theta \cdot v[y + \psi(q^1)] + (1 - \theta) \cdot v[y + \psi(q^0)] = v[y + E^{q\theta} + \psi(q^0)]. \qquad (3.72b)$$

In general with (3.72a, b), $C^{q\theta} \neq E^{q\theta}$. But (3.72) is ordinally equivalent to (3.19b) with the price argument suppressed, and that implies that $C = E$.

What accounts for the difference between results that apply to C and E and those that apply to $C^{q\theta}$ and $E^{q\theta}$? Do results on the WTP/WTA disparity such as Proposition 3.6 still hold for $C^{q\theta}$ and $E^{q\theta}$? It turns out that there are two crucial differences between C or E and $C^{q\theta}$ or $E^{q\theta}$. The first is that the model in section 3.2 assumes *ordinal* preferences whereas that in (3.71a, b) or (3.72a, b) treats $v(q, y)$ as a *cardinal* utility function. The second is that $C^{q\theta}$ and $E^{q\theta}$ are *ex ante* welfare measures, whereas C and E are *ex post* welfare measures. Once these differences are recognized, especially the latter, the framework underlying Proposition 3.6, appropriately modified, carries over to $C^{q\theta}$ and $E^{q\theta}$.

With regard to preferences, if, instead of (3.72), the utility function is

$$u = y + \psi(q), \qquad (3.73)$$

---

[39] As Evans and Viscusi observe, this formulation implies that the marginal utility of income increases with ill-health, rather than decreasing as in (3.70), implying more than full income insurance.

then, indeed, one obtains $C^{q\theta} = E^{q\theta}$. In terms of ordinal utility, (3.19b), (3.72), and (3.73) are all *the same* preference ordering; assuming a given change in q (but no change in p), they all yield the same value of C or E. In terms of cardinal utility, however, they are *different* preference orderings; for example, (3.73) implies risk neutrality, while (3.72) could imply risk aversion or risk proneness. Moreover, when used for *ex ante* valuation, as already noted, they yield different measures of $C^{q\theta}$ or $E^{q\theta}$. The role of cardinal preferences is highlighted when one rewrites (3.71a,b) in the form

$$\theta \cdot [v(q^0, y - C^{q\theta}) - v(q^1, y - C^{q\theta})] = v(q^0, y - C^{q\theta}) - v(q^0, y), \quad (3.74a)$$

$$\theta \cdot [v(q^0, y) - v(q^1, y)] = v(q^0, y) - v(q^0, y + E^{q\theta}). \quad (3.74b)$$

The utility differences in (3.74a,b) are invariant with cardinal utility but not with ordinal utility.

With regard to the distinction between *ex ante* and *ex post* welfare evaluation, observe that when there is no uncertainty and the reduction in q occurs for sure (i.e. $\theta = 1$), it follows from (3.4a,b) and (3.71a,b) that $C^{q\theta} = C \leqslant 0$ and $E^{q\theta} = E \leqslant 0$. Conversely, if the change can absolutely be ruled out, i.e. if $\theta = 0$, or, equivalently, if $q^1 = q^0$, then $C^{q\theta} = E^{q\theta} = 0$.[40] Thus, C and E measure the welfare effect of a reduction in q *conditional on that change occurring*. In Ulph's (1982) terminology, following Harsanyi (1955), the *ex ante* expectations of C and E are the *ex post* welfare measures for the reduction in q—the *ex post* WTA to endure the change is $-\theta C$, and the *ex post* WTP to avoid it is $-\theta E$—while $C^{q\theta}$ and $E^{q\theta}$ are the *ex ante* welfare measures for this change. It is known that the two welfare measures are generally different. Indeed, the difference between them constitutes what is known as *option value* in the environmental economics literature (Cicchetti and Freeman 1971):

$$OV_C \equiv \theta C - C^{q\theta} \quad \text{and} \quad OV_E \equiv \theta E - E^{q\theta}. \quad (3.75)$$

Cicchetti and Freeman saw OV_C and OV_E as a kind of risk premium, analogous to π in (3.61a), and they assumed that it would be positive if the individual were risk-averse (i.e $v_{yy} \leqslant 0$). However, first Schmalensee (1972) and then Bohm (1974) and Graham (1981) proved that OV_C and OV_E could be negative despite risk aversion. Therefore, OV_C and OV_E do not behave like a conventional risk premium. As noted in Hanemann (1984), there is a related finding in the literature on multivariate risk aversion (e.g. Kihlstrom and Mirman 1974; Duncan 1977; Karni 1983). This literature uses the utility model (3.1) cast in a cardinal, expected utility framework, but with uncertainty in the quantities, x, or prices, p, of market commodities rather than in q. It establishes that there is no correspondence between concavity of the direct utility function in x, or the indirect utility function in y, and a positive

[40] More generally, it can be shown that $C^{q\theta}$ and $E^{q\theta}$ are non-increasing in θ.

risk premium to avoid uncertainty, so that the usual definition of risk aversion does not carry over to the multivariate utility setting. An exception is when the utility function has the form in (3.73), where the marginal utility of income, v_y, is a constant, independent not only of y but also of q and θ. Application of (3.4a,b) and (3.71a,b) yields $C = E = \psi(q^1) - \psi(q^0)$, $E^{q\theta} = C^{q\theta} = \theta C$, and $OV_C = OV_E = 0$. In this case, there is risk neutrality, and it makes option value zero. But, when the marginal utility of income varies with q, even if not y, the link between *ex ante* and *ex post* valuation is more complex.

One way to think of this is as follows. I showed above that the combination of *univariate* utility and income risk implies a *bivariate* objective function, $V(\mu, s)$, as defined in (3.64). Correspondingly, when *bivariate* preferences, $v(q, y)$, are combined with riskiness for q, this essentially implies a *trivariate* objective function defined over money income, y, the level of q, and θ, the degree of risk associated with q. Let W denote expected utility:

$$W(y, q^1, \theta; q^0) \equiv \theta \cdot v(q^1, y) + (1 - \theta) \cdot v(q^0, y)$$
$$= \theta[v(q^1, y) - v(q^0, y)] + v(q^0, y); \tag{3.76}$$

the welfare measures $C^{q\theta}$ and $E^{q\theta}$ can then be represented as

$$W(y - C^{q\theta}, q^1, \theta; q^0) = W(y, q^0, 0; q^0), \tag{3.77a}$$

$$W(y, q^1, \theta; q^0) = W(y + E^{q\theta}, q^0, 0; q^0). \tag{3.77b}$$

Compared with C^z and E^z, which are welfare measures for a change in one item in Proposition 3.6, $C^{q\theta}$ and $E^{q\theta}$ value a change in two items: they value the change in q combined with—one might say, confounded by—the presence of risk (θ) as opposed to certainty.

With respect to the properties of $C^{q\theta}$ and $E^{q\theta}$, (3.71a,b) generates a result equivalent to (3.37a,b):

$$E^{q\theta}(y, q^0, q^1, \theta) = C^{q\theta}[y + E^{q\theta}(y, q^0, q^1, \theta), q^0, q^1, \theta], \tag{3.78a}$$

$$C^{q\theta}(y, q^0, q^1, \theta) = E^{q\theta}[y - C^{q\theta}(y, q^0, q^1, \theta), q^0, q^1, \theta]. \tag{3.78b}$$

Since $C^{q\theta} \leqslant 0$ and $E^{q\theta} \leqslant 0$, $E^{q\theta} - C^{q\theta} = \text{WTA} - \text{WTP}$. Then, (3.78a,b) implies that

$$E^{q\theta} \gtrless C^{q\theta} \Leftrightarrow \partial C^{q\theta}/\partial y \lessgtr 0 \Leftrightarrow \partial E^{q\theta}/\partial y \lessgtr 0. \tag{3.79}$$

Thus, part 2 of Proposition 3.6 holds for $C^{q\theta}$ and $E^{q\theta}$. As noted above, the utility model in (3.73) is the counterpart of part 5 under cardinal utility. However, there is no exact analogue of parts 3 and 4, because these assume a single z, rather than the two shift variables involved here. Nevertheless, a weaker version of the result carries over. Differentiation of (3.71b) yields

$$\text{sign}\{\partial E^{q\theta}/\partial y\} = \text{sign}\{[v_y(q^0, y) - v_y(q^0, y + E^{q\theta})] + \theta \cdot [v_y(q^1, y) - v_y(q^0, y)]\}.$$
$$(3.80)$$

Hence, risk aversion (i.e. $v_{yy} < 0$) or risk neutrality (i.e $v_{yy} = 0$) combined with (3.70) (i.e. $v_{yq} \geqslant 0$) is sufficient to ensure that $\partial E^{q\theta}/\partial y \leqslant 0.$[41] From (3.79), this implies that WTA $\geqslant$ WTP (i.e., $-C^{q\theta} \geqslant -E^{q\theta}$). This is consistent with part 3 of Proposition 3.6, since $v_{yy} \leqslant 0$ and $v_{yq} \geqslant 0$ imply that $\{v_y v_{yq} - v_q v_{yy}\} \geqslant 0$, but here they are a sufficient rather than necessary condition for the WTP/WTA disparity to occur.

Besides changes in q, one can also value changes in θ. Using the expected utility function $W(\cdot)$ in (3.76), the compensating and equivalent variations for a change from θ^0 to θ^1, are $C^\theta = C^\theta(\theta^0, \theta^1, y; q^0, q^1)$ and $E^\theta = E^\theta(\theta^0, \theta^1, y; q^0, q^1)$, where

$$W(y - C^\theta, q^1, \theta^1; q^0) = W(y, q^1, \theta^0; q^0), \tag{3.81a}$$

$$W(y, q^1, \theta^1; q^0) = W(y + E^\theta, q^1, \theta^0; q^0). \tag{3.81b}$$

Given $q^1 \leqslant q^0$, W(.) is decreasing in θ. Therefore, if $\theta^1 < \theta^0$, $C^\theta > 0$ measures WTP to obtain the reduction in risk, while $E^\theta > 0$ measures WTA to forgo the reduction in risk. If $\theta^1 > \theta^0$, C^θ and E^θ are negative, $-E^\theta$ is WTP to avoid the increase in risk, and $-C^\theta$ is WTA to endure it. Either way, WTA $-$ WTP $= E^\theta - C^\theta$.

For fixed q^0 and q^1, the expected utility function $W(.)$ as a function of (y, θ) is isomorphic to V(x,z), with y playing the role of x and θ that of z. Hence, C^θ and E^θ in (3.81a,b) are equivalent to C^z and E^z in (3.11a,b), and they are covered by Propositions 3.3, 3.6, and 3.8. With regard to the WTP/WTA disparity, from Proposition 3.6

$$\text{sign}(E^\theta - C^\theta) = \text{sign}(W_\theta W_{yy} - W_y W_{y\theta}). \tag{3.82}$$

With regard to results on the gain/loss disparity in Proposition 3.8 and the results on the elasticity of WTP in Proposition 3.3, these all hinge on the quasi-concavity or quasi-convexity of $W(y, \theta)$ in (y, θ). From (3.76), $W_\theta \leqslant 0$ and $W_{\theta\theta} = 0$; therefore, $W(y, \theta)$ is quasi-concave (quasi-convex) in (y, θ) according to whether

$$W_\theta W_{yy} - 2W_y W_{y\theta} \geqslant (\leqslant)0. \tag{3.83}$$

Since $W_{yy} = \theta v_{yy}(q^1, y) + (1 - \theta)v_{yy}(q^0, y)$ and $W_{y\theta} = v_y(q^1, y) - v_y(q^0, y)$, one obtains:

PROPOSITION 3.11.   For a reduction in risk ($\Delta^\theta \equiv \theta^0 - \theta^1 \geqslant 0$), risk aversion ($v_{yy} < 0$) or risk neutrality ($v_{yy} = 0$) combined with (3.70) ($v_{yq} \geqslant 0$) are sufficient conditions to ensure that:

---

[41] These assumptions about the signs of derivatives presume cardinal rather than ordinal utility.

1. the elasticity of E^θ with respect to Δ^θ exceeds unity;
2. $E^\theta \geqslant C^\theta$; and
3. $\partial E^\theta / \partial y \geqslant 0$, and $\partial C^\theta / \partial y \geqslant 0$.

Moreover, these conditions are sufficient to ensure that the WTA to avoid an *increase* in risk from θ^0 to $(\theta^0 + \Delta)$, for some $\Delta > 0$, exceeds the WTP to secure a symmetric *reduction* in risk from θ^0 to $(\theta^0 - \Delta)$.

Note that the results described in Proposition 3.11 can occur even with $v_{yq} \leqslant 0$ provided that there is *not* risk neutrality and the inequalities in (3.82) and (3.83) are appropriately satisfied—these latter provide the necessary and sufficient conditions for the occurence of the WTP/WTA or gain/loss disparities in the valuation of changes in risk.

To summarize, in a setting of choice under uncertainty, there are at least two mechanisms that can drive a wedge between observed WTP and observed WTA. One operates in what Hoehn and Randall (1987) call the value statement process and involves a gap between the individual's true WTP or WTA and what she expresses to the investigator. It arises from preference uncertainty, strategic behaviour, or satisficing. If the individual believes that what she tells the investigator affects both what she has to pay and whether or not the item is provided, as assumed in the model leading to (3.60a,b), the implication is that she will *understate* her true WTP and *overstate* her true WTA in an open-ended elicitation format. The second mechanism operates in the value-formation process and involves a disparity between the individual's true WTP and her true WTA. With deterministic choice, as discussed in Section 3.6 and 3.7, these disparities can arise because of income and substitution effects. I have shown here that similar disparities can arise in a setting of choice under uncertainty, and for similar reasons.

3.10. THE EFFECTS OF SUBSTITUTION ON WTP AND WTA

I now return to deterministic choice based on the ordinal utility model in (3.1), for the case where q is a vector, and consider the question of how a change in *one* component of q affects the WTP or WTA for a change in *another* component. Given any two components, say q_1 and q_2, I define q_2 as being a *substitute* for q_1 if an increase in q_2 *lowers* the individual's WTP for an increase in q_1, and a complement of q_1 if an increase in q_2 *raises* her WTP for an increase in q_1.

The person's WTP for an increase in q_1—i.e. q_1 changes from q_1^0 to $q_1^1 \geqslant q_1^0$ while q_2, p, and y stay the same—is measured by her compensating variation, C_1, where

$$C_1 = y - m[p, q_1^1, q_2, v(p, q_1^0, q_2, y)]. \tag{3.84}$$

Table 3.1   Implications of q_2 being a substitute or complement for q_1

	q_2 IS A SUBSTITUTE FOR q_1		q_2 IS A COMPLEMENT OF q_1	
	Valuing an increase in q_1	Valuing a decrease in q_1	Valuing an increase in q_1	Valuing a decrease in q_1
Panel A				
An increase in q_2	lowers WTP	lowers WTA	raises WTP	raises WTA
A decrease in q_2	raises WTP	raises WTA	lowers WTP	lowers WTA
Panel B: Assuming $\partial(m_{q_2}/m_u)/\partial q_1$ does not change sign				
An increase in q_2	lowers WTA	lowers WTP	raises WTA	raises WTP
A decrease in q_2	raises WTA	raises WTP	lowers WTA	lowers WTP

By my definition, q_2 is a substitute for q_1 if $\partial C_1/\partial q_2 < 0$ when $C_1 > 0$, and a complement of q_1 if $\partial C_1/\partial q_2 > 0$ when $C_1 > 0$.[42] From (3.8a), C_1 in (3.84) also measures the person's WTA for a *reduction* in q_1 from q_1^1 to q_0^1; this falls as q_2 increases when q_2 is a substitute for q_1, and rises as q_2 increases when q_2 is a complement of q_1. With a decrease in q_2, the change in WTP or WTA reverses direction. Panel A in Table 3.1 summarizes these implications.

Differentiating (3.84) yields

$$\frac{\partial C_1}{\partial q_2} = -m_{q_2}[p, q_1^1, q_2, v(p, q_1^0, q_2, y)]$$
$$- m_u[p, q_1^1, q_2, v(p, q_1^0, q_2, y)] \cdot v_{q_2}(p, q_1^0, q_2, y). \tag{3.85}$$

From (3.3c),

$$v_{q_2}(p, q_1^0, q_2, y) = -\frac{m_{q_2}(p, q_1^0, q_2, u^0)}{m_u(p, q_1^0, q_2, u^0)}, \tag{3.86}$$

where $u^0 \equiv v(p, q_1^0, q_2, y)$. Substituting (3.86) into (3.85) yields

$$\frac{\partial C_1}{\partial q_2} < (>)0 \Leftrightarrow \frac{m_{q_2}(p, q_1^0, q_2, u^0)}{m_u(p, q_1^0, q_2, u^0)} < (>) \frac{m_{q_2}(p, q_1^1, q_2, u^0)}{m_u(p, q_1^1, q_2, u^0)}. \tag{3.87}$$

Setting $q_1^1 \geqslant q_1^0$, q_2 is a substitute (complement) for q_1 if and only if, for fixed u^0, $m_{q_2}(p, q_1, q_2, u^0)/m_u(p, q_1, q_2, u^0)$ is increasing (decreasing) in q_1.[43] It follows that, when $C_1 \geqslant 0$,

$$\frac{\partial C_1}{\partial q_2} < (>)0 \Leftrightarrow m_{q_2}m_{uq_1} - m_u m_{q_2 q_1} < (>)0. \tag{3.88}$$

[42] It can be shown that this is essentially what Madden (1991) calls *R-substitutes* and *R-complements*.
[43] Since $m_{q_2} < 0$, this implies that the *absolute value* of (m_{q_2}/m_u) is decreasing (increasing) in q_1.

Recall that $m_{q_2} \leqslant 0$ and $m_u \geqslant 0$; also, if q_1 is normal, $m_{uq_1} < 0$. Thus, if q^1 is normal, a sufficient condition for q_2 to be a complement of q_1 is that $m_{q_2 q_1} < 0$, while, if q_2 is a substitute for q_1, it is necessary that $m_{q_2 q_1} > 0$.[44]

If q_2 is a substitute or complement for q_1, how does an increase in q_2 affect the individual's WTA for an increase in q_1? The equivalent variation for a change in q_1 is

$$E_1 = m[p, q_1^0, q_2, v(p, q_1^1, q_2, y)] - y. \qquad (3.89)$$

Hence,

$$\begin{aligned}
\frac{\partial E_1}{\partial q_2} = \; & m_{q_2}[p, q_1^0, q_2, v(p, q_1^1, q_2, y)] \\
& + m_u[p, q_1^0, q_2, v(p, q_1^1, q_2, y)] \cdot v_{q_2}(p, q_1^1, q_2, y).
\end{aligned} \qquad (3.90)$$

From (3.3c)

$$v_{q_2}(p, q_1^1, q_2, y) = -\frac{m_{q_2}(p, q_1^1, q_2, u^1)}{m_u(p, q_1^1, q_2, u^1)}, \qquad (3.91)$$

where $u^1 \equiv v(p, q_1^1, q_2, y)$. Substituting (3.91) into (3.90) yields

$$\frac{\partial E_1}{\partial q_2} < (>)0 \Leftrightarrow \frac{m_{q_2}(p, q_1^0, q_2, u^1)}{m_u(p, q_1^0, q_2, u^1)} < (>) \frac{m_{q_2}(p, q_1^1, q_2, u^1)}{m_u(p, q_1^1, q_2, u^1)}. \qquad (3.92)$$

Hence, setting $q_1^1 \geqslant q_1^0$, an increase in q_2 lowers (raises) the individual's WTA for an increase in q_1 if and only if, for fixed $u^1, m_{q_2}(p, q_1, q_2, u^1)/m_u(p, q_1, q_2, u^1)$ is increasing (decreasing) in q_1. Except for the fact that the derivatives are evaluated at u^1 instead of u^0, (3.92) is identical to the condition in (3.87) for q_2 to be a substitute (complement) of q_1. Therefore, unless an increase in u reverses the sign of $\partial(m_{q_2}/m_u)/\partial q_1$, the presumption is that, when q_2 is a substitute for q_1, an increase in q_2 lowers the WTA for an increase in q_1 and raises the WTP for a reduction in q_1; see Panel B of Table 3.1 for further details.

---

[44] If q_2 is a substitute (complement) for q_1, this does *not* necessarily make q_1 a substitute (complement) for q_2. The argument leading to (3.88) yields

$$\frac{\partial C_2}{\partial q_1} < (>)0 \Leftrightarrow m_{q_1} m_{uq_2} - m_u m_{q_1 q_2} < (>)0. \qquad (3.88a)$$

In general, $m_{q_2} m_{uq_1} - m_u m_{q_2 q_1} < (>)0$ does not imply that $m_{q_1} m_{uq_2} - m_u m_{q_1 q_2} < (>)0$. However, if q_1 and q_2 are both normal, $m_{q_2 q_1} < 0$ is a necessary condition both for q_2 to be a substitute for q_1 and for q_1 to be a substitute for q_2. Madden asserts that R-substitution is a symmetric relation, but his argument is incorrect; he bases his conclusion on the symmetry of $m_{q_2 q_1}$, but he overlooks the terms $m_{q_2} m_{uq_1}$ and $m_{q_1} m_{uq_2}$, which are *not* symmetric. The only exception to the asymmetry of substitution / complementarity is when there are zero income effects for *both* q_1 and q_2 (i.e. the indirect utility function takes the form given in (3.19b) with respect to q_1 and q_2), in which case $m_{uq_1} \equiv m_{uq_2} \equiv 0$.

It is natural to define q_1 as being *independent* of q_2 if $\partial C_1/\partial q_2 \equiv 0$. It follows from (3.87) that this happens when, for fixed u, $\partial(m_{q_2}/m_u)/\partial q_1 \equiv 0$. From (3.88) and (3.92), this implies

$$\frac{\partial C_1}{\partial q_2} \equiv 0 \;\Leftrightarrow\; \frac{\partial E_1}{\partial q_2} \equiv 0 \;\Leftrightarrow\; m_{q_2} m_{uq_1} - m_u m_{q_2 q_1} \equiv 0. \tag{3.93}$$

Sufficient conditions for it to occur are that there is a zero income effect for q_1 ($m_{uq_1} \equiv 0$) and $m_{q_2 q_1} \equiv 0$. For the reason mentioned in footnote 44, having q_1 independent of q_2 does not necessarily make q_2 independent of q_1.

Assuming that q_1 is *not* independent of q_2, what is the effect of substitution on the WTP/WTA disparity? In principle, this can go either way. Combining (3.85), (3.86), (3.90), and (3.91), one obtains

$$\frac{\partial(E_1 - C_1)}{\partial q_2} = m_u(p, q_1^0, q_2, u^1)\left[\frac{m_{q_2}(p, q_1^0, q_2, u^1)}{m_u(p, q_1^0, q_2, u^1)} - \frac{m_{q_2}(p, q_1^1, q_2, u^1)}{m_u(p, q_1^1, q_2, u^1)}\right]$$
$$- m_u(p, q_1^1, q_2, u^0)\left[\frac{m_{q_2}(p, q_1^0, q_2, u^0)}{m_u(p, q_1^0, q_2, u^0)} - \frac{m_{q_2}(p, q_1^1, q_2, u^0)}{m_u(p, q_1^1, q_2, u^0)}\right]. \tag{3.94}$$

Observe that, if q_1 is normal and $m_{uu} \geq 0$, $m_u(p, q_1^0, q_2, u^1) \geq m_u(p, q_1^0, q_2, u^0) \geq m_u(p, q_1^1, q_2, u^0)$. If, in addition, $\partial(m_{q_2}/m_u)/\partial q_1$ is sufficiently strongly increasing in u, this would imply that, when q_2 is a substitute for q_1, an increase in q_2 *widens* the WTP/WTA disparity.[45]

The results in Table 3.1 have several implications for the effects of sequencing on WTP and WTA. Suppose that several components of q change, all in the same direction, and that they are all substitutes for one another. Carson *et al.* (1992) show that, while valuing an item *later* in the sequence *lowers* WTP (and WTA) if the change is an improvement, it *raises* WTA (and WTP) if the change is a deterioration. Other implications of Table 3.1 for sequencing and embedding effects will be presented elsewhere.

3.11. CONCLUSIONS

My aim in this chapter has been to identify the observable implications for the WTP and WTA welfare measures of alternative preference structures for q, especially in the context of the Generalized Lancaster utility model, (3.1). Table 3.2 summarizes some of the results of this analysis. I have focused particularly on the issue of whether economic theory can provide an explanation for empirically observed divergences between WTP and WTA, whether observed in contingent valuation surveys, economic experiments, or

---

[45] When q_2 is a substitute for q_1, $\partial(m_{q_2}/m_u)/\partial q_1 < 0$. Therefore, the requirement is that *the absolute value* of $\partial(m_{q_2}/m_u)/\partial q_1$ be sufficiently strongly decreasing in u.

Table 3.2 Some special utility functions

Equ.	Utility model	Comments
(3.10)	$u = T[\phi(p,y) + \psi(p) \cdot q, p]$	C and E depend on $(q^1 - q^0)$
(3.21a)	$u = T\left(\left[y^{1-\eta_\pi} + (1-\eta_\pi)G(p,q)\right]^{\frac{1}{1-\eta_\pi}}, p\right)$	η_π is a constant $\neq 1$
(3.22a)	$u = T(G(p,q) + \ln y, p)$	$\eta_C \equiv \eta_E \equiv \eta_\pi \equiv 1$
(3.29a)	$u = T\left(\left[y^{1-\eta} + K(p) \cdot q^{1-\eta})\right]^{\frac{1}{1-\eta}}, p\right)$	$\eta_q \equiv 1, \eta_\pi \equiv \eta \neq 1$
(3.28)	$u = T[\ln y + K(p) \cdot \ln q, p]$	$\eta_q \equiv \eta_\pi \equiv \eta_C \equiv \eta_E \equiv 1$
(3.19b)	$u = T[y + \psi(p,q), p]$	$m_{qu} = 0; C = E;$ $\eta_\pi \equiv \eta_q \equiv \eta_C \equiv \eta_E \equiv 0$
(3.43c)	$u = T[y + \psi(q)p_1, p]$	x_1 is a perfect substitute for q
(3.43d)	$u = T[y + \sum \psi_i(q)p_i, p]$	each x_i is a perfect substitute for q
(3.47)	$m(p,q,u) = \phi(p,u) - \psi(p,u)q$	$m_{qq} = 0; \text{WTA}^- = \text{WTP}^+$
(3.48a)	$u = T[y + \psi(p)q, p]$	$C^+ = E^+ = C^- = E^-$
(3.50)	$u = T[\Phi(p,y) + \psi(p,q), p]$ $\psi(p,q)$ concave in q	Sufficient for gain/loss disparity > WTP/WTA disparity
(3.51)	$u = T[\phi(p,y) \cdot \psi(p,q), p]$ $\psi(p,q)$ log-concave in q	Sufficient for gain/loss disparity > WTP/WTA disparity

real-life behaviour. For this purpose I am assuming static, unchanging preferences—I do not doubt that preferences may change in real life, and that this could explain some of the observed phenomena, but I believe that some degree of divergence between WTP and WTA can arise with purely static preferences. Two types of mechanism may be involved. One type, involving preference uncertainty, strategic behaviour, or satisficing by survey respondents, can drive a wedge between true WTP and expressed WTP, or true WTA and expressed WTA, in a manner that creates a greater disparity between stated WTP and WTA than exists between true WTP and WTA. Another type of mechanism can create a disparity between true WTP and true WTA. Transaction costs are an example. Another example is less than perfect substitution between market goods and the elements of q that change. This by itself is sufficient to account for the gain/loss disparity. Indeed, I have argued that, while people may well possess reference-dependent preferences, in a static setting these can be subsumed under my explanation based on substitution effects. With regard to the disparity between WTP and WTA, the substitution effect combines with the income effect to determine the sign and magnitude of this disparity. However, even if there is only a small income effect and the budget share of q is small, there still can be a substantial disparity between true WTP and WTA if the elasticity of substitution between q and market goods is sufficiently low. Finally, I have shown that this framework based on income and substitution effects carries over to choice under uncertainty, where it can explain phenomena such as the divergence between the buying and selling price for a lottery, or that between WTP and WTA for a change in risk.

REFERENCES

Apostol, T. M. (1957), *Mathematical Analysis*, Addison-Wesley, Reading, Mass.

Arrow, K. J. (1974), 'Optimal Insurance and Generalized Deductibles', *Scandinavian Actuarial Journal*, 1–42.

Bewley, T. F. (1986), 'Knightian Decision Theory, Part I', Cowles Foundation Discussion Paper, Yale University.

Bohm, P. (1974), 'Option Demand and Consumer's Surplus: Comment', *American Economic Review*, 65: 733–6.

Brookshire, D. S., Randall, A., and Stoll, J. R. (1980), "Valuing Increments and Decrements in Natural Resource Service Flows", *American Journal of Economics*, 00: 478–88.

Carson, R. Flores, N. E., and Hanemann, W. M. (1992), "On the Nature of Compensable Value in a Natural Resource Damage Assessment", paper presented at the American Economic Association Annual Meeting, New Orleans, January.

Cicchetti, C. J., and Freeman, A. M. (1971), "Option Demand and Consumer Surplus", *Quarterly Journal of Economics*, 85: 523–7.

Cook, P. J., and Graham, D. A. (1977), "The Demand for Insurance and Protection: The Case of Irreplaceable Commodities", *Quarterly Journal of Economics*, 91: 143–56.

Diamond, P. A., Hausman, J. A., Leonard, G. K., and Denning, M. A. (1993), "Does Contingent Valuation Measure Preferences? Experimental Evidence", in J. A. Hausman (ed.), *Contingent Valuation: A Critical Assessment*, North-Holland, New York City, pp. 41–85.

Duncan, G. T. (1977), "A Matrix Measure of Risk Aversion", *Econometrica*, 45: 895–903.

Ebert, U. (1993), "A Note on Willingness to Pay and Willingness to Accept", *Social Choice and Welfare*, 10: 363–70.

Evans, W. N. and Viscusi, W. K. (1991), "Estimation of State-Dependent Utility Functions Using Survey Data", *Review of Economics and Statistics*, 73: 94–104.

Graham, D. A. (1981), "Cost–Benefit Analysis under Uncertainty", *American Economic Review*, 71: 715–25.

Hanemann, W. M. (1982), "Quality and Demand Analysis", in G. C. Rausser (ed.), *New Directions in Econometric Modelling and Forecasting in US Agriculture*, North-Holland, Amsterdam, pp. 55–98.

—— (1984), "On Reconciling Different Concepts of Option Value", Working Paper 295, Department of Agricultural and Resource Economics, University of California, Berkeley, July.

—— (1987), "WTP and WTA as Benefit Measures: How Do They Differ? How Can They Be Measured?" In P. A. Meyer and S. O. Anderson (eds.), *Proceedings of a Workshop on Economic Non-Market Evaluation of Losses to Fish, Wildlife and Other Environmental Resources*, Bay Institute of San Francisco, Sausalito, Calif., pp. 20–42.

Hanemann, W. M. (1991), "Willingness to Pay and Willingness to Accept: How Much Can They Differ?" *American Economic Review*, 81: 635–47.

Hardie, B.G.S., Johnson, E. J., and Fader, P. S. (1993), "Modeling Loss Aversion and Reference Dependence Effects on Brand Choice", *Marketing Science*, 12: 378–94.

Harris, M. and Raviv, A. (1981), "Allocation Mechanisms and the Design of Auctions", *Econometrica*, 49: 1477–99.

Harsanyi, J. C. (1955), "Cardinal Welfare, Individualistic Ethics, and Interpersonal Comparisons of Utility", *Journal of Political Economy*, 63: 297–320.

Hicks, J. R. (1943), "The Four Consumers' Surpluses", *Review of Economic Studies*, 11: 31–41.

Hoehn, J. P., and Randall, A. (1987), "A Satisfactory Benefit Cost Indicator from Contingent Valuation", *Journal of Environmental Economics and Management*, 14: 226–47.

Hurwicz, L. and Uzawa, H. (1971), "On the Integrability of Demand Functions", in J. S. Chipman, L. Hurwicz, M. K. Richter, and H. F. Sonnenschein (eds.), *Preferences, Utility and Demand*, Harcourt Brace, New York, pp. 47: 114–48.

Kahneman, D., and Tversky, A. (1979), "Prospect Theory: An Analysis of Decision Under Risk", *Econometrica*, 47: 263–91.

——Knetsch, J. L. and Thaler, R. (1990) "Experimental Tests of the Endowment Effect and the Coase Theorem", *Journal of Political Economy*, 98: 1325–48.

Karni, E. (1983), "On the Correspondence between Multivariate Risk Aversion and Risk Aversion with State-Dependent Preferences", *Journal of Economic Theory*, 30: 230–42.

Kihlstrom, R. E., and Mirman, L. J. (1974), "Risk Aversion with Many Commodities", *Journal of Economic Theory*, 8: 361–88.

Knetsch, J. L. (1989), "The Endowment Effect and Evidence of Nonreversible Indifference Curves", *American Economic Review*, 79: 1277–84.

——and Sinden, J. A. (1984), "Willingness to Pay and Compensation Demanded: Experimental Evidence of an Unexpected Disparity in Measures of Value", *Quarterly Journal of Economics*, 99: 507–21.

——and—— (1987), "The Persistence of Evaluation Disparities", *Quarterly Journal of Economics*, 102: 691—5.

Kolstad, C. D., and Guzman, R. M. (1995), "Information and the Divergence between Willingness-to-Accept and Willingness-to-Pay", Working Paper 9–95, Department of Economics, University of California, Santa Barbara.

Kriström, B. and Riera, P. (1996), "Is the Income Elasticity of Environmental Improvements Less than One?" *Environmental and Resource Economics*, 7: 45–55.

Krosnick, J. A. (1991), "Response Strategies for Coping with the Cognitive Demands of Attitude Measurement in Surveys", *Applied Cognitive Psychology*, 5: 213–36.

Lancaster, K. (1966), "A New Approach to Consumer Theory", *Journal of Political Economy*, 74: 132–57.

LaValle, I. H. (1978), *Fundamentals of Decision Analysis*, Holt, Rinehart and Winston, New York.

Loehman, E. (1991), "Alternative Measures of Benefit for Nonmarket Goods which are Substitutes or Complements for Market Goods", *Social Choice and Welfare*, 8: 275–305.

Loomis, J. B., Hanemann, W. M., and Wegge, T. C. (1990), *Environmental Benefits Study of San Joaquin Valley's Fish and Wildlife Resources*, Jones & Stokes Associates, Sacramento, Calif.

Madden, P. (1991), "A Generalization of Hicksian q Substitutes and Complements with Application to Demand Rationing", *Econometrica*, 59: 1497–1508.

Magat, W. A., Viscusi, W. K. and Huber, J. (1988), "Paired Comparison and Contingent Valuation Approaches to Morbidity Risk Valuation", *Journal of Environmental Economics and Management*, 15: 395–411.

Mäler, K-G. (1971), "A Method of Estimating Social Benefits from Pollution Control", *Swedish Journal of Economics*, 73: 121–33.

——(1974), *Environmental Economics: A Theoretical Inquiry*, published for Resources for the Future by Johns Hopkins University Press, Baltimore.

McConnell, K. E. (1990), "Models for Referendum Data: the Structure of Discrete Choice Models for Contingent Valuation", *Journal of Environmental Economics and Management*, 18: 19–35.

McFadden, D. and Leonard, G. K. (1993), "Issues in the Contingent Valuation of Environmental Goods: Methodologies for Data Collection and Analysis", in J. A. Hausman (ed.), *Contingent Valuation: A Critical Assessment*, North-Holland, New York, pp. 165–215.

Pecaric, J. E., Proschan, F., and Tong, Y. L. (1992), *Convex Functions, Partial Orderings, and Statistical Applications*, Academic Press, San Diego.

Pratt, J. W. (1964), "Risk Aversion in the Small and in the Large", *Econometrica*, 32: 122–36.

Putler, D. S. (1992), "Incorporating Reference Price Effects into a Theory Consumer Choice", *Marketing Science*, 11: 287–309.

Randall, A., and Stoll, J. R. (1980), "Consumer's Surplus in Commodity Space", *American Economic Review*, 71: 449–57.

Rothschild, M., and Stiglitz, J. E. (1970), "Increasing Risk I: A Definition", *Journal of Economic Theory*, 2: 225–43.

Samuelson, W. (1983), "Bargaining under Asymmeric Information", *Econometrica*, 31: 835–51.

——and Zeckhauser, R. (1988), "Status Quo Bias in Decision Making", *Journal of Risk and Uncertainty*, 1: 7–59.

Schmalensee, R. (1972), "Option Demand and Consumer's Surplus", *American Economic Review*, 62: 814–24.

Sileo, P. W. (1995), "Intransitivity of Indifference, Strong Monotonicity, and the Endowment Effect", *Journal of Economic Theory*, 66: 198–223.

Simon, H. A. (1986), "Rationality in Psychology and Economics", in R. Hogarth and M. W. Reder (eds.) *Rational Choice: The Contrast between Economics and Psychology*, University of Chicago Press, pp. 25–40.

Thaler, R. (1980), "Toward a Positive Theory of Consumer Choice", *Journal of Economic Behavior and Organization*, 1: 39–60.

Tversky, A. and Kahneman, D. (1974), "Judgment under Uncertainty: Heuristics and Biases", *Science*, No. 185: 124–31.

——and——(1991), "Loss Aversion in Riskless Choice: A Reference-Dependent Model", *Quarterly Journal of Economics*, 106: 1039–61.

Ulph, A. (1982), "The Role of *Ex Ante* and *Ex Post* Decisions in the Valuation of Life", *Journal of Public Economics*, 18: 265–76.

Viscusi, W. K., and Evans, W. N. (1990), "Utility Functions that Depend on Health Status: Estimates and Economic Implications", *American Economic Review*, 80: 353–74.

Willig, R. D. (1976*a*), "Consumer's Surplus without Apology", *American Economic Review*, 66: 589–97.

—— (1976*b*), "Integrability Implications for Locally Constant Demand Elasticities", *Journal of Economic Theory*, 12: 391–401.

Zeckhauser, R. J. (1970), "Medical Insurance: A Case Study of the Tradeoff between Risk Spreading and Appropriate Incentives", *Journal of Economic Theory*, 2: 10–26.

4

The Theory and Measurement of Passive-Use Value

RICHARD T. CARSON
NICHOLAS E. FLORES
ROBERT C. MITCHELL

4.1. INTRODUCTION

Essays on passive-use values rarely, if ever, fail to mention contingent valuation.[1] Primary reliance upon contingent valuation as a means of including passive-use values in valuation estimates makes it difficult to disentangle passive-use value issues from contingent valuation issues in any discussion or analysis of either. Authors seldom emphasize that passive-use values and contingent valuation are separate, although related issues. In particular, passive-use values can be discussed independently and few, if any, contingent valuation issues are specific to passive-use values. Moreover, passive-use values apply to a more inclusive set of goods than environmental goods only. A wide variety of public projects such as education, family assistance, and national defence can all be viewed as potentially generating substantial passive-use values.[2] Although our analysis is relevant to a more general set of goods, we will confine our discussion to environmental goods. In this chapter we attempt to disentangle passive-use value and contingent valuation and present them in what we believe is a useful perspective.

In Section 4.2 we provide a theoretical exposition of passive-use values. We begin by introducing a definition of passive-use value that is oriented toward the researcher in that it relates to what is potentially observable or estimable. Our approach differs from earlier definitions that rely on motives; relying on motives to define passive-use values results in an *ad hoc* taxonomy

---

[1] 'Passive-use value' is the term adopted by the 1989 US Federal Court of Appeals decision in *Ohio* v. *US Department of Interior* to refer to what many authors in the environmental economics literature call non-use or existence value. Other terms which have been used include 'preservation value', 'stewardship value', 'bequest value', 'inherent value', 'intrinsic value', 'vicarious consumption', and 'intangibles'. 'Option value' in the sense of possible future use is also included in the Court's definition of passive-use values, although it has often been categorized as a special type of direct-use value.

[2] One of the earliest papers suggesting that the set of valuers be expanded to a larger set than current users (Weisbrod, 1964) was based on a public transportation example.

because values are generally driven by multiple motives which are insepar-able. Furthermore, researchers are generally ignorant of consumers' motives in any given economic decision, market or non-market. When motives are elicited, the way in which these motives interact while influencing values is indeterminable.

Our analysis emphasizes different levels of error that may occur from relying exclusively on indirect techniques. One level of error is the failure to identify correctly the population of all relevant resource valuers.[3] This failure may result from valuers lacking a behavioural trail from which to infer values or from researchers' inability to identify relevant linkages when they do exist. A second level of error concerns those individuals whose market demands exhibit responses to resource changes.

In Section 4.3, we address six issues concerning the measurement of total value which are frequently advanced as criticisms of contingent valuation and are thought to be related to passive-use value. The first issue is com-modity definition. We begin by outlining the challenge facing contingent valuation researchers: portraying projects in a way that is meaningful to respondents and that provides the information that is important to respond-ents. We then explain how commodity definition may influence researchers' interpretations of how sensitive respondents are to the good being provided. The second issue is the effect of different means of project provision and payment aspects on goods' values. By recognizing that contingent valuation studies generally provide public or quasi-public goods, one can easily under-stand how a project's implementing details might influence respondents' values. The third issue is resource familiarity. We analyse the reasoning in support of the claim that agents' values for environmental projects lack content when they have limited knowledge of the affected resource. The fourth issue is the claim that passive-use values are an issue only in cases of irreversible changes to unique resources. While uniqueness and irrevers-ibility are important factors, the terms 'irreversible' and 'unique' are relative in that their meanings are contextually derived. The fifth issue is how to deal with substitutes in a valuation analysis. We point out that substitutes can be viewed from three perspectives which make this issue manageable: (1) the opportunities available to the public; (2) the information that respondents already possess; and (3) the amount of information which can realistically be conveyed to the respondent by the survey. Finally we discuss incentive compatibility structures of contingent valuation questions and note that only by carefully considering the incentive structures of a given contingent valuation question can we accurately evaluate the study's results. We reflect on the salience of this issue with respect to recent experiments claimed to have demonstrated biases in contingent valuation surveys.

---

[3] Kopp and Smith (1993) refer to this error as failure to recognize the extent of the market; Mitchell and Carson (1989) refer to this error as population choice bias.

4.2. A THEORETICAL INVESTIGATION OF PASSIVE-USE VALUES

We begin by considering the individual value that we would like to measure. At a general level, broadly defined environmental goods are acted upon collectively and therefore the level or quality of environmental goods is outside of the consumer's choice set. In the environmental goods valuation problem, we are interested in the value, in monetary terms, of changing the level or quality of environmental goods. The measures of individual value that we adopt in this chapter are the maximum amount of money an individual is willing to pay for an increase and the minimum amount of money an individual is willing to accept for a decrease in the environmental goods.[4] These are the standard utility-constant measures of value described in standard texts on applied welfare economics such as Just *et al.* (1982). In order to keep notation and terminology simple, we will consider only the willingness to pay for an increase in the environmental good.

Taking as given the improvement as understood by the individual, we would like to know at what price the individual would no longer desire the improvement.[5] What we wish to measure is not a philosophically deep concept and in principle is no more enigmatic than in the case of private goods, with the exception of the lack of a market.[6] In a market one can observe the point of trade-off and then infer an economic value. However, there is no absolute value for a market good, as some claim should be the case for an environmental good. Rather the specific context (income, other prices, and other factors) motivates the choice. As economic theory predicts, measures of value (consumer surplus) for market goods will differ under different circumstances, which is also true for measures of value for environmental goods. These differences can be with respect to prices of market goods, levels of other environmental goods, and a host of other factors. If a market in environmental goods existed which had proper incentives, value could be revealed similarly to a market good. Instead we are faced with either inferring value for the environmental good from market purchases which may be related to the levels of environmental goods or constructing a market with proper incentives. The fundamental question that makes

[4] One can also consider willingness to pay to avoid a loss and willingness to accept compensation in order to forgo an increase, which are analytically equivalent to those defined above. The willingness-to-pay measures fix utility at the level obtainable with the lower level of environmental goods and unadjusted income; the willingness-to-accept measures fix utility at the higher level with unadjusted income. The two differ only in their reference utility levels.

[5] Part of this choice is an explicit (implicit) set of rules regarding provision and payment. Included in these rules are issues such as the distribution of costs (perceived distribution of costs) and enforcement procedures (perceived enforcement procedures). These issues are discussed at greater length in S. 4.3.

[6] Some authors (e.g. Sagoff, 1994) reject the approach of using pecuniary measures for changes in environmental goods to make decisions. However, environmental changes generally *do* involve economic trade-offs and policy-makers are generally interested in how much the relevant population is willing or not willing to pay.

passive-use value an issue is: How accurately can we measure the value described above without actually constructing a market for the environmental good? While there is no definitive answer, our theoretical exposition is directed toward understanding this question.

In the two most influential papers on passive-use values, Weisbrod (1964) and Krutilla (1967), considerable space is devoted to a discussion of motives. Both papers tell their economic stories without the aid of specific models predicted on particular sets of assumptions.[7] Essentially their forte lies in their choices of examples, which proved sufficiently thought-provoking to illuminate a new line of enquiry in environmental economics. These motivational examples struck a chord with many readers, who may personally identify with these motives. Motives provide a necessary story-line when arguing in favour of expanding the population of valuers, but at the same time cannot be considered the cornerstone of a positive theory of passive-use values.

In the literature, a tradition of defining passive-use value by motivation or lack of motivation has emerged.[8] However, from an operational stand-point, using motivations as a means of defining passive-use values results in an *ad hoc* taxonomy since motivations in any economic decision are generally multifold, inseparable, and unavailable to the researcher.[9] We instead propose a definition that is understandable and operational from the researcher's perspective and does not require knowing agents' motives.

Definition: Passive-use values are those portions of total value (*WTP* or *WTA*) that are unobtainable using indirect measurement techniques which rely on observed market behaviour.

Our definition encompasses the motivational examples provided in the literature while avoiding certain inconsistencies such as whether today's value for future use is a use value or a non-use value.[10] More importantly, the definition has meaning to the researcher who will never have knowledge of all of the many motivations that influence individuals' preferences.

At the core of any prospective model of environmental goods is an examination of the trade-off between those goods to which agents are able

[7] The longevity of these two papers is undoubtedly enhanced by their lack of formal details and their focus on sensible, realistic examples.

[8] For examples see Mitchell and Carson (1981), Randall and Stoll (1983), Fisher and Raucher (1984), Smith and Desvousges (1986), Madariaga and McConnell (1987), Bishop and Welsh (1990), and Shechter and Freeman (1994).

[9] Many contingent valuation researchers ask respondents to apportion elicited total value by motivation. Carson and Mitchell (1991) and Cummings and Harrison (1995) point out that in addition to being cognitively difficult, such decompositions are generally not unique, as the portion of value assigned to a particular motivation may differ depending on the other elicited motivations. Moreover, given all of the potential motivations, no list could ever be exhaustive for *all* individuals. McConnell (1997) addresses a number of technical issues specifically related to welfare economics and altruism.

[10] After completion of our initial draft of this chapter, we discovered that in their discussion of the limitations of the household production function valuation methodology, Mäler *et al.* (1994) employ an approach identical to ours in defining use values.

to allocate scarce resources and environmental goods. In order to represent this trade-off mathematically, assume that preferences over environmental goods, Q, and market goods, X, can be represented by a utility function, $U = f(X, Q)$, where f is increasing in both arguments.[11] Income, y, is allocated toward the purchase of market goods in a way that obtains the highest level of utility given market price vector, p, and the level of environmental goods, Q. The choice of X that maximizes U can be thought of as a function of prices, income, and the level of $Q : X(p, Q, y)$. The highest level of obtainable utility given income, prices, and level of Q can now be written as $v(p, Q, y) = f[X(p, Q, y), Q]$, which is called the indirect utility function. Willingness to pay for an increase in environmental goods from Q^0 to Q^1 satisfies the equation $v(p, Q^0, y) = v(p, Q^1, y - WTP)$. In words, willingness to pay is the most income that would be forgone in order to get the environmental improvement before preferring to keep Q at the initial level, Q^0, with income y. Although this model is very stylized and does not explicitly address important elements such as uncertainty and time, it captures the essential trade-offs (market goods for Q) at a very simplistic level.[12]

Another mathematical concept that is useful in analysing changes in environmental goods is the set of compensated or Hicksian demands. Recall that in the maximization problem, maximum obtainable utility was given by the indirect utility function, $v(p, Q, y)$. If we redefined the objective as minimizing expenditures on market goods while maintaining the utility level $v(p, Q, y)$, then the same combination chosen in the utility maximization problem, $X(p, Q, y)$, will be chosen in the expenditure minimization problem, with the minimum amount of expenditures equal to y. We could consider changing Q or p while maintaining the same utility level $v(p, Q, y)$ and again solve for the minimum expenditures. The bundle of market goods that solves this minimization problem is called the set of compensated or Hicksian demands, which are functions of prices, environmental goods, and the level of utility: $X^h(p, Q, U)$.[13] Total minimized expenditures (the analogue to indirect utility) are given by $e(p, Q, U) = p \cdot X^h(p, Q, U)$. Introduction of the compensated demand/expenditure minimization framework is useful because if we refer back to the equation that defined willingness to pay, $v(p, Q^0, y) = v(p, Q^1, y - WTP)$, we have a utility-constant world. Willingness to pay can be written $WTP = e(p, Q^0, U) - e(p, Q^1, U)$ where $U = v(p, Q^0, y)$. In the utility-constant world, compensated demands respond *even* in cases when the ordinary demands do not.

---

[11] Q and X are vectors of environmental goods and market goods respectively. We assume that U is quasi-concave in X.

[12] Although our model does not explicitly address time and uncertainty, the utility-constant concepts used with respect to uncertainty in the option value literature (see Smith, 1987) and time with uncertainty found in the quasi-option value literature (Arrow and Fisher, 1974; Hanemann, 1989) can be handled by adapting U and the income constraint set.

[13] We will denote compensated demands by the h superscript $X^h(p, Q, U)$; ordinary demands will contain no superscript, $X(p, Q, y)$.

In most applications, we are interested in the values of a population whose members may have very different positions *vis à vis* the resource being affected. While some differences in the choices of market goods may be explained by differences in income, the decision to use or ability to appreciate an environmental resource is undoubtedly influenced by resource proximity and other factors such as socialization. These differences translate into different utility representations and implicit in our analysis is the notion that there are possibly as many utility representations as individuals in the population.

In applications of economic theory where Q is not being varied, measurements of welfare changes (for example for a price change) are possible via the informational triad: prices, income, and market goods chosen. The environmental goods problem is inherently more difficult because we are interested in the inverted relationship (Flores, 1994) of how individual prices respond to changes in the level of Q, or at least a specified change.[14] Note that in the formulation given above, observable market demands are functions of Q. Therefore, at least in theory, it seems that valuing the change in Q may be possible via reflections in the changes in purchases of market goods. From a theoretical stand-point, the ability to pick up reflections of the value of Q from the observation of an individual's market goods choices is the essence of the passive-use value puzzle.

To help illustrate this point, we consider a simple example. Suppose that we are considering improving the environmental quality of a given recreational site. Even though this example deals with a very specific resource, a recreation site, it generates the interesting elements in the passive-use value problem. One subset of the population, site users, leaves behind an easily identified behavioural trail which provides a reflection of the value of Q through market responses—they visit the site. Users of a nearby site may value the site on which quality is being improved not for their own use, but as a way of reducing congestion at their preferred site, enhancing their preferred site through ecosystem linkages, or because the improved site will provide habitat for species important to them. Inferring values from observable behaviour is possible for this group as well, but identification must precede measurement. There may also be other individuals who value the site for a variety of reasons, but it is not possible to identify the behavioural link or there simply is no behavioural link. The modelling strategy and degree of measurement success when using observable behaviour will differ in each case. Taking these cases in reverse order, consider those individuals whose observable decisions are not readily linked to Q.

---

[14] Major difficulties arise because there is rarely much variation in Q to which agents may respond (historical observations) and the agents' private prices (*WTP*) are unobservable. Even in cases where resource-use demand is observable, such as travel-cost modelling, prices inferred for usage by the researcher may be poor estimates of the price inferred by the agent (Randall, 1994).

This case can be represented mathematically as the f function being separable in Q and X.[15] Utility takes the form $f(X, Q) = T[g(X), Q]$, where $g(X)$ is increasing and quasi-concave in X; T is increasing in $g(X)$ and Q. Note that maximization with respect to g is the same as maximization with respect to T because Q is not in the agent's choice set. Therefore the observable demands are not affected by changes in Q.[16] Because T is increasing in Q, the change in Q is still valued although undetectable in the observable demands.

Now consider the second group, users of a nearby site who do not use the site for which quality is being changed, but have positive values due to congestion externalities and other possible considerations such as ecosystem linkages. The utility function for this group has the form $f(X, Q) = T[g(X, Q), Q]$.[17] In this case, Q enters the utility function twice, once in g and once as the second argument of T.[18] This form implies that some of the value is detectable though interactions with market goods, such as costly trips to their preferred site, and some of the value is not detectable from market goods due to the second, separable entry of Q in T. The separable portion precludes ruling out the possibility of value in addition to the congestion externality value, such as ecosystem values related to the site to be improved. Some of the value with utility increment related to g may be obtained by indirect techniques such as the travel-cost method if there is sufficient variation in existing data and, more importantly, if the linkage is recognized. Even when linkages between the change in Q and market goods exist, failure of the researcher to identify the set of goods that interact has the effect of reverting back to the completely separable case for practical purposes.

For the last group, recreational site users, utility takes the same general form as for nearby site users: $f(X, Q) = T[g(X, Q), Q]$. The primary difference between the two groups is that some of the linkages are much easier to identify and the population of users is easier to access. Even for the group of users, there may be values in addition to those picked up through the interaction of Q with the market goods due to the second argument in T. With respect to the values resulting from g (those possibly detectable through market responses), as in the case of nearby site users, failure to recognize all relevant market linkages may lead to over- or underestimation.[19]

[15] For a discussion of the role of separability, see Deaton and Muellbauer (1980) or Varian (1992). Examples of separable preferences are the linear-logarithmic class of utility functions (Cobb-Douglas) and the Stone-Geary class.

[16] Freeman (1979) refers to this as the hopeless case.

[17] This specification is suggested in McConnell (1983) and Hanemann (1988, 1995).

[18] This form is sufficiently flexible in that it encompasses the separable case discussed above (g constant in Q) as well as the common representation $f = h(X, Q)$ (T constant in the second entry).

[19] The evolution of travel-cost models has been greatly influenced by recognizing the importance of including all linkages, such as shifts in demand at other sites (Bockstael et al., 1991; Smith, 1991). Multiple-site models such as random-utility models evolved in response to this issue.

With these three groups in mind, we now turn to some of the theoretical issues involved in the measurement of value with respect to each group. We begin by considering the class of preferences for which some value is recoverable through market responses, utility of the form $f(X, Q) = T[g(X, Q), Q]$. Considering this class allows us to discuss the theoretical basis of some of the measurement techniques used in the literature, address theoretical definitions of passive-use value, and consider potential errors associated with the techniques.

With respect to measuring values for changes in environmental goods from observable market behaviour, we introduce the time-honoured price/quantity decomposition found throughout the literature.[20] Recall that willingness to pay can be written using the expenditure representation: $WTP = e(p, Q^0, U) - e(p, Q^1, U)$. One can add and substract the terms $e(p^*, Q^0, U)$ and $e(p^*, Q^1, U)$ to rewrite WTP:

$$WTP = e(p, Q^0, U) - e(p^*, Q^0, U) + e(p^*, Q^0, U) - e(p^*, Q^1, U)$$
$$+ e(p^*, Q^1, U) - e(p, Q^1, U), \tag{4.1}$$

which holds for any price vector, p^*. Using this mathematical trick allows one to express the change in expenditure in three moves: $(p, Q^0) \rightarrow (p^*, Q^0); (p^*, Q^0) \rightarrow (p^*, Q^1); (p^*, Q^1) \rightarrow (p, Q^1)$. Using the fundamental theorem of calculus and Shephard's Lemma, WTP can be rewritten as

$$WTP = \int_p^{p^*} \sum_{i=1_j}^{nj} [X_i^h(s, Q^1, U) - X_i^h(s, Q^0, U)]ds + [e(p^*, Q^0, U) - e(p^*, Q^1, U)]$$

$$\tag{4.2}$$

X_i^h are elements of the vector of Hicksian demands X^h; s represents the level of prices; the goods that coincide with the price changes in the integral term are denoted by the j subscript, with n_j the number of prices being changed. This first term measures the difference in the area under the compensated demand curves, between the old price and new price, at the initial and subsequent levels of Q. The second term is willingness to pay for the change in Q, but when facing higher prices, p^*. When p^* is high enough to choke off demand in the j subset of goods (assuming they are non-essential), the first term is the change in consumer surplus for each good in subset j resulting from the change in Q.[21]

Early work concerning the measurement of economic value of non-market goods used the weak complementary condition (Clawson, 1959; Mäler, 1974) to derive WTP exclusively from observable goods. Some subset j of market goods is weakly complementary to Q if the marginal utility of Q is

---

[20] Prominent examples include McConnell (1983) and Freeman (1993a, b).
[21] For the different levels of environmental goods, Q^0, Q^1, the choke price may differ. It suffices that p^* be the higher choke price which will choke off demand at both levels of Q.

zero when the complementary goods are not consumed.[22] In our example, travelling to the site for users of the site for which quality is being varied and travelling to the nearby site for its respective users would be candidates for the j subset for the two groups respectively. Suppose that the goods associated with travelling to the two sites became prohibitively expensive and at price p^* demand before and after the quality change at the first site was driven to zero. Then in such a case, (4.2) can be rewritten as the change in consumer surplus for the weakly complementary set before and after the change in the first site's quality:

$$WTP = \int_p^{p^*} \sum_{i=1j}^{nj} [X_i^h(s, Q^1, U) - X_i^h(s, Q^0, U)]ds \qquad (4.3)$$

The second term disappears due to the weak complementary condition. The consumer surplus change above is a Hicksian (compensated) measure which, when estimating from observable behaviour, leads to some difficulty because the Hicksian demands are unobservable. Recovering the Hicksian measure from the ordinary demands requires that one first estimate the ordinary demands as functions of prices, income, and Q, and then derive the constants of integration for each complementary good (Hanemann, 1980; Hausman, 1981).

Several observations are in order with respect to weak complementarity. First, the weak complementary condition is an unverifiable assumption (LaFrance, 1993) and when the assumption is incorrect, some value is neglected. Second, even if such a weak complementary set exists, the researcher must correctly identify the set in order to avoid incorrect estimation. Third, if preferences are represented by a utility function of the form $f(X, Q) = T[g(X, Q), Q]$, the estimated Hicksian demands will correspond to $g(X, Q)$ rather than the entire utility function because value associated with the second argument in T is undetectable. Therefore there can be a correctly identified, weakly complementary set and yet the separable part of T still leaves a portion that is immeasurable from market demand data. The usage of the T function, which allows for both separable and non-separable characteristics in Q, has important implications for interpreting earlier definitions of passive- or non-use values. By allowing for both of these characteristics, values arise in addition to those identified by the definitions presented below. We turn now to a brief discussion of three suggested passive-use value definitions that use decompositions and forms of utility in defining these values.

First, McConnell (1983), Freeman (1993a), and others use the price/quantity decomposition of WTP as a way of defining passive-use value. This

---

[22] Perfect complementarity is said to occur when the subset j of market goods and Q must be consumed in fixed proportion to provide utility.

approach defines the integral term of the decomposition as use value and the second term as passive-use value.

$$WTP = [e(p^*, Q^1, U) - e(p, Q^1, U)] - [e(p^*, Q^0, U) - e(p, Q^0, U)]$$
$$+ [e(p^*, Q^1, U) - e(p, Q^1, U)] \qquad (4.4)$$
$$= UV + PUV.$$

This approach explicitly rejects the weak complementary assumption as a means of determining value. The j subset is given by the goods that differ with Q and are non-essential. The non-essential condition allows for choking off demands and examining changes in consumer surplus resulting from the change in Q. The estimation problems concerning the T utility form still apply. Therefore, after estimating the use term from observable behaviour, part of the use value (as defined by the price/quantity decomposition) is overlooked since estimation will reflect g-compensated demands rather than T-compensated demands. This leaves researchers that are exclusively using indirect methods to measure WTP with two sources of error (for the group with market responses): error from the PUV term and errors associated with measuring Hicksian consumer surplus from g rather than T; both errors are positive.

Larson (1992) introduces the Hicks neutral condition as a way of measuring the PUV term in the price/quantity decomposition from market information. A good is Hicks-neutral to Q if the derivative of its compensated demand with respect to Q is zero. By using the rationed-quantity analogue of the Slutsky equation and budget constraint adding-up conditions, Larson shows how the PUV term can be recovered from market responses. Flores (1996) shows that the condition itself requires a very delicate balance of income and quantity effects which are rarely satisfied, and exact measures are only possible for very restrictive sets of demand systems.[23] Despite these failings, the method may be useful because in some cases the resulting biases are recognizable (ibid.). Therefore by using Hicks neutral techniques, some of the downward measurement bias from the PUV term may be recoverable.

Hanemann (1988, 1995) suggests another way of partioning total value into a use and passive-use component. Considering the increase from Q^0 to Q^1, we can use a sequence approach to separate out the values as follows:

$$C^p \text{ solves } T\{g[X(p, Q^0, y - C^p), Q^1]\} = T\{g[X(p, Q^0, y), Q^0]\} \qquad (4.5)$$

and

$$C^u \text{ solves } g[X(p, Q^1, y^* - C^u), Q^1] = g[X(p, Q^0, y), Q^0], \qquad (4.6)$$

---

[23] As in the case of weak complementarity, the inability to verify the Hicks neutral assumption (LaFrance, 1993) applies here as well.

where $y^* = y - C^p$. Note that $WTP = C^p + C^u$. As Hanemann points out, C^p is a reasonable candidate for passive-use value since it is the portion of total value that is not at all detectable from market goods; C^u is use value or the value that interacts with market goods and generates a market goods response. Hanemann's definition differs from the use value as defined by the price/quantity decomposition. Use value from the decomposition is Hicksian consumer surplus for T although estimation will yield consumer surplus for g. Hanemann's C^u explicitly takes into account that from observable behaviour, the T consumer surplus is unobtainable; C^u is related to g only. Hence Hanemann's use/passive-use value definition is derived in relation to the extent that Q interacts with market goods and therefore the theory coincides more closely with our definition than does the price/quantity definition. In relation to our own definition, Hanemann's definition of use value may still have a passive-use value error.[24]

A third way of defining passive-use values is to consider the value of a proposed change given that access to the resource is denied.[25] This definition, proposed by Bohm (1977) and elaborated on by Gallagher and Smith (1985), coincides with the notion of existence values discussed in the literature since usage is not possible for some or perhaps all individuals.[26] Therefore it seems reasonable that all value must be attributable to considerations other than usage. The conditioning of *whose* access is denied is important, as the following example illustrates.

Suppose that a federal project for wilderness preservation is being considered; currently the land is privately held, inaccessible to the public, and logging is imminent. One possibility is to propose a project X that will preserve the area, but keep it inaccessible to all. Since no one may potentially use the area, we are valuing a good that has no direct service to humans. In the traditional sense, individuals who value the programme do so because they value the mere existence of the area. Another possibility is to preserve the area with access limited to hikers, project Y. This would effectively deny access to all non-hikers. Some non-hikers may value both projects. However, the values they hold for the good provided by X may differ from those they hold for the good provided by Y. Group A non-hikers may believe that preservation of species found in the area is important, but prefer preservation with sensible access for hikers. Group B non-hikers may prefer preservation with access over logging, but prefer preservation without access over preservation with access. The values for both projects are passive-use

[24] Although C^u is defined by interaction with market goods, this does not imply that all of C^u can be recovered from indirect techniques. If one thinks of optimization in g only, there would still be a second term as in the price/quantity decomposition; the second term will generally not be recoverable.

[25] See Zhang (1993) for an empirical application that uses this approach.

[26] Some of the 'existence' value in this case may be detectable through secondary market responses due to linkages with the preserved area. Therefore some of the value may not be passive-use value by our definition.

values for both groups A and B, but group A will have a greater project-X value than project-Y value while for group B project-Y values will be greater.[27]

We raise this issue to emphasize that individuals can have legitimate 'existence' values for a particular good which differ because the access attributes differ. The fact that the attributes differ makes this definition more difficult to represent theoretically than either the price/quantity decomposition or Hanemann definitions. In contrast to these definitions, which basically decompose a single value, the access definition compares values for what are essentially two distinct projects. For example, the access definition should be modelled as different changes in $Q : Q \rightarrow Q^{na}$ in the case of no access, and $Q \rightarrow Q^{ha}$ in the case of hiking access. It is particularly important to recognize that hikers' non-access passive-use value (value of project X) may have nothing to do with non-hikers' hiker-access passive-use value (project Y). In defining existence values by access, one must concede that, while the values of both projects are of interest, the values are for different projects.

The definitions provided above are useful in examining and understanding potentially overlooked values that result from exclusively using indirect methods for measuring WTP. Ideally we would like to know what each individual would be willing to pay for the change in Q in the manner in which it is being provided.[28] By examining the problem using simple mathematical representations, it is apparent that there are multiple sources of error (missed value) that may result when exclusively using indirect techniques to measure total value.

The first and most potentially significant error is the failure to identify correctly the relevant population of valuers. Although it is not always the case, passive-use values can be crucial in decisions involving the allocation of environmental goods, particularly when the number of individuals holding passive-use values is very large. The insight provided by Weisbrod (1964) and Krutilla (1967) emphasized the importance of searching for all resource 'valuers' as a means of enhancing efficiency; this is the population issue. The exclusive use of indirect techniques equates the values for this segment of the population with zero.

The second source of error results from the last term in the price/quantity decomposition given in equation (4.2). This error applies only to the population whose market demands are sensitive to changes in Q. Referring to this term as passive-use value fails to recognize the failure to identify relevant

---

[27] One could conduct similar analyses using other conditions that would have different effects on values for some individuals, such as: no access to all, access to hikers, access to hikers/bikers/off-road vehicles.

[28] The manner in which the change is being provided is important because alternatives to what is being proposed matter as well as the means of provision and the subsequent distributional effects.

non-users, the first source of error discussed above, and has been a source of confusion in the literature. The third source of error results from failing to recognize that there may be separable and non-separable characteristics of preferences. Mixed preferences that possess both characteristics will result in the incorrect estimation of compensated demands because part of the value is not reflected in the observable market response.

The simple mathematical representations of preferences used above capture the essential elements in the passive-use value problem. Preferences which are separable in Q or contain a separable element in Q (mixed preferences) produce the behaviour suggested by Weisbrod and Krutilla. If researchers rely exclusively on estimating value from behaviour observed in the past, they will undoubtedly overlook relevant values, which may lead to inefficient decision-making.[29] In order to pursue efficient environmental resource-allocation decisions, researchers and policy-makers need to utilize the total-value concept for all relevant valuers.

4.3.   THE MEASUREMENT OF PASSIVE-USE VALUE

4.3.1.   Background

Much of the early history of cost–benefit analysis of environmental projects can be written in terms of searching for ways to measure projects' total benefits, benefits that often involve a significant passive-use value component.[30] To many resource economists, the development of a method by which to construct a previously non-existent market in a survey context – the contingent valuation method – effectively ended this search. Although some economists (e.g. Desvousges *et al.*, 1993) continue to question the contingent valuation method's effectiveness, especially its ability to measure passive-use values, its development during the past two decades has removed discussions of estimating economic values for environmental goods from the intangibles or inherently immeasurable category to that of guide-lines for conducting such studies (Arrow *et al.*, 1993).

Although contingent valuation is by far the most popular current technique for measuring total value for goods having significant passive-use values, any technique capable of constructing the missing market for these types of goods is potentially capable of obtaining total-value estimates. The two other approaches which have been used and are capable of measuring total value are the examination of the results of an actual referendum concerning the good (Deacon and Shapiro, 1975) and the construction of a

---

[29] The term 'may lead' is used instead of 'will lead' because in many cases, users' values alone will lead to the same decision as including all relevant values; that is to say, often passive-use values are not decisive.

[30] See Hanemann (1992) for an interesting overview of the development of cost–benefit analysis for environmental projects.

simulated market in which actual purchases of the good can be made (Bishop and Heberlein, 1979).[31] Both of these approaches have substantial drawbacks relative to contingent valuation. Referenda on environmental goods involve only a small subset of the goods for which society would like to have values; they are infrequently held; and when they are held, there is generally an insufficient variation of price for drawing inferences regarding the underlying distribution of *WTP*. Realistic simulated markets are difficult to construct and their effective use with a random sample of the general public is difficult to accomplish and implement. Furthermore, as Kopp (1992) notes, goods with substantial passive-use values have the characteristics of a very pure public good. Therefore implementation of an appropriate incentive structure in a simulated market is substantially more difficult than in the case of quasi-public goods where possible exclusion (Moulin, 1994) makes the task feasible.[32] Contingent valuation's relative flexibility and range of use has made it a more attractive technique and as a result, most of the evidence on passive-use values has been generated using this approach.

The Randall *et al.* (1974) study of air quality improvements in the Four Corners area of the south-western United States is recognized as a landmark because it is the first major study that measured a significant passive-use value benefit. Other contingent valuation studies that measured benefits with a significant passive-use value component quickly followed in the late 1970s and early 1980s.[33] These include studies of air quality issues in national parks (Schulze *et al.*, 1983), air quality issues in national forests (Crocker and Vaux, 1983), regional water quality issues (Greenley *et al.*, 1982; Desvousges *et al.*, 1983), national water quality (Mitchell and Carson, 1981),

---

[31] Another approach discussed in the public finance literature is to infer public preferences for a good from government decisions (Borcherding and Deacon, 1972). While possible in some instances where an electoral campaign is essentially run on the issue in question, inference often involves a circular logic: the politician or bureaucrat assigns the social scientist the task of determining public preferences about an issue under consideration; a decision is made on that information; preferences are determined on the decision. A recent set of papers by Cropper (1994), Oates (1994), and Shapiro and Deacon (1994) examine the relationship between the public finance literature and contingent valuation. The stated-preference approach (Adamowicz *et al.*, 1994) is sometimes mentioned as another possibility. A stated-preference model cast in terms of some collective action to provide the good directly, such as a vote, does allow one to obtain a welfare estimate which incorporates passive-use values. However, in this case, the stated-preference and contingent valuation approaches are essentially identical. The stated-preference approach, cast in terms of some contingent private behaviour, does not allow one to obtain a welfare estimate which incorporates passive-use values.

[32] The importance of incentive structure when providing public goods is noted in the early public goods literature (Samuelson, 1954). As a result, a real (simulated) market for a pure public good with a non-coercive payment scheme should underestimate, and often grossly so, willingness to pay for the good. This issue is discussed at more length below with respect to specific empirical examples.

[33] Particularly informative is the title of a conference volume, *Proceedings of a Workshop on the Measure of Intangible Environmental Impacts*, in which a 1977 paper by the prolific contingent valuation researcher David Brookshire appears.

protection of ecosystems from acid rain (Bishop and Heberlein, 1984), and preservation of wilderness areas in the United States (Barrick, 1983) and in other countries (Bennett, 1984).

The method's use for policy-making purposes was advanced by official acceptance. In 1979, the US Water Resources Council explicitly allowed for the use of contingent valuation in project evaluation to measure passive-use values and prescribed procedures for doing so. These and the subsequent 1983 US Water Resources Council guide-lines had a substantial influence on the US Department of Interior's (DOI's) development of rules for valuing damages to natural resources. However, after receiving industry comments opposing the use of contingent valuation, DOI (1986) promulgated rules placing contingent valuation at the bottom of a hierarchy of valuation methods and allowed for the measurement of passive-use values only in instances where there were no measurable use values. The 1989 US Federal Appeals Court decision in *Ohio* v. *US Department of Interior* subsequently rejected DOI's limitations on the use of contingent valuation, saying that Congress had clearly intended for the Government to collect lost interim-use values, including passive-use values, in natural resource damage cases if they could be reliably measured.[34] Congress later passed the Oil Pollution Act of 1990 and signalled its agreement with the Court's interpretation by directly quoting the language from the *Ohio* decision on this point in the preamble to the bill. In 1992, the US National Oceanic and Atmospheric Administration (NOAA) convened a panel of prominent academic experts chaired by Kenneth Arrow and Robert Solow to examine the issue of whether passive-use values could be reliably measured using contingent valuation. The panel concluded 'that contingent valuation studies can produce estimates reliable enough to be the starting point for a judicial or administrative determination of natural resource damages—including lost passive-use value' (Arrow *et al.*, 1993: 4610).

In what follows, we address a number of key issues regarding the estimation of total value when passive-use considerations may be involved. First we take up the issue of commodity definition. Next we consider the influence of a project's payment and provision characteristics on the estimated total value of the provided good. We then take up two issues which are sometimes said to restrict the measurement of goods with passive-use value: lack of familiarity with the good, and a requirement that the good must be unique and the change must be irreversible for passive-use values to be present. We then address the issue of which substitute goods, if any, should be considered in a contingent valuation survey. Finally, we look at the incentive structure of contingent valuation questions when substantial passive-use values are involved.

---

[34] A comprehensive discussion of the *Ohio* decision and its implications can be found in Kopp and Smith (1993).

4.3.2. Commodity Definition

Much of the 'art' in designing a contingent valuation survey is taking the physical changes of an environmental project, usually given to the survey designer in biological and engineering terms, and translating those into a form understandable to survey respondents. This challenging task is sometimes referred to as the commodity definition problem. One aspect of this problem is the difficulty of portraying the commodity in the survey in a way in which respondents can grasp its relevant attributes. First, the physical changes are often expressed in a highly technical manner and cannot be used in a contingent valuation survey without being first expressed in lay terms. Second, they are typically depicted with respect to what will actually be built or restored and not in terms of the flow of services from the project that respondents are likely to understand and potentially care about.

Another aspect is that once an adequate translation is made and the changes are described in terms of service flows, the interpretation of the change in environmental resources, denoted as a change in Q in our theoretical section, can be problematic. Specifically, what the respondents perceive as the change in Q does not always coincide with what the researcher has in mind. The source of this problem is that Q is typically a multi-attributed object. Consider a project that enhances a degraded wetland area by increasing fresh water flows by 100 per cent in times of drought. Scientists believe that the increased water flows will reduce the probability of extinction of two sensitive bird species and several sensitive plant species to near zero. An alternative enhancement project will increase water flows by only 50 per cent in times of drought. Scientists believe the alternative project will still reduce the probability of extinction of the two sensitive bird species to near zero, but the non-trivial probability of extinction for the plant species will be unchanged. What is the relevant interpretation of the change in Q to which the respondent is expected to be sensitive? For instance, should the change in Q be defined as the change in water flow, which differs by a factor of two under the two projects? Or should the change in Q be interpreted in terms of the number and types of affected species?

Another consideration is how damage actually occurs. For instance, in the wetland enhancement project presented above, it may matter to respondents that water shortages are occurring due to drought or that water shortages are occurring due to the diversion of water for water-intensive crops grown under a federal subsidy programme.[35] Which case requires a more expeditious response depends upon respondents' perspectives. Differing perspect-

---

[35] A market analogy is the purchase of products made with child labour (or labour from political prisoners). Although a given product can be physically non-differentiable, some consumers avoid the purchase of such goods even when this choice is costly. Essentially the product is differentiated by the labour characteristic, which matters little to some and very much to others.

ives will in turn elicit potentially different value responses under the two scenarios.

Projects that affect environmental resources are often complex and respondents are likely to vary in how they weigh the importance of a project's purported accomplishments. Some may care little about any aspect of the project; some may value saving the bird species only; and others may be concerned about birds, plants, and water flow. There are no apparent reasons why understanding respondents' interpretations of the change in Q will necessarily be more difficult for individuals whose values are primarily or exclusively passive-use value than for those who use the resource on a regular basis. However, the factors involved may vary and require different approaches in conveying a project's attributes.

The multi-attribute character of Q can lead to other complications. The choice of which attributes should receive a full description in a contingent valuation scenario requires careful attention, because if the researcher downplays or does not mention attributes that are important to some respondents, the study may either undervalue or overvalue the good. Although this problem can never be completely avoided, the risk of such an error can be reduced by studying respondent beliefs and concerns about the good and its provision during the development of the survey instrument.

Additional issues arise in conducting a benefits transfer. Here judgement on the part of the analyst is required about which attributes of a Q whose benefits are measured in a contingent valuation survey map on to some new Q. If the coverage is imperfect, as is usually the case, then judgements must be made and defended about how the benefits measured in the contingent valuation survey should be allocated to the shared attributes. Yet another complication, which we will discuss in the next section, results from the fact that characteristics of the institutional setting in which the Q is offered to respondents in a contingent valuation survey are also a legitimate part of its multi-attribute set.

4.3.3. Project Provision and Payment Aspects

A common misconception held by some contingent valuation critics is that a respondent's willingness to pay for an environmental good should be unaffected by the manner in which that good is provided and the means of payment. This line of reasoning, although appealing in the abstract, is not true of private consumer goods or public goods. The principal problem with this reasoning is that no consumer good is sold in the abstract and no public good is provided in the abstract. Consumers care about the convenience and reputation of the store where they purchase many of their market goods. They also care about the manner in which they are required to pay for the good. Similarly for environmental goods, the Government usually cannot provide the good directly, such as increasing a bird population. Instead, the

Government undertakes a project which increases the bird's habitat. This action in turn is expected to lead to an increase in the bird population.[36] The project that implements the change also carries with it a particular payment mechanism.[37] Both payment and provision mechanisms can substantially influence respondents' willingness to pay for the project (Mitchell and Carson, 1989).

One seemingly attractive way of dealing with this issue in the contingent valuation scenario is to adopt what appears to be a neutral position and not provide any details of provision and payment. When respondents receive inadequate information regarding the good's provision and payment, they are left to infer important details from the information that is provided or simply guess when no clues are provided. Inference and guessing may take one or both of two predictable forms.

The first form is constructing a subjective probability of provision and/or payment. Basically respondents who are not informed of provision and/or payment means may infer that the good may not even be provided or that they may not be required to pay for it. This inference occurs because respondents discount the possibility of payment and provision because the project is so nascent that the most important details have yet to be determined. The second form, which usually interacts with the first, is to respond according to the respondent's guess as to the most likely means of provision and payment. Therefore respondents may infer a subjective probability of provision/payment as well as the means of provision/payment. Because different respondents will draw different inferences, leaving out important implementing details makes it impossible to have confidence that the respondents are valuing the good that the researcher intends them to value. At some point the lack of details may cause the entire scenario to lose credibility with the respondent, in which case the answers to the contingent valuation questions are likely to become meaningless with respect to the question asked.

In order to avoid this ambiguity, the necessary information should be provided. However, it must also be recognized that the details themselves do and *should* influence values. For instance in our bird habitat example, it may matter to some respondents whether a privately held power company is providing the project or the Federal Government is providing the project. In such a case some respondents may believe that the Federal Government fails to live up to promises and that if it is the provider the probability of

---

[36] Such explanations are often given for the extremely wide range of prices observed in the same city for the same common private consumer goods (Pratt *et al.*, 1979).

[37] Projects presented in contingent valuation surveys often have negative as well as positive effects, at least for some respondents. If the negative impacts are well-known or easily discernible, many respondents will recognize and incorporate them into their decision. In such instances it will often be desirable to incorporate these explicitly into the scenario description so that it will be clear what good was valued. Telling respondents to ignore particular effects in their evaluation of a project is generally not a feasible contingent valuation design strategy.

implementation is low. An equally plausible scenario would be animosity toward a local utility which has been thought to engage in frequent unnecessary rate increases.

As these examples suggest, it is individually rational for the provision mechanism to affect respondents' values. With respect to the payment mechanism, the distribution of project costs may matter to individuals. Respondents generally have clear preferences over forms of taxation. This may be a fairness issue, a belief that some forms of taxation generate unnecessary costs in terms of economic efficiency, or a belief that a particular type of tax has the potential for diverting funds from other projects that are considered important. In any case, changing the payment mechanism may influence values for reasons which are well understood by the respondent, yet poorly understood by the researcher.

Currently unfolding in the United States is an example that stresses the importance of provision and payment mechanisms in a public project which has nothing to do with contingent valuation. The legislative and executive branches of the US Government have been contemplating the expansion of health-care coverage for US citizens. While most parties advocate the same goal, eventual universal health-care coverage for all, the debate revolves almost exclusively around the provision and payment mechanisms. Despite the shared goals, differences over the provision and payment mechanisms have created an impasse. Provision and payment mechanisms, such as those noted in the health-coverage debate, are important issues to citizens included in contingent valuation samples. Therefore it is naïve to expect values to be uninfluenced by the implementing project's details.

4.3.4.   Resource Familiarity

The issue of resource familiarity is frequently represented as problematic for contingent valuation (Cummings *et al.*, 1986; Freeman, 1986; Diamond and Hausman, 1993).[38] The claim is often made that contingent valuation respondents cannot give meaningful values for unfamiliar goods and particularly for those whose values are primarily passive-use values. The supporting rationale for this claim is that consumers of market goods develop well-defined values for these goods by buying and using them. In contrast, many respondents in a contingent valuation survey have very limited or no direct knowledge of the good they are asked to value, nor do they have prior experience in making allocation decisions involving the resource. They therefore must lack well-defined values.

There are several weaknesses in this line of reasoning. First, they offer an idealized, yet incomplete, picture of consumer transactions. A multitude of

---

[38] A few authors such as Milgrom (1992) have advanced the extreme position that in such instances experts should be consulted on behalf of the public, even if it is known that experts' opinions diverge substantially from the public's preferences.

new products become available each year, creating completely new markets in which consumers regularly make purchase decisions involving goods for which they have no prior experience or even understanding.[39] Moreover for a significant portion of the population, each year's purchase of these new products constitutes a significant portion of disposable income expenditures.[40] The practice of cost–benefit analysis is of little practical import if its scope is to be limited to routine consumer purchases such as toilet paper and toothpaste.

Second, contingent valuation respondents' unfamiliarity is, in our opinion, exaggerated. For example, most respondents in the Exxon Valdez contingent valuation study (Carson *et al.*, 1992) who made judgements about preventing damage to Prince William Sound from another large oil spill had never been to Alaska, much less to Prince William Sound. However, with the help of visual aids and a carefully developed description of the situation, most, if not all, respondents were able to envision Prince William Sound, the bird species found there, the potential spill damage, and the project being presented.

Third, as it is information, not familiarity, which lies behind consumers making informed choices, these criticisms fail to appreciate the degree to which a well-designed contingent valuation scenario can inform respondents of the good's salient features. Provided care is taken in conducting sufficient pre-testing to understand the barriers to communication and test ways to overcome them, ways can be found to communicate most goods, even ones with which respondents are unfamiliar. This effort is facilitated by the fact that contingent valuation surveys are centred around the choice between having a good and not having it. This format serves to concentrate the respondent's attention on the distinguishing characteristics. In-person surveys can use visual aids such as photographs, maps, and diagrams, which we have found to be very helpful in conveying this information.

Fourth, the key feature which leads respondents to pay attention to the scenario in any contingent valuation survey is independent of familiarity. This feature is the *plausibility* of the choice situation. When asked to value a good that is presented in a vague, illogical, or excessively hypothetical way, respondents are unlikely to take the exercise seriously and may give a meaningless value no matter how much experience they have with the good.[41] Asked the same question in a survey that describes a credible market for the

[39] With respect to economic theory, the modelling of new-product demand does not treat consumers' decisions as lacking content. For example, see Hausman (1994) for a discussion of consumer surplus resulting from the introduction of new products

[40] 'New' can mean products newly introduced or products which the consumer has never purchased.

[41] In some cases, respondents familiar with the resource may have more difficulty understanding proposed changes than those unfamiliar with the resource. This occurs when the change is significant yet has not received public attention. Such a change may be less plausible to the person who is familiar with the resource and its routine provision.

good, a method of providing it that has a good chance of succeeding, and a credible payment method, respondents are likely to be willing to expend the effort necessary to understand the implications of the choice and to search their preferences in making their decision. Provided it is plausible and understandable, a contingent valuation survey often communicates more information than respondents would typically use in making market or voting decisions involving comparable expenditures.

It is often alleged by critics that responses to contingent valuation surveys where the good involves substantial passive-use values are somehow substantially different than those where the good involves only use values, with the former being unreliable and the latter reliable. As noted above, poorly conceived and improperly designed surveys can generate information that lacks content. However, our position is that *quality* contingent valuation surveys valuing goods with significant passive-use values are every bit as valid as *quality* contingent valuation studies valuing goods where little passive-use value is involved.

A related hypothesis that has received much attention is that contingent valuation respondents holding passive-use values are insensitive to the scope of the good they are being asked to value. The most conspicuous study which tests this hypothesis is the Exxon-sponsored study of Boyle *et al.* (1994). The authors base their claim mainly on a split-sample design in which different subsamples were told that different numbers of birds would be saved from death due to contact with open oil ponds in the US Rocky Mountain Flyway. The data used in the study was gathered in an Atlanta shopping mall using self-administered, intercept surveys.[42]

In order to evaluate the Boyle *et al.* and Kahneman and Knetsch (1992) claim that scope insensitivity is endemic in contingent valuation studies involving passive-use considerations, one must look at the existing body of contingent valuation studies. If the scope insensitivity hypothesis is true, then rarely should one see a contingent valuation study that rejects this hypothesis. Carson (1997) provides a review of the existing literature and notes over thirty studies that conduct split-sample tests and yet reject the scope insensitivity hypothesis. Over half of these studies involve goods where the total value is primarily passive-use value.[43] If one examines the studies which fail to reject the insensitivity hypothesis, most cases can be explained by details regarding survey design, implementation, or analysis.

One can look at other possible comparisons between goods involving principally passive-use values and those believed to involve principally use values by considering reliability in the sense of replicability or test-retest. Carson *et al.* (1997) show that contingent valuation studies generally

---

[42] For a critique of this study, see Hanemann (1995).

[43] See Carson and Mitchell (1995) for a formal presentation of the framework for testing the scope insensitivity hypothesis as well as an empirical example that provides a rejection of this hypothesis in a case of substantial passive-use value.

perform well on this dimension and that there is no apparent pattern with respect to the passive-use value characteristic of the good valued. Another possible comparison is with respect to the construct validity of contingent valuation estimates, particularly in the estimation of valuation functions.[44] Two successful valuation functions of the authors can be found in the State of Alaska's contingent valuation study of the Exxon Valdez oil spill (Carson et al., 1992) and in the Carson et al. (1994) paper reporting on the results of the Australian Resource Assessment Commission's Kakadu study. The valuation functions found in these papers have a large number of statistically significant predictor variables, which one would expect a priori should predict respondent willingness to pay. However, both studies used highly developed surveys and sample sizes which were large enough to yield statistical tests with reasonable power.

The only area where one can find consistent indications of a difference between goods with principally use and principally non-use values is with respect to comparisons between different response modes (e.g. Boyle et al., 1996; Kealy and Turner, 1993). However, these differences are potentially explained by the questions' incentive structures, an issue which is discussed subsequently.

4.3.5.   Irreversibility and Uniqueness

When Krutilla (1967) raised the issue of expanding the set of relevant valuers, he referred to an 'area with some unique attribute – a geomorphic feature such as the Grand Canyon, a threatened species, or an entire eco-system'. Some authors (e.g. Cicchetti and Wilde, 1992) have inferred from this passage that if resources are not unique and changes are not irreversible, then Krutilla's concerns do not apply.[45] We first note that 'unique' and 'irreversible' are relative terms and it is necessary to consider how the relevant population is affected.

With respect to irreversibility, consider the example of an oil spill that kills 10 per cent of the spill area's sea-bird population. Scientists predict the population will completely recover in eight years. Some individuals from the spill area as well as some individuals outside of the spill area care about birds in the sense that it upsets them that any birds are unnecessarily killed by humans. Others in and out of the area are concerned only with the long-range prospects of the bird species' survival. The first group clearly considers the 10-per-cent bird kill irreversible (short of a miracle) since the birds are dead. The second group may consider the 10-per-cent bird kill as nothing to worry

---

[44] In the case of passive-use valuers, one may see more heterogeneity of preferences than in the case of users because the motivating factors may be more diverse.

[45] Krutilla's analysis was not all-inclusive in that while it illuminated a line of enquiry by providing a powerful example, it did not address whether these concerns did or did not apply to non-unique resources.

about as long as the number of birds killed is within the regenerative capacity of the population. Individuals from this group would consider the injury significant only if it adversely affected the bird's population in the future.

Like reversibility, uniqueness is in the eye of the beholder. Consider the example of creating an urban park or green belt which may be unique to nearby residents and highly valued. Residents on the other side of the city who share the same tax-base may recognize this uniqueness and favour creating the park or green belt for a variety of reasons. However, from a global or even regional perspective, if one ignores location there will always be ample substitutes. If one were to issue an edict deeming passive-use values relevant only to irreversible changes of unique resources, the question is who defines the terms 'uniqueness' and 'irreversible'. Moreover, nothing in our theoretical analysis indicates that an irreversible change in a unique resource is either a necessary or sufficient condition for passive-use values to be present in any given situation. The question of whether or not passive-use values are important for a given resource can only be answered empirically. Both are better seen and easier understood in the context of substitute availability and possibilities.

4.3.6.   Substitute Availability

An issue always facing the designer of a contingent valuation study is what substitute goods, if any, should be clearly discussed in the survey instrument.[46] In answering this question, it is useful to consider three perspectives: (1) the choice opportunities which are actually available; (2) the information that respondents already possess; and (3) the amount of information which can realistically be conveyed to the respondent by the survey. By considering these three perspectives, the question of which substitutes are relevant becomes manageable.

With respect to (1), once again consider the park/green belt example. One respondent may prefer upgrading the local sewage treatment facility in order to improve water quality over the preservation of the park. Another respondent may prefer providing light rail from downtown to a suburban area as a means of reducing air pollution over park preservation. One could plausibly think of as many projects preferred over provision of the park as there are residents. As economic theory predicts (Hoehn and Randall, 1989; Carson et al., 1995), the simultaneous availability of other projects will generally affect the value for preservation of the park.[47] Neo-classical theory

---

[46] The issue of which goods should be considered as substitutes applies to any valuation analysis and is therefore not exclusively a contingent valuation issue. For instance, the number of substitute sites included in travel-cost analyses has received considerable attention (Bockstael et al., 1991).

[47] In the rationed goods literature, this phenomenon is referred to as the existence of q-substitution or q-complementarity (Madden, 1991). In the public choice literature, it is called the bundling effect (Mackay and Weaver, 1983).

(Flores, 1994) predicts this effect can be quite large even if one is considering providing a few other goods which are not close substitutes at the same time.[48] The value of the project may become arbitrarily small if enough projects are considered and the projects are substitutes with respect to valuation.[49] Because any possible combination of projects could conceivably be considered, does this imply that values are demonstrably arbitrary, as Kahneman and Knetsch (1992) suggest when discussing this issue in the context of contingent valuation?

While Kahneman and Knetsch's conclusion has received much attention in the literature, we note that while it is true that any combination of projects may be considered, it is never the case that arbitrary combinations of projects are considered. Researchers need only consider other projects that will actually be undertaken at the same time, rather than all potential projects.[50] While researchers are always obliged to inform policy-makers of potential project interactions, practical considerations will usually serve as the best guide to deciding which other projects, if any, should be discussed.

With respect to (2), respondents considering the provision of the pocket park or green belt may not be aware of parks and green belts in other areas of the city. Therefore, other similar available resources are potentially crucial pieces of information that may affect respondents' values. This example emphasizes that these sorts of substitutes are part of the relevant information needed by respondents to make an informed decision. In some cases, respondents will possess most of this knowledge and in other cases, respondents will have hardly any of the requisite information.

Due to (3), this set should generally be limited to close substitutes of which respondents are unaware, because there are limitations to the information that respondents can absorb and more importantly want to have provided.[51] These limitations may differ according to survey mode. For example, in a telephone survey there are very real communicative limitations. Without in-person contact, it is difficult to adapt the interview to respondents' needs. In particular, it is difficult to gauge how well respondents are understanding the scenario. More importantly, telephone surveys rule out the use of the visual aids such as maps and photographs which are commonly used for emphasiz-

---

[48] Flores (1994) shows that demand and virtual-price (e.g. willingness to pay) substitution elasticities are inversely related. Therefore goods which are poor demand substitutes may have large virtual-price substitution properties when quantity-rationed.

[49] It is important to note that this is a purely theoretical issue which does not involve either contingent valuation or passive-use values *per se*.

[50] While there are potentially very large numbers of projects that could be considered in a given year, only a handful of major projects are actually implemented even at the US federal level. Furthermore, for some of the largest government endeavours, the per-capita expenditure is often fairly small. For example, President Clinton's health-care plan would purportedly provide health care to all and will change health-care costs by less than $50 annually for most taxpayers.

[51] Included in this set are spatial as well as temporal substitutes, such as the quick recovery of an injured bird population.

ing substitutes. Mail surveys are able to incorporate such aids, but are plagued by both literacy and question-ordering problems. Respondents often read ahead before answering questions and skip sections considered difficult to read, which can render a complex mail-survey instrument ineffective. Finally, even with the preferred in-person mode, there are limitations to how many substitutes can be effectively conveyed. In most cases, the number of potential relevant and unknown substitutes is small and as such represents little problem in designing and administering the survey. However, if one were to consider the extreme position that all potential projects (assuming a finite number) should be considered, then respondents will quickly be overwhelmed and lose interest.[52] In summary, the decision regarding which substitutes to include in a scenario is an important issue which any contingent valuation researcher must address. However, it does not represent a paralysing issue and is generally manageable.

4.3.7   Passive-Use Values and Incentive Structures

An examination of the incentive properties of a given contingent valuation question is crucial when evaluating the study's results. In the most general sense, for a contingent valuation question to be incentive-compatible, the respondent must be presented with a single binary discrete choice question offering a specified amount[53] and a credible mechanism for carrying out the project described. For users of many quasi-public goods, these two conditions are easily satisfied. However, this is not true of pure public goods, of which pure passive-use value is a special case. Pure public goods require the additional element of a coercive payment structure.

To see this, consider a camper who is offered a contingent valuation choice between the current *status quo*, paying a fee of $2 to camp at a forest site offering few amenities, and an alternative which involves improving the site by adding running water, toilet facilities, and cooking facilities while charging a $5 fee. The camper will pick the alternative offering the higher level of utility and will never pick the improved alternative unless the value of the improvements to the camper is at least $3. We know this because the unimproved campsite with a $2 fee and the improved campsite with a $5 fee will never simultaneously exist. Essentially the choice set has been altered so that, under the new regime, the camper will have to pay the additional fee

[52] For example, in their Exxon-sponsored study, Kemp and Maxwell (1993) require respondents to allocate expenditures in a top-down fashion into as many as thirty-two different categories of public expenditure.

[53] A number of other elicitation methods such as double-bounded discrete choice questions, payment cards, and open-ended questions offer the possibility of achieving more information about a respondent's willingness to pay at the expense of introducing a downward bias. This may be a desirable trade-off under a mean square error criterion if the reduction in variance is large and the bias small. See Alberini (1995) for an examination of the double-bounded elicitation method in this context. See also Langford *et al.* (1994) for a discussion of a triple-bounded dichotomous format.

in order to use the site.[54] Consider an alternative proposal that will provide a new site nearby with these amenities, assuming away congestion externalities, and the old site at the old price were still available. In this case, the incentive structure for provision of the new site is not the same, because the old choice is still available. The camper can increase the choice set at no cost by responding positively to the question of provision of the new site with a $5 fee.

Pure public goods are similar to the last example because one is almost always dealing with an addition to the existing choice set. As long as the respondent has the option of not paying and the addition to the choice set is desirable, then the agent should always prefer the addition.[55] As clearly laid out in his classic paper on public goods and free-riding, Samuelson (1954) shows that an agent typically has a clear incentive to misrepresent his or her preferences in the pure public goods case. With a payment mechanism such as a voluntary trust fund, the incentives underlying a request for an actual payment and a contingent valuation request will diverge in opposite directions.[56]

In the first instance, which Samuelson's analysis directly addresses, the agent has an incentive to say 'no' even if the provision of the good is worth the amount requested. This is done in hopes that other people will pay into the fund and provide the good at no personal cost to the respondent. Unfortunately, this strategy is available to all and mass underreporting may result, implying that the payment into the trust fund will underestimate actual willingness to pay.

For the contingent valuation request, saying 'yes' encourages the creation of the trust fund, thereby increasing the likelihood that the good will be eventually provided. However, because of the voluntary nature of the trust fund, the agent knows she can later renege on the response when the actual request comes if she believes the good will still be provided without her contribution. Basically, the respondent hopes to expand the choice set by including the option to free-ride later. Therefore in the case of a survey trust fund the incentive is to overreport, which is the opposite result of actual

---

[54] Another way to put this is that the respondent is indicating preferences over non-nested choice sets.

[55] A similar situation is seen in many marketing surveys where users of an existing product are asked if they would switch to a new product if it were available at a given price. The incentive structure of this question is to give whatever response increases the likelihood that the new product will be produced as long as the addition of that product to the choice set provides positive utility. As a result, such questions provide estimates of potential rather than actual demand.

[56] Voluntary trust funds have a number of other undesirable properties which may influence the amounts empirically observed in actual payment requests and in contingent valuation surveys. For example, respondents may perceive a lower probability that the good will be provided than with a tax mechanism (Bateman et al., 1993) and in the extreme case, an insufficient amount will be paid into the fund to actually provide the good with any amount paid into the fund non-recoverable by the respondent (Twight, 1993).

payments into a trust fund. Neither the response to the actual payment request nor the response to the contingent valuation request will reveal the agent's true preference if agents take advantage of the incentives for mis-representation offered by the two questions. This divergence in incentives is likely to lie behind the results of experiments such as those conducted by Duffield and Patterson (1992), Navrud (1992), Seip and Strand (1992), and Champ *et al.* (1997), who show hypothetical contingent valuation pledges to be larger than actual payments.

The condition necessary to restore incentive compatibility in the pure public goods case is a coercive payment mechanism. Many tax mechanisms such as income taxes, sales taxes, value-added taxes, and property taxes satisfy this requirement, as do increases in utility bills and increases in specific taxes on universally used commodities. As long as the Government's decision to provide the good and implement the payment is perceived by the respondent as increasing with the percentage who respond with a yes on an actual vote or to a contingent valuation question, the agent will have an incentive to indicate a yes response only if the good is preferred given the specified payment and to indicate 'no' otherwise. The enhanced incentive structure arises because there is a credible coercive mechanism by which to extract payments from all agents if the good is provided. As a result, there is no incentive to wait and see if others will first pay for providing the good.

4.4. CONCLUSION

When making environmental resource allocation decisions, the correct mea-sure of economic welfare is total value aggregated over the entire relevant population. Assessment methods which are dependent on observable behav-iour will fail to include passive-use values in their estimates of total value. We have chosen to base our definition of passive-use values directly on this property rather than to continue defining passive-use values by motivation. However, our analysis provides theoretical representations which are con-sistent with the behaviour described in the many motivational examples found throughout the literature. More importantly, these representations allow us to emphasize ways in which passive-use values can occur with respect to the population of interest.

Turning from economic theory to issues of empirical measurement, we have focused on six conceptual issues which have been advanced as proble-matic for contingent valuation when passive-use values are present: (1) commodity definition; (2) the effect of provision and payment aspects; (3) resource familiarity; (4) uniqueness and irreversibility; (5) substitute avail-ability; and (6) the incentive structure of valuation questions involving passive-use values. Upon a careful examination of these issues, it can be seen that some have little to do with passive-use values *per se*, some have little to do with contingent valuation *per se*, and others are neither contingent valuation issues nor passive-use value issues, but deeper philosophical concerns regarding the theoretical foundations and relevance of welfare economics. Problems related to commodity definition, resource familiarity, and substitute availability are essentially contingent valuation design issues which can be overcome or avoided by ensuring that the respondent clearly understands the nature of the good being offered and is thus able to make an informed decision. People making decisions in private goods markets and in the voting booth are typically forced to deal with these problems with less information than they receive in a high-quality contingent valuation survey. Economic theory provides relatively simple answers to issues regarding the uniqueness of a good and irreversibility of changes in its provision; neither are necessary or sufficient conditions for the presence of passive-use values. Economic theory also provides guidance on the issue of whether payment or provision aspects of the good can influence an agent's value for the good. The answer is yes—consumers are free to care about any aspect of the good. Such concerns are a major force behind much of the product differentiation seen in private goods markets. With respect to the last issue, the incentive structure of contingent valuation questions, one must endeavour to provide questions with a proper incentive structure that elicit a truthful response. Thus we would conclude that none of these conceptual issues should discourage the analyst who wants to stay within the standard cost–benefit framework of neo-classical economics from using contingent value of a valuation to measure the total non-marketed good. However, this is not the same thing as concluding that such an undertaking is an easy or inexpensive task if reliable estimates are to be obtained.

REFERENCES

Adamowicz, W. L., Louviere, J., and Williams, M. (1994), 'Combining Revealed and Stated Preference Methods for Valuing Environmental Amenities', *Journal of Environmental Economics and Management*, 26: 271–92.
Alberini, A. (1995), 'Efficiency *v.* Bias of Willingness to Pay Estimates: Bivariate and Interval Data Models', *Journal of Environmental Economics and Management*, 29: 169–80.
Arrow, K. J., and Fisher, A. C. (1974), 'Environmental Preservation, Uncertainty, and Irreversibility', *Quarterly Journal of Economics*, 88: 312–19.
——Solow, R., Portney, P. R., Leamer, E. E., Radner, R., and Schuman, H. (1993), 'Report of the NOAA Panel on Contingent Valuation', Federal Register, 58 4602–4614.
Barrick, K. A. (1983), 'Measurement of Wilderness Benefits and Option Value, with an Application to the Washakie Wilderness, Northwest Wyoming', Ph.D. dissertation, DAI, 45, Southern Illinois University, Carbondale.

Bateman, I. J., Langford, I. H., Willis, K. G., Turner, R. K., and Garrod, G. D. (1993), 'The Impacts of Changing Willingness to Pay Question Format in Contingent Valuation Questions: An Analysis of Open-Ended, Iterative Bidding and Dichotomous Choice Formats', CSERGE Working Paper GEC 93–05, Centre for Social and Economic Research on the Global Environment, UEA Norwich and UCL London.

Bennett, J. W. (1984), 'Using Direct Questioning to Value the Existence Benefits of Preserved Natural Areas', *Australian Journal of Agricultural Economics*, 28: 136–52.

Bishop, R. C. and Heberlein, T. A. (1979), 'Measuring Values of Extra-Market Goods: Are Indirect Measures Biased?' *American Journal of Agricultural Economics*, 61: 926–30.

—— and—— (1984), 'Contingent Valuation Methods and Ecosystem Damages from Acid Rain', Department of Agricultural Economics Staff Paper no. 217, University of Wisconsin, Madison.

—— and Welsh, M. P. (1990), 'Existence Value in Resource Evaluation', paper presented at the USDA W-133 Annual Meeting. Molokai, Hawaii, February.

Bockstael, N. E., McConnell, K. E., and Strand, I. (1991), 'Recreation', in J. B. Braden and C. Kolstad (eds.), *Measuring the Demand for Environmental Commodities*, North-Holland, Amsterdam, pp., 227–270.

Bohm, P. (1977), 'Estimating Access Values', in L. Wingo and A. Evans (eds.), *Public Economics and the Quality of Life*, Johns Hopkins University Press, Baltimore, pp. 181–95.

Borcherding, T. and Deacon, R. (1972), 'The Demand for the Services of Non-Federal Governments', *American Economic Review*, 62: 842–53.

Boyle, K. J., Johnson, R., McCollum, D. W., Desvousges, W. H., Dunford, R., and Hudson, S. (1996), 'Valuing Public Goods: Discrete versus Continuous Contingent Valuation Responses', *Land Economics*, 72: 381–96.

—— Desvousges, W. H. Johnson, R., Dunford, R., and Hudson, S. (1994), 'An Investigation of Part–Whole Biases in Contingent Valuation Studies', *Journal of Environmental Economics and Management*, 27: 64–83.

Brookshire, D. S. (1977), 'Some Results and Problem Areas in the Application of Bidding Games', *Proceedings of a Workshop on the Measure of Intangible Environmental Impacts*, Electric Power Research Institute, Palo Alto, Calif.

Carson, R. T. (1997), 'Contingent Valuation Surveys and Tests of Scope Insensitivity', in R. J. Kopp, W. Pommerhene, and N. Schwartz (eds), *Determining the Value of Non-Marketed Goods: Economic, Psychological, and Policy Relevant Aspects of Contingent Valuation Methods*, Kluwer, Boston.

—— and Mitchell, R. C. (1991), 'Nonuse Values and Contingent Valuation', paper presented at the annual meeting of the Southern Economic Association, Nashville, Tenn., November.

—— and—— (1995), 'Sequencing and Nesting in Contingent Valuation Surveys', *Journal of Environmental Economics and Management*, 28: 155–73.

—— Mitchell, R. C., Hanemann, W. M., Kopp, R. J., Presser, S., and Ruud, P. A. (1992), *A Contingent Valuation Study of Lost Passive Use Values Resulting from the Exxon Valdez Oil Spill*, Report to the Attorney General of the State of Alaska, Natural Resource Damage Assessment, Inc., La Jolla, Calif., November.

——Wilks, L., and Imber, D. (1994), 'Valuing Preservation of Australia's Kakadu Conservation Zone', *Oxford Economic Papers*, 46: 727–49.

——Flores, N. E., and Hanemann, W. M. (1995), 'On the Creation and Destruction of Public Goods: The Matter of Sequencing', Discussion Paper 95–21, Department of Economics, University of California, San Diego, April.

——Hanemann, W. M., Kopp, R. J., Krosnick, J. A., Mitchell, R. C., Presser, S. and Ruud, P. A. (1997), 'Temporal Reliability of Contingent Valuation Estimates', *Land Economics*, 73: 151–63.

Champ, P., Bishop, R. C., Brown, T. C., and McCollum, D. W. (1997), 'Using Donation Mechanisms to Value Nonuse Benefits from Public Goods', *Journal of Environmental Economics and Management*, 33: 151–62.

Cicchetti, C. J. and Wilde, L. L. (1992), 'Uniqueness, Irreversibility, and the Theory of Nonuse Values', *American Journal of Agricultural Economics*, 74: 1121–5.

Clawson, M. (1959), 'Methods of Measuring the Demand for and Value of Outdoor Recreation', reprint 10, Resources for the Future, Washington.

Crocker, T. D., and Vaux, H. (1983), *Some Economic Consequences of Ambient Oxidant Impacts on a National Forest*, Report to the Environmental Protection Agency, Washington.

Cropper, M. L. (1994), 'Comments on "Estimating the Demand for Public Goods: the Collective Choice and Contingent Valuation Approaches" ', paper presented at the DOE/EPA Workshop. Washington, May.

Cummings, R. G., and Harrison, G. W. (1995), 'The Measurement and Decomposition of Nonuse Values: A Critical Review', *Environmental and Resource Economics*, 5: 225–47.

——Brookshire, D. S., and Schulze, W. D. (1986), Valuing Environmental Goods: an Assessment of the Contingent Valuation Method, Rowman and Allanheld, Totowa, NJ.

Deacon, R., and Shapiro, P. (1975), 'Private Preference for Collective Goods Revealed through Voting on Referenda', *American Economic Review*, 65: 943–55.

Deaton, A., and Muellbauer, J. (1980), *Economics and Consumer Behaviour*, Cambridge University Press, New York.

Desvousges, W. H., Smith, V. K., and McGivney, M. P. (1983), *A Comparison of Alternative Approaches for Estimating Recreation and Related Benefits of Water Quality Improvements*, EPA Report 230–05–83–001, US Environmental Protection Agency, Office of Policy Analysis, Washington.

——Gable, A. R., Dunford, R. W. and Hudson, S. P. (1993), 'Contingent Valuation: the Wrong Tool for Damage Assessment', *Choices*, 2: 9–11.

Diamond, P. A. and Hausman, J. A. (1993), 'On Contingent Valuation Measurement of Nonuse Values', in J. A. Hausman (ed.), *Contingent Valuation: A Critical Assessment*, North-Holland, Amsterdam, pp. 3–38.

DOI (US Department of Interior) (1986), 'Final Rule for Natural Resources Damage Assessments under the Comprehensive Environmental Response Compensation and Liability Act of 1980 (CERCLA)', *Federal Register*, 51: 27674–753.

Duffield, J. W., and Patterson, D. (1992), 'Field Testing Existence Values: Comparison of Hypothetical and Cash Transaction Values', paper presented at the USDA W-133 Annual Meeting, South Lake Tahoe, Nev., February.

Fisher, A., and Raucher, R. (1984), 'Intrinsic Benefits on Improved Water Quality: Conceptual and Empirical Perspectives', in V. K. Smith and A. D.

White (eds.), *Advances in Applied Microeconomics*, iii, JAI Press, Greenwich, Conn., pp. 37–66.

Flores, N. E. (1994), 'The Effects of Rationing and Virtual Price Elasticities', unpublished paper, Department of Economics, University of California, San Diego, November.

——(1996), Reconsidering the Use of Hicks Neutrality to Recover Total Values', *Journal of Environmental Economics and Management*, 31: 49–64.

Freeman, A. M. III (1979), *The Benefits of Environmental Improvements: Theory and Evidence*, Johns Hopkins University Press, Baltimore.

——(1986), 'On Assessing the State of the Arts of the Contingent Valuation Method of Valuing Environmental Changes', in Cummings *et al.* (1986), pp. 148–61.

——(1993*a*), 'Nonuse Values in Natural Resource Damage Assessment', in R. J. Kopp and V. K. Smith (eds.), *Valuing Natural Assets: the Economics of Natural Resource Damage Assessment*, Resources for the Future, Washington.

——(1993*b*), *The Measurement of Environmental and Resource Values: Theory and Methods*, Resources for the Future, Washington.

Gallagher, D. R. and Smith, V. K. (1985), 'Measuring Values for Environmental Resources Under Uncertainty', *Journal of Environmental Economics and Management*, 12: 132–43.

Greenley, D. A., Walsh, R. G., and Young, R. A. (1982), *Economic Benefits of Improved Water Quality: Public Perceptions of Option and Preservation Values*, Westview Press, Boulder, Colo.

Hanemann, W. M. (1980), 'Measuring the Worth of Natural Resource Facilities', *Land Economics*, 56: 482–90.

——(1988), 'Three Approaches to Defining "Existence" or "Non-Use" Value Under Certainty', unpublished paper, Department of Agricultural and Resource Economics, University of California, Berkeley, July.

——(1989), 'Information and the Concept of Option Value', *Journal of Environmental Economics and Management*, 16: 23–37.

——(1992), Preface to S. Navrud (ed.), *Pricing the European Environment*, Oxford University Press, pp. 9–35.

——(1995), 'Contingent Valuation and Economics', in K. G. Willis and J. T. Corkindale (eds), Wallingford, UK: CAB International.

Hausman, J. A. (1981), 'Exact Consumer's Surplus and Deadweight Loss', *American Economic Review*, 71: 662–76.

——(1994), 'Valuation of New Goods under Perfect and Imperfect Competition', paper presented at the NBER Conference on Income and Wealth: The Economics of New Products, Williamsburg, Va, April.

Hoehn, J. P., and Randall, A. (1989), 'Too Many Proposals Past the Benefit Cost Test', *American Economics Review*, 79: 544–51.

Just, R. E., Hueth, D. L., and Schmitz, A. (1982), *Applied Welfare Economics and Public Policy*, Prentice-Hall International, Englewood Cliffs, NJ.

Kahneman, D., and Knetsch, J. (1992), 'Valuing Public Goods: the Purchase of Moral Satisfaction', *Journal of Environmental Economics and Management*, 22: 57–70.

Kealy, M. J., and Turner, R. W. (1993), 'A Test of the Equality of Close-Ended and Open-Ended Contingent Valuations', *American Journal of Agricultural Economics*, 75: 321–31.

Kemp, M. A., and Maxwell, C. (1993), 'Exploring a Budget Context for Contingent Valuation Estimates', in J. A. Hausman (ed.), *Contingent Valuation: A Critical Assessment*, North-Holland, Amsterdam, pp. 217–70.

Kopp, R. J. (1992), 'Why Existence Value Should Be Used in Cost–Benefit Analysis', *Journal of Policy Analysis and Management*, 11: 123–30.

—— and Smith, V. K. (1993*a*), 'Understanding Damages to Natural Assets', in Kopp and Smith (1993*b*), pp. 6–22.

—— and —— (eds.) (1993*b*), *Valuing Natural Assets: The Economics of Natural Resource Damage Assessment*, Resources for the Future, Washington.

Krutilla, J. V. (1967), 'Conservation Reconsidered', *American Economic Review*, 57: 777–86.

LaFrance, J. (1993), 'Weak Separability in Applied Welfare Analysis', *American Journal of Agricultural Economics*, 75: 770–5.

Langford, I. H., Bateman, I. J., and Langford, H. D. (1994), 'Multilevel Modelling and Contingent Valuation. Part I: A Triple Bounded Dichotomous Choice Analysis', CSERGE Working Paper GEC 94–04, Centre for Social and Economic Research on the Global Environment, UEA Norwich and UCL London.

Larson, D. M. (1992), 'Further Results on Willingness to Pay for Nonmarket Goods', *Journal of Environmental Economics and Management*, 23: 101–22.

MacKay, R. J., and Weaver, C. (1983), 'Commodity Bundling and Agenda Control in the Public Sector', *Quarterly Journal of Economics*, 98: 563–87.

Madariaga, B., and McConnell, K. E. (1987), 'Exploring Existence Value', *Water Resources Research*, 23: 936–42.

Madden, P. (1991), 'A Generalization of Hicksian Substitutes and Complements with Application to Demand Rationing', *Econometrica*, 59: 1497–1508.

Mäler, K. (1974), *Environmental Economics: A Theoretical Inquiry*, Johns Hopkins University Press, Baltimore.

—— Gren, I., and Folke, C. (1994), 'Multiple Use of Environmental Resources: A Household Production Function Approach to Valuing Natural Capital', in A. Jansson, M. Hammer, C. Folke, and R. Costanza (eds.), *Investing in Natural Capital: The Ecological Economics Approach to Sustainability*, Island Press, Washington.

McConnell, K. E. (1983), 'Existence and Bequest Value', in R. D. Rowe and L. G. Chestnut (eds.), *Managing Air Quality and Scenic Resources at National Parks and Wilderness Areas*, Westview Press, Boulder, Colo.

—— (1997), 'Does Altruism Undermine Existence Value', *Journal of Enviromental Economics and Management*, 32: 22–37.

Milgrom, P. (1992), 'Benefit–Cost Analysis, Bounded Rationality and the Contingent Valuation Method', comment no. 34 submitted to the National Oceanic and Atmospheric Administration Blue Ribbon Panel on Contingent Valuation, 29 September.

Mitchell, R. C., and Carson, R. T. (1981), *An Experiment in Determining Willingness to Pay for National Water Quality Improvements*, Report to the US Environmental Protection Agency, Washington, June.

—— and —— (1989), *Using Surveys to Value Public Goods: The Contingent Valuation Method*, Resources for the Future, Washington.

Moulin, H. (1994), 'Serial Cost-Sharing of Excludable Public Goods', *Review of Economic Studies*, 61, 305–25.

Navrud, S. (1992), 'Willingness to Pay for Preservation of Species: An Experiment with Actual Payments', in S. Navrud (ed.), *Pricing the European Environment*, Oxford University Press, pp. 230–57.

Oates, W. E. (1994), 'Estimating the Demand for Public Goods: The Collective Choice and Contingent Valuation Approaches', paper presented at the DOE/EPA Workshop, Washington, May.

Pratt, J. W., Wise, D. A., and Zeckhauser, R. (1979), 'Price Differences in Almost Competitive Markets', *Quarterly Journal of Economics*, 93: 189–211.

Randall, A. (1994), 'A Difficulty with the Travel Cost Method', *Land Economics*, 70: 88–96.

——and Stoll, J. R. (1983), 'Existence Value in a Total Valuation Framework', in R. D. Rowe and G. Rowe (eds.), *Managing Air Quality and Scenic Resources at National Parks and Wilderness Areas*, Westview Press, Boulder, colo.

——Ives, B., and Eastman, E. (1974), 'Benefits of Abating Aesthetic Environmental Damage from the Four Corners Power Plant, Fruitland, New Mexico', Agricultural Experiment Station Bulletin no. 618, New Mexico State University, May.

Sagoff, M. (1994), 'Should Preferences Count?' *Land Economics*, 70: 127–44.

Samuelson, P. A. (1954), 'The Pure Theory of Public Expenditure', *Review of Economics and Statistics*, 36: 387–9.

Schulze, W. D., Brookshire, D., Walther, E., MacFarland, K., Thayer, M., Whitworth, R., and Ben-David, S. (1983), 'The Economic Benefits of Preserving Visibility in the National Parklands of the Southwest', *Natural Resources Journal*, 23: 149–73.

Seip, K., and Strand, J. (1992), 'Willingness to Pay for Environmental Goods in Norway: A Contingent Valuation Study with Real Payment', *Environmental and Resource Economics*, 2: 91–106.

Shapiro, P., and Deacon, R. (1994), 'Estimating the Demand for Public Goods: Comments and Extensions', paper presented at the DOE/EPA Workshop. Washington, May.

Shechter, M., and Freeman, S. (1994), 'Some Reflections on the Definition and Measurement of Non-Use Value', in R. Pethig (ed.), *Valuing the Environment: Methodological and Measurement Issues*, Kluwer, Boston, pp. 171–94.

Smith, V. K., (1987), 'Uncertainty, Benefit–Cost Analysis, and the Treatment of Option Value', *Journal of Environmental Economics and Management*, 14: 283–92.

——(1991), 'Household Production Functions and Environmental Benefit Estimation', in J. B. Braden and C. Kolstad (eds.), *Measuring the Demand for Environmental Commodities*, North-Holland, Amsterdam, pp. 41–76.

——and Desvousges, W. H. (1986), *Measuring Water Quality Benefits*, Kluwer, Boston.

Twight, C. (1993), 'Urban Amenities, Demand Revelation, and the Free-Rider Problem: A Partial Solution', *Public Choice*, 77: 835–54.

US Court of Appeals for the District of Columbia. *Ohio* v. *United States Department of Interior*, 880 F.2nd 432 (DC Cir. 1989).

US Water Resources Council (1979), 'Procedures for Evaluation of National Economic Development (NED) Benefits and Costs in Water Resources Planning (Level C), Final Rule', *Federal Register*, 44: 72892–976.

——(1983), *Economic and Environmental Principles and Guidelines for Water and Related Land Resource Implementation Studies*, US Government Printing Office, Washington.

Varian, H. R. (1992), *Microeconomic Analysis*, W. W. Norton, New York.

Weisbrod, B. A., (1964), 'Collective-Consumption Services of Individual-Consumption Goods', *Quarterly Journal of Economics*, 78: 471–7.

Zhang, X. (1993), 'Integrating Resource Types, Payment Methods, and Resource Using Status to Model Use and Nonuse Values: Valuing Marine Debris Control', Ph.D. dissertation, North Carolina State University, Raleigh, NC.

5
Public Goods and Contingent Valuation

ROBERT SUGDEN

5.1. PUBLIC GOODS

Many applications of the contingent valuation (CV) method are concerned with public goods. This chapter considers some of the special problems involved in eliciting preferences for such goods.

In economic theory, the distinction between public and private goods is clear-cut. What is now the standard definition of a public good derives from a classic paper, only three pages long, by Paul Samuelson (1954); this encapsulates some of the key elements of a tradition of public finance which can be traced back to Lindahl (1919/1958) and Wicksell (1896/1958). The defining characteristic of a public good is that *the same* units of the good are consumed by, or give utility to, more than one individual.

For example, consider the benefits that the residents of a suburban area derive from an expanse of open-access woodland. One way of modelling these benefits would be to define a good, 'open-access woodland', measured in hectares. A typical resident, we may assume, prefers more of this good to less, just as she prefers to have more rather than less of private consumption goods, such as food and clothing. But there is a crucial difference between food and clothing on the one hand and the woodland on the other. In relation to food and clothing, individual consumers are *rivals*: if any given unit of one of these goods (say, a particular packet of frozen peas or a particular coat) is consumed by one person then, necessarily, it is not consumed by another person. In contrast, in the case of the woodland, there is *non-rivalry*: each hectare of woodland is giving benefits to many people simultaneously. Thus, when we specify the utility functions of a set of individuals, the level of provision of each public good is represented by a single variable, which is an argument in each individuals' utility function, while the level of consumption of each private good is represented by a separate variable for each individual.

This chapter was written as part of a research project supported by the Economic and Social Research Council, through its Transport and the Environment Programme (Award No. W 119 25 1014). Thanks go to Ian Bateman, Alistair Munro, and Chris Starmer for their help.

At first sight, it may seem odd that the theoretical distinction between public and private goods should be so categorical. Isn't there a continuum stretching from almost pure private goods (such as frozen peas) to almost pure public goods (such as national defence)? The answer is that Samuelson's distinction between public and private goods is not so much a classification of goods as a classification of ways of modelling them. Indeed it is often possible to choose whether to model a given source of benefits as a private good or as a public one.

Take the case of the woodland. In an informal sense, open-access woodland in a suburban area is not a 'pure' public good. Beyond a certain point, the more visitors there are to a wood, the poorer is each visitor's experience. Thus, one might say, visitors *are* rivals. But this factor can be incorporated within a model in which woodland is a public good in Samuelson's sense. The effects of congestion come through as properties of individuals' valuations of the public good; one of the reasons why an increase in quantity (i.e. an increase in the area of woodland) is valued is because this reduces congestion. However, the same real-world state of affairs could be modelled, with equal legitimacy, in private-good terms. We could define 'visits to woodland areas' as a good, measured in (say) numbers of visits per year. Visits to woodland are private goods, even if there is open access: each visit is made *by* a particular person. In this framework, an increase in the area of woodland would appear as an improvement in the quality of the good 'visits', and thus as an outward shift of the demand curve for that good.

Whether a given source of benefits should be analysed as a public good or as a private good is a question of modelling strategy. If we wish to elicit individuals' valuations of some benefit, we can often choose between alternative ways of setting up the problem; some ways of setting it up call for valuations of private goods, others for valuations of public goods. In the case of the woodland, for example, we might try to elicit valuations of the private good 'visits', perhaps by asking people about their willingness to pay different hypothetical entry charges, or (if they travel to the woodland by car) different charges for parking.

The strategy of valuing visits has some obvious limitations: it fails to pick up some of the ways in which individuals derive benefits from woodland. Expanses of woodland make a suburban area look more attractive, and this can be a source of benefit even to residents who never set foot in a wood. But these benefits, too, can be valued through private goods. If what people value is the amenity benefits of having trees *near their homes*, then it is equally true to say that they value homes that are near trees. Here we can try to find out how much extra people are willing to pay to buy or rent houses in well-wooded areas. This could be investigated either by using a hedonic pricing method (i.e. identifying differences in market prices for houses in different areas) or by using a CV survey to elicit individuals' housing preferences.

However, the more diffuse the nature of the benefit, the more difficult it becomes to find an appropriate private good. An extreme case is the *existence value* that a person may derive merely from the knowledge that something – a wildlife habitat, a landscape, an historic monument – exists. One of the apparent strengths of the CV method is that it can be used to elicit preferences both for private and for public goods. This chapter will be concerned with applications of the CV method to public goods.

5.2. THE THEORY OF PUBLIC GOODS

For the purposes of exposition, it is convenient to start with a very simple model in which there are just two goods, one private and one public. The public good is supplied under conditions of constant costs; the cost of supplying each unit is p. There are n individuals, labelled by $i = 1, \ldots, n$, each of whom consumes the quantity y_i of the private good. The quantity of the public good is x; this quantity is consumed by, or is made available to, every individual. Thus individuals' preferences can be represented by the utility functions:

$$u_i = u_i(x, y_i) \quad i = 1, \ldots, n. \tag{5.1}$$

Preferences over combinations of public and private consumption are assumed to have the conventional neo-classical properties; thus, each person's preferences can be represented by a family of smooth, strictly convex, downward-sloping indifference curves in (x, y_i) space. I shall also make the very weak assumption that the private good is a normal good.

For any individual i, we may define the *marginal valuation* of the public good as $v(x, y_i)$, where

$$v(x, y_i) = [\partial u_i / \partial x] / [\partial u_i / \partial y_i] \quad i = 1, \ldots, n. \tag{5.2}$$

Thus, starting from any given bundle (x, y_i), the value of $v(x, y_i)$ represents the individual's valuation of a marginal increase in the quantity of the public good, expressed in units of the private good. If the private good is treated as the *numéraire* (i.e. if quantities of the private good are measured in money units), $v(x, y_i)$ can be interpreted as the individual's willingness to pay (WTP) for a marginal increase in the quantity of the public good. Since the private good is normal, $v(x, y_i)$ is decreasing in x. Since more of each good is preferred to less, $v(x, y_i)$ is strictly positive for all values of x and y_i.

It is easy to see that Pareto efficiency will be achieved if and only if

$$\sum_i v(x, y_i) = p. \tag{5.3}$$

That is, the sum of all individuals' marginal valuations of the public good must be equal to the marginal cost of that good. If the sum of marginal valuations was greater than marginal cost, it would be possible to make everyone better off by increasing the quantity of the public good and divid-ing the extra cost between individuals in proportion to their marginal valuations. Conversely, if the sum of marginal valuations was less than marginal cost, it would be possible to make everyone better off by reducing the quantity of the public good and distributing the cost saving between individuals in proportion to marginal values.

Unfortunately, market economies contain no mechanisms which can be relied on to ensure that (5.3) is satisfied. Under conditions of constant costs, competitive firms will supply a good at a price equal to its marginal cost; thus, p may be interpreted as the competitive market price of units of the public good. In a market economy, the public good will be supplied only to the extent that it is bought by individuals. Thus, we need to ask how much of it would be bought at the price p.

One apparently natural assumption is that each person maximizes utility, taking as given both the price of the public good and the quantities bought by all other individuals. I shall call this assumption *parametric instrumental rationality*. 'Instrumental' signifies that the individual treats her choices among goods as means, her ends being given by her preferences over final outcomes. 'Parametric' signifies that she treats other people's decisions as given, rather than seeing herself as engaged in strategic interaction with those other people. Consider the implications of this assumption.

For each person i, let z_i be the value of i's endowments, and let w_i be the total quantity of the public good bought by people other than i (i.e., $w_i = \sum_{j \neq i}[z_j - y_j]/p$). Then i faces two budget constraints:

$$p(x - w_i) + y_i = z_i \tag{5.4}$$

and

$$x \geq w_i. \tag{5.5}$$

The market is in equilibrium (analogous with a market-clearing equilibrium in a private-good economy) if x and $y_1, \ldots, y_n$ are such that, for each person i, the combination (x, y_i) maximizes i's utility subject to the constraints (5.4) and (5.5).

In such an equilibrium, the following must be true for each person i:

$$\text{either } v(x, y_i) = p \text{ and } x \geq w_i \tag{5.6a}$$

$$\text{or } v(x, y_i) < p \text{ and } x = w_i. \tag{5.6b}$$

Condition (5.6a) is the case in which i buys just enough of the public good to ensure that marginal valuation is equal to price. Condition (5.6b) is the case in which, even if she buys none of the good, marginal valuation is less than price; in this case, the utility-maximizing solution is to buy nothing.

It is immediately obvious that, if the Pareto-efficient solution requires *any* positive quantity of the public good to be supplied, Pareto efficiency cannot be achieved consistently with (5.6*a*) or (5.6*b*) being true for all persons *i*. Since $v(x, y_i) = p$ for any person *i* who chooses to buy any of the public good, and since $v(x, y_i) > 0$ for all *i*, the sum of $v(x, y_i)$ across all *i* must be greater than *p*; and this is incompatible with the Pareto-efficiency condition (5.3). If in equilibrium the public good is supplied at all, the sum of individuals' marginal valuations of the public good will be greater than the good's marginal cost.

Thus, the implication of this model is that if the supply of public goods is left to the market, there will be undersupply. Intuitively, the source of the problem is easy to see: each individual buys the good (if at all) with a view to the benefits to herself; but each unit that *any* individual buys supplies benefits to *all* individuals.

5.3. INCENTIVE COMPATIBILITY: THE THEORETICAL PROBLEM

Welfare economists have generally argued that public policy should aim at achieving Pareto efficiency in the supply of public goods. The problem, then, is to find a procedure for discovering enough about individuals' preferences to allow us to identify Pareto-efficient levels of provision for public goods. Samuelson was pessimistic about the prospects; in a section of his classic paper with the title 'Impossibility of Decentralized Solution', he argued that no decentralized pricing system could identify Pareto-efficient solutions because 'it is in the selfish interest of each person to give *false* signals, to pretend to have less interest in a given collective consumption activity than he really has' (1954: 338–9).

Subsequent theoretical work has shown that this problem is slightly less intractable than Samuelson thought. Clarke (1971), Groves (1973), and Groves and Ledyard (1977) have proposed a *demand-revealing mechanism* for public goods which tailors each individual's tax payment to his preferences as reported by him. The essential idea is that each person is invited to 'vote' by reporting his WTP for a public good; the supply of that good is then set at a Pareto-efficient level, relative to the reported preferences of all voters; finally, each voter is required to pay a tax equal to the marginal net cost that he has imposed on other individuals by voting rather than abstaining. Under reasonable assumptions about preferences, this mechanism can be shown to be *incentive-compatible* – that is, no individual can benefit by misrepresenting his preferences if no one else is misrepresenting theirs. Unfortunately, however, the demand-revealing mechanism is very vulnerable to strategic behaviour by small coalitions of voters, and for this reason probably cannot be regarded as a practical proposal.

In any case, it is clear that Samuelson's claim about the 'impossibility of decentralized solutions' applies to CV: if the CV method is used to elicit individuals' preferences for a public good, and if the findings are then used to determine the supply of that good, then each individual typically has a selfish interest in giving a false signal. To see why, consider a simple case in which a collective decision has to be made between two options – either not to supply a particular public good (option *A*) or to supply it (option *B*). If the good is supplied, it will be paid for from taxes; each individual's share of the increase in tax will be independent of how he or she responds to the CV survey. Assume that each individual has preferences of the kind described in Section 5.2. After taking account of taxes, each individual must either prefer *A* to *B*, or prefer *B* to *A*, or be indifferent between the two. Now consider what response it would be rational for a self-interested individual to make to a CV survey. Subject to her response being credible, the larger the WTP a person reports, the more likely it is that *B* will be chosen. Thus if she prefers *B* to *A*, her best strategy is to report the highest WTP that would be credible. Conversely, if she prefers *A* to *B*, her best strategy is to report the lowest WTP that would be credible.

Some commentators have suggested that CV respondents believe that the responses they make *as individuals* may determine the tax payments they make *as individuals*, and that this discourages the overstating of WTP (Hoehn and Randall, 1987; Mitchell and Carson, 1989: 153–70). It is possible that some respondents *do* believe this; but since the belief is false, it would be unwise for CV researchers to count on it and unethical for them to try to induce respondents to hold it. I know of no CV survey in which individual responses have been used to determine individual tax payments. Furthermore, it is standard practice in surveys to assure respondents that the information they give will be treated anonymously. Any respondent who understands and believes this assurance must realize that she cannot be taxed according to her reported willingness to pay.

It is sometimes implied that the CV method can be made incentive-compatible by using a *referendum format*, in which each respondent is presented with just two options and asked to report which she prefers. For example, the 'Blue Ribbon' Panel on Contingent Valuation argues that the referendum format is preferable to the use of open-ended WTP questions, because the latter encourage the overstatement of true valuations as 'a costless way to make a point' (Arrow *et al.*, 1993: 29; see also Mitchell and Carson, 1989: 148–9). The truth, however, is that *any* CV study which elicits preferences for a public good offers respondents a costless way to make a point.

It is important to distinguish between a real referendum and a CV survey which uses a referendum format. It is easy to see that if there are only two options *A* and *B*, and if a collective decision is to be made between them by majority voting, then no voter has any incentive to misrepresent her preferences. But such a referendum will not elicit the distribution of WTP in the population, which is the whole point of the CV method. A CV study which uses a referendum format presents different respondents with different pairs of options, and uses the resulting data to estimate the distribution of WTP in the population. Thus, a respondent who understands what is going on has exactly the same incentive to misrepresent her preferences as if she had answered an open-ended question. For example, if she really prefers *B* (the public good's being supplied at its true cost) to *A* (its not being supplied), she should 'vote' for the public good in a CV survey, whatever hypothetical cost she is asked to consider.

I can see no escape from the conclusion that, *if* survey respondents are motivated solely by rational self-interest, the CV method is fatally flawed. Like other forms of social-survey research, CV studies cannot work unless the vast majority of respondents can be relied on to give honest answers to well-formulated questions. But whether surveys elicit honest responses or strategic ones is ultimately an empirical question; it cannot be settled by *a priori* deduction from the axioms of rational choice theory.

5.4. INCENTIVE COMPATIBILITY: IS IT A PROBLEM FOR SURVEY RESEARCH?

The possibility that responses may be self-interested rather than honest is not a problem that is peculiar to CV studies. Almost all social surveys offer some incentives for strategic behaviour. Consider, for example, a survey of voting intentions before an election. A respondent who was motivated solely by rational self-interest might choose his answer by thinking about the effects of the publication of the survey on other voters; thus, a supporter of party *X* might pretend to be intending to vote for party *Y* so as to induce complacency among the supporters of *Y*. Or consider a survey of the extent of unreported crime. If someone would like to see more public spending on the police, it might be in her interest to pretend to have been the victim of non-existent crimes. In these examples, of course, the self-interested benefits to be gained by answering dishonestly are tiny. But the same is true of CV surveys, provided the sample size is sufficiently large.

In many social surveys, self-interest provides no obvious incentive to respondents to answer in one way rather than another. For example, this is typically the case in the censuses and panel surveys on which econometricians rely for their data. If respondents are motivated solely by rational self-interest, we have no reason to expect honest answers to such questions. Conversely, if there are forces at work which can generate systematic honesty in the absence of positive incentives to be honest, the same forces might be expected to have some influence even when there are weak incentives to be dishonest. For example, it might be hypothesized that, other things being equal, honesty involves less cognitive strain than dishonesty, or that the social setting of interviewer and interviewee evokes norms of honesty. These hypotheses might explain honesty in the absence of incentives; but they would also imply a tendency for respondents to give honest answers rather than strategic ones when the incentives for strategic behaviour are sufficiently weak.

Thus, when assessing the validity of the assumption that CV surveys elicit honest responses, it is legitimate to draw on evidence from social-survey research in general. Social psychologists have done a great deal of research into the relationships between attitudes (as reported in surveys) and actual behaviour. The balance of evidence, drawn from many studies, is that behaviour and attitudes are positively correlated (Schuman and Johnson, 1976; Hill, 1981). Of course, the mere demonstration of such a correlation is a relatively weak result, but attitudes are more remote from behaviour than the intentions into which CV surveys enquire. For example, compare the attitude 'I agree strongly that the Government should spend more money on national parks' with the intention 'If there were a referendum on the issue, I would vote for more spending on national parks.'

Experimental psychology and experimental economics offer another source of evidence. Many investigations of decision-making behaviour were first carried out by asking subjects to make hypothetical choices, and have subsequently been replicated in settings with financial incentives. In most cases, the same patterns of behaviour—often patterns that are inconsistent with received economic theory—are found in both types of experiment. For example, this is the case for the preference-reversal experiments discussed in Chapter 6 (Grether and Plott, 1979; Slovic and Lichtenstein, 1983). Notice, however, that such similarities in patterns of behaviour across experiments does not imply that incentives do not affect behaviour at all. For example, psychological effects such as response compatibility and anchoring might come into play irrespective of incentives, and these might generate preference reversals (see Chapter 6), but subjects might still be more risk-averse in the presence of incentives.

Further evidence comes from experiments which compare responses to hypothetical questions about willingness to trade with real trading behaviour. Bishop, Heberlein, and their associates have carried out a series of investigations of individuals' valuations of hunting permits in cases in which these are strictly rationed (Bishop and Heberlein, 1979, 1986; Bishop et al., 1983; Heberlein and Bishop, 1986). A typical experiment is conducted with two random samples drawn from a population of applicants for hunting permits. Subjects in one sample are treated as in a normal CV survey: WTP or willingness to accept (WTA) is elicited by using hypothetical questions. Subjects in the other sample are offered genuine opportunities to buy or sell permits. The results are mixed, but the general picture seems to be that hypothetical responses overstate real WTP and WTA. In one typical case, mean hypothetical WTA was $101 and mean real WTA was $63 (Bishop and Heberlein, 1979). In another, mean hypothetical WTP was $32 and mean real WTP was $24 (Bishop and Heberlein, 1986).

Thus, it seems that there may be a systematic discrepancy between hypothetical responses and real behaviour. If such a discrepancy exists, it undoubtedly poses a problem for CV research; but it need not be interpreted as evidence that responses are casual or insincere. People may be honestly reporting their beliefs about how they would respond to trading opportunities, were these to arise; but those beliefs may be systematically biased (for example, in a hypothetical context people may underestimate their aversion to giving up money). I suggest that observed differences between hypothetical responses and real behaviour are more plausibly explained by such effects than by assuming that survey respondents act strategically. It seems reasonable to proceed on the working assumption that respondents in CV surveys make honest attempts to answer the questions they are confronted with.

5.5. THE LINK BETWEEN PREFERENCE AND CHOICE

Respondents in CV surveys are typically presented with hypothetical scenarios within which they are asked to make choices. Even if we can assume that responses are honest, two difficulties must be overcome if we are to make inferences about individuals' preferences from the data generated by CV surveys. (A further problem, that preferences with the properties postulated by economic theory might not exist at all, will be considered in Chapter 6.)

The first difficulty is that the scenario has to represent a conceivable situation in which the respondent chooses between alternative combinations of money and the relevant good. In the case of a private good, the scenario can be based on the market. For example, a respondent may be asked to imagine that hunting permits are on sale at a price of $30, and to say whether or not he would buy one at that price. Most people have a vast amount of experience of buying private goods, and at least some experience of selling them; thus, they will find a market scenario quite familiar. But the design of scenarios for public goods is less straightforward. The problem is to find a context in which people make decisions *as individuals* about the supply of public goods. There seem to be two obvious candidates: voluntary contributions to public goods, and voting on issues concerned with the supply and finance of such goods.

The second difficulty is to find a theory which connects preferences to choices of the kind described by the scenario. For private goods and market settings, economics offers a simple theory—that each individual maximizes utility, taking prices as given. Using this theory, we can infer preferences from choices made in markets, or from hypothetical choices made in market scenarios. If we are to elicit valuations of public goods, we need a corresponding theory of how individuals' decisions about voluntary contributions to public goods, or about how to vote, connect with their preferences.

5.6. VOLUNTARY CONTRIBUTIONS TO PUBLIC GOODS

Some significant goods are financed by the voluntary contributions of many individuals: think of the activities of humanitarian, educational, medical and environmental charities and pressure groups. Donors to such organizations make decisions which involve giving up private consumption in order to increase the supply of public goods. Decision contexts of this kind might seem to offer suitable scenarios for eliciting preferences for public goods. However, it is surprisingly difficult to explain such voluntary contributions in terms of conventional economic theories of decision-making. In this section I shall examine these difficulties and the problems they create for CV research.

A number of economists have tried to explain voluntary contributions to public goods by using variants of the model presented in Section 5.2. Each individual is assumed to have preferences over combinations of private and public goods; each individual chooses how much to contribute to public goods, maximizing her utility while taking prices and other individuals' contributions as given. The equilibrium state of the model is taken to be a representation of the real world (e.g. Schwartz, 1970; Becker, 1974; Arrow, 1981).

More recent work, however, has shown that this type of theory yields implications which are clearly inconsistent with the facts of voluntary giving. These implications are generated because, in the model, each individual regards other people's contributions to a public good as perfect substitutes for her own. Thus, each individual's contribution is highly sensitive to changes in other people's contributions. Under reasonable assumptions about preferences, we should expect to find that each individual reduces her own contribution by almost one dollar for every extra dollar contributed by others; but we do not find anything like this degree of responsiveness in reality (Sugden, 1982; Warr, 1982; Roberts, 1984). If real people behaved like the individuals of the model, virtually no one would contribute anything to public goods in a large economy (Andreoni, 1988). And if individuals became aware of the extent to which their contributions were interdependent, the prospects for the voluntary supply of public goods would be still worse. Since each would know that a reduction in her own contributions would be almost wholly made up by increases in others' contributions, rational self-interest would lead each to try to take a free ride (Sugden, 1985).

A further challenge to the conventional theory of public goods has come from experimental research. In a classic series of experiments, Marwell and Ames (1979, 1980, 1981) investigated the extent to which individuals are willing to contribute to public goods. In a typical experiment, subjects were assigned to groups, within which interaction was anonymous (groups did not meet; all interactions were via the experimenters). Each subject was endowed with tokens to be allocated between a private activity and a collective activity; the subject was given a money pay-off which depended on the amount that he had allocated to the private activity and on the total amount that all group members had allocated to the public activity. This set-up corresponds very closely with the model described in Section 5.2, and thus provides a direct test of the conventional theory that individuals act according to parametric instrumental rationality. The typical result was that subjects contributed less to the collective activity than would be necessary for Pareto efficiency, but much more than was implied by the conventional theory (an interesting exception occurred when the experiment was carried out with economics graduate students: these subjects acted according to the dictates of rational self-interest).

Vernon Smith and his associates have carried out a different kind of investigation into the voluntary provision of public goods (e.g. Smith, 1980). Smith's concern is not to test any particular theory, but to try to design a mechanism for decentralized decision-making about public goods which will be as efficient as possible. The mechanism which Smith has developed is a form of auction; as the auction proceeds, each individual receives feedback about the bids made by others. The basic set-up is similar to that in Marwell and Ames's experiments, but instead of requiring each individual to make a unilateral decision about how much to contribute to the collective activity, Smith runs an auction.

In Smith's auction, each individual i makes a two-part bid: he states some contribution b_i which he is (provisionally) willing to make, and he proposes some amount t_i to be the total of everyone's contributions. The auctioneer then calculates the mean of everyone's proposal for the total (i.e., $\sum_j t_j / n$, where n is the number of individuals) and reports this back to everyone. The auctioneer also calculates, for each person i, his proposed contribution as a proportion of total proposed contributions (i.e., $b_i / \sum_j b_j$) and reports this back to that person. New bids are invited, and the process continues until there is unanimous agreement (that is, everyone proposes the same total t_i, and this is equal to the sum of all b_i proposals). If no agreement is reached after some predetermined number of rounds, the public good is not supplied at all. This mechanism turns out to be able to reach outcomes which are reasonably close to Pareto efficiency, at least for fairly small groups (up to nine individuals).

The puzzle is to explain why Smith's auction mechanism works so well. It seems to be in each individual's self-interest to act as if the public good is of little value to him, in the hope that it will be provided at other people's expense. Of course, if everyone tries to take a free ride, the public good will not be supplied at all, and everyone will be a loser. But why should this consideration be relevant to rational *individual* decisions? We know from the Prisoner's Dilemma that individually rational actions can aggregate to Pareto-inefficient outcomes. Smith's results, then, seem to provide further evidence against theories that explain private contributions to public goods in terms of rational self-interest.

So how are we to explain private contributions to public goods? Two alternative lines of approach seem particularly worth following. One emphasizes the moral norms of fairness and reciprocity; the other emphasizes the expressive or symbolic aspects of decisions.

A number of economists have proposed theories of moral behaviour which can be characterized as broadly rule-utilitarian or Kantian in flavour (e.g. Laffont, 1975; Collard, 1978; Harsanyi, 1982). These theories model preferences in a conventional way, but do not make the usual assumption that individuals maximize utility: the connection between preference and choice is more complex than this. Roughly, the individual considers alternative *rules* which could be followed by everyone, and which satisfy certain criteria of anonymity or fairness. The individual chooses the rule which, if followed by everyone, would lead to the outcome that she most prefers; then she follows that rule. I have proposed a variant of the rule-utilitarian approach, in which each individual accepts a moral obligation to act on her optimal rule only to the extent that other people follow that rule too; this amounts to a norm of reciprocity which forbids free-riding but which does not require anyone to provide free rides for others (Sugden, 1984).

In these theories, private contributions to public goods are motivated by people's moral commitment to rules which they see as fair. Thus, contributions to public goods do not reveal the donors' preferences in the same direct way that decisions to buy private goods do. What is revealed is the combined effect of the donor's own preferences, her beliefs about fair rules for cost-sharing, and (in the version which emphasizes reciprocity) other people's contributions.

An alternative approach to explaining voluntary contributions to public goods is proposed by Andreoni (1990). Andreoni suggests that contributions may be motivated by the desire for the 'warm glow' of believing that one has done a good deed (perhaps compounded by the belief that other people know this too). He models this warm glow by making each person's utility a function not only of the total quantity of each public good, but also of her own contribution to it. Thus, private contributions to public goods become private goods in their own right.

A theory of this kind has little content unless it can explain why some acts generate a warm glow while others do not. If the answer is that the warm glow is associated with following moral norms of fairness or reciprocity, then we need to model those norms; and this takes us back to the first approach. But there is an alternative way of developing the theory: acts may generate a warm glow through their expressive content.

Consumption goods are desired, not only for instrumental reasons, but also as expressions of the consumer's sense of identity (Douglas and Isher-wood, 1979; Hargreaves Heap, 1989). The distinction between *expressive value* and *instrumental value* is imprecise, but nevertheless useful. Consider a sports car. This has instrumental value as a means of transport. But by buying a sports car, a person can also express—or try to bolster—a self-image of being young, rich, and carefree: this is the expressive value of the car. Similarly, a bicycle has instrumental value as a means of transport and as a way of getting exercise; it has expressive value by expressing or bolstering a self-image of being fit and environmentally responsible. In the context of private goods, economic theory has no need to distinguish between expressive and instrumental value; both are subsumed under the concept of preference (that is why, for an economist, the distinction seems to lack precision). But in the context of public goods, this distinction is much more significant.

Contributions to public goods can have expressive value. By sending a donation to Greenpeace, for example, a person can express a self-image of being public-spirited, environmentally conscious, and mildly radical. The instrumental value of the donation (that it allows Greenpeace to do marginally more campaigning) is non-rival, but its expressive value is private to the contributor. Thus, expressive value can be used to explain private contributions to public goods (Kahneman and Knetsch, 1992). One implication of this explanation is that decisions about private contributions to public goods may reveal much more about the expressive value of contributions than they do about the instrumental value of those goods.

Whether voluntary contributions are motivated by norms of fairness or by expressive value, we should not expect responses to questions about such contributions to reveal preferences in any straightforward way. A telephone survey reported by Kahneman and Knetsch (1992) provides an illustration. In this survey, respondents were asked to think about the environmental services provided by federal and provincial governments in Canada. Then they were asked questions such as the following: 'If you could be sure that extra money collected would lead to significant improvements, what is the most you would be willing to pay each year through higher taxes, prices, or user fees to go into a special fund to improve environmental services?' Notice that there is no reference to any specific improvement in environmental services which respondents might try to evaluate. Nor is the respondent told how many other individuals will pay the 'higher taxes, prices, or user fees' which he is being invited to consider. He is being asked to decide how much to contribute to a special fund; the general purpose of the fund is known, but how much it will be able to do will depend on its total income, which is not known; there is a suggestion that others will match his contributions in some way, but no details are given. For most respondents, I guess, such a scenario will evoke thoughts about voluntary contributions to charitable funds. Kahneman and Knetsch seem to think so too, suggesting that responses to their questions 'express a willingness to acquire a sense of moral satisfaction ... by a voluntary contribution to the provision of a public good' (1992: 64).

In Kahneman and Knetsch's survey, different respondents were asked about different classes of environmental services, some classes being subsets of others. For example, some respondents faced the question presented in the previous paragraph, involving a special fund 'to improve environmental services'; they were told that 'environmental services' included 'preserving wilderness areas, protecting wildlife, providing parks, preparing for disasters, controlling air pollution, insuring water quality, and routine treatment and disposal of industrial wastes'. Other respondents were asked a similar question, but in relation to 'a special fund to improve preparedness for disasters'. In the first case, the mean WTP was $136 and the median was $50; in the second case, the mean was $152 and the median was again $50. Kahneman and Knetsch interpret this and other similar results as evidence of an *embedding effect*: reported WTP for a whole (environmental services) is no greater than reported WTP for a small part of that whole (preparing for disasters).

Such embedding effects are not surprising if respondents are thinking in terms of voluntary contributions. In the case of voluntary contributions, the distinction between superset and subset is far from clear. Suppose, for example, that I give £5 to the Woodland Trust—a charity which maintains woodlands throughout Britain. Should I think of the effect of this donation as an infinitesimal increase in the quality of thousands of acres of woodland, or should I think of it as one new tree planted somewhere? Either interpretation seems legitimate, and there seems no obvious reason why I should give more if I think in terms of the thousands of acres than if I think in terms of the single tree. Most fund-raisers, incidentally, seem to expect the opposite, encouraging potential donors to think in terms of something specific that can be paid for from a small donation.

This irrelevance of scale can readily be understood if voluntary contributions are motivated by expressive value. As Kahneman and Knetsch (1992: 64–5) argue, the expressive value of a contribution to an inclusive cause, and the expressive value of a contribution to a representative subset of that cause, are likely to be similar to one another. Alternatively, the irrelevance of scale can be understood as part of a theory in which voluntary contributions are motivated by norms of fairness and reciprocity. If there is a moral norm that each person should contribute a certain amount to some inclusive public good, then it would seem that an individual can discharge that obligation by contributing the required amount of money to any representative component of that good. For example, if everyone has an obligation to contribute a certain amount towards tree-planting, and if this amount is equal to the cost of planting one tree, then a person who pays to plant a specific tree has 'done his bit'.

So where does this leave us? Given the limitations of current knowledge about why individuals contribute to public goods, and the lack of consensus on a theory linking contributions to preferences, scenarios involving voluntary contributions to public goods seem unlikely to be useful as a means of eliciting preferences. Similarly, scenarios (like that of Kahneman and Knetsch's telephone survey) which prompt respondents to think in terms of voluntary contributions should be avoided.

5.7. VOTING

An alternative approach to eliciting preferences for public goods is to use scenarios based on decisions about how to vote. The referendum format is often recommended for CV surveys which involve public goods (Mitchell and Carson, 1989: 94–7, 148–9; Arrow *et al.*, 1993: 18–25). In a survey with this format, each respondent considers just two options, although different respondents may consider different pairs of options. The options in any pair differ in two respects: the level of provision of the relevant public good and the level of taxation. The respondent is asked to say which option he prefers. Notice that the options are descriptions of states of affairs that, were they to come about, would affect everyone in the community, and not just the individual respondent. Ordinary people do not have experience of taking decisions of this kind as individuals; but typically they have experience of participating in collective decision-making about public affairs. Thus the question 'Which option do you prefer?' can be construed as: 'If a collective choice had to be made between these two options, which would you vote for?'

I have argued that we are entitled to assume, as a working rule, that respondents give honest answers to the questions they face (see Section 5.4). So if we ask respondents to say how they think they would vote in a referendum between *A* and *B*, we should interpret their answers as honest statements of their intentions or inclinations. When a collective decision has to be made between two options, there is nothing to be gained by strategic voting (see Section 5.3). Thus, it might seem obvious that the referendum format will elicit individuals' true preferences: a person who prefers *A* to *B* would vote for *A* rather than *B* in a real referendum, and so, if asked to imagine such a referendum, would say that he would vote for *A* rather than *B*.

But to reach this conclusion, we need to make a particular assumption about how voting behaviour connects with preferences: we need to assume that voters are instrumentally rational. That is, we have to assume that the voter thinks of the act of voting as a means of trying to bring about the outcome that he prefers. Unfortunately, as Brennan and Buchanan (1984) and Brennan and Lomasky (1985) have argued, this assumption is questionable.

Many public-choice theorists have noticed that instrumentally rational individuals would not vote in elections with large electorates (see, e.g., Mueller, 1989: 348–69). This is just another instance of the public goods problem. For example, consider a presidential election with two candidates,

X and Y, and an electorate of, say, 20 million. If approximately 10 million electors prefer X to Y, then every vote cast for X is a public good for a group of 10 million individuals. For any individual who prefers X, the cost of voting (perhaps giving up half an hour in front of the television) is borne by that individual privately, but the benefit (a tiny increase in the probability that X will be elected) is spread among 10 million people. Although the value to the individual of X's being elected rather than Y may be quite large, this has to be discounted by the infinitesimally small probability that an election involving 20 million voters will be decided by the margin of a single vote. Thus, if the act of voting involves any significant costs, an instrumentally rational individual who expected many other people to vote would choose not to vote himself. Since we repeatedly observe elections in which large numbers of people vote, the hypothesis that voters are instrumentally rational must be rejected.

It is natural to try to explain the act of voting in much the same way that voluntary contributions to public goods are explained: either in terms of norms or in terms of expressive value. Public-choice theorists often invoke notions of civic duty for this purpose. Civic duty might be construed as a principle of fairness, prescribing that everyone bears her share of the costs of maintaining an institution—democracy—that everyone values. Or it might be construed in more expressive terms: by voting, a person expresses a self-image of being concerned with public affairs and proud to be a citizen of a democratic country. But if these are the sorts of motivations that get people as far as the polling station, why should we assume (as public-choice theorists usually do) that the same people become instrumentally rational when choosing how to cast their votes?

First, consider the possibility that, as Brennan, Buchanan, and Lomasky suggest, voting for one option rather than another has expressive content. For example, imagine two options A and B, where A is the *status quo* and B is a policy of cleaning up a marine oil spill at the cost of an increase in taxation. In a referendum between A and B, the act of voting for B may be a way of expressing a self-image of being concerned about the environment. The same act has instrumental value in making it marginally more likely that the oil spill will be cleaned up, and instrumental disvalue in making it marginally more likely that taxes will be increased. But because the expressive value is private to the individual voter, while the instrumental values and disvalues are public goods, we should expect voting behaviour to reveal more about expressive value than it does about instrumental value.

Discussing the implications of this argument for CV surveys, Mitchell and Carson express unconcern. In response to Brennan and Buchanan (1984), they say:

We regard their arguments as another way of saying that people may behave in a more public-spirited manner in political markets than they do in private goods markets. Brennan and Buchanan are disturbed by the implications of this type of behaviour for the use of voting outcomes to reveal economic preferences; we are not (1989: 149).

But Mitchell and Carson ought to be disturbed. The whole CV method depends on the assumption that individuals have well-defined preferences which are independent of the context in which those individuals act. It is this assumption that allows us to use preferences elicited in one context (the hypothetical scenario of the CV survey) to guide decisions in another context (public policy-making). If Brennan, Buchanan, and Lomasky are right, then CV surveys will elicit different valuations of the same benefit, depending on whether they use a private-good format (e.g. eliciting valuations for entry permits) or a public-good referendum format.

A further possibility, not considered explicitly by Brennan, Buchanan, and Lomasky, is that voters may be influenced by norms of fairness and reciprocity. When people make voluntary contributions to public goods, they may be motivated by moral rules which prescribe, for each individual, a fair share of the total cost of providing a public good (see Section 5.6). Thus, when comparing two alternative options A and B, where A is the *status quo* and B is some mix of increased public-good provision and increased taxation, an individual might ask two distinct questions: 'Do I prefer B to A?' and 'Is B a fair proposal?' The first of these questions is the one that is relevant for a CV survey. But it may not be the only one that is relevant for a person who is deciding how to vote.

To answer the first question, the individual has to consider the benefits that she would derive from the increased provision of the public good, and then to compare these benefits with the extra taxes that she would have to pay; how much other people would have to pay is irrelevant. To answer the second question, she has to make other comparisons too; in particular, she needs to compare the extra taxes that she would have to pay with the extra taxes that other people would have to pay. It is quite possible that she would prefer B to A, and yet also believe that B imposed on her an unfairly large share of the costs. If so, how would she vote in a referendum to decide between A and B?

An instrumentally rational voter would, of course, vote according to her preference (provided she believed that A and B really were the only two options available). But we know that the instrumental benefits of voting one way rather than another are extremely small. The kind of person who was sufficiently lacking in instrumental rationality to take the trouble to cast a vote in the first place might well use that vote as a means of expressing her sense of fairness.

There is a body of experimental evidence which suggests that people are prepared to incur some costs rather than acquiesce in arrangements which, in their view, treat them unfairly. This evidence comes from studies of *ultimatum games*—a type of game first analysed by Güth *et al.* (1982). In the classic ultimatum game, two players have to agree on how to divide a fixed sum of money between them. One player is assigned the role of 'allocator', the other that of 'recipient'. The allocator proposes a division of the money between the two players. The recipient can either accept this proposal or reject it. Either way, the game ends immediately. If the recipient rejects the proposal, neither player gets anything. An instrumentally rational recipient would accept any proposal which gave her a positive amount of money. However, in experiments involving ultimatum games, allocations which give the recipient a very small share are often rejected (Güth *et al.*, 1982; Thaler, 1988).

A related item of evidence comes from CV studies which have tried to elicit individuals' willingness to accept money in return for giving up public goods. CV researchers often suggest that respondents find questions about their WTA for public goods morally objectionable. For example, consider: 'Would you accept $100 as compensation for the destruction of wildlife by this oil spill?' Such questions seem to presuppose that each respondent has a property right in the public good, which he is entitled to exchange for private consumption if he chooses; respondents may refuse to answer such questions, or give extreme responses, as a way of signalling their rejection of this conception of property rights (e.g. Mitchell and Carson, 1989: 34). In such cases, respondents are revealing their judgements about fairness, not their preferences. (In contrast to the previous examples, however, the concern here is with fairness *tout court*, rather than with fairness to the respondent herself.)

Thus, it is not always clear how answers to questions about hypothetical referenda can be mapped on to the conventional model of preferences. Suppose a person is asked a question of the form 'Would you vote for a proposal which supplied this public good and imposed x extra taxes on you?' An answer of 'yes' might indicate the expressive value of the act of voting for that proposal; but the respondent who gives this answer might (in the instrumental sense) prefer the *status quo* to the package of public good plus x tax bill. Conversely, a respondent who answers 'no' may be expressing the judgement that, given the likely cost of providing the good, it would be unfair to call on him to pay as much as x—even though he may prefer the package of public good plus tax bill to the *status quo*. The referendum format does not provide an easy solution to the problem of eliciting preferences for public goods.

5.8. CONCLUSION

The main message of this chapter can be summed up in a sentence: Preferences for public goods are much more difficult to elicit than are preferences for private goods.

Suppose we can assume that individuals have well-defined preferences over private goods, and that these preferences have the properties postulated by economic theory (whether we *can* assume this is a big question, to be considered in Chapter 6). Then there is a straightforward and fairly uncontroversial theory of the connection between preference and action in competitive markets: each individual maximizes her own utility, taking prices as given. Using this theory, we can infer preferences from choices made in market settings. Similarly, CV researchers can set up market scenarios in which respondents make hypothetical decisions, and then infer preferences from those decisions.

If, however, we are prepared to make the corresponding assumption that individuals have well-defined preferences over *public* goods, and that these preferences have the properties postulated by economic theory, we find that we still need a theory of how preferences connect with actions. A satisfactory method for eliciting preferences must be able, for some readily understandable scenario, to isolate the effects of preferences on choices. But it seems that in order to explain individual behaviour in relation to public goods— whether private contributions to public goods, or voting behaviour—we have to take account of factors other than preference. In particular, we have to take account of the expressive value of actions, and of the moral norms to which individuals subscribe. Thus, we need a theory of decision-making which can explain how these factors work together, and which can allow a CV researcher to disentangle them. As yet, no theory of choice seems sufficiently well-developed to do this reliably. Until these fundamental theoretical problems have been solved, attempts to elicit preferences for public goods must be treated with caution.

REFERENCES

Andreoni, J. (1988), 'Privately Provided Public Goods in a Large Economy: the Limits of Altruism', *Journal of Political Economy*, 35: 57–73.

——(1990), 'Impure Altruism and Donations to Public Goods: a Theory of Warm-Glow Giving', *Economic Journal*, 100: 464–77.

Arrow, K. (1981), 'Optimal and Voluntary Income Distribution', in S. Rosenfielde (ed.), *Economic Welfare and the Economics of Soviet Socialism: Essays in Honor of Abram Bergson*, Cambridge University Press.

——Solow, R., Portney, P., Leamer, E., Radner, R., and Schuman, H. (1993), *Report of the NOAA Panel on Contingent Valuation*, Report to the General Counsel of the US National Oceanic and Atmospheric Administration, Resources for the Future, Washington.

Becker, G. S. (1974), 'A Theory of Social Interactions', *Journal of Political Economy*, 82: 1063–93.

Bishop, R. C., and Heberlein, T. A. (1979), 'Measuring Values of Extra-Market Goods: Are Indirect Measures Biased?' *American Journal of Agricultural Economics*, 61: 926–30.

——and——(1986), 'Does Contingent Valuation Work?' in R. G. Cummings, D. S. Brookshire, and W. D. Schulze (eds.), *Valuing Environmental Goods*, Rowman and Allanheld, Totowa, NJ.

——Heberlein, T. A., and Kealy, M. J. (1983), 'Hypothetical Bias in Contingent Valuation: Results from a Simulated Market', *Natural Resources Journal*, 23: 619–33.

Brennan, G., and Buchanan, J. M. (1984), 'Voter Choice', *American Behavioral Scientist*, 28: 185–201.

——and Lomasky, L. (1985), 'The Impartial Spectator Goes to Washington: Toward a Smithian Theory of Electoral Politics', *Economics and Philosophy*, 1: 189–211.

Clarke, E. H. (1971), 'Multipart Pricing of Public Goods', *Public Choice*, 11: 19–33.

Collard, D. (1978), *Altruism and Economy*, Martin Robertson, Oxford.

Douglas, M., and Isherwood, I. (1979), *The World of Goods*, Basic Books, New York.

Grether, D. M. and Plott, C. R. (1979), 'Economic Theory of Choice and the Preference Reversal Phenomenon', *American Economic Review*, 69: 623–38.

Groves, T. (1973), 'Incentives in Teams', *Econometrica*, 41, 617–31.

Groves, T. and Ledyard, J. O. (1977), 'Optimal Allocation of Public Goods: a Solution to the Free Rider Problem', *Econometrica*, 45: 783–809.

Güth, W., Schmittberger, R., and Schwarze, B. (1982), 'An Experimental Analysis of Ultimatum Bargaining', *Journal of Economic Behavior and Organization*, 3: 367–88.

Hargreaves Heap, S. P. (1989), *Rationality in Economics*, Blackwell, Oxford.

Harsanyi, J. C. (1982), 'Morality and the Theory of Rational Behaviour', in A. Sen and B. Williams (eds.), *Utilitarianism and Beyond*, Cambridge University Press.

Heberlein, T. A., and Bishop, R. C. (1986), 'Assessing the Validity of Contingent Valuation: Three Field Experiments', *Science of the Total Environment*, 56: 99–107.

Hill, R. J. (1981), 'Attitudes and Behavior', in M. Rosenberg and R. H. Turner (eds.), *Social Psychology: Sociological Perspectives*, Basic Books, New York.

Hoehn, J. P. and Randall, A. (1987), 'A Satisfactory Benefit–Cost Indicator from Contingent Valuation', *Journal of Environmental Economics and Management*, 14: 226–47.

Kahneman, D., and Knetsch, J. L. (1992), 'Valuing Public Goods: the Purchase of Moral Satisfaction', *Journal of Environmental Economics and Management*, 22: 57–70.

Laffont, J.-J. (1975), 'Macroeconomic Constraints, Economic Efficiency and Ethics: An Introduction to Kantian Economics', *Economica*, 42: 430–7.

Lindhal, E. (1919/1958), 'Just Taxation: A Positive Solution', in R. A. Musgrave and A. T. Peacock (eds.), *Classics in the Theory of Public Finance*, Macmillan, London, 1958. (First published in German in 1919.)

Marwell, G., and Ames, R. E. (1979), 'Experiments on the Provision of Public Goods, I. Resources, Interest, Group Size, and the Free Rider Problem', *American Journal of Sociology*, 84: 1335–60.

——and——(1980), 'Experiments on the Provision of Public Goods, II. Provision Points, Stakes, Experience, and the Free Rider Problem', *American Journal of Sociology*, 85: 926–37.

—— and—— (1981), 'Economists Free-Ride: Does anyone Else? Experiments on the Provision of Public Goods, IV', *Journal of Public Economics*, 15: 295–310.

Mitchell, R. C., and Carson, R. T. (1989), *Using Surveys to Value Public Goods: The Contingent Valuation Method*, Resources for the Future, Washington.

Mueller, D. C. (1989), *Public Choice II*, Cambridge University Press.

Roberts, R. D. (1984), 'A Positive Model of Private Charity and Public Transfers', *Journal of Political Economy*, 92: 136–48.

Samuelson, P. A. (1954), 'The Pure Theory of Public Expenditure', *Review of Economics and Statistics*, 36: 387–9.

Schuman, H., and Johnson, M. P. (1976), 'Attitudes and Behavior', in A. Inkeles (ed.), *Annual Review of Sociology*, ii, Annual Reviews, Palo Alto, Calif.

Schwartz, R. A. (1970), 'Personal Philanthropic Contributions', *Journal of Political Economy*, 78: 1264–91.

Slovic, P., and Lichtenstein, S. (1983), 'Preference Reversals: a Broader Perspective', *American Economic Review*, 73: 596–605.

Smith, V. (1980), 'Experiments with a Decentralized Mechanism for Public Good Decisions', *American Economic Review*, 70: 584–99.

Sugden, R. (1982), 'On the Economics of Philanthropy', *Economic Journal*, 92: 341–50.

—— (1984), 'Reciprocity: the Supply of Public Goods through Voluntary Contributions', *Economic Journal*, 94: 772–87.

—— (1985), 'Consistent Conjectures and Voluntary Contributions to Public Goods: Why the Conventional Theory Does Not Work', *Journal of Public Economics*, 27: 117–24.

Thaler, R. H. (1988), 'Anomalies: the Ultimatum Game', *Journal of Economic Perspectives*, 2: 195–206.

Warr, P. G. (1982), 'Pareto Optimal Distribution and Private Charity', *Journal of Public Economics*, 19: 131–8.

Wicksell, K. (1896/1958), 'A New Principle of Just Taxation', in R. A. Musgrave and A. T. Peacock (eds.), *Classics in the Theory of Public Finance*, Macmillan, London, 1958. (First published in German in 1896.)

6

Alternatives to the Neo-classical Theory of Choice

ROBERT SUGDEN

INTRODUCTION

The contingent valuation (CV) method is often described as a technique for *eliciting* preferences. The idea of eliciting—of drawing out—seems to presuppose the existence of preferences; the suggestion is that a well-conducted survey *discovers* those preferences. CV practitioners normally assume that individuals have preferences and that those preferences have the properties that are postulated in Hicksian consumer theory (Hicks, 1943, 1956). Preferences over bundles of goods are assumed to be complete, transitive, continuous, and convex; thus, in a two-good case, they can be represented by a map of downward-sloping indifference curves, convex to the origin. These assumptions are so basic to economics that they often are not even stated. Given these presuppositions, the results of a CV study may be understood as propositions, which may be more or less accurate, about individuals' Hicksian preferences. CV practitioners recognize that the accuracy of their results may be affected by various systematic biases in survey instruments, but they try to use instruments which reduce these biases as far as possible.

However, the concepts of 'accuracy' and 'bias', like that of elicitation, presuppose that there are true answers to the questions which CV studies address. This chapter will review a body of research which raises doubts about that presupposition. It will focus on two issues in CV methodology: divergences between willingness-to-pay and willingness-to-accept valuations, and the sensitivity of reported valuations to the elicitation method (for example: open-ended questions, binary choices, iterated bidding, auctions, referenda).

Section 6.1 discusses the status of Hicksian consumer theory. Sections 6.2 and 6.3 investigate how far the valuations elicited by CV surveys might be expected to differ between willingness-to-pay and willingness-to-accept

This chapter was written as part of a research project supported by the Economic and Social Research Council, through its Transport and the Environment Programme (Award No. W 119 25 1014). Thanks go to Ian Bateman, Alistair Munro, and Chris Starmer.

formats, and between different elicitation methods, *if* respondents had Hicksian preferences, and *if* survey instruments were unbiased. Section 6.4 considers the possibility that, although respondents do have Hicksian preferences, certain CV survey designs are systematically biased. Sections 6.5 and 6.6 look at some non-Hicksian theories of decision-making, and draw out their implications for the valuations generated by CV surveys. Sections 6.7 and 6.8 review the evidence generated by CV and experimental research, and ask whether this can best be explained by Hicksian theory alone, by Hicksian theory combined with hypotheses about bias, or by non-Hicksian theories. Section 6.9 draws some tentative conclusions.

6.1. HICKSIAN THEORY: TRUTH OR MODEL?

If we are to think clearly about the elicitation of preferences, we must begin with a recognition that the individual who appears in Hicksian consumer theory *is a model*. By a 'model', I mean a well-defined, internally consistent theoretical construct, whose properties have been chosen by the modeller. A model must be distinguished from the reality that it represents. The consumer of Hicksian theory—the *Hicksian consumer*—is offered as a model of those real consumers who shop in supermarkets and who respond to CV surveys. But how closely real consumers resemble Hicksian ones is an open question.

Thus, we must distinguish between questions that are asked within a model and questions that are asked about the real world. When we ask a question within a model, we seek to explore the logical implications of the model's properties. Within the Hicksian model, for example, we may ask whether the quantity that an individual demands of a good will change if her income and all prices increase in the same proportion. The answer is that there will be no change in the quantity demanded. As it stands, this answer is not a statement about real consumers; it is a statement about Hicksian consumers.

Of course, if a model is to be *useful*, there has to be some correspondence between it and the real world: a model is a model *of* something. Economists use the Hicksian model to help them organize data generated by real consumers, and to predict the future behaviour of those consumers. For example, the Hicksian model gives us the concept of a demand function and imposes certain restrictions on that function. If we *assume* that real consumers behave like the individuals of the Hicksian model, we can use data from a real market to estimate a demand function for a group of real consumers. Having estimated such a function, we can use it to predict the effects of price and income changes on the quantities demanded of different goods. To the extent that the estimated demand function fits the data, and to the extent that the predictions we derive from it are confirmed, the underlying model has demonstrated its usefulness.

Within the Hicksian model, we may also ask the kind of questions that are often asked in contingent valuation studies. For example, consider our theoretical Hicksian consumer who has preferences over combinations of a private good ('private consumption') and a public good ('environmental quality'). Let her current level of private consumption be y_0, and let the current level of provision of environmental quality be x_0. Let x_1 be some higher level of environmental quality. We may then pose the question: what reduction in private consumption, if combined with an increase in environmental quality from x_0 to x_1, would leave the individual just as well off (in terms of her preferences) as she is currently? *Within the model*, this is a well-defined question: if the model consumer's preference map has been fully specified, the question has a correct answer.

But this is not to say that the same question, addressed to a *real* survey respondent, has a correct answer. When the question is asked within the model, it is formulated in terms of concepts (in particular, that of preference) which are themselves defined within the model. The question that the real respondent answers must be formulated in words, such as: 'What is the maximum amount of money that you would be willing to pay to....?' or 'Would you be willing to pay at least...to ...?'. A CV analysis *assumes* that real respondents have the same kind of preferences as the individuals of the Hicksian model, and then uses that model to organize the data generated by their responses.

But what if the model does not fit the data? Suppose that a CV survey generates data in which there are regularities that are not consistent with the Hicksian model. What are we to make of this? There seem to be two main ways in which we might respond to such evidence: we can either blame the survey instrument or blame the Hicksian model.

The first kind of response may often be reasonable. Survey research is subject to a wide range of problems, and the design of surveys calls for considerable skill and judgement. Anomalous findings may be the result of biases unintentionally imparted by the survey instrument. Taking an example from outside CV research, consider a survey which asks each member of a random sample of the British population how many cigarettes he or she smoked in the preceding seven days. For any given individual, this question has a correct answer; in this case, the concept of elicitation—of seeking to discover something that already exists—seems entirely appropriate. From the results of the survey, and on the assumption that it is unbiased, we can estimate the weekly consumption of cigarettes in Britain. Suppose the resulting estimate is significantly less than the weekly sales of cigarettes in Britain. There are various ways of explaining this anomaly. For example, people may be stockpiling cigarettes, or taking them abroad and selling them. But the most plausible explanation is in terms of the well-known tendency of survey respondents to give answers that they would like to be true, or that they think the interviewer or survey designer wants them to give. If this interpretation is accepted, the implication is that the survey instrument is biased. Similarly, if a CV survey generates data that are inconsistent with Hicksian theory, this *may* be a signal that the survey instrument is subject to some kind of bias.

Notice, however, an important difference between the cigarette survey and the CV survey. In the case of the cigarette survey, what we are seeking to elicit is a matter of objective fact: how many cigarettes each respondent smoked in the preceding seven days. In principle, at least, we can conceive of a completely accurate survey instrument—one which elicits the truth. Given this bench-mark, we can speak unambiguously of the biases or errors associated with different survey instruments. In contrast, the CV survey is seeking to 'elicit' a value which has merely been *assumed* to exist; the survey is looking for something in the real world which can be mapped on to a theoretical concept within a Hicksian model. If the survey results contain regularities which cannot be mapped on to the model, it may be the model that is at fault. The survey may have elicited regularities which exist in the real world, but which the model fails to take account of.

At this stage, I wish only to make a plea for open-mindedness. In this chapter, I shall be reviewing evidence of systematic divergences between, on the one hand, the results of CV surveys and of laboratory experiments, and on the other, the Hicksian theory of preference. In thinking about this evidence, we must keep open the two main possible explanations: survey instruments and experimental methods may be subject to bias, and real individuals may be systematically different from Hicksian ones.

6.2. IMPLICATIONS OF HICKSIAN THEORY: WILLINGNESS TO PAY AND WILLINGNESS TO ACCEPT

Apparent disparities between *willingness-to-pay* (WTP) and *willingness-to-accept* (WTA) valuations are a well-known problem for CV surveys. In this section, I shall examine the implications of the Hicksian model for the relative magnitude of WTP and WTA. The conclusions that I shall draw will be conclusions about the properties of the model; whether these also apply to real consumers or real survey respondents will remain an open question.

Consider an individual in a world in which there are two infinitely divisible goods, X and Y. X is the good for which we are trying to elicit valuations; it may be a public good (such as environmental quality) or a private good (such as chocolate). The quantity of X that is consumed by or enjoyed by the individual is x. Y is a 'composite commodity', representing all private consumption goods other than X. The prices of the various goods which make up this composite are held constant throughout the analysis, and so we may measure quantities of Y in money units. The quantity of Y consumed by the individual is y. Since the individual is taken to be a Hicksian consumer, she

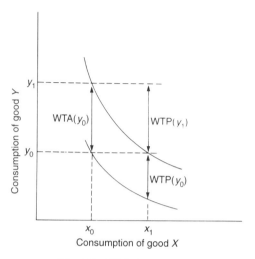

Fig. 6.1   Hicksian preference

has preferences over the set of all non-negative consumption bundles (x, y). These can be represented by an indifference-curve map with the usual properties, as in Figure 6.1.

Let x_0 and x_1 be two levels of consumption of good X, with $x_1 > x_0$. The object is to measure the value to the individual of a change in consumption of X from x_0 to x_1 (in the case of WTP) or from x_1 to x_0 (in the case of WTA). Suppose the individual is currently endowed with y_0 of good Y. To arrive at a WTP measure, we take the bundle (x_0, y_0) as a notional starting-point. We then ask what the maximum amount is of good Y (i.e. the maximum sum of money) that the individual would be willing to give up in return for an increase in her consumption of good X from x_0 to x_1. That is, we find the amount of money, v, such that she is indifferent between the bundles $(x_1, y_0 - v)$ and (x_0, y_0). This value of v is the WTP measure of the value of the increase in the consumption of X, given that the consumer's endowment of good Y is y_0. This measure, which I shall write as 'WTP (y_0)', is known in economic theory as a *quantity-compensating variation* or *compensating surplus* (Hicks, 1943).

To arrive at a WTA measure of the value of a change in consumption of good X from x_1 to x_0, we take the bundle (x_1, y_0) as a starting-point. Here we start from a position in which the individual is consuming the higher level of good X. We then ask what is the minimum amount of good Y that the individual would be willing to accept in return for a reduction in her consumption of good X from x_1 to x_0. That is, we find the amount of money v such that she is indifferent between the bundles $(x_0, y_0 + v)$ and (x_1, y_0). This value of v is the WTA measure of the value of the change in the consumption of X, given that the consumer's endowment of good Y is y_0. This measure, which I shall write as 'WTA (y_0)', is a *quantity-equivalent variation* or *equivalent surplus*.

A glance at Figure 6.1 is enough to show that Hicksian theory does not imply WTA (y_0) = WTP (y_0). But how far can the WTP and WTA measures diverge? Comprehensive answers to this question about the properties of the Hicksian model have been given by Randall and Stoll (1980) and Hanemann (1991). Randall and Stoll show that the divergence between WTP and WTA depends on the value of a term that they call the *price flexibility of income* (ξ). For any x, y, we may define the *marginal valuation* of good X as the negative of the marginal rate of substitution between Y and X at the point (x, y). In other words, the marginal valuation of good X measures the individual's WTP for a marginal change in the quantity of good X, if the individual is initially consuming the combination (x, y). The price flexibility of income is the elasticity of marginal valuation with respect to y, that is, with respect to the endowment of good Y, or to 'income'. Randall and Stoll show that if the price flexibility of income is not very far from zero (say, in the range $-2 \leq \xi \leq 2$), then the divergence between WTA and WTP will normally be small.

Hanemann shows that ξ is equal to the income elasticity of demand for X divided by the elasticity of substitution (roughly, a measure of the curvature of the indifference curves). Thus, the divergence between WTA and WTP will be relatively small if the income elasticity of demand for X is not very far from zero and if, in addition, the elasticity of substitution is not too close to zero. Why are these two terms relevant? It is easy to show that, if the income elasticity of demand for X is positive (that is, if X is a *normal good*), then the vertical distance between any two given indifference curves decreases as x increases, which in turn implies that WTA is greater than WTP. Since positive income elasticities are indeed normal (in the everyday sense of 'normal'), this result implies that we should typically expect WTA to be greater than WTP. For any given positive income elasticity, the greater the divergence between WTA and WTP, the less the elasticity of substitution, that is, the 'more curved' the indifference curves are. Hanemann (ibid. 646) uses this result to argue that 'large empirical divergences between WTP and WTA' might be expected when X is a public good for which private consumption goods are imperfect substitutes.

But how large is 'large'? Since it is not easy to have intuitions about typical values of the elasticity of substitution, it may be helpful to think in terms of a magnitude which will be more familiar to CV researchers. For given values of x_0 and x_1, I shall define

$$\beta = \partial WTP(y)/\partial y. \qquad (6.1)$$

Thus β measures the rate at which WTP increases with respect to increases in the endowment of good Y. Notice that β is similar to ξ in that both terms represent relationships between WTP and endowments of Y. However, ξ refers to marginal WTP, while β refers to WTP for a given increment of good X; and β is a rate of change, while ξ is an elasticity. In CV studies, it is standard practice to include individual (or household) income in the set of variables which explain differences in WTP between individuals (or households); β corresponds to the coefficient on income in a linear regression equation with WTP as the dependent variable. I shall assume that, for the consumer in the model, β is a constant over the relevant range of values of y. This is an approximation,[1] but provided we work within a small range of values of y, any errors can be expected to be small.

To see the significance of β, consider again the consumer whose preferences are shown in Figure 6.1, but suppose that her endowment of Y is now y_1, where $y_1 = y_0 + WTA(y_0)$. Consider what effect this additional endowment will have on her WTP for an increase in her consumption of X from x_0 to x_1. In this case, WTP(y_1) is given by the amount of money v such that she is indifferent between (x_0, y_1) and $(x_1, y_1 - v)$. It is easy to work out, or to see from Figure 6.1, that WTA(y_0) = WTP (y_1): WTP based on a Y-endowment of y_1 is equal to WTA based on a Y-endowment of y_0. Since $y_1 = y_0 +$ WTA (y_0), we can write:

$$\text{WTA}(y_0) = \text{WTP}(y_0 + \text{WTA}[y_0]). \tag{6.2}$$

But since β is the rate at which WTP increases as the Y-endowment increases,

$$\text{WTP}(y_0 + \text{WTA}[y_0]) = \text{WTP}(y_0) + \beta\,\text{WTA}(y_0). \tag{6.3}$$

Thus

$$\text{WTA}(y_0) = \text{WTP}(y_0) + \beta\,\text{WTA}(y_0). \tag{6.4}$$

Rearranging (6.4), we arrive at:

$$\text{WTA}(y_0) = \text{WTP}(y_0)/(1 - \beta). \tag{6.5}$$

Equation (6.5) establishes a relationship between WTA, WTP, and the readily observable parameter β.

Notice that β measures a kind of income effect: the responsiveness of WTP to changes in income. Equation (6.5) tells us that the divergence between WTA and WTP will be small if income effects, of the kind measured by β, are small. This result holds whatever the degree of substitutability between the two goods: if the elasticity of substitution is so low as to generate a large divergence between WTA and WTP, it will also generate a high value of β.

To get some sense of the extent of divergence between WTA and WTP that is consistent with (6.5), here is a back-of-the-envelope example.

---

[1] This assumption is equivalent to approximating WTP (y) by the first two terms of a Taylor series.

Consider a Hicksian consumer with an income of £10,000 per year, whose WTP for a given increase in good X is £20 per year. Now suppose her income were to increase to £10,100. By how much might we expect her WTP to increase? If WTP increased in proportion to income, it would increase to £20.20. This would imply $\beta = 0.002$, and so (6.5) tells us that WTA would be equal to 1.002 times WTP—a divergence of only 0.2 per cent. If WTP increased more than in proportion to income, the divergence would be slightly larger—but only slightly. Consider the absurdly extreme assumption that WTP increases with the *fifth* power of income. Even in this case, the value of β would be only 0.01, and so the divergence between WTA and WTP would be only 1 per cent.

More generally, we can draw the following conclusion. If WTP is only a small fraction of income (as it is in most CV studies), then for a Hicksian consumer, the divergence between WTA and WTP can be expected to be very small—at most, a few per cent.

6.3. IMPLICATIONS OF HICKSIAN THEORY: DIFFERENT RESPONSE MODES

A wide range of elicitation methods have been used by CV researchers. Among the ways in which elicitation methods differ is in terms of their *response modes*—that is, in terms of the kind of response that is required from the individual whose preferences are being elicited. The most direct method is the *open-ended question*. Here, for example, if the object is to elicit WTP for an entry permit to a wilderness area, each respondent might be asked 'What is the largest amount of money that you would be willing to pay for a permit?' Another method is to present each respondent with a single *binary choice*, such as: 'Would you be willing to pay £20 for a permit?' A third method is *iterated bidding*. Here, a respondent is first asked, say: 'Would you be willing to pay £20 for a permit?' If the answer is 'Yes', the question is repeated, but with a higher price, say £40; if the answer is 'No', it is repeated with a lower price, say £10. This process continues until the respondent's WTP has been bracketed in a sufficiently narrow band (for example, he is willing to pay £35, but not £40). A fourth method is a *sealed-bid auction*. For example, m permits are auctioned among a group of n potential buyers (with $n > m$). Each participant states a reservation price (for example, 'I wish to buy a permit if and only if the price is no more than £22') and the permits are then sold to the m highest bidders.

In this section, I am concerned with the responses that a Hicksian consumer would give to such questions. I shall add two further idealizing assumptions about the respondent. First, she fully understands whatever scenario she is presented with, and whatever questions she is asked. Second, she responds honestly to any well-formulated question about her preferences. These assumptions neutralize a range of potential biases which could result, for example, from respondents' failure to understand what they are expected to do; from their attempts to manipulate the survey to their own advantage; from their attempts to give the answer that they believe the interviewer or survey designer wants; or from their unwillingness to co-operate with the survey. Such biases will be considered in Section 6.4. For the moment, I wish to focus on the properties of *unbiased* responses.

For the purposes of exposition, I shall consider the elicitation of WTP valuations, but the discussion can easily be adapted to the case of WTA. Consider the Hicksian consumer of Section 6.2, who currently consumes y_0 of the composite good Y. We wish to elicit her WTP for an increase in her consumption of good X from x_0 to x_1.

For a Hicksian consumer, the open-ended question 'What is the largest amount of money that you would be willing to pay to increase your consumption of good X from x_0 to x_1?' has a well-defined true answer; this is the value WTP (y_0) we are trying to elicit. By assumption, the respondent gives an honest answer to any well-formulated question about her preferences. Thus the open-ended question elicits true WTP. In the present context, in which strategic motivations are absent, a sealed-bid auction is equivalent to an open-ended question: the respondent is asked to state the highest price she is willing to pay, and her true WTP is elicited. Similarly, the binary-choice question 'Would you be willing to pay £z to increase your consumption of good X from x_0 to x_1?' has a well-defined true answer (except in the case in which the consumer is exactly indifferent between paying and not paying). If $\text{WTP}(y_0) > z$, the answer is 'Yes'; if $\text{WTP}(y_0) < z$, the answer is 'No'. Thus, in the non-indifferent case, the binary-choice question elicits one of two pieces of information about true WTP: either that it is no less than z, or that it is no greater than z. Iterated bidding may be interpreted as a series of binary choices, each of which elicits one piece of information about true WTP. Summing up: in the absence of biases resulting from misunderstanding or deliberate misrepresentation, WTP and WTA valuations elicited from Hicksian consumers will not vary according to the response mode.

6.4. STRATEGIC BIASES

In Sections 6.2 and 6.3 I have shown that Hicksian consumer theory implies strict limits to the extent of divergence between WTA and WTP, and that it gives us no reason to expect valuations to differ according to the response mode used to elicit them. If, in practice, CV surveys produce results which are inconsistent with these implications of Hicksian theory, the explanation may be that there are biases in the survey instruments used; or it may be that the theory is at fault. In this section I shall consider the first possibility.

Many sources of bias are specific to the valuation of public goods. Mechanisms which elicit valuations of public goods are particularly vulnerable to the strategic misrepresentation of preferences. In addition, questions concerning preferences for public goods can easily become entangled with questions about moral obligations and rights. These biases were considered in Chapter 5. However, there is plenty of evidence that large divergences between WTA and WTP, and differences in valuations across response modes, are *not* specific to public goods (this evidence will be reviewed in Section 6.7). Thus, if these anomalies are to be explained as the product of biases in survey instruments, at least some of those biases must be ones that affect the elicitation of preferences for private goods. In this chapter, therefore, I shall restrict my attention to private goods.

This section will focus on biases which result from the strategic misrepresentation of preferences for private goods. I shall work within the Hicksian model, in which the concept of 'true preferences' is not problematic; whether that model is adequate will be considered later, in Sections 6.5 and 6.6.

Consider any mechanism which is designed to elicit a particular piece of information about a person's preferences (for example, how much the person is willing to pay for some quantity of a good). The mechanism is *incentive-compatible* if, whatever a respondent's true preferences, he has an incentive to respond in a way that correctly reveals the desired information. An incentive-compatible mechanism will not induce strategic biases—provided that the respondent has sufficient understanding of the mechanism.

In Section 6.3 I discussed four different response modes. Each can be used as part of an incentive-compatible mechanism for eliciting preferences for private goods.

Binary choices are incentive-compatible if the respondent is made a take-it-or-leave-it offer. For example, suppose we wish to discover whether a person is willing to pay at least £20 for some permit. We simply make him a non-negotiable offer: he can have a permit if he pays £20. If his true WTP is greater than £20, he has an incentive to accept; if it is less than £20, he has an incentive to refuse.

Open-ended questions and *iterated bidding procedures* can be made incentive-compatible by combining them with a mechanism proposed by Becker, DeGroot, and Marschak (1964). Suppose someone is asked to state the maximum amount he is willing to pay for a permit. After he has responded, a price is generated at random from some given probability distribution of prices. If the randomly generated price is less than or equal to the person's stated maximum, he is required to pay that price, and receives the permit in exchange. If the price is greater than the stated maximum, no trade takes place. Given the standard assumptions of expected-utility theory, it is in the individual's interest to report his true WTP.

A *sealed-bid auction* can be made incentive-compatible by using the *second-price* rule. If there are n participants in an auction for permits, each of the m highest bidders (where m is some number in the range $0 < m < n$) is given a permit, and each pays an amount equal to the $(m + 1)$th highest bid.

It is well-known that, in a second-price sealed-bid auction, it is a dominant strategy for each individual to set his bid equal to his true WTP (Vickrey, 1961).

Clearly, the concept of incentive-compatibility does not apply directly to preference-elicitation mechanisms which present respondents with hypothetical scenarios (as most CV surveys do). But we may say that a mechanism is *hypothetically incentive-compatible* if the respondent is presented with a scenario in which, were it real, preferences would be elicited by an incentive-compatible mechanism. For example, a hypothetical take-it-or-leave-it offer ('Suppose you were offered the opportunity to buy this permit at a cost of £20: would you buy?') is hypothetically incentive-compatible. CV researchers typically try to ensure that the survey instruments they use are at least hypothetically incentive-compatible.

This, however, is not to say that respondents always *understand* the incentive-compatibility of the mechanism they are presented with. In particular, the Becker–DeGroot–Marschak mechanism and the second-price sealed-bid auction are quite complicated, and their incentive-compatibility is not immediately obvious. Further, respondents may wonder whether a mechanism is exactly as it has been described to them. For example, a respondent who is presented with a purportedly take-it-or-leave-it offer may wonder whether the offer really is non-negotiable. After all, in real bargaining, 'final offers' are not always final. Thus, respondents might misrepresent their preferences in the mistaken belief that it was to their advantage to do so.

It is conventional for bargaining to begin with each party stating some terms on which he or she is willing to trade; there is then a process in which the parties make concessions. A buyer begins by offering to pay less than the maximum he would be willing to pay; a seller begins by suggesting a price greater than the minimum she would be willing to accept. And in most bargaining situations, it is good tactics to try to give the impression that you are less eager to trade than you really are. ('A lot of other people have expressed interest in buying this house.' 'If I can't get a good price for this car, I'll be quite happy to keep it.' 'I really can't afford to pay any more.') The point of these manœuvres is to try to influence the other party's belief about your reservation price; you want the other party to underestimate your maximum WTP, or to overestimate your minimum WTA. Respondents in a CV survey may fail to recognize that the elicitation mechanism is incentive-compatible. Consciously or unconsciously, they may use mental routines that, although not appropriate in the particular circumstances of a CV survey, are well-adapted to real-life bargaining situations. Such routines can be expected to lead to the understatement of WTP and to the overstatement of WTA (Knez et al., 1985).

Since such understatement and overstatement result from misunderstanding, we might expect the extent of these biases to be sensitive both to the response mode and to the detailed design of the survey instrument. For example, it is probably much easier for a respondent to understand why the take-it-or-leave-it-offer mechanism is incentive-compatible than to understand why the same is true of the Becker–DeGroot–Marschak mechanism or of the second-price sealed-bid auction. For any given response mode, respondents' understanding of its incentive-compatibility may depend on the clarity of the instructions they are given and on the opportunities they are allowed for gaining experience of how the elicitation mechanism works.

6.5. REFERENCE-DEPENDENT PREFERENCES

In Section 6.2 I showed that, within the Hicksian model, divergences between WTP and WTA would normally be very small. The large divergences observed in many CV studies *might* result from strategic biases of the kind considered in Section 6.4; but equally, they might be signs of the limitations of the Hicksian model as a representation of real decision-making. In this section, I shall consider an alternative model of decision-making which permits much larger divergences between WTP and WTA than the Hicksian model does—the *reference-dependent preference theory* of Tversky and Kahneman (1991). This is an extension of the same authors' earlier theory of choice under risk: *prospect theory* (Kahneman and Tversky, 1979).

A fundamental idea in both of these theories is that individuals understand the options in decision problems as *gains or losses relative to a reference point*. The reference point is normally the current asset position of the individual. Tversky and Kahneman allow certain exceptions to this rule, but in this chapter, these exceptions will be ignored. In contrast, the Hicksian model has no concept of a reference point.

Consider, for example, an individual who is given £0.50 and then offered the opportunity to exchange that £0.50 for a bar of chocolate. In the Hicksian framework, we may think in terms of bundles of good X (chocolate bars) and good Y (the composite commodity, measured in money units). Let (x', y') be the individual's wealth, in chocolate and other goods, before she is given the £0.50. Then if she keeps the £0.50, she has the bundle $A = (x', y' + 0.50)$. If she exchanges the £0.50 for the chocolate, she has the bundle $B = (x' + 1, y')$. Thus, in the Hicksian model, her decision will be determined by her preference between A and B. Now suppose instead that the same individual is given a bar of chocolate, and then offered the opportunity to sell it for £0.50. This amounts to a choice between exactly the same two bundles A and B as in the previous case, and so the individual's decision will be determined by the same preference. If in the first case, she would prefer *not* to exchange the £0.50 for the bar of chocolate, then Hicksian theory implies that in the second case, she *would* prefer to exchange the bar of chocolate for the £0.50.

In Tversky and Kahneman's model, however, the two decision problems are quite distinct. In the first case, the individual chooses between (1) the *status-quo* bundle $(x', y' + 0.50)$ and (2) *gaining* one bar of chocolate and *losing* £0.50. In the second case, she chooses between (3) a different *status-quo* bundle $(x' + 1, y')$ and (4) *losing* one bar of chocolate and *gaining* £0.50. If in the first case she prefers (1) to (2), we cannot infer that she also prefers (4) to (3). If she is particularly averse to losses, she may prefer the *status quo* in each case.

Tversky and Kahneman present their model for the case of two goods. As in the Hicksian model, we can consider the set of all non-negative consumption bundles; the goods are X and Y, and a typical bundle is (x, y). Let the bundle R be the individual's current asset position and reference point. Then the individual has a preference ordering over bundles, *conditional on the reference point*; the relation 'is at least as preferred as, evaluated in relation to the reference point R' (or 'is at least as preferred as, viewed from R') is written as $\succcurlyeq_R$. Strict preference, viewed from R, will be denoted by $\succ_R$; indifference will be denoted by $\sim_R$. It is assumed that this reference-dependent preference relation can be represented by a family of downward-sloping indifference curves, but (for reasons which will emerge shortly) these curves are not required to be convex to the origin.

Preferences conditional on one reference point may be different from preferences conditional on a different reference point. Tversky and Kahneman impose two conditions on the way in which preferences can change as the reference point changes.

One of these conditions is *diminishing sensitivity*. The idea behind this condition is that 'marginal value decreases with the distance from the reference point' (Tversky and Kahneman, 1991: 1048). If we are working in the *gain domain* (i.e. if we are evaluating bundles which dominate the reference point), diminishing sensitivity is analogous with the familiar assumption of diminishing marginal utility in conventional consumer theory. In contrast, in the *loss domain* (i.e. if we are evaluating bundles which are dominated by the reference point), diminishing sensitivity is analogous with *increasing* marginal utility. Thus, diminishing sensitivity imparts a tendency for reference-dependent preferences to be convex in the gain domain but non-convex in the loss domain.

In the present context, Tversky and Kahneman's second condition is much more significant. This is the condition of *loss aversion*, which represents the psychological intuition that 'losses ... loom larger than corresponding gains' (ibid. 1047). Consider any two bundles $A = (x_0, y_1)$ and $B = (x_1, y_0)$, such that $x_1 > x_0$ and $y_1 > y_0$. And consider any two potential reference points $R = (x_0, y^*)$ and $S = (x_1, y^*)$, where y^* may take any fixed value (see Figure 6.2). Notice that R and S differ only on the X-dimension, and that this is the dimension on which B is superior to A. Viewed from R, the difference between A and B on the X-dimension is that A gives the

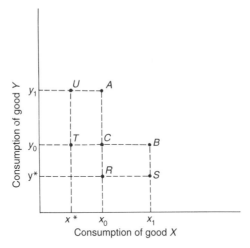

Fig. 6.2 Bundles and reference points

reference level of good X, while B gives a gain of $x_1 - x_0$ above that level. Viewed from S, in contrast, B offers the reference level of good X, while A gives a loss of $x_1 - x_0$ below that level. If losses on any given dimension loom larger than corresponding gains, we should expect B's superiority on the X-dimension to have more impact on overall preference when the reference point is S than when it is R. Thus we arrive at the loss-aversion condition, that $B \sim_R A$ implies $B \succcurlyeq_S A$.[2] Notice that, since preferences are complete, this condition can be written equivalently as: $A \succcurlyeq_S B$ implies $A \succcurlyeq_R B$.

A symmetrical condition is imposed on the Y-dimension. Defining A and B as before, consider the potential reference points $T = (x^*, y_0)$ and $U = (x^*, y_1)$. In this case, A's superiority on the Y-dimension has more impact on overall preference when the reference point is U (i.e. when y_1 is the reference level for good Y and y_0 is below) than when it is T (i.e. when y_0 is the reference level and y_1 is above). Thus $A \succcurlyeq_T B$ implies $A \succcurlyeq_U B$.

To see the implications of loss aversion for divergences between WTP and WTA, consider an individual for whom $A \sim_B B$ is true. That is, she is indifferent between A and B when the reference point is B. Let C be the bundle (x_0, y_0). It follows from the loss-aversion condition for the X-dimension that $A \sim_B B$ implies $A \succcurlyeq_C B$.[3] Similarly, it follows from the loss-aversion condition for the Y-dimension that $A \succcurlyeq_C B$ implies $A \succcurlyeq_A B$. Combining these two results: $A \sim_B B$ implies $A \succcurlyeq_A B$. In other words, reference-dependent theory implies that if, starting from B, the individual would be

---

[2] Tversky and Kahneman explicitly require only that $B \sim_R A$ implies $B \succ_S A$, but the condition I have stated seems to express better what they have in mind.

[3] To see why, set $y^* = y_0$ so that $S = B$ and $R = C$.

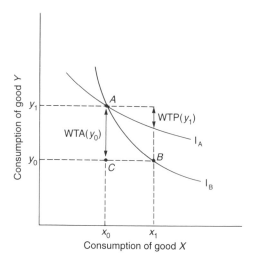

Fig. 6.3   Reference-dependent preferences

indifferent between keeping B and exchanging it for A, then, starting from A, she would *not* be willing to exchange A for B. This case is illustrated in Figure 6.3. Here I_A is an indifference curve for preferences based on the reference point A, while I_B is an indifference curve for preferences based on the reference point B.

To say that A and B are indifferent, viewed from B, is to say that, if the individual's initial endowment of good Y is y_0, her WTA (in units of good Y) for a decrease in her consumption of good X from x_1 to x_0 will be exactly $y_1 - y_0$. This WTA valuation is shown in Figure 6.3 as WTA (y_0). To say that A is strictly preferred to B, viewed from A, is to say that, if the individual's initial endowment of good Y is y_1, her WTP for an increase in consumption of good X from x_0 to x_1 will be *less than* $y_1 - y_0$. This WTP valuation is shown in Figure 6.3 as WTP (y_1). Figure 6.1 shows the corresponding case in the Hicksian model, in which WTP $(y_1) =$ WTA(y_0).

Thus, reference-dependent preference theory implies that WTA will exceed WTP, even if income effects have been controlled for. How large can this divergence be? Tversky and Kahneman do not require reference-dependent indifference curves to be smooth: given the assumption of loss aversion, it would be quite natural to expect these curves to be kinked at the reference levels of X and Y (Tversky and Kahneman, 1991: 1051). But if there are such kinks, the calculus-based approach of Randall and Stoll and Hanemann cannot be used to establish bounds for the divergence between WTA and WTP. Thus, even very large divergences can be consistent with reference-dependent theory if the relevant individual is sufficiently loss-averse.

6.6. RESPONSE COMPATIBILITY AND IMPLIED VALUE CUES

If individuals have Hicksian preferences, then the valuations that are elicited by CV studies ought not to be different for different response modes. If such differences *are* found, and if the Hicksian model is to be retained, the explanation of the differences must be sought in survey-instrument bias. As in the case of divergences between WTA and WTP, however, there is an alternative way of explaining anomalous findings: it may be that respondents do not have Hicksian preferences.

In the Hicksian model (and, indeed, in Tversky and Kahneman's model of reference-dependent preferences) an individual comes to a decision problem equipped with a complete preference map, from which decisions can be 'read off'. But do *real* individuals have such preferences? An alternative approach, favoured by some psychologists, is to think of the individual as *constructing* her preferences in response to specific decision problems. Summarizing this *constructive processing* approach, Payne *et al.* write:

> It appears that decision-makers have a repertoire of methods for identifying their preferences and developing their beliefs. Descriptive research on decision-making processes has shown that the information and strategies used to construct preferences or beliefs appear to be highly contingent upon and predictable from a variety of task, context, and individual-difference factors. (1992: 89–90)

Thus, different ways of presenting what, in a Hicksian perspective, is the same decision problem may evoke different strategies for constructing preferences. As a result, the preference that is constructed may differ according to the way the problem has been presented. It is important to notice that, from a constructive processing viewpoint, such differences are *not* the result of biases. To think in terms of bias is to presuppose that there are 'true' preferences which an ideal, unbiased elicitation mechanism would discover. But the constructive processing approach rejects this presupposition.

One dimension of problem presentation which is particularly significant for CV research is the distinction between *choice tasks* and *valuation tasks*. In a choice task, a respondent is offered a number of options and asked to choose one of them. In a valuation task, the respondent is shown one option and is asked to value it in money terms. In CV surveys, open-ended WTP or WTA questions are valuation tasks, while binary-choice questions are choice tasks (iterated bidding might be thought of as a hybrid of choice and valuation).

A number of hypotheses have been proposed about the difference between choice tasks and valuation tasks. The guiding idea behind these hypotheses is *response compatibility*. Different strategies for constructing preferences, and different pieces of information which might be used in the construction process, vary in the extent to which they are compatible with the kind of response that is required. Here, 'compatibility' is understood in terms of ease of mental processing; it is hypothesized that individuals tend to use decision-making strategies which economize on mental processing.

Much of the discussion of the differences between choice and valuation has centred on the phenomenon of *preference reversal*. The classic preference-reversal experiment involves two lotteries, the '$ bet' and the '*P* bet'. The $ bet offers a relatively large money prize with low probability (say, a 0.2 chance of winning £10) while the *P* bet offers a smaller prize with higher probability (say, a 0.8 chance of winning £2.50). In the choice task, subjects are asked to choose between the two bets. In the valuation tasks, they are asked to state a WTA valuation for each bet. This results in two rankings of the bets, one elicited by the choice task (which bet is chosen?) and the other elicited by the two valuation tasks (which bet has the higher valuation?). If a subject has a fixed set of (reference-independent) preferences, these two rankings should agree. But experiments show a consistent tendency for the rankings to differ in a systematic way: the *P* bet is more likely to be ranked above the $ bet in the choice task than in the valuation tasks.

One explanation of preference reversal is in terms of response compatibility (Slovic and Lichtenstein, 1983; Tversky *et al.*, 1988; Tversky *et al.*, 1990). Certain processes for coping with choice problems economize on mental effort, but cannot be applied to valuation tasks. In particular, for a binary choice between two options which differ on two attributes,

If neither option has a decisive advantage, the decision maker seeks a procedure for resolving the conflict. Because it is often unclear how to trade one attribute against another, a common procedure for resolving conflict is to select the option which is superior on the more important attribute. This procedure, which is essentially lexicographic, has two attractive features. First, it does not require the decision maker to assess the trade-off between the attributes, thereby reducing mental effort and cognitive strain. Second, it provides a compelling argument for choice that can be used to justify the decision to oneself as well as to others.   (Tversky *et al.*, 1988: 372)

In the case of the two bets, it is hypothesized that there are two relevant attributes, 'probability of winning' and 'amount to be won', with probability of winning being more important for most subjects. Thus the lexicographic procedure tends to favour the P-bet.

This procedure, however, is not compatible with valuation tasks, which call for a response in the form of a sum of money. Tversky *et al.* (1988) hypothesize that any attribute is given more weight in determining a response if the required response is on the same scale as the attribute than if the scales are different (*scale compatibility*). In support of this hypothesis, they present evidence from experiments using *matching tasks*. In a typical experiment, subjects consider two alternatives (say, applicants for a job) and two desirable attributes of those alternatives (say, literacy and numeracy). Each applicant has been given a numerical score for each attribute. Subjects are shown three of these scores and are asked to fill in the fourth score so that the two applicants are equally good for the job. A response can be interpreted as indicating the relative importance that the subject attaches to the two attributes. Subjects appear to give relatively greater weight to the attribute which is the response mode; thus, they attach more importance to literacy if the missing score is for literacy than if it is for numeracy.

Extending this hypothesis to the case of preference reversal, giving a WTA valuation of a bet may be understood as a form of matching task. A subject who is giving such a valuation knows the bet's scores on the two attributes, 'probability of winning' and 'amount to be won'. In effect, she is asked to consider a second option for which the probability of winning is 1, and to fill in the amount to be won so that she is indifferent between the two options. The scale-compatibility hypothesis implies that, because the response mode is an amount of money, the 'amount to be won' attribute will be given particular weight in valuation tasks; and this will tend to favour the $ bet.

A related, but slightly different, explanation of the relatively high valuation of the $ bet can be derived from the *anchor-and-adjustment hypothesis* (Tversky and Kahneman, 1974). Roughly: if an individual faces a task which requires him to respond on some given scale, he will begin by looking for some point on that scale that can serve as an 'anchor', and then arrive at a response by 'adjusting' from that point. Adjustment does not completely eliminate the influence of the original anchor: the higher the anchor point, the higher the response. If, say, the individual is asked to value a 0.2 chance of winning £10, he will look for a salient money value which is in some way related to the required response. Since £10 has been brought to his attention, this value is likely to be used; he will then adjust downwards to allow for the risk that the £10 will not be won. If the amount to be won is used as the anchor when evaluating bets, this will tend to favour the $ bet relative to the *P* bet.

In a typical CV survey, the options can be thought of as having two main attributes: monetary cost and non-monetary benefit. Discussing choice tasks involving public programmes to improve road safety and to clean up beaches, Tversky *et al.* (1988: 373–4) hypothesize that non-monetary benefit (safety or health) is viewed as a more important attribute than monetary cost. If this is generally true, then the theory of response compatibility implies that binary-choice CV questions ('Would you be willing to pay £y for...?') will tend to evoke affirmative answers. Thus, the binary-choice response mode might be expected to elicit responses which imply relatively high money valuations of non-monetary benefits.

If the scale-compatibility hypothesis is correct, open-ended CV questions ('How much would you be willing to pay for...?') will tend to focus respondents' attention on the attribute of monetary cost. Thus, open-ended questions might be expected to elicit responses which imply relatively *low* money valuations of non-monetary benefits.

The anchor and adjustment hypothesis has a different implication. If this hypothesis is correct, responses to open-ended CV questions will be particularly vulnerable to what Mitchell and Carson (1989: pp. 240–6) call *implied value cues*. The common feature of implied value cues is that respondents make inappropriate use of information that happens to be salient for them at the time. For example, an iterated bidding procedure might start by asking a respondent whether she would be willing to pay £20 for some permit. The respondent might then think of £20 as a potential answer, and ask herself how much more or less than £20 she is willing to pay. If respondents use this kind of anchor-and-adjustment process, WTP and WTA valuations elicited by iterated bidding may be positively related to the amount of money referred to in the opening question: this is *starting-point bias*. Or consider a sealed-bid auction that is repeated several times (this is a standard experimental technique: see Section 6.7). Respondents might use market prices generated by earlier auctions as anchors when choosing their bids for later auctions; this would create a tendency for stated reservation prices to converge on the market price.

Should response-compatibility effects be regarded as biases, or as components of a coherent (but non-Hicksian) theory of decision-making? Recall that, according to the theory of response compatibility, decision-making strategies are more likely to be adopted the more economical they are of mental effort. Thus, we *might* assume that individuals have 'true' Hicksian preferences, which they can retrieve with sufficient mental effort. On this view, response-compatibility effects will occur only when respondents take mental short cuts, and can properly be thought of as biases. Mitchell and Carson (ibid. 240) seem to take this line in their discussion of implied value cues, pointing to the 'significant effort' required of CV respondents and arguing that this 'creates an incentive to adopt strategies to lighten the task'.

It is important to recognize, however, that the interpretation of implied value cues as biases depends on the assumption that individuals have consistent preferences to 'consult' or 'retrieve'. *If* such preferences exist, there is a clear sense in which it is inappropriate to allow one's response to (say) an iterated bidding mechanism to be influenced by the starting-point. But the assumption might be false: respondents might simply not have the preferences which Hicksian theory attributes to them. If, for example, I am asked how much I would be willing to pay for some good in a counterfactual situation ('If you could enter this area only with a permit, would you be willing to pay £20 for one?'), I may genuinely *not know*. If I am confronted with a real decision problem ('We are offering you a permit at a price of £20: do you want to buy?'), then I may have to *decide*—rather than check out or discover—which option I prefer. If I do not have a pre-existing preference ordering to consult, it is not at all obvious that my separate responses to tasks of different kinds will turn out to be consistent with such an ordering—however much mental effort I devote to each task.

6.7. WILLINGNESS TO PAY AND WILLINGNESS TO ACCEPT: THE EVIDENCE

When CV surveys elicit both WTP and WTA valuations of the same good, the mean and median values of WTA are often found to be several times higher than the corresponding WTP values. An entirely typical example is Rowe et al.'s (1980) study of the value of visibility to the residents of an area in New Mexico. Respondents were asked to compare visibilities of 75 miles (the existing state of affairs) and 50 miles (the potential impact of a coal-fired power station). When they were asked to state their WTP to retain high visibility, the mean response was $4.75 per week; when they were asked to state their WTA for accepting low visibility, the mean response was $24.47 per week. Another example is Bishop and Heberlein's (1979) study of the value of goose-hunting permits; in their sample, mean WTP for a permit was $21, and mean WTA was $101. Many similar results could be quoted (Kahneman et al., (1990) review some of this evidence). Such large divergences between WTA and WTP, when WTP is a relatively small proportion of total income, are not remotely compatible with Hicksian theory: this is obvious from a glance at Equation (6.5).

Equally extreme divergences between WTP and WTA have been found in surveys of attitudes to risks. Two typical examples are Jones-Lee et al.'s (1985) investigation of the value of road safety and Viscusi et al.'s (1987) investigation of the value of safety in household products. Each of these studies found that respondents were extremely unwilling to accept even small increases above their current level of risk, while being willing to pay only quite modest amounts for further risk reductions.

The studies I have quoted so far have been 'field' surveys which asked hypothetical questions about WTP and WTA. An alternative way of investigating apparent anomalies in preferences is to carry out 'laboratory' experiments in which subjects make real decisions, usually about goods whose value is relatively low. A typical example is an experiment reported by Knetsch and Sinden (1984: 514–16), in which the good to be valued was a lottery ticket. The subjects in the experiment were divided at random into two groups. In one group, each subject was endowed with a lottery ticket and then invited to sell it back to the experimenters; in the other group, each subject was invited to buy a lottery ticket. A binary-choice format was used, each subject making a decision in relation to one take-it-or-leave-it offer. The estimated mean value of WTP for a ticket was $1.28, while the mean WTA was $5.18. Another example is an experiment conducted by Eisenberger and Weber (1993), in which subjects stated their WTP and WTA for various lotteries. Valuations were elicited through open-ended questions, with a Becker–De Groot–Marschak incentive mechanism (see Section 6.4). WTP valuations were of the order of DM4.00, and ratios of WTA to WTP were typically in the range 1.5 : 1 to 2 : 1.

In all the experiments and field surveys I have described up to now, WTP and WTA valuations are small in relation to subjects' incomes. In such cases, Hicksian theory implies that divergences between WTA and WTP will be very small (see Section 6.2); the observed divergences are far too large to be compatible with that theory. However, if any readers are still tempted to try to explain these divergences in terms of income effects, they should notice that some experimenters have used designs which control for these effects. For example, Knetsch and Sinden (1984: 512) report an experiment in which subjects were divided at random into two groups. In one group, each subject was endowed with $3[4], and then offered the opportunity to buy a lottery ticket for $3. In the other group, each subject was endowed with a lottery ticket and then offered the opportunity to sell the ticket for $3. Notice that, in each case, the subject has a choice between exactly the same two options: $3, and a lottery ticket. According to Hicksian theory, each subject has a preference ranking of these two options, and will choose whichever of the options he or she prefers. Clearly, this implication does not depend on any assumption about income effects. Since the two groups have been formed at random from a common pool of individuals, there should be no systematic difference in preferences between the groups. Thus, apart from random variation, there should be no difference between (1) the proportion of subjects in the first group who choose to buy lottery tickets and (2) the proportion of subjects in the second group who choose not to sell their tickets. In the experiment, however, the proportions were 38 per cent and 82 per cent respectively. This may be interpreted as an instance of the usual divergence between WTA and WTP: 38 per cent of subjects report a WTP of $3 or more, while 82 per cent report a WTA of $3 or more.

Knetsch (1989) reports another experiment with the same basic design, involving trades between candy bars and coffee mugs. In a group of subjects endowed with candy bars, 11 per cent chose to exchange candy bars for mugs; in a 'comparable' group which had been endowed with mugs, 90 per cent chose to keep their mugs rather than exchanging them for candy bars.

Several experiments have tried to discriminate between two alternative explanations for divergences between WTA responses and WTP responses: strategic bias and reference-dependent preferences. Much the same basic experimental design has been used by Coursey et al. (1987), Kahneman et al. (1990), and Shogren et al. (1994). Here subjects participate in groups. The elicitation mechanism is a sealed-bid auction. In any one *trial*, each subject in the group makes a bid, and then a market-clearing price is calculated and reported back to each subject. This procedure is repeated several times, but only one of the trials (the *binding trial*) is used to determine the trades that actually take place. The idea behind this design is that, with repeated experience of a market mechanism, people might learn to avoid certain

---

[4] The currency seems to have been Australian dollars.

kinds of mistake or bias. For example, a person who at first thought that it was in his interest to overstate his true WTA in an auction might learn from experience that this was not so. With this design, we can investigate whether there is any tendency for WTA and WTP bids to increase or decrease over the series of trials, and whether there is still a significant divergence between WTA and WTP at the end of the series.

In Coursey et al.'s experiment, subjects faced the possibility of having to taste an unpleasant substance (sucrose octa-acetate, or SOA). Auctions were run for eight groups of eight subjects each. In the WTP format, faced by four of the groups, all the subjects were endowed with $10 plus the obligation to taste SOA, and then bid money to avoid tasting; if the trial was binding, the four highest bidders won the right not to taste, and each paid the fifth-highest bid. In the WTA format, faced by the other four groups, subjects were given no endowments, and their bids represented payments in return for which they would taste SOA. If the trial was binding, the four lowest bidders were required to taste SOA, and each was paid the fifth-lowest bid. For each group there were four non-binding trials. After this, trials were repeated until all four of the subjects who had submitted 'winning' bids in a trial agreed to accept that trial as binding.

The results can be summarized roughly as follows. There was no obvious trend either in WTP bids or in WTA bids over the four non-binding trials; mean WTP bids were of the order of $2 to $3, and mean WTA bids of the order of $10 to $12.[5] After the non-binding trials, mean WTP remained roughly constant, but mean WTA fell sharply; for binding trials, mean WTP was about $3, and mean WTA about $4.60. Finding that the difference between these final means is not statistically significant at the 99-per-cent confidence level, Coursey et al. conclude that 'we can accept the hypothesis that willingness to accept and willingness to pay measurements...are equivalent' (687). What they should have said, of course, is that they cannot reject that hypothesis with 99 per cent confidence. A more natural interpretation of these results is that WTA is greater than WTP throughout the trials, but the divergence is smaller in later, potentially binding trials than in the earlier trials, which are known in advance to be non-binding. This difference might be the result either of the subjects' greater experience in later trials or of the incentive effect of a trial's being potentially binding.

Kahneman et al. ran four experiments which were very similar to one another and which generated very similar results; I shall describe one of these. A group of 44 subjects participated in this experiment, which had three parts. The first part of the experiment consisted of an auction with three trials, in which subjects traded induced-value tokens. An induced-value token is a token which is redeemable for money. Each subject is told how much she will be paid for a token, but this amount may differ between

---

[5] Coursy et al. report their results by using diagrams; the reader is not told the exact means.

subjects. One would not expect to find loss aversion for induced-value tokens. For example, if a token is redeemable for $5, one would expect a subject to be willing to pay up to $5 to get it, and to be willing to sell it at any price above $5. Thus, an induced-value auction can be used to test subjects' understanding of the auction mechanism itself; if they understand it, reservation prices will be equal to token values.

The second and third parts of the experiment consisted of two auctions, each with four trials. In each auction, one trial was selected at random after all four trials had taken place; this trial was binding. This feature of Kahneman *et al.*'s design is an improvement on Coursey *et al.*'s, since it ensures that incentives are constant across trials. For the auction in the second part of the experiment, half of the subjects (the 'sellers') were endowed with coffee mugs, and the others (the 'buyers') were given no endowments. Each subject stated a reservation price; a seller's reservation price is a WTA valuation, while a buyer's is a WTP valuation. From these bids, a market-clearing price was calculated and reported to the subjects. If the trial was binding, trades took place at the market price, according to subjects' stated willingness to trade. The auction in the third part of the experiment was just like the one just described, except that the roles of buyer and seller were switched round, and the endowments were boxes of ball-point pens. Assuming that income effects are negligible, Hicksian theory implies that there should be no systematic difference between the reservation prices of buyers and sellers.

Behaviour in the induced-value auction was consistent with a high degree of understanding of the auction mechanism. Nevertheless, in the mug and pen auctions, median reservation prices were between 2 and 2.5 times higher for sellers than for buyers, with no obvious trend over the trials.

In Shogren *et al.*'s experiment, there were two types of good: 'market' and 'non-market'. The market good was an upgrade from a small piece of candy to a regular-size candy bar. The non-market good was an upgrade from a normal food item to one which had been stringently tested for some food-borne pathogen. Second-price sealed-bid WTA and WTP auctions were run separately, as in Coursey *et al.*'s experiment, except that there was only one 'winner' in each auction.[6] Each subject took part in a market good auction with five trials, followed by a non-market good auction with twenty trials. As in Kahneman *et al.*'s experiment, one trial of each auction, selected at random after all trials had been completed, was binding.

In the case of candy bars, bids made in the first trial of the WTA auction were significantly greater than those made in the first trial of the WTP auction (an average of $0.51 compared with $0.40). WTP bids stayed

---

[6] Notice that the 'market price' is the second-*highest* valuation in a WTP auction but the second-*lowest* in a WTA auction. If the market price provides an anchor or cue for valuations (see Section 6.6), this feature of Shogren *et al.*'s design will tend to increase WTP bids and decrease WTA ones relative to Kahneman *et al.*'s more neutral design.

constant over the five trials; WTA bids fell over the first three trials, converging on $0.40 by the third trial. This is broadly the pattern of observations that we should expect to find if subjects have Hicksian preferences but are affected by strategic bias.

In the case of the screened food, in contrast, WTA bids were much higher than WTP bids throughout the twenty trials, with no apparent tendency towards convergence. Different pathogens were used for different groups of subjects, and the extent of the WTA–WTP divergence differed between pathogens. The *lowest* ratio of WTA to WTP was 2.95 : 1 (for screening against salmonella). In this case, the average WTP bid in the final four trials was $0.55, while the average WTA bid was $1.62.

Shogren *et al.* interpret these findings as providing support for Hanemann's explanation of WTA–WTP divergences as the result of low elasticities of substitution (see Section 6.2 above). They argue that the crucial difference between the two types of goods is that, outside the experiment, their subjects have ready access to a market in candy bars, but not to a market in stringently-screened food. Thus money is a much closer substitute for candy bars than it is for screened food. Hanemann's analysis then implies that we should expect a larger WTA–WTP divergence in the case of screened food. So far, this argument is entirely reasonable. But notice how tiny WTP is for screened food, relative to subjects' wealth. As the analysis of Section 6.2 shows, we should expect the difference between WTA and WTP to be no more than a few per cent in such a case. It is inconceivable that a difference of 195 per cent (still less the 6,590 per cent difference observed in the case of screening against *Staphylococcus aureus*) could be consistent with Hicksian theory. Thus, Shogren *et al.*'s findings in the case of screened food seem to support the hypothesis of reference-dependent preferences.

Considered as a whole, the results reported by Coursey *et al.*, Kahneman *et al.*, and Shogren *et al.* do not allow us to draw any firm conclusions about the effects of market experience on WTA–WTP divergences. Coursey *et al.*'s results, and Shogren *et al.*'s results for market goods, suggest that these divergences are eroded by market experience. Kahneman *et al.*'s results, and Shogren *et al.*'s results for non-market goods, suggest the contrary. These differences between the results of similar experiments are puzzling.[7]

What can be said is that there is overwhelming evidence of a systematic divergence between WTA responses and WTP responses, both in hypothetical CV surveys and in one-off experiments involving real transactions. This divergence cannot be accounted for by Hicksian theory. How far this divergence is due to strategic bias and how far to reference-dependent preferences remains an open question.

---

[7] Among the factors which might be considered as possible explanations for this difference are differences in incentive mechanisms, and the implied value cues given by the market price (see fn. 6).

6.8. RESPONSE COMPATIBILITY AND IMPLIED VALUE CUES: THE EVIDENCE

There is a good deal of evidence that, when used in CV surveys, binary-choice questions elicit higher valuations than open-ended questions. For example, Bateman et al. (1995) report a very large CV survey designed to elicit valuations of the prevention of salt-water flooding of the Norfolk Broads. Open-ended and binary-choice WTP questions were given to independent samples of respondents. Each format can be used to construct a WTP survival function, i.e. for each positive amount of money, v, the proportion of the sample for whom WTP is greater than or equal to v. At all values of v, the binary-choice survival function lies above the open-ended survival function. Similar discrepancies are reported by Sellar et al. (1985) and Kriström (1990). Starting-point bias is another well-attested property of CV surveys. This effect has most often been reported in the context of iterated bidding: respondents' final valuations are found to be positively correlated with the first amount of money they are asked to consider (Boyle et al., 1985; Roberts et al., 1985). A striking example is reported by Loomes (1994). Piloting a CV questionnaire to elicit valuations of vehicle safety features, Loomes used a visual aid which consisted of a plain card with a window cut out to reveal a single sum of money. This sum could be changed by rotating a disc. The interviewer rotated the disc until the respondent was just willing to pay the amount shown in the window. For half the respondents, the first amount displayed in the window was £25; for the other half, it was £75. Depending on the risk-reduction scenario being valued, the mean WTP elicited with the £75 starting-point was between 1.9 and 2.9 times greater than that elicited with the £25 starting-point.

One explanation of the discrepancy between open-ended and binary-choice responses is in terms of strategic bias. Some commentators have argued that, in hypothetical CV surveys, open-ended valuation questions encourage respondents to behave as free-riders, understanding their true WTP for public goods (Hoehn and Randall, 1987). Others have argued the opposite: that open-ended questions encourage the over-statement of true valuations as 'a costless way to make a point' (Arrow et al., 1993: 20). These kinds of strategic bias, which are specific to public goods, were discussed in Chapter 5.

An alternative explanation of these response-mode and starting-point effects is provided by the theory of response compatibility (see Section 6.6). CV surveys which use binary-choice questions correspond with choice tasks, while those which use open-ended questions correspond with valuation tasks. If it is assumed that environmental quality is seen as more important than monetary cost as an attribute of policies, CV surveys should be expected to elicit higher valuations of environmental public goods if they use binary-choice questions than if they use open-ended ones.

There is a large body of experimental evidence which supports the theory of response compatibility. In particular, the evidence is overwhelming that the classic form of preference reversal, described in Section 6.6, does indeed occur (see, e.g., Grether and Plott, 1979; Slovic and Lichtenstein, 1983; Tversky *et al.*, 1990). Some economists have suggested that preference reversal might be an artefact of the incentive devices used in experiments (Holt, 1986; Karni and Safra, 1987), but this seems implausible, since the same pattern of reversals has been found in experiments both with and without incentives. It has also been suggested that preference reversal might be the result of non-transitive preferences (Loomes and Sugden, 1983), but in the light of a diagnostic study by Tversky *et al.* (1990) it seems that reversals are primarily the result of discrepancies between choices and valuations—particularly the valuation of the $ bet.

A significant discovery has been that the classic preference-reversal phenomenon can be replicated for options which involve time rather than risk (ibid.). In this case, one option *L* (the long-term option, analogous with the $ bet) gives a relatively large sum of money at a relatively distant date; the other option *S* (the short-term option, analogous with the P bet) gives a smaller sum of money at an earlier date. There is a systematic difference between choices and valuations; individuals tend to attach a higher valuation to *L*, but to choose *S* rather than *L* in a binary-choice task. The close similarity between this observation and the classic form of preference reversal provides further evidence that choice tasks and valuation tasks elicit different kinds of response, as implied by the theory of response compatibility.

Starting-point bias can be interpreted as an instance of a more general implication of the theory of response compatibility: that respondents give disproportionate attention to information—whether relevant or not—that is compatible with the response mode. As one of many possible examples of the evidence for this effect, consider an experiment reported by Slovic *et al.* (1990). Subjects were told the 1986 market value of twelve companies, in billions of dollars, and the rank of each of these companies, among the top 100 companies, with respect to 1987 profits. Half the subjects were asked to predict each company's 1987 market value in billions of dollars, while the other half were asked to predict each company's rank with respect to 1987 market value. Notice that both groups are predicting 1987 market values, but for the first group the response mode is a dollar value while for the second it is a ranking. Relative to subjects in the first group, subjects in the second group gave more weight to the information that had been presented as rankings and less weight to the information that had been presented as dollar values.

6.9. CONCLUSIONS

In the light of the evidence, there can be little doubt that the responses elicited by CV surveys show systematic patterns that are not compatible with Hicksian theory. In particular: willingness-to-accept valuations are greater than willingness-to-pay valuations to a degree that cannot be explained by income and substitution effects; responses can be strongly influenced by what (from the perspective of a theory of rational choice) is irrelevant information, such as the starting-point for iterated bidding; and binary-choice questions tend to elicit higher valuations than open-ended ones.

It also seems clear that these disparities are not specific to CV surveys. Similar effects can be generated in controlled experiments in which subjects make decisions involving real trades in private-consumption goods. Thus these disparities cannot be attributed solely to the hypothetical nature of the questions in CV surveys, or to the difficulties in eliciting preferences for public goods. The best available explanations, I suggest, are provided by psychologically based theories of decision-making, such as the theories of reference-dependent preferences and response compatibility.

It remains an open question, however, how wide the domain is in which such theories apply. One possibility is that these theories apply to economic behaviour in general, and that the Hicksian theory which economists have used to model consumer choice is fundamentally flawed. An alternative possibility is that the learning and feedback mechanisms which operate in real markets tend to induce behaviour which is consistent with Hicksian theory, and that it is only in the absence of these mechanisms that non-Hicksian psychological effects come into play.

Two lines of enquiry thus suggest themselves. One is to investigate the learning and feedback mechanisms in markets, and to try to discover whether these mechanisms tend to reward some decision-making routines or heuristics more than others. The investigations outlined in Section 6.6, of how WTP and WTA bids are revised in repeated auctions, are examples of this research strategy. *If* it emerged that the mismatch between behaviour and Hicksian theory is eliminated or greatly reduced by market forces, it could be argued that individuals do indeed have Hicksian preferences; the challenge for CV researchers would then be to design survey methods which could elicit those preferences in the absence of real markets.

The other line of enquiry starts from the thought that the non-Hicksian regularities that are found in responses to CV surveys may be properties of decision-making in general. Thus, the aim is to build new theories of decision-making which can account for the main disparities between observations and Hicksian theory, but which still model individuals' preferences in a way that can be tested against observations of market behaviour and that permits some form of cost–benefit analysis. CV techniques would then need to be adapted so as to elicit non-Hicksian preferences.

For what it is worth, my own hunch is that both lines of research will be productive, and that they will converge. Market experience will be found to induce some kinds of decision-making consistency, but these will not always be the kinds of consistency that economists have come to expect.

REFERENCES

Arrow, K., Solow, R., Portney, P., Leamer, E., Radner, R., and Schuman, H. (1993), *Report of the NOAA Panel on Contingent Valuation*, Report to the General Counsel of the US National Oceanic and Atmospheric Administration, Resources for the Future, Washington.

Bateman, I. J., Langford, I. II., Turner, R. K., Willis, K. G., and Harrod, G. D. (1995), 'Elicitation and Truncation Effects in Contingent Valuation Studies', *Ecological Economics*, 12: 161–79.

Becker, G. M., DeGroot, M. H., and Marschak, J. (1964), 'Measuring Utility by a Single-Response Sequential Method', *Behavioral Science*, 9: 226–32.

Bishop, R. C., and Heberlein, T. A. (1979), 'Measuring Values of Extramarket Goods: Are Indirect Measures Biased?' *American Journal of Agricultural Economics*, 61: 926–30.

Boyle, K. J., R. C., Bishop, and M. P. Welsh, (1985), 'Starting Point Bias in Contingent Valuation Surveys', *Land Economics*, 61: 188–94.

Coursey, D. L., Hovis, J. L., and Schulze, W. D. (1987), 'The Disparity between Willingness to Accept and Willingness to Pay Measures of Value', *Quarterly Journal of Economics*, 102: 679–90.

Eisenberger, R., and Weber, M. (1993), 'Willingness-to-Pay and Willingness-to-Accept for Risky and Ambiguous Lotteries', mimeo, Lehrstuhl für ABWL, University of Mannheim.

Grether, D. M. and Plott, C. R. (1979), 'Economic Theory of Choice and the Preference Reversal Phenomenon', *American Economic Review*, 69: 623–38.

Hanemann, W. M. (1991), 'Willingness to Pay and Willingness to Accept: How Much can they Differ?' *American Economic Review*, 81, 635–47.

Hicks, J. R. (1943), 'The Four Consumer Surpluses', *Review of Economic Studies*, 8: 108–16.

——(1956), *A Revision of Demand Theory*, Clarendon Press, Oxford.

Hoehn, J. P., and Randall, A. (1987), 'A Satisfactory Benefit–Cost Indicator from Contingent Valuation', *Journal of Environmental Economics and Management*, 14: 226–47.

Holt, C. A. (1986), 'Preference Reversals and the Independence Axiom', *American Economic Review*, 76: 508–15.

Jones-Lee, M. W., Hammerton, M., and Philips, P. R. (1985), 'The Value of Safety: Results of a National Sample Survey', *Economic Journal*, 95: 49–72.

Kahneman, D., and Tversky, A. (1979), 'Prospect Theory: An Analysis of Decision under Risk', *Econometrica*, 47: 263–91.

——Knetsch, J. L., and Thaler, R. H. (1990), 'Experimental Tests of the Endowment Effect and the Coase Theorem', *Journal of Political Economy*, 98: 1325–48.

Karni, E., and Z. Safra, (1987), ' "Preference Reversal" and the Observability of Preferences by Experimental Methods', *Econometrica*, 55: 675–85.

Knetsch, J. L. (1989), 'The Endowment Effect and Evidence of Nonreversible Indifference Curves', *American Economic Review*, 79: 1277–84.

——and Sinden, J. A. (1984), 'Willingness to Pay and Compensation Demanded: Experimental Evidence of an Unexpected Disparity in Measures of Value', *Quarterly Journal of Economics*, 99: 507–21.

Knez, M., Smith, V. L., and Williams, A. W. (1985), 'Individual Rationality, Market Rationality, and Value Estimation', *American Economic Review*, Papers and Proceedings, 75: 397–402.

Kriström, B. (1993), 'Comparing Continuous and Discrete Valuation Questions', *Environmental and Resource Economics*, 3: 63–71.

Loomes, G. (1994), 'Valuing Health and Safety: Some Economic and Psychological Issues', paper presented at Seventh International Conference on the Foundations of Utility, Risk and Decision Theory, Oslo, July.

——and Sugden, R. (1983), 'A Rationale for Preference Reversal', *American Economic Review*, 73: 428–32.

Mitchell, R. C., and Carson, R.T. (1989), *Using Surveys to Value Public Goods: The Contingent Valuation Method*, Resources for the Future, Washington.

Payne, J. W., J. R., Bettman, and E. J. Johnson, (1992), 'Behavioral Decision Research: A Constructive Processing Perspective', *Annual Review of Psychology*, 42: 87–131.

Randall, A., and Stoll, J. R. (1980), 'Consumer's Surplus in Commodity Space', *American Economic Review*, 70: 449–55.

Roberts, K. J., Thompson, M. E., and Pawlyk, P. W. (1985), 'Contingent Valuation of Recreational Diving at Petroleum Rigs, Gulf of Mexico', *Transactions of the American Fisheries Society*, 114: 214–19.

Rowe, R. D., d'Arge, R. C., and Brookshire, D. S. (1980), 'An Experiment on the Economic Value of Visibility', *Journal of Environmental Economics and Management*, 7: 1–19.

Sellar, C., Stoll, J. R., and Chavas, J. P. (1985), 'Validation of Empirical Measures of Welfare Change: A Comparison of Nonmarket Techniques', *Land Economics*, 61: 156–75.

Shogren, J. F., Shin, S. Y., Hayes, D. J., and Kliebenstein, J. B. (1994), 'Resolving Differences in Willingness to Pay and Willingness to Accept', *American Economic Review*, 84: 255–70.

Slovic, P. and Lichtenstein, S. (1983), 'Preference Reversals: A Broader Perspective', *American Economic Review*, 73: 596–605.

—— Griffin, D., and Tversky, A. (1990), 'Compatibility Effects in Judgement and Choice', in R. M. Hogarth (ed.), *Insights in Decision Making: Theory and Applications*, Chicago University Press.

Tversky, A., and Kahneman, D. (1974), 'Judgment under Uncertainty: Heuristics and Biases', *Science*, no. 185: 1124–31.

——and——(1991), 'Loss Aversion in Riskless Choice: A Reference-Dependent Model', *Quarterly Journal of Economics*, 106: 1039–61.

——Sattath, S., and Slovic, P. (1988), 'Contingent Weighting in Judgment and Choice', *Psychological Review*, 95: 371–84.

——Slovic, P. and D. Kahneman, (1990), 'The Causes of Preference Reversal', *American Economic Review*, 80: 204–17.

Vickrey, W. (1961), 'Counterspeculation, Auctions, and Competitive Social Tenders', *Journal of Finance*, 16: 8–37.

Viscusi, W. K., Magat, W. A., and Huber, J. (1987), 'An Investigation of the Rationality of Consumer Valuations of Multiple Health Risks', *RAND Journal of Economics*, 18: 465–79.

PART II

Methodology

7

Doubt, Doubts, and Doubters: The Genesis of a New Research Agenda?

KEVIN J. BOYLE
JOHN C. BERGSTROM

7.1. INTRODUCTION

The first contingent valuation (CV) study was conducted in the early 1960s (Davis, 1963), a small number of studies were conducted in the 1970s (Hammack and Brown, 1974; Randall *et al.*, 1974; Brookshire *et al.*, 1976; Bishop and Heberlein, 1979), and the 1980s and 1990s have experienced an explosion of contingent valuation studies (Carson *et al.*, 1992). Doubters have not been reticent in expressing their concerns about CV. Early concerns were succinctly expressed by Scott when he characterized CV with the statement 'ask a hypothetical question and you will get a hypothetical response' 1965: 37.

While research exploring the validity and reliability of CV estimates has evolved through a sometimes focused and sometimes random process over the last two decades, criticisms of CV have generally been sporadic, with the same doubts being rehashed over and over again. This evolution changed dramatically with the Exxon Valdez oil spill in 1989. No longer was CV an intellectual curiosity of practitioners or a tool of Government economists where the results of a cost–benefit analysis would only indirectly affect a broad segment of society. CV became the focal point in determining a liability payment by a single, but large, corporation, Exxon. Exxon brought a number of economists together to attack the credibility of CV, focusing on the measurement of non-use values to support their legal defence in the natural-resources damage litigation ensuing from the Exxon Valdez oil spill.[1] The focus of the critiques was on non-use values because this component of value was expected to be a large portion of any monetary damage claim put forward by the federal and state trustees responsible for protecting the damaged resources. After the case was settled out of court Exxon documented its major critiques of CV estimates of non-use values in a

---

[1] The senior author of this paper, Boyle, worked for Exxon as a paid consultant in the natural-resource damage litigation arising from the Exxon Valdez oil spill.

book edited by Hausman (1993) entitled *Contingent Valuation: A Critical Assessment*. Although the experiments presented in the Hausman book focused specifically on the application of CV to the measurement of non-use values, the doubts expressed were implicitly extended, perhaps not accidentally, to CV measurements of use values.

In response to this book, which many considered to express the jaded opinions of consultants to Exxon, the United States National Oceanic and Atmospheric Administration (NOAA) commissioned an independent 'Contingent Valuation Panel . . . to evaluate the use of [contingent valuation] . . . in determining nonuse values' (NOAA, 1993: 4610). The NOAA Panel concluded that CV estimates of non-use values do 'convey useful information' (ibid.) when their proposed guide-lines for conducting a CV study are followed. The outcome of the Exxon-funded critique and NOAA response clearly sent the message that conditions for conducting CV studies had changed. Doubters now had a solid foothold to express their doubts and supporters of CV were forced to recognize a well-organized and -financed attack on CV methodologies.

CV research, as a cohesive investigation, is incomplete and many hard questions remain. By focusing on these questions, rather than taking prematurely fast and firm positions, it may be possible to facilitate a more constructive debate. In the mean time, a healthy dose of concern is important in the application, use, and interpretation of CV. This is true for any empirical methodology, but doubts and scepticism are not sufficient to dismiss any analytical tool. The current debate helps to focus the issues of concern in the application of CV. In the remainder of this chapter we identify what we believe are some of the more important issues facing CV applications today. Before turning to these specific issues, we attempt to set the current debate over the validity of CV in a broader context.

7.2. A BROADER VIEW OF THE ISSUE OF CONCERN

The Hausman book is not the first assessment of the 'state of the art' of CV, and the NOAA Panel's report is not the first attempt to develop guide-lines for conducting CV studies. Cummings *et al.* (1986) did the first assessment of CV and proposed some very restrictive 'reference operating conditions' where CV was deemed to work well. The Cummings book, like the Hausman book, was denigrated by some critics but for the opposite reason. The US Environmental Protection Agency (EPA) provided funding for the assessment that led to the book and some viewed this as an attempt to deem CV as good enough for government work and to avoid additional funding of costly validation studies.

Fischoff and Furby proposed conditions for a 'satisfactory (CV) transaction' where respondents 'are fully informed, uncoerced, and able to identify their own best interests' (1988: 148). The Fischoff and Furby contribution has some credibility because they are generally deemed to be outsiders to the CV debate. They explicitly acknowledged the hypothetical nature of CV and asserted that 'specifying all relevant features and ensuring they have been understood, is essential to staging transactions. Unless a feature is specified explicitly and comprehensively, [CV respondents]...must guess' (ibid. 179–80). They go on to state that 'ensuring understanding is the responsibility of those who pose the transaction' (ibid. 180). At this juncture, Fischoff and Furby implicitly appear to be judging CV against an absolute criterion, establishing a satisfactory transaction. Two sides to this debate arise. A pragmatic approach would reveal that consumers do not have full information when making market decisions, so why should such an ideal be applied to CV applications? On the other hand, consumers can choose among the information when making market decisions, and we do not know what information they use, so we must provide as much information as possible. This position does not, however, recognize potential cognitive overload by respondents and the heuristics they may employ when answering CV questions in this context.

Despite the fact that three decades have elapsed since the publication of Scott's article, the basic critique of CV has changed little. Hausman states in the preface to his edited book that 'CV...differs significantly from most empirical research in economics, which is based on market data caused by real-world decisions made by consumers and firms' (1993: vii). The basic concern still centres around the hypothetical nature of CV; money is not actually exchanged. Although revealed behaviour results in the estimation of Marshallian surplus, which is not the desired Hicksian compensating or equivalent welfare measure (Mäler, 1974; Just et al., 1982; Freeman, 1993), the doubters are more confident in economic theory and econometrics to unravel Hicksian surplus than they are in individuals' statements of value. The doubters appear readily to accept the use of economic theory to establish Willig (1976) bounds or a combination of theory and econometrics to derive exact (Hicksian) welfare measures (McKenzie and Pearce, 1976; Hausman, 1981).

CV practitioners, on the other hand, have confidence that responses to hypothetical questions will approximate behaviour when money is actually exchanged, yielding acceptable estimates of Hicksian welfare. In the domain of use values a number of field and laboratory experiments lend credence to this confidence (Bishop et al., 1983; Dickie et al., 1987; Kealy et al., 1988). These comparisons of CV estimates with actual cash transactions are known as tests of criterion validity (Carmines and Zeller, 1979). No criterion validity studies exist to provide a comparable level of confidence in CV applications to the estimation of non-use values.

Fundamental problems exist with both the Hausman and NOAA Contingent Valuation Panel positions. The Hausman book and the NOAA

Panel report do not clearly distinguish applications of CV to measuring use values from applications to measuring non-use values. There has been much more research conducted to investigate CV applications to use values than to non-use values (Cummings *et al.*, 1986; Mitchell and Carson, 1989; Carson *et al.*, 1992) and, consequently, there is less controversy surrounding the use of CV to measure use values. People who are unfamiliar, or casually familiar, with the CV debate have construed the Hausman book and NOAA Panel report to criticize all applications of CV, not just those to measuring non-use values. Both works, however, are concerned with potential problems associated with attempting to use CV for measuring non-use values. The issue of concern is also clouded by many CV studies estimating total values or option prices that include both use and non-use components.

Critiques in the Hausman book implicitly evaluate CV on an absolute scale where the outcome is either right or wrong, not in the context of errors involved in the application of other empirical methodologies. The NOAA Panel recognized this inconsistency when they deemed CV acceptable 'by the standards that seem to be implicit in similar contexts' (1993: 4610). For example, one line of criticism follows from the fact that CV estimates may be inconsistent with what is suggested by economic theory (Desvousges *et al.*, 1992; Diamond *et al.*, 1993). These inconsistencies also arise in the analysis of market data, but the conditions of economic theory (e.g., adding up, homogeneity, symmetry) are often imposed on the data to ensure estimates are consistent with theory (Deaton and Muellbauer, 1980). The Hausman critique also overlooks the fact that market data are collected by some type of survey and can be subject to some of the same concerns expressed regarding CV. The NOAA Panel position on CV standards is of concern because it proposed guide-lines that in many cases are without citations to document the recommended protocol and to place it in context with the literatures on economic welfare theory, survey research methodologies, existing valuation research, or comparable empirical analyses.

Within a research agenda, practical applications aside, objective rules must be employed to evaluate the credibility of any empirical methodology, and CV is no exception. The usefulness of a methodology for practical applications arises from the extent to which the methodology is capable of meeting a desired theoretical construct. In CV research, this is generally evaluated in terms of the validity and reliability of value estimates (Carmines and Zeller, 1979; Mitchell and Carson, 1989). Within this context, Fischoff and Furby proposed a conceptual framework for the conduct of CV studies, but they do not delve substantially into the context for accomplishing their proposals.

The NOAA Panel considered more of the details of accomplishing a CV study of non-use values. They addressed sample type and size, minimizing non-response, using personal interviews, pre-testing for interviewer effects, reporting of sampling procedures, questionnaire pre-testing, conservative design, using willingness to pay, using referendum questions, accurate commodity descriptions, pre-testing photographs, reminders of substitutes, and various other issues (1993: 4611–14). Despite the prognostications of this esteemed group of economists, hard questions remain. For example, CV applications have typically employed mail surveys and the Panel did not discuss in detail why mail surveys are inappropriate and personal interviews are more appropriate. Referendum questions are simply dichotomous-choice questions with the payment vehicle posed as a referendum. Considering Fischoff and Furby's conceptual protocol, a referendum is not the right payment vehicle for all social contexts, i.e. respondents may know the decision or payment will be not be established by referendum vote. What if reminding respondents of substitutes does not affect value estimates? Does this mean that CV is fundamentally flawed because respondents do not consider substitutes when formulating value responses, or did the investigator specify the wrong set of substitutes, or do respondents consider substitutes without prompting? Thus, while helpful in raising questions for the CV research agenda, the NOAA Panel's recommendations also do not go far enough in answering the hard questions that must be addressed when designing a CV study.

In the ensuing discussion we focus on selected issues associated with applying CV which appear to us to be of greatest current concern in the literature. This is done within the context of the CV literature. Issues that affect CV values estimates, but are not unique to the method, such as the choice of a functional form in data analyses, will not be extensively discussed. The discussion is organized around value conceptualization, questionnaire design (information issues and CV methodology), and data analysis.

7.3. VALUE CONCEPTUALIZATION

Defining the value to be estimated is a necessary prerequisite of any valuation study regardless of whether CV, some other non-market valuation methodology, or market data are to be employed. Three issues rise to the forefront in CV studies: (1) understanding option price; (2) sorting out non-use values; and (3) the relationship between estimates of willingness to pay (WTP) and willingness-to-accept compensation (WTA). Option price and non-use values are interrelated because non-use values can be components of option prices. Option price and non-use values can also be measured as either WTP or WTA. Given that option price is the measure of an individual's value under conditions of uncertainty, this provides a useful starting-point for the discussion. The non-use value issue, however, is simmering close below the surface.

7.3.1.   Option Price

Let us start with a simple example where

$$V(p_{gw}, P_s, I; GW) \qquad (7.1)$$

is an indirect utility function representing an individual's optimal choices regarding consumption of groundwater; p_{gw} is the price of potable groundwater, P_s is a vector of prices of substitute sources of potable water, I is income, and GW is a vector of non-use arguments relating to groundwater quality. All other terms are suppressed for notational convenience. Let us assume that there are a variety of discrete threats to the groundwater resource and we wish to measure the value of reducing the probability of contamination. The appropriate measure of value is option price (Bishop, 1982; Smith, 1983; Freeman, 1993; Ready, 1993). Option price (*op*) can be defined by

$$\sum_i \pi_i' V(p_{gw,i}, P_s, I_i - op; GW_i) = \sum_i \pi_i V(P_{gw,i}, P_s, I_i; GW_i) \quad i = 1, \ldots, n$$

$$(7.2)$$

where π_i is the probability of alternative groundwater conditions, and $p_{gw,i}$, I_i, and GW_i are indexed by i to indicate that they may be influenced by the groundwater condition. The effects on p_{gw} and GW are obvious, while it is assumed that I (income) is net of health expenditures resulting from the consumption of contaminated groundwater. Option price (*op*) in this example, which assumes supply uncertainty and demand certainty, is a state-independent payment to reduce the probability of contamination. If π_j is the subset of probabilities associated with groundwater contamination, then $\pi_i' \leqslant \pi_i$ for at least one i.[2]

Three issues can be developed from this simple example. The first arises from a recognition that option price depends critically on the change in the probability of contamination. In the CV literature, practitioners have tended to overlook probabilities in the design of CV questions and in the analyses of CV data (Boyle and Bishop, 1987; Desvousges *et al.*, 1987; Loomis, 1987). Some notable exceptions do exist, including studies which attempt to incorporate the role of subjective probabilities into CV survey design and data analyses (Smith and Desvousges, 1987; Edwards, 1988; Loomis and duVair, 1993; Bergstrom and Dorfman, 1994). If option price is to be estimated, the CV question should be framed to include both the baseline (π_i') and alternative (π) probabilities. This information is subsequently utilized to analyse and interpret CV responses. This is particularly true for applications of dichotomous-choice questions where estimated

[2] Option value is not considered here because it is simply the difference between option price and expected consumer surplus (Bishop, 1982). It is an artefact of uncertainty that does not arise from arguments in individuals' preferences.

equations, based on the value definition, provide the basis for deriving estimates of central tendency (Hanemann, 1984; Cameron, 1988; McConnell, 1990).

If information regarding the change in the likelihood of contamination is missing from the CV question, respondents guess at the current and future likelihoods of contamination, and there is no assurance that all respondents will impose the same assumptions (Lindell and Earle, 1983). When different respondents impose different assumptions, then CV responses can only be assumed to be loosely associated with the desired policy value and aggregating individual CV responses may be akin to adding apples and oranges, whereas under the best of conditions, perhaps, the problem may be no worse than aggregating different varieties of apples. The absence of probability information appears to be an act of accidental omission in many cases. In some cases, however, CV exercises are not well-linked to physical changes that are occurring in the resource. In the case of groundwater contamination, CV studies have been hindered by the absence of dose-response models that reveal how the policy being valued will affect groundwater contamination (Boyle *et al.*, 1994). Thus, physical scientists may not be providing all of the information needed to effectively apply CV value estimates to assess specific environmental policy and management actions.

The second issue also relates to uncertainty—even if information on the likelihood of contamination is provided in a CV question, respondents may reject this information in favour of their own subjective perceptions of contamination. In a classic study, Lichtenstein *et al.* (1978) demonstrate that people tend to overestimate the likelihood of low-probability events and underestimate the likelihood of higher-probability events (see also Kask and Maani, 1992). If this is the case, providing information on the likelihood of contamination in the CV question may not be sufficient; it may also be necessary to elicit respondents' subjective perceptions of the likelihood of contamination in the survey. Doing this, however, opens other potentially undesirable doors. Should subjective probabilities be elicited prior or subsequent to the CV question? The former can be used as exogenous regressors, but may not represent those used in answering the CV question if important information is contained in the question itself. Subjective probabilities elicited immediately subsequent to the CV question may be more representative of the information respondents used in answering the CV question, but this data is endogenous to the valuation exercise. These issues have not been explored in the CV literature, and if they have been explored by social psychologists in other contexts, this literature has not been brought to bear on CV. If respondents employ subjective probabilities when answering CV questions, the resulting value estimates are only appropriate for valuing a policy that actually reduces the probability of contamination, for example, by the proportion that respondents subjectively employ. Different respondents may employ different subjective probabilities, further complicating the interpretation of CV data unless this issue is explicitly addressed in the analysis.

Another implication of subjective editing is that CV studies which attempt to measure values under certainty may actually be measuring values under uncertainty—that is, option price. For example, many CV studies are framed to estimate values under conditions of supply certainty. However, the description of potential effects of a proposed policy in a CV question may not be clear to respondents or respondents may not believe that the outcome of the policy will occur with certainty. The consequence is that respondents may edit the information presented, transforming the CV exercise to valuation under uncertainty. Even if supply is certain and the CV description is completely clear, respondents may be providing option prices if their demand is uncertain. Thus, changes in probabilities, whether objective or subjective, are fundamental to CV studies and the ramifications of this theme are relatively unexplored in the CV literature.

The third issue relates to the components of option price. Since option price can be interpreted as economic value under uncertainty (Randall, 1991), it can include both use and non-use values as components. An ongoing debate among researchers and decision-makers is the relative importance of these two component values while the interrelationship of these components remains unknown (Fisher and Raucher, 1984). For example, are use and non-use values complementary or substitutes?

The bottom line is that although option price is perhaps the most widely estimated value in the CV literature, this value is generally treated as a black box, without concern for the component parts. Such benign neglect may be acceptable in a policy context where option price is the desired welfare measure, but this state of affairs is simply unacceptable from a research perspective when considering the validity and reliability of CV estimates.

7.3.2.   Non-Use Values

This is not the place to debate the validity of non-use values and their relevance for public policy (Kopp, 1992); rather, non-use values are accepted for this discussion and the estimation of these values is considered (Bishop and Welsh, 1992; Carson *et al.*, Chapter 4 of this volume). We consider here two main areas of investigation in the literature: alternative CV approaches for measuring non-use values and explorations of revealed-preference techniques for measuring non-use values.

With respect to CV approaches for measuring non-use values, one line of research starts with the estimation of option price, or total value under conditions of certainty, and then estimates non-use values conditioned on the absence of any use opportunities (Boyle and Bishop, 1987). An alternative approach asks respondents for total values and to allocate their responses to a menu of component values, which includes several types of non-use value 'motivations' (altruism, bequest, etc.) (Walsh *et al.*, 1984; Loomis, 1987). The debate over these two approaches has been going on for over a decade without any resolution, or any solid research to support either position.

The former approach has the advantage that non-use values are conditioned on a specific set of circumstances—but is this set of circumstances correct for the policy question at hand? If embedding does occur as suggested by Kahneman and Knetsch (1992), then this approach may reduce the potential for respondents to provide responses composed of use and non-use values when only non-use values are requested. If use and non-use values are complementary, then non-use values are overestimated if use truly would not be precluded. The converse occurs if they are substitutes. Conditioning non-use values on the absence of use values would be irrelevant if these component values are neither complements nor substitutes.

The menu approach avoids having non-use values conditioned on the absence of use values, but has a comparable drawback. Unless value components each arise from weakly separable components of individuals' preferences, the component values will not be additive. If preferences for component values are not separable, estimates for individual components are conditioned on the sequence in which the researcher designs the menu of responses. In addition, questions arise regarding whether the components of the non-use menu are appropriate or whether respondents are answering the valuation question in the only way possible given the framing of the response options.

In a recent article, Larson (1993) challenges the conventional wisdom that CV is the only game in town when it comes to measuring non-use values, and develops a conceptual framework for revealed-preference measures of non-use values. For opponents of CV this makes the method obsolete whereas for proponents it provides an empirical testing-ground for validation of non-use value measures. Larson's conceptual framework draws upon such activities as money and time committed to environmental NGOs as revealed-behaviour linkages to non-use values. While these activities are likely indicators of non-use values, they may also contain a use component which is difficult to separate out from the non-use component. Environmental-NGO members, for example, may receive publications to read and other services which contribute to use values (Portney, 1994). In addition, individuals holding non-use values who have not demonstrated any choice-based behaviour are omitted.

Another more general problem exists in much of the non-use value literature—non-use values are not well understood and defined. Misunderstandings begin with the label ('non-use', 'existence', 'bequest', and 'passive use') and carry through to empirical estimates. All that appears to be clearly

known is that non-use values do not *require* any revealed-preference behaviour or direct interaction with the environmental resource. Beyond this
point the waters become murky rather quickly, precluding progress regarding the validation of economic estimates of non-use values using CV or some
other technique. Since explorations of alternatives to CV for measuring non-
use values are in their infancy, the spotlight has been on CV as the sole
technique for measuring non-use values. Issues surrounding the definition,
measurement, and application of non-use values, however, are much larger
than concerns one might have about CV as an economic valuation technique, but at this time the two (CV and non-use values) appear to be
systemically rather than fraternally connected.

7.3.3.   WTP and WTA Disparity

The CV literature has a number of studies demonstrating substantial empirical differences between WTP and WTA (Bishop *et al.*, 1983; Knetsch and
Sinden, 1984; Brookshire and Coursey, 1987; Coursey *et al.*, 1987). Economic theory suggests that the difference between WTP and WTA should be
small if income effects are small (Just *et al.*, 1982; Freeman, 1993) or close
substitutes exist for the commodity being valued (Hanemann, 1991). However, even when these conditions appear to be met in empirical studies,
unreasonably large disparities between WTP and WTA have been observed.
Kahneman and Tversky (1984) use 'prospect theory' to suggest that the large
disparities between WTP and WTA might be explained by respondents
shifting reference points when valuing gains and losses of equal magnitudes.
At this point, however, the disparity between WTP and WTA observed in
empirical CV studies remains an enigma. Problems with adequately explaining observed disparities between WTP and WTA, and unrealistically large
estimates of WTP relative to WTA, prompted the NOAA Panel to recommend the use of WTP.

In many natural resource and environmental situations, WTA is the
theoretically correct welfare measure (Vatn and Bromley, 1994). This
includes situations, for example, where an individual may suffer the loss of
use of a natural resource over which they hold initial rights. In such a case,
the correct Hicksian welfare measure is the minimum compensation it would
take to bring the individual back up to his or her pre-loss utility level (Just
et al., 1982; Freeman, 1993). Because of the theoretical relevance of WTA
under certain property-right structures, it seems inconsistent simultaneously
to advocate the use of CV and exclude applications to WTA. For example,
Coursey *et al.* (1987) found that WTP is stable in repeated trials, while WTA
declines over repeated trials and asymptotically approaches WTP. These
experimental results, although not directly transferable to CV applications,
do suggest possible means for reducing the disparity between WTP and
WTA in CV surveys.

In this section we first discuss issues surrounding the question format used to elicit CV responses. Implicit in the Fischoff and Furby article is the recognition that the design of CV questions for eliciting values contains two different, but related, components. The first is the description of the commodity to be valued (commodity description) and the second is the description of the institutional setting for valuing the commodity (contingent market). Neither component stands alone, but each raises separate issues to be considered.

7.4.1.   Commodity Description

The commodity description constitutes the bridge between the theoretical definition of value and respondents' value responses. As such, this is the crucial component of any CV study, because it tells respondents what they are buying and flaws in this information can undermine the entire valuation exercise. The concerns here can be succinctly expressed with three questions. What information do respondents need to answer CV questions? What information unduly influences CV responses, i.e. leads respondents to understate or overstate their values? And is it possible to create information overload by providing respondents with an overly detailed commodity description?

Referring back to the groundwater option price in Equation (7.2), the commodity description would detail the contaminants and the effects of contamination. The baseline likelihood of contamination would be presented along with its proposed change. The availability and cost of substitute sources of potable water would also be provided, as advocated by the NOAA Panel. This collective information is what Fischoff and Furby refer to as the 'good'. They state that 'achieving ... clarity in [the commodity description] ... is a craft, but one that can be aided by the scientific study of potential pitfalls' and 'has been part of the research methodology of every social science that asks people to answer unfamiliar questions' (1988: 154). A number of studies have found the addition or deletion of information in commodity descriptions can have statistically significant effects on CV responses (Bergstrom and Stoll, 1989; Bergstrom et al., 1989, 1990; Boyle, 1989; Poe, 1993; Munro and Hanley, Chapter 9 of this volume), highlighting the need to investigate appropriate commodity descriptions.

Bergstrom et al. (1990) group information used to describe an environmental commodity under two broad headings, characteristic and service information. Characteristic information describes the objective physical attributes of an environmental commodity (e.g. groundwater quantity and quality). Service information describes how changes in commodity characteristics affect use and non-use service flows (e.g. drinking-water services and existence value of clean aquifers). This may be less important for the estimation of use than non-use values because users may be relatively more familiar with the implications of a change in the resource. If users have not experienced the proposed condition of the resource, service information may still be of primary importance when individuals are answering CV questions designed to elicit use values (Boyle *et al.*, 1993).

Identifying appropriate types and amounts of characteristic and service information to describe an environmental commodity adequately is a difficult task. Additionally, relevant information is not limited to that regarding the characteristics and services of the environmental commodity *per se*. The NOAA Panel, for example, stresses the need to include substitute information in a CV survey. But the literature is not clear as to how much substitute information is 'enough'. In a meta-analysis of CV studies of groundwater value (Boyle *et al.*, 1994), information regarding the cost of substitutes significantly reduced WTP responses while information about substitute availability did not. Cummings *et al.* (1994) have also shown that the provision of information on substitutes can influence values in a laboratory setting. Considering the research agenda, particularly in the context of field experiments, addressing substitutes is not easy. If CV estimates are not statistically sensitive to information on substitutes, a number of plausible explanations arise: respondents neglected to consider substitutes so the CV estimates are flawed, likely overestimating the true value; the investigator provided the wrong set of substitutes so the study design is flawed; or respondents were already considering substitutes so the provision of this information in the CV experiment was redundant.[3]

The NOAA Panel proposed a 'burden of proof' test where, in the absence 'of reliable reference surveys, ... pretesting and other experiments', practitioners must show that each CV 'survey does not suffer from the problems that their guidelines are intended to avoid' (1993: 4614). As the example in the preceding paragraph illustrates, the burden of proof can constitute a formidable obstacle. Statistical results, whether from a CV study or a study using market data, can be subject to multiple interpretations and identifying appropriate conclusions can often be difficult at best. The correct set of substitutes may vary across goods and sample populations, making it difficult to establish a set of reference surveys. These concerns are not unique to substitutes, but may be pervasive throughout commodity descriptions.

Ferreting out an appropriate commodity description has generally been based on the issue to be valued, discussions with individuals knowledgeable with the valuation issue, the theoretical definition of value, previous studies of similar topics, and the investigators' experience. This is where the 'craft'

---

[3] It is assumed that the CV experiment would have a design where respondents would be randomly stratified into those who do, and those who do not, receive information on substitutes.

that Fischoff and Furby discuss plays a crucial role in the design process. Refining the survey instrument typically involves the use of focus groups, one-on-one pre-tests, and more recently verbal protocols allowing the survey instrument to be tailored to the specific application (Desvousges *et al.*, 1992; McClelland *et al.*, 1993).

One criticism of such an individualized, interactive approach to survey design is that information provision may become endogenous to the survey process. How does this repeated interaction affect the researchers' perceptions of the valuation problem (e.g. does the nature of the commodity to be valued change)? Furthermore, the iterative nature of such an approach invites the CV researchers to decide, on an *ad hoc* basis, to add or drop information based on insights gained from focus groups, pre-tests, etc. If statistical tests are not conducted to investigate the effects of adding or deleting information, how do we know what the final effects of such changes will be on CV responses?

Simply put, we do not know what information respondents need, so information provision often appears to be a hit-or-miss attempt to provide accurate and complete information, perhaps subject to the whims of individual investigators. In addition, commodity descriptions are often constrained by the availability of technical details regarding proposed changes in provision. Progress demands a systematic research programme to identify and classify the specific types of information respondents commonly use when answering CV questions and how this varies across applications and/or respondents. Furthermore, such a research process must be conducted in an interdisciplinary context to improve the technical information that often constitutes the basis of commodity descriptions.

7.4.2. Contingent Market or Referendum Description

Four issues are explored in this subsection: (1) choice of CV question format; (2) selection of a payment vehicle; (3) treatment of zero, protest, and misstated bids; and (4) mode of data collection. The NOAA Panel's recommendation of referendum questions provides an underlying linkage of these topics. Referendum questions are dichotomous-choice questions with the payment vehicle posed as a referendum vote.

7.4.2.1. *Dichotomous-Choice Questions*

A number of different formats have been used to frame CV questions, with dichotomous-choice, open-ended, and unanchored payment cards being most commonly employed in the literature today (for more discussion of CV question formats, see Langford and Bateman, Chapter 12 of this volume). The most important questions, however, centre on dichotomous-choice (DC) questions. A generic DC question, given a commodity description and appropriate payment vehicle, might be posed as:

Would you pay $ —— per year to reduce groundwater contamination so drinking water meets US Environmental Protection Agency safety standards?

The blank is filled in with a randomly assigned monetary amount (Cooper, 1993). This question can be modified to a referendum format:

Would you vote 'yes' on a referendum to reduce groundwater contamination so drinking water meets US Environmental Protection Agency safety standards and your personal cost would be $ ——?

The referendum format has been advocated by Hoehn and Randall (1987) using incentive-compatibility arguments. The referendum format is not universally applicable. Mitchell and Carson (1989) have argued that payment vehicles must be believable and neutral in the elicitation of values. The referendum framing of DC questions is not likely to satisfy the believability condition in the elicitation of many use values because referenda are not typically used to make money from these decisions. Thus, although DC questions are universally applicable, the referendum format is only applicable in narrower contexts.

The primary concern with DC questions is whether the monetary amount provides a value clue, thereby inadvertently affecting responses. Cooper and Loomis (1992) provide tentative evidence of these effects, and Shapiro (1968) has shown that this type of anchoring can arise even with the amount individuals pay for market goods. These effects can occur for traditional DC questions or for DC questions posed as a referendum, and may be more pronounced with multiple-bounded DC questions (McFadden, 1994). If the tentative evidence on anchoring proves to true, will DC maintain its current status as the fair-haired CV question format?

The anchoring concern in DC questions, however, is a prime example of the issue of relative errors discussed in the Introduction. If posting a price for a market good can influence what consumers will pay for a market good, this influence would be reflected in Marshallian estimates of consumer surplus. Is the anchoring effect in DC questions any worse than for market goods with posted prices? Within this context, a statistically significant anchoring effect is not sufficient to dismiss DC questions, but it is necessary to assess the extent of this impact relative to any similar effect in revealed-behaviour measures. Future research on CV questions should focus on the selection and effect of monetary amounts in DC questions, and the relative errors of value estimates derived from DC questions versus competing question formats (open-ended and unanchored payment cards).

7.4.2.2.   Payment Vehicle

Despite early evidence that payment vehicles can influence responses to CV questions (Rowe and Chestnut, 1983; Mitchell and Carson, 1985) no published research has been conducted to address this concern. The guiding principle has been the Mitchell and Carson (1989) believability and neutrality conditions, and with the extensive use of DC questions, the Hoehn and Randall (1987) incentive-compatibility argument is often invoked. In reality, payment vehicles are generally customized to each study and are refined in survey pre-testing, with no checks for undesirable effects of the payment vehicle on value estimates. The selection of payment vehicles would not pass the NOAA Panel's 'burden of proof' test of content validity (Carmines and Zeller, 1979), leaving a large hole in the CV literature.

Even DC questions posed as referenda are not without problems. The first is that 'DC' and 'referendum' are often used as synonyms to describe CV questions eliciting a yes/no response to a fixed monetary amount. This confusion has led some investigators to pose DC questions that do not use a referendum, while appealing to the Hoehn and Randall incentive-compatibility argument. As noted above, the referendum format does not always pass the Mitchell and Carson believability condition for some applications of DC questions. Finally, and most important, the institutional context of CV requires that respondents know how the payments will be collected. The referendum format must include an explanation of how the payments will be collected, e.g. per household fee on water bills, property taxes, income tax, etc. This brings us full circle to the conditions where payment vehicle effects were initially identified. The referendum format of DC questions may have desirable incentive properties for eliciting values, but the inclusion of a payment mechanism may have concurrent undesirable effects. The effects of payment vehicles simply can not continue to be overlooked from either a conceptual nor an empirical perspective.

7.4.3.3. *Zero, Protest, and Misstated Responses*

These are not issues that have been neglected in the CV literature, but they are far from being resolved. Given the discussion above, the initial focus here is with DC questions. 'No' responses to DC questions are generally probed for invalid responses, searching for free-riders, individuals protesting about the payment vehicle, etc. If the data are to be screened for invalid responses, 'yes' responses must also be examined, for example, to identify individuals who support the project behaving strategically. Beyond this consistency in the treatment of the data, no established theoretical criteria or generally accepted protocols exist for excluding observations from data analyses. It appears that a consensus exists that some observations may be invalid, but the exclusion of observations is generally undertaken using *ad hoc* criteria.

The NOAA Panel recommended allowing respondents the option of answering 'do not know' in addition to 'yes'/'no' when answering DC questions. An additional issue relates to individuals who do not value the good. Individuals who answer 'no', but hold a positive value, are treated the same as individuals who answer 'no' and hold a value of $0. Consideration of response distributions to other question formats, such as open-ended questions, suggests that a discrete spike might occur at $0 in the distribution of values. Perhaps individuals who answer 'no' to a DC question should be given the opportunity to answer '$0' and these responses should be modelled in the data analyses.

Concerns regarding data screening also apply to open-ended, unanchored payment cards, and other questioning formats. Open-ended questions typically result in zero bids and these bids are screened for protests and other types of invalid responses. Non-zero bids are also sometimes screened for invalid responses (e.g. a bid representing 25 per cent or more of someone's income might be interpreted as unreasonable or an error). Some investigators have used statistical routines to search for data outliers (Desvousges *et al.*, 1987). The fundamental concern remains; no established theoretical criteria or established protocols exist for excluding responses. Although the issue of zero values does not arise with most other question formats because an answer of '$0' is allowed, the NOAA Panel's concern of allowing 'do not know' responses applies to all questioning formats.

The issue of screening CV data for invalid responses cuts to the heart of the critique that CV is not based on actual consumers' actual market decisions (Diamond and Hausman, 1994). CV practitioners, by screening CV data, implicitly acknowledge that there is some merit to this critique (Stevens *et al.*, 1994). The implicit agreement does not extend beyond this initial acknowledgement. Critics appear to be arguing that the absence of cash transactions makes all CV responses flawed or that the share of invalid responses in the data makes it useless for statistical analyses. CV practitioners appear to believe that the share of individuals providing invalid CV responses is small and these responses can be identified and addressed in data analyses. This process is not easy. Why would someone who is behaving strategically reveal this motive to an interviewer? If direct revelation of ulterior motives is not possible, is there an objective way to identify strategic responses?

These concerns also apply to accidental misstatements of value when, for example, a respondent does not fully understand the valuation task. Respondents' misunderstandings of CV scenarios, from either incomplete or unclear commodity descriptions, may be the key reason for the embedding problem, which is on the 'front burner' in the current debate over the application of CV to measuring non-use values (Diamond and Hausman, 1994; Hanemann, 1994).

It is not an easy task to establish conditions for excluding responses from CV data. A profitable line of investigation, perhaps, involves identifying groups of individuals who are likely to misstate their values either purposely or inadvertently. The focus would be on whether responses by these individuals significantly influence estimated statistics. This is not substantially different to what some investigators have done when they use the data with and without invalid responses, but the investigations could be more focused in terms of economic theory and more rigorous in terms of statistical analyses. Researchers should investigate the appropriateness of the NOAA Panel's 'do not know' recommendation. This issue was already being invest-igated prior to the NOAA recommendation (Ready *et al.*, 1995). Zero-bidders in DC data also need to be investigated, as do other influential observations such as 'outliers' (Mitchell and Carson, 1989).

As a matter of perspective, it is important to recognize that screening of data occurs in all empirical analyses, even market data. For example, the US Department of Agriculture's Market News Service collects data on the sale prices and volumes of agricultural commodities. Data reported by sellers and buyers that is deemed to be misstated in an attempt to influence market conditions is excluded from reported market statistics.[4] The exclusion deci-sion is made by the individual who collects the market data and the indi-vidual's superior; no explicit theory or econometric analyses are used as a basis for exclusion. Some valid data may be excluded and some invalid data may be included. It is also important to recognize that individuals operating in wholesale markets might have more knowledge, ability, and incentives to influence survey outcomes than do respondents to CV surveys. Market data, like CV data, are often collected in a survey format, with all of the associated data-collection problems and with a greater likelihood of respondents behaving strategically. Again, we are back to the issue of relative errors.

7.4.3.4. *Mode of Data Collection*

The NOAA Panel's recommendation of personal interviews, and its state-ment that they believe that it is unlikely that reliable estimates of values could be elicited with mail surveys' (1993: 4608), hit a raw nerve among CV researchers and survey researchers who work with mail surveys. This is an example where a strong position has been taken without adequate reference to the literature. What is known in the literature on personal interviews and mail surveys that supports the NOAA Panel's position? Using personal interviewers allows an investigator more control over respondents' CV responses, but also introduces a potential interviewer effect. How should these countervailing effects be considered?

The vast majority of CV studies have been conducted using mail surveys because the per-observation cost is less than that of personal interview surveys and most university researchers do not have access to trained inter-viewers. These pragmatic considerations, however, are not sufficient to justify the extensive use of mail surveys; it must be demonstrated that mail surveys are capable of providing valid and reliable CV estimates. There are only a few studies in the literature that investigate alternative

---

[4] This information was received from Mr John Boyle (Kevin Boyle's father), who is a former employee of the Market New Service.

CV administrative modes, and these studies produce mixed or inconclusive results (Randall and Kriesel, 1990; Mannesto and Loomis, 1991; Loomis and King, 1994). Because of the dearth of research investigating the relative merits of different modes of administrating CV surveys, we believe this issue deserves high priority on the CV research agenda. With personal interviews being the most expensive form of primary-data collection, the benefits of establishing mail surveys as a credible mode for conducting CV surveys can be substantial.

7.4.4.   Analysis of CV Responses

Many contributions have been made to the CV literature in recent years in terms of analysing DC data (Cameron, 1988), functional form of valuation equations (Boyle, 1990), developing bid amounts for DC questions (Cooper, 1993), computing confidence intervals for DC means (Park *et al.*, 1991)—and the list goes on and on. Looking at the future research agenda, contributions in this area might be reaching diminishing returns. Sophisticated econometric models are intended primarily to recover information from poor data. Many of the recent contributions to the CV literature accept the quality of whatever data is available and concentrate on new econometric twists to develop what may be questionable insights. However, the greatest future pay-offs may lie in two areas: (1) better understanding of individual preferences for environmental commodities, with insights from a wide variety of disciplines including economics, psychology, marketing, and philosophy (Portney, 1994), and (2) improving CV data-collection efforts to enable clearer and more robust insights from empirical analyses of these data.

7.5.   CONCLUSIONS

The title of this chapter was posed as a question, so it is only appropriate to answer the question. The answer is implicit in the arguments presented within the chapter. The current debate surrounding CV has changed the rules of the game, suggesting the need for a more focused research agenda and improved study designs leading to clearer insights. This conclusion is emphasized by the NOAA Panel's 'burden of proof' condition. Rather than CV being innocent until proven guilty, the lasting impact of the Panel may be their judgement that CV estimates are guilty until proven innocent. Although the context for their pronouncement dealt with CV applications to non-use values in natural-resource damage litigation, it is clear that their guide-lines are being generally applied to all applications of CV. The loosely evolving nature of CV research and the lack of a revealed-preference connection for non-use values made the application of CV to the measurement of non-use values susceptible to criticism.

The basic argument against CV, that transactions involving cash do not occur, comes very close to rejecting the sovereignty of consumer demand in suggesting that consumers cannot decide what is in their best interest unless money changes hands. This seems to be a relatively strict and arbitrary condition. In fact, if CV did not exist, Exxon would have looked for another weak link to reduce their potential liability payment, even if the only opportunities were revealed-preference measurements. Thus, the issue that brought CV to its current contentious position might have focused on a revealed-preference measure within another context.

Hard-and-fast positions on any issue appear to shut off the research agenda prematurely. Research is about asking hard questions and subjecting these questions to objective and rigorous study. Researchers are trained to raise doubts and act as if we were all from Missouri—that is, before we reject or accept something as 'fact', we say, 'Show me!' A healthy dose of scepticism is important in the application, use, and interpretation of any empirical methodology. However, any empirical methodology, whether it deals with estimating economic values or testing an accused criminal's DNA, cannot be rejected out of hand by unsubstantiated doubt and scepticism.

REFERENCES

Bergstrom, J. C., and Dorfman, J. H. (1994), 'Commodity Information and Willingness-to-Pay for Groundwater Quality Protection', *Review of Agricultural Economics*, 16: 413–25.

—— and Stoll, J. R. (1989), 'Applications of Experimental Economics Concepts and Precepts to CVM Field Survey Procedures', *Western Journal of Agricultural Economics*, 14: 98–109.

—————— and Randall, A. (1989), 'Information Effects in Contingent Markets', *American Journal of Agricultural Economics*, 71: 683–91.

—————— and—— (1990), 'The Impact of Information on Environmental Commodity Valuation Decisions', *American Journal of Agricultural Economics*, 72: 614–21.

Bishop, R. C. (1982), 'Option Value: an Exposition and Extension', *Land Economics*, 58: 1–15.

—— and Heberlein, T. A. (1979), 'Measuring Values of Extra-Market Goods: Are Indirect Measures Biased?' *American Journal of Agricultural Economics*, 61: 926–30.

—— and—— (1990), 'The Contingent Valuation Method', in R. L. Johnson and G. V. Johnson (eds.), *Economic Valuation of Natural Resources*, Westview Press, Boulder, Colo.

—— and Welsh, M. P. (1992), 'Existence Values in Benefit–Cost Analysis and Damage Assessments', *Land Economics*, 68: 405–17.

—— Heberlein, T., and Kealy, M. J. (1983), 'Contingent Valuation of Environmental Assets: Comparison with a Simulated Market', *Natural Resources Journal*, 23: 619–34.

Boyle, K. J. (1989), 'Commodity Specification and the Framing of Contingent-Valuation Questions', *Land Economics*, 65: 57–63.

——(1990), 'Dichotomous-Choice, Contingent-Valuation Questions: Functional Form is Important', *Northeastern Journal of Agricultural and Resource Economics*, 19: 125–31.

——(1994), 'A Comparison of Contingent-Valuation Studies of Groundwater Protection', Staff Paper REP 456, Department of Resource Economics and Policy, University of Maine.

——and Bishop, R. C. (1987), 'Valuing Wildlife in Benefit–Cost Analyses: a Case Study Involving Endangered Species', *Water Resources Research*, 23: 943–50.

——Welsh, M. P., and Bishop, R. C. (1993), 'The Role of Question Order and Respondent Experience in Contingent-Valuation Studies', *Journal of Environmental Economics and Management*, 25: 80–99.

——Poe, G. L., and Bergstrom, J. C. (1994), 'What Do We Know About Groundwater Values? Preliminary Implications from a Meta-Analysis of Contingent-Valuation Studies', *American Journal of Agricultural Economics*, 76: 1055–61.

Brookshire, D. S., and Coursey, D. L. (1987), 'Measuring the Value of a Public Good: An Empirical Comparison of Elicitation Procedures', *American Economic Review*, 77: 554–66.

——Ives, B. C., and Schulze, W. D. (1976), 'The Valuation of Aesthetic Preferences', *Journal of Environmental Economics and Management*, 3: 325–46.

Cameron, T. A. (1988), 'A New Paradigm for Valuing Non-Market Goods using Referendum Data: Maximum Likelihood Estimation of Censored Logistic Regression', *Journal of Environmental Economics and Management*, 15: 355–79.

Carmines, E. G., and Zeller, R. A. (1979), *Reliability and Validity Assessment*. Beverly Hills, Calif. Sage.

Carson, R. T., Wright, J., Alberini, A., Carson, N., and Flores, N. (1992), 'A Bibliography of Contingent Valuation Studies and Papers', Natural Resource Damage Assessment, Inc., La Jolla, Calif.

Cooper, J. C. (1993), 'Optimal Bid Selection for Dichotomous-Choice Contingent Valuation Surveys', *Journal of Environmental Economics and Management*, 24: 25–40.

——and Loomis, J. (1992), 'Sensitivity of Willingness-to-Pay Estimates to Bid Design in Dichotomous Choice Contingent Valuation Models', *Land Economics*, 68: 211–24.

Coursey, D. L., Hovis, J. J., and Schulze, W. D. (1987), 'On the Supposed Disparity between Willingness to Accept and Willingness-to-Pay Measures of Value', *Quarterly Journal of Economics*, 99: 679–90.

Cummings, R. G., Brookshire, D. S., and Schulze, W. D. (eds.) (1986), *Valuing Environmental Goods: An Assessment of the Contingent Valuation Method*, Rowman & Allanheld, Totowa, NJ.

——Ganderton, P. T., and McGuckin, T. (1994), 'Substitution Effects in CVM Values', *American Journal of Agricultural Economics*, 76: 205–14.

Davis, R. K. (1963), 'Recreation Planning as an Economic Problem', *Natural Resources Journal*, 3: 239–49.

Deaton, A., and Muellbauer, J. (1980), *Economics and Consumer Behaviour*, Cambridge University Press.

Desvousges, W. H., Smith, V. K., and Fisher, A. (1987), 'Option Price Estimates for Water Quality Improvements: a Contingent Valuation Study for the Monongahela River', *Journal of Environmental Economics and Management*, 14: 248–67.

——Johnson, F. R., Dunford, R. W., Boyle, K. J., Hudson, S. P., and Wilson, K. N. (1992), *Measuring Nonuse Damages Using Contingent Valuation: an Experimental Evaluation of Accuracy*, Research Triangle Institute Monograph 92–1, Research Triangle Park, NC, prepared for Exxon Company.

Diamond, P. A., and Hausman, J. A. (1994), 'Contingent Valuation: Is Some Number better than No Number?' *Journal of Economic Perspectives*, 8(4): 45–64.

Diamond, P. A., Hausman, J. A., Leonard, G. K., and Denning, M. A. (1993), 'Does Contingent Valuation Measure Preference? Experimental Evidence', in J. A. Hausman (ed.), *Contingent Valuation: A Critical Assessment*, Elsevier Science Publishers BV, Amsterdam.

Dickie, M., Fisher, A., and Gerking, S. (1987), 'Market Transactions and Hypothetical Demand Data: a Comparative Study', *Journal of the American Statistical Association*, 81: 69–75.

Edwards, S. F. (1988), 'Option Prices for Groundwater Protection', *Journal of Environmental Economics and Management*, 15: 465–87.

Fischoff, B., and Furby, L. (1988), 'Measuring Values: a Conceptual Framework for Interpreting Transactions with Special Reference to Contingent Valuation of Visibility', *Journal of Risk and Uncertainty*, 1: 147–84.

Fisher, A., and Raucher, R. (1984), 'Intrinsic Benefits of Improved Water Quality: Conceptual and Empirical Perspectives', in V. K. Smith and A. D. Witte (eds.), *Advances in Applied Micro-Economics*, iii, JAI Press, London.

Freeman, A. M. III (1993), *The Measurement of Environmental and Resource Values: Theory and Methods*, Resources for the Future, Washington.

Hammack, J., and Brown, G. M. Jr (1974), *Waterfowl and Wetlands: Towards Bioeconomic Analysis*, Johns Hopkins University Press, Baltimore.

Hanemann, W. M. (1984), 'Welfare Evaluations in Contingent Valuation Experiments with Discrete Responses', *American Journal of Agricultural Economics*, 66: 332–41.

——(1991), 'Willingness to Pay and Willingness to Accept: How Much can they Differ?' *American Economic Review*, 81: 635–47.

——(1994), 'Valuing the Environment through Contingent Valuation', *Journal of Economic Perspectives*, 8(4): 19–43.

Hausman, J. A. (1981), 'Exact Consumer's Surplus and Dead Weight Loss', *American Economic Review*, 71: 662–76.

——(ed.) (1993), *Contingent Valuation: A Critical Assessment*, Elsevier Science Publishers BV, Amsterdam.

Hoehn, J. P., and Randall, A. (1987), 'A Satisfactory Benefit–Cost Indicator from Contingent Valuation', *Journal of Environmental Economics and Management*, 14: 226–47.

Just, R. E., Hueth, D. L., and Schmitz, A. (1982), *Applied Welfare Economics and Public Policy*, Prentice-Hall, Englewood Cliffs, NJ.

Kahneman, D., and Knetsch, J. (1992), 'Valuing Public Goods: the Purchase of Moral Satisfaction', *Journal of Environmental Economics and Management*, 22: 57–70.

——and Tversky, A. (1984), 'Choices, Value and Frames', *American Psychologist*, 39: 341–50.

Kask, S. B., and Maani, S. A. (1992), 'Uncertainty, Information, and Hedonic Pricing', *Land Economics*, 68: 170–84.

Kealy, M. J., Dovidio, J. F., and Rockel, M. L. (1988), 'Accuracy in Valuation is a Matter of Degree', *Land Economics*, 64: 158–71.

Knetsch, J. L., and Sinden, J. A. (1984), 'Willingness to Pay and Compensation Demanded: Experimental Evidence of an Unexpected Disparity in Measures of Value', *Quarterly Journal of Economics*, 100: 507–21.

Kopp, R. J. (1992), 'Why Existence Value *Should* be Used in Cost–Benefit Analysis', *Journal of Policy Analysis and Management*, 11: 123–30.

Larson, D. M. (1993), 'Efficient Multiple-Use Forestry May Require Land-Use Specialisation', *Land Economics*, 69: 377–87.

Lichtenstein, S., Slovic, P., Fischhoff, B., Layman, M., and Canbs, B. (1978), 'Judged Frequency of Lethal Events', *Journal of Experimental Psychology: Human Learning and Memory*, 4: 551–78.

Lindell, M., and Earle, T. (1983), 'How Close is Close Enough? Public Perceptions of the Risks of Industrial Facilities', *Risk Analysis*, 3: 245–53.

Loomis, J. B. (1987), 'Balancing Public Trust Resources of Mono Lake and Los Angeles Water Rights: An Economic Approach', *Water Resources Research*, 23: 1449–56.

——(1989), 'Test–Retest Reliability of the Contingent Valuation Method: a Comparison of General Population and Visitor Responses', *American Journal of Agricultural Economics*, 71: 76–84.

——(1990), 'Comparative Reliability of the Dichotomous Choice and Open-Ended Contingent Valuation Techniques', *Journal of Environmental Economics and Management*, 18: 78–85.

——and duVair, P. J. (1993), 'Evaluating the Effect of Alternative Risk Communication Devices on Willingness to Pay: Results from a Dichotomous-Choice Contingent Valuation Experiment', *Land Economics*, 69: 287–98.

——and King, M. (1994), 'Comparison of Mail and Telephone-Mail Contingent Valuation Survey', *Journal of Environmental Management*, 41: 309–24.

Magat, W. A., and Viscusi, W. K. (1992), 'Informational Approaches to Regulation', Massachusetts Institute of Technology Press, Cambridge, Mass.

Mäler, K-G. (1974), *Environmental Economics: a Theoretical Inquiry*, Johns Hopkins University Press, Baltimore, for Resources for the Future.

Mannesto, G., and Loomis, J. (1991), 'An Evaluation of Mail and In-Person Contingent Valuation Surveys', *Journal of Environmental Management*, 32: 177–90.

McClelland, G. H., Schulze, W. D., Lazo, J. K., Waldman, D. M., Doyle, J. K., Elliott, S. R., and Irwin, J. R. (1993), 'Methods for Measuring Non-Use Values: A Contingent-Valuation Study of Groundwater Cleanup', Final Report, US Environmental Protection Agency, Cooperative Agreement no. CR-815183, Washington.

McConnell, K. E. (1990), 'Models for Referendum Data: the Structure of Discrete Choice Models for Contingent Valuation', *Journal of Environmental Economics and Management*, 18: 19–34.

McFadden, D. (1994), 'Contingent Valuation and Social Choice', *American Journal of Agricultural Economics*, 76: 689–708.

McKenzie, G. W., and Pearce, I. F. (1976), 'Exact Measures of Welfare and the Cost of Living', *Review of Economic Studies*, 43: 465–8.

Mitchell, R. C., and Carson, R. T. (1985), 'Comment on Option Value: Empirical Evidence from a Case Study of Recreation and Water Quality', *Quarterly Journal of Economics*, 100: 291–4.

——and—— (1989), *Using Surveys to Value Public Goods: the Contingent Valuation Method*, Resources for the Future, Washington.

NOAA (National Oceanic and Atmospheric Administration) (1993), 'Natural Resource Damage Assessments under the Oil Pollution Act of 1990', *Federal Register*, 58: 4601–14.

Park, T., Loomis, J. B., and Creel, M. (1991), 'Confidence Intervals for Evaluating Benefits Estimates from Dichotomous Choice Contingent Valuation Studies', *Land Economics*, 68(4): 64–73.

Poe, G. L. (1993), 'Information, Risk Perceptions and Contingent Values: the Case of Nitrates in Groundwater', unpublished Ph.D. dissertation, Department of Agricultural Economics, University of Wisconsin, Madison.

Portney, P. R. (1994), 'The Contingent Valuation Debate: Why Economists should Care', *Journal of Economic Perspectives*, 8(4): 3–17.

Randall, A. (1991), 'Total and Nonuse Values', in J. B. Braden and C. D. Kolstad (eds.), *Measuring the Demand for Environmental Quality*, Elsevier Science Publishers BV, Amsterdam.

——and W. Kriesel, (1990), 'Evaluating National Policy Proposals by Contingent Valuation', in R. L. Johnson and G. V. Johnson (eds.), *Economic Valuation of Natural Resources: Issues, Theory, and Applications*, Westview Press, Boulder, Colo.

——Ives, B., and Eastman, C. (1974), 'Bidding Games for Evaluation of Aesthetic Environmental Improvement', *Journal of Environmental Economics and Management*, 1: 132–49.

Ready, R. C. (1993), 'The Choice of a Welfare Measure under Uncertainty', *American Journal of Agricultural Economics*, 75: 896–904.

——J. C., Whitehead, and G. C. Bloomquist, (1995), 'Contingent Valuation when Respondents are Ambivalent', *Journal of Environmental Economics and Management*, 00: 181–96.

Rowe, R. D., and Chestnut, L. G. (1983), 'Valuing Environmental Commodities Revisited', *Land Economics*, 59: 404–10.

Scott, A. (1965), 'The Valuation of Game Resources: Some Theoretical Aspects', *Canadian Fisheries Report*, iv, Department of Fisheries of Canada, Ottawa, Ontario.

Shapiro, B. P. (1968), 'The Psychology of Pricing', *Harvard Business Review*, 46: 14–25.

Smith, V. K. (1983), 'Option Value: a Conceptual Overview', *Southern Journal of Economics*, 49: 654–68.

——and Desvousges, W. H. (1987), 'An Empirical Analysis of the Economic Value of Risk Changes', *Journal of Political Economy*, 95: 89–114.

Stevens, T. H., More, T. A., and Glass, R. J. (1994), 'Interpretation and Temporal Stability of CV Bids for Wildlife Existence: a Panel Study', *Land Economics*, 70: 355–63.

Vatn, A., and Bromley, D. W. (1994), 'Choices without Prices without Apologies', *Journal of Environmental Economics and Management*, 26: 129–48.

Walsh, R. G., Loomis, J. B., and Gillman, R. A. (1984), 'Valuing Option, Existence and Bequest Demands for Wilderness', *Land Economics*, 60: 14–29.

Walsh, R. G., Johnson, D. M., and McKean, J. R. (1992), 'Benefit Transfer of Outdoor Recreation Demand Studies, 1968–1988', *Water Resources Research*, 28: 707–13.

Willig, R. D. (1976), 'Consumers' Surplus without Apology', *American Economic Review*, 66: 589–97.

8

A Psychological Perspective

COLIN GREEN
SYLVIA TUNSTALL

8.1. INTRODUCTION

From the perspective of psychology, any social survey should be seen first as an experiment to test one or more hypotheses derived from some theory. In general, psychology does not accept the axiomatic claim made for the assumptions upon which the neo-classical economic model is built. It also sees people as more fallible and complex than is assumed in neo-classical economics. Secondly, psychology differs in its model of the person. The neo-classical model is essentially static: an individual has both pre-existing preferences and perfect information. Conversely, the psychological model is a process model where the emphasis is upon how beliefs and preferences are formed or learnt, and how information is acquired. Thirdly, an interview, like any form of interpersonal communication, is regarded as fraught with the potential for misunderstanding, misdirection, mistakes, and incomprehension. Instead of having the economist's concerns for strategic bias and incentive-compatibility, the psychologist worries about whether the task asked of the respondent is one which they can do and about the likelihood that the respondent will give the answer that they feel they ought to give: socially acceptable responses or answers that others (interviewer, experimenter, sponsor, or others present) want to hear. These potential respondent effects we shall refer to as 'compliance bias' (Groves et al., 1992), using this term in a somewhat broader definition than that adopted by Mitchell and Carson (1989). Fourthly, in psychology an experiment is increasingly defined as a form of discourse, an interaction between several groups of people (Figure 8.1) in which the respondent has demands and has demands placed upon him or her by the experimenter. Thus, whilst much of psychology shares with economics a focus on the behaviour of the individual in isolation, social psychology treats individual behaviour as emerging from the individual's interaction in a social context.

The task, from the psychological perspective, of the experimenter in developing a contingent valuation (CV) study, and it is here assumed that the study will involve interviews carried out face to face, as recommended by

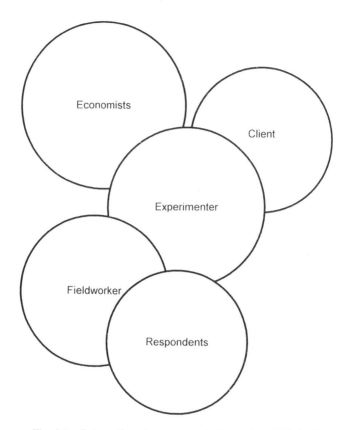

Fig. 8.1   Interactions between participants in a CV study

the NOAA Panel (NOAA, 1993), rather than a mail or telephone survey, is therefore fourfold:

- to exactly convert theory into a survey design and interview schedule, and to do this in a way which conveys meanings exactly to the respondents;
- to avoid incorporating implicit theory;
- to begin with the needs and perceptions of the other participants in the discourse; and
- to enable the respondent to learn what his or her preferences are in the course of the experiment.

From the experimenter's standpoint, the purpose of the discourse is to test some hypotheses derived from theory. In order for the theory to be testable, the theory must be detailed and specific. Since the experiment is a test of theory, it follows that the process of converting the theory underlying the CV study into a survey instrument must be exact. A CV study consequently involves a rigorous process of converting theory into a survey instrument, survey design, and plan for statistical analysis. The starting-point of development must be a rigorous, articulated model which defines all of the variables expected to be involved and the relationships between them. Since economic theory is thin, the Fishbein–Ajzen (1975) attitude model is often adopted as the starting-point for this process of model development.

Theory, however, can be in the form of implicit assumptions as well as explicit; thus, different forms of statistical analysis all impose theoretical assumptions on the data. It is consequently necessary to determine what the appropriate theoretical concerns are and to avoid introducing implicit assumptions. In particular, before a CV study can be designed, it is necessary to determine *what* is the good for which respondents have a preference and a willingness to pay. When we ask someone how much they are prepared to pay for some good, we assume that the good can be meaningfully located in their cognition of the world, their mental representation of the world. We have argued (Green and Tunstall, 1993*a*, *b*; Green *et al.*, 1993*b*) that CV studies often embody strong implicit theories of cognition, and that the embodiment of these implicit theories often determines the results of the studies.

An explicit motivational assumption of neo-classical economics is that value is solely given by the individual and reflects individual preferences. Since such a claim has been explicitly rejected by both deep ecologists (Devall and Sessions, 1985; Naess, 1993) and others (Sagoff, 1988), we cannot rely upon Robbins's (1935) claim for an axiomatic status for this assumption. Once some people reject it, it has ceased to be a self-evident truth. Similarly, the economic concept of non-use value is essentially a rather speculative theory of motivation, of the reasons or drives which give rise to particular forms of behaviour.

It is therefore essential to determine *why* people want the good as well as *what* people want as part of a CV study, to determine whether willingness to pay solely reflects the individual's personal preferences or is motivated by other concepts of value. It is the understanding gained from the experiment as to why the respondents are prepared to pay which gives meaning to the values obtained; without that understanding the values elicited have no meaning.

This model must then be converted into questions which the respondents will understand and be able to answer. The barriers to the respondent being able to give the answers which the experimenter is seeking have been summarized by Sudman and Bradburn (1982) as:

- *memory*: the respondent may have forgotten or may remember incorrectly;
- *motivation*: the respondents may be afraid to tell the truth because they are afraid of the consequences of so doing or because they want to

present themselves in a favourable light, or they may be insufficiently interested to make the effort to respond accurately;

- *communication*: the respondents may not understand what they are being asked; and
- *knowledge*: they may not know the answer.

The participants in the experimental discourse all bring to it perceptions and expectations about the motives and behaviours of others and of their own role. A CV study is consequently more than the interview schedule and a sampling design and must be based upon an understanding of what each participant brings to the discourse. For example, Orne (1962) described the role of the subject in a psychology experiment, as seen by the subject, as follows:

The subject's performance in an experiment might almost be conceptualised as problem-solving behaviour; that is, at some level he sees it as his task to ascertain the true purpose of the experiment and respond in a manner which will support the hypotheses being tested

Orne here argued that the participant, in the context of academic psychology experiments, positively seeks to be a 'good' participant having positive expectations about the purpose of the experiment. Thus, the experiment itself is a stimulus the interpretation of which evokes a response.

However, the key word in this quote is 'task': the respondent must determine how to respond, the difficulty of the task being influenced by the nature of the survey. The outcome of the study is then the outcome of this complex interaction and exchange in which information flows between the participants through both formal and informal channels, such as body language, and where the information that is received by the respondent is partly planned and sometimes unplanned. However, a CV study, or any form of social survey, as a form of social interaction or discourse, is typically highly restricted, wherein that which is sayable is largely defined by the experimenter. The experimenter creates a conceptual and procedural corset which the fieldworkers and respondents are then expected to wear. This places a heavy responsibility on the experimenter to set out the terms of the discourse in a form which is meaningful to, and comprehensible by, the respondent. Questions which fail to satisfy these criteria will, at best, result in different interpretations by the respondents, adding spurious variance. At worst, the respondents will answer an entirely different question to that which the experimenter intended to ask them.

A CV study also involves difficult questions about issues to which respondents may previously have given little or no attention. Whilst babies are born with some inherited instincts, it is implausible to argue that they are born with demand schedules for such things as video recorders. Consequently, we form and learn our preferences over time. A CV study may well, therefore, be the first time an individual has had to decide or choose how much they are prepared to pay for the good that is the focus of the study.

Thus, Fischhoff (1991) argues 'that people lack well-differentiated values for all but the most familiar evaluation questions, about which they have had the chance, by trial, error, and rumination to settle on stable values. In other cases, they must derive specific valuations from some basic values through an inferential process.'

Therefore the design of the willingness-to-pay question itself must be such as to enable the respondent to decide how much he or she is prepared to pay: the design and format of this question must be such that the respondent has the best chance of getting it right. That is, it must enable them to have the best chance of expressing their true willingness to pay. The balder the question asked, the less opportunity there is for the respondent to learn what they are prepared to pay. A single open-ended question, therefore, relies wholly upon the unobserved cognitive processes of the individual to construct an answer or upon prior knowledge by the respondent as to how much they are prepared to pay.

8.2.   WHAT IS THE GOOD?

To begin a study, it is necessary to define the good which is to be evaluated; this definition must be shared by all of the respondents and by the experimenter. Since the cues are provided by the experimenter, the respondents have to locate these cues within their cognitive structure in order to decide what is the good which they are being asked to value. The cues provided by the experimenter may be vague, ambiguous, or even meaningless in the context of the respondents' cognitive structures. It is, therefore, the job of the experimenter to determine how respondents construe the world so as to ensure that the defined good has a meaning. In CV studies we are typically concerned with evaluating complex and abstract goods, which makes more difficult both the respondents' task and, equally, the experimenter's task of identifying what it is that they value.

The five crucial lessons from research on cognition (Lakoff 1987; Rosser 1994) are that:

- the individual structures their beliefs about reality in terms of categories;
- these categories are located in a hierarchical structure (e.g. corgi, dog, mammal);
- some categories, like 'dog', are basic and are the 'natural' level at which that individual construes reality;
- each category is a Gestalt, or pattern; and
- each category has some sort of organizing structure although this may be very simple.

Since cognition is based upon categorization, it is also reasonable to expect preferences, hence willingness to pay, to be held for categories (Green *et al.*, 1993*b*). The value of an individual instance of that category may depend upon the structure of that category.

Although the idea is somewhat complex, the implications can be easily illustrated. Figure 8.2 is a reproduction of Leonardo da Vinci's *Mona Lisa*; in each case, a strip has been removed. If you were asked how much you were prepared to pay for either of the two individual strips without seeing the whole painting, few people would probably be able to identify the source. Those unable to identify the strip as part of the *Mona Lisa* are likely to express a zero or low willingness to pay since what they appear to be asked to value is only a meaningless bit of a painting. The value as a strip of paint is different from its value as a piece of the *Mona Lisa*. Now, suppose instead that you were asked how much you required in compensation for the proposed sale by the Louvre of either of the two strips taken from the painting seen as a whole. Although the two strips are of equal area, the location of the central strip, its structural context, might well lead you to demand greater compensation for it over the border strip, the value of each strip depending upon its context. Some people will also protest that the sale of a strip of the painting destroys the whole painting and that therefore

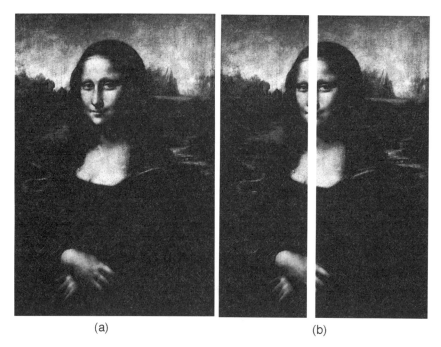

(a)   (b)

Fig. 8.2   Part versus whole

the value of the central strip is equal to the value of the whole painting. In this instance the basic category level at which individuals hold a preference is likely to be the painting as a whole. Furthermore, the organizing structure for the category of 'painting' is not simply the sum of the parts.

This example is probably self-evident. However, it is quite possible that individuals think in the same terms about many of the environmental goods to which it sought to apply CV and where neither the basic category nor the organizing structure is self-evident. Thus, a species may be regarded as a strip when biodiversity is the painting, in which case it will be a meaningful question to ask people how much they are prepared to pay to preserve the full range of species including all endangered species—but not meaningful instead to ask them simply how much they are prepared to pay for this species and that species. Given the scientific definition of biodiversity, a species-based approach would also be singularly inappropriate. The same principle may apply to stretches of rivers, to landscapes, and to habitats. We have consequently argued that the effect found in some CV studies which is variously labeled 'embedding' or 'part–whole' bias (Hoevenagel, 1990; Strand and Taraldset, 1991; Kahneman and Knetsch, 1992) is the result of asking questions which are essentially meaningless to the respondents because they make false assumptions about the cognitions of the respondents.

Consequently, it is necessary to start a CV study by discovering how the good which it is desired to evaluate fits into the cognitive structures of potential respondents and the nature of the structure of the relevant category. Various methods, including focus groups (Stewart and Shamdasani, 1990; Krueger, 1994), can be used to aid in this process in the exploratory stage in study development; it is essential that the experimenter fully report the process whereby it was discovered what it is that respondents value.

Where the basic category is higher than the target good, then willingness to pay needs first to be elicited at the basic-category level. Respondents then need to be asked essentially to prioritize the target good within the overall category. For example, in studies of water quality, we have asked respondents their willingness to pay to improve river-water quality in general. They have then been asked to decide how this amount should be allocated between different types of rivers, or which attributes of rivers should be used to determine priorities (Green et al., 1990; Green, 1993).

8.3. THE DEMANDS OF THE PARTICIPANTS

All the different participants in the experimental discourse have demands and place demands upon the other participants. However, the participants differ markedly in their power, because of their role in the discourse, to enforce their demands on the other participants. Thus, the respondents and fieldworkers are largely the recipients of the demands placed upon them by the experimenter. If their demands are not met, however, then the study is likely to fail. Therefore, the experimenter must satisfy their demands in the design of the experiment. In turn, the experimenter, to a greater or lesser extent, is driven by the demands of his or her peer group of economists.

8.4. THE DEMANDS OF ECONOMISTS

The theoretically most interesting area is economists' initial expectations of the respondents, particularly the implicit assumptions which are made. Norbert Weiner penetratingly remarked that the assumptions a scientist brings to the design of an experiment are invariably more interesting than any conclusions s/he draws from that experiment. Overstatement, even parody, is often a useful way of identifying the implicit assumptions which a discipline makes so that these assumptions can be examined.

The neo-classical economic starting-point is that we know what people want and how they choose. Respondents are treated as passive subjects who react to a stimulus defined by economic theory in the ways predicted by economic theory. It follows that it is merely a question of reliably eliciting the correct responses. The respondent is reduced to a dog jumping through a hoop and, since there are no theoretical problems, the only problem is the methodological one of developing better observational methods so that we can measure more reliably how far and how high they jump.

Essentially, respondents are expected to comply with neo-classical theory and to exhibit no responses beyond those which neo-classical theory demands. Any possible component of a stimulus which is not required by economic theory is regarded as irrelevant and respondents are expected to ignore it. Any unexpected effect, any systematic deviation by respondents from the theoretical expectations, is defined as a 'bias' and ascribed to experimental error. Conversely, in psychology, 'bias' refers to a characteristic of the experimental or survey context which influences respondents to answer in a particular way (Roiser, 1974). For example, a four-point scale whose points are labelled 'poor', 'acceptable', 'satisfactory', and 'very satis-factory' is likely to give results biased towards the satisfactory end of the scale.

'Bias' is an interesting piece of economic labelling; it carries with it the presumption that if the results differ from theory, then it is the results, the respondents, or the experimental methods which are wrong. In the case of 'strategic bias', this is an effect which is predicted from theory (Samuelson, 1954) but which is defined as a deviation from the theoretically 'true' will-ingness to pay. Thus, the term 'bias' is used promiscuously in economic discussions of CV to describe both theoretically unexpected and theoretically expected, but undesirable, effects. Because it is a value-laden term, like much of economic terminology, 'bias' is also a very dangerous term and should be used with extreme caution.

Conversely, psychology capitalizes upon unexpected effects as a way to theoretical development; Fischhoff (1991) quotes McGuire (1969) as arguing that the history of psychology is one of the conversion of unexpected effects into theoretically expected effects.

Neo-classical theory also assumes a basic consensus: whilst individuals may differ somewhat in the strength of their preference, they all want the same things for the same reasons. This is a strong claim which requires to be tested, not least because it is different from our everyday experience.

The basic economic theory upon which a CV study is based is usually expressed in the following form (McFadden and Leonard, 1992):

$$\text{WTP} = y - C_0 - M[V(y - C_0, p, m_0, r_0; \varepsilon), p, m_1, r_1; \varepsilon] \qquad (8.1)$$

where WTP is willingness to pay; y is before-tax income; C is a tax to finance the public goods; p is the vector of market prices of private goods; M is the expenditure function dual of the indirect utility function V; m is a vector of user fees; r is a vector denoting the allocation of public goods; ε equals tastes; and the subscripts $_0$ and $_1$ stand respectively for the situation now and after the proposed change.

8.5. THE DEMANDS OF THE EXPERIMENTER: THE ARTICULATION OF A THEORETICAL MODEL

The experimenter is faced with the task of converting this somewhat vague equation first into a testable model and thence in a series of unambiguous and intelligible questions. Without a testable model, we would be compelled to accept the results at their face value, since we would not have any way of testing the validity of the underlying hypotheses. Equation (8.1) can be re-expressed in simple terms as:

$$\text{WTP} = \text{preference (or taste)}^* \text{ ability to pay}, \qquad (8.2)$$

the interactive form being necessary to constrain willingness to pay to zero in the absence either of a desire or an ability to pay for that good. It is this theoretical hypothesis which must be translated into an interview schedule and survey design; it must also form the basis of the statistical analysis which is required to determine the validity of the results.

The difficulty in converting Equation (8.2) into an experimental method is that the two terms are respectively theoretically unobservable and undefined. Conventionally the reason why we measure willingness to pay is that we do not believe that it is possible to measure preference on an interpersonal, cardinal basis. However, as Coombs (1964) notes, psychologists routinely make the assumption that such a comparison is possible. If the economic model is to be subjected to any test of construct validity, then it is necessary to assume that we can make interpersonal comparisons at some level of measurement with some degree of measurement error. In fact, it is possible to tolerate a significant degree of measurement error, resulting from differences in the way individuals use a scale of preference, for the purposes of statistical analysis, since all it will do is reduce the power of our tests of validity.

If preference is hypothesized to be constrained by ability to pay, then we need to measure the force of this income constraint. Unfortunately, the elegant Hicksian definition of income does not help in designing a question which will tap the degree to which the respondent feels constrained by their ability to pay. Consequently, it is necessary to define the income in terms both of its force as a constraint and in a way which can be measured.

However, whilst Equation (8.2) is sufficient to test the construct validity of the derived willingness-to-pay values, it is also necessary to test the validity of the measures of preference and income we use to test the construct validity of the willingness-to-pay values. Thus, validity is a Russian doll in which the validity of the estimate of any one variable depends upon the validity of the variables used to predict it. As a result we need to develop a model which predicts, in particular, differences in preferences or tastes. Furthermore, unless we develop and apply such a model we will not be in a position to understand why people differ in their willingness to pay.

The basic approach which is adopted in developing such a theoretical model is to keep on asking *why* differences between individuals might occur.

8.6. THE DEMANDS OF THE EXPERIMENTER: THE FISHBEIN–AJZEN ATTITUDE MODEL

One common way (Tunstall *et al.*, 1988; Mitchell and Carson, 1989; Green *et al.*, 1990; Wilks, 1990; Bateman *et al.*, 1992*a*) to formalize the development of this model is to base it upon the Fishbein–Ajzen attitude model (Figure 8.3). The Fishbein–Ajzen model is not usually followed in a formally exact way, But it does offer a basis for identifying the components of the model, and the relationships between them.

In this model, beliefs determine attitudes. Attitudes are regarded as evaluative beliefs towards an act, event, or object, classically defined by Allport (1935) as follows:

Attitudes are learned predispositions to respond to an object or class of objects in a consistently favorable or unfavorable way

In turn, attitudes are predicted to influence behavioural intentions—an intention to behave in a particular way. Willingness to pay is considered to be one such possible behavioural intention. A key word embedded in All-

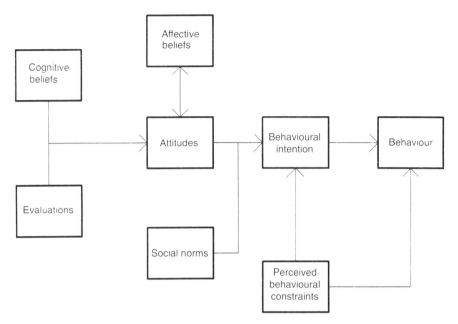

Fig. 8.3   The Fishbein–Ajzen Attitude model

port's definition is 'learned'; thus, an attitude is considered to be formed in some way rather than to be innate, and consequently may also change.

There are, however, important differences between attitude theory and economic theory. The Fishbein–Ajzen model has a number of limitations. For this reason, we have developed a more elaborate model which includes preferences and values as the basis for the design of CV studies in which the Fishbein–Ajzen model forms the core (Figure 8.4). Central to this model are the relationships between beliefs, attitudes, and behavioural intentions.

8.6.1.   Cognitive Beliefs

Cognitive beliefs are the individual's opinions about the object and, in the case of a possible behaviour, about the consequences of that act (Table 8.1). Fishbein and Ajzen further differentiate between an opinion or belief about the magnitude of the consequences of an act and the desirability of that characteristic. Formally, they predict an attitude towards an object or act as $\sum e_i b_i$, where b_i is a belief about the object's attributes or about the act's consequences and e_i is the evaluation of the attribute or consequence.

These beliefs can be positive or negative. Since the behavioural intention is towards an act with several facets (Fischhoff and Furby, 1988), it is usually

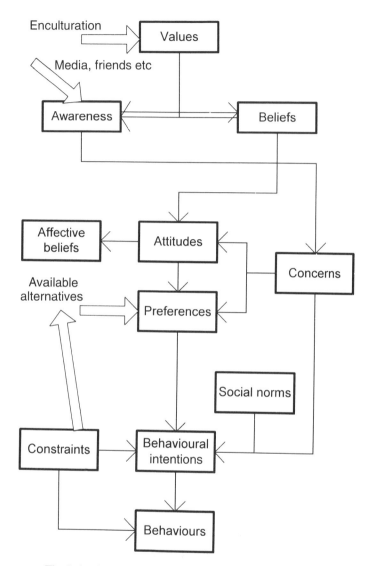

Fig. 8.4   An elaborated Fishbein–Ajzen Attitude model

appropriate to include measures of beliefs about the *means* of payment proposed; on the form of *action* to be undertaken; and about the *organiza-tion* who would undertake that action, as well as on the consequences of the *change* in the *good* itself.

For example, in a study on willingness to pay to protect different types of sites from coastal erosion, beliefs about the methods adopted for coast protection (do engineers simply want to pour concrete everywhere?); about

Table 8.1   Illustrative examples of questions used to measure the variables in an extended Fishbein–Ajzen model

Cognitive belief	Would you please tell me how often the water from your kitchen cold tap is: flat-tasting, has a chlorine taste, ...
Attitude	Overall, how acceptable for drinking is the cold water from your kitchen tap? How satisfied are you with a risk of 1 in 10 each year of a hosepipe ban?
Social norm	Can you tell me how important each factor was to your decision [as to whether or nor they were prepared to pay and how much they were prepared to pay]: What other people would expect us to pay
Preference	What priority should be given to improvements in the following services? Taking each of these conservation measures in turn, how strongly do you oppose or favour——in order to reduce the risk of a hosepipe ban?
Value	Here are a number of things people have said about the way we use water and about the environment. How strongly do you agree or disagree with each of the following statements: 'Each of us has a duty to other people as well as to ourselves' 'We shouldn't have to pay for improvements to other people's water' 'Everyone ought to receive the same quality of water' 'It is the responsibility of the individual householder to insure their homes properly against flooding'
Awareness	Are there any restrictions on the use of water in this area at present (e.g. a ban on the use of hosepipes)? Do you think that you use more water, less water, or about the same amount of water as an average household of your size?
Affective beliefs and concerns	The media are irresponsible to spread so many scare stories about the environment

Source: Green *et al.* (1993*b*)

the desirability of central government intervention; and towards different ways in which the costs of any such works would be funded (e.g. income tax, user charges, VAT, charitable donation) were all included (Green and Tunstall, 1991*b*). It is usually found, for example, that individuals do have strong preferences as to the method by which costs should be recouped (Mitchell and Carson, 1989).

8.6.2.   Attitudes

Thus, attitude is a preference-like measure although there are some important differences between attitude theory and economic theory.

Attitudes towards the object, or good, are usually found to be inferior as predictors of behavioural intentions to attitudes towards the act itself. It follows that, when willingness to pay is elicited in one form, it cannot necessarily be assumed that willingness to pay towards the same good would be the same if another payment mechanism were to be used.

Thus, an attitude measure towards the desirability of the proposed change must be included in the study. Since the behavioural intention is tightly bounded, so too should be the attitude measure or measures.

8.6.3. Social Norms

Fishbein and Ajzen also include the effect of social norms into their model. A social-norm effect will occur when the respondent gives an answer which the respondent believes that others would expect of him or her rather than what the individual himself or herself believes. Thus, a distinction is drawn between an internalized, or shared, normative belief and a social norm. What the respondent believes that some other people would expect the respondent to do has been found to be significant in determining behavioural intentions in a number of contexts. Although found in such contexts as intentions to visit church or use contraception (Ryan and Bonfield, 1975; Ajzen, 1988), it has also been found to be a significant influence in relation to purchasing intentions for consumer goods (Assael, 1992). It might also be argued that social norms influence the decision to participate in a social survey since the respondent is unlikely to obtain any pleasure from the experience.

Social norms are also one explanation of 'compliance bias', a problem which will worry the psychologist far more than the possibility of 'strategic bias' (Samuelson, 1954). Several hypotheses have been put forward to explain compliance bias: that respondents seek to be good respondents and give those answers which they believe the experimenter or sponsor wants; that they defer to the social status of the interviewer; or that they give what they believe to be socially acceptable responses (Bradburn, 1983).

Compliance bias may be a partial explanation of what has been called 'hypothetical bias' in CV studies. For example, Seip and Strand (1990) found that the proportion of respondents who stated that they would be willing to pay to join a Norwegian environmental organization was significantly greater than the proportion who, in a follow-up study, had joined that organization. A similar difference between what people say and what they do has also been found after the event. Thus, Sudman and Bradburn (1982) quote from a 1949 study in which residents of Denver were asked whether they had contributed to the last Community Chest campaign. They report that twice as many respondents claimed to have given as were recorded as having given. They attribute this overreporting by respondents to the effects of the social desirability of giving to this charity making respondents reluctant to say that they had not done so; some part of the difference found by Strand may thus occur for similar reasons. A 'hypothetical bias' must then be defined as the difference between before- and after-event overreporting of behaviours.

In most instances the good at the centre of the CV study will be socially desirable; implicitly, therefore, the individual will feel under a social norm pressure to be prepared to pay, particularly with the interviewer standing there. Compliance bias is not necessarily a complete explanation for hypothetical bias, since in conjoint-analysis studies of consumer goods it is generally found that respondents overestimate their likelihood of making a purchase whilst underestimating the amount they would be willing to pay (S. Trussler, personal communication, 1994).

The discussion of social norms above has, to some extent, trivialized it as some sort of exogenous force which affects individual responses. However, if there was not some degree of social agreement as to the appropriate forms of behaviour, then organized societies would not be possible. The economic concept of property rights is but a limited component of these socially agreed forms of behaviours. The form of a CV study may therefore make assumptions which violate the socially negotiated and agreed norms governing decisions about the provision of public goods. The neo-classical economic model certainly makes assertions about how such choices should be made which are not part of our everyday experience as to how those decisions are made (Tunstall *et al.*, 1988). Everyday experience of the ways that societal decisions about the provision of such goods are taken is not that the amount that individuals are prepared to pay is simply aggregated and compared to the costs of provision.

There are two possible problems that may then be experienced in a CV study. First, there may be social norms which associate particular payment vehicles with the provision of particular forms of goods. Trust funds, or other forms of charities, have been a popular form of payment vehicle in CV studies. However, this raises the question of what, in a particular society, is the socially defined role for charities; for instance, the provision of national defence through a charitable fund is a proposal which peace campaigners make in jest. Certainly, how the costs of some public goods should be paid for is a matter of political and ideological argument.

Secondly, respondents may consider that, in deciding how much they are prepared to pay for the provision of a public good, a different framework of reference is appropriate to that for personal choices about private goods (Margolis, 1982). In the studies of Marwell and his associates (Marwell and Ames, 1979, 1980, 1981), respondents, when asked how they decided how much they were prepared to pay, often referred to what they thought it was 'fair' for them to pay.

Consequently, it is important to explore in the pre-tests which payment vehicle it is appropriate to adopt and to test in the main survey whether individual respondents have preferences for alternative payment mechanisms. Similarly, the reasons why respondents were prepared to pay, their motives, need also to be explored in the survey.

8.6.4.   Behavioural Intentions

A stated intention to perform an act at a later date, a behavioural intention, is considered to be a consequence of the attitude towards that act. However, other factors intervene between the attitude and the intention to adopt that behaviour. Thus, the influence of social norms may be greater over an action than over expressing an opinion. Similarly, the physical and other limitations on behaviour that the individual perceives to constrain his/her actions will limit that individual's capability to adopt a particular behaviour. A behavioural intention is also an expectation about a future behaviour and thus based upon expectations about the circumstances in which that behaviour will be appropriate. These expectations may change, as beliefs about the consequences of the action change, perhaps because of new information. Equally, so may perceived behavioural constraints change over time, rendering the original behavioural intention out of date. An intention to take a holiday in the Seychelles next summer could, for example, be rendered void either by redundancy or pregnancy.

As tests of convergent validity, behavioural intentions towards other acts which are logically dependent on the same attitudes can be included in a CV study (e.g. an individual is prepared to pay for an improvement, subject to other constraints). For construct validity, measures relating to beliefs as to the consequences of the act, and the desirability of those consequences, also should be included.

8.6.5.   Preferences

The major difference between economic theory and attitude theory is that in economics we are concerned with choices between alternatives whereas attitude theory is couched in terms of the desirability of a single action or object. The distinction is twofold. First, the economic concept of preferences is that these are held between actions. Thus, the weakness of attitude theory is that whereas someone may have a very positive attitude towards a particular action, they may prefer and choose another action.

Secondly, choices involve sacrifices either of the specified alternative options which will not now be undertaken or from some generalized pool of resources. This second aspect of preferences is of prioritization within limited resources. An attitude towards an action does not necessarily include a conceptualization of a sacrifice being necessary to undertake that action except in so far as the particular individual chooses to select such a belief. Part of the test of construct validity of the study is indeed to determine whether the respondent did select an ability to pay or affordability belief amongst those considered in deciding his/her willingness to pay.

Therefore, the parallel between an attitude and preference is not exact. Consequently, it is desirable to include measures of the strength of preference as well as of attitudes towards the proposed action. Preferences, however, may be defined either in terms of choices between alternatives or in terms of priorities: at the simplest level, between specific options that may be adopted in a specific instance. For example, in a CV study of alleviating low flows in the River Wey, House et al. (1994) described four different options, including the do-nothing option, and asked respondents how strongly they favoured each option. Questions may also be asked as to the priority which the respondent attaches to the area under study relative to other issues. Thus, Kemp and Maxwell (1992) asked respondents to indicate whether they believed that public expenditure on each of nine broad categories of public expenditure should be increased or decreased before respondents were asked how much they were prepared to pay. Green et al. (1993b) asked respondents to rate eight water and sewerage services in terms of the priority which should be given to improvements in each, after respondents had been asked their willingness to pay for improvements in three of these service areas.

8.6.6. Values

Fishbein and Ajzen do not address the question of why some particular beliefs should be engaged by a particular act or object—in other words, why an individual should decide that some beliefs about the consequences of that act are relevant and not others (Green, 1986), so locating the act within his or her cognitive structure.

Consequently, the first issue is to determine *which* beliefs to include in the survey instrument. Focus groups (Merton and Kendall, 1946; Krueger, 1994), or the use of repertory grids (Kelly, 1955), are two approaches to the identification of the relevant beliefs. The purpose of the focus groups, and other methods adopted, is to determine the boundaries of the discourse, not to seek a representative view. Therefore, any focus-group study should include subpopulations who are expected to have extreme views.

The second issue is theoretical: the results of focus groups may tell us *which* beliefs respondents consider to be relevant but they do not tell us *why* those beliefs were engaged *now*: why the respondents consider those beliefs to be relevant to the choice in question. For this reason, it is undesirable to stop at simply measuring the beliefs; rather, hypotheses should be developed to explain why people differ in the importance they attach to each of these beliefs, and indeed, in the beliefs which are so engaged. In this sense, the weakness of the Fishbein–Ajzen model is the same as that of the neo-classical economic model. It is a static model that does not provide an explanation of how those beliefs came to be engaged by the choice.

To the issue of *which* beliefs will be engaged must be related the question of *the strength of* belief that a respondent comes to hold. For example, an individual has to decide that effects upon wildlife is a relevant belief in making a choice about reducing the risks of pollution. Then they have to decide how much of an effect on wildlife pollution has now and what will be the effect of the proposed action. In the Fishbein–Ajzen model, the *b* variable measures the magnitude of the effect and the *e* variable the desirability of the effect. The *b* variable is an informational factor whereas the *e* variable identifies the importance of the effect in relation to the individual's core beliefs.

Rokeach (1973) defined a value as

an enduring belief that a specific mode of conduct or end-state of existence is personally or socially preferable to an opposite or converse mode of conduct or end-state of existence.

Cognitive theories (Rosser, 1994) conclude that beliefs are organized in a hierarchical form, higher-order beliefs being more wide-ranging and generalized, lower-level beliefs being very specific in their frame of reference, such as a belief that this dog is a corgi. Kelly (1955) further argued that since we are purposive, this hierarchy of beliefs is organized so that we can operate on the world. At the top of the hierarchy then are core beliefs which relate to our purposes or, in everyday speech, values. These core beliefs are so central that they have been argued to constitute the concept of personality. The function of engaging beliefs to a particular action or object is then to identify this action or object within the cognitive structure so that we can decide what to do.

Some beliefs appear to be mainly associative or descriptive ('hot' or 'cold', 'insect' or 'mammal'); however, even here there are evaluative connotations. Many people, for example, don't like insects but do like mammals. Similarly, 'hot' is often associated with good things and 'cold' with bad things. 'Clean' and 'dirty', and particularly 'polluted', have obvious resonances.

Those beliefs which are engaged by a choice then are those which identify within the individual's cognitive structure the nature of the action and its desirability. The beliefs selected will then in part derive from the individual's higher-order beliefs or core values.

How far the selection of beliefs needs to be pursued depends upon the experimenter's belief as to the extent to which everyone shares the same core beliefs and same cognitive structure. If everyone shares the same beliefs, and we know what these are, then we need not explore their values. However, if there is reason to believe that respondents differ in their core beliefs, or the relative importance they attach to each, then these differences should be expected to show up in the beliefs engaged by a choice. There is indeed a substantial body of evidence (Rokeach, 1973) to show that there are significant differences between individuals in their core beliefs, particularly those which relate to the environment (McKechnie, 1972, 1977; van Liere and Dunlap, 1981; Cotgrove, 1982). Therefore, it will often be useful to include questions which seek to tap these deeper core values. A number of studies (Green and Tunstall, 1993a; Green et al., 1993a) have found that such measures are highly predictive of other beliefs, attitudes, and behaviours, including willingness to pay. Such questions are particularly useful in order to clarify what reasons respondents have for expressing a non-use value; indeed, what non-use value really means. There is some evidence which suggests that non-use values are driven by wider ethical concerns which relate to beliefs about duties to others and to other species (Green and Tunstall, 1993a).

Furthermore, since the neo-classical assumption as to the nature of value cannot claim axiomatic status, it is desirable to include questions which explore what concepts of value motivated the respondents. For example, the willingness-to-pay question can be followed by statements (Fouquet et al., 1991) which respondents are asked to rate in terms of their importance in their decision as to whether or not they were prepared to pay (e.g. 'the value to me of——').

These core values themselves are formed through the process of enculturation. Indeed, cultural theorists (Rayner, 1984; Douglas, 1985; Schwartz and Thompson, 1990) argue that the cultural background of the individual will determine their attitudes and behaviours.

8.6.7. Awareness

If an individual has engaged some beliefs by the choice presented in the CV study, that individual still has to decide the magnitude of the effect which will result from the action being considered. In economics, the assumption of perfect information normally allows us to ignore this question: we assume that everyone knows everything which is relevant to their choice. In reality, we usually operate under conditions of imperfect information and have developed a cognitive structure so that we are still able to make choices in these conditions. For example, you can answer the question 'Would you like some fruit?' without being shown the fruit in question.

The respondents have only two sources of information available to them in a CV study: that prior awareness which they bought to the experiment and that information presented to them in the course of the experiment. They will then have to fill any gaps in the information that they have by a process of cognitive inference, as does the individual in the example of being offered fruit. The greater the extent to which the individual must make cognitive inferences, the greater the scope both for differences between individuals in what they infer and between the experimenter's own inferences and the respondent's. For example, if the individuals were to be asked how much they would be prepared to pay for some fruit, and differed in their preferences between types of fruit, then they would have to infer what fruit is likely to be on offer. In real life, they have the option of asking what fruit is being offered but in a CV study, the fieldworker will only repeat the original question back to them. In the case of an offer of fruit, the respondent might, for example, infer the type of fruit on offer on the basis of what is usually offered or what is in season.

Gill's (1947) anecdote that respondents were able to express an opinion on the fictitious Metallic Metals Act illustrates this inferential process. Subsequent experiments indicate that substantial minorities of the public will provide an opinion on a proposed law about which they necessarily know nothing if the question is asked without an explicit 'don't know' option being provided. Although some respondents may have responded randomly in this situation, others made an educated guess, drew an inference, as to what the proposed Act represented (Schuman and Presser, 1981).

In a world of imperfect information, a cognitive structure which enables such inferences to be drawn is essential. The interesting question in such circumstances is how the respondent integrates the issue into his or her cognitive structure, which beliefs are selected. But in a CV study, the requirement is to ensure that the respondents and the experimenter share the same frame of reference, and that this is what the respondents consider to be appropriate. This applies in particular to the wording of the questions, an issue on which the survey research literature provides detailed insights (for example, Payne, 1951; Oppenheim, 1966; Moser and Kalton, 1971; Belson, 1981; Sudman and Bradburn, 1982).

Respondents can be expected to use all the cues provided in the experimental situation as a basis for inference, including the names of the organization undertaking the study and that sponsoring it. The questions asked prior to the willingness-to-pay question are also a potential basis for inference. Unless the respondent expects the experimenter to include purposeless and meaningless questions, to be irrational, then the questions asked earlier must have had some relevance to the later questions. Consequently, the shorter the interview schedule, the less cues that the respondent has from which to draw inferences, potentially leaving respondents with ill-defined and differing expectations as to the nature of the good for which they are being asked how much they are prepared to pay.

In designing a CV study, it is desirable, therefore, to include questions which tap pre-existing knowledge: what and how much do they know about the issue in question and where did they get that information? Secondly, the information needs of the respondents must be identified and addressed in the design of the interview schedule. Since the respondents are not allowed to make the reasonable request for more information before stating their preferences, it is the experimenter's responsibility to find out what those needs are and satisfy them in the design of the CV study. The information needs of individual respondents or categories of respondent may vary and the experimenter then has to balance the different requirements. In the Exxon Valdez study by Carson *et al.* (1992), the researchers took great care to feed information to the respondents about the consequences of the spill in digestible amounts, interspersing the information delivery with questions to maintain interest and to check understanding. The procedure adopted to feed this information to the respondents was itself the result of an extensive programme of exploratory studies and pre-testing.

Since the theoretical definition of information is that which removes uncertainty and changes decisions (Cherry, 1966), the so-called 'information bias' in CV studies is an expected effect. The only question is: what is information to individual respondents and what data is merely noise?

8.6.8. Affective Beliefs and Concerns

Fishbein and Ajzen argue that affective, or emotional, beliefs essentially mirror evaluative beliefs: attitudes. Those emotions associated with pleasure or pain (e.g. 'I like chocolate', 'I love lobster', and 'I hate fat') are clearly almost inseparable from evaluative beliefs. In a hierarchical cognitive structure, such links are both inherent and part of the functionality of the system. Consequently, to include measures of such affective beliefs in a CV survey is to gain little knowledge or understanding. However, not all affective beliefs appear to be so similar to evaluative beliefs.

In particular, there is one group of affective beliefs which is not associated with the magnitude of the consequences of the action but with the direction of the action, and the degree to which this direction is consistent with expectations as to what is right and proper. For example, classically, we get angry when someone does something wrong; that is, different from what we intended or believe ought to be done. Thus, this group of affective beliefs seems to be associated with the extent to which an action deviates from the desired or preferred direction. This group of affective beliefs may be labelled as 'concern'. People have, for example, been found to be 'angry' at the levels of noise they experience (Grimwood, 1993), rather than simply dissatisfied or annoyed. Consequently, such beliefs have two referents: the desired direction and the perceived current direction of action.

The action for which a behavioural intention is sought may then be seen as wrong in direction or as correcting a present wrong. For example, you may believe that shipping companies skimp on the maintenance and operation of oil tankers so as to endanger sea life. You therefore perceive a deficit between how you believe that the companies ought to behave and how they do behave. A change in their behaviour is therefore necessary: a present wrong is to be corrected. In this case, then, you may be angry about the companies' behaviour. On the other hand, the change proposed may be seen as wrong: in the past, nuclear power stations were a strong focus of objection, as new roads are increasingly so being viewed. Rather than simply 'disliking', or being 'unhappy' about, such proposals, opponents often hold much stronger affective beliefs about them.

The distinction being made between affective beliefs such as 'like' and 'love' and 'concern' is between 'wants' and 'oughts'; between those relating to 'more' or 'less' of something 'different'. Children may throw a tantrum, expressing extreme emotions of anger, if they do not get an ice-cream but such behaviour is in itself seen as 'wrong'. Whilst in part it is seen as wrong to give way to anger, it is also that anger is regarded as inappropriate over a mere selfish want. It is more acceptable, for example, to be angry about child abuse or politicians. Thus, for example, indignation is defined by the *Shorter Oxford Dictionary* as 'anger at what is unworthy or wrongful'.

Therefore, where either the present situation or the proposed change is contentious, it can be helpful to include measures of negative affective beliefs such as anger as an aid to understanding both differences between respondents in their answers and in the ways in which they construe the choice. Moreover, when some people are angry about the issue with which the study is concerned, then if the interview schedule does not allow them to express their rage, the interview distorts their response.

8.6.9.   Income and Other Constraints

Economic theory predicts that income will constrain willingness to pay. Unfortunately, theory is silent upon what is the appropriate measure of income as perceived by the respondent to limit their ability to pay.

First, household rather than individual income is generally taken to be the constraint, it being assumed that forming a household involves some degree of pooling or sharing of income. Secondly, logically, the appropriate measure should be of short-term disposable or discretionary income rather than gross or net income. A perceptual measure of discretionary income has been reported by Green *et al.* (1992).

We can't avoid or reduce some of our household's spending (e.g. on mortgages or rent). How far do you feel that all your household's income has to be spent on necessities rather than you having a choice about how to spend it?

Whilst a monetary measure of disposable income is desirable, we have been unable to devise a single reliable question as opposed to a series of questions to measure this which can be answered easily and accurately. Therefore, some monetary measure of total household income is also required. It is usually best to follow the advice of the fieldwork organization as to whether respondents can give more accurate answers to a question on gross or net income, per week or per month; the fieldwork organization will have a customary and preferred approach.

In households, expenditure decisions are also taken for the household rather than wholly independently by each household member. A household may share both resources and decisions. It is possible, therefore, that the member of the household who is the respondent in the survey has no responsibility for expenditure decisions for the payment vehicle adopted or would expect to consult other household members before taking that decision. Equally, the bill-payer may be influenced by what they believe to be the preferences of other members of the household.

Pahl (1989, 1990) reports a survey of 102 married couples on the control of household income and expenditure decisions. This showed wide variations in patterns of control: the traditional British working-class pattern of the husband handing over his pay packet to the wife, who then took all spending decisions, other than over the husband's pocket money, persisting in low-income households.

More generally, control of different categories of expenditure also varied, and the pattern of control showed significant differences with income. Different payment vehicles also would affect different budget controllers: sales taxes, such as Value Added Tax, would typically affect the wife's expenditure more than the husband's, while the impact of property taxes varies according to the financial status of the household (Pahl, 1990). Consequently, it is desirable to include in the CV study a question as to whether or not the respondent is responsible for paying bills for the payment mechanism adopted.

Apart from who pays the particular bill, there is also the question of how expenditure decisions are taken in that household. If decisions are taken jointly, then to ask the respondent without giving them a chance to consult other members is to misrepresent the normal decision process. In particular, Tannen (1991) hypothesizes that men and women have different approaches to household decision-making. She argues that

Many women feel it is natural to consult with their partners at every turn, while many men automatically make more decisions without consulting their partners. This may reflect a broad difference in conceptions of decision making. Women expect decisions to be discussed first and by consensus.

A pragmatic approach is currently the best one to adopt to these problems. To ask a respondent to reply as an individual is to assume that individuals can detach themselves wholly from their family and social context. Conversely, to ask them to answer on behalf of their household, or a family or social group such as a visitor group, is to assume that the individual both knows the preferences of the other members and can synthesize their views, since different members may hold different beliefs and attitudes. It is generally not regarded as advisable to ask respondents in surveys to express opinions on behalf of a group. Moreover, validity studies, in particular, require the matching of attitudes to behavioural intentions. Consequently, the role context in which the respondent answers—as an individual or on behalf of the household or group—must be identical for both.

A pragmatic, and conservative, solution is to ask respondents to reply as individuals to the questions on attitudes and willingness to pay, but then to estimate total benefits as if the WTP sums applied per household. In addition, a question may be asked as to how expenditure decisions are made in the household: by the respondent, jointly, or by the partner or other household member.

In particular instances, constraints in addition to income are likely to operate: lack of access to a car may constrain recreational choices, as may stage in the life-cycle; disability might similarly constrain behaviour or reduce sensitivity to the good in question (e.g. hearing acuity and noise). Both time (Soule, 1955) and the costs of information (Phipps and Carter, 1985) may be argued to be significant constraints upon individual choice.

8.7. THE DEMANDS OF FIELDWORKERS AND THE DEMANDS PLACED UPON THEM

Fieldworkers are often lowly-paid, figures of $5 an hour having been cited for the USA, often working unsociable hours, sometimes in risky areas, yet they perform a critical role in the interaction. The interviewers are required:

- to contact respondents and persuade them to participate;
- to interview those, and only those, respondents specified in the sample;
- to ask all the questions exactly as written and in the order specified in the schedule;
- to ensure that respondents attempt to answer all the questions in the schedule;
- to probe inadequate answers in a non-directive way;
- to record the answers without using their discretion; and
- to be professional and non-judgemental regarding the questions and answers given.

In particular, it is the interviewers who are likely to be important determinants of whether or not a respondent agrees to participate in the survey through the initial impression they make and the skill with which they introduce the survey. Equally, they are expected to edit out almost all the non-verbal cues which we normally expect in a conversation, whilst showing that intelligent interest which will maintain the participant's involvement. They have to do this consistently and to do so irrespective of their own or the respondents' expressed opinions of the intelligibility of the survey which they are undertaking.

In some respects CV surveys might be expected to be particularly vulnerable to interviewer effects, because of, for example, the novelty, length, and complexity of valuation questions, and the probing required to obtain answers. Ideal tests for interviewer effects require respondents to be randomly allocated to interviewers and this condition does not appear to have been met in many CV studies to date. Where possible interviewer effects have been investigated, evidence of interviewer bias has not been found but these results were obtained in surveys carried out by highly trained professional interviewers from leading survey organizations (Mitchell and Carson, 1989). However, one general finding on the effects of interviewer characteristics on response is that young interviewers, usually students, produce much larger response effects than other interviewers, probably because of their age, lack of training, and inexperience (Bradburn, 1983).

There is some evidence that interviewers' expectations about the difficulty of interviewing on topics may have an effect on the responses obtained and an effect of this kind might operate with valuation questions (Singer *et al.*, 1989). There is also evidence that the standards that interviewers communicate to respondents for how they should perform their role in the interview, how interviewers 'train' respondents, has an effect on the quality of the information that comes out of an interview (Fowler and Mangione, 1990). Interviewer briefing is important in ensuring that appropriate standards are set for answering valuation questions. Furthermore, instructions to the respondent as to how the respondent should perform in answering, for example, instructions to give time and thought to the questions in order to arrive at as honest and accurate answer as possible can be written into the schedule, for the interviewer to read out to give emphasis to what is required (Cannell *et al.*, 1977).

In designing a CV study, it is important to consider the interviewers' needs. It must be recognized too that the fieldworkers have a wealth of practical experience in conducting interviews to contribute to CV research. The involvement of interviewers in the development of the survey instrument—the pre-testing and piloting of the schedule, through briefing, debriefing sessions, and through their written comments or questionnaire responses on pilot interviews—is a way of drawing on this valuable experience and ensuring that the schedule meets their needs (Converse and Presser, 1986).

CV studies are usually new to, and are certainly more demanding for, interviewers than the average social survey, and are viewed as being more difficult by interviewers. There is usually more introductory text and often longer questions to read out to the respondent than is usually the case in surveys. Interviewers may regard CV questionnaires as 'wordy' and may be tempted to paraphrase or cut text to be read out. Belson (1986) has found that lengthy instructions to the respondent such as those that may precede a valuation question are often altered or cut by interviewers and that alterations by interviewers may affect the response. However, long introductions may be needed to convey essential information and signal importance and may also be beneficial in allowing respondents time to consider and focus on the valuation issue (Bradburn, 1983).

Furthermore, the CV survey material is often physically difficult to handle, as it usually includes photos or drawings as well as the conventional show cards. Interviewers also may prefer surveys involving questions such as simple verbal-scale questions to which respondents can give quick, easy answers ('Are you: very dissatisfied; dissatisfied; satisfied; or very satisfied?') rather than the more complex procedures that may be required in a CV survey. A CV study requires thought by the respondent and the WTP question, in particular, should be designed to help the respondent form an opinion rather than for speedy administration.

Again, CV studies are usually about interesting and sometimes controversial subjects; the respondents may consequently want to talk about the subject outside the framework provided by the interview schedule although piloting the questionnaire should ensure that respondents' main concerns are catered for in the questions. A problem for the interviewer may be to control the respondent. Interviewers may be tempted to probe directively or to change question order or wording as a result. Interviewer training, project briefing, and good fieldwork control and, perhaps, payment by the hour rather than by completed interview are ways to counteract any such tendencies.

Thus, a first requirement is to convince the interviewers of the validity and legitimacy of the CV approach: considerable scepticism may be felt about the approach initially. Hence, it is essential to brief the interviewers on the main survey in detail; the full interview, and in particular the WTP question, should be practised by the fieldworkers in the session to ensure that they both understand what is required and have confidence that the question is a sensible one. A useful check upon the interviewers' perceptions of the difficulty of the valuation questions and on possible effects of such perceptions is to include a set of questions to the interviewers eliciting their views on the response to the questionnaire and, in particular, the CV section, to be completed after the interview.

The recommendations of the NOAA Panel (NOAA, 1993) are likely to result in the use of non-professional interviewers being largely limited to academic research; here, both a high level of fieldwork supervision and testing for interviewer effects will be particularly necessary. Strictly, however, the issue is not one of a commercial fieldwork organization being used, versus student interviewers but the quality of the fieldwork. It is essential that trained interviewers be used and it is highly desirable that these fieldworkers have previous experience in carrying out interview studies. The two basic options are, then, to recruit, train, and supervise a fieldwork force or to contract with a commercial survey organization to undertake the fieldwork. In either case, fieldwork must be conducted in accordance with established quality-assurance standards (for example, in the UK, the standards set by the Interviewer Quality Control Scheme, to which most major market research companies offering fieldwork subscribe) and also according to the established ethical guide-lines governing social surveys (for example, the Code of Conduct of the Market Research Society, the codes of the Association of Market Survey Organizations in the UK, and the European Society for Opinion and Market Research).

The time and resources required to set up, train, and supervise a special field force must not be underestimated; it is essential, for example, that validation through call-back checks be undertaken for at least 5 per cent, and preferably 10 per cent, of those interviewed to confirm that they were interviewed in the prescribed manner at the reported time and place. It is essential that the experimenters, at a minimum, brief the fieldwork supervisors in person where the survey is geographically widely spread. Ideally, all of the interviewers should attend a main survey briefing session with the experimenters present. A necessary part of the development of the survey instrument is preparation of the instructions to interviewers.

Since the way in which the interviewer administers the interview schedule is critical, it is essential that these instructions, along with the interview schedule itself, form part of the survey report. These instructions can also be useful in understanding the responses.

A fieldwork report is required and this should be annexed to the study report. This report should include the fieldwork specification issued to the fieldwork company along with: the interviewers' instructions; details of response rates both for the sample as a whole and for question non-response; and reports of questions which caused problems.

It is easy to neglect the physical layout of the interview schedule itself, particularly in an interview survey where it will not be shown to the respondent. However, if the interviewers are confused by the layout then the result will be, at best, an excessive number of missing values. Routing instructions in particular, need, to be clear.

8.8. DEMANDS UPON AND BY THE RESPONDENT

A standardized survey interview imposes certain demand characteristics on a potential respondent. Equally, the respondents also have demands and rights. We want the respondent to:

- agree to take part in the survey and to answer all the questions asked;
- give attention to the questions and to give considered answers;
- answer only the questions asked and, for most questions, answer within the restricted range of response categories provided; and
- give those answers which best represent their true opinions.

Their demand is the mirror image of this set of demands: why should they give up the time and effort required? The experimenter must somehow convince the respondent that this expenditure of effort is worthwhile and to adopt the required response mode of giving both attention and true opinions. The obvious economist's answer to obtaining participation is to pay the respondents in cash or in kind and this approach has been adopted in some CV studies (Green *et al.*, 1994), as it is in many undergraduate or postgraduate psychology studies and also for focus groups.

Payment is not usually adopted in large-scale social surveys, where different incentives are used. These centre essentially on convincing the respondent that the survey has a worthwhile and legitimate purpose and that the interview will be an interesting and enjoyable experience. An interest in being of service and the chance to interact with the interviewer have been identified as the main perceived benefits of participating in an interview (Cannell *et al.*, 1965). Unfortunately, the increased use of social surveys in market research, or bogus surveys as part of a marketing exercise, has reduced the public's expectations as to the legitimacy of social surveys and increased their suspicions. Therefore, it is essential to assuage potential respondents' suspicions as to the nature and purpose of the survey, since those who reject the legitimacy of the exercise will refuse to take part, so biasing the sample. The interviewer's introduction plays a key role in legitimating the survey and it must also engage respondents' interest. Interest and the perceived legitimacy of the survey have been shown to be amongst the determinants of response decisions (Young and Morton-Williams, 1986; Goyder, 1988; Groves *et al.*, 1992). Perhaps surprisingly, in Britain generally, research and interviewer training on ways of introducing and securing participation in a survey has been limited and 'doorstep' introductions are often unscripted and at interviewers' discretion (Morton-Williams, 1993).

The use of experienced fieldworkers who have a professional manner; the appearance and quality of material shown to the respondent; and in some cases, the way in which the research is being funded by and carried out for a 'client' body, the name of this client, may all help to establish a serious setting. Then, the nature of questions, and particularly the order in which they are given, help to establish trust and confidence and the context for the valuation questions. Again, if the respondents are not informed of the purpose and nature of the study, then they will guess: the differences in their guesses will result in random variance.

Mentioning the client in the introduction may serve to focus attention on the research topic at too early a stage or may lead respondents to give answers which they believe will fit in with the views of the sponsors. Carson *et al.* (1992) report that they did not mention the research sponsor at all or state the main topic of the research in the early stages of their interviews in their study of lost passive-use values from the Exxon Valdez oil spill. Conversely, respondents may start with the initial expectation, given the client, that the survey is intended to provide a spurious legitimacy to an improper decision which has already been taken. In this case, there is little the analyst can do other than to recommend that project oversight and control should be shifted to researchers or managers who will be recognized as legitimate. In one study of willingness to pay for water and sewerage services, public beliefs about the service providers, in particular a belief that the profits made by the water companies were too high, were associated with unwillingness to pay for selected services. In particular, this belief was a discriminating factor in whether or not people were prepared to pay for reductions in the risk of sewage flooding (Green *et al.*, 1993*b*). In this study, the service providers were not the clients and sponsors of the research, which was undertaken for the regulatory body for the water industry, the Office of Water Services (OFWAT). Thus, public confidence in the institutional arrangements for environmental management and service provision may affect response to a CV survey and this effect may be particularly significant where the service provider or environmental manager is also the sponsor of the research.

More damaging, given the importance of a CV study as a communications exercise, is when the survey instrument is interpreted by the respondents as biased: as designed to ensure that respondents give particular views. Such an interpretation should be picked up in pre-testing and the draft instrument altered accordingly (Green *et al.*, 1993*b*).

This argues against the use of the willingness-to-pay form when the willingness-to-accept-compensation form is the theoretically correct approach to use (Mitchell and Carson, 1989). The real problem with the WTA formulation is not that the numbers are too high, but that too large a proportion of the sample typically makes a protest bid, such as a demand for infinite compensation, or refuses to participate. Thus, they appear to reject the entire definition of the problem. Consequently, it is important to find out why those who do not state a value make this choice. A significant refusal rate will delegitimize the CV study. In addition, since a CV study is partially a communications and public relations exercise in which respondents derive a view of what the client defines the problem to be about, those respondents will have gained the impression, at best, that the client totally misunderstands the problem.

Consequently, the NOAA Panel's (1993) conclusion that the WTP format should be used in such circumstances is not acceptable either for theoretical or public relations reasons. Where a WTA format is theoretically required, then an alternative to the CV method, such as conjoint analysis, should be used. In both a small exploratory study (Brown and Green, 1981), and in a current computer-moderated interview survey in which a conjoint analysis exercise is followed by a CV question, we have found that respondents will make compensatory trade-offs in the conjoint analysis exercise, albeit at rates consistent with CV studies, demonstrating a large difference between WTP and WTA (Coursey *et al.*, 1987). However, they state a refusal to be compensated in the equivalent CV context.

The experimenter wants the respondent to give their attention to the interview and to give considered answers, particularly to the willingness-to-pay question. The interview setting and the interviewer have a major role to play in this. However, whilst these features can all help to establish an initial setting of importance and significance, background factors can reduce the respondent's attention: screaming children are a notable distraction. The length of the interview needs to be limited for this reason, not least because the CV question itself must be fairly late in the sequence of questions. If the interview is too long, then attention may be fading just when the CV question is asked.

Other measures have also been tried such as stressing that a decision hangs upon the outcome of the survey. Unless this is true, then it is not ethical to use such an approach. Or, respondents may be advised of the importance of complete and accurate responses or instructed to 'think hard' about a question. A variant which has been used in some CV studies is a preamble to the willingness-to-pay question in the form of 'This is a difficult question' (Garner et al., 1994), or 'You probably will not have thought about this before and may want some time to think about it' (Green et al., 1993b). Rather than being heard as an instruction to 'think hard', such wording was intended to imply the presumption that the respondent would naturally want to think hard, and that the purpose of the question was to help them to do so. Interviewers have also been trained to positively reinforce desired respondent behaviour which, in the context of CV studies, might be taking time to consider material presented to them and their responses. In research in the United States, the process of setting standards for the respondent has been taken further: respondents have been asked for a signed or verbal commitment that they would answer completely and accurately as a condition of continuing the interview (Fowler and Mangione, 1990). All of these approaches may have something to offer to CV studies.

If the experimenters do not appear to be taking the study seriously, there is no reason why the respondent should decide to do so and devote attention to it. Some CV study questionnaires are brutally short; it is not clear that respondents necessarily always value brevity over content. Instead, very brief interviews and questions may be seen by the respondent as indicating that the experimenter has only a superficial or restricted interest in the research topic and in the respondent's opinions and as providing little or no satisfaction to the respondent.

The standardized interview using a structured questionnaire is a very restricted form of social discourse within a narrowly constrained universe of discourse. The interviewer is trained to respond to the respondent in a standardized, non-directive, and neutral way. Equally, the respondent's responses are, for the most part, structured and limited to, for example, agreement or disagreement to statements; stating that she or he is willing to pay; and other equally narrow ranges of responses. There is often no formal scope for the respondent to say 'but what I really mean' or 'what I really want'; the only option for a respondent who believes the survey does not address his or her real concerns is to refuse to respond to particular question items or at the most extreme to refuse to continue to participate altogether. Having engaged their attention, the interview may then ignore their interests and concerns.

It is not surprising, therefore, that qualitative researchers (Burgess *et al.*, 1987) will argue that such a restricted form of discourse does not yield meaningful answers, that the only way of discovering what people think is to listen to them by engaging in an open and less structured discussion over a longer period of time. Again, they argue that asking individuals to respond as individuals is to denude individuals of the social context, further removing meaning from the answers. Such an argument, of course, fundamentally rejects the neo-classical economic assumption of individual values individually considered.

Therefore, it is essential that the survey instrument be based on a prior understanding of the potential universe of responses which respondents may wish to make, and that this checked in pre-testing. Secondly, it is desirable to include some open-ended questions to ensure that respondents have an opportunity to express their views freely and that respondents feel their opinions to be valued. Thirdly, as well as asking the fieldworkers at the end of the survey how much attention the respondent gave to answering the questions, how 'good' the respondent was against some concept of the ideal respondent, we might also ask the respondent how good the survey was. For example: was the study interesting? were the questions meaningful? was adequate information provided? could realistic answers be given to the questions? was the survey biased? were the questions intrusive? and did the survey address what the respondent considers to be the real questions in relation to the issue under study? Equally, explicit response options to individual questions might include 'This is a silly/meaningless question.' Although initial exploratory research using unstructured interviews and focus groups and pre-testing of the questionnaire should have avoided such questions being introduced in the first place, and any remaining examples should have been weeded out, it may be a useful check.

We want respondents to tell us their true opinions. There is little evidence of a systematic 'free-riding' effect except amongst students of economics (Marwell and Ames, 1980, 1981). However, the possibility of other response effects associated with the respondent such as 'acquiescence bias', and social desirability bias—a tendency of some respondents to give answers which are socially acceptable—has been extensively investigated and interpreted by psychologists and survey researchers (Schuman and Presser, 1981; Bradburn, 1983). The presumed acquiescence tendency has been variously interpreted as reflecting personality characteristics (Couch and Keniston, 1960), as social deferral to the higher social status of the interviewer, as reflecting the norms governing communications in a situation such as the interview: norms of politeness and co-operation (Bradburn *et al.*, 1978). The effect may be a desire to conform to what the respondent believes to be what the experimenter or interviewer wants to hear. Therefore, it is necessary that the survey setting define a 'good' respondent as one who gives his/her own views rather than those s/he believes that the survey is seeking or those that other people will expect them to express. This means that the CV setting must legitimate all views. Equally, extra care must be taken to avoid loaded questions and to present information in a balanced neutral way. Those features which encourage respondents to stay in the survey, by indicating that it is serious and unbiased, also help show that what is wanted is for respondents to express their true opinions. By drawing upon the full range of issues which the respondents want to bring to the discourse, the survey also legitimates all views, making it socially acceptable for a respondent to express them.

8.9.   THE DESIGN OF THE INTERVIEW SCHEDULE

The interview schedule is both a formalization of the theoretical model and the main means of communication between interviewer and respondent, given the restrictions on the role of the fieldworker in a structured interview survey. All of the issues which have been discussed earlier must be embodied in the interview schedule. In terms of asking respondents to express their beliefs and opinions, it is the form of the questions and, particularly, the words used in the questions that are important. However, the data collected also have to be analysed and validity checks undertaken; for this purpose, it is the form of the scales used that is important.

An interview schedule has a beginning, a middle, and an end. The standard advice is to start with easy and non-threatening questions closely related to the declared topic of the survey; in the middle, to put the questions which enhance the respondent's confidence in the legitimacy of the survey and their interest and, importantly, provide the context for the valuation questions; and to follow these with the willingness-to-pay questions. Questions on socio-economic and demographic status which are seen as personal in nature are conventionally asked at the end of the interview. The questions on income, usually seen as particularly sensitive, naturally fall into this last section.

One of the main problems in questionnaire design and a particularly acute problem for site surveys is that of condensing the survey to within the allowable length for an interview. The conventional advice of survey research organizations is that interviews with general population samples should not normally exceed twelve to fifteen minutes for site-visitor surveys. However interesting the survey may be to the respondents, it is considered that this is the maximum time for which people will generally be prepared to interrupt their activities on site to participate in an interview usually standing in the open air. Furthermore, refusal rates are likely to be higher for long interviews, increasing the risk of a biased sample with only those with nothing else to do being prepared to be interviewed.

8.9.1. Communicating to the Respondent

There is a wealth of experience, conventional wisdom, and some research findings on the effects of question form, wording, order, and context of questions, which are summarized in the literature (Payne, 1951; Belson, 1981, 1986; Schuman and Presser, 1981; Converse and Presser, 1986; Singer and Presser, 1989).

The researcher will obviously start from an understanding of these texts and will consequently be aware of the importance of, for example, using plain English and avoiding ambiguous words, or double negatives. An example of a recent notoriously badly worded question is: 'Does it seem possible or does it seem impossible to you that the Nazi extermination of the Jews never happened?', which can be much better expressed as 'Do you believe that the Holocaust happened?' Equally mangled language can often be found in CV surveys, often in the WTP question itself. The researcher must keep trying to make every sentence simpler and clearer, free from both technical and colloquial language; every CV survey should aim to win a 'Plain English' Award. It is also necessary to remember that an interview involves spoken English, and not written English, where the two involve different styles: it needs to be written in a way that the interviewer can read out fluently.

Attention must be paid to even apparently small details of language. For example, the economic term 'willing to pay' may not mean the same thing to non-economists. In a pre-test of one study, a respondent told the interviewer that they were willing to pay but they could not afford to pay (Green *et al.*, 1993*b*). The problem in designing questionnaires is that it is the richness of the language which gives words nuances. Exactly the right words, with shared and understood nuances, must be used.

A range of techniques, which might be used to explore how respondents understand and respond to the valuation and other questions and survey materials, are available for developing and testing interview schedules and survey materials: in-depth interviews and focus groups, double interviews (Belson, 1981), observed or tape-recorded pilot interviews, cognitive research techniques in which respondents think aloud about their thought processes as they go through the interview (Fowler and Mangione, 1990). Draft interview schedules should be tested on colleagues and family, particularly those of a robust disposition, before being put out for pre-testing. The researchers will first have tested that they can answer their questions themselves. Software which tests the reading level required to understand a particular piece of text is widely available: it is worth using such programs to test the comprehension level required by a draft survey instrument.

At least one pilot study using part of the field force should be undertaken and the interviewers then debriefed. Carson *et al.* (1992) provide good examples of the use of careful pre-testing and extensive pilot survey work to throw light on key questionnaire design issues. The purpose of the debrief is explore both the reactions of the respondents to the survey and the problems experienced by the fieldworkers. It is logical to use a sample from the least literate part of the population for the pilot (Green *et al.*, 1993*b*) although ideally the full range of types of respondent in the population should be covered in the pilot surveys. The pilot also provides an opportunity to check on the average duration of the survey interview and on sample and respondent selection procedures. Besides the detailed debriefing, as a minimum Exploratory Data Analysis (Tukey, 1977; Erickson and Nonsanchuk, 1979) should be undertaken of the resulting data.

An area where there is a lack of general research results is in the layout of the interview schedule, show cards, and informational materials for the respondent, which are of particular importance in CV surveys. Survey organizations will have a house style for the layout of the interview schedule which it is advisable to adopt because the fieldworkers will be familiar with it. But, as an exercise in communication, there is little research which enables specific recommendations (Sanchez, 1992) to be made as to the layout of the often substantial quantities of material which will be shown to respondents.

Having begun the CV study by defining the good which is to be evaluated, it is necessary to describe to the respondents, in unambiguous terms, the exact change which they are being asked to evaluate. How this may be done depends upon what is to be evaluated; the more abstract the change, the greater is likely to be the difficulty in describing it and the more limited is the possible range of techniques for communication. Available methods include: verbal or written description, drawings, maps, photographs (including computer-modified photographs), and such techniques as water-quality ladders (Mitchell and Carson, 1981; Smith and Desvouges, 1986; Green *et al.*, 1989). The interpretation of pictorial material seems to be reasonably accurate provided that when photographs are used, these are in colour and a wide-angled lens is used (Shuttleworth, 1980). Navrud (1994) has successfully used video although this requires the fieldworker to transport a combination TV and video recorder with them in order to ensure a standard picture quality.

It is desirable to explore response to materials in qualitative research and to test all such material. Particular challenges with graphic material, especially photographs, are the suppression of extraneous material and bringing out those features which are significant in terms of preferences, but small in scale compared to other features. Respondents will be selectively perceiving and interpreting such material in the same way that they do in real life.

One check which can be made is to ask respondents to value the current situation as known to them and also the supposedly similar situation as depicted in the visual or verbal material presented to them. Thus, for example, Penning-Rowsell *et al.* (1992) asked respondents to value both the visit to the beach which they were visiting and a visit to supposedly the same beach as depicted in a drawing.

A choice has to be made whether to describe the change that will occur or the state of the good before and after the change: for instance, to specify an increase of 50 per cent in the probability of survival of the species or to compare a survival probability before the change of 20 per cent to a post-change survival probability of 30 per cent. It is usually easier, and arguably more neutral, to describe the two states rather than the change. In the development of the theoretical model, the experimenter will have given attention to the question of what statistical techniques are to be used to test it. This question must also be considered in the development of the interview schedule. In general, multi-point rating scales are preferable to ranking or categorical scales for analysis purposes. With the former, the more powerful multivariate parametric statistical procedures and smaller samples can be used. The greater the number of points in a rating scale, the more likely it is to approximate to an interval scale. However, how many scale points are feasible depends upon the question: multi-statement questions in which respondents are essentially making relative judgements can generally employ longer scales than single-statement questions.

The labels on the ends of the scale, and labels on intermediary points, may bias the results. One rule is to use mirror-image terms such as 'very satisfied' and 'very dissatisfied'. Using different words to define the end-points and qualifications such as 'somewhat' and 'quite' to describe intermediary points can cause problems. There is a substantial literature on the effects of varying both the scale length and the labelling of the points making up the scale (McKelvie, 1978).

Where a measure of an attitudinal or other cognitive variable is required, it is more reliable to use a multi-item scale: one, for example, consisting of many statements all of which are believed to tap the belief or attitude in question. Usually the respondent is asked to indicate how strongly she or he agrees with each statement. These statements should, however, be so phrased that some statements read in the opposite direction to others. In addition, the order in which the statements are read out to the respondents should be rotated. Finally, the number of statements should be kept down.

These statements can then be combined to form a single scale which measures the belief or attitude in question. A variety of scaling procedures are available (Dawes, 1972; van Schur, 1977); the most commonly used is the Likert scale. In a Likert scale, an individual's scores for the individual statements comprising the scale can be summed to provide an overall scale for the attitude or belief in question, after allowing for any necessary reversals of scoring on individual statements.

The derivation of a Likert scale from a set of statements requires a factor analysis (Harman, 1967) to determine whether the hypothesis of a single common underlying belief or attitude fits the pattern of correlation in the strengths of agreement between statements. Usually, it will be necessary to drop one or more statements in order to establish a unidimensional scale, or scales if the factor analysis indicates that more than one latent belief is involved. Cronbach's Alpha (Carmines and Zeller, 1979) is then used to determine the degree of internal agreement between respondents' scores on the statements forming the scale.

8.9.2. The Willingness-to-Pay Task

That we assume in economics by axiom that individuals are rational, in the particular sense of achieving optimality when making purchasing decisions, has meant that the question of *how* people do this has not been a question which economics has addressed. Consequently, quite bald questions have been asked in CV studies on the assumption that respondents could give accurate responses: it is effectively assumed that the task asked of respondents is trivially easy. Not much attention has been given to the question of under what conditions people are able to give the most accurate responses. Indeed, discussions about the format of willingness-to-pay questions now centre upon the issue of incentive compatibility rather than upon the difficulty of the task asked of the respondents.

The axiomatic assumption that individuals do invariably, whenever there is perfect information somehow defined, optimize in the market is one which psychologists would argue is somewhat sweeping. The results of CV studies of private goods, such as strawberries (Dickie *et al.*, 1987) and chocolate bars (Kealy *et al.*, 1988), where one might expect the market prices to be approximately known to the respondents, may be interpreted as showing a surprising lack of knowledge and rather poor performance. Similarly, in conjoint analysis studies of consumer products, willingness to pay is typically less than the current market price of the product (Trussler, personal communication, 1994).

Nevertheless, if people are assumed to perform perfectly in a perfectly competitive market, the question is how they are able to do this—what enables them to do it? This is a particularly demanding question since the evidence is that people do most other tasks rather poorly. If only 32 per cent of sixteen-year-olds in the USA are able to give the date of the American Civil War to the nearest half-century, why should those same sixteen-year-olds be any better at recalling their preferences about, say, rain forests? We cannot argue that an incentive to get it right is sufficient to ensure that it is got right, since the incentive in other tasks (e.g. to preserve one's life, to get a degree) is often greater than in a purchasing decision, yet a significant number of failures occur in those tasks.

Similarly, we do not know how people approach the decision in a CV study. Thus, in bidding games (Randall *et al.*, 1974), starting-point bias

(Cummings *et al.*, 1986) is normally found to a greater or lesser extent: the final sums stated by respondents are anchored upon the first sum they are asked whether they are prepared to pay. Unfortunately, we do not know why this effect occurs or even which of two starting bids is the more accurate. In the absence of knowledge as to the reason why anchoring occurs, there is no basis for selecting between the different willingness-to-pay formats in terms of accuracy since we cannot assess the degree of anchoring which occurs in other formats.

The economic axiom of rationality is essentially composed of two assumptions:

- that people know what their preferences are for a particular good relative to other goods; and
- they are able accurately to translate this into money terms.

The starting-point of psychologists in addressing these questions will inevitably be a learning model. The questions that psychologists would seek to address are, therefore: how are preferences formed or learnt? how do people learn about money? and how can people be best enabled to learn their preferences? In particular, psychologists will query whether people will have any preferences before they are offered a choice, particularly where that choice involves a good which is entirely new to them.

Secondly, as Fischhoff (1991) notes, psychologists will expect practice to improve performance, as will attention. Consequently, psychologists will not be surprised if a short CV study, about an issue to which respondents have not previously given any attention, involving a bald open-ended willingness-to-pay question, fails to yield any accurate or, indeed, meaningful results.

Instead, they will look to survey designs which direct respondents' attention to the issue, enable them to form preferences, and practice their willingness to pay. Two possible virtues of conjoint analysis (Green and Srivinasan, 1978; Louviere, 1988) are then that it focuses respondents' attention on specific trade-offs and is an iterative process, wherein respondents have an opportunity to learn their preferences through practice. Similarly, the advantage of the Vickrey auction model (Harrison, 1989) may have less to do with its incentive compatibility than with the learning that is involved, since it is normally necessary to train the respondents in the procedure before they understand it. The virtue of the market-place, psychologists will argue, is that the incentive directs attention to the issue: thus, that it is attention rather than paying real money which is important. Psychologists will have no trouble in accepting that some purchasing decisions that people make in the market are, as the market research literature indicates, suboptimal because people make some purchasing decisions on a habitual basis without thought (Assael, 1992).

It is also arguable that, in addition to sampling problems, telephone interviews will be inferior to in-person interviews because there is less scope for the interviewer to train the respondent and fewer stimuli available with which to engage the attention of the respondent. Thus, the respondent is likely to pay less attention to the questions asked. Similarly, mail or postal questionnaires might be argued to produce such low response rates because they fail to attract enough attention against competing stimuli.

Psychologists may also suggest that starting-point bias is partly a consequence of a learning process which is interrupted before it is complete. However, they will also suspect a social-desirability bias because the goods for which CV studies are typically undertaken are usually ones for which there is a social expectation that they are good things. To minimize such bias, it is desirable in a CV study to legitimate a refusal to pay by an explicit statement which identifies all of the reasons why the respondent might be unable or unwilling to pay. A filter question asking the respondent whether or not they are prepared to pay before asking them how much they are prepared to pay is desirable for the same reason. A bald question on how much they are prepared to pay can imply to the respondent the expectation by the experimenter that everyone is prepared to pay, the only question being how much.

Anchoring is a standard problem in psychometric studies. The most sophisticated measurement technique used in psychometrics outside of CV studies is magnitude or ratio scaling (Stevens, 1975; Lodge, 1981). Poulton (1968, 1977, 1979, 1982) has argued that that procedure is bedevilled by both anchoring and range effects. Faced with a task in the form of a question, be this a simple rating scale, or willingness-to-pay question, the respondent has to start somewhere, unless it is assumed that they already know the answer to that question. Consequently, Hamblin (1974) argues that it is the anchoring point which is important and particularly the reason why the respondent chooses a particular anchoring point.

Indeed, in a CV study, we are expecting and requiring respondents to anchor since we require a willingness to pay relative to other goods; what we are then looking for is anchoring on the values they place upon other goods and services, particularly those that they would have to sacrifice in order make resources available for the good in question. Anchoring is only a problem, therefore, if it is an irrelevant anchor, one simply adopted by the respondent in an attempt to provide an answer.

Two options that have been adopted, therefore, are to remind respondents how much they have to pay for some other goods, or to ask them what consumption they would give up to obtain the good which is the focus of the study. However, the basis for selecting this as an appropriate anchoring point is the hypothesis that an individual determines their willingness to pay on the basis of the value of the good to him/herself. If, in reality, individuals decide how much they are prepared to pay on another basis, such as what their fair share of the cost would be, then they will want to use a different anchoring point, such as the cost of the provision of the good, and will require the appropriate information. More research is required in order to understand how respondents approach the willingness-to-pay task and, consequently, what anchoring points they seek to use.

The starting point for the design of a CV study should, therefore, be that we are asking respondents a difficult question and one which they are unlikely to have previously considered. The form of the social interaction needs to be structured so as to direct their attention to the issue—Carson *et al.*'s (1992) Exxon Valdez study being a good example of this practice. It should also be designed to enable them to learn what their preferences are and what their willingness to pay is. Only when the respondent has discovered or formed their preferences can we expect them to give an answer.

Unfortunately, there is no comparative material on which formats are most successful in this task although conjoint analysis (Louviere, 1988) and extended bidding games (Green *et al.*, 1993*b*) might be expected to be more successful than straight open-ended questions or single-offer referendum formats. The NOAA Panel's (1993) arguments in favour of the referendum format on grounds of familiarity are also culturally biased and not generally applicable outside of the United States. Referenda on public expenditure decisions are not common except in the United States and fixed-offer prices are also not universal even in developed economies, particularly when variations in prices between outlets are considered.

8.9.3. Willingness-to-Pay Format

The willingness-to-pay question itself has five components:

- the introduction;
- the payment vehicle;
- a filter question on whether the respondent is prepared to pay anything extra at all;
- a way of eliciting how much those who are prepared to pay are prepared to offer; and
- a follow-up question which asks respondents the reasons which led them to the answer they gave.

8.9.3.1. *Introduction*

In the introduction, it is necessary to do three things:

- legitimate a refusal to pay by reason of an inability to pay or lack of any preference for the good;
- remind respondents of other current and actual calls on their resources; and
- arguably, inform them of how much they are already paying for the good in question.

As discussed earlier, it is essential to legitimate a refusal to pay.

Secondly, concerns have been expressed about whether respondents take into account other actual and potential calls on their resources (Brunton, 1991; Quiggin, 1991). It is conservative, therefore, to remind them of these other calls.

Thirdly, and most arguably, the introduction may remind the respondents how much they are already paying towards the good in question. However, there are some indications that respondents use the amount that they are told they are already paying as an anchor in deciding how much extra they are prepared to pay (Green et al., 1993b). In one study Bateman (unpub. diss., 1996) found that informing respondents of their current payments appeared to have the effect of depressing the WTP expressed when current payments are low. However, Bateman (forthcoming) also found in another study of recreational users of Thetford Forest that including a question on recreational budgets prior to the valuation question had the effect of more than doubling WTP because annual recreational budgets are large and they anchored up WTP. Given that information on budgets or on current payments can have a striking effect on and may act as an anchor to WTP, the real question is which measure is the more valid WTP measure: WTP with or without the budget question.

8.9.3.2.   Payment Vehicle

The choice of the payment vehicle should be governed by three considerations:

- the appropriateness of the payment to the elicitation of use and/or non-use values;
- the credibility of the payment vehicle; and
- the acceptability of the payment vehicle.

The format of the payment vehicle used (e.g. entry fee, tax payment, donation to charity, water charge, price increase) is likely itself to influence the motivations which are elicited (where such motivations include 'non-use' values). This is a hypothesis since the point has not been adequately tested. In a pilot study of the recreational and preservation value of the Norfolk Broads, Bateman et al. (1993) found taxes to be a more credible payment vehicle than a payment via a charitable donation or trust fund. Markedly more people refused to pay via a trust fund and, particularly, a charitable donation because they thought that all should pay and because they were not confident that payment via donation or trust fund would be fully channelled effectively towards preservation work.

It is reasonable to suspect that when a payment vehicle such as a donation to charity is used, then the respondent is likely to consider a wider range of, and probably different, factors than if, say, an entry-charge vehicle is used. In the former case, it is plausible that the respondent will respond in a social-role context, considering more than his or her narrow self-interest. Conversely, an entry charge probably defines a narrower context but one still not necessarily limited to pure self-interest as exemplified in terms of use value.

Therefore, where use values alone for a recreational site are required, a payment vehicle which is specific to use values must be used. There are two options for recreational value:

- an entry charge; and
- enjoyment per visit.

The entry-charge payment vehicle (Stabler and Ash, 1978; Hanley, 1989) has several disadvantages compared to the enjoyment-per-visit approach (Penning-Rowsell *et al.*, 1992). In using an entry-charge payment vehicle some assumption has to be made about the degree to which respondents can substitute between time and income. If perfect substitution is assumed, the conventional assumption, then the resource costs of visiting, any entry charge, and the opportunity cost of time are additive. Consequently, the effect of any entry charge is necessarily to reduce the frequency with which the individual respondent makes visits, as Stabler and Ash (1978) noted. Bateman (unpub. diss., 1996) has repeatedly found a strong negative relationship between WTP entrance fees and frequency of visiting.

For an improvement to the site, the respondent can be asked what entry charge she or he would be prepared to pay whilst continuing to visit with the same frequency as at present:

What entrance fee would you be prepared to pay at which you would visit (the site in question) no more or less often than you do now? (Green *et al.*, 1992)

For those who might visit the site after the improvement, but do not do so at present, no such easy option can be defined.

If the change involves a decrease in the recreational value of the site, then, where there is no entry charge at present, there is no entry charge at which the respondent would continue to visit at the same frequency as at present.

A potential problem with payment mechanisms is the degree of trust the respondent may have that money raised that way will go to the good in question. In the UK and in most countries, no formal link is possible (because of the 'Treasury Rules' which prohibit restricting the use of tax monies raised in one way to a specific purpose). So the respondent may make some judgement about the risk that a WTP for one good will simply be raised through a tax and then that sum will be applied to a different purpose.

Equally, the respondent will have to make a judgement about the probability that the good will be provided. A respondent asked about his/her WTP for, say, the preservation of a woodland via a donation to the National Trust or English Nature for its purchase may be aware that its acquisition will not necessarily preserve it. A number of bodies, mainly governmental, will reserve the right to take over or change that land. In the context of a road proposal, the knowledgeable respondent would be aware that the

Department of Transport, for example, could still exercise compulsory purchase rights over that land.

Respondents typically have quite strong positive or negative attitudes towards the payment vehicle. This will cause potential problems if the logically appropriate method of paying for the provision of the good is through an unpopular payment mechanism. Equally, there may be times when the policy issue is as much about *how* the good should be paid for as about *how much* it is worth paying for the good.

Care needs to be taken that attitudes towards the payment vehicle do not overwhelm attitudes towards the good. Entry charges, for example, appear to be an obvious payment vehicle for visits to a recreational amenity. However, Simmonds (1976) found that visitors to one beach, who were asked how much they were willing to pay through an entrance charge to maintain that beach, answered that the amount they offered was partly determined as a level sufficient to 'keep the yobs away'. The good being valued by the respondent was different to that which the experimenter intended; the good actually valued included a reduction in congestion by undesirables. Entry charges are in principle used to ration the availability of resources, and respondents appear to have recognized this. Conversely, that prices serve to ration goods is a potential problem: respondents may react more to the implied proposal to ration the good than to the request for valuation.

Consequently, the survey instrument should include a question on attitudes towards payment for the good via the payment mechanism used in the CV question and towards alternative payment mechanisms. Ideally, pre-testing will have explored the perceived appropriateness of different payment mechanisms. However, it should be noted that some payment mechanisms will not result in costs to all individuals (e.g. not everyone pays income tax). Thus, some general reference to payment via taxes may be appropriate when public expenditure is involved. There are indications that basic value differences amongst respondents are associated with differences in preferences between alternative payment mechanisms (Green and Tunstall, 1993*a*).

A further, associated question is how payments should be distributed over time: for example, as a one-off sum, an annual payment, or a monthly payment. In part this issue will be settled by the payment vehicle chosen. However, sums elicited as one-off or annual sums are usually less than the capitalized value of the amounts that individuals are willing to offer on a monthly basis (Green and Tunstall, 1991*a*). This may simply imply a very high individual time preference or say something about the way households prefer to organize their budgets.

Bateman *et al.* (1992*b*) found in a study of the recreation and preservation value of the Norfolk Broads that respondents had more difficulty in answering and offered a lower WTP in an open question on a one-off lump-sum payment compared with an annual payment and its capitalized value. It appears that because the good valued, the Norfolk Broads, was an important one facing a significant change and, therefore, attracting high annual payments, budget constraints operated on the lump sums offered. In two experiments relating to the perception of payments over time, 84 per cent of respondents were prepared to make payments for a period of ten years; 45 per cent of respondents, when asked to state for how long they were prepared to make annual payments, stated that they would pay for as long as necessary or for ever. In contrast, Carson *et al.* (1992) concluded that people had some difficulty in accepting long-term payment obligations and that a lump-sum payment avoids recontracting problems: the tendency for respondents to feel that they can recontract for annual sums and decisions on the appropriate discount rate.

8.9.3.3. Filter Question

The need was specified earlier for a filter question as to whether the respondent is willing to pay at all to precede the question on how much the respondent is willing to pay. In addition, the attitudes which determine whether or not an individual is prepared to pay may differ from those which determine how much those who are prepared to pay then offer.

This filter question should allow a 'don't know' and/or 'protest vote' option. It is important to be able to distinguish between respondents who find the question too difficult and those who object to the principle of attaching monetary values to the good in question. Both those who say 'yes' or 'maybe' should be routed on to the question on the amount they are prepared to pay. It is conservative to make no reference to likely size of the amount respondents would pay—to avoid terms like 'small amount'.

8.9.3.4. The Willingness-to-Pay Question

The choice of the willingness-to-pay formats would ideally be based upon an understanding of the advantages and disadvantages of the different formats. The ideal instrument would be highly reliable and of proven validity, yield easy-to-analyse data and not require very large sample sizes. The criteria probably impose requirements which are antagonistic, and inadequate comparative work has been undertaken to enable comparisons to be made based on these criteria.

In the absence of such a comparison, the experimenter must make a deliberate choice of the format and set out the reasons for the choice of the form used. Similarly, the design must be such that they can test for different possible factors which may influence the respondent's decision. Nevertheless, for the reasons given earlier, the psychologist's preferred format is unlikely to be either a referendum type or open-ended question.

8.9.3.5. Follow-up Questions

After completion of the CV question, respondents should be asked either why they were not prepared to pay for the good or what factors they took into account in deciding how much they were prepared to pay: for example, how much they, as individuals, could afford; how much they thought it was fair they should pay; how much their household could afford; and how difficult they thought it was to put a money value on the goods in question. Although this approach risks the respondent simply post-justifying his/her willingness-to-pay sum, explicable differences have been found between identifiable subgroups in responses to this question. Moreover, the responses are also found to be correlated with the willingness-to-pay offers made (Fouquet *et al.*, 1991; Costa *et al.*, 1993; Green *et al.*, 1993*b*). Similarly, respondents should also be asked about their preferences between different payment vehicles; differences have been found between identifiable subgroups (Green *et al.*, 1993*a*).

8.10. CONCLUSIONS

To develop the CV method requires a multidisciplinary approach; economists have to draw upon the theoretical knowledge of psychology and the other disciplines. The alternative is for economists to continue, without recognizing it, to design CV studies using implicit, and consequently untestable, theories of cognition and motivation and in general to invent naïve theories of psychology and sociology. To continue to do so will waste time and effort. The researcher cannot afford to be limited to the horizons of his or her own discipline, whatever that discipline may be. Secondly, the CV researcher must be ruthless in adopting and adapting the experimental methods of those other disciplines which have specialized in social surveys. It is wasteful to have to relearn those lessons through trial and error which those other disciplines have acquired over eighty to one hundred years of experience.

Each application of the CV method is truly an experiment wherein we increase our understanding of what people want and why. It is not yet an 'off-the-shelf' procedure which can be simply used to go out and get some values. There is, consequently, no such thing as a 'consultancy' CV study. Each application is potentially a process of discovery, 'unexpected effects' being a rich source of new theory. We have shown that there are questions for which there are as yet no clear theoretical or methodological solutions; a purpose of each CV study is to find them.

Consequently, whilst it is possible to set out the principles for the design of a CV survey, it is not possible to set out a recipe book. The NOAA (1993) guide-lines are thus premature. Paramount amongst these principles is rigour not only in designing the survey itself and the fieldwork, but especially in articulating the theoretical model which it is intended to test. A second principle is caution; it is not possible to design a CV study until it is known what people want and why, and often this is precisely what we do not know at the beginning of a study. In consequence, there are important issues to which the cautious CV researcher will not yet seek to apply the CV method. A third principle is disbelief; any experiment is a test of theory and the results of the experiment may lead to the refutation of the theory: the researcher must be prepared to reject standard theory if it does not work. More especially, the researcher must constantly test their developing model for implicit assumptions and convert these into hypotheses. A fourth principle is to examine all possible alternative explanations both in the design of the model and in the analysis of the results. This includes listening to the arguments of those who reject the whole basis of economics: until we understand them, we cannot test those arguments. Finally, it is necessary to remember that the purpose of economics is to aid in the making of choice, not least by clarifying what those choices are about. It is the understanding gained from the experiment as to why the respondents are prepared to pay which gives meaning to the values obtained; without that understanding the values elicited have no meaning.

It is precisely these difficulties which make the CV method one of the most exciting research areas in economics.

REFERENCES

Ajzen I., (1988), *Attitudes, Personality and Behaviour*, Open University Press, Milton Keynes, Bucks.

Allport, G. W., (1935), 'Attitudes', in C. Murchison, (ed.), *A Handbook of Social Psychology*, Clark University Press, Worcester, Mass.

Assael, H. (1992), *Consumer Behavior and Marketing Action*, PWS-Kent, Boston.

Bateman, I. J. (1996), 'Comparison of Forest Recreation, Timber, and Carbon Fixing Values with Agriculture in Wales: A GIS/CBA Approach', unpublished Ph.D. thesis, University of Nottingham.

——Green, C. H., Tunstall, S. M., and Turner, R. K. (1992*a*), *The Contingent Valuation Method*, Report to the Transport and Road Research Laboratory, Flood Hazard Research Centre, Enfield, Middx.

——Willis, K. G., Garrod, G. D., Doktor, P., Langford, I. H., and Turner R. K. (1992*b*), *Recreational and Environmental Preservation Value of the Norfolk Broads: A Contingent Valuation Study*, Environmental Appraisal Group, University of East Anglia, Norwich.

——Langford, I. H., Willis, K. G., Turner, R. K., and Garrod, G. D. (1993), *The Impact of Changing Willingness to Pay Question Format in Contingent Valuation Studies: An Analysis of Open-Ended, Iterative Bidding and Dichotomous Choice Formats*, CSERGE Working Paper GEC 93–05, Centre for Social and Economic Research on the Global Environment, London.

Belson, W. A. (1981), *The Design and Understanding of Survey Questions*, Gower Press, Aldershot.

—— (1986), *Validity in Survey Research*, Gower Press, Aldershot.

Bradburn, N. M. (1983), 'Response Effects', in P. H. Rossi, J. D. Wright, and A. B. Anderson (eds.), *Handbook of Survey Research*, Academic Press, Orlando, Fla., pp. 289–328.

—— Sudman, S., Blair, E., and Stocking, C. B. (1978), 'Question Threat and Response Bias', *Public Opinion Quarterly*, 42: 221–34.

Brown, R. A., and Green, C. H. (1981), 'Threats to Health and Safety: Perceived Risk and Willingness-to-Pay', *Social Science and Medicine*, 15c: 67–75.

Brunton, R. (1991), *Will Play Money Drive out the Real Money? Contingent Valuation Surveys and Coronation Hill*, Environmental Backgrounder no. 2, Environmental Policy Unit, Institute of Public Affairs, Deakin, ACT.

Burgess, J., Limb, M., and Harrison, C. M. (1987), 'Exploring Environmental Values through the Medium of Small Groups, 1. Theory and Practice', *Environmental and Planning Series* A, 20: 309–26.

Cannell, C. F., Fowles, F. T., and Marquis, K. H. (1965), 'Respondents Talk about the National Health Survey Interview', mimeo, Survey Research Centre, University of Michigan, Ann Arbor.

—— Marquis, K. H., and Laurent, A. (1977), 'A summary of Studies', *Vital and Health Statistics*, Series 2(69), US Government Printing Office, Washington.

Carmines, E. G., and Zeller, R. A. (1979), *Reliability and Validity Assessment*, Reston, Va.

Carson, R. T., Mitchell, R. C., Hanemann, W. M., Kopp, R. J., Presser, S., and Ruud, P. A. (1992), *A Contingent Valuation Study of Lost Passive Use Values Resulting from the Exxon Valdez Oil Spill*, Report to the Attorney General of the State of Alaska, Long Beach, Calif.

Cherry, C. (1966), *On Human Communication*, MIT Press, Cambridge, Mass.

Converse, J. M., and Presser, S. (1986), *Survey Questions*, Sage, Beverly Hills, Calif.

Coombs, C. H. (1964), *A Theory of Data*, John Wiley, New York.

Costa, P., Green, C. H., and Tunstall, S. M. (1993), *St Mildreds Bay: Assessment of Coast Protection Benefits*, Report to Thanet District Council, Flood Hazard Research Centre, Enfield, Middx.

Cotgrove, S. (1982), *Catastrophe and Cornucopia*, John Wiley, Chichester.

Couch, A., and Keniston, K. (1960), 'Yeasayers and Naysayers: Agreeing Response Set as a Personality Variable', *Journal of Abnormal and Social Psychology*, 60: 151–74.

Coursey, D. L., Hovis, J. L., and Schulze, W. D. (1987), 'The Disparity between Willingness to Accept and Willingness to Pay Measures of Value', *Quarterly Journal of Economics*, 102: 679–90.

Cummings, R. G., Brookshire, D. S., and Schulze, W. D. (1986), *Valuing Environmental Goods: An Assessment of the 'Contingent Valuation Method'*, Rowman and Allanheld, Totowa, NJ.

Dawes, R. M. (1972), *Fundamentals of Attitude Measurement*, John Wiley, New York.

Devall, B., and Sessions, G. (1985), *Deep Ecology*, Peregrine Smith, Layton, Utah.

Dickie, M., Fisher, A., and Gerking, S. (1987), 'Market Transactions and Hypothetical Demand Data: A Comparative Study', *Journal of the American Statistical Association*, 82: 69–75.

Douglas, M. (1985), *Risk Acceptability according to the Social Sciences*, Routledge and Kegan Paul, London.

Erickson, B. H., and Nonsanchuk, T. A. (1979), *Understanding Data*, Open University Press, Milton Keynes.

Fischhoff, B. (1991), 'Value Elicitation: Is There Anything in There?', *American Psychologist*, 46: 835–47.

——— and Furby, L. (1988), 'Measuring Values: a Conceptual Framework for Interpreting Transactions with Special Reference to Contingent Valuation of Visibility', *Journal of Risk and Uncertainty*, 1: 147–84.

Fishbein, M., and Ajzen, I. (1975), *Belief, Attitude, Intention and Behavior*, Addison-Wesley, Reading, Mass.

Fisher, A., McClelland, G. H., and Schulze, W. D. (1988), 'Measures of Willingness to Pay versus Willingness to Accept: Evidence, Explanations, and Potential Reconciliation', in G. L. Peterson, B. L. Driver, and R. Gregory, (eds.), *Amenity Resource Evaluation: Integrating Economics with Other Disciplines*, State College, Pa.: Venture, pp. 127–34.

Fouquet, M.-P., Green, C. H., and Tunstall, S. M. (1991), *Evaluation of the Benefits of Coast Protection for Hurst Spit*, Report to New Forest District Council, Flood Hazard Research Centre, Enfield, Middx.

Fowler, F. J., and Mangione, T. W. (1990), *Standardized Survey Interviewing*, Sage, Newbury Park, Calif.

Garner, J. L., Tunstall, S. M., and Green, C. H. (1994), *Cliftonville: an Assessment of Coast Protection Benefits*, Report to Thanet District Council, Flood Hazard Research Centre, Enfield, Mass.

Gill, S. (1947), 'How do you Stand on Sin', *Tide*, 14 March: 72.

Goyder, J. (1988), *The Silent Minority: Non-Respondents on Sample Surveys*, Polity Press, Cambridge.

Green, C. H. (1986), 'Reason, Choice and Risk', paper given at the Colloque internationale de recherche, evaluer et matriser les risques, Chantilly.

——— (1993), *The Evaluation of the Nonuse Value of Improvements to River Water Quality*, Report to the Foundation for Water Research, Flood Hazard Research Centre, Enfield, Middx.

——— and Tunstall, S. M. (1991*a*), 'The Evaluation of River Water Quality Improvements by the Contingent Valuation Method', *Applied Economics*, 23: 1135–46.

——— and ——— (1991*b*), 'Is the Economic Evaluation of Environmental Goods Possible?' *Journal of Environmental Management*, 33: 123–41.

——— and ——— (1992), 'The Recreational and Amenity Value of River Corridors', in P. J. Boon, P. Calow, and G. E. Petts (eds.), *River Conservation and Management*, John Wiley, Chichester, pp. 425–41.

——— and ——— (1993*a*), 'The Ecological and Recreational Value of River Corridors: An Economic Perspective', paper given at conference on The Ecological Basis for River Management, Leicester.

——— and ——— (1993*b*), 'The environmental value and attractiveness of river corridors', paper given at conference on Les Paysages de l'eau aux portes de la ville: Mise en valeur écologique et intégration sociale, Lyons.

——— ——— and House, M. A. (1989), 'Investment Appraisal for Sewerage Schemes: Benefit Assessment', in H. Laikari (ed.), *River Basin Management*, v, Pergamon Press, Oxford, pp. 45–57.

——— ——— N'Jai, A., and Rogers, A. (1990*a*), 'The Economic Evaluation of Environmental Goods', *Project Appraisal*, 5(2): 70–82.

————Fouquet, M.-P., and Coker, A. C. (1992), 'Estimating the Recreational Value of an Environmental Resource', paper given at the Civil Service College, London.

————Herring, M., and Herring, A. (1993a), *CVM: A Social Science Kaleidoscope*, paper presented at the ESRC Seminar on Environmental Evaluation, London.

————Herring, M., and Sawyer, J. (1993b), *Customer Preferences and Willingness to Pay for Selected Water and Sewerage Services*, technical report, Office of Water Services, Birmingham.

Green, D. P., Kahneman, D., and Kunreuther, H. (1994), 'How the Scope and Method of Public Funding Affects Willingness to Pay for Public Goods', *Public Opinion Quarterly*, 58: 49–67.

Green, P. E., and Srinivasan, V. (1978), 'Conjoint Analysis in Consumer Research: Issues and Outlook', *Journal of Consumer Research*, 5: 103–23.

Grimwood, C. J. (1993), 'A National Survey of the Effects of Environmental Noise on People at Home', *Proceedings of the Institute of Acoustics*, 15(8): 69–76.

Groves, R. M., Cialdini, R. B., and Couper, M. P. (1992), 'Understanding the Decision to Participate in a Survey', *Public Opinion Quarterly*, 56: 475–95.

Hamblin, R. L. (1974), 'Social Attitudes: Magnitude Measurement and Theory', in H. M. Blalock (ed.), *Measurement in the Social Sciences*, Aldine, Chicago, pp. 61–120.

Hanley, N. D. (1989), 'Problems in Valuing Environmental Improvements resulting from Agricultural Policy Changes', in A. Dubgaard, and A. Nielson (eds.), *Economic Aspects of Environmental Regulation in Agriculture*, Wissenschaftsverlag Vauk Kiel, Kiel.

Harman, H. H. (1967), *Modern Factor Analysis*, University of Chicago.

Harrison, G. W. (1989), 'Theory and Misbehavior of First-Price Auctions', *American Economic Review*, 79: 749–62.

Hoevenagel, R. (1990), 'The Validity of the Contingent Valuation Method: Some Aspects on the Basis of Three Dutch Studies', paper presented at congress on Environmental Cooperation and Policy in the Single European Market, Venice.

House, M. A., Tunstall, S. M., Green, C. H., Portou, J., and Clarke, L. (1994), 'The Evaluation of the Recreational Benefits and Other Use Values from Alleviating Low Flows', R&D Note 258, National Rivers Authority, Bristol.

Kahneman, D., and Knetsch, J. (1992), 'Valuing Public Goods: the Purchase of Moral Satisfaction', *Journal of Environmental Economics and Management*, 22: 57–70.

Kealy, M. J., Dovidio, J. F., and Rockel, M. L. (1988), 'Accuracy in Valuation is a Matter of Degree', *Land Economics*, 64(2): 159–71.

Kelly, G. A. (1955), *The Psychology of Personal Constructs*, W. W. Norton, New York.

Kemp, M. A., and Maxwell, C. (1992), 'Exploring a Budget Context for Contingent Valuation', in Cambridge Economics Inc., *Contingent Valuation: A Critical Assessment*, Cambridge Economics Inc., Cambridge, Mass., sec. 4.

Krueger, R. A. (1994), *Focus Groups: A Practical Guide for Applied Research*, Sage, Beverly Hills, Calif.

Lakoff, G. (1987), *Women, Fire, and Dangerous Things*, University of Chicago Press.

Lodge, M. (1981), *Magnitude Scaling: Quantitative Measurement of Opinion*, Sage, Beverly Hills, Calif.

Louviere, J. L. (1988), *Analyzing Decision Making: Metric Conjoint Analysis*, Quantitative Applications in the Social Sciences 67, Sage, Newbury Park.

Margolis, H. (1982), *Selfishness, Altruism and Rationality*, University of Chicago Press.

Marwell, G., and Ames, R. E. (1979), 'Experiments on the Provision of Public Goods, I: Resources, Interest, Group Size, and the Free Rider Problem', *American Journal of Sociology*, 84: 1335–60.

—— and —— (1980), 'Experiments on the Provision of Public Goods, II: Provision Points, Stakes, Experience and the Free Rider Problem', *American Journal of Sociology*, 85: 926–37.

—— and —— (1981), 'Economists Free Ride, Does Anyone Else? Experiments on the Provision of Public Goods, IV', *Journal of Public Economics*, 15: 295–310.

McFadden, D. L., and Leonard, G. K. (1992), 'Issues in the Contingent Valuation of Environmental Goods: Methodologies for Data Collection and Analysis', in Cambridge Economics Inc., *Contingent Valuation: A Critical Assessment*, Cambridge Economics Inc. Cambridge Mass., sec. 8.

McGuire, M. (1969), 'Suspiciousness of the Experimenter's Intent', in R. Rosenthal, and R. L. Rosnow, (eds.), *Artifact in Behavioral Research*, Academic Press, New York.

McKechnie, G. (1972), *The Environmental Response Inventory*, University of California Press, Berkeley.

—— (1977), 'The Environmental Response Inventory in Application', *Environment and Behavior*, 9: 255–76.

McKelvie, S. J. (1978), 'Graphic Rating Scales: How Many Categories?' *British Journal of Psychology*, 69: 185–202.

Merton, R., and Kendall, P. (1946), 'The Focused Interview', *American Journal of Sociology*, 51: 541–57.

Mitchell, R. C., and Carson, R. T. (1981), *An Experiment in Determining Willingness to Pay for National Water Quality Improvements*, Draft Report to the US Environmental Protection Agency, Washington.

—— and —— (1989), *Using Surveys to Value Public Goods: the Contingent Valuation Method*, Resources for the Future, Washington.

Morton-Williams, J. (1993), *Interviewer Approaches*, Dartmouth, Aldershot.

Moser, C. A., and Kalton, G. (1971), *Survey Methods in Social Investigation*, Heinemann Educational, London.

Naess, A. (1993), 'The Deep Ecological Movement: Some Philosophical Aspects', in S. J. Armstrong and R. G. Botzler (eds.), *Environmental Ethics: Divergence and Convergence*, McGraw-Hill, New York, pp. 411–21.

NOAA (National Oceanic and Atmospheric Administration) (1993), 'Natural Resource Damage Assessments under the Oil Pollution Act of 1990', *Federal Register*, 58: 4601–14.

Navrud, S. (1994), 'Does the Presentation of Information Matter in Contingent Valuation Studies? Experimenting with Video', paper given at conference on Determining the Value of Non-Marketed Goods: Economics, Psychological and Policy Relevant Aspects of Contingent Valuation, Bad Homburg.

Oppenheim, A. N. (1966), *Questionnaire Design and Attitude Measurement*, Heinemann, London.

Orne, M. T. (1962), 'On the Social Psychology of the Psychology Experiment', *American Psychologist*, 17: 776–89.

Pahl, J. M. (1989), *Money and Marriage*, Macmillan, London.

——(1990), 'Household Spending, Personal Spending and the Control of Money in Marriage', *Sociology*, 24: 634–65.

Payne, S. L. (1951), *The Art of Asking Questions*, Princeton University Press.

Penning-Rowsell, E. C., Green, C. H., Thompson, P. M., Coker, A. M., Tunstall, S. M., Richards, C., and Parker, D. J. (1992), *The Economics of Coastal Management*, Belhaven, London.

Phipps, A. G., and Carter, J. E. (1985), 'Normative versus Heuristic Models of Residential Search Behaviour: An Empirical Comparison', *Environment and Planning A*, 17: 761–76.

Pollak, R. A. (1994), 'For Better or Worse: the Roles of Power in Models of Distribution within Marriage', *AEA Papers and Proceedings*, 84: 148–52.

Poulton, E. C. (1968), 'The New Psychophysics: Six Models for Magnitude Estimation', *Psychological Bulletin*, 69: 1–18.

——(1977), 'Quantitative Subjective Assessments are almost always Biased, sometimes Completely Misleading', *British Journal of Psychology*, 68: 409–25.

——(1979), 'Models for Biases in Judging Sensory Magnitude', *Psychological Bulletin*, 86: 777–803.

——(1982), 'Biases in Quantitative Judgments', *Applied Ergonomics*, 13: 31–42.

Quiggin, J. (1991), *Total Valuation for Kakadu National Park*, Department of Agricultural and Resource Economics, University of Maryland, College Park, Md.

Randall, A., Ives, B., and Eastman, C. (1974), 'Bidding Games for Valuation of Aesthetic Environmental Improvements', *Journal of Environmental Economics and Management*, 1: 132–49.

Rayner, S. (1984), 'Disagreeing about Risk: the Institutional Cultures of Risk Management and Planning for Future Generations', in S. G. Haddon, (ed.), *Risk Analysis, Institutions and Public Policy*, Associated Faculty Press, Port Washington, NY.

Robbins, L. (1935), *An Essay on the Nature and Significance of Economic Science*, 2nd edn., Macmillan, London.

Roiser, M. (1974), 'Asking Silly Questions', in N. Armistead (ed.), *Reconstructing Social Psychology*, Penguin, Harmondsworth, pp. 101–14.

Rokeach, M. (1973), *The Nature of Human Value*, Free Press, New York.

Rosser, R. (1994), *Cognitive Development: Psychological and Biological Perspectives*, Allyn and Bacon, Boston.

Ryan, M. J., and Bonfield, E. H. (1975), 'The Fishbein Extended Model and Consumer Behaviour', *Journal of Consumer Research*, 2: 118–36.

Sagoff, M. (1988), *The Economy of the Earth*, Cambridge University Press.

Samuelson, P. A. (1954), 'The Pure Theory of Public Expenditure', *Review of Economics and Statistics*, 36: 387–89.

Sanchez, M. E. (1992), 'Effects of Questionnaire Design on the Quality of Survey Data', *Public Opinion Quarterly*, 56: 206–17.

Schuman, H., and Presser, S. (1981), *Questions and Answers: Attitude Surveys: Experiments on Question Forms, Wording and Context*, Academic Press, New York.

Schwartz, M., and Thompson, M. (1990), *Divided we Stand: Redefining Politics, Technology and Social Choice*, Harvester Wheatsheaf, London.

Seip, K., and Strand, J. (1990), *Willingness to Pay for Environmental Goods in Norway: A Contingent Valuation Study with Real Payment*, Memorandum no. 12, Department of Economics, University of Oslo.

Shuttleworth, S. (1980), 'The Use of Photographs as an Environment Presentation Medium in Landscape Studies', *Journal of Environmental Management*, 11: 61–76.

Simmonds, A. (1976), *The Recreational Value of Beaches*, East Anglian Coastal Research Programme, Report no. 4, University of East Anglia, Norwich.

Singer, E., and Presser, S. (eds.) (1983), *Survey Research Methods: A Reader*, Chicago University Press.

——Frankel, M. R., and Glassman, M. B. (1989), 'The Effect of Interviewer Characteristics and Expectations on Responses', pp. 272–87, in Singer and Presser (1989).

Smith, V. K., and Desvousges, W. H. (1986), *Measuring Water Quality Benefits*, Kluwer Nijhoff, Boston.

Soule, G. (1955), *Time for Living*, Viking, New York.

Stabler, M. J., and Ash, S. E. (1978), *The Amenity Demand for Inland Waterways*, Amenity Waterways Study Unit, University of Reading.

Stevens, S. S. (1975), *Psychophysics: Introduction to its Perceptual, Neural and Social Prospects*, John Wiley, New York.

Stewart, D. W., and Shamdasani, P. N. (1990), *Focus Groups: Theory and Practice*, Sage, Newbury Park, Calif.

Strand, J., and Taraldset, A. (1991), *The Valuation of Environmental Goods in Norway: A Contingent Valuation Study with Multiple Bias Testing*, Memorandum no. 2, Department of Economics, University of Oslo.

Sudman, S., and Bradburn, N. M. (1982), *Asking Questions: A Practical Guide to Questionnaire Design*, Jossey-Bass, San Francisco.

Tannen, D. (1991), *You Just Don't Understand: Women and Men in Conversation*, Virago, London.

Trussler, S. (1994), personal communication.

Tukey, J. W. (1977), *Exploratory Data Analysis*, Addison-Wesley, Reading, Mass.

Tunstall, S. M., Green, C. H., and Lord, J. (1988), *The Evaluation of Environmental Goods by the Contingent Valuation Method*, Flood Hazard Research Centre, Enfield, Middx.

van Liere, K. D., and Dunlap, R. E. (1981), Environmental Concern: Does it Make a Difference how it's Measured? *Environment and Behavior*, 13: 651–76.

van Schur, W. H., and Niemoller, K. (1977), *Basic Scaling*, ECPR Summer School at the University of Essex Monographs on Social Science Data Analysis, University of Essex, Wivenhoe.

Wilks, L. C. (1990), *A Survey of the Contingent Valuation Method*, Resource Assessment Commission, Research Paper no. 2, Australian Government Publishing Service, Canberra, ACT.

Young, P., and Morton-Williams, J. (1986), 'Co-operation and Participation in Surveys: an Analysis of the Doorstep Interaction between Interviewer and Respondent', *Survey Methods Newsletter*, Autumn, SCPR, London.

9

Information, Uncertainty, and Contingent Valuation

ALISTAIR MUNRO
NICK D. HANLEY

9.1. INTRODUCTION

Uncertainty occurs when individuals have less than full knowledge of the true state of the world. Information is then the stock of knowledge the individual has of the true state, but it also usually means any increments to that stock via news or messages from other individuals.[1] The values individuals attach to goods depend on the information available to them, but in the context of contingent valuation (CV) studies this dependency is often referred to as *information bias*. Yet the word 'bias' has pejorative overtones that do not seem appropriate when an individual's valuation is correct given the information available.[2] Even if it is not a true 'bias', nevertheless information creates its own difficulties for CV analysis. In this chapter we shall view these problems from a purely neo-classical viewpoint, using expected utility theory. However, there are strong reasons for suspecting that information cannot be treated solely in this manner, but must also be viewed from the perspective of psychological theories of information-processing. In particular, the impact of information will depend on the way it is 'framed' (see, for instance, Thaler (1980) or Slovic *et al.* (1982)).[3] The reader is therefore directed elsewhere in this book, particularly to Green and Tunstall (Chapter 8), for a complementary approach to the issue. We say 'complementary' rather than 'alternative', since in practice both viewpoints produce insights about the effects of information on CV.

The chapter is organized around two important questions. First, what are the consequences for CV of the fact that subjects are likely to bring a wide variety of beliefs to the issue being discussed? Second, what is the optimal amount of information that should be given in CV? This is an issue which

---

[1] This pattern of usage follows Hirshleifer and Riley (1992).
[2] We will therefore usually omit the word 'bias' in this chapter, confining its use to the discussion of biased probabilities.
[3] The 'frame' refers to the way in which information is presented; for instance whether stopping the construction of a road will lead to fewer amphibians dying or more surviving.

need not be faced if information has no effect on valuation, so we first provide a short survey of the empirical work done to date on the impact of the provision of information on the results of CV studies. We move on to consider the theoretical ideas underlying valuation under uncertainty and the effects of giving extra information, before returning to the problem of the optimal level of information.

9.2. EVIDENCE ON THE EFFECTS OF INFORMATION: A SHORT SURVEY

One of the first CV studies specifically to address the impact of information is that of Bergstrom and Dillman (1985), who considered willingness to pay for prime-land preservation in the USA. Here participants were divided into two groups, one of which received messages from the organizers on the scenic and environmental benefits from preservation, and then asked to state bids for the protection of prime land. Mean willingness to pay (WTP) was then compared across the two groups, with the informed group having an average bid a significantly different $5.29 above the uninformed group. This paper set the pattern for many subsequent studies, results from which are summarized in Table 9.1. Except where mentioned, responses were elicited via face-to-face interviews.

In all these studies the researchers had clear prior expectations regarding the impact which the information provided would have upon WTP and, in general, the changes recorded matched expectations, although the observed effects were not always significant. Where there is a strong use value for the good in question and therefore respondents (if they are users) have made the decision to enjoy the commodity, it is reasonable to expect that values will be less sensitive to new information compared to commodities lacking a use value. Therefore, it is not surprising that information had no significant impact in two out of the three experiments involving users (Bergstrom *et al.*, 1989; Boyle, 1989; and Boyle *et al.*, 1991).

The other articles in the table investigated existence value or a combination of existence and use value. All the studies, except for Hanley and Munro (1992), show clear evidence of significant changes in mean WTP. Moreover, as would be expected, positive information (i.e. news which emphasizes good attributes) on substitutes lowers WTP, while, in the only study which considered complements (Whitehead and Blomquist, 1991), WTP rose in the wake of positive information. The results reported in Samples *et al.* (1986) are especially interesting, since they suggest that changes in WTP may be due to experimenter effects rather than information *per se*. Individuals given extra information typically spend longer with the experimenter and build more of a relationship. If they then judge that the interviewer 'wants' a higher bid, this may make them willing to pay more for a good. This does not mean that information does not have an impact itself (two of the three

Table 9.1   The Impact of Information on WTP: Some recent studies

Study	Good	Information	Results
Bergstrom and Dillman, 1985	Prime farmland (USA)	One group told of environmental and scenic values of farmland.	$5.29 mean difference in bids, significant at 99% level.
Samples *et al.*, 1986	Humpback whale (USA)	One group shown film on humpbacks; control shown film on making TV ads.	Both groups increase WTP during film, but difference between groups not significant.
Samples *et al.*, 1986	Three species (rabbit, monkey, and rat) (USA)	4 levels: (1) none; (2) physical appearance; (3) endangered status; (4) all.	Subjects asked to allocate $30 between the 3 species. Significant changes at 99% level with endangered status having most impact.
Boyle, 1989	Wisconsin Trout fishery (USA)	3 groups: (1) basic; (2) current stocking activity; (3) 2 + costs of same.	Mail survey (84% response rate) produced no significant differences, but estimated variances and percentage of zero bids fell.
Bergstrom *et al.*, 1989	Recreation in freshwater wetlands (USA)	2 groups: (1) control; (2) service information on daily bag of catch, scenery, isolation.	Mail survey (62% response rate) yielded positive change in mean, significant at 99% level.
Boyle *et al.*, 1991	Hunting in Maine (USA)	2 groups: (1) control; (2) information on prices of substitute species (deer, upland birds, and sea-ducks).	No significant impact.
Whitehead and Blomquist, 1991	Kentucky Wetlands (USA)	4 groups: information on substitute and complementary goods.	Mail survey (31% response rate) with dichotomous choice. $5.81 fall in median bid when substitutes information given; $5.71 rise for complements, but estimated bid curve not integrable, so mean WTP figures unavailable.
Hanley and Munro, 1992	Dorset Heathland (UK)	4 groups: (1) control; (2) site-specific; (3) endangered habitat; (4) all.	Estimated bid curves showed positive impact, but with significance dependent on bid vehicle. Information had no overall impact on protest bids.

mail surveys reported here did produce significant changes in WTP), but it does suggest that the appropriate control in face-to-face interviews is not zero information, but irrelevant information, the presentation of which lasts a similar length of time.

Two studies consider the effect of new information on other aspects of CV results. Boyle (1989) reports a fall in the dispersion of bids, while Hanley and Munro (1992) report no overall pattern in the sample variances, but find that information is more likely to have an impact on bids if subjects feel that they have some familiarity with the information prior to the interview. This study also considers information effects upon the number of protest bids. When asked, no interviewees who had refused to bid stated that lack of information was the reason.[4]

There are clear lessons to be learnt from the empirical evidence to date. First, the influence of the level of information on a subject's WTP for an environmental amenity is potentially significant, particularly when non-use values are being elicited. Secondly, the impact on other measures, such as the dispersion of bids or the number of protest bids, is unclear, although little research has been done on these issues.

9.3. MEASURING SURPLUS UNDER UNCERTAINTY

In order to understand how information affects measures of consumer surplus we must first consider valuation under uncertainty. Following Hoehn and Randall (1987) and Bergstrom et al. (1989, 1990), it is helpful to split the reporting of CV estimates by respondents to researchers into two stages: the value formulation stage, where individuals decide their valuation of a good; and then the value statement, where the individual must report a figure to the researcher. Under traditional economic approaches to choice under uncertainty, namely the expected-utility model, this separation is justified, but in many psychological models of decision-making (see Beach and Mitchell (1978) for instance) it would not be.

In the context of uncertainty there ceases to be a single measure of value, because the amount the consumer is willing to pay will depend on the state of the world. For instance, suppose that there is a 50 per cent chance of rain tomorrow and I am risk-neutral. If it is sunny I will be willing to pay nothing for an umbrella; if it pours the maximum I will pay is £10. Since I am risk-neutral, when viewed *ex ante* I am actually indifferent between paying nothing when it is sunny, plus £10 when it rains, and paying £5 whatever the state of the world. Indeed there is a whole locus of values between which I am indifferent as long as the expected loss is equal to £5. Graham (1981; see

---

[4] Instead most were protesting either against the bid vehicle employed or against the principle of paying anything for an open-access common.

also Bishop, 1982), provides a clear guide through the possibilities in terms of a 'willingness-to-pay' locus and it is his approach that we summarize below.

Suppose that a bird-watcher is considering visiting a reserve. If it rains (the probability of this is $1-p$), visibility will be low and this will reduce the benefits of the visit. Expected utility (V) is given by

$$V = pU^1(y, \alpha) + (1-p)U^2(y, \alpha), \qquad (9.1)$$

where U is utility and superscripts 1 and 2 indicate sun and rain respectively, y is income and $\alpha = 1$ if the watcher visits the site[5] and $\alpha = 0$ otherwise. The surplus, $S^i (i = 1, 2)$, in each state of the world is defined as the *ex-post* WTP for $\alpha = 1$, that is:

$$U^i(y - S^i, 1) = U^i(y, 0). \qquad (9.2)$$

Expected surplus, $E[S]$, is then simply

$$E[S] = pS^1 + (1-p)S^2. \qquad (9.3)$$

Define $x^i (i = 1, 2)$ as the payment made by the individual in state of the world i. The willingness-to-pay locus is then defined as the pairs of payments (x^1, x^2) by the bird-watcher such that expected utility with the site available and payments being made is equal to expected utility with the site unavailable and no payments made. That is, the locus is given by all pairs (x^1, x^2) satisfying

$$pU^1(y - x^1, 1) + (1-p)U^2(y - x^2, 1) = pU^1(y, 0) + (1-p)U^2(y, 0) = U. \qquad (9.4)$$

Figure 9.1 illustrates this locus (the curve BS^2), for the simple case where there is no value in a visit when it is raining, so $S^2 = 0$. Risk aversion implies that the curve is concave, i.e. as income decreases so the marginal utility of income rises such that the curve becomes steeper as the payment, x^2, increases.

When CV is usually carried out, subjects are asked to state a WTP that is constant across all states of the world. In other words, $x^1 = x^2$, which is the point on the WTP locus where it cuts the 45-degree line. This is the *option price* for the good, *OP*, more formally defined as

$$pU^1(y - OP, 1) + (1-p)U^2(y - OP, 1) = U. \qquad (9.5)$$

Option price minus the expected surplus is known as *option value* (*OV*) and may be positive or negative. In Figure 9.1, for instance, the line DS^2,

---

[5] Describing the options in this way makes the use of the site a private good for the visitor, removing the extra difficulties posed by public goods.

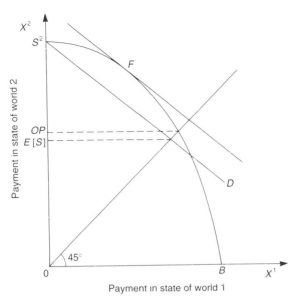

Fig. 9.1 Valuation under uncertainty

drawn through $(0, S^2)$ on the vertical axis, is the set of all points with the same expected value as the expected surplus. As an example, in Figure 9.1, this line cuts the 45-degree line below OP, so the option value is positive.

There are several possible appropriate measures of consumer surplus under uncertainty: $E[S]$, OP, and the 'fair-bet' point—the position where the consumer is indifferent between not having the good and being fully insured against rain[6]—are all candidates. A priori, there is no reason to prefer any of the measures. Rather it depends upon the context in which the cost–benefit analysis will be made. If markets for all contingent commodities are available and the consumer can therefore buy the good 'go to the site if it rains', then expected surplus is the appropriate measure. If there are no contingent markets, but the consumer can insure against rain, then the fair-bet measure is correct. However, in many cases, there are neither contingent nor insurance markets and the consumer must pay the same whatever the state of the world. The appropriate measure in that case is option price—the yardstick usually employed in environmental cost–benefit analysis.

[6] If fully insured then they are also indifferent between rain and sun, hence the marginal utility of income will be the same in both states of the world. The contingent payments are therefore given by F—the point on the willingness-to-pay locus where its slope is equal to the slope of the expected surplus line.

9.4. INFORMATION AND UNCERTAINTY

Information is news; a signal or a message that potentially changes the probabilities attached by individuals to the likelihood of events occurring.[7] In the standard expected-utility model, there are three main ways in which a consumer's formulated WTP is affected by the information provided. First, information will affect the probabilities attached to different possible benefits. Secondly, their hypothetical nature can make the questions used in interviews confusing and often unbelievable for many participants. Information can therefore improve the credibility of the CV process. Thirdly, to the extent that responses to surveys may be strategically biased, the level of information may alter the link between individuals' formulated and revealed WTP.

9.4.1. Bayes' Theorem

It is worth while being precise about how messages (i.e. new information) affect beliefs in the rational consumer model. Suppose that there are S possible states of the world (e.g. the number of otters on a site). An agent's prior beliefs that $s(=1,\ldots,S)$ is the true state of the world is represented by π_s. The subject then receives a message, m (one of M possible messages) which carries some information about the true state of the world. He or she will then revise beliefs in the light of Bayes' Theorem,[8] which states that

$$\text{prob. of } s \text{ being the true state given message } m \text{ is received} = \frac{(\text{prob. } m \text{ is received given } s \text{ is true state})(\pi_s)}{\text{prob.} m \text{ is received}}.$$

We can see from this that prior beliefs are likely to remain unaltered if the probability that m is received is similar across all states of the world. Conversely, if the chances of m being received are low, then its receipt is more likely to lead to significant revision in beliefs about the true state of the world. Giving full and complete information to a subject in a CV study therefore means supplying a message such that the recipient would not expect it in any other state of the world. However, when an individual invests in further information acquisition he or she cannot anticipate the message that will be received. If, for instance, we knew that by watching the weather

---

[7] In this chapter we make the implicit assumption that the marginal benefit of information is always declining. In an important paper, Stiglitz and Radner (1984) argue that the returns to information may be convex for small amounts of information, so that, even with a price of zero, there will be no net benefit from small amounts of information. In their case the decision variable is continuous and hence their argument does not necessarily carry over. Nevertheless it remains possible that there may also be returns to scale in information even when the decision variable is dichotomous.

[8] See Hirshleifer and Riley (1992: part ii) for a more detailed exposition of Bayes' Theorem and the impact of information on beliefs.

news, we would attach a higher probability to it raining tomorrow, then we could update our prior beliefs even without switching on the television. We can therefore see that it is fundamentally improbable that two individuals, even if they have the same prior beliefs and make the same investment in information acquisition, will end up with identical posterior beliefs about the world.

There are mechanisms by which beliefs may end up being shared, but typically these do not apply to non-marketed goods. With marketed goods the price conveys information about the good and may, in certain circumstances, equalize information sets across all individuals (see Grossman and Stiglitz, 1981). If one stock-market trader learns something significant about Acme PLC, this information may be transmitted to others on the market when the trader buys stock. Even with traded goods such an outcome may be rare, but the crucial point is that, by definition, information disclosure in this way is not possible with non-marketed goods. Similarly, in markets with asymmetric information about the quality of goods, reputation effects can lead to higher-quality goods having higher prices than their competitors (Klein and Leffler, 1981) and this enables new consumers to judge quality. Of course with environmental goods, reputations can still be passed on by word of mouth, but not via prices. There is scope for intermediation in information through complementary goods (e.g. wildlife books and videos), but there are still strong reasons for suspecting that information transmission for non-marketed goods is far less effective than that for their marketed counterparts, so that the information held by individuals will vary systematically across the community.[9]

Generally, therefore, the response to information will vary a priori. Someone who emphatically believes that there are many otters in a nature reserve, for example, may revise their formulated WTP to visit the site downwards when told that otters are actually rare. Someone else who did not know of the otters may raise their valuation upwards when given the same message.

9.4.2. Information and Valuation

Consequently there is no necessary expectation that formulated WTP will rise after information is received, even on average. Suppose that individuals are given a message which reveals the true state of the world. *Ex ante*, the expected value of the *ex-post* formulated WTP is simply the expected surplus ($E[S]$) described above. As we have already shown, this may be higher or

---

[9] This does not mean that the information held by any one individual will be any less accurate if the good is non-marketed: as long as information is transmitted via prices then it becomes a public good and therefore underprovided in a private market. Consumers may therefore invest more in information acquisition for non-marketed goods than for marketed goods—provided, of course, that either a decision is to be made or information has some intrinsic value. This issue is taken up in Section 9.5.

lower than the option price elicited prior to the provision of information.[10]
The implications of this can be seen if we consider a naïve test of the impact
of information where we divide subjects into two groups and give information (i.e. a message) to one group and not to the other. With dispersion in the
priors and in the impact of the message itself, estimates of formulated WTP,
derived from aggregated responses, may change little. However, small
changes in aggregate stated WTP may hide large shifts in individual formulated WTP. As with estimates of the mean, the impact of new information
on other summary measures is also unclear. At first sight, for instance, we
might think that the variance of bids would fall as all individuals became
informed about the true state of the world, but again this may be mistaken if
prior beliefs differ across individuals. Suppose, for instance, that there are
two types of agents: one type values the good highly ('High'), while the other
places a low valuation on the good ('Low'). If the information received raises
the valuation of the good for the High agents and lowers it for Low agents,
then the variance of formulated WTP will rise. Furthermore, just as the
mean stated WTP may rise or fall, so too might the number of zero bids. All
in all, therefore, there is no reason to suppose that the provision of information will actually alter the results of CV studies.

9.4.3.   Testing for the Effects of Information

The fact that information may have no impact on aggregate measures of
formulated WTP is good news for researchers wishing to discover WTP, but
bad news for those wishing to investigate the impact of information on
individual WTP. The consequences of simply supplying information may
disappear when aggregated across individuals; so, in order to test whether
information has an effect at the individual level using aggregated data, we
therefore have to supply messages where the researchers have strong priors
about the impact. For instance, if we assume that subjects are risk-averse, a
message which reduces uncertainty about the benefits of an environmental
amenity, while keeping the expected level of benefits constant, will raise its
valuation (see Rothschild and Stiglitz, 1971). Suppose that prior beliefs are
that there is a 25 per cent chance of seeing no otters, a 50 per cent chance of
seeing two otters and a 25 per cent chance of seeing four otters at the nature
reserve. Information is given which leads the agent to revise his or her
probabilities to 20 per cent, 60 per cent and 20 per cent respectively. The
expected number of animals remains unchanged, but the riskiness of visiting
the reserve has been reduced, which implies that a risk-averse agent will raise
his or her formulated WTP to see otters.

---

[10] Actually for supply uncertainty (and forms of demand uncertainty where income effects are
known to be small), option value is positive and hence average willingness to pay *ex post* will lie
above its *ex-ante* value. However, this result depends on prior beliefs being unbiased and there is
no reason why this should be true for unmarketed goods with non-use values.

Hoehn and Randall (1987) analyse such a case in a path-breaking article which attempts to model the impact of information formally. Nevertheless, as Section 9.4.2 has indicated, there is a crucial problem with their approach. If, as would normally be the case, individuals do not share the same prior beliefs, then it is almost impossible to imagine a single message which simultaneously keeps the mean level of benefits constant for all agents and reduces uncertainty surrounding those benefits. For instance, suppose there was another agent who believes that there are no otters in the reserve. The message which transforms the first agent's probabilities to 20 per cent, 60 per cent and 20 per cent must leave the second agent still believing that there are no otters in the river.[11]

It follows that if we want to test for the effects of information on valuation, messages have to be provided where the effect on beliefs is more clear-cut. Since we are only testing the effects, it does not necessarily matter that the information is accurate (although there are clear dangers in providing misleading information, not least for the credibility of the CV industry as a whole). For instance suppose that information is *positive*. Then it should raise the valuations of all respondents; but what do we mean by 'positive'? The simplest approach is that information is positive if valuation rises for all individuals, but this is too circular. If a film was shown to one subsample and not to the other and valuations of the amenity shown in the film did not differ between the samples, we could either conclude that information had no impact, or that the film was not informative. We therefore need a stronger notion of positive (or even negative) information, more along the lines of Milgrom's (1981) 'good news'.

Suppose that we can list the attributes of an environmental asset in a vector z. In the case of a woodland these may include, for example, the area of the site and the variety and abundance of flora and fauna. Even for regular visitors to the site the scale and availability of the characteristics of the site and other, substitute sites will be uncertain. For simplicity we can suppose there is only one dimension along which characteristics may vary. So let the set of possible attributes for both the goods be Z—a subset of the real numbers, R. A bundle may not have much of the attribute, and it may be that many people believe that a particular good does not have particular features, but both aspects of the problem can be incorporated in the probabilities rather than the characteristics themselves. This formulation allows certainty and allows for the fact that some goods may be known (or just believed, since probabilities are subjective) to have none of a particular characteristic. If, for instance, the attribute z was 'having a volcanic

---

[11] More formally, if the likelihood matrix (the matrix which lists the probability of message m occurring given the state of the world is s for all combinations of m and s) is allowed to differ across individuals, then it is mathematically possible to devise messages which can overcome this problem. The practical problems of creating such a message for agents with different priors would still remain insuperable, however.

mud-pool', a rural English healthland could have a probability of 1 that $z = 0$, and zero probabilities for all strictly positive values of z.

Following Hanley and Munro (1992) let the individual have a *cumulative density function*, $G(z)$—which is the probability that the commodity has at least z of the attributes. For instance, in the example of the otters in the previous section, the probability that there were no more than two otters would be 75 per cent. Preferences are of the form $U(y, z)$, where y is income. U is twice differentiable, concave, and it is assumed that U is increasing in income and z. Defining expected utility (V), as before, then

$$V = \int_{z_{min}}^{z_{max}} U(y, z)g(z)dz. \qquad (9.6)$$

where g is the probability density function for z, and z_{min} and z_{max} are the lower and upper limits to possible values for z. Integrating by parts yields

$$V = U(y, z_{max})G(z_{max}) - U(y, z_{min})G(z_{min}) - \int_{z_{min}}^{z_{max}} U_z(y, z)G(z)dz. \qquad (9.7)$$

But $G(Z_{max}) = 1$, while $G(z_{min}) = 0$, so

$$V = U(y, z_{max}) - \int U_z(y, z)G(z)dz. \qquad (9.8)$$

Willingness to pay, or more specifically, the option price of the amenity, is given implicitly by

$$\int_{z_{min}}^{z_{max}} U(y - \text{WTP}, z)gdz = U(y, 0). \qquad (9.9)$$

As with all definitions of consumer surplus, the choice made in the absence of the original good is optimal given this constraint and the extra income represented by WTP.[12] Using (9.8), Equation (9.9) becomes

$$U(y - \text{WTP}, z_{max}) - \int_{z_{min}}^{z_{max}} Uz(y - \text{WTP}, z)G(z)dz = U(y, 0). \qquad (9.10)$$

In complex environments it is difficult, if not impossible, to quantify information. It is not like measuring work time, oil, or other tangible inputs. Moreover, the effects of information, like information itself, are hard to formalize and there is no consensus on the functional form of an increase in information on the distribution of benefits as represented by $G(z)$. For that reason we propose the following, very general, definition of what constitutes

---

[12] Thus the formulation can either be interpreted as the WTP for a particular site or for a quality change in the attributes available. In the characteristics approach, the two views are equivalent since goods (here, 'sites') are merely specific bundles of attributes. To take an extreme example, both cars and coffee could be drawn in characteristic space, a car having less of the beverage qualities of coffee, but more transport potential.

positive information that seems to accord with the view taken in most empirical studies.[13]

DEFINITION: Information is positive if it raises the subjective probabilities that a particular bundle has more of the good attributes. More formally, if after receiving information the cumulative density function is G' such that $G'(z) \leqslant G(z)$ for all z and all individuals and the inequality is strict for at least one point in Z for all individuals, then the information is positive for all individuals.

In the example of the otters, positive information means that it is less likely that there are only a small number of the animals, which in turn means that it is more likely that a large number are present. It amounts to saying that G' first-order-stochastically dominates G, but more importantly, it is empirically testable provided that we can agree on the positive attributes of a bundle of goods. Suppose that the positive information provided is specific to the actual bundle the consumer chooses. For instance, if the good was an area of woodland, we could provide information about the varieties of trees in that particular wood, but information applicable to woodlands generally would not be specific. With increased information, the formula for WTP' (i.e. the *ex-post* formulated WTP) is given by

$$\int_{z_{min}}^{z_{max}} U(y - \text{WTP}', z)g'dz = U(y, 0) \tag{9.11}$$

where a $'$ attached to variables indicates an *ex-post* value. Putting (9.11) in the form of (9.10) and combining them yields

$$U(y - \text{WTP}, z_{max}) - U(y - \text{WTP}', z_{max})$$
$$+ \int_{z_{min}}^{z_{max}} U_z(y - \text{WTP}, z)(G' - G)dz \tag{9.12}$$
$$+ \int_{z_{min}}^{z_{max}} U_z(y - \text{WTP}', z) - U_z(y - \text{WTP}, z)G'dz = 0.$$

But if we take the first two terms on the left-hand side and the second integral over to the right-hand side and reverse the integration by parts we get

$$\int_{z_{min}}^{z_{max}} U_z(y - \text{WTP}, z)(G' - G)dz$$
$$= \int_{z_{min}}^{z_{max}} (U(y - \text{WTP}', z) - U(y - \text{WTP}, z))g'dz. \tag{9.13}$$

[13] Papers which discuss the effects of information make no attempt to specify functional form beyond identifying the sign of derivatives of probability functions with respect to increased information. See Feder and Slade (1984) or Kislev and Shchori-Bachrach (1973) for example. Evidence from advertising (see Lambin (1976)) suggests that there may be threshold effects: a little information may have no impact, but with repetition agents' valuations may undergo large changes. However, this is a very tentative idea, which also requires us to be able to measure units of information.

Since U is concave in y and z, the left-hand side of this equation is negative, but the right-hand side has the opposite sign to the change in WTP. In other words, formulated WTP rises if positive information is given. However, positive information may also raise an individual's valuation of alternative goods. If this is the case, there is an extra term to add to the right-hand side of (9.13) and WTP′ may be lower than WTP. Hence only with information specific to the good should we expect formulated WTP to rise.[14]

The second way that information may alter the results of a CV study is through the credibility of the hypothetical questions asked of respondents.[15] Thus the value statement may alter as well as the value formulation. This is particularly true where the subjects are asked to contribute towards the preservation of an environmental amenity that they themselves may not believe to be under threat. If they do not pay for the good, the threatened loss may not occur and so there is less reason to state a high WTP for what may be a wasted payment. For instance, in Hanley and Munro (1992), based on a survey at the kind of Dorset heathland featured in the novels of Thomas Hardy, some of the subjects were shown graphs depicting the decline of the area covered by heathland in the last 150 years. This device would help convince subjects of the real possibility of further inroads on the habitat.

If p is the subjective probability that the threat is real, then formulated WTP is defined implicitly by

$$\int_{z_{min}}^{z_{max}} U(y - \text{WTP}, z)gdz = pU(y, 0) + (1 - p)\int_{z_{min}}^{z_{max}} U(y, z)gdz. \quad (9.14)$$

If information raises the credibility of the conditional statement 'suppose this good will be unavailable to you', then the probability, p, rises. From (9.14) the right-hand side falls, so WTP′ is higher than WTP. Furthermore, the effect should be reflected not just in the mean WTP scores, but also in the number of zero bids, since one of the prime reasons usually given for these bids is the interviewee's lack of belief in the credibility of the questions posed.

In addition, because of its consequences for average measures of WTP and for the credibility of the framework, some authors (e.g. Boyle, 1989) have suggested that measures of dispersion should be affected by the provision of information. In particular, it can be argued that as more information is received, those who are already informed will adjust their formulated WTP only marginally, while those who were relatively ignorant will raise their valuations substantially. This should narrow the gap between the ignorant and the informed and hence reduce measures of the dispersion of WTP. This requires not only adopting a specific functional form for the relationship

---

[14] See also Bergstrom et al. (1990) and Hanley and Munro (1992).
[15] Mitchell and Carson (1989: 237) include the problem of the 'probability of provision' in their list of amenity misspecification biases.

between G and information (which we have already argued is not realistic), but also assuming a functional form that applies across individuals. To see that in general nothing can be predicted about the variance or the standard error, consider the effect of providing positive information on the good chosen and suppose that individual WTP and hence the mean WTP rises. If there are H individuals (the superscripts $h = 1, \ldots, H$ are omitted for simplicity), the change in the variance is given by

$$\left(\frac{1}{H}\right) \sum_{h=1}^{h=H} [\text{WTP}' - \overline{\text{WTP}}']^2 - \left(\frac{1}{H}\right) \sum_{h=1}^{h=H} [\text{WTP} - \overline{\text{WTP}}]^2, \qquad (9.15)$$

where a bar above WTP indicates the mean value. Equation (9.15) can be rewritten as

$$[\text{WTP}^2 - \overline{\text{WTP}}'^2] + \left(\frac{1}{H}\right) \sum_{h=1}^{h=H} [(\text{WTP}' - \text{WTP})(\text{WTP}' + \text{WTP})]. \qquad (9.16)$$

The first term is negative since WTP is increased by information. The second term is negative if the *change* in formulated WTP, following the receipt of information, is negatively correlated with the average of value of formulated WTP before and after information. For small changes in information, we would expect the two means to be close, hence provided that information increases formulated WTP, a sufficient condition for the variance of bids to fall is that the size of increases in formulated WTP are negatively correlated with actual WTP. Conversely, if the correlation is positive, the variance may rise in the wake of information. How likely is this result?

Essentially, if those with the highest initial valuation are either the most ignorant or the most receptive to new information, then the variance will rise. The first alternative does not seem likely—after all if the good is a visit to a nature reserve then the set of those visiting the site is not random, but will tend to consist of those with the highest valuation and those most informed about the site attributes. However, the second suggestion is plausible: these people may also be the most receptive to new information because they have already chosen to consume the environmental good. Ultimately, therefore, no predictions can be made about changes in measures of dispersion.

9.4.4. Summary

Table 9.2 summarizes the impact of the provision of information. Positive, good-specific information should raise the mean WTP figures, while negative information about other alternative goods should also increase the bids to preserve a specific good. General information about all possible environmental bundles should raise the formulated WTP for the preservation of all goods together. Meanwhile, if the credibility of the whole process is

Table 9.2   The Effects of Positive Information

	Valuation	Willingness to pay	Variance of bids	Number of zero bids
Good-specific	+	+	?	—
Non-specific	+	?	?	?

enhanced by the provision of information, then the number of zero (non-protest) bids should fall. However, there is no clear-cut prediction of the effects of information on measures of dispersion.

9.5.   THE OPTIMAL LEVEL OF INFORMATION

Section 9.4 has shown that providing information will often affect the results of CV analysis. This prompts a fundamental question: how much information should be given? There are two quite distinct views. One is that information is a good like any other: individuals will buy or search for information up to the point where its marginal value is equal to the marginal cost of further effort. If I wish to buy a car I may telephone round local dealerships, test-drive different makes, and buy magazines that tell me which brands are the most reliable. Providing extra information therefore either means that the social benefit of information exceeds the private benefit,[16] or it implies rejecting consumer sovereignty and viewing environmental goods as 'merit wants' along the lines of health-care or education. Since Musgrave (1959) first proposed the notion of merit wants, economists have been very uneasy about the concept, remaining wary about overriding the preferences of individuals. However, there are reasons why the social benefit of information may differ from and, in some cases, exceed the private marginal benefits.

The second approach, associated with Sagoff (1988), rejects the view of information as just another economic good. Sagoff gives the example of a jury asked to decide on the fate of a prisoner. He argues that the economic view would have the jurors reaching their decision before they sit through the trial and receive evidence from witnesses. Uninformed views would be unacceptable in this instance, he argues, because another person's life might depend on our decision. In a similar way, it would be wrong to accept uninformed views about the value of the environment.

Obviously, the two views have widely divergent implications. Under the first approach, if the social benefit of extra information does not differ from the private benefit, any information passed between the conductor of the study and the subjects is a form of contamination. Under the second, the

---

[16] Or that the social marginal cost is less than the private marginal cost. Given that any cost is simply a negative benefit, for the purposes of what follows we shall refer only to the case where social benefits exceed their private counterpart.

researcher must give as much information to the respondents as is possible. We have already seen in Section 9.2 that information can affect valuation significantly. We need, therefore, to examine the extent to which private benefits from information fall below public benefits and then to see if the result squares with Sagoff's argument.

9.5.1. The Private Value of Information

Information is sometimes valued for its own sake: some people enjoy memorizing train timetables or the capital countries of the world. However, usually information is a means to an end—making a decision—and it only has value in that context. If extra information will not change a decision then it is worthless. Similarly, if there is no decision to be made, then information has no value. If by checking a real-ale guide I can discover which beer has the highest alcohol content, but this will not alter my choice of beers, then there is no point in obtaining the information. Furthermore, even if such information would sway my choice of beers, if I am in a wine bar with no beer available, then again acquisition of such knowledge seems pointless. Only if I am thinking of driving home or might face a choice of beers in the future does the information have a value.

To illustrate the private value of information, suppose an individual is faced with an option to buy a good which costs £2.50. She is uncertain of the good's value: there is a 50 per cent chance that it is worth £3 and an equal probability that she will value it at only £2. Her decision rule is: buy the good if its expected value is greater than or equal to its cost. In this case, therefore, she will buy the good and her expected gain is zero. However, suppose that she could buy information, in the form of a message which will tell her which state of the world she is in without doubt. If the message says '£3' she will buy the good, if it says '£2' she will hold on to her money. The probability she will receive either message is 0.5 so, excluding the cost of the information, her expected gain (prior to the perfect information being revealed) is £0.25. Therefore, the expected value of perfect information[17] for her is £0.25.

9.5.2. The Divergence between Social and Private Values of Information

Clearly if the individual mentioned above is not going to make a decision about buying the good, or her decision-rule is unaffected by any information, then information is valueless. Thus the first and most important source of the divergence between social and private values of information in CV arises from the fact that respondents to the survey are not primed to make a

---

[17] For simplicity, we concentrate on the case where the message is perfectly informative. If the message is less than perfectly informative, some residual uncertainty remains. One message service can be ranked as less informative than a second if it can be represented as a garbling of the second. See Blackwell (1953) or Hirshleifer and Riley (1992).

decision and, therefore, will not have made the necessary investment in information. This statement has to be qualified somewhat if the CV study focuses on users of an environmental amenity where the good enjoyed is essentially private. If the users are rational consumers then they will have invested the appropriate amount of time and money in information acquisition prior to using the good; thus there is no special reason for giving extra information unless the good under analysis differs substantially from the good they have already chosen. For instance, suppose that boating is allowed on a lake, but not fishing. A question of the form 'what are you willing to pay for a fishing licence?' would justify the provision of extra information in a way that 'what are you willing to pay for boating?' would not.[18]

The second and third reasons for the divergence between private and social values of information within CV arise because typically the good is public and furthermore, information itself often has public-good attributes. However, these do not necessarily imply that the social value of information is greater than its private value. Consider a project which will supply a public good to two risk-neutral agents, A and B, at a cost of £2.50 per person. Both A and B are uncertain of the benefits. A believes there is a 0.5 chance that the project is worth £4 and an equal chance that she values it at only £3. Similarly, B assigns 0.5 to the probability of valuing it at £2 and an equal chance of valuing it at £1. The decision rule is as before, so in the absence of further information the project proceeds with an expected net pay-off to A of £1 and of −£1 to B. In this situation, the private value of information depends on the other player's choice of whether to invest in information or not, irrespective of whether information is non-rival or not. The social value differs from the private value in either case, because the information has a value to the other agent. To see this, suppose A can purchase a message service which reveals the true state of her preferences.[19] B, meanwhile, remains ignorant. If A's valuation is £3 the project will not proceed; if it is £4 it will go ahead. *Ex ante*, her expected surplus with the message is therefore £0.75 (a 0.5 chance of 0 if the message is £3 plus a 0.5 chance of £4 - £2.5 otherwise); and so her expected value of information is −£0.25. She would therefore prefer to stay ignorant. If A buys the message service, however, B's expected surplus is −£0.50, yielding an expected value of A's information to B of £0.50. Overall, the expected social value of perfect information (ESVPI)—defined as the sum of the expected private values of perfect information (EPVPI)—is £0.25.

Fundamentally, therefore, group decisions create external effects from information acquisition between members of the group. Moreover, as the

---

[18] It is difficult to be more precise than this, since there is necessarily a gap between the formal theory and the practicalities of fieldwork.

[19] At this stage, we are supposing that states of the world are independent, so a message about A's preferences provides no information on B's.

example illustrates, agents who lose from a decision made under ignorance (defined here as the absence of the extra information) will place a higher value on information than agents who win, precisely because information may reverse the decision in their favour. It is also apparent that, though the social value of information will differ from its private equivalent, we cannot conclude that there will be underinvestment. However, suppose, as would normally be the case, that under the state of ignorance, the expected value of the project is strictly positive or negative. Suppose also that there are many individuals, each of whom has a wide range of possible valuations, with at least some tendency for extreme valuations to be less likely than those in the centre of the range. As the number of agents involved became larger, the impact of any one person's valuation on the decision would become smaller. In these circumstances, the EPVPI for any individual would decline since it would take a more and more extreme valuation for the decision to be affected. For the same reason, the ESVPI would tend to zero for all individuals. Moreover, if we were considering investing in information acquisition for a proportion of the population, then as this subsample became larger, the *ex-ante* mean valuation for the subgroup would become a more and more reliable predictor of the *ex-post* mean. Again, therefore, the value of information would decline. It follows that the fact that the good is public[20] does not necessarily imply underinvestment in information by private individuals.

However, information is a non-rival good, so surely this means that private individuals will underinvest compared to the social optimum? Note that the arguments of the preceding two paragraphs hold equally well whether or not the cost of supply of already acquired information to an extra individual is zero. The conclusions are transformed, though, if states of the world are correlated, so that information on A's preferences also provides information on B's. There are many reasons why this might be so: if we know that costs are to be shared in some fixed proportion across individuals, but we are uncertain about those costs, then any cost information acquired will have an impact on all individual valuations. Similarly, if the benefits from an environmental amenity depend on some objective measure for all individuals, then any information on this measure will have an effect on all individual valuations.[21] For instance, suppose all agents will produce a higher formulated WTP for a wildlife sanctuary the greater the number of otters present. Then a message on otter numbers will have consequences for all individual valuations of the resource.

Let us take a final numerical example: suppose two individuals each value an amenity at either £2 or £4. There is an equal probability of either

---

[20] Note that private goods subject to group decision-making also come under this heading.

[21] We cannot say that these effects will be correlated without knowing more about the distribution of prior beliefs in the population.

valuation, but on this occasion valuations are perfectly positively correlated, while the cost of the amenity per person is once more £2.50. Prior to receiving information, therefore, the project should proceed with an expected gain per person of £0.50. Suppose that an individual can invest in a message service which reveals his or her true valuation. Now clearly such a service also reveals the other person's valuation as well, but suppose that it is too costly for the individual receiving the message to convey it to the other individual. If the message states '£2' then the decision is unchanged (on the basis that the other person's expected valuation is still £3), as it is if the message states '£4'. Thus the private value of information is zero. However, if the information was available to both players, a message of '£2' would halt the project and the ESVPI is £0.25 per person. We therefore have a clear case where the social value of information lies above the private value, a second clear justification for supplying information to subjects in a CV survey which does not rely on the merit-wants view.

Unfortunately, the fact that respondents in a CV survey will typically come to the survey with less than the socially optimal level of information does not tell us what that level is. The thrust of the economic argument suggests that it will rarely be optimal for someone to be fully informed about an issue: if the acquisition of further information is costly then optimality dictates that the marginal social value of information should equal its marginal cost. Sagoff (1988) argues that the jury ought to be fully informed, but even in the extremes of criminal cases, society does not take the view that full information is optimal: juries have to convict when they believe the defendant is guilty 'beyond all reasonable doubt'—not when they are certain. Moreover, if we are to take a literal view of the injunction to ensure respondents are fully informed, then it behoves the researcher to inform subjects fully about the alternative uses of their income—so that no uncertainty surrounds the opportunity cost of their money. The example of the trial by jury is still potentially useful, though. While the cost of information already gathered may approximate to zero within the trial, prior to the trial both prosecuting and defending actors face a positive cost for gathering extra information. Similarly the researcher will often have a body of information which can be passed on to respondents at something close to zero marginal cost.[22] In this sense 'full' information should be provided, but it remains an unresolved issue as to whether researchers should go beyond this point and invest in the acquisition of further information which would then be transmitted to subjects.[23]

---

[22] Although even this is an approximation since information transmission and absorption takes time, which has an opportunity cost for each respondent.

[23] Note though, that if too much information is given, this does not undermine the results of the CV analysis; it simply means that excessive resources have been poured into discovering the correct result.

9.6. DISCUSSION

This chapter has one central message: information is a scarce resource like any other. Therefore, within the confines of neo-classical economics there is no particular reason why WTP (or willingness to accept compensation) statements should only be acceptable if based on full information. Thus when the good is marketed, or when CV is designed purely to elicit use values from current users, so that there is no reason to expect a divergence between the social and private values of information, then there is no reason for contaminating the information sets held by individuals.

This is not the usual case in CV: often we are interested in finding WTP for the kind of goods where citizens are unlikely to have prepared themselves for decision-making. In this case the provision of information is justifiable. Nevertheless, this simple statement creates two major problems. First, what is the optimal extent of information provision?[24] Secondly, what is 'true and accurate' information? Putting responsibility onto the researcher for the supply of information creates ethical dilemmas. To the extent that subjects view interviewers as unbiased sources, the possibility of altering the information set gives the unscrupulous researcher the opportunity to produce CV results which reflect the experimenter's preferences rather than those of the respondents. To the extent that this occurs, the whole process of CV will be undermined.

Work to date on the impact of information is mixed. Moreover, it appears that in most of the face-to-face studies conducted to date, the wrong notion of the control has been employed. Even if this defect is remedied by, for instance, following Samples *et al.* (1986) and giving the control group irrelevant information, an underlying problem is that we have no functional form for the effect of increased information on subjective probabilities. Perhaps what is required of future work is a more controlled environment in which researchers can clearly see how information affects valuation and place limits on the extent to which WTP figures are manipulable. This requires more detailed information from respondents, so that we are not just eliciting WTP, but also assessing beliefs as well.[25] We then run into other difficulties, not least the growing body of experimental evidence which casts doubt on both the expected-utility hypothesis and the Bayesian approach to information processing as predictors of human behaviour (see Machina (1989) or Schoemaker (1982) for the former and Grether (1980) or Kahneman *et al.* (1982) for the latter). One implication of this literature is

---

[24] Formally this is equivalent to the problem of deciding the optimal size of any non-rival good, which means the experimenter gathering information up to the point where the marginal cost of new information is equal to the sum of the marginal values of information for the subjects.

[25] One promising development is the use of verbal protocol analysis, in which subjects are asked to explain their thought processes. See Schkade *et al.* (1994) for an example of its use in CV.

that while further research is required into the effects of information on CV studies, there is an equally pressing need for tests of the consequences of using different frames of reference for the same information.

REFERENCES

Beach, L., and Mitchell, T. (1978), 'A Contingency for the Selection of Decision Strategies', *Academy of Management Review*, 3: 439–49.

Bergstrom, J., and Dillman, B. (1985), 'Public Environmental Amenity Benefits of Private Land: the Case of Prime Agricultural Land', *Southern Journal of Agricultural Economics*, 17: 139–50.

——Stoll, J., and Randall, A. (1989), 'Information Effects in Contingent Markets', *American Journal of Agricultural Economics*, 00: 685–91.

——— and—— (1990), 'The Impact of Information on Environmental Commodity Valuation Decisions', *American Journal of Agricultural Economics*, 00: 615–21.

Bishop, R. C., (1982), 'Option Value: an Exposition and an Extension', *Land Economics*, 58: 1–15.

Blackwell, D. (1953), 'Equivalent Comparison of Experiments', *Annals of Mathematics and Statistics*, 24: 265–72.

Boyle, K. (1989), 'Commodity Valuation and the Specification of Contingent Valuation Questions', *Land Economics*, 55: 57–63.

——Reiling, S., and Philips, M. (1991), 'Species Substitution and Question Sequencing in Contingent Valuation Surveys', *Leisure Sciences*, 12: 103–18.

Cummings, R., Brookshire, D., and Schulze, W. (eds.) (1986), *Valuing Environmental Goods: an Assessment of the Contingent Valuation Method*, Rowman and Allanheld, Totowa, NJ.

Feder, G., and Slade, R. (1984), 'The Acquisition of Information and the Adoption of New Technology', *American Journal of Agricultural Economics*, 66: 312–20.

Graham, D. A. (1981), 'Cost–Benefit under Uncertainty', *American Economic Review*, 71: 715–25.

Grether, D. M. (1980), 'Bayes Rule as a Descriptive Model: the Representativeness Heuristic', *Quarterly Journal of Economics*, 95: 537–57.

Grossman, S., and Stiglitz, J., (1980), 'On the Impossibility of Informationally Efficient Markets', *American Economic Review*, 70: 393–408.

Hanley, N., and Munro, A. (1992), 'The Effects of Information in Contingent Markets for Environmental Goods', *Queen's University Discussion Papers*, Queen's University, Ontario.

Hirshleifer, J., and Riley, J. (1992), *The Analytics of Uncertainty and Information*, Cambridge University Press.

Hoehn, J., and Randall, A. (1987), 'A Satisfactory Benefit–Cost Indicator from Contingent Valuation', *Journal of Environmental Economics and Management*, 14: 226–47.

Kahneman, D., Slovic, P., and Tversky, A. (1982), *Judgement under Uncertainty: Heuristics and Biases*, Cambridge University Press.

Kislev, Y., and Shchori-Bachrach, L. (1973), 'The Process of an Innovation Cycle', *American Journal of Agricultural Economics*, 55: 28–37.

Klein, B., and Leffler, K. B. (1981), 'The Role of Market Forces in Assuring Contractual Performance', *Journal of Political Economy*, 89: 615–41.

Lambin, J. J. (1976), *Advertising, Competition and Market Conduct in Oligopoly Over Time*, North-Holland, Amsterdam.

Machina, M. (1989), 'Choice under Uncertainty: Problems Solved and Unsolved', pp. 12–46 in J. Hey, (ed.), *Current Issues in Microeconomics*, Macmillan, Basingstoke.

Milgrom, P. R., (1981), 'Good News and Bad News: Representation Theorems and Applications', *Bell Journal of Economics*, 00: 380–91.

Mitchell, R., and Carson, R., (1989), *Using Surveys to Value Public Goods: the Contingent Valuation Method*, Resources for the Future, Washington.

Musgrave, R. A. (1959), *Public Finance in Theory and Practice*, McGraw-Hill, Maidenhead, Berks.

Rothschild, R., and Stiglitz, J. (1971), 'Reductions in Risk and Risk Aversion', *Journal of Economic Theory*, 2: 225–43.

Sagoff, M. (1988), 'Some Problems with Environmental Economics', *Environmental Ethics*, 10: 55–74.

Samples, K., Dixon, J., and Gower, M. (1986), 'Information Disclosure and Endangered Species Valuation', *Land Economics*, 62: 306–12.

Schkade, D., and Payne, J. W. (1994), 'How People Respond to Contingent Valuation Questions', *Journal of Environmental Economics and Management*, 26: 88–110.

Schoemaker, P. J. (1982), 'The Expected Utility Model', *Journal of Economic Literature*, 20: 529–63.

Slovic, P., Fischoff, B., and Lichtenstein, S. (1982), 'Response Mode, Framing and Information Processing Effects in Risk Assessment', pp. 21–40 in R. Hogarth, (ed.), *New Directions for the Methodology of Social and Behavioural Science: Question Framing and Response Consistency*, Jossey-Bass, San Francisco.

Stiglitz, J., and Radner, R. (1984), 'A Nonconcavity in the Value of Information', pp. 33–52 in M. Boyer and R. Kihlstrom (eds.), *Bayesian Models in Economic Theory*, Elsevier Science Publications, Amsterdam.

Thaler, R. (1980), 'Towards a Positive Theory of Consumer Choice', *Journal of Economic Behaviour and Organization*, 1: 39–60.

Whitehead, J., and Blomquist, G. (1991), 'Measuring Contingent Values for Wetlands: Effects of Information about Related Environmental Goods', *Water Resources Research*, 27: 2523–31.

10

A Monte Carlo Comparison of OLS Estimation Errors and Design Efficiencies in a Two-Stage Stratified Random Sampling Procedure for a Contingent Valuation Study

KYEONGAE CHOE
WILLIAM R. PARKE
DALE WHITTINGTON

10.1. INTRODUCTION

A reliable, cost-efficient sampling design is an important first step in obtaining accurate estimates from a contingent valuation (CV) study. For simple random sampling, standard statistical theory predicts a square-root relation between the sample size and the standard deviations of estimation errors. Mitchell and Carson (1989) extend this general relation to contingent valuation analysis.[1]

Important practical limitations, unfortunately, confront simple random sampling, especially in the developing countries. In such settings, a reliable, complete sampling framework is often non-existent, making simple random sampling cost-inefficient, if not completely impossible. As a consequence, fieldwork for the implementation of contingent valuation studies is often based on a two-stage stratified random sample. In the first stage, a number of enumeration areas are selected to reduce the geographic area of the survey. In the second stage, observations are drawn from within each enumeration area. Little attention has been paid, however, to efficiency gains or losses that might result from varying the number of selected sample units at either of the two stages of such a stratified sampling strategy.

---

[1] Mitchell and Carson (1989) give the formula

$$n = \frac{Z\hat{\sigma}}{\delta \overline{RWTP}}$$

where n is the sample size needed, $\overline{RWTP}$; is the mean of the estimated WTP bids, δ is the percentage difference between the true willingness to pay and $\overline{RWTP}$, $\hat{\sigma}$ is the estimated standard deviation the WTP response, and Z represents the critical values for t-statistics.

The focus of this chapter is on sampling design issues for contingent valuation analysis based on two-stage stratified random samples. The practical aspects of this problem are emphasized by evaluating alternative sampling designs based on actual data obtained during a contingent valuation study designed to estimate household demand for improved sanitation services in Kumasi, Ghana. The effects of using different numbers of enumeration areas in the first stage and different sample sizes in the second stage are assessed by repeating the experiment for simulated data based on the original coefficient estimates. The results provide some guidance in approaching the sampling design problem for other settings.

Choosing an effective sampling design requires achieving a balance between the nature of the research problem, research costs, time to completion, and the desired level of precision in the results. Consequently, no single principle is a sufficient guide to choosing a sampling strategy in all circumstances. For example, a purely random sampling design based on a complete enumeration of the population is impossible in most survey research projects in developing countries. The major reason is that in such contexts a complete list of sampling units is rarely available, and constructing one is apt to involve a great deal of time and expense.

When a reasonably complete population listing is not available and the population covers a wide area, a two-stage stratified sampling strategy is often adopted. This involves first selecting a number of sampling units, often referred to as enumeration areas, from which sample households (usually called 'elementary sampling units') are randomly selected at the second stage. At both stages a decision has to be made on how many sampling units to select. That decision is usually governed by the degree of accuracy required and the funds available, not by the size of the population. That is, the minimum sample size for a study is calculated on the basis of how much error can be tolerated. A larger sample will be more expensive, but yield more precise estimates. Because of this trade-off between accuracy of estimates and expenditures of time and money, determining what percentage of sampling units should be selected at each stage is a major concern among field practitioners using the contingent valuation method (CVM).

For example, if the study area is a city, the first-stage sampling unit is often the city's smallest-level administrative unit/district or census block; the second-stage unit is the individual household. Sometimes the city's population can be divided into groups or strata according to some chosen criteria, and a number of census blocks can be randomly selected within each group or stratum. From these census blocks, sample households can be randomly selected for study.

During the first-stage sampling process, field representatives are sent out to the selected enumeration areas (EAs) to prepare a complete list of households for the second stage of sampling. The more EAs selected at the first stage, the greater the cost and time spent listing households. But reducing the number of EAs selected at the first stage of sampling may lead to biased or inefficient estimation results in the end. Few studies have investigated the impact on estimation results of varying sampling units at either the first or the second stage of sampling (Rossi *et al.*, 1983). This study explores this issue.

Monte Carlo simulation from the case study presented here suggests that increasing second-stage sample size within a limited number of EAs selected at the first stage of sampling will result in a greater return in statistical and sampling design efficiency than will increasing the number of EAs with a limited second-stage sample size. In both approaches, though, the marginal return diminishes as the number of sampling units increases. These findings hold true even when the sampling strategy includes stratification of the population.

Since the objective of this study is to demonstrate the magnitude of estimation errors caused by sampling design, not by the type of estimator itself, a classical Ordinary Least Squares (OLS) model is used to present the analysis. In Monte Carlo experiments on real data from the Kumasi contingent valuation study, different sampling schemes were simulated to determine their effect on OLS estimation errors.

10.2. THE MODEL AND ANALYTICAL FRAMEWORK

10.2.1   The Economic Model

The study focuses on estimating an inverse compensated demand function for an improved sanitation system from consumers' willingness-to-pay (WTP) bids recorded during a CV survey. WTP bids arise from the difference between two expenditure functions, with consumers minimizing their expenditure $E(\cdot)$ subject to a prespecified level of utility U_0 for levels Q_0 and Q_1 of the service being evaluated. This is expressed as

$$\text{WTP} = E(P_0, Q_0, U_0) - E(P_0, Q_1, U_0), \tag{10.1}$$

where P is a vector of prices, Q is the 'service level' (perhaps degree of technical sophistication) of the sanitation system, and U is the prespecified utility level. A subscript 0 represents the initial level, and a subscript 1 represents some subsequent (improved) level. Our empirical version of this concept takes the form of a linear regression model:

$$\text{WTP} = \beta_0 + \beta_d D + \beta_h H + \beta_s S + \varepsilon, \tag{10.2}$$

where D is the vector for controlling the effects of survey design, H is the vector of household socio-economic characteristics representing consumer preferences, S is the vector describing households' sanitation situation, $\beta_0, \beta_d, \beta_h$, and β_s are the parameters of the variables for respective vectors, and ε is the random error term. β is used to denote the vector ($\beta_0, \beta_d, \beta_h$, and β_s) combining these coefficients.

10.2.2. Sampling Distribution Properties of the Estimator

There are four features of a sampling distribution that are crucial to the assessment of an estimator.[2] They are the mean, the bias, the variance, and the mean squared error (MSE). The expected value of the $\hat{\beta}$ is

$$E[\hat{\beta}] = \beta \tag{10.3}$$

and the bias is defined as

$$\text{Bias}(\hat{\beta}) = E[\hat{\beta}] - \beta. \tag{10.4}$$

Unbiasedness means that as the sample size increases, a correct estimate is received on the average. Unbiasedness is desirable although not always attainable. In this study, the fact that the dependent variable is truncated at zero (negative responses were not allowed) for a small number of cases implies that the data do not strictly speaking satisfy the assumptions needed to establish unbiasedness.[3] The numerical results show that the bias, for our particular case, was a small factor.

The two concepts related to the dispersion of the distribution of $\hat{\beta}$ are

$$\text{Var}(\hat{\beta}) = E[(\hat{\beta} - E(\hat{\beta}))^2] \tag{10.5}$$

measures the magnitude of deviations about the expected value. The mean squared error, defined as

$$\text{MSE}(\hat{\beta}) = E[(\hat{\beta} - \beta)^2], \tag{10.6}$$

measures the magnitude of deviations about the true, unknown parameter value. These two measures and the bias are linked by the relation

$$\text{MSE}(\hat{\beta}) = \text{Var}(\hat{\beta}) + [\text{Bias}(\hat{\beta})]^2. \tag{10.7}$$

If the average to unbiased estimator $\hat{\beta}$ has a smaller variance than another unbiased estimator $\tilde{\beta}$, then an analyst using $\hat{\beta}$ will be closer on the correct parameter than if using $\tilde{\beta}$.

The distinction between the variance of an estimator and its MSE is that while variance measures the dispersion around the $E(\hat{\beta})$, MSE measures the dispersion around the true value of the parameter, β. Thus any difference between them, i.e. subtracting (10.5) from (10.7), is due to bias. The smaller the difference between $\text{Var}(\hat{\beta})$ and $\text{MSE}(\hat{\beta})$, and the smaller the size of $\text{MSE}(\hat{\beta})$, the better are the estimates of the estimators from a specified sample.

---

[2] The discussion in this section requires a preliminary understanding of certain properties of the OLS estimator. Appendix A, drawn largely from Kmenta (1986), supplies the relevant background.

[3] OLS estimates were tried with and without the zero truncation of the dependent variable in order to see the effects of normal random-error terms on the estimator. However, it did not make any differences to the estimation results.

The variance of β as described in Equations (A5) and (A6) in the Appendix is affected by three factors: the variances of random-error term ε; the sample size n; and the total variation in X from the sample at hand. First, the small size of the σ_ε^2 could make $\mathrm{Var}(\hat{\beta})$ smaller (see Equation (A5) in Appendix). However, analysts cannot do anything about this random-error term because they are unobservable random disturbances. Second, increasing the sample size n will make the variance of β smaller. Because the σ_ε^2 is unknown, the variances of errors in Formula (A6) is replaced by its estimated values $s^2 = \varepsilon'\varepsilon/n$. Thus analysts usually like to increase sample sizes as much as time and costs allow. Third, if the total variation in X values is more widely dispersed, $\mathrm{Var}(\hat{\beta})$ will be smaller. However, analysts cannot arbitrarily select X values so that they are widely dispersed. The variation in X values is given according to the population. Analysts can only attempt to have a representative distribution of X values in a sample which is close to that in the study population. Thus, the total variation in X values varies to some extent from sample to sample. If a random sampling design can provide a variance of X values close to that in a population, $\mathrm{Var}(\hat{\beta})$ could be further reduced by adding more observations.

10.2.3. Measuring the Design Efficiency of Sampling Strategy

The design efficiency ratio is used to assess sample-design efficiency for various sample sizes and designs (Frankel 1983). The design efficiency ratio is the ratio of the standard errors of an estimate from a specified sample design to the standard errors for the corresponding estimate from the standard (base) sample design:

$$\text{Design efficiency ratio} = \frac{\mathrm{SE}(\hat{\beta}^{mn})}{\mathrm{SE}(\hat{\beta}^{base})}. \tag{10.8}$$

The greater this ratio, the less effective the specified sample design. In this study, the original sampling design is the one used in the Kumasi project.[4]

10.3. DATA AND DESIGN OF THE EXPERIMENTS

10.3.1. Description of the Data

The data used in this study were drawn from a 1989 contingent valuation survey of households in Kumasi, Ghana (see Whittington et al., 1993a, b).

---

[4] Frankel (1983) suggested basing the denominator on a simple random sample with the same number of observations. However, since the purpose of this exercise was to assess the design effect of varying the number of the sample size at either the first or the second stage of stratified sampling strategy, the sampling variance for the estimate is adopted from the initial sample design used in the Kumasi data set as the base design.

This study used a two-stage stratified sampling procedure to select a random sample. The 373 enumeration areas (EAs) in Kumasi were first stratified according to household density per building (very low, low, medium, high). Then, 26 EAs were randomly selected from the 373 in proportion to the number of EAs in each stratification, and a random number of households were selected from those 26 EAs in proportion to the size of each EA. This resulted in about 1,600 households to be interviewed. After locating and identifying the selected sample households, the enumerators completed interviews with a total of 1,224 households.

This study used the subsample of 769 households who did not have a water closet and who were asked their willingness to pay (WTP) for a Kumasi Ventilated Improved Pit Latrine (KVIP). These households were found in 23 of the 26 EAs: 7 EAs from the high-density, 9 from the medium-density, 6 from the low-density, and 1 from the very-low-density stratification.

To implement the economic model in Equation (10.2) above, 10 exogenous variables were selected (see Tables 10.1 and 10.2). Households' WTP bids for KVIPs were regressed against these 10 exogenous variables. Since most of the exogenous variables in Table 10.2 are binary dummy variables, the means of these dummies indicate the percentage of households that had the respective characteristic. The OLS estimates of the coefficients, standard errors, and t-ratios for each variable are reported in Table 10.1. These estimates were used as baseline coefficients for the Monte Carlo experiments.

10.3.2   The Monte Carlo Experimental Design

To explore the nature of the relationship between sample designs and the performance of the estimators, two approaches were adopted for resampling the Kumasi data set. In the first approach, the number of EAs was varied while holding constant the number of households selected at the second stage of sampling, maintaining the same proportions of EAs selected from each density stratification as in the original, real-case data set. For this 'EA approach', the numbers of EAs selected were 23, 14, 7, and 3. In the second approach, the number of households selected at the second stage was varied, maintaining the number of EAs selected at the first stage of sampling as constant. For this, the 'S approach', sample sizes of 50, 200, 400, and 600 households were tested.

Sixteen experiments [(23, 14, 7, and 3 EAs) × (50, 200, 400 and 600 households)] were conducted to evaluate all possible combinations of these sampling-design choices. Table 10.3 gives identification names for each experiment with the notation $\{EA = m, S = n\}$, where m is 23, 14, 7, or 3, and n is 50, 200, 400, or 600. Each experiment consisted of 40 replications of OLS estimation with the given sample design.

Table 10.1 Description of the exogenous variables and the 'baseline' estimates from the entire sample (769 households)

Type of variable Name	Variable description	Coefficients (β)	Standard errors (SE (β))	t-ratio
INTERC	Intercept	198.57	32.96	6.02**
Questionnaire design				
START	1 = bidding game used high starting point	53.35	18.99	2.81**
	0 = low starting point			
TIMETT	1 = respondent was given time to think about WTP	−9.43	26.73	−0.35
	0 = no time to think			
Household socio-economic characteristics				
INCOMER	Monthly household income in 10,000 cedis	43.74	5.85	7.48**
YRSEDUC	Years of education of respondent	4.17	1.96	2.14*
TRADER	1 = primary worker's occupation is trader	−19.65	20.26	−0.97
	0 = otherwise			
STORY	1 = house is multi-story building	−83.87	26.68	−3.14**
	0 = otherwise			
LANDLORD	1 = landlord lives in the house	42.09	19.32	2.17*
	0 = otherwise			
Water and sanitation practices				
WATERTAP	1 = private water tap is primary water source	97.11	22.79	4.26**
	0 = otherwise			
SANEXPNR	Monthly sanitation expenditure per household (in 100 cedis)	26.87	3.05	8.80**
SATISFY	1 = respondent was very satisfied with current sanitation system	−111.72	49.68	−2.24*
	0 = otherwise			

* Significant at $\alpha \leq 0.05$
** Significant at $\alpha \leq 0.01$

For each of the forty replications, the following three steps were repeated:
1. A subsample of size $n(= 50, 200, 400,$ or $600)$ was randomly drawn from the 769 observations according to the two-stage stratified sampling strategy.

- Stage 1: the EAs (3, 7, 14, or 23 according to the given experiment design) were selected, maintaining the same proportions of EAs selected from each density stratification as in the original Kumasi data set.
- Stage 2: from the households contained in the EAs selected at the first stage, households were randomly sampled to achieve the final sample size of either 50, 200, 400, or 600 according to the experiment design.

Table 10.2 Descriptive statistics of the exogeneous variables by stratification

Stratification	START	TIMETT	INCOMER	YRSEDUC	TRADER	STORY	LANDLORD	WATERTAP	SANEXPNR	SATISFY
High density (no. of EA = 7, N = 169)										
Subtotal										
min	0	0	0.25	0	0	0	0	0	0	0
max	1	1	10.00	21.00	1	1	1	1	18.00	1
mean	0.50	0.27	2.45	7.79	0.42	0.30	0.47	0.46	3.45	0.02
var	0.50	0.44	1.94	5.07	0.50	0.46	0.50	0.50	3.63	0.13
Med. density (no. of EA = 9, N = 209)										
Subtotal										
min	0	0	0.25	0	0	0	0	0	0	0
max	1	1	12.50	19.00	1	1	1	1	25.00	1
mean	0.48	0.21	2.41	7.68	0.35	0.10	0.54	0.59	2.98	0.08
var	0.50	0.41	1.91	4.96	0.48	0.30	0.50	0.49	3.14	0.27
Low density (no. of EA = 6, N = 328)										
Subtotal										
min	0	0	0.25	0	0	0	0	0	0	0
max	1	1	6.25	19.00	1	1	1	1	20.00	1
mean	0.51	0.17	1.97	7.79	0.32	0.16	0.52	0.60	1.87	0.02
var	0.50	0.37	1.27	4.99	0.47	0.37	0.50	0.49	2.81	0.12
Very low density (no. of EA = 1, N = 3)										
Area 5 only										
min	0	0	0.75	0	0	0	0	0	0	0
max	1	1	1	10	0	0	0	0	5	1
mean	0.67	0.33	0.83	3.33	0	0	0	0	2.67	0.33
var	0.33	0.33	0.02	33.33	0	0	0	0	6.33	0.33
Total (no. of EA = 23, N = 769)										
min	0	0	0.25	0	0	0	0	0	0	0
max	1	1	12.50	21.00	1	1	1	1	25.00	1
mean	0.50	0.20	2.22	7.74	0.35	0.17	0.51	0.56	2.61	0.04
var	0.25	0.16	2.84	24.99	0.23	0.14	0.25	0.25	10.13	0.04

Table 10.3   Design of the experiments and identification name of the subsamples

Number of sample households at the second stage of sampling	Number of selected sample units (EAs) at the first stage of sampling			
	3	7	14	23
50	{EA=3, S=50}	{EA=7, S=50}	{EA=14, S=50}	{EA=23, S=50}
200	{EA=3, S=200}	{EA=7, S=200}	{EA=14, S=200}	{EA=23, S=400}
400	{EA=3, S=400}	{EA=7, S=400}	{EA=14, S=400}	{EA=23, S=400}
600	{EA=3, S=600}	{EA=7, S=600}	{EA=14, S=600}	{EA=23, S=600}

Note: Because of the proportional distribution of selected EAs in each stratification, the experiment design with 14 and 23 EAs included the very-low-density EA at the first stage, whereas the design with 3 and 7 EAs did not.

2. For each household in the sample, a value was calculated for the dependent variable Y (simulated WTP bids for KVIPs) using the 'baseline' coefficients (β in the third column of Table 10.1), the set of exogenous explanatory variables X for that household, and the normal random-error term $\varepsilon \sim N(O, \sigma^2)$. Because negative values of WTP bids are impossible in real observations, the simulated values of Y were controlled such that Y was always greater than or equal to zero.

3. The WTP model was estimated using OLS and the simulated Y values from the second step.

These calculations yield 40 sets of parameter estimates for each experimental design. These 40 parameter estimates then serve as data for evaluating the efficiency of the respective sampling designs.[5]

10.4.   RESULTS

Three types of results are reported from these experiments: sampling distributions measuring the performance of OLS in estimating the coefficients for each sampling design; differences in the standard errors of $\hat{\beta}$ (SE ($\hat{\beta}$)) and t-statistics among the experiments; and efficiency of sampling design in different experiments.

10.4.1.   Sampling Distributions

Tables 10.4 and 10.5 provide summary statistics of the sampling distribution of the estimated coefficients for the experiment designs $\{EA = 23, S = n\}$

---

[5] However, in the sample size $n = 50$, some of the OLS replications did not result in full rank because no variability existed in the variable SATISFY. In such cases, only the full-rank samples were used rather than replacing those ineligible replications with new random samples.

Table 10.4. Sampling distribution of estimated coefficients: {EA = 23, S = n} (varying the no. of obs. while holding the no. of EAs = 23)

Dependent variable: simulated maximum WTP bids for KVIP (SIMBKMAX)

Sample ID	INTERC	START	TIMETT	INCOMER	YRSEDUC	TRADER	STORY	LANDLORD	WATERTAP	SANEXPNR	SATISFY
Baseline: beta	198.6	53.35	−9.43	43.74	4.17	−19.65	−83.87	42.09	97.11	26.87	−111.72
No. of obs. = 600											
mean	214.76	51.49	−7.14	41.89	3.84	−16.73	−74.79	39.45	89.26	26.12	−97.31
STD	33.46	20.95	25.04	6.40	2.09	22.14	29.77	23.56	21.04	3.57	57.53
RMSE	37.17	21.03	25.15	6.66	2.11	22.33	31.13	23.71	22.46	3.64	59.30
Relative bias (%)	0.08	−0.03	−0.24	−0.04	−0.08	−0.15	−0.11	−0.06	−0.08	−0.03	−0.13
No. of obs. = 400											
mean	225.38	59.49	−11.23	42.72	3.14	−27.72	−74.11	29.73	88.36	25.31	−100.13
STD	42.00	27.79	28.74	7.13	2.36	24.71	33.66	25.53	27.38	3.98	54.53
RMSE	49.83	28.45	28.79	7.20	2.58	25.99	35.05	28.36	28.74	4.27	55.75
Relative bias (%)	0.14	0.12	0.19	−0.02	−0.25	0.41	−0.12	−0.29	−0.09	−0.06	−0.10
No. of obs. = 200											
mean	216.33	51.58	−10.41	39.83	3.97	−17.93	−81.98	47.12	102.92	25.13	−112.84
STD	59.67	35.03	58.29	10.13	4.47	36.19	55.02	30.79	45.22	5.02	101.75
RMSE	62.26	35.07	58.29	10.86	4.48	36.23	55.06	31.20	45.59	5.31	101.76
Relative bias (%)	0.09	−0.03	0.10	−0.09	−0.05	−0.09	−0.02	0.12	0.06	−0.06	0.01
No. of obs. = 50*											
mean	155.78	53.88	−2.34	47.55	6.81	−28.34	−111.91	67.23	95.69	29.52	−93.04
STD	137.06	68.33	107.59	19.14	8.79	70.77	114.46	61.58	73.12	13.93	176.56
RMSE	143.58	68.33	107.83	19.51	9.18	71.31	117.84	66.51	73.13	14.18	177.55
Relative bias (%)	−0.22	0.01	−0.75	0.09	0.63	0.44	0.33	0.60	−0.01	0.10	−0.17

* Out of 40, only 33 replications resulting in full rank, and were used for analyzing sampling distribution of the OLS estimator.

Table 10.5. Sampling distribution of estimated coefficients: {EA = m, S = 600} (varying the no. of EAs while holding the no. of obs = 600)

Dependent variable: simulated maximum WTP bids for KVIP (SIMBKMAX)

Sample ID	INTERC	START	TIMETT	INCOMER	YRSEDUC	TRADER	STORY	LANDLORD	WATERTAP	SANEXPNR	SATISFY
Baseline: beta	198.6	53.35	−9.43	43.74	4.17	−19.65	−83.87	42.09	97.11	26.87	−111.72
No. of EAs = 23											
mean	214.76	51.49	−7.14	41.89	3.84	−16.73	−74.79	39.45	89.26	26.12	−97.31
STD	33.46	20.95	25.04	6.40	2.09	22.14	29.77	23.56	21.04	3.57	57.53
RMSE	37.17	21.03	25.15	6.66	2.11	22.33	31.13	23.71	22.46	3.64	59.30
Relative bias (%)	0.08	−0.03	−0.24	−0.04	−0.08	−0.15	−0.11	−0.06	−0.08	−0.03	−0.13
No. of EAs = 14											
mean	222.92	49.66	−13.90	42.42	3.84	−19.62	−80.05	39.62	86.99	25.41	−104.58
STD	31.39	17.68	26.69	5.21	1.96	17.45	26.21	20.38	21.73	3.89	63.97
RMSE	39.73	18.06	27.06	5.38	1.99	17.45	26.49	20.53	23.97	4.15	64.36
Relative bias (%)	0.12	−0.07	0.47	−0.03	−0.08	0.00	−0.05	−0.06	−0.10	−0.05	−0.06
No. of EAs = 7											
mean	212.96	53.06	−18.96	42.37	3.76	−22.26	−67.32	41.94	96.19	25.59	−85.95
STD	36.12	25.17	23.10	6.72	2.47	19.41	31.66	20.28	21.14	4.18	82.58
RMSE	38.88	25.17	24.99	6.86	2.51	19.59	35.72	20.28	21.16	4.37	86.51
Relative bias (%)	0.07	−0.01	1.01	−0.03	−0.10	0.13	−0.20	0.00	−0.01	−0.05	−0.23
No. of EAs = 3**											
mean	207.97	50.42	−5.92	41.59	3.91	−15.39	−64.48	44.90	98.89	27.09	−91.18
STD	35.59	17.18	33.04	5.07	2.54	26.51	33.76	23.19	23.13	3.81	89.37
RMSE	36.81	17.42	33.23	5.51	2.55	26.85	38.93	23.36	23.19	3.82	91.70
Relative bias (%)	0.05	−0.05	−0.37	−0.05	−0.06	−0.22	−0.23	0.07	0.02	0.01	−0.18

** Out of 40, only 35 replications resulting in full rank, and were used for analyzing sampling distribution of the OLS estimator.

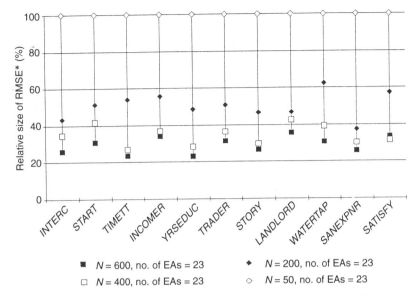

Fig. 10.1   The relative size of RMSE as sample size changes (EA = 23, S = n)

* The ratio of RMSE from the various sample size to the RMSE of the smallest sample size, for each respective parameter.

and $\{EA = m, S = 600\}$.[6] These include mean, standard deviation, RMSE (root of MSE), and relative bias. The relative bias of a coefficient is presented as a percentage of biasedness to the respective baseline coefficient. The relative RMSEs are reported in Figures 10.1 and 10.3, and the ratios of STD to RMSE are in Figures 10.2 and 10.4. The relative size of RMSE for each respective parameter is expressed as a ratio to that parameter's RMSE for the smallest sample size in the table.

Table 10.4 shows the results for varying the second-stage sample size (n) while the number of EAs selected at first-stage sampling remains the same. These results are in accordance with the experimental designs listed in column 4 of Table 10.3. As discussed above (Section 10.2), the mean value of $\hat{\beta}$ is little affected by the actual number of observations, n.

As would be expected, distribution of the estimates around the baseline parameter values, as measured by the RMSE, narrows as the sample size increases. Figure 10.1 shows how much the relative RMSE is reduced by increasing n, in this case for experiment design $\{EA = 23, S = n\}$. Keeping the given 23 EAs at the first stage but increasing n from 50 to 200 reduces

---

[6] For simplicity, only the results from $\{EA = 23, S = n\}$ and $\{EA = m, S = 600\}$ are presented. The results of the experiments $\{EA = 14, S = n\}$, $\{EA = 7, S = n\}$, and $\{EA = 3, S = n\}$ were very similar to $\{EA = 23, S = n\}$ (Table 10.4). Experiments $\{EA = m, S = 400\}$, $\{EA = m, S = 200\}$, and $\{EA = m, S = 50\}$ showed patterns similar to $\{EA = m, S = 600\}$ (Table 10.5).

RMSE approximately 50 per cent; from 200 to 400, by a further 20 per cent; and from 400 to 600, by 5 per cent more.

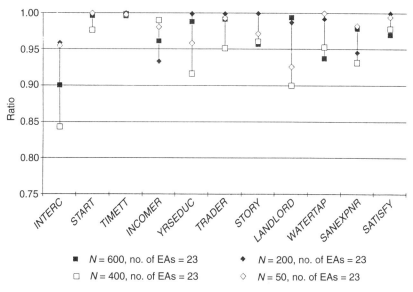

Fig. 10.2   The ratio of STD to RMSE (EA = 23, S = n)

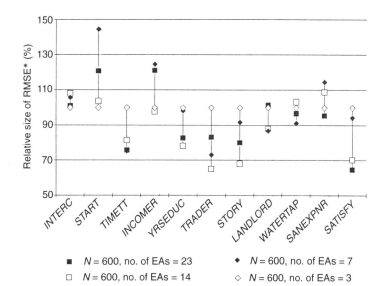

Fig. 10.3   The relative size of RMSE as the number of EAs changes (EA = m, S = 600)

* The ratio of RMSE from the various sample size to the RMSE of the sample size EA = 3, for each respective parameter.

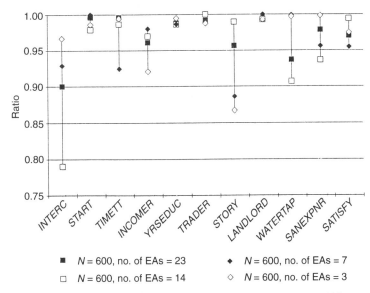

Fig. 10.4   The ratio of STD to RMSE (EA = m, S = 600)

Figure 10.2 shows the ratio of STD to RMSE for each $\hat{\beta}$ from the sampling design {EA = 23, S = n}. Considering that the square of this ratio is

$$(\text{STD/RMSE})^2 = \text{Var}(\hat{\beta})/\text{MSE}(\hat{\beta}) = \text{Var}(\hat{\beta})/\{\text{Var}(\hat{\beta}) + [\text{Bias}(\hat{\beta})]^2\}$$

from Equation (10.7). This ratio differs from unity to the extent that the mean of $\hat{\beta}$ deviates from its baseline value. Generally the ratios from sample sizes 50 and 200 stay above 0.97, whereas those from sample sizes 400 and 600 are lower for a few variables. It should be noted that even though the ratios from sample sizes 50 and 200 are much closer to 1, this is mainly due to the large variances relative to the squared biases, and also the variances in these smaller sample sizes are greater than for sample sizes 400 or 600.

Table 10.5 reports the results when the number of EAs at the first stage of sampling varies, but the number of households selected at the second stage of sampling remains the same (in this case, {EA = m, S = 600}). The results in Table 10.5 show that when the number of EAs at the first stage is reduced while the number of second-stage observations remains the same, relative sizes of RMSE do *not* decrease significantly, nor decrease predictably (in contrast to the experiment designs in which the size of n varies as reported in Table 10.4). The relative RMSE decreases by about 20 to 30 per cent when the number of EAs is increased from 3 to 14 (Figure 10.3). This indicates that, at least in this case study, when sample size is maintained at a specific constant, increasing the number of EAs at the first stage of sampling would achieve only a modest gain in efficiency.

As shown in Figure 10.4, ratios of STD to RMSE are generally above 0.95 for the various EA approaches, and show a similar pattern across the variables. Moreover, these patterns do not differ greatly between the S approach (shown in Figure 10.2) and the EA approach (shown in Figure 10.4).

10.4.2.   Statistical Inferences

Tables 10.6 and 10.7 report the means of SE $(\hat{\beta})$, the means of estimated t-statistics, and the percentages of cases rejecting the null hypothesis, $\hat{\beta} = 0$, out of the 40 replications. Notice that all the baseline estimates except for TIMETT and TRADER rejected the null hypothesis of $\hat{\beta} = 0$, and were statistically significant at a 5 per cent α level in explaining the variances of the dependent variable (see the t-ratio column of Table 10.1). Thus, the per cent of rejecting the null hypothesis for each variable in each experiment should be close to 100.

In Table 10.6 the mean of SE $(\hat{\beta})$ increases more than four times the baseline SE (β) when sample sizes are reduced to 50 while keeping EAs at the first stage constant at 23. With $n = 200$, the mean of SE $(\hat{\beta})$ is almost twice as large as SE (β). Since t-statistics are calculated as $(\hat{\beta})$ divided by SE $(\hat{\beta})$, it is clear that reducing the sample size (n) at the second stage results in smaller t-statistics. In return, estimates from small sample sizes (especially $n = 50$ or 200) would produce a situation where analysts might make incorrect interpretations regarding the significance of key variables. Rejection of the null hypothesis, $\hat{\beta} = 0$, is generally less than 50 per cent for sample sizes 50 and 200, regardless of the number of EAs selected at the first stage. (Figure 10.5 shows only the case when $EA = 23$.)

Table 10.7 (and Figure 10.6) shows corresponding statistics for various numbers of EAs at the first stage while holding the number of second-stage observations constant. With the size of n fixed, varying the number of EAs at the first stage of sampling had very little effect on the mean of SE $(\hat{\beta})$. The reason why the mean of SE $(\hat{\beta})$ does not decrease much when number of EAs increases (compared to increasing n in the S approach) may be largely due to the stratification sampling strategy adopted. Because that strategy tends to select representative population characteristics regardless of the number of EAs selected, variability in X was relatively homogeneous across the sampling designs. And because the number of EAs in each stratification was always kept approximately the same as in the original data set in these experiments, variability of X here would reflect population characteristics even if the number of EAs selected at the first stage of sampling was small. In that sense, the increase or decrease in SE $(\hat{\beta})$ is primarily a function of sample size (n) rather than the variances in X values. This implies that stratification in the first-stage EA selection plays an important role in sampling design and in estimating parameters.

Table 10.6. Sampling distribution of estimated standard errors and t-ratio: {EA = 23, S = n}
(varying the no. of obs. while holding the no. of EAs = 23)

Dependent variable: simulated maximum WTP bids for KVIP (SIMBKMAX)

Sample ID	INTERC	START	TIMETT	INCOMER	YRSEDUC	TRADER	STORY	LANDLORD	WATERTAP	SANEXPNR	SATISFY
Baseline values: SE(beta)	32.96	18.99	26.73	5.85	1.96	20.26	26.68	19.32	22.79	3.05	49.68
Baseline values: t-ratio	6.02	2.81	−0.35	7.48	2.14	−0.97	−3.14	2.17	4.26	8.80	−2.24
No. of obs. = 600											
Avg. of estimated SE(beta)	35.48	20.42	28.71	6.31	2.10	21.82	28.67	20.76	24.55	3.26	53.97
Efficiency ratio	1.08	1.08	1.07	1.08	1.07	1.08	1.07	1.07	1.08	1.07	1.09
Avg. of estimated t-ratio	6.06	2.52	−0.24	6.64	1.83	−0.76	−2.62	1.90	3.64	8.03	−1.82
% rejected Ho***	100	80	8	100	53	28	80	63	100	100	55
No. of obs. = 400											
Avg. of estimated SE(beta)	44.00	25.20	35.83	7.78	2.60	26.95	35.69	25.68	30.40	4.07	66.37
Efficiency ratio	1.34	1.33	1.34	1.33	1.33	1.33	1.34	1.33	1.33	1.33	1.34
Avg. of estimated t-ratio	5.13	2.36	−0.32	5.51	1.21	−1.03	−2.08	1.15	2.91	6.27	−1.52
% rejected Ho***	100	68	5	100	33	25	68	25	93	100	40
No. of obs. = 200											
Avg. of estimated SE(beta)	63.12	36.54	51.69	11.34	3.79	39.16	51.84	37.17	43.92	5.91	97.86
Efficiency ratio	1.92	1.92	1.93	1.94	1.94	1.93	1.94	1.92	1.93	1.94	1.97
Avg. of estimated t-ratio	3.45	1.42	−0.19	3.53	1.03	−0.48	−1.60	1.28	2.37	4.30	−1.16
% rejected Ho***	95	38	20	100	30	10	53	28	73	100	38
*No. of obs. = 50**											
Avg. of estimated SE(beta)	138.79	79.73	114.68	24.87	8.35	83.93	111.17	80.79	95.85	12.76	215.31
Efficiency ratio	4.21	4.20	4.29	4.25	4.27	4.14	4.17	4.18	4.21	4.18	4.33
Avg. of estimated t-ratio	1.16	0.67	−0.03	2.01	0.84	−0.34	−1.07	0.82	0.99	2.38	−0.41
% rejected Ho***	30	12	−9	61	21	9	24	15	12	76	3

*** The number of replications in which the estimated t-ratio was rejected at 10% significance level divided by the total number of replications in each experimental design.

* Out of 40, only 33 replications resulting in full rank, and were used for analyzing sampling distribution properties of the OLS estimator.

Table 10.7. Sampling distribution of estimated standard errors and t-ratio: {EA = m, S = 600} (varying the no. of EAs. while holding the no. of obs. = 600)

Dependent variable: simulated maximum WTP bids for KVIP (SIMBKMAX)

Sample ID	INTERC	START	TIMETT	INCOMER	YRSEDUC	TRADER	STORY	LANDLORD	WATERTAP	SANEXPNR	SATISFY
Baseline values: SE(beta)	32.96	18.99	26.73	5.85	1.96	20.26	26.68	19.32	22.79	3.05	49.68
Baseline values: t-ratio	6.02	2.81	−0.35	7.48	2.14	−0.97	−3.14	2.17	4.26	8.80	−2.24
No. of EAs = 23											
Avg. of estimated SE(beta)	35.48	20.42	28.71	6.31	2.10	21.82	28.67	20.76	24.55	3.26	53.97
Efficiency ratio	1.08	1.08	1.07	1.08	1.07	1.08	1.07	1.07	1.08	1.07	1.09
Avg. of estimated t-ratio	6.06	2.52	−0.24	6.64	1.83	−0.76	−2.62	1.90	3.64	8.03	−1.82
% rejected Ho***	100	80	8	100	53	28	80	63	100	100	55
No. of EAs = 14											
Avg. of estimated SE(beta)	35.42	20.50	28.55	6.35	2.12	21.92	29.17	20.91	24.34	3.35	57.28
Efficiency ratio	1.07	1.08	1.07	1.09	1.08	1.08	1.09	1.08	1.07	1.10	1.15
Avg. of estimated t-ratio	6.30	2.43	−0.50	6.71	1.81	−0.89	−2.77	1.90	3.58	7.63	−1.94
% rejected Ho***	100	83	15	100	58	18	85	48	100	100	58
No. of EAs = 7											
Avg. of estimated SE(beta)	39.22	21.49	31.96	6.61	2.24	22.80	31.16	21.77	27.40	3.61	76.14
Efficiency ratio	1.19	1.13	1.20	1.13	1.15	1.13	1.17	1.13	1.20	1.18	1.53
Avg. of estimated t-ratio	5.45	2.46	−0.57	6.49	1.69	−0.97	−2.18	1.93	3.58	7.17	−1.29
% rejected Ho***	100	75	5	100	45	15	63	50	100	100	40
No. of EAs = 3*											
Avg. of estimated SE(beta)	40.24	21.91	33.24	7.16	2.30	23.63	32.52	22.78	28.26	3.72	102.11
Efficiency ratio	1.22	1.15	1.24	1.22	1.18	1.17	1.22	1.18	1.24	1.22	2.06
Avg. of estimated t-ratio	5.33	2.32	−0.14	5.93	1.70	−0.66	−2.12	1.98	3.60	7.37	−1.22
% rejected Ho***	100	80	11	100	46	23	66	60	94	100	31

*** The number of replications in which the estimated t-ratio was rejected at 10% significant level divided by the total number of replications in each experimental design (normally 40 runs, otherwise specified).

* Out of 40, only 35 replications resulted in full rank, and are used for analyzing sampling distribution properties of the OLS estimator.

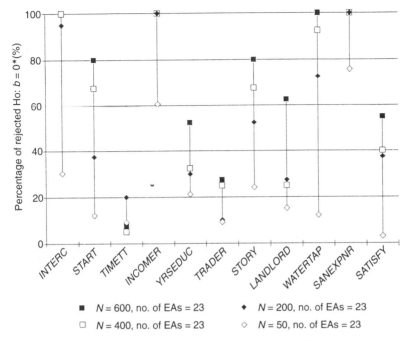

Fig. 10.5 Percentage of the replications in which the null hypotheses, $b = 0$, is rejected (EA = 23, S = n)

* At 10% significance level.

Interestingly, there is not much noticeable difference in hypothesis rejection percentages among the different numbers of EAs, as long as sample sizes are the same (Figure 10.6). But rejection rates do differ greatly from variable to variable. When sample size was limited to 50, most variables had a low percentage of rejection rates for this sample t-statistics. This means that, when sample size is controlled at 50, analysts may be led to the incorrect statistical inference that the exogenous variables do not explain the variances in WTP bids.

10.4.3.   Efficiency of Sampling Design

This section assesses the various sample designs used in the experiments from the practical standpoint of statistical design efficiency. Table 10.8 documents the efficiency of sampling design in terms of the design efficiency ratio (described in Equation (10.8) above) for the experiments, as compared to the original sample design taken from the Kumasi data set. Four distinct groups emerge. The most efficient are $\{EA = 23, S = 600\}$ and $\{EA = 14, S = 600\}$, whose ratios have almost the same very low values (less than 1.10). The next level is found among $\{EA = 3, S = 400\}$,

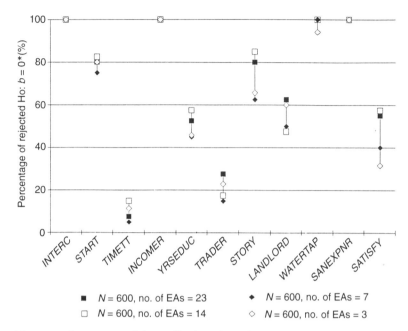

Fig. 10.6   Percentage of the replications in which the null hypothesis, $b = 0$, is rejected (EA $= m$, S $= 600$)

{EA $= 7$, S $= 400$}, {EA $= 14$, S $= 400$}, {EA $= 23$, S $= 400$}, {EA $= 3$, S $= 600$}, and {EA $= 7$, S $= 600$}, where the ratios are generally above 1.10 but less than 1.60; {EA $= 7$, S $= 400$} is the most efficient (lowest ratio) within this group. A third level is represented in {EA $= m$, S $= 200$}, at approximately 2.00, where m is the number of EAs selected, i.e. 3, 7, 14, or 23. The least efficient group centre on {EA $= m$, S $= 50$}: ratios from all designs with $n = 50$ range above 4.00.

Generally, these results indicate that gains in statistical efficiency can be quite considerable when second-stage sample size is increased from 50 to

Table 10.8   Design efficiency ratios by sample design

Stage 2: varying the no. of sample households	Stage 1: varying the no. of selected sample units (EAs)*			
	3	7	14	23
50	4.62	4.25	4.30	4.22
200	2.30	1.99	1.98	1.93
400	1.56	1.14	1.35	1.33
600	1.28	1.19	1.09	1.08

* These are the average of the efficiency ratios across over the estimated coefficients for each sampling design.
Note: Tables 10.6 and 10.7 show the average of efficiency ratios for each coefficients in case of the sampling design {EA $= 23$, S $= n$}.

200. That is, average standard errors of $\hat{\beta}$ from $\{EA = m, S = 50\}$ are more than four times those of SE (β^{base}), whereas those of $\hat{\beta}$ from $\{EA = m, S = 200\}$ are only about twice those of SE (β^{base}). Doubling n from 200 to 400 improves the ratio, not quite as dramatically, by a further 0.60 to 0.80 points; tripling n from 200 to 600 results in a gain of about 0.10 to 0.30 points further, at ratios increasingly close to 1.00.

Gains realized by increasing EAs are small by comparison. Increasing EAs more than fourfold (for example, from 3 to 14) in the first stage of sampling improves (reduces) efficiency ratios by only 0.32 or less: at $n = 50$ they all remain above 4.00; at $n = 600$ they are all less than 1.30.

To summarize, though the rate at which marginal gains accured slowed as second-stage sample size (n) increased, the greatest efficiency was clearly achieved with the largest sample size considered ($n = 600$), with the next largest ($n = 400$) not far behind. The statistical efficiency gained by increasing the number of EAs at the first stage was more modest, but still noticeable.

10.5. CONCLUSIONS

Although statistical theory provides some guidance for determining sample size, the trade-offs between design efficiency and the accuracy of OLS estimation that a researcher can comfortably tolerate in two-stage stratified sampling have received little attention in the literature. This study investigates this trade-off by testing a variety of possible sampling strategies based on actual data obtained from a contingent valuation survey for improved sanitation in Kumasi, Ghana.

The results of these experiments suggest that increasing the number of enumeration areas (EAs) at the first stage of sampling while maintaining a specified sample size (n) for second-stage observations will generate small marginal gains in statistical efficiency. By contrast, increasing second-stage sample size (n) generates a predictable rate of gain in statistical efficiency, regardless of the number of EAs selected at the first stage of sampling. As statistical theory suggests, increasing the number of observations fourfold decreases standard deviations in estimates by approximately one-half. Our findings specifically show that performance of OLS estimators, as well as sample-size efficiency, from sample sizes EA = 3 or S = 50 (the smallest categories in our first-and second-stage approaches, respectively) are lower compared to those from the other, larger experimental sample sizes, especially when the sample size n is limited to 50.

The practical implications depend, of course, on the problem at hand. The prospective researcher must choose between gain in statistical efficiency and the increase in cost: for example, she must consider whether increasing n from 400 to 600 is worth while from the stand-point of research or policy purposes.[7] In this light it might be useful to remember that, to judge from our experimental designs, performances at $\{EA = 14, S = 600\}$ could be as efficient as at $\{EA = 23, S = 600\}$. That is, a reasonable choice might be to increase second-stage sample size (n) without enlarging the number of first-stage enumeration areas.

These Monte Carlo findings indicate that gains in statistical efficiency as well as design effectiveness attained by increasing the number of EAs are small compared to gains achieved by increasing second-stage sample size (n). Though the decision on how large a sample should be depends on the nature of the research problems, the desired level of precision in the results, and the time and cost factors involved, these findings indicate that smaller sample size (in this experiment, limiting sample size to 50) increases the risk of making incorrect inferences from the OLS estimations.

Two important caveats remain for researchers contemplating a small EA strategy. First, because an alternative sampling strategy without stratification of EAs was not examined, it is not possible to state categorically whether increasing the number of EAs at the first stage without stratification would still result in very little gain in statistical efficiency. A poorly balanced choice of a limited number of EAs could certainly produce an unrepresentative sample. Second, if the cost of expanding the number of EAs is not great compared to the basic cost of increasing the total sample size, there are modest efficiency gains available from increasing the number of EAs.

APPENDIX PROPERTIES OF THE OLS ESTIMATOR

To obtain the OLS estimate of β, equation (10.2) can be written in matrix notation as

$$Y = X\beta + \varepsilon, \tag{10A.1}$$

where β is a k-element-column vector of the unknown coefficients and ε is an $n \times 1$-column vector of i.i.d. random errors, $\varepsilon \sim N(0, \sigma^2 I)$. The OLS estimates are given by

$$\hat{\beta} = (X'X)^{-1}X'Y. \tag{10A.2}$$

---

[7] From a practical point of view, it may be more appealing to compare the statistical efficiency of sampling design with the design cost efficiency. It is defined as

design cost efficiency = design efficiency ratio* .
(cost per case for a specified sample design/cost per case for the standard design).

If this factor is equal to 1, the specified sample design has the same cost efficiency as the standard design. If the factor is greater than 1, the specified design is less cost-efficient than the standard design. Since the costs per case for CV surveys differ greatly from study to study, we do not attempt to show this calculation. However, it should be noticed that the gains (or losses) in design efficiency may be reduced (or enhanced) depending on the results of this cost efficiency calculation.

Substituting (10A.1) into (10A.2) gives

$$\hat{\beta} = \beta + (X'X)^{-1}X'\varepsilon. \tag{10A.3}$$

Taking the expectation of (10A.3) yields

$$E(\hat{\beta}) = \beta. \tag{10A.4}$$

The variance of $\hat{\beta}$ is

$$\text{Var}(\hat{\beta}) = E[(\hat{\beta} - \beta)(\hat{\beta} - \beta)'] = E[(X'X)^{-1}X'\varepsilon\varepsilon'X(X'X)^{-1}]. \tag{10A.5}$$

For non stochastic X's,

$$\text{Var}(\hat{\beta}) = \sigma^2(X'X)^{-1}. \tag{10A.6}$$

The square roots of the diagonal elements are the estimated standard errors of $\hat{\beta}$, SE $(\hat{\beta})$. For normally distributed errors, hypothesis tests are based, $\hat{\beta} \sim N[\beta, \sigma^2(X'X)^{-1}]$.

REFERENCES

Frankel, M. (1983), 'Sampling Theory', ch. 3 in Rossi *et al.* (1983).

Greene, W.H. (1990), *Econometric Analysis*, Macmillan, New York.

Kmenta, J. (1986), *Elements of Econometrics*, 2nd edn., Macmillan, New York.

Mitchell, R.C. and Carson, R.T. (1989), *Using Surveys to Value Public Goods: the Contingent Valuation Method*, Resources for the Future, Washington, DC.

Rossi, P. Wright, J.D., and Anderson, A.B. (1983), *Handbook of Survey Research*, Academic Press, New York.

Whittington, D. D.T., Lauria, Choe, K., Hughes, J.A., Swarna, V., and Wright, A.M. (1993a), 'Household Sanitation in Kumasi, Ghana: a Description of Current Practices, Attitudes, and Perceptions', *World Development*, 21: 733–48.

————Wright, A.M., Choe, K., Hughes, J.A. and Swarna, V. (1993b), 'Household Demand for Improved Sanitation Services in Kumasi, Ghana: a Contingent Valuation Study', *Water Resources Research*, 29: 1539–60.

11

The Statistical Analysis of Discrete-Response CV Data

MICHAEL HANEMANN
BARBARA KANNINEN

11.1 INTRODUCTION AND OVERVIEW

In recent years, increasing attention has been given to the statistical aspects of contingent valuation (CV) survey design and data analysis. The main reason for the growing interest in statistical issues is the shift in CV practice from using an open-ended question to ask about willingness to pay (WTP) to using a closed-ended question. The open-ended format confronts respondents with a question on the lines of 'What is the most you would be willing to pay for...?' The closed-ended format uses a question like 'If it cost x to obtain..., would you be willing to pay that amount?' The closed-ended format was introduced into CV by Bishop and Heberlein (1979). Since the mid-1980s it has gained widespread acceptance as the preferred way to cast the valuation question, a position that was recently endorsed by NOAA's Blue Ribbon Panel on CV (Arrow *et al.*, 1993). For reasons mentioned in Section 11.4, we share this preference against the open-ended approach and in favour of the closed-ended approach. However, the closed-ended approach creates a heavy demand for statistical technique. Statistical issues are not pressing with the open-ended format because the data essentially speak for themselves—the survey responses yield a direct measure of WTP which requires little or no further analysis. With the closed-ended format, by contrast, the CV responses are not dollar amounts but answers of 'yes' or 'no', and one obtains a WTP value from these responses by introducing a statistical model that links them to the dollar amounts that people faced in the survey.

Since the CV responses are binary variables, one needs a statistical model appropriate for a discrete dependent variable. Such models have come to play an important role in many areas of microeconomics since the 1970s. A

We gratefully acknowledge helpful comments and suggestions from Anna Alberini, Ian Bateman, Richard Carson, Anni Huhtala, and Kerry Smith, as well as excellent research assistance by Craig Mohn. We are deeply indebted to Ian Bateman for his editorial kindness and forbearance.

major reason for this was the growth in availability of disaggregated survey data on specific choices by individual agents—when economic behaviour is observed at that level, the outcomes often turn out to be discrete variables, or mixed discrete/continuous variables, rather than purely continuous variables. Some of the most important statistical models for discrete dependent variables used in field like labour economics were first developed in the field of biometrics—logit and probit are obvious examples—but they found ready application to microeconomic data. Discrete-response CV is no exception—logit and probit play a key role in the analysis of CV data. Moreover, there is a direct analogy between the response-generating mechanism in some biometrics applications and that in a CV survey. A common setting in biometrics is the dose–response study, where the stimulus is an administered dose of some substance and the outcome is a discrete measure of health status (e.g. alive or dead). The aim is to measure the probability distribution of susceptibility to the substance in question. In a CV survey, the monetary amount presented to subjects (the 'bid') can be thought of as the dose, and the yes/no reply as the response; the equivalent of susceptibility is the WTP amount.

Another fruitful analogy is with reliability analysis and life testing in industrial engineering, where equipment is stressed until it fails. Sometimes one does not know when it failed, only that it failed after more than 7,000 hours, say, or less than 10,000 hours. The aim is to estimate a probability distribution for the true life of the item—analogous to the true WTP in a CV setting—using information on upper or lower bounds. Statistically, the data look just like responses from a discrete-response CV survey. In CV the bids are subject to the control of the researcher, just as the dose or stress are subject to control by the researcher in dose–response and life-testing experiments. Thus, one can apply to the selection of CV bids statistical techniques for optimal experimental design that have been developed in biometrics and reliability analysis. These analogies with other branches of applied statistics have substantially transformed the statistical side of CV research in recent years.

In this chapter we survey the statistical issues associated with discrete-response CV. Our aim is to make the reader aware of the recent developments in the design and analysis of CV surveys. A major theme is the close interplay between economics and statistics. The CV responses are analysed using statistical models. But the models must make sense from the point of view of economic theory. This places significant restrictions on the statistical models that can be used. These implications were first developed by Hanemann (1984a), but his analysis was incomplete and incorrect in some particulars. Here we extend his analysis and correct the errors. We show that many of the models in the current literature violate some of the restrictions of economic theory. Another major theme is the value of richness in the statistical models in order to accommodate heterogeneity of preferences in the population of interest and, also, heterogeneity of response behaviour in a survey setting. Richness typically requires introducing additional parameters into the model; the question is how this should be done. Again, there are interesting interactions between the statistics and the economics. Structural models provide the most information from an economic point of view, but they can be fragile if the structure is misspecified. Non-parametric models are more robust and offer greater flexibility in the shape of the response function, but they provide less economic information. Moreover, which economic welfare measure one wants to use can affect the choice of statistical methodology; for example, non-parametric models generally have more trouble providing an estimate of mean than median WTP.

This chapter consists of three main sections. Section 11.2 presents the economic theory of responses to CV survey questions, set within the framework of a random utility maximization model, and shows how this generates statistical models for the survey responses. Section 11.3 reviews the statistical issues that arise in the estimation of economic welfare measures from data on CV responses using the maximum likelihood method; it also describes procedures for selecting the bids to be used in CV surveys and for interpreting the results after the data have been collected, based on the principles of optimal experimental design. Section 11.4 considers some advanced topics in the statistical design and analysis of discrete-response CV data that are both of practical interest and on the current frontiers of research. Section 11.5 offers some brief conclusions.

11.2 ECONOMIC THEORY AND STATISTICAL MODELS

11.2.1 Types of discrete response format

We start by reviewing the different types of closed-ended question that could be used in a CV survey. In what follows, we denote the object of the valuation by q.[1] The CV study could involve just two levels of q or multiple levels of q, depending on whether the goal is to value a single programme, to value multiple programmes, or indeed to estimate an entire valuation function.

When valuing a single programme, one asks people about their WTP to obtain a change from q^0 (the status quo) to some particular alternative q^1. With closed-ended questions, there are *single-bounded* and *multiple-bounded* ways to do this. The single-bounded approach is the original format of Bishop and Heberlein (1979), where respondents are presented with a specific dollar cost to obtain the change and asked whether they would be willing to pay this amount. With a public programme, the question can be framed in terms of whether they would vote for or against the programme if

---

[1] Depending on the circumstances, q could be a scalar or a vector.

it involved a specific increase in their taxes.[2] Their response provides qualitative information in the form of a bound on their WTP for the change—a
lower bound if they answer 'yes', and an upper bound if they answer 'no'.
The double-bounded format, proposed by Hanemann (1985) and Carson
(1985) and first applied by Carson and Steinberg (1990) and Hanemann *et al.*
(1991), follows up on the initial question with a second question, again
involving a specific dollar cost to which they can respond with a 'yes' or a
'no'. The amount presented in this second bid depends on the response to the
first bid: if the respondents answered 'no' to the first bid, the second bid is
some lower amount, while if they answered 'yes' it is some higher amount.
Consequently, if they answer 'yes' to one of the questions and 'no' to the
other, this provides both upper and lower bounds on their WTP for the
change. Similarly, the triple-bounded format has an additional follow-up
question with a bid amount that depends on the responses to the first two
questions (Chapter 15 below; Cooper and Hanemann, 1995). The additional
bids can lead to sharper bounds on the estimate of WTP.

Other formulations of the survey question also generate bounds on WTP.
For example, subjects can be shown a *payment card* listing various dollar
amounts and asked to circle the one that comes closest to their own value
(Mitchell and Carson, 1981). The response can be interpreted not as an exact
statement of WTP but, rather, as an indication that the WTP lies somewhere
between the highest number below the amount circled and the smallest
number above it (Cameron and James, 1987). Equivalently, they can be
shown a list of dollar amounts and asked to mark off the amounts they are
sure they would be willing to pay and those they are sure they would not
(Welsh and Bishop, 1993). Similarly, they can be presented with alternative
dollar *ranges* and asked to identify the one that comes closest to their own
value. These approaches all yield upper and lower bounds on WTP for the
change in q.

When dealing with multiple programmes, one can proceed similarly, comparing each programme q^1, q^2, q^3,... in turn with the baseline status quo, q^0,
using either a single- or multiple-bounded format. This is like valuing a single
programme, but repeated many times over. Alternatively, one can ask
respondents to assess several programmes simultaneously. With *contingent
ranking*, introduced by Beggs *et al.* (1981) and Chapman and Staelin (1982),
respondents are presented with a set of programmes each involving a specific
action and a specific cost, and asked to rank them.[3] For example, they might
be offered programs to save 5,000 acres of wetlands at a cost of $30

---

[2] Because of this, the close-ended format is sometimes called *referendum* CV. Strand
(1981) appears to have been the first CV study to use the frame of voting.

[3] If q is a vector, one must ask about not only different *levels* of q but also different
combinations of the elements of q, in order to span the full range covered by the multi-attribute
valuation function. When valuing a single programme, by contrast, it matters little whether q is
a scalar or a vector because one is simply asking for a global valuation of q^1 versus q^0.

per taxpayer, 10,000 acres at a cost of $60 per taxpayer, and 15,000 acres at a cost of $150 per taxpayer, and asked to rank these from most to least preferred.

In each case, whether it is yes/no or a ranking, the response to the CV question provides only qualitative information about WTP. Thus, from the raw responses alone, one cannot obtain a quantitative measure of WTP. To obtain that, one must embed the data in a model relating the responses to the monetary stimuli that induced them. How this is done—what models to use, and how then to derive quantitative measures of value—is the subject of this section.

11.2.2   The economic foundations of a statistical model

Statistically, the CV responses are discrete dependent variables since they are measured on a nominal or ordinal scale. There is a variety of statistical models for analysing such data.[4] While we consider specific models below, their common structure can be summarized as follows. In the general case, the CV responses can assume a finite number of values, which we index $j = 1, \ldots, M$. For the ith observed response, the probability that it takes a particular value can be expressed as some function

$$\Pr\{\text{response}_i = j\} = H_j(A_i; Z_i; \gamma) \tag{11.1}$$

where A_i is the bid on that occasion, Z_i represents other covariates describing the subject, the item being valued, or any other pertinent aspect of the survey, and γ is a vector of parameters to be estimated from the data. In order for the probabilities to be well defined, the right-hand side (RHS) of (11.1) must return a value between zero and one, and it must sum to unity over all possible outcomes $j = 1, \ldots, M$. In binary response models where there are just two possible outcomes, 'yes' and 'no', (11.1) reduces to

$$\begin{aligned}
\Pr\{\text{response is 'yes'}\} &= H(A; Z; \gamma) \equiv H(A) \\
\Pr\{\text{response is 'no'}\} &= 1 - H(A; Z; \gamma) \equiv 1 - H(A).
\end{aligned} \tag{11.1'}$$

It is common to write the $H(\cdot)$ function as the composition of two subfunctions,

$$H(A; Z; \gamma) \equiv 1 - F[T(A; Z; \gamma)], \tag{11.2}$$

which then permits the statistical response model to be cast in the form

$$\begin{aligned}
\text{Response} &= \text{'yes' if } T(A; Z; \gamma) - \eta \geq 0 \\
&= \text{'no' otherwise,}
\end{aligned} \tag{11.3}$$

---

[4] Econometric texts with good coverage of these models include Maddala (1983), Amemiya (1985), and Greene (1993). More specialized references include Santner and Duffy (1989), Collett (1991), and Morgan (1992); the latter calls these 'quantal response' models.

where $T(\cdot)$ is some real-valued function of A and Z, η is some random variable with cumulative distribution function (c.d.f.) $F(\cdot)$, and γ represents both coefficients associated with $T(\cdot)$ and parameters of the cdf. The composition ensures that the RHS of (11.1′) returns a value within the range $[0, 1]$. As we show below, different discrete-response models involve different formulas on the RHS of (11.1) or (11.1′).

This statistical perspective can be distinguished from what might be called the economic perspective, which requires that the survey responses be economically meaningful in the sense that they constitute a utility-maximizing response to the survey question. To satisfy both perspectives, one wants to formulate a statistical model for the CV responses that is consistent with an economic model of utility maximization. In this section, we sketch how that is done.

We assume an individual consumer with a utility function like that considered in Chapter 3 above, which is defined over both market commodities, denoted x, and some non-market item which is to be valued, denoted by q. The corresponding indirect utility function depends on the individual's income, y, the non-market item q, and various other arguments including the prices of the market goods, perhaps attributes of the market goods, and attributes of the individual that shift her preferences.[5] For now, however, we suppress all of these arguments except (q, y). The other key component of the indirect utility function is a stochastic component representing the notion of random utility maximization (RUM). It is the RUM concept that provides the link between a statistical model of observed data and an economic model of utility maximization. In a RUM model it is assumed that, while the individual knows her preferences with certainty and does not consider them stochastic, they contain some components that are unobservable to the econometric investigator and are treated by the investigator as random (Hanemann, 1984b). These unobservables could be characteristics of the individual and/or attributes of the item; they can stand for both variation in preferences among members of a population and measurement error. For now, we represent the stochastic component of preferences by ε without yet specifying whether it is a scalar or a vector, and we write the indirect utility function as $v(q, y, \varepsilon)$.

To fix ideas, we focus on the valuation of a single programme using the single-bounded approach.[6] Thus, the individual is confronted with the possibility of securing a change from q^0 to $q^1 > q^0$. We assume she regards this as an improvement, so that $v(q^1, y, \varepsilon) \geqslant v(q^0, y, \varepsilon)$. She is told this change will

---

[5] Following the suggestion in McFadden and Leonard (1993), the variable y could be *supernumerary* income that remains after allowing for committed expenditures on market or non-market goods; i.e., $y \equiv \bar{y} - \kappa$, where $\bar{y}$ is full income and κ is committed expenditure. The parameter κ could be known exogenously or it could, in principle, be estimated from the CV responses along with the other model parameters.

[6] The double-bounded approach and the valuation of multiple items are taken up in Section 11.4.

cost A, and she is then asked whether she would be in favour of it at that price. By the logic of utility maximization, she answers 'yes' only if $v(q^1, y - A, \varepsilon) \geqslant v(q^0, y, \varepsilon)$, and 'no' otherwise. Hence,

$$\Pr\{\text{response is 'yes'}\} = \Pr\{v(q^1, y - A, \varepsilon) \geqslant v(q^0, y, \varepsilon)\}. \qquad (11.4)$$

An equivalent way to express this same outcome uses the compensating variation measure, which is the quantity C that satisfies

$$v(q^1, y - C, \varepsilon) = v(q^0, y, \varepsilon). \qquad (11.5)$$

Thus, $C = C(q^0, q^1, y, \varepsilon)$ is her maximum WTP for the change from q^0 to q^1. It follows that she answers 'yes' if the stated price is *less* than this WTP, and 'no' otherwise. Hence, an equivalent condition to (11.4) is

$$\Pr\{\text{response is 'yes'}\} = \Pr\{C(q^0, q^1, y, \varepsilon) \geqslant A\}. \qquad (11.6a)$$

In a RUM model, $C(q^0, q^1, y, \varepsilon)$ itself is a random variable—while the respondent's WTP for the change in q is something that she herself knows, it is something that the *investigator* does not know but treats as a random variable. Let $G_c(\cdot)$ be what the investigator assumes is the cdf of C, and $g_C(\cdot)$ the corresponding density function (the investigator will estimate the parameters from the CV data); then (11.6a) becomes[7]

$$\Pr\{\text{response is 'yes'}\} = 1 - G_c(A). \qquad (11.6b)$$

Equations (11.4) and (11.6a, b) constitute not only an economic model of respondent behaviour but also a statistical model, since the RHS defines a particular form of the $H(\cdot)$ function in (11.1'). Specifically, $H(A) \equiv 1 - G_C(A)$. In effect, this represents the integrability condition for the single-bounded case: the statistical model (11.1') is consistent with an economic model of maximizing behaviour if and only if the RHS of (11.1') can be interpreted as the cdf of a random WTP function, $C(q^0, q^1, y, \varepsilon)$.

There are two ways to formulate a statistical model with this property. One approach, associated with Cameron (1988), is to directly specify a particular cdf for the individual's random WTP. Let $E\{C\} = \mu$ (in a regression model one would have $\mu = X\beta$), let $\text{var}\{C\} = \sigma^2$, and let $G(\cdot)$ be the c.d.f of the standardized variate $z = (C - \mu)/\sigma$; then

$$\Pr\{\text{response is 'yes'}\} = 1 - G_C(A) = 1 - G\left(\frac{A - \mu}{\sigma}\right). \qquad (11.7)$$

For example, when $G(x) = \Phi(x)$, the standard normal cdf, one has a probit model

$$\Pr\{\text{response is 'yes'}\} = \Phi\left(\frac{\mu - A}{\sigma}\right), \qquad (11.8)$$

---

[7] It follows that $\partial\Pr\{\text{'yes'}\}/\partial A = -g_C(A) \leqslant 0$: regardless of the particular form of the utility function, the 'demand function' for the change in q is downward-sloping.

while $G(x) = (1 + e^{-x})^{-1}$, the standard logistic, yields a logit model

$$\Pr\{\text{response is 'yes'}\} = \frac{1}{1 + \exp[(A - \mu)/\theta]}, \tag{11.9}$$

where $\theta \equiv \sigma\sqrt{3}/\pi.$[8]

The other approach, emphasized by Hanemann (1984a), starts by specifying a particular indirect utility function $v(q, y, \varepsilon)$ and a particular cdf for ε, and then constructs the corresponding $G_c(\cdot)$. For example, the following Box–Cox utility function nests many of the models used in the existing literature:

$$u_q = \alpha_q + \beta_q \left(\frac{y^\lambda - 1}{\lambda}\right) + \varepsilon_q, \quad q = 0 \text{ or } 1, \tag{11.10a}$$

where $\alpha_1 \geqslant \alpha_0$ and $\beta_1 \geqslant \beta_0 > 0.$[9] This can be regarded as a form of CES utility function in q and y. The corresponding formula for WTP is

$$C = y - \left(\frac{\beta_0 y^\lambda}{\beta_1} - \frac{\lambda\alpha}{\beta_1} + \frac{\beta_1 - \beta_0}{\beta_1} - \frac{\lambda\eta}{\beta_1}\right)^{\frac{1}{\lambda}}, \tag{11.10b}$$

where $\alpha \equiv \alpha_1 - \alpha_0$ and $\eta \equiv \varepsilon_1 - \varepsilon_0.$[10] McFadden and Leonard (1993) proposed a restricted version of this model with $\beta_1 = \beta_0 \equiv \beta > 0$, yielding

$$C = y - \left(y^\lambda - \frac{\alpha}{b} - \frac{\eta}{b}\right)^{\frac{1}{\lambda}}, \tag{11.11}$$

where $b \equiv \beta/\lambda$. This includes as special cases the two utility models used by Hanemann (1984a), i.e. the linear model where $\lambda = 1$,

$$u_q = \alpha_q + \beta y + \varepsilon_q$$
$$C = \frac{(\alpha + \eta)}{\beta}, \tag{11.12}$$

and the logarithmic model where $\lambda = 0$

$$u_q = \alpha_q + \beta \ln y + \varepsilon_q$$
$$C = y(1 - \exp[-(\alpha + \eta)/\beta]). \tag{11.13}$$

The model is completed by specifying a probability distribution for η. Let $G_\eta(\cdot)$ be this c.d.f; the response probability formulas for the models (11.10)–(11.13) are given by:[11]

---

[8] The c.d.f of a logistic with scale parameter $\tau > 0$ and location parameter μ is $F(x) = (1 + \exp[-(x - \mu)/\tau])^{-1}$; this has a mean and median of μ, and a variance of $\tau^2\pi^2/3$. In the standard logistic, $\mu = 0$ and $\tau = 1$. In (11.9), $G(\cdot)$ is taken to be the c.d.f of $z = (C - \mu)/\theta$.
[9] Since $y > 0$, the problems raised by Burbidge et al. (1988) with the Box–Cox transformation do not arise.
[10] Note that α_1 and α_0 are not separately identifiable here, only their difference α. Similarly, in this model the cdfs of ε_1 and ε_0 are not separately identifiable, only the c.d.f of η. Depending on the model structure, there will generally be some identifiability restrictions such as these.

$$\Pr\{\text{response is 'yes'}\} = 1 - G_\eta\left[\frac{\beta_0 y^\lambda}{\lambda} - \frac{\beta_1(y-A)^\lambda}{\lambda} + \frac{\beta_1 - \beta_0}{\lambda} - \alpha\right] \quad (11.10')$$

$$\Pr\{\text{response is 'yes'}\} = 1 - G_\eta[by^\lambda - b(y-A)^\lambda - \alpha]. \quad (11.11')$$

$$\Pr\{\text{response is 'yes'}\} = 1 - G_\eta[-\alpha + \beta A] \quad (11.12')$$

$$\Pr\{\text{response is 'yes'}\} = 1 - G_\eta\left[-\alpha - \beta\ln\left(1 - \frac{A}{y}\right)\right]. \quad (11.13')$$

The linear and logarithmic models have been widely used in CV because of their simplicity. However, they impose quite stringent restrictions on the shape of the WTP function: the linear model (11.12) implies that the income elasticity of C is zero; the logarithmic model (11.13) implies that it is unity. The Box–Cox models are more flexible in this regard, since they permit other values for the income elasticity of C. The income elasticity is negative when $\lambda > 1$, positive when $\lambda < 1$, and is approximately equal to $(1 - \lambda)$. Though more flexible than the linear and logarithmic models, the Box–Cox models provide a relatively restricted shape for the graph of WTP against income; more flexible functional forms (with additional parameters) may be needed. Nevertheless, for convenience we will frequently use (11.11) in this chapter to illustrate points of modelling methodology.

Observe that, when one uses the linear model with $G_\eta(\cdot)$ a standard normal c.d.f, (11.12') becomes

$$\Pr\{\text{response is 'yes'}\} = \Phi(\alpha - \beta A), \quad (11.14)$$

which is a probit model that becomes identical to the model in (11.8) when $\alpha = \mu/\sigma$ and $\beta = 1/\sigma$. This can be verified by inspection of the formula for C: since η has zero mean and unit variance, it follows directly from (11.12) that $E\{C\} \equiv \mu = (\alpha/\beta)$ and $\text{var}\{C\} \equiv \sigma^2 = 1/\beta^2$. Similarly, when $G_\eta(\cdot)$ is the standard logistic c.d.f, (11.12') becomes

$$\Pr\{\text{response is 'yes'}\} = \frac{1}{1 + \exp(-\alpha + \beta A)}, \quad (11.15)$$

which is a logit model that becomes identical to the model in (11.9) when $\alpha = \mu/\theta$ and $\beta = 1/\theta$.[12, 13] These examples illustrate the point that, with an

---

[11] The models in this paragraph all involve an additively random structure, of the general form $u_q = \bar{v}(q, y) + \varepsilon_q, q = 0$ or 1. Given this structure, the individual responds 'no' if $\Delta\bar{v} - \eta \geqslant 0$ where $\Delta\bar{v} \equiv [\bar{v}(q^0, y) - \bar{v}(q, y - A)]$ and $\eta \equiv (\varepsilon_1 - \varepsilon_0)$. Hanemann (1984a) called $\Delta\bar{v}$ a *utility difference*; it corresponds to $T(A; Z; \gamma)$ in (11.3). This utility difference formulation does *not* apply when the random term enters the utility model nonlinearly, as in (11.19) below.

[12] In this case, since η has a variance of $\pi^2/3$, (12) implies that $\text{var}\{C\} \equiv \sigma^2 = \text{var}\{\eta\}/\beta^2 = \theta^2\pi^2/3$.

[13] The probit model arises if ε_1 and ε_0 are normally distributed; if they are i.i.d. normal with mean zero and variance 0.5, their difference, η, is standard normal. Similarly, the logit model arises if the ε's are extreme value variates. The cdf of an extreme value variate with location parameter ζ and scale parameter $\tau > 0$ is $F(\varepsilon) = \exp[-\exp(-\varepsilon - \zeta)/\tau)]$; the mean is $\zeta + 0.5772\tau$

appropriate choice of distributions, the two alternative approaches to generating a statistical model for the CV responses yield the same formula. This result holds generally. There is no essential difference between the two approaches because any formula for an indirect utility function, $v(q, y, \varepsilon)$, implies a corresponding formula for WTP, $C(q^0, q^1, y, \varepsilon)$. The converse is also true since, from (11.5), one has

$$
\begin{aligned}
C &= y - m[q^1, v(q^0, y, \varepsilon), \varepsilon] \\
  &\equiv y - K(q^0, q^1, y, \varepsilon),
\end{aligned}
\tag{11.16}
$$

where $m(q, u, \varepsilon)$ is the expenditure function associated with $v(q, y, \varepsilon)$, and $K(q^0, q^1, y, \varepsilon)$ is the income-compensation function which, as Hurwicz and Uzawa (1971) showed, provides a complete representation of consumer preferences. Thus, $C(\cdot)$ and $v(\cdot)$ are alternative representations of the same preference ordering; any probability distribution of u implies a corresponding probability distribution of C, and conversely.

There are two important implications. First, just as economic theory places certain restrictions on $v(\cdot)$, it also places restrictions on $C(\cdot)$. These must be reckoned with whatever the approach to model formulation. The existing literature—our own work included—has not always paid adequate attention to these restrictions. We discuss them further in the next section.

Second, an essential feature of RUM models is that the stochastic and deterministic components are commingled. In conventional economic analysis, one generally formulates a deterministic economic model and then adds a random term for the purpose of statistical estimation. The random term is assumed to arise outside the economic model and it plays no role in the economic analysis once the model has been estimated. In a RUM model, by contrast, the stochastic component is an essential part of the economic model and it plays a substantive role in the use of the model for both prediction of behaviour and evaluation of welfare.

We have already seen an example of this in connection with the variance parameter $\sigma^2 \equiv \text{var}\{C\}$. Assuming a regression setting where $\mu_i = X_i\beta$ for the ith respondent, the response probability formula in (11.7) can be written

$$
\Pr\{i\text{th respondent says 'yes'}\} = 1 - G\left(\frac{A_i}{\sigma} - \frac{X_i\beta}{\sigma}\right),
\tag{11.7'}
$$

which implies that the term $1/\sigma$ serves as the 'coefficient' of the bid amount in the statistical model of respondent behaviour. Thus, what might have been thought a purely statistical parameter also has a behavioural significance. This is a general result, not limited to any particular RUM

and the variance is $\tau^2\pi^2/6$. In the standard extreme value, $\zeta = 0$ and $\tau = 1$. If ε_1 and ε_0 are independent extreme value variates with separate location parameters ζ_1 and ζ_0 and a common scale parameter τ, $\eta = \varepsilon_1 - \varepsilon_0$ has a logistic distribution with location parameter $\mu = \zeta_1 - \zeta_0$ and scale parameter τ. The standard logistic arises when $\zeta_1 = \zeta_0$ and $\tau = 1$.

specification.[14,15] Some insight into the reason for it can be obtained from the Box–Cox utility model; (11.10b) implies that var$\{C\}$ is a function not only of the stochastic terms in the utility function but also of the structural parameters, such as α, β_q, or λ. Moreover, in (11.10), (11.11), and (11.13), var$\{C\}$ is a function of income, y, so that C has a heteroscedastic distribution. It is inappropriate, therefore, to think of var$\{C\}$ as merely a statistical constant. Many other examples of the commingling of stochastic and deterministic components in RUM models will be encountered below.

In their original paper, Bishop and Heberlein (1979) used the following model for the CV responses:

$$\text{Pr}\{\text{response is 'yes'}\} = \frac{1}{1 + \exp(-\alpha + \beta \ln A)}. \qquad (11.17)$$

Like (11.15), this is a logit model where the response probability is independent of income; the difference is that (11.15) uses A, whereas (11.17) uses (ln A). Hanemann (1984a) asserted that (11.17) was not consistent with economic theory because it was not a valid RUM model. As we now show, that assertion was incorrect.

The definition in (11.16) implies that $C(q^0, q^1, y, \varepsilon)$ is independent of y if and only if $m_u(q^1, u^0, \varepsilon) = m_u(q^0, u^0, \varepsilon)$. As shown in Chapter 3, this comes about if

$$u = T[y + \theta(q, \varepsilon), \varepsilon] \qquad (11.18a)$$

for some increasing function $T(\cdot)$. The resulting formula for C is

$$C = \theta(q^1, \varepsilon) - \theta(q^0, \varepsilon), \qquad (11.18b)$$

which implies response probabilities of the form

$$\text{Pr}\{\text{response is 'yes'}\} = \text{Pr}\{C \geqslant A\} = \text{Pr}\{\theta(q^1, \varepsilon) - \theta(q^0, \varepsilon) \geqslant A\}. \quad (11.18')$$

---

[14] Holding all else constant, changes in σ affect response behaviour since, from (11.7), $\partial \text{Pr}\{\text{'yes'}\}/\partial \sigma \geqslant (\leqslant)0$ according as $A_i \geqslant (\leqslant)\mu_i$. Note that (11.7') assumes a homoscedastic distribution of WTP where σ is the same across all survey responses. This is not a necessary feature of RUM models; one can formulate models where σ varies as a function of attributes of the individuals, attributes of the item being valued, and/or attributes of the survey administration. Examples appear in several parts of this chapter.

[15] Assuming a homoscedastic WTP distribution, Cameron (1988) points out that σ can be identified from the CV responses only because there is variation in A_i. If the same bid were used for all respondents, σ would be unidentified. In that case, one could still identify the ratio β/σ if X_i varied across respondents; but one needs variation in A_i to obtain separate estimates of σ and β. Even with variation in A_i, there still can be circumstances that create an identification problem. Suppose subjects believe that the price of the item will actually turn out to be different from what is stated in the CV survey, and their subjective perception of price is some function of A, denoted $\psi(A)$. Then, the RHS of (11.7) becomes $1 - G[\psi(A_i)/\sigma - (\mu_i/\sigma)]$. Depending on the form of $\psi(\cdot)$, it may not be possible to identify σ. This happens, for example, if $\psi(A) = \theta A$ for some $\theta > 0$. If something like this is possible, it reinforces the behavioural interpretation of the parameter σ.

Any RUM model with response probabilities independent of income must be nested within this structure. By inspection, the linear model (11.12) fits the structure in (11.18a), but not other versions of the Box-Cox model. The Bishop–Heberlein model (11.17) corresponds to the particular version of (11.18) where

$$C = \exp[(\alpha + \varepsilon)/\beta] = \exp(\alpha/\beta)v, \qquad (11.19a)$$

where $v \equiv \exp(\varepsilon/\beta)$. This formula for C is generated by the utility model

$$v(q^0, y, \varepsilon) = y + \delta$$
$$v(q^1, y, \varepsilon) = y + \delta + \exp\left[\frac{(\alpha + \varepsilon)}{\beta}\right] \qquad (11.19b)$$

for some arbitrary δ. The resulting response probability is

$$\Pr\{\text{response is 'yes'}\} = 1 - G_\varepsilon(-\alpha + \beta \ln A), \qquad (11.19')$$

where $G_\varepsilon(\cdot)$ is the c.d.f of ε. This model (11.19) combined with various distributions for $G_\varepsilon(\cdot)$ appears commonly in the CV literature. To obtain (11.17), Bishop and Heberlein used the logistic distribution for $G_\varepsilon(\cdot)$, which makes v and C log-logistic. If ε is standard normal, v and C are lognormal, and (11.19') becomes

$$\Pr\{\text{response is 'yes'}\} = \Phi(\alpha - \beta \ln A). \qquad (11.20)$$

If $(-\varepsilon)$ has the standard extreme value distribution, v and C have a cdf that corresponds to the two-parameter Weibull distribution, so that (11.19') becomes[16]

$$\Pr\{\text{response is 'yes'}\} = \exp[-\exp(-\alpha + \beta \ln A)]. \qquad (11.21)$$

The utility model (11.19), especially in its log-logistic, lognormal, and Weibull versions (11.17), (11.20), and (11.21) respectively, appears frequently in the CV literature.[17] Another very common model is the linear Box-Cox model, (11.12), in its probit and logit versions (14) and (15). These particular models are so popular because they can readily be estimated with canned programmes available in well-known statistical packages such as LIMDEP, SAS, STATA and SYSTAT.[18] While the models (11.12) and (11.19) may seem somewhat similar, they are fundamentally different

---

[16] The two-parameter Weibull with scale parameter $\theta > 0$ and shape parameter $\gamma > 0$ has a survivor function $S(x) = \exp[-(x/\theta)^\gamma]$. Setting $\gamma = 1$ produces the exponential distribution; setting $\gamma = 2$ produces the Rayleigh distribution. When $(-\varepsilon)$ has the standard extreme value distribution, the cdf of C corresponds to a Weibull with $\theta = e^{\alpha/\beta}$ and $\gamma = \beta$.

[17] In the literature on reliability and life testing, these are referred to as survival or life distributions (Kalbfleisch and Prentice, 1980; Nelson, 1982). Being distributions for a non-negative random variable, they are commonly used to model the length of life; hence the name.

[18] Those packages parameterize the log-logistic, lognormal, and Weibull distributions in terms of $\mu \equiv E\{\ln C\} = \alpha/\beta$ and $\sigma = 1/\beta$. In order to convert the parameter estimates reported by those packages to our parameterization, one sets $\alpha = \mu/\sigma$ and $\beta = 1/\sigma$.

because the random term η enters (11.12) *additively*, whereas the random term ε enters (11.19) *nonlinearly*. Thus, if one uses a log-logistic, lognormal, or Weibull cdf for $G_\eta(\cdot)$ in (11.12), the result is *not* (11.17), (11.20), or (11.21) but, rather, models with a different response probability formula. Those are indicated in Appendix Table 1, which summarizes the various parametric statistical models that have been discussed in this section. For reasons we now explain, these models must be modified further in order to make them fully consistent with economic theory.

11.2.3   Utility theoretic restrictions

For convenience of exposition, we continue to focus on the valuation of a change from q^0 to q^1 using the single-bounded approach. We showed in the previous section that the statistical model for these CV responses can be cast in the form of (11.1) or (11.6). The economic integrability condition is that the RHS in these equations must be interpretable as the survivor function of a random WTP distribution. We now examine some of the implications for the stochastic specification of the RUM models, focusing in particular on the upper and lower bounds on C that are implied by economic theory.

Economic theory implies that a person's maximum willingness to pay for an item is bounded by her income; in terms of the WTP function, the constraint is that[19]

$$C(q^0, q^1, y, \varepsilon) \leqslant y. \qquad (11.22a)$$

In terms of the response probability formula, the constraint is that

$$\Pr\{\text{response is 'yes'}\} = 0 \quad \text{when} \quad A \geqslant y. \qquad (11.22b)$$

In terms of the RUM indirect utility function, conditions sufficient to ensure (11.22) are that

$$\lim_{y \to 0} v(q, y, \varepsilon) = -\infty \qquad (11.23a)$$

or that, given any q' and any $y' > 0$, there exists no q'' such that[20]

$$v(q'', 0, \varepsilon) = v(q', y', \varepsilon). \qquad (11.23b)$$

However, most of the models in the existing CV literature violate these restrictions. In the Box–Cox family, only the logarithmic model (11.13) satisfies (11.22). To make the other Box–Cox models satisfy (11.22) one needs to modify the c.d.f of η so that, focusing on (11.11),

$$\eta \leqslant \eta^{\max} \equiv -\alpha + by^\lambda. \qquad (11.24)$$

---

[19] Two qualifications should be noted. First, we observed earlier that the relevant income variable could be *supernumerary* income rather than full income. Second, the individual's preferences could be such that her WTP has an upper bound that is *less* than y : $C \leqslant C^{\max} < y$. If so, $C^{\max}$ should be substituted for y in the discussion below. In principle, $C^{\max}$ could be estimated from the data along with the other model parameters—see, e.g. Ready and Hu (1995).

[20] This implies that the market goods x in the underlying direct utility function $u(x, q, \varepsilon)$, taken as a group, are essential.

Similarly, the nonlinear model (11.19) fails to satisfy (11.22) unless one modifies the c.d.f of ε so that

$$\varepsilon \leqslant \varepsilon^{\max} \equiv -\alpha + \beta \ln y. \tag{11.25}$$

There are two ways to generate a c.d.f that satisfies (11.24) or (11.25): truncating the distribution, and inserting a probability mass (a 'spike'). We illustrate these for the nonlinear model (11.19).[21] Truncating at $\varepsilon^{\max}$ means changing the distribution of ε from whatever it was originally, say $G_\varepsilon(\cdot)$, to a new c.d.f., say $\bar{G}_\varepsilon(\cdot)$, defined by[22,23]

$$\bar{G}_\varepsilon(\epsilon) = \begin{cases} G_\varepsilon(\epsilon)/G_\varepsilon(-\alpha + \beta \ln y) & \varepsilon \leqslant -\alpha + \beta \ln y \\ 1 & \varepsilon > -\alpha + \beta \ln y. \end{cases} \tag{11.26}$$

Inserting a probability mass means replacing ε with a new random term $\bar{\varepsilon} \equiv \min(\varepsilon, \varepsilon^{\max})$, which has a c.d.f $\bar{G}_\varepsilon(\cdot)$ defined by

$$\bar{G}_\varepsilon(\epsilon) = \begin{cases} G_\varepsilon(\epsilon) & \varepsilon < -\alpha + \beta \ln y \\ 1 & \varepsilon \geqslant -\alpha + \beta \ln y. \end{cases} \tag{11.27}$$

This is also called *censoring* the distribution $G_\varepsilon(\cdot)$. The censored distribution has a spike at $\varepsilon^{\max}$ since, by construction, $\Pr\{\bar{\varepsilon} = \varepsilon^{\max}\} = 1 - G_\varepsilon(-\alpha + \beta \ln y)$.[24] In both cases, the response probability formula becomes

$$\Pr\{\text{response is 'yes'}\} = 1 - G_\varepsilon(-\alpha + \beta \ln a). \tag{11.28}$$

A graphical illustration of truncation and censoring may be useful. Figure 11.1(a) shows the graph of the response probability as a function of the bid amount, A. It has been drawn for a model that fails to satisfy (11.22b). Figure 11.1(b) illustrates how this is remedied by truncating the distribution, thus 'shrinking' the response probability graph to the horizontal axis at $A = y$. Figure 11.1(c) illustrates censoring via the insertion of a spike at $A = y$. While both approaches produce a response function that satisfies

---

[21] For the Box–Cox model, substitute η for ε, $\eta^{\max}$ for $\varepsilon^{\max}$, and (b_{y^λ}) for $\beta \ln y$.

[22] This was suggested by Boyle *et al* (1988) for the Bishop–Heberlein model (11.17), which they proposed truncating from above at some value $C^{\max} < y$.

[23] Ready and Hu (1995) suggest an alternative to truncation which they call 'pinching'. They pinch the WTP distribution down to some $C^{\max} < y$ by replacing the original response probability function, which lacks a finite upper bound, denoted by Pr, with a new response probability, denoted by $\overline{\text{Pr}}$, defined by

$$\overline{\text{Pr}}\{\text{response is 'yes'}\} = [1 - (A/C^{\max})] \cdot \tilde{\text{Pr}}\{\text{response is 'yes'}\}.$$

They apply this to the Bishop–Heberlein model (11.17) and find that it fits their data better than the truncated model. However, when one does this, the utility model is no longer given by (11.17). The shrinking factor implicitly changes both the utility model and the formula for C, not just the c.d.f of ε.

[24] Replacing ε by $\bar{\varepsilon}$ is equivalent to replacing C by $\bar{C} \equiv \min\{\exp[(\alpha + \varepsilon)/\beta], y\}$, a Tobit-like model. There is some confusion over terminology in the CV literature; Ready and Hu (1995) refer to (11.27) as a truncated model, and to the truncated model (11.26) as a normalized truncated model.

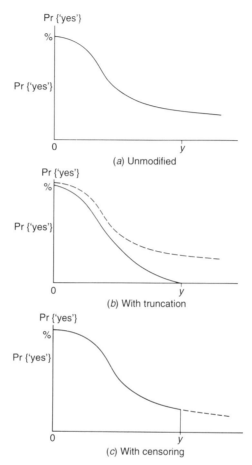

Fig. 11.1   Response probability models and the upper bound on WTP
(a) Unmodified, *(b)* With truncation, *(c)* With censoring

(11.22b), they have different implications for model estimation. Inserting a spike at $\varepsilon^{\max}$ is a simple adjustment that can be performed *after* the original response model has been estimated, whereas truncation (and, for that matter, pinching) requires re-estimation of the modified response probability model.[25]

Turning from the upper to the lower bound on C, when we defined WTP in (11.5) we assumed that the increase in q would be viewed as an *improvement*. Of course, it is an empirical question how people feel about the change in q. For the purpose of further analysis, we now consider three

---

[25] If the CV survey used bids that exceeded respondents' incomes, then even under censoring it would be necessary to re-estimate the response probability function; but not otherwise.

cases: (1) the individual views the change as an improvement; (2) the individual views the change as an improvement or is indifferent to it (i.e., places zero value on it); (3) the individual could view the change as a good thing, or as a bad thing, or be indifferent. We start with the first case which we refer to as the *canonical case*. This is because, as shown below, models for the other two cases can always be constructed by appropriate modification of this canonical case.

In the canonical case, the individual sees the change as an improvement and, with probability 1,

$$C(q^0, q^1, y, \varepsilon) \geqslant 0. \qquad (11.29a)$$

In terms of the response probability formula, the constraint is that

$$\Pr\{\text{response is 'yes'}\} = 1 \quad \text{when} \quad A = 0. \qquad (11.29b)$$

In terms of the RUM indirect utility function, this is equivalent to requiring that $u^1 \equiv v(q^1, y, \varepsilon)$ *first-order stochastically dominates* $u^0 \equiv v(q^0, y, \varepsilon)$. This stochastic dominance is automatically satisfied by the nonlinear model (11.19), given that $\alpha > 0$. For the nonlinear family, therefore, the response probability formula (11.28) meets both of the restrictions on the range of C that are imposed by economic theory. However, the Box–Cox family fails to satisfy (11.29) unless the lower support of the additive stochastic term η is adjusted appropriately. Existing Box–Cox models use distributions for $G_\eta(\cdot)$ that are defined over either $(-\infty, \infty)$ or $[0, \infty)$. The former give C a lower support of $C^{\min} = -\infty$. The latter make $C^{\min}$ positive. Neither produces $C^{\min} = 0$.

With (11.11), for example, when η has a lower support of $\eta^{\min} = 0$, then $C^{\min} = y - [y^\lambda - (\alpha/b)]^{(1/\lambda)} > 0$; in this case, therefore, it is necessary to restrict $G_\eta(\cdot)$ so that $\eta^{\min} = -\alpha$.[26] There are two ways to accomplish this, both involving truncation. One is to employ a distribution for η with a finite, negative lower support, such as the beta. The beta density function is

$$g_\eta(\eta) = \frac{1}{B(r, s)} \frac{(\eta - \eta^{\min})^{r-1}(\eta^{\max} - \eta)^{s-1}}{(\eta^{\max} - \eta^{\min})^{r+s-1}},$$

where $r > 0$ and $s > 0$ are parameters, and $B(r, s)$ is the beta function.[27] In this case, one sets $\eta^{\min} = -\alpha$ in order to satisfy (11.29), while setting $\eta^{\max} = -\alpha + by^\lambda$ to satisfy (11.22). Then, instead of (11.11'), the response probability formula becomes, for $0 \leqslant A \leqslant y$,

$$\Pr\{\text{'yes'}\} = \int_{by^\lambda - b(y-A)^\lambda - \alpha}^{by^\lambda - \alpha} \left(\frac{(\eta + \alpha)^{r-1}(by^\lambda - \alpha - \eta)^{s-1}}{B(r, s)(by^\lambda)^{r+s-1}} \right) d\eta. \qquad (11.30)$$

---

[26] More generally, with any additively random model $\bar{v}(q, y) + \varepsilon_q$, where $\eta \equiv \varepsilon_1 - \varepsilon_0$, it is necessary to restrict $G_\eta(\cdot)$ so that $\eta^{\min} = \bar{v}(q^0, y) - \bar{v}(q^1, y) < 0$ in order to have $C^{\min} = 0$.

[27] Special cases include the uniform distribution $(r = s = 1)$, the arcsine $(r = s = 0.5)$, and the half triangular $(r = 1$ and $s = 2$, or $r = 2$ and $s = 1)$.

The other way is truncation of a c.d.f defined over $(-\infty, \infty)$ such as the normal or logistic.[28] In order to satisfy (11.22), the c.d.f. would already have been modified at the upper end by truncation or censoring, as in (11.26) or (11.27). To satisfy (11.29), it would now be truncated from below at $-\alpha$. If truncation had been used at the upper end to satisfy (11.22), the c.d.f would now be *doubly* truncated to satisfy (11.29) as well. If $G_\eta(\cdot)$ is the untruncated c.d.f, the doubly truncated c.d.f is $[G_\eta(\eta) - G_\eta(-\alpha)]/[G_\eta(-\alpha + by^\lambda) - G_\eta(-\alpha)]$ and, instead of (11.11′), the response probability formula becomes, for $0 \leqslant A \leqslant y$,

$$
\begin{aligned}
\Pr\{\text{response is 'yes'}\} = 1 - \{&G_\eta[-\alpha + by^\lambda - b(y - A)^\lambda] \\
&- G_\eta(-\alpha)/[G_\eta(-\alpha + by^\lambda) - G_\eta(-\alpha)]\}.
\end{aligned}
\tag{11.31}
$$

If censoring had been used at the upper end to satisfy (11.22), the c.d.f would be truncated at the lower end to satisfy (11.29). With the combination of censoring and truncation, the response probability formula becomes

$$
\Pr\{\text{'yes'}\} = \begin{cases}
1 - \{[G_\eta(-\alpha + by^\lambda - b(y - A)^\lambda) \\
\quad - G_\eta(-\alpha)]/[1 - G_\eta(-\alpha)]\} & 0 \leqslant A < y \\
0 & A \geqslant y
\end{cases}
\tag{11.32}
$$

To summarize, in the canonical case where the individual sees the change as an improvement, economic theory imposes the restriction that $0 \leqslant C \leqslant y$. One way or another, this is violated by most of the RUM models in the existing literature, including those listed in Appendix Table 1. Appendix Table 2 presents some models that do satisfy this requirement, based on (11.28) and (11.30)–(11.32); we shall refer to these as canonical models.

Now suppose one wants to allow for indifference—with some positive probability, the individual has a zero WTP for the change in q. Indifference is equivalent to a probability mass at $C = 0$. There are at least two ways to introduce this. One is to combine a canonical model, denoted $G_c(\cdot)$, with a degenerate distribution for C consisting of a spike at zero, γ, so as to form the mixture distribution[29]

$$
\Pr\{C \leqslant x\} \equiv \bar{G}_c(x) = \gamma + (1 - \gamma)G_c(x), \quad x \geqslant 0.
\tag{11.33}
$$

---

[28] There does not appear to be any way to adjust a $G_\eta(\cdot)$ defined over $[0, \infty)$, such as the lognormal, log-logistic, or Weibull, so that it generates a Box–Cox model satisfying (11.29).

[29] For a CV application, see Kriström *et al.* (1992). Schmidt and Witte (1989) apply this model to recidivism, calling it a 'split population' survival model. In one version of their model, γ is treated as a constant to be estimated from the data; in another, they make γ a function of covariates, Z, by writing $\gamma = [1 + e^{\theta z}]^{-1}$, where θ are coefficients to be estimated. Werner (1994) shows that, if γ does depend on covariates in the true model, and the canonical WTP distribution also depends on the same covariates (e.g. through α), estimating a misspecified model that treats γ as a constant seriously biases both the estimate of γ and the coefficient estimates for the covariates in the canonical WTP distribution.

By construction, $\gamma \equiv \Pr\{C = 0\}$. This formulation can be interpreted as representing a population that consists of two distinct types: a group of people, amounting to $100\gamma\%$ of the population, who are simply indifferent, for whom $\Pr\{C = 0\} = 1$; and another group, which has a varying but positive WTP for the change in q, with a c.d.f given by $G_c(\cdot)$. For the mixture to make sense, the lower support of $G_c(\cdot)$ should be zero. Hence, $G_c(\cdot)$ should be a canonical model like those listed in Appendix Table 2, rather than a model like those listed in Appendix Table 1.[30] With the mixture approach, the response probability created by the mixture model, which we denote $\overline{\Pr}$, is related to the response probability associated with the canonical model, which we denote $\widetilde{\Pr}$, as follows:

$$\overline{\Pr}\{\text{response is 'no'}\} = \gamma + (1 - \gamma)\,\widetilde{\Pr}\,\{\text{response is 'no'}\}$$
$$\overline{\Pr}\{\text{response is 'yes'}\} = (1 - \gamma)\,\widetilde{\Pr}\,\{\text{response is 'yes'}\}. \tag{11.33'}$$

Any of the formulas in Appendix Table 2 could be used as the formula for $\widetilde{\Pr}$. The 'downweighting' in the response probability $\overline{\Pr}$ is illustrated in Figure 11.2; Figure 11.2(a) depicts the response probability graph associated with a canonical model, while Figure 11.2(b) shows the response probability graph associated with the mixture model.

The other way to introduce indifference is to use a response probability model with censoring at $C = 0$. In the case of the Box–Cox model (11.11), for example, truncation generated the response probability formula in (11.31). Now, one starts with a random term η defined over $(-\infty, -\alpha + by^\lambda]$—for example a normal or logistic distribution that has been modified at the upper end by truncation or censoring, as in (11.26) or (11.27)—and one censors rather than truncates this from below. Thus, one replaces η with $\bar{\eta} \equiv \max(\eta, -\alpha)$. The distribution of $\bar{\eta}$ has a spike at $-\alpha$ since, by construction, $\Pr\{\bar{\eta} = -\alpha\} = G_\eta(-\alpha)$. This is equivalent to replacing C as defined in (11.11) with $\bar{C} \equiv \max(C, 0)$. This use of censoring to represent indifference is illustrated in Figure 11.2 (c). Response probability formulas for such censored models are given in Appendix Table 3.

The first of these methods for putting a spike at $C = 0$, the mixture approach (11.33), can be applied to the nonlinear utility model (11.19) as well as the Box–Cox model (11.11); the second approach, based on censoring, requires an additive error and thus can be applied only to the Box–Cox model. The difference is that the former introduces an extra parameter, γ, to account for the spike, while the latter uses the model parameters α, β, and λ to represent both the spike and the rest of the response probability function. The first approach implies a population consisting of two distinct types, as

---

[30] This is violated by McFadden and Leonard (1993), who use mixture models that combine a spike at zero with a c.d.f $G_c(\cdot)$ having a lower support of $\alpha > 0$, which results from using the Box–Cox model (11.11), with a c.d.f $G_\eta(\cdot)$ defined over $[0, \infty)$. The consequent WTP distribution $G_c(\cdot)$ 'jumps' from 0 to α, leaving $\Pr\{0 < C < \alpha\} = 0$.

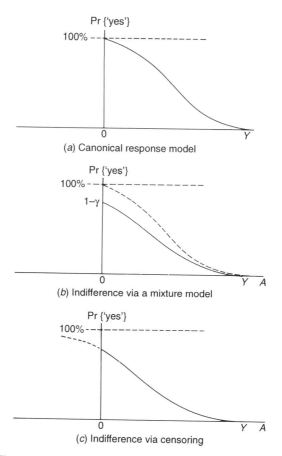

Fig. 11.2 Response probability models with indifference
(a) Canonical response model, *(b)* Indifference via a mixture model, *(c)* Indifference via censoring

described above, while the second assumes a single group with homogeneous preferences.

Lastly, we consider the case where the individual could view the change in q as either good or bad. As in the previous case, there are several ways to model this. One approach uses a mixture distribution combining *two* models, one representing positive preferences $(C \geqslant 0)$ and the other negative preferences $(C \leqslant 0)$. The positive preferences are represented by a canonical c.d.f $G_+(\cdot)$ defined over $[0, y]$ with $G_+(0) = 0$. The negative preferences are represented by a c.d.f $G_-(\cdot)$ defined over the negative domain with $G_-(0) = 1$.[31]

---

[31] If one takes the Box–Cox model (11.11) and sets $\alpha < 0$ instead of $\alpha > 0$, this would generate a model of negative preferences. This does not work with the nonlinear model (11.19), since that formula yields $C \geqslant 0$ regardless of the sign of $(\alpha + \varepsilon)/\beta$.

In addition, there can be a spike at zero to allow for indifference. The resulting mixture distribution is

$$\Pr\{C \leqslant x\} \equiv G_c(x) = \gamma_1 G_-(x) + \gamma_2 G_+(x) + (1 - \gamma_1 - \gamma_2). \qquad (11.34)$$

Here, one can think of the population as consisting of three groups: a fraction γ_1 who dislike the change, a fraction γ_2 who like it, and the remainder who are indifferent.[32]

It is important to note that, when the individual dislikes the change, $-C$ as defined in (11.5) represents minimum *willingness to accept* to suffer the change, rather than maximum WTP to avoid it.[33] The exception is any utility model like (11.18) that has no income effects, such as the linear Box–Cox model (11.12). With no income effects, the (negative) WTP and WTA coincide. Therefore, with dispreference in that model, $-C$ must satisfy the restriction that $-C \leqslant y$ since it measures WTP as well as WTA. Otherwise, in models with non-zero income effects such as the general Box–Cox model (11.11), when $C < 0$, there is no restriction that $-C \leqslant y$ since $-C$ measures only WTA. Hence, C is potentially unbounded from below in the negative domain.

Therefore, another approach to modelling both positive and negative preferences is to use the Box–Cox family with a distribution for η that ranges from $-\infty$ to $-\alpha + by^{\lambda}$. This ensures $C^{\max} \leqslant y$ while leaving C unbounded in the negative left tail. This model is intermediate between the Box–Cox models listed in Appendix Tables 1 and 2—like those in Appendix Table 2, η is bounded from above while, like those in Appendix Table 1, it is unbounded from below. Response probability formulas for such models are presented in Appendix Table 4.[34]

The two approaches to modelling both positive and negative preferences are illustrated in Figure 11.3. The upper panel illustrates the mixture approach, (11.34); the lower panel illustrates the modified Box–Cox model. In general, when one uses a mixture distribution, the mixing parameters—γ in (11.33), γ_1 and γ_2 in (11.34)—are either known exogenously or else treated as unknowns to be estimated from the response data along with the other model parameters. The mixture approach provides the most flexibility—it allows for *different* parameters (and different covariates) in the nonstochastic component of the RUM, depending on whether the individual likes or

---

[32] The parameters γ_1 and γ_2 can be taken as constants or made functions of covariates, in the manner described in fn. 29 above.

[33] As defined in (11.5), C is the Hicksian compensating variation measure. When $C < 0$, WTP to avoid the change is measured by the equivalent variation, rather than the compensating variation. The equivalent variation is the quantity E that satisfies $v(q^1, y, \varepsilon) = v(q^0, y + E, \varepsilon)$. It is shown in Ch. 3 above that, if C' is the compensating variation for a change from q' to q'', and E'' the equivalent variation for the reverse change from q'' to q', then $E'' = -C''$

[34] We have noted that, in these models, $C < 0$ measures WTA rather than WTP. Using the result mentioned in the previous fn, one obtains the equivalent variation measure, E, that corresponds to WTP when $E < 0$ by replacing $(\alpha + \eta)$ in these formulas with $-(\alpha + \eta)$.

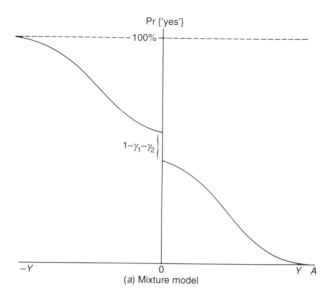

(a) Mixture model

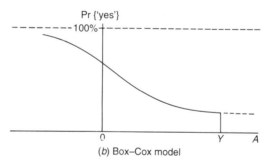

(b) Box–Cox model

Fig. 11.3 Response probability models with positive and negative preferences
(a) Mixture model, *(b)* Box–Cox model

dislikes q. By contrast, the modified Box–Cox model imposes the *same* deterministic tastes on the whole population, leaving the burden of differentiating between preference and dispreference to the distribution of the stochastic component, η.

In this section, we have emphasized the importance of modifying statistical models for CV responses to incorporate restrictions imposed by economic theory on the range of C. Without this, the statistical models are not in fact consistent with the economic hypothesis of utility maximization. As outlined in Appendix Tables 2–4, there are several different possible restrictions, depending on what one assumes about indifference or negative preferences. Two points should be emphasized. First, it is an empirical question which is the appropriate set of restrictions to impose—economic theory *per se* cannot prescribe whether people like, dislike or are indifferent to the change in q. The analyst either has to know ahead of time which of these to assume, taking it as a maintained assumption, or she has to make a point of collecting data that can resolve this, for example by asking respondents directly whether they like or dislike the change.[35] Indeed, if there is a chance that respondents dislike the change, one should ask about this *at the beginning of the survey*, since this permits the CV question to be framed appropriately—those who like the change can be asked their WTP to secure it, while those who dislike the change can be asked their WTP to avoid it.[36] The responses to the initial question can be used to estimate γ_1 and γ_2 in (11.34). Similarly, if one believes that people either like the change or might be indifferent, as in (11.33), one could start off assuming that respondents like it but then ask those who say "no" to the CV bid a follow-up question on the lines of "would you be willing to pay anything at all for this change in q?"[37] The proportion who say 'no' provides a direct estimate of γ in (11.33).

Second, the restrictions are inherently non-parametric. As illustrated in Figures 11.1–11.3, they constrain the lower and upper ends of the empirical response probability function. Therefore, once one has decided which restrictions to impose, they are consistent with many different statistical models. Although we have focused so far on the particular *parametric* models in Appendix Tables 1–4, other parametric models can be used as long as they satisfy (11.22b) and, if one assumes positive preferences, (11.29b). Moreover, semi-parametric and non-parametric models can also be used. As discussed in Section 11.4.5, these models effectively censor the WTP distribution at the lowest and highest observed bids, which has the effect of guaranteeing that they satisfy (11.22b) and (11.29b).

What are the practical consequences if one disregards the restrictions on the range of C? As shown below, there are two possible effects: the formulas for welfare measures may be wrong, and/or the estimates of model parameters may be biased owing to the incorrect specification of the response probability model. The welfare measures are discussed in the following section. Estimation of model parameters is discussed in Section 11.3.

---

[35] Failure to allow for the possibility of negative preferences towards the item being valued has figured in several CV disputes (e.g. Cameron and Quiggin, 1994).

[36] Duffield (1993) and Huhtala (1994) are examples of CV studies that follow this approach. Note that it entails asking the compensating variation for those who like the change, and the equivalent variation for those who dislike it. This difference should be reflected in the response probability models applied to the data.

[37] In practice, finding a way to ask this requires some care, since one wants to avoid any appearance of pressuring the respondent to express a positive value.

11.2.4   Welfare evaluation

So far we have discussed how to formulate statistical models for the CV responses that are consistent with utility theory. We turn now to the question of how to derive useful measures of monetary value once the statistical models have been estimated.[38] As we noted earlier, by virtue of the RUM hypothesis, rather than being a fixed number, a person's WTP for the change is actually a random variable with a c.d.f given by $G_c(\cdot)$. The survey responses permit one to estimate this WTP distribution. Indeed, this is a basic difference between conventional regression models for continuous dependent variables (e.g., responses to open-ended CV questions) and quantal response models. Conventional regression models estimate the *conditional mean* of the dependent variable given the regressors. Quantal response models for discrete dependent variables estimate the *conditional distribution* of the dependent variable given the regressors, i.e. the entire cdf. The question then arises how one might summarize this distribution for practical purposes. As we show in this section, that is a nontrivial question.

The literature has generally focused on two summary statistics. One is the *mean* of the estimated WTP distribution,

$$C^+ \equiv E\big[C(q^0, q^1, y, \varepsilon)\big]. \tag{11.35}$$

The other, advocated by Hanemann (1984a), is the *median* of the estimated WTP distribution, i.e. the quantity C^* such that

$$1 - G_c(C^*) = 0.5. \tag{11.36}$$

It follows from (11.6a) that Pr {response is 'yes'} $= 0.5$ when $A = C^*$, i.e. there is a 50–50 chance that the individual would be willing to pay at least C^*. In addition, Hanemann (1989) has suggested giving consideration to other quantiles of the $G_c(\cdot)$ distribution. The θ-percentile of the WTP distribution, C_θ, satisfies

$$\theta = 1 - G_c(C_\theta); \tag{11.37}$$

i.e., there is a $100\theta\%$ probability that the individual would be willing to pay at least C_θ.[39] By way of example, for the Box–Cox model (11.11), the mean is

$$C^+ = y - E\left\{ \left(y^\lambda - \frac{\alpha}{b} - \frac{\eta}{b} \right)^{\frac{1}{\lambda}} \right\}, \tag{11.38}$$

while the median is

---

[38] In this section, when we refer to parameters such as α and β, we mean the *estimates* of these parameters. The statistical properties of these parameter estimates are discussed in Section 11.3.
[39] The analogs of C_θ in the biometrics literature are what is known as the $ED_{100\theta}$ or $LD_{100\theta}$. These are the dose levels or concentrations at which, on average, $100\theta\%$ of subjects respond; E denotes 'effective', and L denotes 'lethal'. The distribution of which they are the quantiles is called a tolerance distribution. Much of the attention in the biometrics literature is focused on the medians ED_{50} or LD_{50}.

$$C^* = y - \left(y^\lambda - \frac{\alpha}{b} - \frac{\eta^*}{b}\right)^{1/\lambda}, \tag{11.39}$$

where η^* is the median of distribution of η. In the linear model (11.12) where $\lambda = 1$, one has $C^+ = (\alpha + E\{\eta\})/\beta$ and $C^* = (\alpha + \eta^*)/\beta$. If $E\{\eta\} = \eta^*$ in that model, $C^+ = C^*$. Otherwise, the two welfare measures are numerically different.

Deciding which measure is appropriate involves considerations of both statistics and economics. Suppose that the survey data came from repeated questioning of a single individual—while this is fairly impractical, one could imagine it happening. In that case, even though we were estimating a single individual's WTP, it still would be a random variable for us as outside observers because of the RUM hypothesis. The issue would then be just one of representation—what is the best way to summarize the probability distribution? The answer depends on the statistical loss function: with a sum-of-squared-errors loss function, the mean is the optimal measure of central tendency; with a sum-of-absolute errors loss function, the median is optimal. For this reason, the mean is more sensitive to skewness or kurtosis in the WTP distribution (Stavig and Gibbons, 1977). This could be important because most RUM models with non-negative preferences imply a skewed distribution of WTP. As shown below, it can often happen that the point estimate of the median is more robust, or has a much smaller sampling error, than the point estimate of the mean.

Now consider the more realistic situation where the survey data come from questioning different individuals in a population. In that case, the summary measure of the WTP distribution would be multiplied by the number of people in the population to produce an estimate of aggregate value. Thus, the choice of a summary statistic implies a particular approach to the aggregation of welfare across the population. The mean, C^+, is equivalent to adopting the Kaldor–Hicks potential compensation principle. Suppose there are both positive and negative preferences for the change in q, as in the response probability models listed in Appendix Table 4. Then, $C^+ > 0$ if and only if those who are better off as a result of the change in q could fully compensate those who are worse off, and still gain by it. The Kaldor–Hicks criterion is commonly used, but it can lead to logical inconsistencies and it has been severely criticized on ethical grounds (Little, 1957). As a means of aggregating values, the median C^* is equivalent to applying the principle of majority voting: the change is desirable if a majority of the population would vote for it. Using a lower quantile of the WTP distribution would correspond to super-majority voting; for example, $C_{0.67}$ would correspond to requiring a two-thirds majority vote. It is known that majority voting rules do not satisfy Pareto efficiency; but they still may be considered ethically superior. In view of these welfare-theoretic implications, choosing a measure of central tendency is essentially a value judgement. Moreover, different circumstances may call for different welfare measures. For example, Carson *et al.* (1992) make a distinction between benefit–cost analysis and natural resource damage assessment, recommending the use of median WTP for the former and mean WTA for the latter because of the difference in the implied property right and the legal requirement in the latter case (but not the former) to restore all those who were injured to their original position. These are judgements that the researcher must make.

The reason why C^+ is more sensitive than C^* to skewness in the WTP distribution becomes evident when one considers graphical representations of these welfare measures. The graphical approach permits one to calculate the welfare measures even with a non-parametric model that has no closed-form representation for the response probability function. The median, C^*, can be read directly from the empirical response probability function—it is the dollar amount that corresponds to a 50% probability of saying 'yes' (see Figure 11.4(a)). The graphical representation of C^+ comes from a standard result in statistics about the relation between the mean of a random variable and the integral of its c.d.f (Parzen, 1960):

$$C^+ = \int_{-\infty}^{0} G_c(A)dA + \int_{0}^{\infty} [1 - G_c(A)]dA. \qquad (11.40a)$$

This corresponds to the shaded areas over/under the empirical response probability function in Figure 11.4(b). When C is restricted to being non-negative, the formula for the mean reduces to

$$C^+ = \int_{0}^{\infty} [1 - G_c(A)]dA, \qquad (11.40b)$$

which corresponds to the shaded area under the response probability function in Figure 11.4(c).

Two implications follow from the graphical representation of welfare measures. The first concerns the relationship between the two welfare measures. Whereas the median depends on the location of the response probability graph at a particular point, viz. the 50% probability level, the mean depends on the location of response probability graph throughout its entire length, from tail to tail. When $C \geqslant 0$, while small differences in the right tail of the distribution have essentially no effect on the median, they can affect the mean greatly.[40] This explains why the relation between the mean and median can vary with the specification of the WTP distribution. By way of illustration, consider the various versions of the nonlinear utility model (11.19). With the lognormal model (11.20), application of (11.36) and (11.40b) yields the following formulas for median and mean:

---

[40] Boyle *et al.* (1988) refer to this as the 'fat tails' problem.

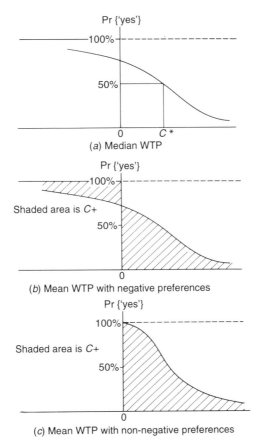

Fig. 11.4   Graphical representation of median and mean of WTP distribution
(a) Median WTP, *(b)* Mean WTP with negative preferences, *(c)* Mean WTP with
non-negative preferences

$$C^* = e^{\alpha/\beta} \tag{11.41a}$$

$$C^+ = e^{\alpha/\beta} \exp\left[\frac{1}{\beta^2}\right]. \tag{11.41b}$$

With the log-logistic model (11.17), while the formula for the median is the
same as for the lognormal

$$C^* = e^{\alpha/\beta}, \tag{11.42a}$$

the mean turns out to be

$$C^+ = \begin{cases} e^{\alpha/\beta}\Gamma[1 + (1/\beta)]\Gamma[1 - (1/\beta)] & \text{if } \beta > 1 \\ \infty & \text{if } \beta \leqslant 1. \end{cases} \tag{11.42b}$$

With the Weibull model (11.21), one has

$$C^* = e^{\alpha/\beta}(\ln 2)^{-1/\beta} \tag{11.43a}$$

$$C^+ = \begin{cases} e^{\alpha/\beta}\Gamma[1 - (1/\beta)] & \text{if } \beta > 1 \\ \infty & \text{if } \beta \leqslant 1. \end{cases} \tag{11.43b}$$

In each case, the ratio C^+/C^* depends crucially on the value of β, which is related to $\omega^2 \equiv \text{var}\{\ln C\}$. In the lognormal case, $\beta = 1/\omega$, and C^+ grows larger with ω but remains finite as long as $\beta > 0$. In the log-logistic case, $\beta = \pi/\omega\sqrt{3}$ and C^+ blows up if $\beta \leqslant 1$, i.e. if $\omega^2 \geqslant \pi^2/3 \approx 3.29$. In the Weibull case, $\beta = \pi/\omega\sqrt{6}$ and C^+ blows up if $\omega^2 \geqslant \pi^2/6 \approx 1.65$. In terms of Figure 11.4(c), the integral corresponding to the shaded area fails to converge when $\beta \leqslant 1$. This is yet another example of the fact that the stochastic specification of a RUM can have substantive economic implications, since different probability distributions constrain the relation between mean and median in such different ways.

The second implication concerns the restrictions on the range of C. Welfare formulas such as those in (11.41a, b) and (11.42a, b), which were first presented in Hanemann (1984a), or in (11.43a, b) are in fact incorrect since they ignore the restriction that $C \leqslant y$. When this restriction is imposed, as in Appendix Table 2 or 3, it will probably not affect the formula for the median, C^*, but it certainly will affect the formula for the mean, C^+.[41] This can be seen by decomposing the formula in (11.40b):

$$C^+ = \int_0^y \Pr\{\text{'yes'}\}dA + \int_y^\infty \Pr\{\text{'yes'}\}\,dA \tag{11.44a}$$

$$= \int_0^y \Pr\{\text{'yes'}\}\,dA. \tag{11.44b}$$

When one takes account of the restriction that $C \leqslant y$, the second term on the RHS of (11.44a) vanishes by virtue of (11.22b). Equivalently, (11.40b) can be manipulated into the form

$$C^+ = y - \int_0^y \Pr\{\text{'no'}\}\,dA. \tag{11.45}$$

Hence, C^+ is always finite and bounded from above by the person's income. Corrected formulas for C^+ and C^* that incorporate the restrictions on the range of C are included along with the response probability formulas in Appendix Tables 2–3.

Although the existing analytic formulas for C^+ in Hanemann (1984a, 1989) incorrectly ignore the restrictions on the range of C, not all of the empirical estimates of C^+ in the literature should be considered erroneous,

---

[41] The discussion in this paragraph focuses on the case where $C \geqslant 0$. Analogous results hold for the case of negative preferences (i.e. for the probability response models in Appendix Table 4).

because some researchers used other formulas or procedures when calculating C^+. This started, in fact, with Bishop and Heberlein, who truncated the WTP distribution at the highest bid in their survey, $A^{\max}$, when estimating mean WTP. Instead of (11.44a), they calculated

$$\tilde{C}^+ \equiv \int_0^{A^{\max}} \Pr\{\text{'yes'}\}\, dA. \tag{11.46}$$

Since $A^{\max} < y$, $\tilde{C}^+$ is a conservative estimate of C^+. Computer programs to calculate C^+ are quite readily available, and this welfare measure has been used quite widely in the literature. We show in Section 11.4.5 that non-parametric estimators of the response probability function estimate the mean in essentially the same way, since they truncate the c.d.f of C at the highest observed data point. Instead of $A^{\max}$, other researchers have proposed truncating the c.d.f at some amount, $C^{\max}$, that represents the analyst's assessment of an upper bound on individuals' WTP, perhaps based on non-sample data.[42, 43]

A different type of approach was adopted by Werner (1994), who advocated partitioning the population into groups and computing the average of the medians for each group. The groups could be identified in various ways—according to administrative or political criteria, for example, or on the basis of socio-demographic, behavioural, or attitudinal covariates. Suppose there are K groups; each group has a WTP distribution with a cdf, $G_k(C_k)$, that has a mean C_k^+ and a median C_k^*. Depending on how the groups are defined, these distributions would be obtained by fitting response probability functions to the data for each group separately or by fitting a single response probability function to data pooled over all groups but parameterized on group indicator covariates. Werner's statistic, the average of group (conditional) medians, is $C^W \equiv (1/K)\Sigma C_k^*$. Of course, if there is only one group, this measure corresponds to the overall median, C^*; if each group has only a single member, it corresponds to the overall mean, C^+. Otherwise, she establishes that C^W generally lies between C^* and C^+ and that, for a given sample size, while estimates of C^W do not have quite as low a variance as C^*, they have a considerably lower variance than estimates of C^+.

11.2.5   Summary

Most of the existing CV literature uses response probability models based on either the Box–Cox utility model (11.11), including its linear and logarithmic

---

[42] See Boyle *et al.* (1988), and Ready and Hu (1995). Carson *et al.* (1992) test for the presence of a $C^{\max} < y$ and find they cannot reject the hypothesis that $C^{\max} = 0.02y$ with their data.

[43] Related approaches are constrained estimation and Bayesian estimation where, at the stage of model estimation rather than when calculating the welfare measure, one imposes a constraint on the location of the right-hand tail of the response probability function, or one introduces prior information about the location of this tail.

versions, or the nonlinear utility model (11.19). As summarized in Appendix Table 1, depending on the stochastic specification, the former gives rise to probit and logit response probability models, while the latter generates lognormal, log-logistic, and Weibull models. Most of these models violate restrictions on the range of C from economic theory. This problem can be avoided by using the modified response probability models listed in Appendix Tables 2–4. These generally satisfy the economic restrictions by either censoring (introducing a spike) or truncating the corresponding response probability model in Appendix Table 1. Censoring may not affect parameter estimation—one can get the same parameter estimates for the censored and uncensored models—but it does change the formula for the mean WTP and it could affect the median. Truncation invariably affects both parameter estimation and the formulas for mean as well as median WTP. How much difference this makes in practice is an empirical question that remains to be investigated. The choice between the response probability models listed in Appendix Tables 2, 3, and 4 involves a judgement by the analyst as to whether to allow for indifference and/or dispreference for the item in question. The choice of welfare measure—mean, median, or some other quantile of the WTP distribution—also calls for a judgement by the analyst that can involve both ethical and statistical considerations. The mean is the conventional measure in benefit–cost analysis and reflects the Kaldor–Hicks potential compensation criterion; the median may be more realistic in a world where decisions are based on voting and there is concern for the distribution of benefits and costs. From a statistical point of view, the mean is generally far more sensitive than the median to the choice of a response probability model or the method of estimation.

11.3. STATISTICAL ESTIMATION AND DESIGN

This section discusses practical issues in the estimation of CV data based on the maximum likelihood method. Section 11.3.1 reviews maximum likelihood procedures. Section 11.3.2 discusses the asymptotic properties of maximum likelihood estimators and approaches for calculating the variance of estimated WTP. Section 11.3.3 discusses procedures for checking model misspecification including hypothesis testing and goodness of fit. Section 11.3.4 discusses optimal experimental design.

11.3.1 The maximum likelihood approach

The method of maximum likelihood seeks the values of the unknown parameters that are most likely to have generated the data that were observed. In the present context, the data consist of yes/no responses from survey participants. Let y_i denote the response of the ith individual—we can think of

$y_i = 1$ as 'yes', and $y_i = 0$ as 'no'. In addition, we observe a vector of explanatory variables for each respondent that includes the bid amount presented to her, A_i, and any covariates that might have been recorded, such as income (if the utility model exhibits non-zero income effects), socio-demographic variables, attitudinal variables, etc. We now follow the notational convention in statistics by expressing all the exogenous variables for the ith respondent as a vector x_i. Finally, we represent the unknown parameters, such as α, β, and λ, in a single vector θ. The response probability formulas discussed in Section 11.2, including those in Appendix Tables 1–4, can each be thought of as a likelihood function for the ith observation—they express the likelihood (or probability) of observing the response that was observed, y_i, given the exogenous variables x_i and the (unknown) parameters, θ. Following the convention in statistics, we now refer to these response probabilities using the notation $P(y_i \mid x_i, \theta)$. Since the responses from a random sample represent independent observations, the likelihood function for the overall set of responses $\{y_1, \ldots, y_n\}$, given the corresponding set of explanatory variables $\{x_1, \ldots, x_n\}$ and the true but unknown parameters θ, is simply the product of the individual likelihood functions for each observation in the sample. Taking the logarithm, the log-likelihood function for the sample is the sum of the individual likelihoods[44]

$$L(\theta \mid y_1, \ldots, y_n, \ x_1, \ldots, x_n) = \sum_{i=1}^{n} \ln P(y_i \mid x_i, \theta). \qquad (11.47)$$

In forming (11.47), one substitutes for $P(y_i \mid x_i, \theta)$ the specific formula for the response probability function that the analyst has selected. Maximum likelihood estimation of the model parameters involves maximizing (11.47) with respect to θ; the maximum likelihood estimator is denoted $\hat{\theta}$.

With the single-bounded approach, the CV survey collects one response from each participant, and the log-likelihood function can be expressed as a series of Bernoulli trials:

$$L = \sum_{i=1}^{n} y_i \ln P_i + (1 - y_i) \ln (1 - P_i), \qquad (11.48)$$

where $P_i = P(y_i \mid x_i, \theta)$, the ith individual's response probability. Maximization of the log-likelihood function (11.48) yields a set of first-order conditions:

$$\frac{\partial L(\theta)}{\partial \theta} = \sum_{i=1}^{N} \frac{\partial \ln P(y_i \mid x_i, \theta)}{\partial \theta} = 0 \qquad (11.49)$$

---

[44] In what follows, we use $L = L(\theta)$ to denote the *log*-likelihood function.

In general, these first-order conditions are a set of nonlinear equations that require iterative numerical solution techniques. Solution algorithms are discussed further in the appendix to this chapter.[45]

Two practical issues that the researcher must address when using maximum likelihood estimation are the choice of starting values for the parameter vector θ, and the convergence criterion. There is no generally accepted procedure for determining starting values. Fortunately, logit and probit models are well behaved and generally converge quite quickly regardless of the starting values. With more complicated models, such as those in Appendix Tables 2–4 or some of the models to be discussed in Section 11.4, it may be useful to first estimate a simpler version of the model that takes the form of a logit or probit model and use the resulting coefficients as starting values for the more complicated model. Otherwise, starting values can be set on the basis of the researcher's intuition and knowledge of the data. In some cases, trial and error is the only option.

The iterative estimation procedure ends when a convergence criterion is met. The best criterion is usually based on evaluating the first derivative vectors: when they are zero, the maximum has been reached. Some software packages assume convergence when there is only a very small change between successive estimates of the value of the likelihood function, or successive estimates of the vector of parameters. However, this can halt estimation prematurely. Even with fairly simple likelihood functions, it may be difficult to obtain convergence, especially in models with a large number of parameters. In this case, one can try changing the starting values for the parameters. When starting values are far from the true values, the algorithm for picking the next iteration may move in a direction that leads away from the optimum, or sometimes the function is flat in the region of the starting values and the algorithm cannot find an improving direction so that parameters barely change at each iteration. Another useful trick is to scale the data so that the parameters are expected to be of the same order of magnitude. The GAUSS manual states that 90% of technical support calls about failure to converge are solved by re-scaling the data appropriately.

Many econometric software packages offer a variety of binary response specifications, including logit, probit, and Weibull, that use analytical derivatives and converge quite quickly. Estimation of these models involves little more on the part of the user than a one-line command. Some packages, such as GAUSS, LIMDEP and STATA, allow the user to programme his or her own likelihood function and derivatives, and to specify the starting points, algorithm, and convergence criterion. The main reason for programming one's own likelihood function is to estimate models that are more complex

---

[45] See Judge *et al.* (1988, App. B) or W. H. Greene (1993, Ch. 12) for discussions of numerical optimization algorithms. Gill *et al.* (1981) provide an excellent general reference for the issues discussed in the next few paragraphs.

than those in the standard software packages, such as those in Appendix Tables 2–4 or the models to be discussed in Section 11.4.

11.3.2   Asymptotic properties of maximum likelihood estimators

Once we leave the world of the standard normal linear model, properties such as unbiasedness are very difficult to evaluate. The linear model allows straightforward evaluation of the distributions of estimators and test statistics. For most other situations, however, we resort to Monte Carlo simulations or asymptotic evaluations of the limiting distributions of estimators at sample sizes of infinity. Two asymptotic properties of maximum likelihood estimators are of particular interest to us: one is the asymptotic behaviour of the estimator itself; the second is the asymptotic behaviour of the estimator standardized by sample size so that its limiting behaviour is non-degenerate.

11.3.2.1   Consistency

The maximum likelihood estimator $\hat{\theta}$ converges in probability to the true parameter value, θ, a property known as *consistency*.[46] This is a large sample property and does not ensure unbiasedness, especially in small samples.[47]

Small-sample results are available from Copas (1988) for the logit model (11.15). He uses a Taylor expansion to derive analytically the bias of maximum likelihood parameter estimates (D.R. Cox and Hinkley, 1974). The bias of the jth parameter estimate can be defined implicitly using a Taylor expansion of the jth element of the score vector of a log-likelihood function:

$$L_{\theta j} = L_{\hat{\theta} j} + H_j(\theta - \hat{\theta}) + \tfrac{1}{2}(\theta - \hat{\theta})' M_j(\theta - \hat{\theta}) = 0, \qquad (11.50)$$

where H_j is the jth column of the Hessian matrix and M_j is the jth matrix of third derivatives of the log-likelihood function. The bias is equal to the expected value of $(\hat{\theta} - \theta)$. In general, the expectation of the expressions in (11.50) involve covariances between H and $\hat{\theta}$ cannot be simplified. In the case of the logit model, and only for this case, however, H is a constant and is not dependent on the particular response vector. Using this property, Copas obtains an approximate expression for the bias of the sth maximum likelihood parameter estimate for the logit model:

$$b_s \cong \frac{1}{2} \sum_j \sum_k \sum_l H^{sj} H^{kl} M_{jkl}, \qquad (11.51)$$

where H^{jk} is the inverse of $H = \{H_{jk}\}$. Expressions for H and M are presented in Kanninen (1995).

---

[46] See Amemiya (1985) or Huber (1981) for discussions of the asymptotic properties of maximum likelihood estimators.

[47] J. A. Anderson and Richardson (1979) and Griffiths *et al.* (1987) found biases in numerical simulations of logit and probit models with small samples.

The bias is a function of the maximum likelihood estimate, $\hat{\theta}$, and the bid vector. Equation (11.51) provides an analytical formula for the small-sample bias of the maximum likelihood estimator in the logit model. This can be used to examine the effect of the choice of bids on the bias of the maximum likelihood estimator. However, analytical formulas for small-sample bias do not appear to be available for other binary response models besides logit. We might surmise that probit models would have similar bias properties to those of the logit model, but we are not aware that this has yet been proven in the literature, nor are we aware of small-sample results for any of the other models listed in Appendix Tables 1–4.

11.3.2.2   Efficiency

The second asymptotic property of maximum likelihood estimators is the convergence of $\hat{\theta}$ scaled by the sample size, N : $\sqrt{N}(\hat{\theta} - \theta)$ converges in distribution to a normal distribution with mean 0 and variance $[I(\hat{\theta})/N]^{-1}$, where $I(\hat{\theta})$ is the Fisher Information matrix (the negative of the expectation of the Hessian matrix), also known as the *Cramer–Rao Lower Bound*. For the binary response model, the Fisher information matrix is:

$$I(\theta) = \sum_{i=1}^{N} \frac{f^2}{F(1-F)} x_i x_i' \tag{11.52}$$

where f is the p.d.f. and F the c.d.f. of the response vector, and x_i is the vector of independent variables including the bid value and a 1 for the constant term. The Cramer–Rao inequality states that no consistent estimator can have lower variance than the inverse of the Fisher information matrix. This implies that $\hat{\theta}$ is an *efficient* estimator. We refer to the inverse of $[I(\hat{\theta})/N]$ as the asymptotic variance of the maximum likelihood estimator.

11.3.2.3   Calculating the variance of WTP

Although we know the asymptotic distribution of the maximum likelihood estimator for θ, we do not necessarily know the asymptotic distribution of the maximum likelihood estimator of the welfare measures C^* or C^+, since those are *functions* of the elements of θ. For example, we might be interested in the parameter $\mu = \alpha/\beta$, which corresponds to both C^* and C^+ for the simple logit and probit models (11.14) and (11.15), and to C^* for censored versions of those models as well as for nonlinear models based on (11.19). While the maximum likelihood estimators of α and β are asymptotically normal, the distribution of a function of them such as μ is *not* asymptotically normal. Sometimes this can be tackled by re-parameterizing the likelihood function; as noted earlier, the logit and probit models can be parameterized in terms of $\mu = \alpha/\beta$ and $\sigma = 1/\beta$ instead of α and β (Cameron, 1988). Because the maximum likelihood estimator satisfies an invariance principle, both parameterizations yield exactly the same estimate of$(\hat{\mu})$.[48] But this does not apply to the *variance* of the maximum likelihood estimate of$(\hat{\mu})$. One obtains different estimates of this variance depending on whether the model is parameterized in terms of (μ, σ) or (α, β). The former provides a direct estimate of var$(\hat{\mu})$ via the appropriate element of the inverse of the information matrix; the latter provides an asymptotic variance matrix for $(\hat{\alpha}, \hat{\beta})$ from which one must somehow extract an estimate of var$(\hat{\mu})$.[49]

When one cannot obtain the asymptotic distribution of the welfare measure via reparameterization, there are three ways to proceed. One approach is to apply the delta method based on a truncated Taylor series expansion which yields the following convergence in distribution of a function $f(\theta)$:

$$\sqrt{N}[f(\hat{\theta}) - f(\theta)] \to N[0, f'(\hat{\theta})I(\hat{\theta})^{-1}f'(\hat{\theta})'].\qquad(11.53)$$

For the logit or probit models (11.14) and (11.15), the resulting asymptotic variance of $\mu = \alpha/\beta$ is

$$\text{Var}\left(\frac{\alpha}{\beta}\right) \cong \frac{1}{\beta^2}\left[\sigma_{\alpha\alpha} + \left(\frac{\alpha}{\beta}\right)^2 \sigma_{\beta\beta} - 2\left(\frac{\alpha}{\beta}\right)\sigma_{\alpha\beta}\right],\qquad(11.54)$$

where $\sigma_{\alpha\alpha}$ and $\sigma_{\beta\beta}$ are the variances of α and β and $\sigma_{\alpha\beta}$ is their covariance. In practice, one uses the maximum likelihood estimates of the coefficients $\hat{\alpha}$ and $\hat{\beta}$ and the variance matrix $[I(\hat{\theta})/N]^{-1}$. Cox (1990) shows that the resulting estimate of the var$(\hat{\theta})$ is the same as that which arises from asymptotic theory if the model is parameterized directly in terms of (μ, σ). However, two qualifications should be noted. First, since it is an asymptotic approximation, this variance formula may be unreliable with small samples. Second, it forces the confidence intervals for $(\hat{\mu})$ or other quantiles of the WTP distribution to be symmetric, which may be implausible. The other methods discussed below do not possess this feature.

In the biometrics literature, Finney (1964) popularized the use of Fieller's (1954) theorem on ratios of normally distributed random variables to obtain a confidence interval for the ED_{50}. Fieller's theorem generates the following $100(1 - \gamma)\%$ confidence interval for $\mu = \alpha/\beta$, $ci_{\gamma}(\mu)$,

$$ci_{\gamma}(\mu) = \frac{1}{1-g}\left[\left(\frac{\alpha}{\beta} - g\frac{\sigma_{\alpha\beta}}{\sigma_{\beta\beta}}\right) \pm \frac{z_{\gamma/2}}{\beta}\left\{\sigma_{\alpha\alpha} - 2\sigma_{\alpha\beta}\frac{\alpha}{\beta} + \sigma_{\beta\beta}\left(\frac{\alpha}{\beta}\right)^2 - g\left(\sigma_{\alpha\alpha} - \frac{\sigma_{\alpha\beta}^2}{\sigma_{\beta\beta}}\right)\right\}^{\frac{1}{2}}\right]\quad(11.55)$$

---

[48] The invariance principle states that the maximum likelihood estimator of a function is the function of the maximum likelihood estimator.

[49] Many standard software packages force one to parameterize the response probability model in terms of (α, β) rather than (μ, σ), which could be an argument against using them. Note that, in cases where the welfare measure is a more complicated function of the model coefficients than the simple ratio (α/β), there may be no convenient reparameterization that permits direct estimation of the welfare measure even if one does programme one's own likelihood function.

where $z_{\gamma/2}$ is the upper $(\gamma/2)$ point of the standard normal distribution and $g \equiv (z_{\gamma/2})^2 \sigma_{\beta\beta}/\beta^2$. Again, one uses maximum likelihood estimates of coefficients and variance/covariance terms to construct the confidence interval. The more β is significantly different from zero, the smaller is the term g. If g were zero, the confidence interval for $\hat{\mu}$ generated by (11.55) would be exactly the same as that generated by the asymptotic variance in (11.54). When g is small (say $g < 0.05$) the two confidence intervals are similar. They become different as g increases, and the confidence interval in (11.55) becomes increasingly asymmetric. Recent literature, summarized by Morgan (1992), suggests that the Fieller interval is generally preferable to the confidence interval generated by (11.54).

The Fieller approach to confidence intervals has been relatively neglected in the CV literature in favour of other methods involving Monte Carlo simulation or bootstrapping. The former simulates the asymptotic distribution of the coefficients (i.e., a multivariate normal distribution with means given by the maximum likelihood estimates of the coefficients and a variance–covariance matrix given by $[I(\hat{\theta})/N]^{-1}$), taking repeated random draws of coefficient vectors from this distribution and using them to generate an empirical distribution for the welfare measure, from which a confidence interval is computed. This approach was proposed by Krinsky and Robb (1986) and first applied to CV by Park et al. (1991). Bootstrapping and jackknife procedures (Effron and Tibshirani, 1993) simulate the distribution of the explanatory variables in the data set (i.e. the CV bid and any other covariates), using the actual data sample of N observations to simulate this distribution. Bootstrapping creates multiple simulated data sets, each formed by sampling N times with replacement from the actual data. The jackknife creates N simulated data sets, each formed by dropping one observation from the actual data. Given N simulated data sets for the explanatory variables, both approaches use the actual estimated maximum likelihood coefficients to generate a set of N quantal responses, and then apply maximum likelihood to these simulated data to obtain a new set of coefficient estimates, from which the welfare measure is computed. This is repeated over many simulated data sets to generate an empirical distribution for the welfare measure from which a confidence interval is computed. This was first applied to CV by Duffield and Patterson (1991). Cooper (1994) compares these methods for constructing confidence intervals for the welfare measure μ, along with the delta method (11.54) and finds they all perform fairly well, with the ranking of methods varying according to the size of the sample, the specification of the response probability distribution (e.g. logistic versus Weibull), and whether or not one allows for dispreference or indifference in the formula for the welfare measure. Poe et al. (1994) use bootstrapping to test for differences in WTP distributions (obtained, for example, through different elicitation procedures); they bootstrap the convolution distribution of the difference $\Delta \equiv (WTP_1 - WTP_2)$ and use the resulting confidence interval to test the null hypothesis that $\Delta = 0$.

11.3.3 Checking model misspecification

Fitting a response probability model and estimating a welfare measure is often only part of the work. The researcher may want to know whether the results are vulnerable to misspecification in the fitted model. This could arise in several ways, including specifying the wrong response probability model, omitting relevant regressors, or errors in variables used as regressors. Moreover, there could be heterogeneity of preferences among the respondents so that different observations correspond to different response probability models. Since the true model is unknown, misspecification is always a possibility. But its consequences are considerably more severe in nonlinear models such as logit or probit than in conventional linear regression models. In the linear model, the ordinary least squares estimator possesses a robustness that makes it still consistent (although biased) even if the model is misspecified. In nonlinear models, by contrast, the maximum likelihood estimator is not consistent if the model is misspecified. This could undermine the reliability of both point estimates and confidence intervals for model coefficients and welfare measures. How serious this is depends on the circumstances.

Given misspecification of the form of the response probability model, Ruud (1983) showed analytically that, despite this, maximum likelihood estimates of slope coefficients in a quantal response model (but not the intercept) could still be consistent under fairly general conditions, except for a common scaling factor. Hence, *ratios* of slope coefficients could be estimated consistently. This result, however, would not help with welfare measures, since those depend on the intercept α as well as the slope coefficient β. A simulation analysis by Horowitz (1993) suggests that errors in estimating these are likely to be small as long as the assumed WTP distribution has the same *qualitative* shape as the true distribution, e.g. they both are unimodal and homoskedastic. But otherwise—for example when one fits a logit model (11.15) to data generated from a true distribution that departs significantly from an ogive (S-shaped) curve because it is bimodal or heteroscedastic—maximum likelihood estimation of a misspecified model can bring large errors in coefficient estimates and response predictions.[50,51]

Heteroscedasticity in quantal response models was considered by Yatchew and Griliches (1985) who found that, for small departures from homoscedasticity in a probit model, there is only a rescaling effect as long as the variance is uncorrelated with the explanatory variables. But they found that

[50] Bimodality can arise from heterogeneity of preferences. Heteroscedasticity can arise for reasons discussed in notes 14 and 15.

[51] We showed in S.11.2 that most of the response probability models in the existing literature fail to satisfy bounds on the WTP distribution imposed by economic theory and therefore are misspecified to some degree. Horowitz's findings suggest that the consequences might not be too severe since the response probability models in Appendix Table 1 and those in Appendix Tables 2–4 have similar shapes.

there could be a substantial bias in coefficient estimates when the variance is correlated with the explanatory variables in question.

Omitting relevant regressors affects the estimates of both the intercept and the slope coefficients. With the latter, Yatchew and Griliches (1985) show that there is a combination of two effects. The first effect, as in linear regression, is that the coefficients of the included variables are in general biased, the bias being equal to the true coefficient of the omitted variable multiplied by the coefficient from a regression of the omitted variable on the included variable. In addition, unlike linear regression, there is a second effect resulting from the nonlinearity of the quantal response model. This is a rescaling of the slope coefficient which applies regardless of the first effect. Thus, with missing variables in a quantal response model the coefficients of the included variables may be biased even if the omitted variables are uncorrelated with included variables (see also Lee, 1982). Moreover, in contrast to linear regression, the biases depend on the shape of the conditional distribution of the omitted variable, not just the conditional mean.

Errors in variables in quantal response models have been investigated by Yatchew and Griliches (1985), Carroll *et al.* (1984), Kao and Schnell (1987), and many others; Carroll *et al.* (1995) provide a comprehensive review of the recent literature. When explanatory variables are measured with error, the maximum likelihood estimates of the intercept and slope coefficients are inconsistent. While the bias depends on the specific distribution of the measurement errors, there is a general tendency for maximum likelihood estimation to *attenuate* the coefficient of the variables measured with error, i.e. to shrink them towards zero. The coefficients of other variables not measured with error will also be affected, often in an offsetting manner. In the case of a probit model with normal measurement errors, the maximum likelihood coefficient estimates are scaled down in a manner that leads to a consistent estimate for α/β but not for the mean and other quantiles of the WTP distribution. In small samples, however, even the estimate of α/β may be seriously biased.

11.3.3.1   Model checking

While it is well known that there exists a variety of diagnostic techniques for checking model adequacy in the case of linear regression (Cook and Weisberg, 1982, 1994), it is less well known that analogous techniques exist for logit and other quantal response models. These have so far received too little attention from CV researchers. In both linear and nonlinear models, the two main pillars of diagnostic testing are the analysis of residuals and the assessment of influence.

Residuals are used to identify ill-fitting data—observations that do not gibe with the estimated model. There are several ways to define residuals for nonlinear models. The raw residual is $r_i = [y_i - E(y_i)] = [y_i - P(y_i|x_i, \theta)]$. For a binary response model where $y_i = 0$ or 1, r_i takes one of two possible values, $P(y_i|x_i, \theta)$ or $1 - P(y_i|x_i, \theta)$. Since a large difference between y and $E(y)$ should matter less when y has low rather than high precision, it is conventional to divide r by the standard deviation of y, producing the standardized residual

$$r_s = [y - E(y)]/\text{s.e.}(y). \tag{11.56}$$

In the binomial case with n_j observations per bid, the standardized residual is simply

$$r_{sj} = \frac{y_j - n_j \hat{P}_j}{\sqrt{n_j \hat{P}_j (1 - \hat{P}_j)}}, \tag{11.56a}$$

the normalized difference between the observed and predicted number of 'yes' responses at the jth bid. This is known as the *Pearson residual*, since the sum of the squares of these residuals,

$$X^2 = \sum_j r_{sj}^2, \tag{11.57}$$

is Pearson's chi-squared statistic for measuring the goodness of fit of a quantal response model. These residuals thus measure the contribution that each observation makes to the overall fit of the model. An alternative is the *standardized Pearson residual*, in which the raw residual r is normalized by its standard error in order to allow for the variation in $E(y)$ as well as y:

$$r_p = [y - E(y)]/\text{s.e.}[y - E(y)]. \tag{11.58}$$

By construction, these residuals have unit variance. Another approach is to find some transform of the responses, $T(y)$, which renders them approximately normally distributed and then to construct the analogue of the standardized Pearson residual, which is known as the *Anscombe residual*:[52]

$$r_A = [T(y) - E(T(y))]/\text{s.e.}[T(y) - E(T(y))]. \tag{11.59}$$

A different type of residual can be formed from the *deviance statistic*,

$$D = -2(L^c - L^f), \tag{11.60}$$

where $L^c \equiv \sum_i l_i^c$ is the log-likelihood function for the 'current' model that is being estimated, with l_i^c the log-likelihood term for the ith (grouped) observation, and $L^f \equiv \sum_i l_i^f$ is the log-likelihood for the 'full' model, i.e. a model that would have as many parameters as observations and therefore would fit the data perfectly. D measures the model's overall discrepancy with the data and thus can be considered an alternative to Pearson's chi-squared statistic. The signed square root of the ith observation's contribution to this statistic,

---

[52] Formulas for the standard errors in the denominators of (11.58) and (11.59) as well as for the transformation $T(y)$ are discussed in Pierce and Schafer (1986) and Collett (1991).

$$d_i = -\text{sgn}\,[y_i - E(y_i)]\, 2(l_i^c - l_i^f)^{1/2}, \qquad (11.60a)$$

where $D = \sum_i d_i^2$, is known as the *deviance residual*. The *standardized deviance residual* is

$$r_{Di} = d_i/\text{s.e.}(d_i), \qquad (11.61)$$

where s.e.(d_i) is (an approximation to) the standard error of d_i. Another way of using the deviance statistic to define a residual is to compare the change in the value of the deviance when each of the observations in turn is omitted from the data set. The signed square root of the change in deviance for the *ith* observation, known as the *likelihood residual*, can be approximated by a linear combination of the standardized Pearson residual and the standard-ized deviance residual for that observation (Collett, 1991).

Although the Anscombe residuals, standardized deviance residuals, and likelihood residuals have very different formulas, the values that they take are often remarkably similar, and they tend to rank extreme observations in the same way (Pierce and Schafer, 1986). By contrast, the standardized Pearson residuals are not as closely approximated by a normal distribution and may not rank extreme observations correctly. Since the Anscombe residuals are much more difficult to compute than others, there is no great advantage in using them. The standardized deviance residuals or the like-lihood residuals do not suffer from this disadvantage and should routinely be considered.

Residuals are used for two main purposes—model checking, and the identification of outliers (observation checking). First, by plotting residuals in various ways, one can check for the omission of relevant variables, the inclusion of inappropriate variables, the use of inappropriate transforma-tions for included variables, or the use of an inappropriate functional form or probability distribution in the quantal response model. Second, through plots or statistical tests of residuals, one can identify observations that are discordant with the rest of the data with a view to investigating the causes of the discrepancy or handling them as outliers. Chesher and Irish (1987) and Collett (1991) are useful sources on this topic.

An observation is influential if its deletion from the data would cause major changes in coefficient estimates, confidence intervals, or other statis-tics of interest. An observation that is an outlier need not be influential, and vice versa. An influential observation that is not an outlier occurs when the observation distorts the form of the fitted model so much that there is only a small residual for that observation. (The classic example is extreme observa-tions in ordinary least squares regression.) Since residuals *per se* do not necessarily reveal the presence of influential observations, additional diag-nostic techniques are needed. In linear regression, the key tool for assessing influence is the *hat* matrix $H = X(X'X)^{-1}X'$, where X is the matrix of observations on the explanatory variables, and H maps the observed value of the dependent variable, y, into the predicted value, $\hat{y} : \hat{y} = Hy$. Its diagonal elements, h_{ii}, measure the effect that the observed y_i has on the fitted y_i, and are known as the *leverage* of the *ith* observation (Cook and Weisberg, 1982). In nonlinear models estimated by maximum likelihood there is no analogous exact formula linking y to $E(y|\hat{\theta})$, but Pregibon (1981) obtained some useful results based on the *case deletion* principle, which considers the change in the maximum likelihood coefficients when one observation is omitted. Pregibon developed a convenient approximation analogous to the hat matrix which can be used to measure the leverage of an observation on the estimated coefficients or some linear combination of them. The details can be found in Collett (1991), Morgan (1992), or Santner and Duffy (1989). Another approach uses infinitesimal perturbation of the maximum likelihood normal equations rather than case deletion to assess influence. This has been applied by James and James (1983) to assess influence on the estimate of the ED_{50} in a logit dose–response model, and is discussed in Morgan (1992).

In summary, despite its desirable asymptotic properties, maximum likelihood is still sensitive to errors in the data or deviations from the assumed model. There are three main ways to deal with this: modifying the estimation procedure to make it less sensitive to influential or outlying observations, dropping outliers from the data, or modelling the outlier generating process itself.

Approaches that offer better protection than maximum likelihood against violations of the model assumptions include robust estimation (Huber, 1981), bounded-influence estimation (Hampel, 1974), and resistant fitting (Hoaglin, Mosteller, and Tukey, 1983). Technically, *robust estimation* refers to techniques that are robust against deviations from the assumed stochastic distribution (e.g. the random elements come from a distribution with a much heavier tail than the normal distribution), while the other two terms refer to techniques that are robust against more general violations of the assumptions such as gross errors in the variables or misspecification of the functional form. In *M-estimation*, one of the main methods of robust regression, coefficient estimates are chosen so as to minimize $\sum_i \Psi(r_i)$ for some loss function $\Psi(\cdot)$. Ordinary least squares and least absolute deviations are special cases where $\Psi(r) = r^2$ and $\Psi(r) = |r|$, respectively; the first is highly sensitive to large values of r_i, the latter highly insensitive. Most *M*-estimates use some loss function that is a compromise between those two; the Huber loss function is equal to r^2 when r is near 0, but close to $|r|$ when r is far from 0. This has the effect of downweighting observations that are discordant with the rest of the data. The limiting form of downweighting is deleting the observation entirely. *M*-estimation can thus be regarded as a generalization of more traditional approaches in statistics such as removing outliers when they are detected or *trimming*, in which one automatically removes a fixed proportion of the sample from one or both tails. The *influence function* of an estimator measures the rate of change in the estimator with respect to the proportion of observations that come from a contamination point rather than from the assumed model. Robust estimators generally have an influence function that is continuous and bounded. *Bounded-influence estimators* are those with minimum variance subject to a specified upper bound on the value of the influence function.

Robust and resistant estimators were first developed for linear regression but have subsequently been extended to nonlinear models. Early applications to logit were Hamilton *et al.* (1977) for trimmed estimation of the LA_{50}, Miller and Halpern (1980) for robust estimation, and Pregibon (1981, 1982) for bounded influence estimation. See Kunsch *et al.* (1989) and Morgan (1992) for some more recent developments. Non-parametric estimation, discussed below in Section 11.4.4, can be seen as yet another way of estimating a probability response model that protects against error in specifying a parametric model.

Finally, Copas (1988) has explored the possibility of dealing with outliers by modelling the contamination process explicitly. With a binary dependent variable, outliers must take a simple form—the recorded response is 'yes' when the model yields a high probability of 'no', or conversely. Thus, Copas proposes a 'transposition' model where some fraction of the responses, γ, is mis-classified:

$$\Pr\{\text{recorded response is 'yes'}\} = (1 - \gamma)\Pr\{\text{true response is 'yes'}\} \\ + \gamma\Pr\{\text{true response is 'no'}\}, \quad (11.62)$$

where γ is a parameter to be estimated from the data along with the parameters of the true response probability model.[53] This may be regarded as a structural approach to the problem of contamination, as opposed to that of resistant estimation.[54]

11.3.3.2 Hypothesis tests

Given maximum likelihood coefficient estimates, formal hypothesis tests can be used to test the inclusion of a set of variables in the model. The classical approaches to hypothesis testing are the Wald test, which relies on parameter estimates from the unrestricted model only, the likelihood ratio test, which relies on parameter estimates from the restricted and unrestricted models, and the Lagrange multiplier test, which relies only on parameter estimates from the restricted model. The choice of test is generally based on ease of computation, which for most practitioners depends on the statistics provided by the software package used.

---

[53] Observe that this is a mixture model like (11.33′), but with a different structure.

[54] There is some debate in the literature as to which is preferable. Copas (1988) and Jennings (1986) argue that the techniques of resistant estimation do not carry over well from the linear model to quantal response models; Pregibon (1988) disagrees.

Most software packages provide t-statistics for each estimated coefficient. The t-test is equal to the square root of the Wald test and is used to test the null hypothesis that a coefficient, β_0, is equal to some value, z:

$$t = \frac{\hat{\beta}_0 - z}{\text{s.e.}(\hat{\beta}_0)}, \qquad (11.63)$$

where s.e.$(\hat{\beta}_0)$ is equal to the asymptotic standard error of $\hat{\beta}_0$. The critical value for a two-tailed t-test with 95% confidence is 1.96; for a one-tailed t-test with 95% confidence it is 1.645.

The likelihood ratio test compares the maximized log-likelihood function under the hypothesized restriction (L_R) with the unrestricted maximized likelihood function (L). The greater the difference between these two values, the less likely the restriction is to be true. This test is more flexible than the t-statistic because it can be used to compare any number of restrictions simultaneously. The test statistic is:

$$LRT = -2(L_R - L), \qquad (11.64)$$

which has a χ^2 distribution under the null hypothesis with the number of degrees of freedom equal to the number of restrictions. Rejection of the null hypothesis simultaneously rejects the set of restrictions being tested. The likelihood ratio test can be used to test for a variety of misspecification problems such as the inclusion of variables, functional specifications, or heteroscedasticity of known form.[55]

Lagrange multiplier tests, or score tests, have also been shown to be useful for testing a variety of misspecification problems. These tests compare the value of the score function, or the first derivative of the likelihood function, to see if it is significantly different from zero; they are convenient because they require only estimates of the score function under the null hypothesis (the restricted model). Davidson and MacKinnon (1984) and McFadden (1987) show that Lagrange multiplier tests for binary response models can be computed using linear regressions of the residual values from the restricted models.

11.3.3.3 Goodness of fit measures

Goodness of fit measures are used to assess how well a model fits the observed data. We have already mentioned the Pearson chi-square statistic (11.57), which compares fitted and observed response frequencies, and the deviance statistic (11.60), which compares the maximized loglikelihood function with the 'full' model, as measures of goodness of fit. Under the null

---

[55] Note that this procedure cannot be used to compare different model specifications that are non-nested. Horowitz (1983) specifically addresses non-nested hypothesis testing for discrete choice models. See also Gourieroux et al. (1983), Kent (1986), Pesaran and Deaton (1978), MacKinnon (1983) and Davidson and MacKinnon (1981).

hypothesis that the fitted model is the true one, both test statistics are asymptotically distributed χ^2 with $M - K$ degrees of freedom, where M is the number of groups defined by the bid values and categorical variables and K is the number of estimated parameters in the model. The test statistics are attractive as goodness of fit measures because they can use statistical inference to test the fitted model explicitly. Unfortunately, when a large number of groups are defined, with a limited number of observations per group, the asymptotic χ^2 distribution is a poor approximation to the true distribution and statistical inference cannot be used. The approximation is especially poor when the data are ungrouped, i.e. when there is a single observation per group (Collett, 1991, McFadden, 1976).[56]

Other approaches to measuring goodness of fit do not provide statistical tests but can be used as indicators of model adequacy, perhaps for comparing different models. The McFadden pseudo-R^2 is widely used and is available in most standard software packages. It can be written as:

$$R^2 = 1 - \frac{L_{max}}{L_0},$$ (11.65)

where L_0 is the log-likelihood in the null case (where all coefficients other than the constant are assumed to be zero) and L_{max} is the unrestricted log-likelihood. There is no commonly accepted threshold value for the pseudo-R^2 that denotes a satisfactory or well-specified model; higher values are preferred. Ben-Akiva and Lerman (1985) suggest that a shortcoming of the pseudo-R^2 measure is that it increases, or at least does not decrease, when new variables are added to the model. However, if the new variables do not add sufficient explanatory power to the model, one might prefer a more parsimonious specification. An *adjusted* pseudo-R^2 measure addresses this concern:

$$\bar{R}^2 = 1 - \frac{L_{max} - A}{L_0}.$$ (11.66)

Two proposals for the adjustment factor, A, have been offered. Ben-Akiva and Lerman suggest setting A equal to the number of parameters in the model, K; Horowitz (1982) proposes setting it equal to $K/2$.

The classification procedure is another common approach to evaluating goodness of fit. One generates a 2×2 classification table of hits and misses by comparing the predicted and actual outcomes. Prediction typically uses the simple rule that an outcome is predicted to be positive when the predicted response probability is greater than 0.5, and negative otherwise. The diagonal elements of the table display the numbers of correctly predicted

---

[56] Furthermore, Collett (1991) has shown that in this case the deviance statistic does not measure goodness of fit because the 'full' model will always equal exactly zero. The deviance statistic then depends only on the maximized log-likelihood function and not on the actual observations.

positive and negative outcomes, and the off-diagonal elements contain the numbers of mis-classified outcomes. There is no specific requirement for the minimum number of correct predictions. The main disadvantage of this technique is that the prediction rule is simplistic and can greatly misrepresent situations where the predicted probability is close to 0.5.

11.3.4   Alternatives to maximum likelihood estimation

Alternatives to maximum likelihood estimation that are sometimes used in the CV literature include minimum chi-squared estimation, the generalized linear model and quasi-maximum likelihood estimation. Minimum chi-squared estimation is based on the Pearson chi-square statistic (11.57), or some transformed version of it, taken as an overall measure of goodness of fit. It was first developed by Berkson (1953) for logit, where the transform $z = \Psi(P) \equiv \ln[P/(1-P)]$ applied to (11.15) yields a simple linear model

$$z_j = \alpha - \beta A_j. \tag{11.15'}$$

Let $\hat{z}_j = \Psi(\hat{P}_j)$, where $\hat{P}_j$ is the observed proportion of yes responses for bid A_j. Then, (11.15') suggests an ordinary least squares regression of $\hat{z}_j$ on A_j,

$$\hat{z}_j = \alpha - \beta A_j + v_j, \tag{11.15''}$$

where $v_j \equiv \hat{z}_j - z_j$ is a random error term, with $E\{v_j\} = 0$.[57] However, var (v_j) is not a constant, and therefore the model is heteroscedastic and must be estimated by weighted least squares. Provided that $\hat{P}_j$ is not too near 0 or 1, var(v_j) is asymptotically equal to $V(P_j) \equiv [n_j P_j(1-P_j)]^{-1}$, where n_j is the number of observations associated with bid A_j. A consistent estimate of $V(P_j)$ is given by $V(\hat{P}_j) \equiv [n_j \hat{P}_j(1-\hat{P}_j)]^{-1}$. The weighted least squares estimator of (11.15'') minimizes

$$\sum_j (\hat{z}_j - z_j)^2 / V(\hat{P}_j).$$

The expression being minimized is a transformed version of the Pearson chi-squared statistic (11.57), and the resulting estimate of α and β is known as the minimum chi-squared estimator. This estimator is consistent and asymptotically normal, and has the same asymptotic covariance matrix as the maximum likelihood estimator. Following Berkson, Amemiya (1980) showed that it has a smaller mean square error than the maximum likelihood estimator. Minimum chi-squared estimators have been developed for probit and other quantal response models where there exists some appropriate transform of the response variable that generates a linear (or simple

---

[57] A similar transform can be applied to the logit version of the Box–Cox model (11.11) by substituting $[\alpha - by^\lambda + b(y - A_j)^\lambda]$ for $[\alpha - \beta A_j]$ in (11.15') and (11.15''). This leads to a non-linear least squares regression.

nonlinear) least squares regression like (11.15″); details can be found in Maddala (1983).

By construction, when an appropriate transformation exists, the minimum chi-squared estimator is simpler to estimate than the maximum likelihood estimator, since it involves weighted least squares regressions (sometimes iterated, if either the transformation $\Psi(\cdot)$ or var(v) depend on the parameters to be estimated) and has the same asymptotic covariance matrix as the maximum likelihood estimator. Since the approximation to the asymptotic variance breaks down when $\hat{P}_j = 0$ or 1, the method cannot be applied to individual data, just to grouped data where the observed proportions lie between 0 and 1. This is not a problem with single-bounded CV, where multiple subjects receive the same bid, A_j, unless one wants to include covariates in the response probability model as determinants of α and/or β. In that case, one needs enough data so that there are multiple observations for each given value of the covariates, a requirement that is difficult to satisfy unless covariates take only a small number of discrete values.

In the generalized linear model (GLM), introduced by Nelder and Wedderburn (1972) and discussed in detail in McCullagh and Nelder (1989), it is assumed that the responses $\{y_1, \ldots, y_n\}$ are independent observations drawn from the *exponential family* of distributions. The distribution of a random variable Y belongs to the exponential family if the density function takes the form

$$f_Y(y) = \exp[(y\zeta - b(\zeta))/a(\phi) + c(y, \phi)], \qquad (11.67)$$

where $a(\cdot), b(\cdot)$, and $c(\cdot)$ are specified functions, and ζ and ϕ are parameters. It follows from (11.67) that $E(Y) \equiv \mu = b'(\zeta)$, where b' is the first derivative of $b(\cdot)$, and var$(Y) = a(\phi)b''(\zeta)$, where b'' is the second derivative of $b(\cdot)$. The parameter ζ is known as the natural parameter of the distribution. The parameter ϕ is known as the scale or dispersion parameter. In general, the variance can be a function of the mean, via its dependence on ζ. Different specifications of $a(\cdot), b(\cdot)$, and $c(\cdot)$ give rise to different distributions. For example, if $a(\phi) = \phi \equiv \sigma^2, b(\zeta) = \zeta^2/2$, and $c(y, \zeta) = \{y^2/\sigma^2 + \ln(2\pi\sigma^2)\}/2$, one has the normal distribution with $\mu = \zeta$. Other members of this family include the Poisson, gamma, and binomial distributions. Covariates may enter the model through the natural parameter ζ, which can be written as a function $\zeta = \zeta(X)$. In a GLM, this is assumed to be a linear function, $\zeta = \Sigma X_k \beta_k$, and in this context ζ is referred to as a *linear predictor*. Also, in GLM terminology, the relation between the mean, μ, and the linear predictor, ζ, is known as the *link function*: $\zeta = g(\mu)$. It follows that the inverse of the link function coincides with the derivative of the $b(\cdot)$ function: $\mu = g^{-1}(\zeta) = b'(\zeta)$. The logit model, for example, when viewed as a GLM, has $E\{Y\} \equiv \mu$, the link function is simply the transform $\zeta = \Psi(\mu\pi) = \ln[\mu/(1 - \mu)]$, and the linear predictor is $\zeta \equiv \alpha - \beta A$.

Given the GLM structure, when the method of scoring—see (11A.6) in the Appendix—is applied to a GLM model, the coefficient estimates obtained at each Newton–Raphson iteration turn out to be the same as the regression coefficients that one would obtain in a weighted least squares regression with a certain weight matrix and a certain dependent variable regressed on the covariates $X_1, \ldots, X_K$. Hence, the maximum likelihood estimator can be obtained via a series of weighted least squares regressions, which significantly simplifies the computation.[58] In the case of the logit model, the weighted least squares regression is essentially the same as that in minimum chi-squared estimation.

Since the original work of Nelder and Wedderburn (1972), there have been several refinements and extensions of the GLM structure. The *over-dispersion* model of Williams (1982) provides a generalization of the binomial and Poisson distributions. The binomial distribution imposes a tight link between mean and variance: $\text{var}(Y) = \pi(1 - \pi)$. However, it sometimes happens that data on binary outcomes possess a larger variance than permitted by the binomial model. This extra-binomial variation may be due to the omission of explanatory variables or other forms of misspecification captured in the model's random component. If it is not possible to eliminate the extra-binomial variation by including extra covariates, the alternative is to model it explicitly. For this purpose, Williams introduces an additional parameter, ω, the overdispersion parameter. His model has the same linear predictor $\zeta \equiv \alpha - \beta A$ and the same link function $\zeta = \ln[\pi/(1 - \pi)]$ as in logit, but the variance is specified as $\text{var}(Y) = \omega\pi(1 - \pi)$, where ω is estimated along with α and β within the GLM framework. Williams iterates on ω, α, and β until the extra-binomial variation is eliminated, based on a goodness of fit statistic such as the Pearson chi-square statistic (11.57). Under the assumption of binomial residual dispersion, this statistic has an expected value equal to the degrees of freedom $(N - K)$, where N is the number of distinct groups and K the number of parameters estimated; reaching this value is the convergence criterion.[59]

Another refinement is the method of estimation known as *quasi-likelihood* (Wedderburn, 1974), which extends GLM to statistical models that are *not* members of the exponential family but have first and second moments with the same type of structure, i.e. $E(Y) \equiv \mu = b'(\zeta)$ and $\text{var}(Y) = a(\phi)b''(\zeta)$ where $a(\cdot)$ and $b(\cdot)$ are specified functions. Nothing else is specified about the distribution other than these two moments. Therefore, if one proceeds to estimate the model as though applying maximum likelihood to an

---

[58] This is implemented in the statistical packages GLIM and GENSTAT.

[59] Langford (1994) applies the overdispersion model to (11.15) and finds that, while it has little effect on the point estimate of $\mu = \alpha/\beta$, it increases the covariance matrix for (α, β) and widens the confidence interval for μ. Langford concludes that a conventional logit model ignoring the overdispersion would seriously understate the true confidence interval for median WTP.

exponential family, this would be a form of specification error. Although *in general* the desirable properties of maximum likelihood estimators are lost when a model is incorrectly specified, this turns out to be an exception where applying maximum likelihood in a situation where it is not strictly valid still produces consistent and asymptotically normal estimators.[60] The quasi-likelihood approach has come to serve as the basis for various recent extensions of GLM, including random-coefficient versions of GLM discussed in Section 11.4.1.4.

11.3.5   Optimal experimental design

In quantal response models, the bias and variance of $\hat{\theta}$ are functions not only of the underlying parameters of the WTP distribution and the sample size, but also of the explanatory variables, including the bid values. This is evident from (11.51) and (11.54) for the logit model, but it also applies to other binary response models. This has led researchers to pursue the study of optimal experimental design as an additional technique for improving the efficiency of estimates of welfare measures obtained from discrete response CV studies. The goal of optimal experimental design is to find the bid values that provide the maximum possible information about the parameters of the WTP distribution, given the size of the sample. Similar issues have been studied extensively in the bioassay and applied statistics literatures for some time (Abdelbasit and Placket, 1983; Chaloner, 1986; Finney, 1978; Minkin, 1987; Tsutakawa, 1972, 1980; Wu, 1985, 1988). More recently, a literature has developed on optimal design for CV experiments (Alberini, 1994; Alberini and Carson, 1993; Cameron and Huppert, 1991; Cooper, 1993; Duffield and Patterson, 1990; Kanninen, 1993*a*, *b*; Nyquist, 1992). Most of this literature has focused on the logit model (11.15) because of its simplicity and because, in this case, it is possible to obtain analytical results. None of the existing design literature has dealt with the models presented in Appendix Tables 2–4, but it is reasonable to assume that many of the qualitative properties of the optimal bid design for the logit model would carry over to these other models. Our discussion, therefore, focuses on bid design for the logit model. We start by reviewing the impact of bid values on the bias and variance of estimators and then go on to discuss the broad principles of optimal bid design for this model.

11.3.5.1   *Bias and variance in the logit model*

Table 11.1 presents estimates of bias and variance for parameter values and welfare measures in the logit model for several alternative bid designs. The biases of $\hat{\alpha}$ and $\hat{\beta}$ are calculated using the formulas in (11.51). The bias of estimated median WTP is the difference between estimated and actual

---

[60] For the general theory of quasi-maximum likelihood estimation, see Gourieroux *et al.* (1984), who use the term 'pseudo-maximum likelihood estimation', or White (1994).

Table 11.1 Analytical Bias and Asymptotic Variance of WTP - Single-Bounded Logit Model

($\alpha = 2.5$, $\beta = -0.01$, median WTP = $250, 250 observations)

Bid design (percentile)	% bias in α	% bias in β	% bias in median WTP	Asymptotic variance of median WTP
$200, $300 (38%, 62%)	0.83	−0.83	0.00	170.21
$100, $400 (18%, 82%)	1.14	1.14	0.00	268.19
$5, $500 (8%, 92%)	1.90	−1.90	−0.03	588.60
$5, $200, $300, $500 (8%, 38%, 62%, 92%)	1.94	−1.95	0.00	258.85
$300, $400, $500 (62%, 82%, 92%)	4.15	−3.62	0.51	1779.19

median WTP: $(-\hat{\alpha}/\hat{\beta})-(-\alpha/\beta)$, where $\hat{\alpha} = \alpha + \text{bias}(\hat{\alpha})$ and $\hat{\beta} = \beta+\text{bias}(\hat{\beta})$. The asymptotic variance of estimated median WTP is calculated using (11.54). The true values of the parameters (α, β) are set at $(2.5, -0.01)$, which yields a median WTP value of $250. Five bid designs are compared. In each case, it is assumed that, while respondents in the CV survey are presented with a single bid, this is drawn with equal probability from one of several possible bid values. The first three examples involve two-point bid designs; i.e., there are two possible bid values, half the respondents receive one bid value and half the other.[61] The first design places the bid values fairly close to the median of the WTP distribution at $200 and $300 (38th and 62nd percentiles). The second design has bid values of $100 and $400 (18th and 82nd percentiles). The third design is a 'tails only' design, with bids in the tails of the WTP distribution: $5 and $500 (8th and 92nd percentiles). The fourth design combines the first and third designs to create a four-point design; the aim is to investigate how multiple-point designs perform relative to two-point designs. All of these designs are symmetric, in that the bid values are spaced symmetrically around the median WTP. The fifth design is an asymmetric, one-sided design involving three bid values, all greater than the median.

As Copas (1988) predicted on the basis of (11.51), the maximum likelihood estimates of both parameters tend to be overstated in a small sample. Because the welfare measures involve the ratio of parameters, the bias in the estimates of the welfare measures is substantially smaller than the bias in the estimates of the individual parameters. Consequently, so long as the bid design does not boost the precision of one parameter at the expense of the other, the estimate of the welfare measure may not be too biased.

---

[61] With a two-parameter model like logit, two design points are sufficient to identify the two parameters of the response probability distribution. See Kanninen (1995) for a similar analysis of bias where more than two design points are used. Previous studies of the bias in WTP estimation have involved empirical examples using actual data (Cooper and Loomis, 1992) and Monte Carlo simulations (Kanninen and Kriström, 1993; Cooper and Loomis, 1993) rather than the analytic approach employed here.

The bias and variance of the individual parameters and the welfare measures all increase as the bid values are placed further out into the tails of the distribution. The best design is the first one, where the bid values are fairly close to the middle of the distribution; the worst design is the one that places the bids in the tails.[62, 63] The combined design, where some bids are placed in the middle and others are placed in the tails, performs better than the 'tails only' design in terms of variance but not bias. The one-sided design does not perform well for either bias or variance.

The biases decrease with sample size. Table 11.1 uses a sample size of 250. The effects of increasing sample size are easily calculated by dividing the bias by the proportionate increase in sample size. For example, if sample size were 500, the bias of $\hat{\alpha}$ and $\hat{\beta}$ would be half of the values in the table. The corresponding biases in the estimated welfare measure do not decrease in exactly the same proportion as for the parameter estimates, but in practice they decrease roughly proportionately. It follows that, if there were no financial constraints, the simplest solution for avoiding bias resulting from poor bid design is to have a large sample.

The sample size and the specific value of β play crucial roles in the value of asymptotic variance. As shown in Kanninen (1993a), the asymptotic variance is inversely proportional to $N\beta^2$; this result extends directly to non-optimal bid designs such as those presented here. As sample size increases, the asymptotic variance decreases proportionately. Also, as β increases, the asymptotic variance decreases. This is because β is inversely proportional to the standard deviation of the WTP distribution. If β is small, a large asymptotic variance of WTP is unavoidable.

Provided that one wants to estimate median WTP and the response probability model is correctly specified, these results suggest that choice of bid design may not have much impact on the point estimate of welfare measures. It can, however, have a substantial effect on the variance of the estimated welfare measure. This is especially problematic in small samples. Consequently, our recommendations are: (1) increase the sample size, which has the effect of reducing both bias and variance; and (2) keep the bids away from the tails, because excessively high or low bids inflate the variance of the estimated welfare measure. While the sample size is obviously constrained by the researcher's budget, we would typically recommend samples of at least 500 respondents, and preferably closer to 1,000, to keep confidence intervals down to a reasonable size.

---

[62] In addition to losing statistical information when bid values are located in the tails, excessively high or low bid values may strike respondents as implausible and thereby undermine the credibility of the CV survey. They can also distort welfare estimates if outliers occur in the data (Kanninen, 1995).

[63] Desvousges et al. (1993) is sometimes cited as evidence that about a third of respondents say 'yes' to a bid as high as $1,000. This is extremely unrepresentative of the general experience in CV, and reflects the peculiar circumstances in which that survey was administered (Hanemann, 1996); in fact, such high bids typically receive a very small proportion of 'yes' responses.

11.3.5.2   Basic principles of optimal design

Optimal design may seem odd to an econometrician used to taking the data as given. But, in a discrete-response CV experiment the researcher has the opportunity to influence the data by setting the bids. To do this optimally, she must first make an assumption about the form of the underlying WTP distribution and the value of its parameters. Moreover, she must decide which particular welfare measure she wishes to estimate, and must select a particular criterion for the precision of the estimate. Those decisions will reflect her interests and priorities. For example, she might be concerned to reduce the variance of the estimate of median WTP. This implies minimizing the asymptotic variance of the median, given in (11.54) for the logit model, with respect to the bid values. In the experimental design literature, minimizing a function of parameter estimates is known as a C-optimal design criterion.[64] Alternatively, the researcher could choose a D-optimal design, based on maximizing the determinant of the Fisher information matrix, (11.52). In the case of the logit model, this corresponds to jointly minimizing the confidence intervals around the parameters α and β. This criterion would be of most use for a researcher who is interested primarily in obtaining efficient parameter estimates, perhaps for predictive purposes or for benefits transfer.

Optimal bid designs for the minimum variance (C-optimal) and D-optimal design criteria are presented in Table 11.2. These are expressed in terms of percentiles of the underlying true WTP distribution. Of course, since that distribution is unknown, one has to rely on estimates or guesses of the distribution in order to identify the bid points. This is the basic paradox of optimal experimental design in nonlinear models. The optimal design depends on the true parameter values. Therefore, one must know these in order to engineer the best design for collecting the data. But, there would be no point in collecting the data if one already knew the true parameter values. As indicated, one resolves this paradox in practice by relying on prior information. In addition, it highlights a second important role for optimal design analysis, namely interpreting the results after the data have been collected and analysed, by helping one to understand, *ex post*, which data points were influential or contributed the most statistical information.

The design results in Table 11.2 have several interesting features. For example, the designs are all quite simple, consisting of no more than two different bid values each. The single-bounded C-optimal design is especially simple, consisting of a single bid point located at what one believes to be the median of the WTP distribution. Note that such a design does not identify the two underlying parameters, α and β. But then, it was not the goal of the optimal design to estimate these parameters—the aim was to estimate their ratio, α/β. The result tells us something about where the most informative

---

[64] Other examples of C-optimal designs in the CV literature are the minimization of the variance of a non-parametric estimator of truncated mean WTP, (11.44) (Duffield and Patterson, 1991) and the minimization of the mean squared error of mean WTP (Cooper, 1993).

Table 11.2 Some optimal designs for single bounded CV data

Design criterion	Criterion description	Single bounded design (in percentiles)	
		Logit models	Probit models
D-optimal	Maximize determinant of Fisher information matrix	Half of sample each at: $B = 82.4\%$ $B = 17.6\%$	Half of sample each at: $B = 87.25\%$ $B = 12.75\%$
C-optimal	Minimize variance of median WTP	$B = 50.0\%$ (parameters unidentifiable)	$B = 50.0\%$ (parameters unidentifiable)

Source: Results from Alberini (1994), Minkin (1987), Wu (1988).

bids are located: the bid values near the centre of the WTP distribution are best for obtaining an efficient estimate of median WTP.[65] Conversely, we note that no optimal design contains bids in the outer 12% of each tail of the distribution. The outer tails of the normal and logistic distributions are quite flat, and consequently, responses to bids lying on these parts of the distribution offer very little information about the WTP distribution. If one wanted to obtain reliable point estimates of response probabilities in the tails of the distribution, the sample size would have to be very large; for example, we expect to have to collect 100 observations at the 95th percentile in order to receive just five positive responses. This gets even worse as one moves further out into the tails.

11.3.5.3 Sequential design

One way to resolve the paradox of optimal experimental design is to conduct the survey in stages, using data from the earlier stages to optimize the design in the later stages. Most CV researchers do this, at least to some degree. For example, a common practice is to employ a two-step procedure: first, perform a pre-test to obtain preliminary information about the WTP distribution, then survey the full sample. The pre-test results are used to design optimal bids for the full survey based on the parameter values estimated from the pre-test data. Typically, however, pre-test sample sizes are small relative to the size of main sample; this allocation of survey effort generates only a modest quantity of initial information.[66]

To take better advantage of the optimal design results available, a sequential estimation procedure should be used, preferably with more than two

[65] Alberini and Carson (1993) derived optimal designs for this case using higher order Taylor series approximations to the asymptotic distribution of median WTP. They found that, while a first-order approximation (leading to a one-point design) was generally unreliable, there was little gain from using more than a third-order Taylor series term. They obtained two-point designs that tend to be within one standard deviation of the centre of the WTP distribution.

[66] Pre-testing is also essential for honing the questionnaire and checking its field implementation. In our experience, inadequacies of pre-testing are often the greatest flaw in academic CV studies. Not only should there be a reasonably large sample for a pre-test (say, 100–200 observations), but also there needs to be at least two and perhaps three pre-tests for a high quality survey.

Table 11.3 Performance of simulated sequential single bounded C-optimal logit CV design[a]

No. of survey iterations	No. of observations per iteration	Mean squared error of WTP *relative* to C-optimal design[b]
1	500	101.42
2	250	2.46
3	166	1.34
4	125	1.32
5	100	1.23

[a] These simulations are based on a logistic distribution with parameters $\alpha = 2.5, \beta = 0.01$; expected median WTP $= 250$, $n = 500$.
[b] Based on the specified parameters and sample size, a C-optimal design would produce a mean squared error estimate of $4/n\beta^2$ for the single-bounded model (Kanninen, 1993*b*).
Source: table from Kanninen (1993*a*).

stages (Kanninen, 1993*a*; Nyquist, 1992). After each iteration of the survey, provided the survey instrument has not changed, the WTP distribution can be estimated using all available observations so that a new (optimal) bid design can be derived for use with the subsequent iteration of the survey. This approach can asymptotically attain the efficiency of the theoretical optimal design results.

Kanninen (1993*a*) demonstrates the efficiency of sequentially updating the bid design by performing a simulation where the initial bid design is poor, but is updated after a set number of observations is collected. If, for example, the sample size is 500 and two iterations are performed, then each iteration collects 250 observations; if three iterations are performed, each iteration collects 166 observations; etc. Table 11.3 presents the results of this experiment, comparing the simulated mean squared error with the asymptotic mean squared error that would be obtained from a C-optimal design. For a total sample of 500 observations split equally among iterations, the results show that the mean squared error decreases monotonically with the number of iterations. The rate of improvement slows after three iterations. With five iterations, the single-bounded model has a mean squared error that is only 23% larger than the C-optimal design.

Two lessons can be learned from the CV sequential design literature. First, there are substantial efficiency gains from increasing the number of iterations of data collection and bid design update. Second, the use of a sequential procedure relieves concerns arising from the fact that optimal design results call for just two bid values. With a sequential design, only two bid values are employed at each iteration, but the values change between iterations as information is accumulated. How many bid values are ultimately employed depends on how many iterations are performed.[67] How much the bid values

---

[67] Alberini (1995*a*) investigates how many design points are needed to obtain a powerful Pearson chi-square test.

differ between iterations depends on how close the initial assessment of parameter values was to the true distribution.

11.3.5.4   Concluding comments on optimal design

Because optimal bid designs tend to require only one or two bid points, CV researchers are sometimes reluctant to employ them in practice. There are clearly reasons to be concerned about using two-point designs. First, because there is *a priori* uncertainty about parameter values, it is unwise to limit the range of bid points collected. Second, because optimal bid designs vary depending on the functional form of the underlying distribution, it is risky to base the optimal design on a particular assumption about functional form when it is unknown *a priori*. For both reasons, one wants to modify optimal design results somewhat for practical application.

As discussed above, one solution is to conduct the CV survey sequentially. This approach gives the researcher flexibility for updating the bid designs so that the final bid design, given several iterations, can be close to optimal. The researcher maintains the ability of adapting to new information about the shape and position of the WTP distribution. If several iterations are performed, the data will contain several different bid points because of the different iterations of the survey, but by the end the researcher will have achieved an optimal set of bids to maximize efficiency.

The other solution is to hedge one's bets by making several guesses at the true parameter values, and then using multiple bids corresponding to the optimum designs for the various possible parameter values. By doing this, one might end up with, say, four to six bid points. As a matter of general practice, we would caution against having many more bid points than this. While it may seem attractive to multiply the number of bids in the face of uncertainty about the true WTP distribution, we believe that this is generally an unwise practice for two reasons. First, for a fixed sample size, having more bid points means fewer observations and therefore less information at each point. Second, as noted earlier, bid points from the tails of a distribution are generally uninformative—for the logistic distribution, we observed that this ruled out bid points in the outer 12% tails of the distribution. Collecting observations in those tails typically wastes the observations; to obtain useful and reliable data so far out in the tails of the distribution, one would need an inordinately large sample.

11.4.   ADDITIONAL TOPICS

In this section we consider some additional statistical issues connected with discrete-response CV. We have chosen five topics that interest us and are at the current frontiers of research, although we treat them briefly because of space limitations. The topics are valuing multiple items, the double-bounded CV format, extensions of the response probability model, non-parametric response probability models, and non-response bias.

11.4.1 Valuing multiple items

So far we have focused on valuing a single item. In this section we discuss the statistical issues that arise when respondents value multiple items. We also briefly consider situations where the same individual provides multiple valuations of the same item; this is then considered at greater length in Section 11.4.2.

From one point of view, valuing multiple items adds nothing of substance and raises no new issues: one merely takes each item by itself and fits a separate response probability model for that item, using the methods discussed above. However, if the analyst believes that the response probability models are related because they share parts of the utility function, there is a distinct advantage to treating the items simultaneously. One can obtain a more efficient estimate of the model parameters by pooling the responses, or at least analysing them in a linked manner, thus taking advantage of the additional information embodied in the valuations of the other items. In this section we discuss some ways for doing this. Our discussion is divided into three parts. Section 11.4.1.1 focuses on ways of formulating hedonic models that can be applied to the valuation of multiple items; Section 11.4.1.2 focuses on the stochastic specification of such models; Section 11.4.1.3 deals with the ways in which valuations of multiple items can be elicited, including contingent ranking and related techniques; and Section 11.4.1.4 considers the connection with random coefficient models.

11.4.1.1 Hedonic utility formulations

The various items that respondents are asked to value could be either different things (e.g., preserving forests, preserving wetlands, preserving lakes, etc.) or different quantities of the same thing (e.g., preserving 1 forest, preserving 2 forests, preserving 3 forests, etc.). In either case, the utility function associated with the kth item will be written $u_k = v_k(q^k, y, \varepsilon_k)$. The baseline utility in the absence of the item is $v_0(q^0, y, \varepsilon_0)$, which may or may not vary with k. The elements that are related or shared in common may involve the deterministic or the stochastic components of $v_k(q^k, y, \varepsilon_k)$, or both. We start with models where the commonality involves just the deterministic components of the utility function. In effect, this defines a *hedonic* utility model. Such models can take various forms. For example, suppose that the underlying utility model is the Box–Cox model (11.11), where β and λ are the same for all k, while α varies across programmes according to some function $\alpha_k = \phi(q^k)$. Thus, the utility associated with the kth programme is

$$u_k = \phi(q^k) + \beta\left(\frac{y^\lambda - 1}{\lambda}\right) + \varepsilon_k, \tag{11.68}$$

and the individual's WTP for the kth programme is

$$C_k = y - \left(y^\lambda - \frac{\phi(q^k) - \phi(q^0)}{b} - \frac{\eta_k}{b}\right)^{1/\lambda}, \tag{11.68'}$$

where $\eta_k \equiv \varepsilon_k - \varepsilon_0$ and $b \equiv \beta/\lambda$. Given the specification of a joint distribution for the η_k, response probability formulas can readily be generated from $(11.68')$.[68] If the programmes involve different quantities of the same item, q^k is a scalar and $\phi(\cdot)$ is a univariate, and presumably quasi-concave, function. If the programmes involve different items, q^k is a vector and $\phi(\cdot)$ is a multivariate, quasi-concave function. For this purpose, one could use a standard formula from the literature such as the translog multivariate utility function or some other flexible form. Hoehn (1991) uses a quadratic approximation to represent the change in $\phi(\cdot)$:[69]

$$\phi(q^k) - \phi(q^0) = e + g\Delta^k + \Delta^{k'}H\Delta^k, \tag{11.69}$$

where $\Delta^k \equiv q^k - q^0$ is the vector of changes in q, e and g are vectors of coefficients, and H is a matrix of coefficients whose off-diagonal elements, $h_{ij}, i \neq j$, reflect the utility interactions among the separate programme components. If $h_{ij} < 0, i \neq j$, the ith and j^{th} components of q are substitutes for one another, and an increase in q_j lowers the individual's WTP for an improvement in q_i; if $h_{ij} > 0, i \neq j$, they are complements, and an increase in q_j raises the WTP for an improvement in q_i.

If there are only a few discrete values of the q_i, it may be simpler to replace $\phi(q)$, viewed as a function of continuous variable(s), with a step function consisting of a set of constant terms and dummy variables. Suppose, for example, that the programmes involve three different items (e.g., $i = 1$ is forests, $i = 2$ is wetlands, and $i = 3$ is lakes), each of which can be either left in a baseline condition or improved by some specific amount. The change in an item is represented by a scalar index Δ_i, where $\Delta_i = 1$ if the item is improved and $\Delta_i = 0$ otherwise. The kth programme consists of some combination $\Delta^k = (\Delta_1^k, \Delta_2^k, \Delta_3^k)$. Given that there are three resources and two possible states for each resource, there are $2^3 = 8$ possible programmes. There are several ways to represent $\phi(\cdot)$. One model in the literature sets

$$\phi(q^k) = \sum_i g_i \Delta_i^k + h_{12}\Delta_1^k\Delta_2^k + h_{13}\Delta_1^k\Delta_3^k + h_{23}\Delta_2^k\Delta_3^k, \tag{11.70}$$

where the g_i and h_{ij} are coefficients to be estimated. Another model adds a three-way interaction term,

---

[68] The restrictions on stochastic specification discussed in Section 11.2.3 would still need to be imposed in order to ensure that $0 \leqslant C_k \leqslant y$.

[69] In addition, he uses the version of (11.68) where $\lambda = 1$.

$$\phi(q^k) = \sum_i g_i \Delta_i^k + h_{12}\Delta_1^k\Delta_2^k + h_{13}\Delta_1^k\Delta_3^k + h_{23}\Delta_2^k\Delta_3^k + h_{123}\Delta_1^k\Delta_2^k\Delta_3^k. \qquad (11.71)$$

Both models satisfy the normalization that $\phi(0,0,0) = 0$. The formulation in (11.70) is closer to Hoehn's quadratic approximation in (11.69).[70] The formulation in (11.71) is what is known as a fully saturated model. Using (11.71), the baseline utility associated with no improvement in any resource (denoted $k = 000$) is

$$u_{000} = \beta\left[\frac{y^\lambda - 1}{\lambda}\right] + \varepsilon_{000}, \qquad (11.71a)$$

while the utility associated with a programme that improves just forests ($k = 100$) is

$$u_{100} = g_1 + \beta\left[\frac{y^\lambda - 1}{\lambda}\right] + \varepsilon_{100}, \qquad (11.71b)$$

that associated with a programme that improves both forests and wetlands ($k = 110$) is

$$u_{110} = g_1 + g_2 + h_{12} + \beta\left[\frac{y^\lambda - 1}{\lambda}\right] + \varepsilon_{110}, \qquad (11.71c)$$

and that associated with a programme that improves all three resources ($k = 111$) is

$$u_{111} = g_1 + g_2 + g_3 + h_{12} + h_{13} + h_{23} + h_{123} + \beta\left[\frac{y^\lambda - 1}{\lambda}\right] + \varepsilon_{111}. \qquad (11.71d)$$

The utilities associated with the other four possible programme ($k = 001$, 010, 011, and 101) are calculated similarly. The corresponding formulas for the individual's WTP to have improvement programme $k = xxx$ instead of the baseline $k = 000$ are obtained by substituting (11.71) into (11.68′), from which response probability formulas can be generated.

What is gained by using the step-function hedonic model in (11.71)? Suppose that, instead of using the formulation in (11.71), one simply used (11.68) but with a separate constant $\alpha_k \equiv \phi(q^k)$ for each of the seven improvement programme, yielding

$$u_k = \alpha_k + \beta\left[\frac{y^\lambda - 1}{\lambda}\right] + \varepsilon_k. \qquad (11.72)$$

In this case, it would be natural to impose the normalization that $\alpha_{000} = 0$. Fitting (11.72) to CV data covering all of the improvement programme provides estimates of the constants α_{100}, α_{110}, α_{111}, α_{101}, α_{001}, α_{010}, and α_{011}. A comparison of (11.72) with (11.71b, c) shows that $\alpha_{100} = g_1$, $\alpha_{010} = g_2$,

---

[70] Hoehn and Loomis (1993) use a version of (11.70) where $\lambda = 1$ and apply this to a case where there are *two* discrete levels of q_i^k in addition to the baseline q_i^0.

and $\alpha_{110} = g_1 + g_2 + h_{12}$. Hence, $h_{12} = \alpha_{110} - \alpha_{100} - \alpha_{010}$. The other parameters h_{13}, h_{23}, and h_{123} can similarly be obtained as linear combinations of the α_k. Thus, there is a one-to-one mapping between the seven α_k in (11.72) and the seven parameters (g and h) in (11.71). It follows that (11.72) is equivalent to the fully saturated model in (11.71). By contrast, the model in (11.70) is not equivalent to (11.72) because it has fewer parameters—given estimates of α_k from (11.72), the h's in (11.70) are over-identified.

Within the framework of the Box–Cox model (11.68), the formulation in (11.71) can be regarded as the most general, non-parametric representation of the $\phi(\cdot)$ function that can be estimated from responses to CV questions about the seven programmes. Other formulations such as (11.70) are restrictions of this general model. If the components of q really can take on more than two discrete values associated with the programme in the CV survey, estimating (11.68) with some particular parametric representation of $\phi(\cdot)$ has the advantage that it allows one to predict the individual's WTP for a range of programme different from those covered in the survey. But, this advantage comes at the cost of imposing a particular parametric representation on $\phi(\cdot)$.

11.4.1.2   Multivariate WTP distributions

We have focused so far on ways to model the deterministic component of $v(q^k, y, \varepsilon_k)$ that allow for linkage in preferences for the various items. We have said nothing about the stochastic specification of ε_k. Existing empirical models of multi-item valuation generally assume that these are independently and identically distributed (i.i.d.)—i.e., there is *no* linkage among the stochastic components of preferences for the various items. There are two reasons why this may be inadequate. First, there may be unobserved attributes of the programmes which induce some correlation in preferences for them. (Two programmes which the analyst is treating as separate may actually be related because of factors that the analyst has overlooked, and this will appear to the analyst as inducing correlation among people's preferences for them.) Second, there may be unobserved attributes of the respondents which induce correlation in preferences for programme. (An individual who particularly likes one type of programme may be more inclined to like (or dislike) another type.) In these cases, one needs to introduce some joint density for $\varepsilon_k, f_\varepsilon(\varepsilon_0, \varepsilon_1, \ldots, \varepsilon_K)$, with a non-diagonal covariance matrix. How one might do that is the subject of this section.

Continuing with the Box–Cox model, the dependence among the ε_k in (11.68) carries over to the η_k and the C_k. The joint density $f_\varepsilon(\varepsilon_0, \varepsilon_1, \ldots, \varepsilon_K)$ induces a joint density $f_\eta(\eta_1, \ldots, \eta_K)$ and, via (11.68'), a joint density $g_C(C_1, \ldots, C_K)$. The latter is used to represent the response probability formula for the suite of programme valuations. Suppose, for example, that there are $K = 3$ programs which are evaluated using the single-bounded, discrete-response format. Let A_k denote the dollar cost presented to the individual for the kth programme. Suppose, the individual answers 'no' to programme 1 and 3, but 'yes' to programme 2. From (11.6a,b), the probability of these responses is given by

$$\mathrm{Pr}\{\text{'no' to1 and3, 'yes' to2}\} = \mathrm{Pr}\{C_1 \leqslant A_1, C_2 \geqslant A_2, \text{and} C_3 \leqslant A_3\}$$

$$= \int_0^{A_1} \int_{A_2}^{C_2^{max}} \int_0^{A_3} g_C(C_1, C_2, C_3) dc_1 \, dc_2 \, dc_3,$$

$$(11.73)$$

where $C^{max} \leqslant y$ is the upper bound on the individual's WTP for programme k. Let $G_C(C_1, \ldots, C_K)$ be the joint distribution function associated with the density $g_C(C_1, \ldots, C_K)$, and let $G_{(k)}(C_1, \ldots, C_K)$ denote the partial derivative of this joint distribution with respect to the kth argument: $G_{(k)}(C_1, \ldots, C_K) \equiv \partial G_C(C_1, \ldots, C_K)/\partial C_k$. An equivalent way of expressing (11.73) is

$$\mathrm{Pr}\{C_1 \leqslant A_1, C_2 \geqslant A_2, \quad \text{and} \quad C_3 \leqslant A_3\} = \int_{A_2}^{C_2^{max}} G_{(2)}(A_1, C_2, A_3) dc_2.$$

$$(11.73')$$

As noted above, the existing CV literature on multi-item valuation generally assumes independence among the C_k (Loomis, *et al.*, 1990; Hoehn, 1991; Hoehn and Loomis, 1993). In that case, the response probability formula for the suite of responses is the product of the marginal response probabilities for the individual programmes

$$\mathrm{Pr}\{C_1 \leqslant A_1, C_2 \geqslant A_2, \text{and} C_3 \leqslant A_3\} = \mathrm{Pr}\{C_1 \leqslant A_1\} \mathrm{Pr}\{C_2 \geqslant A_2\} \mathrm{Pr}\{C_3 \leqslant A_3\}.$$

$$(11.74)$$

With stochastic dependence among the C_k, however, the factoring into marginal probabilities does not apply, and one must deal directly with the joint response probability. In general, this involves a K-dimensional integral, as in (11.73). The question is whether there are stochastic specifications that yield tractable formulations for this integral while still allowing for a general covariance structure among the random components of preferences. Achieving this is not simple.

A natural starting point is to look for some multivariate generalization of the logistic distribution that retains a closed-form representation of the multivariate c.d.f. for the η_k. Arnold (1992) reviews a variety of multivariate distributions that have the univariate logistic as their marginal distribution. But most of these entail severe restrictions on the covariance structure. For example, the simplest formulation of a multivariate logistic c.d.f. is

$$F_\eta(\eta_1, \ldots, \eta_k) = \left[1 + \sum_k \exp(-\eta_k)\right]^{-1}, \qquad (11.75)$$

but this imposes a correlation among values for pairs of programmes of $\rho(\eta_k, \eta_l) = 0.5$. Arnold describes some other multivariate logistic distributions, but these still involve correlation coefficients restricted to a subset of the interval $[-1, 1]$ that is likely to be unsuitable for CV applications. Wu *et al.* (1992) use McFadden's (1978) Generalized Extreme Value distribution for ε_k to generate a nested logistic distribution for the η_k. Suppose, for example, that $(\varepsilon_0, \varepsilon_1, \ldots, \varepsilon_K)$ can be partitioned in a two-level clustering. In the top level, there are R groups; in the rth group, there are S_r elements. The multivariate c.d.f. for ε_k then takes the form

$$F_\varepsilon(\varepsilon) = \exp\left[-\sum_{r=1}^{R} \left(\sum_{s=1}^{S_r} \exp(-\varepsilon_s)^{\frac{1}{\theta_r}} \right)^{\theta_r} \right], \tag{11.76}$$

where the θ_r are parameters that determine within-group correlation.[71] The correlation coefficients are (Johnson and Kotz, 1972, p. 256):

$$\text{corr}\,(\varepsilon_k, \varepsilon_l) = \begin{array}{ll} 1 - \theta_r^2 & \text{if } \varepsilon_k \text{ and } \varepsilon_l \text{ are both in the } r\text{th group,} \\ 0 & \text{if } \varepsilon_k \text{ and } \varepsilon_l \text{ are in different groups.} \end{array}$$

Since there is usually a restriction that $\theta_r \leqslant 1$, this does not allow for any negative correlation among the ε_k. More generally, there does not appear to be any multivariate logistic distribution that would allow for a full range of positive or negative correlation among preferences for programmes.

When $K = 2$, the problem can be solved by using Mardia's (1970) method for generating a bivariate distribution with specified marginals and an unrestricted correlation. Let $F_i(\eta_i)$ be the marginal distribution for $\eta_i, i = 1, 2$. Let $G(x, y; \rho)$ be some bivariate c.d.f. with an unrestricted correlation coefficient, ρ, and with marginal distributions, $G_x(x)$ and $G_Y(y)$. One creates the transformed variables $\eta_1^* = G_x^{-1}[F_1(\eta_1)] \equiv J_1(\eta_1)$ and $\eta_2^* = G_Y^{-1}[F_2(\eta_2)] \equiv J_2(\eta_2)$ and endows them with the specified bivariate distribution, thereby inducing a joint distribution for η_1 and η_2, $G[J_1(\eta_1), J_2(\eta_2); \rho]$. For example, one could use the standard logistic distribution, $F_i(\eta) = (1 + e^\eta)^{-1}$, combined with a standard bivariate normal for $G(x, y; \rho)$. This is a convenient way to generate bivariate distributions with a general correlation structure, but it does not readily extend to multivariate distributions for $K > 2$.[72]

In the multivariate case, the best approach is to use a multivariate normal distribution. While this requires numerical evaluation, it permits a general covariance structure that offers maximum flexibility in modelling preferences

[71] The distribution in (11.75) is essentially a special case of (11.76) with $R = 1$. It should be emphasized that the distributions of stochastic components discussed in 11.4.1.2–11.4.1.4 may all need to be modified by censoring or truncation, along the lines described in S. 11.2.3, in order to satisfy the economic restriction that $0 \leqslant C_k \leqslant y$ and perhaps also to ensure some pattern of stochastic ordering among the u_k.
[72] Lee (1983) applies this method to create a generalized selectivity bias model; Ward (1995) uses it for double-bounded CV.

for multiple programmes. Until recently, this would not have been regarded as a feasible option. While many software packages will evaluate a bivariate normal integral, numerical integration methods are required for $K > 2$ which until recently were considered impractical.[73] For multivariate probit models (discussed further in Section 11.4.1.3), numerical approximations were used based on formulas developed by Clark (1961) for the moments of the maximum of (non-i.i.d.) normal random variables; this maximum is not itself a normal variate, but the approximation treats it as though it were. In practice, however, the approximation turns out to be poor when individual variances are highly dissimilar or there are negative correlations (Horowitz, et al., 1984), and this approach is rarely used now. Lerman and Manski (1981) proposed an alternative approach based on sampling from multivariate normal distributions via Monte Carlo simulation and evaluating multinomial choice probabilities based on the proportion of outcomes in the empirical simulation. Since the empirical cumulative distribution (e.c.d.f.) converges to the true c.d.f. (given certain regularity conditions), any function of the e.c.d.f. will converge to the corresponding function of the c.d.f. itself. The Lerman–Manski method combined simulation of the likelihood function for given parameter values with iteration over parameter values to achieve numerical maximization of the likelihood function. In application, this proved to be almost as burdensome as numerical quadrature of the integrals. A breakthrough occurred when McFadden (1989) proposed the use of smoothed frequency simulators for the empirical probabilities that make up the likelihood function, and showed that this requires far fewer simulations yet provides consistent and almost efficient parameter estimates. This led to the development of several highly efficient smooth simulator algorithms, the leading one currently being the Geweke–Hajivassiliou–Keane (GHK) simulator.[74] This has been applied to the analysis of contingent ranking data by Hajivassiliou and Ruud (1994) and Layton (1995).

So far, we have focused on dependent multivariate distributions for ε_k, η_k or C_k. The C_k can be thought of as latent variables which generate the observed binary responses via the crossing of a threshold, as in (11.3) or (11.6a,b). Instead of modelling dependence among these latent continuous variables, an alternative is to model dependence among the binary response variables directly. This type of model, known as multivariate logit or simultaneous logit, was introduced by D.R. Cox (1972), Nerlove and Press (1973), and Schmidt and Straus (1975), and has recently been the focus of much attention in the biometrics literature.

Let Y_k denote the binary response for the kth program in a single-bounded CV format with bid A_k, and let $y_k = 0$ or 1 denote the realization

---

[73] Chapman and Hanemann (1993) use the bivariate normal distribution combined with the Box–Cox model (11.72) in a CV study where $K = 2$.

[74] For further discussion of these approaches, see Hajivassiliou (1993), Keane (1993), and Hajivassiliou and Ruud (1994).

of this variable. The quadratic exponential model (D.R. Cox, 1972; Zhao and Prentice, 1990) characterizes the joint distribution of Y_k as a log-linear model with third-order and higher terms zeroed out:

$$\Pr\{Y_1 = y_1, \ldots, Y_K = y_K\} = (1/\Delta)\exp\left(\sum_k \gamma_k y_k + \sum_{k<1} \gamma_{kl} y_k y_1\right), \quad (11.77)$$

where Δ is a normalization constant which ensures that the probabilities sum to unity. This implies that

$$\ln\left[\frac{\Pr\{Y_k = 1 | Y_l = y_l, \quad Y_{k'} = 0, \quad k' \neq k, l\}}{\Pr\{Y_k = 0 | Y_l = y_l, \quad Y_{k'} = 0, \quad k' \neq k, l\}}\right] = \gamma_k + \gamma_{kl} y_l$$

and

$$\ln\left[\frac{\Pr\{Y_l = 1 | Y_k = y_k, \quad Y_{k'} = 0, \quad k' \neq k, l\}}{\Pr\{Y_l = 0 | Y_k = y_k, \quad Y_{k'} = 0, \quad k' \neq k, l\}}\right] = \gamma_l + \gamma_{kl} y_k$$

Hence, in this model, γ_k is the log of the odds ratio for Y_k conditional on $Y_{k'} = 0$ all $k' \neq k$, which, in the Box–Cox model (11.72), would take the form

$$\gamma_k = \alpha_k + b(y - A_k)^\lambda - by^\lambda.$$

The γ_{kl} term measures the association between Y_k and Y_l; it characterizes how the conditional distribution of Y_k depends on Y_l,

$$\ln\left[\frac{\Pr\{Y_k=1, Y_\ell=1 | Y_{k'}=0, k' \neq k, l\} \bullet \Pr\{Y_k=0, Y_\ell=0 | Y_{k'}=0, k' \neq k, l\}}{\Pr\{Y_k=1, Y_\ell=0 | Y_{k'}=0, k' \neq k, l\} \bullet \Pr\{Y_{k'}=0, Y_\ell=1 | Y_{k'}=0, k' \neq k, l\}}\right] = \gamma_{kl}$$

and, equally, how the conditional distribution of Y_l depends on Y_k. Y_k and Y_l are positively associated if $\gamma_{kl} > 0$, and negatively if $\gamma_{kl} < 0$. The parameters to be estimated are b, λ, the α_k (or an underlying parametric function, $\phi(q^k)$, which generates them) and the γ_{kl}, which may themselves be expressed as functions of covariates. Estimation is by maximum likelihood (Fitzmaurice and Laird, 1993) or the method of moments (Liang *et al.*, 1992).

Though it is relatively tractable, this approach to creating a stochastic dependence among the evaluations of multiple programme has the disadvantage that one cannot directly recover from (11.77) an explicit multivariate distribution of the C_k. Moreover, when applied to different elicitation formats that generate different types of discrete response, such as single-bounded versus double-bounded (discussed in Section 11.4.2) or referendum-style voting versus ranking (discussed immediately below), the approach in (11.77) implies a separate and distinct underlying distribution of the C_k for each format. In effect, this method of modelling stochastic dependence provides a statistical association among the dependent variables but not a structural association, a criticism made in a different context by Heckman (1978) and Maddala (1983). In contrast, directly specifying a dependent multivariate WTP distribution yields a structural model that can be applied consistently across different elicitation formats.

11.4.1.3 Contingent ranking and related techniques

In this section we discuss contingent ranking and two related techniques, contingent choice and mixed contingent voting/ranking. In the pure voting format, the respondent is presented with a set of programs, each offering some set of environmental amenities q^k at a cost A_k, and votes 'yes' or 'no' on each program. An alternative is to have the respondent *rank* the programs from most to least preferred. This is known as contingent ranking. It was introduced by Beggs *et al.* (1981) and Chapman and Staelin (1982) for automobile and college choices, respectively, and was first applied to environmental valuation by Rae (1982, 1983); recent applications are summarized in Layton (1995). In this case, the response is not a set of 1s and 0s but a set of integers from 1 to K giving each program's rank. Index the items so that $k = 1$ is rated highest and $k = K$ lowest. Given the RUM setting, the probability of this ranking is

Pr {item 1 ranked 1st, item 2 ranked 2nd, ..., item K ranked last} =

$$\Pr\{v_1(q^1, y - A_1, \varepsilon_1) \geqslant v_2(q^2, y - A_2, \varepsilon_2) \geqslant \ldots \geqslant v_K(q^K, y - A_K, \varepsilon_K)\}.$$

(11.78)

Suppose the utility functions have an additively random structure as described in fn. 11, $u_k = \bar{v}_k(q^k, y - A_k) + \varepsilon_k$; the Box–Cox models (11.11) and (11.68) would be examples. Define the utility differences $\bar{\delta}_k \equiv \bar{v}_k$ $(q^k, y - A_k) - \bar{v}_{k+1}(q^{k+1}, y - A_{k+1})$ and let $\bar{\eta}_k \equiv \varepsilon_{k+1} - \varepsilon_k, k = 1, \ldots, K - 1$. The ranking response can then be expressed in terms of $f_{\bar{\eta}}(\bar{\eta}_1, \ldots, \bar{\eta}_{k-1})$, the joint density of the $\bar{\eta}_k$, as

Pr{item 1 ranked 1st, item 2 ranked 2nd, ..., item K ranked last} =

(11.79)

$$\int_{-\infty}^{\bar{\delta}_1} \cdots \int_{-\infty}^{\bar{\delta}_{K-1}} f_{\bar{\eta}}(\bar{\eta}_1, \ldots, \bar{\eta}_{K-1}) d\bar{\eta}_1 \ldots d\bar{\eta}_{K-1}.$$

Before discussing the statistical models that can be generated from (11.78) or (11.79), four points should be noted about the economic implications of ranking responses. First, with ranking responses, as with voting choices, the response probabilities depend essentially on differences in utilities. Therefore, there will generally be some identifiability restrictions like those noted in fn. 10. Second, with contingent ranking and related techniques, it is not necessary that the baseline status quo (receive q^0, pay $A_0 = 0$) be included among the items for respondents to consider. There may be practical advantages in doing this, for example with the mixed voting/ranking model to be described below, but it is not required in order to obtain a valid measure of individual preferences. Of course, if the status quo is not included, one cannot recover from (11.78) or (11.79) an estimate of the parameters uniquely associated with the utility function $v_0(q_0, y, \varepsilon_0)$; but one will be able to recover an estimate of those associated with $v_k(q^k, y, \varepsilon_k)$, $k \neq 0$.[75] Third, regardless of whether or not the status quo is included as an item to be ranked, it is *not* generally possible to characterize the ranking response in terms of the multivariate WTP distribution. With referendum responses, as we noted in Section 11.2.2, it makes no difference whether one follows the approach to model formulation associated with Hanemann (1984a), based on the specification of indirect utility functions, or the approach associated with Cameron (1988), which directly specifies a WTP distribution. Both approaches lead to exactly the same response probability formula for referendum responses. This does not carry over to contingent ranking or contingent choice. In those cases, the responses generally cannot be expressed in term of the WTPs for the individual items (the C_k). For example, suppose that $K = 2$ and the individual ranks the items such that

$$v_1(q^1, y - A_1, \varepsilon_1) \geqslant v_2(q^2, y - A_2, \varepsilon_2).$$

This is *not* equivalent to the condition that

$$C_1 - A_1 \geqslant C_2 - A_2.$$

Therefore, the joint density of C_1 and C_2 cannot usefully be employed to characterize the probability of the ranking responses.[76]

Fourth, when one thinks of the observed responses in terms of an underlying RUM model, there is an obvious link between ranking and *choice*. In a standard choice exercise, respondents are presented with K items and asked to choose one of them. Choice thus corresponds to a *partial ranking*, where just one item is ranked, the most preferred:[77]

$$\begin{aligned} \Pr\{k\text{th item chosen}\} &= \Pr\{k\text{th item ranked first}\} \\ &= \Pr\{v_k(q^k, y - A_k, \varepsilon_k) \geqslant v_1(q^1, y - A_1, \varepsilon_1), \ell = 1, \ldots, K\}. \end{aligned} \quad (11.80)$$

Assume the utility functions have an additively random structure like that leading to (11.79). For simplicity, let $k = 1$ be the item chosen. Define the utility differences $\delta_k \equiv \bar{v}_1(q^1, y - A_1) - \bar{v}_k(q^k, y - A_k)$ and let $\eta_k \equiv \varepsilon_k - \varepsilon_\ell$,

---

[75] If one uses some form of hedonic model, it may be possible to extrapolate the parameters of $v_0(q_0, y, \varepsilon_0)$ from those of the utility functions $v_k(q^k, y, \varepsilon_k), k \neq 0$. Freeman's (1991) objection to the use of rating or ranking for preference elicitation is essentially that the omission of a status quo alternative prevents one from recovering $v_0(q_0, y, \varepsilon_0)$.

[76] An exception occurs when there are no income effects, as in (11.18a,b). In that case, the two conditions are equivalent and the ranking response can be characterized in terms of the multivariate WTP distribution. The general non-equivalence of the two characterizations arises because of the non-additivity of WTP (and WTA)—as discussed in Chapter 3, the sum of WTPs (or WTAs) for a change from q^0 to q^1 plus a change from q^1 to q^2 does not equal the WTP (or WTA) for the change from q^0 to q^2.

[77] This equivalence requires a regularity condition which is described in Barbera and Pattanaik (1986).

$k = 2, \ldots, K$; the choice probability can then be expressed in terms of $f_\eta(\eta_2, \ldots, \eta_K)$, the joint density of the η_k, as

$$\text{Pr}\{\text{item 1 chosen}\} = \int_{-\infty}^{\delta_2} \cdots \int_{-\infty}^{\delta_K} f_\eta(\eta_2, \ldots, \eta_K) d\eta_2 \ldots d\eta_K. \qquad (11.81)$$

If there are only two items, item 1 with (q^1, A_1) and item 0 with $(q^0, A_0 = 0)$, (11.81) reduces to (11.4). That is to say, referendum-like voting of the type considered in Sections 11.2 and 11.3 is simply a choice among $K = 2$ alternatives; conversely, the contingent choice model is a generalization of voting to more than two courses of action.[78] If the ε_k are multivariate normal, then $f_\eta(\eta_2, \ldots, \eta_K)$ is also multivariate normal and (11.81) is a multivariate generalization of the probit model in (11.14), known as multinomial probit (Hausman and Wise, 1978). If the ε_k are i.i.d. extreme value variates with scale parameter τ, the η_k are i.i.d. logistic variates with scale parameter τ and (11.81) is a multivariate generalization of the logit model in (11.15), known as multinomial logit (McFadden, 1974). In that case, the joint distribution function, $F_\eta(\eta_2, \ldots, \eta_K)$, takes the form[79]

$$F_\eta(\eta_2, \ldots, \eta_K) = \prod_{k=2}^{K} [1 + \exp(-\eta_k/\tau)]^{-1}, \qquad (11.82a)$$

and the choice probability in (11.81) has a closed-form representation[80]

$$\text{Pr}\{\text{item 1 chosen}\} = \exp[\bar{v}_1(q^1, y - A_1)/\tau] \bigg/ \bigg\langle \sum_{k=1}^{K} \exp[\bar{v}_k(q^k, y - A_k)/\tau] \bigg\rangle$$

$$= \bigg[1 + \sum_{k=2}^{K} \exp\big[\bar{v}_k(q^k, y - A_k)/\tau - \bar{v}_1(q^1, y - A_1)/\tau\big] \bigg]^{-1}$$

$$(11.82b)$$

Let $P(k \mid C)$ denote the probability that item k is the one chosen when the alternatives available are the set C. The multinomial logit choice probabilities possess the property that, for any sets C and T, where $C \subseteq T$, and for any alternatives $i, j \in C$,

$$\frac{P(i \mid C)}{P(j \mid C)} = \frac{P(i \mid T)}{P(j \mid T)}. \qquad (11.83)$$

---

[78] Welfare evaluation in the contingent choice model—e.g. WTP or WTA measures for changes in the prices or attributes of some or all of the alternatives—is based on the *unconditional* indirect utility function, $v(q, A, y, \varepsilon) \equiv \max\{v_1(q^1, y - A_1, \varepsilon_1), \ldots, v_K(q^K, y - A_K, \varepsilon_K)\}$, rather than on the conditional indirect utility functions as in (11.5). This introduces various complexities which are analysed in Hanemann (1983a, 1985b).

[79] Note the difference between this and (11.75), in which the η_k are not independent.

[80] In addition to identification problems with the utility differences, there may also be a problem associated with the scaling parameter τ; conventionally, one imposes the restriction that $\tau = 1$.

This is the *independence of irrelevant alternatives* (IIA) property of choice (Luce, 1959). McFadden (1974) and Yellott (1977) establish that RUM choice probabilities satisfy IIA if and only if the u_k are independent extreme value variates with a common scale parameter. However, as Debreu (1960) first observed, IIA is not necessarily a plausible or reasonable property for choice behaviour since it generates what is known as the 'red bus / blue bus' paradox (Ben Akiva and Lerman, 1985). The generalized extreme value distribution (11.76) relaxes IIA partially, but not within individual groups; the multivariate normal distribution eliminates it entirely.

Just as choice is a form of ranking, the converse also holds: ranking can be seen as a series of choices. Suppose there are four items and the individual ranks items 1, 2, 3, and 4 in descending order. Given some regularity conditions, the joint probability of this ranking response can be expressed as a product of conditional choice probabilities,

$$\text{Pr}\{\text{item 1 ranked 1}^{\text{st}}, \text{ item 2 ranked 2nd}, \text{ item 3 ranked 3rd}, \\ \text{item 4 ranked last}\} = P(1 \mid 1, 2, 3, 4) \bullet P(2 \mid 2, 3, 4) \bullet P(3 \mid 3, 4), \tag{11.84}$$

where the first term on the RHS is the conditional probability that 1 is chosen out of $\{1, 2, 3, 4\}$, conditional on 2 being chosen out of $\{2, 3, 4\}$ and 3 being chosen out of $\{3, 4\}$; the second term is the conditional probability that 2 is chosen out of $\{2, 3, 4\}$ conditional on 3 being chosen out of $\{3, 4\}$; and the third term is the unconditional probability that 3 is chosen out of $\{3, 4\}$. In general, however, these conditional probabilities involve complex expressions because the conditional probability of the utility associated with the most favoured item depends on the ordering of the other items. The *cascading choice theorem* of Luce and Suppes (1965) establishes that, when the u_k satisfy the IIA property, these conditional probabilities are *independent* of the ordering of the less favoured choices. Hence, (11.84) holds as a simple product of *unconditional* choice probabilities on the RHS. This comes about if and only if the individual u_k are independent extreme value variates with a common scale parameter (Strauss, 1979; Yellott, 1980). In that case, the RHS of (11.84) involves the product of a set of multinomial logit choice probabilities; with the additively random formulation used above, this takes the form

$$\text{Pr}\{\text{item 1 ranked 1st}, \text{ item 2 ranked 2nd}, \ldots, \text{item } K \text{ ranked last}\} = \\ \prod_{k=1}^{K-1} \left\langle \exp[\bar{v}_k(q^k, y - A_k)/\tau] \Big/ \sum_{l=k}^{K} \exp[\bar{v}_l(q^l, y - A_l)/\tau] \right\rangle, \tag{11.85}$$

where one conventionally sets $\tau = 1$.[81]

To summarize, if the ε_k in an additively random model have the extreme value distribution, the ranking response probabilities take the form in

---

[81] The ranked probit and logit models in (11.79) and (11.85) are not to be confused with ordered probit and logit models presented below.

(11.85). In all other cases, including additive models where the ε_k follow the normal or generalized extreme value distribution, the ranking response probabilities take the form given in (11.78) or (11.79). Until recently, applications of contingent ranking used the logit formulation. As noted above, the multivariate normal distribution affords a more general covariance structure for the u_k and, while there is no closed-form representation for the choice probabilities in (11.79), Layton (1995) finds that simulation techniques such as GHK are eminently practical.

Compared with contingent choice, contingent ranking offers two advantages. First, some parameters of the utility function not estimable with data on only the single most preferred choice may be estimable with data on the complete ranking; this can occur when the distribution of the most preferred item in the sample data is highly skewed. Second, rankings provide more statistical information than choice, which leads to tighter confidence intervals around parameter estimates.[82] In practice, however, it turns out that the extra information comes at a cost; the general experience is that some rankings are often inconsistent, and they tend to become increasingly noisy as the lower ranked items are included, causing attenuation in the estimated coefficients of explanatory variables. When one thinks of the cognitive burden involved, this should not be a surprise. Ranking every item in the set is harder than identifying the best item. Some items may be easier to rank than others and, as Ben-Akiva *et al.* (1992) suggest, people may use different decision criteria for different rankings (e.g., the weights on attributes change when they are selecting the best item versus lower-ranked items). Growing respondent fatigue could explain why lower rankings might be less reliable. Alternatively, while the top- and bottom-ranked items might be easy to discern, it could be harder to discriminate among the items in the middle.

R. Chapman and Staelin (1982) framed the issue as a trade-off between reducing sampling variance when one incorporates more of the rankings versus greater bias arising from increasing unreliability. They suggested systematically varying the number of ranks included in the analysis and stopping when there was a significant decrease in goodness of fit or a significant evidence of changing estimates of coefficients. In their empirical study, which involved the linear model (11.12) applied to rankings of three or four items, they found it desirable to restrict the analysis to the ranking of the top two items. Hausman and Ruud (1987) estimate a similar utility model for rankings of eight items and apply both a Durbin–Hausman specification test for the IIA property and a consistency test for constant ratios of attribute coefficients; both tests reject the logit ranking model (11.85). The same result was obtained by Ben-Akiva *et al.* (1992) when they analysed rankings of four items. To deal with this, Hausman and Ruud propose a modification of (11.85) whereby the scale parameter, τ,

---

[82] For an exploration of both these issues, see Waldman (1983).

varies across rankings. This allows for differences in cognitive burden, decision criterion, or carefulness among the rankings. Let τ_k be the scaling parameter associated with the kth ranking, $k = 1, \ldots, K - 1$, where τ_{K-1} is normalized to unity; smaller values of τ_k correspond to less noisy rankings. Hausman and Ruud's rank-ordered heteroscedastic logit model is[83, 84]

$$\Pr\{\text{item 1 ranked 1st, item 2 ranked 2nd}, \ldots, \text{item K ranked last} = \prod_{k=1}^{K-1} \left\langle \exp[\bar{v}_k(q^k, y - A_k)/\tau_k] \middle/ \sum_{l=k}^{K} \exp[\bar{v}_l(q^l, y - A_l)/\tau_k] \right\rangle. \quad (11.86)$$

They find that the τ_k significantly increase with k, though not monotically. Ben-Akiva *et al.* (1992) find the same. But, they also find that, while their first two rankings can be combined together, their third is still not consistent with the other two rankings; even after re-scaling, the rankings still violate the IIA property assumed by (11.86). When Layton (1995) analysed partial rankings data, he found that the rank-ordered heteroscedastic logit model was inappropriate; he concluded that the variation in parameter estimates for different rankings was caused not by heteroscedasticity across rankings but rather by a violation of IIA. To handle this, he employed a rank-ordered heteroscedastic multivariate normal model (11.79), derived from a random coefficient version of (11.12). He found that this fitted the data well and eliminated the inconsistency among the rankings.

While more experience is needed, the rank-ordered heteroscedastic multi-variate normal model seems promising since it provides considerable flex-ibility and permits one to model a variety of response phenomena. For example, the variances of the u_k could be made a function of the degree to which the item is similar in its characteristics to other items in the set, as measured by some distance metric. One hypothesis is that greater similarity among items makes it harder to rank them. An alternative hypothesis is that greater *divergence* makes it harder to rank items.[85] One might also be able to obtain from respondents an assessment of how hard they found the rankings, and then parameterize the variances of the u_k as a function of task difficulty.[86]

In addition to changing the stochastic specification of RUM preferences, another way to improve the results from ranking experiments is to modify

[83] It should be noted that (11.86) does not appear to be strictly consistent with the RUM framework. If the u_k are extreme value variates with a common scale parameter, as noted above, (11.85) is equivalent to (11.78). But, if they have *different* scale parameters, one no longer obtains the logistic for the distribution of their differences. We are not aware of a stochastic specification of the u_k that would make (11.86) equivalent to (11.78). In effect, (11.86) implies a separate set of preferences for each ranking activity.

[84] The heteroscedastic logit model is also used for choices where data from separate choice tasks are to be combined in a single estimation; the choice probabilities for each task are given by (11.82b), with the τ_k varying across the data sets. For examples and references, see Chapter 13 above.

[85] The results in Mazzotta and Opaluch (1995) provide some support for the second hypoth-esis; these are consistent with observing a higher variance when items differ on more attributes.

[86] For example, an interesting model by Swait and Adamowicz (1996) makes the variances a function of an entropy measure of the differences in attribute vectors.

the ranking task so as to lighten the cognitive burden on respondents. Since respondent fatigue could be a problem, it may be desirable to limit the number of items in the set to be considered. It may also be useful to mix ranking with choice, in order to limit the number of ranking evaluations. Suppose the survey includes the status quo along with other programmes. One might ask respondents to separate the programmes into those that are better than the status quo, and therefore worth paying for, versus those that are not, and then have them rank the former but not the latter. Ranking items which one does not want may be a futile task (Mitchell and Carson, 1989). Suppose the individual considers that items $1, \ldots, I$ are an improvement over the status quo, while items $I + 1, \ldots, K$ are not, and she ranks the former in descending order; with this mixture of choice and ranking, the response probability is the following blend of (11.78) and (11.80):

Pr{item 1 ranked 1st, item 2 ranked 2nd, $\ldots$, item I ranked Ith,

and items $I + 1, \ldots, K$ deemed unacceptable}

$$= \Pr\{v_1(q^1, y - A_1, \varepsilon_1) \geqslant v_2(q^2, y - A_2, \varepsilon_2) \geqslant \ldots \geqslant v_I(q^I, y - A_I, \varepsilon_I) \geqslant$$
$$v_0(q^0, y, \varepsilon_0), \text{ and } v_0(q^0, y, \varepsilon_0) \geqslant v_k(q^k, y - A_k, \varepsilon_k), \quad k = I + 1, \ldots, K\}.$$

$$(11.87)$$

With the additively random formulation of (11.79) and (11.81), the response probability formula becomes:

Pr{item 1 ranked 1st, item 2 ranked 2nd, $\ldots$, item I ranked Ith,

and items $I + 1, \ldots, K$ deemed unacceptable}

$$= \int_{-\infty}^{\bar{\delta}_1} \cdots \int_{-\infty}^{\bar{\delta}_1} \int_{-\infty}^{\delta_{I+1}} \cdots \int_{-\infty}^{\delta_K} f_{\bar{\eta}\eta}(\bar{\eta}_1, \ldots, \bar{\eta}_1, \eta_{I+1}, \ldots, \eta_K) d\bar{\eta}_1 \cdots$$
$$d\bar{\eta}_I d\eta_{I+1} \ldots d\eta_K, \qquad (11.88)$$

where $\bar{\delta}_k \equiv \bar{v}_k(q^k, y - A_k) - \bar{v}_{k+1}(q^{k+1}, y - A_{k+1}), \; k = 1, \cdots, I - 1, \; \bar{\delta}_I \equiv \bar{v}_I$ $(q^I, y - A_I), \; \delta_k \equiv \bar{v}_k(q^k, y - A_k) - \bar{v}_0(q^0, y - A_0), \; k = I + 1, \cdots, K, \; \bar{\eta}_k \equiv \epsilon_{k+1} - \epsilon_k, \; k = 1, \cdots, I - 1, \; \bar{\eta}_I \equiv \epsilon_I - \epsilon_0, \; \eta_k \equiv \epsilon_k - \epsilon_0, \; k = I + 1, \cdots, K$. While an extreme value distribution for the ε_k yields a closed-form expression for (11.88), a multivariate normal distribution seems preferable for the reasons given above.

Instead of valuing a single item, as in referendum CV, the goal with choice and ranking is to estimate a utility function, or a system of utility functions, that can be used to value *many* items, perhaps including items not covered in the CV survey whose value can be extrapolated from the utility model fitted to the survey responses. Second, contingent choice and ranking break the direct tie between response probabilities and welfare measures that is present in referendum (binary choice) CV. The response probability for ranking or multivariate choice is constructed from a multivariate utility distribution rather than a multivariate WTP distribution (i.e. from the joint distribution of the u_k's rather than the C_k's). Formulation and estimation of monetary measures of value proceeds separately from, and subsequent to, the modelling of survey responses.

In closing, we should mention the connection between the preference elicitation techniques discussed above and what is known as *conjoint analysis*, a term coined by Green and Srinivasan (1978) to cover a variety of preference elicitation techniques used in psychometrics and market research.[87] These include forms of ranking and choice, as well as *rating*, where respondents are asked to rate a set of items on a scale from, say, 1 to 10 or 1 to 100.[88] A distinctive feature is that respondents typically perform multiple tasks, and a separate preference model is often fitted for each respondent.[89] The items to which subjects respond are selected by the researcher to span some attribute space, often with special designs such as fractionated sampling (Green, 1974; Louviere, 1988). Data collected through one form of elicitation may be converted into another equivalent form for the purposes of analysis. For example, subjects may be asked to rate a large set of items but, for model fitting, their ratings are converted into implied rankings or choices. Or, subjects may be asked to make a sequence of choices among pairs of items, but their pairwise choices are then converted into an implied ranking over the entire set of items. The statistical models used to analyse conjoint responses are typically not designed to satisfy the economic restrictions discussed in Section 2.3. They tend to be either linear models of the form $u_k = \sum_r \beta_{kr} x_{kr} + \varepsilon_k$, where x_{kr} is the level of the rth attribute in item k, which is essentially equivalent to (11.12), or *ideal point* models where $u_k = -\sum_r \beta_r (x_{kr} - x_{kr}^*)^2 + \varepsilon_k$, where x_{kr}^* is the individual's ideal level for the rth attribute.[90] Aside from the multiple responses per subject and the form of the statistical model, to the extent that conjoint data are analysed as ranking or choices, there is no essential difference with the contingent ranking or choice techniques described above.

---

[87] For summaries of what is now a vast literature, see Green and Srinivasan (1990) or Carroll and Green (1995). The review by Louviere (1994) emphasizes choice-based conjoint analysis, which we have called contingent choice.

[88] Sometimes, the rating scale is cast in terms of likelihood of purchase—e.g. 1 means 'I would never buy this', while 100 means 'I would definitely buy it'. In that case, it may be possible to apply to the conjoint ratings the statistical models of preference uncertainty discussed at the end of Section 11.4.3.

[89] Some form of cluster analysis may be used to group subjects into market segments for the purposes of demand analysis and projection.

[90] The x_{kr}^*'s may be elicited directly as part of the survey, or they may be estimated from subjects' responses. Another model commonly used in conjoint analysis, besides linear and ideal point utility models, is the *part-worth function*; this posits an additively separable utility function $u_k = \sum_r \Psi_r(x_{kr}) + \varepsilon_k$ where $\Psi_r(\cdot)$ is the sub-utility (part-worth) function for the rth attribute. In practice, $\Psi_r(x_{kr})$ is usually estimated for only a few selected levels of x_{kr}, with the value for other levels of x_{kr} obtained by extrapolation. This corresponds to estimating the step function hedonic model (11.71) without cross-product terms, and then making a piecewise linear approximation to an additively separable function.

The older tradition in conjoint analysis is to take the ratings as a cardinal measure of preference and fit a utility function directly to them, $u_k = v_k(q^k, y - A_k, \varepsilon_k)$, using ordinary least squares regression, linear programming or some other method of estimation.[91, 92] As cardinal measures of utility, ratings have the advantage of providing more information since they convey intensity of preference, unlike the ordinal measures of preference associated with ranking or choice. However, the extra information comes at some cost. Pooling responses across individuals presumes inter-personal comparability of utility, the practical feasibility of which has been debated in economics since the 1930's.[93] For example, a rating of '5' may mean different things to different people. Certainly, it often happens that different subjects centre their ratings on different parts of the scale. Fitting a separate response model for each subject can be viewed as one way of circumventing inter-personal comparisons; but the problem reappears as soon as one extrapolates from individual subjects to market segments. A recent CV application of conjoint analysis by Roe et al. (forthcoming), which pooled ratings across individuals, attempted to control for differences in centering by having one scenario (the status quo) that was rated by everybody and then estimating utility difference functions where the differences in ratings between the common scenario and each other scenario were regressed on the differences in attributes between the scenarios. This appeared to reduce the

---

[91] CV applications of traditional conjoint analysis, where the fitted utility model is used to compute monetary welfare measures for changes in attributes, appear to have started with Magat et al. (1988).

[92] Ordinary least squares and linear programming are known as *decompositional* methods of estimation, since they fit the utility function in one step. *Compositional* methods of conjoint analysis, by contrast, fit the function in stages, first estimating part-worth functions for individual attributes (for example, by asking subjects to scale alternative levels of each attribute taken separately) and then estimating weights for combining the part-worth functions into an overall utility index. The compositional approach is also used in *multiattribute utility assessment* (MAUA) (Keeney and Raiffa, 1976; von Winterfeldt and Edwards, 1986). As with conjoint analysis, the general practice in MAUA is to estimate a separate utility function for each subject. The multivariate utility models used in MAUA generally allow for some interaction among the part-worth functions; the particular form is chosen by testing whether the subject's preferences satisfy certain axioms. To elicit the part-worth functions, MAUA generally uses pairwise choices or *matching* (essentially equivalent to open-ended CV, in which subjects are asked to identify the level of an attribute required to adjust the utility of one item so that it exactly matches that of another); for model fitting, calibration is generally used rather than statistical estimation. MAUA typically involves more intensive data collection from subjects than conjoint analysis. How this affects the results in prediction of behaviour or assessment of value is still an open question. Gregory et al. (1993) advocate switching from conventional CV to MAUA because they consider the compositional approach to preference elicitation more reliable. In our view, the case for a compositional approach is more normative than positive: this may be how individuals *should* make judgments, but we are not sure it is how they *do* make judgments.

[93] Approaches which model behaviour in terms of ordinal preferences, such as referendum CV, contingent ranking and choice, or demand function estimation, avoid inter-personal comparisons of utility because they allow a separate monotone transformation of the utility index for each individual.

noise in the data and it produced the most significant coefficients.[94] But, even if it corrected for differences in centering, it does not preclude other factors, e.g. differences in range or variance, that could invalidate inter-personal utility comparisons.

Aside from the problem of inter-personal comparisons, one may doubt whether subjects can always measure their preferences with the precision implied by a cardinal rating. To ease the burden on respondents, some conjoint researchers employ scales with only a few integer ratings; for example, both Mackenzie and Roe *et al.* use a scale from 1 ('very undesirable') to 10 ('very desirable'). This may be more convenient, but it also can turn the ratings into an *ordinal* measure of preference; it is not clear whether, on this scale, subjects treat an '8' as twice a '4', or a '4' as twice a '2'. With this scale it may be more appropriate to apply *ordered* probit or logit models, due originally to Aitchison and Silvey (1957) and Ashford (1959) and popularized in the social sciences by Zavoina and McElvey (1975), which treat the dependent variable as an ordering and permit one to test whether it is measured on an ordinal or cardinal scale. These models postulate that, while the observed dependent variable is an ordinally-ranked categorical variable, it is derived from a latent continuous variable reflecting the respondent's underlying sentiment. Let the stated rating of the kth item be R_k; in this case $R_k = 1, 2, 3, \ldots, 9$ or 10. In addition to the underlying conditional indirect utility function $u_k = v_k(q^k, y - A_k, \varepsilon_k)$, the model involves a set of thresholds $\bar{r}_1, \ldots, \bar{r}_9$, which can be treated as constants or as functions of covariates. The relation mapping the subject's underlying utility for the item into her stated rating is given by:[95, 96]

$$
\begin{aligned}
R_k &= 1 && \text{if } v_k(q^k, y - A_k, \varepsilon_k) \leqslant \bar{r}_1 \\
R_k &= 2 && \text{if } \bar{r}_1 \leqslant v_k(q^k, y - A_k, \varepsilon_k) \leqslant \bar{r}_2 \\
R_k &= 3 && \text{if } \bar{r}_2 \leqslant v_k(q^k, y - A_k, \varepsilon_k) \leqslant \bar{r}_3 \\
&\;\;\vdots && \qquad\quad \vdots \\
R_k &= 9 && \text{if } \bar{r}_8 \leqslant v_k(q^k, y - A_k, \varepsilon_k) \leqslant \bar{r}_9 \\
R_k &= 10 && \text{if } v_k(q^k, y - A_k, \varepsilon_k) \geqslant \bar{r}_9
\end{aligned}
\tag{11.89}
$$

[94] Faced with the same problem, Mackenzie (1993) simply included the subject's mean rating over all items as an explanatory variable in each rating regression; first differencing is a better solution.

[95] In their analysis, Roe *et al.* use a double-hurdle tobit model for regressions of ratings or ratings differences. This gives R_k a censored normal distribution with spikes at '1' and '10'; within the interval (1, 10), it makes R_k a continuous variable, not an integer.

[96] The model could be adjusted for differences among subjects in the centering of ratings by compressing and relabelling some of the ratings categories. Suppose some subjects' ratings fall in the interval (1,5) while others' fall in the interval (5,9); one could, for example, convert the ratings to a common, five-point scale, making '5' the highest rating and relabelling the second group's ratings so that they range from '1' to '5' instead of "5" to "9."

If ε_k enters $v_k(q^k, y - A_k, \varepsilon_k)$ additively and is normally distributed, this is an ordered probit model; if it is logistic, this is an ordered logit model. The coefficients to be estimated include the parameters of $v_k(\cdot)$, the parameters of the joint distribution of the ε_k's, and the $\bar{r}_k$'s (possibly subject to a normalization restriction);[97] estimation is by maximum likelihood or, if there are grouped data, by minimum chi-squared. If the $\bar{r}_k$'s are *equally spaced*, i.e. $\bar{r}_2 \equiv \bar{r}_1 + \Delta, \bar{r}_3 \equiv \bar{r}_1 + 2\Delta, \ldots, \bar{r}_9 = \bar{r}_1 + 8\Delta$, the R_k's are an approximately cardinal measure of preference. This can be tested as a restriction on the estimated $\bar{r}_k$'s.

In summary, while there is a close relationship at the conceptual level between rating, ranking, and choice, there are important practical differences in terms of the cognitive burden on respondents and the implications for inter-personal comparability of utility. When comparisons have been made among alternative modes of preference expression, the general experience is that inconsistencies appear: different modes imply different preferences even though, in theory, a single utility function should suffice to generate all the various types of response. The differences in welfare measures estimated from the fitted utility functions can be quite substantial (Mackenzie; Roe *et al.*). The evidence suggests that this task-dependence is a general phenomenon, and is not confined to non-use values, environmental goods, or contingent valuation. For researchers, it has two implications. First, it creates a challenge to develop explicit models of task-dependence in the stochastic and/or deterministic components of the response model. Second, it requires the researcher to exercise judgment in deciding which set of results is the most appropriate to her research goal.

11.4.1.4 *Random coefficient models*

So far we have discussed how the deterministic or stochastic components of RUM models can be made to reflect variation in the item being valued. In this section we touch on aspects of model specification dealing with variation *among respondents*. This can arise, for example, from socio-economic differences, or from heterogeneity in preferences for programmes.

From a statistical perspective, the CV evaluations of programmes can be viewed as panel data—we pool observations on individuals over programmes, rather than over time. To illustrate this, we employ the linear model (11.12), adding subscript i to denote the ith individual. Some or all of the programme attributes mentioned in the preceding paragraph may vary across individuals; therefore, let x_{ikr} denote the rth attribute of program k for the ith individual. In addition, x_{is} denotes the sth attribute or socio-demographic characteristic of the ith individual. Thus, we write (11.12) as
$$u_{ik} = \alpha_{ik} + \beta_y y_i + \varepsilon_{ik} \text{ where}$$

[97] To the extent that the $\bar{r}_k$'s are taken to be the same across subjects, this makes the u_k's cardinal utility measures and implies inter-personal comparability of utility.

$$\alpha_{ik} \equiv \text{intercept} + \sum_r \beta_r x_{ikr} + \sum_s \beta_s x_{is};$$

different models correspond to different treatments of the intercept and different stochastic specifications for ε_{ik}. In panel data terminology, many of the models discussed above would be categorized as *one-way fixed effects* models. This applies, for example, to the model in (11.72) with $\lambda = 1$,

$$u_{ik} = \alpha_k + \sum_r \beta_r x_{ikr} + \sum_s \beta_s x_{is} + \beta y_i + \varepsilon_{ik}, \qquad (11.90)$$

where the ε_{ik} are all i.i.d. with mean zero and variance σ_ε^2 and the α_k are fixed parameters to be estimated from the data along with σ_ε^2 and the various β. This formulation is appropriate if preferences for different programmes are viewed as parametric shifts of a utility function. An alternative is the *one-way random effects* model, which treats the programme-specific terms as varying randomly across programmes; this would apply if one saw the sampled programmes as drawn from a larger set of programs. This model takes the form

$$u_{ik} = \alpha + \sum_r \beta_r x_{ikr} + \sum_s \beta_s x_{is} + \beta y_i + v_k + \omega_{ik}, \qquad (11.91)$$

where v_k is a stochastic component which is constant across respondents and represents unmeasured factors specific to the kth programme. We assume that $E\{v_k\} = E\{\omega_{ik}\} = 0$, $E\{v_k^2\} = \sigma_v^2$, $E\{\omega_{ik}^2\} = \sigma_\omega^2$, $E\{v_k v_l\} = 0$ if $k \neq l$, $E\{\omega_{ik}\omega_{jl}\} = 0$ if $i \neq j$ or $k \neq l$, and $E\{v_k \omega_{il}\} = 0$ for all i, k and l; σ_v^2 and σ_ω^2 are to be estimated from the data along with α and the various β. In addition to (11.90) and (11.91), *two-way* fixed- and random effects models are possible, with both programme-specific and individual-specific parameters or variance components. The two-way fixed-effect model is[98]

$$u_{ik} = \gamma_i + \alpha_k + \sum_r \beta_r x_{ikr} + \sum_s \beta_s x_{is} + \beta y_i + \varepsilon_{ik}, \qquad (11.90')$$

where the γ_i and α_k are fixed parameters and, as before, the ε_{ik} are i.i.d. with mean zero and variance σ_ε^2. The two-way random effects model is

$$u_{ik} = \alpha + \sum_r \beta_r x_{ikr} + \sum_s \beta_s x_{is} + \beta y_i + v_i + v_k + \omega_{ik}, \qquad (11.91')$$

where, in addition to the above specification of the variances and covariances of the v_k and ω_{ik} one has $E\{v_i\} = 0$, $E\{v_i^2\} = \sigma_v^2$, $E\{v_i v_j\} = 0$ if $i \neq j$, and $E\{v_i v_k\} = E\{v_i \omega_{jk}\} = 0$ for all i, j, and k. The two-way fixed effects

---

[98] We noted above the common practice in conjoint analysis of eliciting multiple responses from subjects and then fitting a separate response probability model for each subject. That is equivalent to a fixed effects formulation, with individual-specific intercepts and slope coefficients.

formulation is appropriate if individual differences in preferences for a programme are viewed as parametric shifts of the utility function for that programme; the random effects formulation is appropriate if one sees the respondents as drawn from a larger population with randomly varying preferences. It is also possible to have a *mixed* two-way model combining, say, fixed effects over programmes with random effects over individuals:

$$u_{ik} = \alpha_k + \sum_r \beta_r x_{ikr} + \sum_s \beta_s x_{is} + \beta y_i + \nu_i + \omega_{ik}, \qquad (11.92)$$

where $E\{\nu_i^2\} = \sigma_\nu^2, E\{\omega_{ik}^2\} = \sigma_\omega^2$, and $E\{\nu_i\omega_{jk}\} = 0$ for all i, j, and k.

The choice between fixed and random effects formulations has been the subject of much debate. This originally focused on conventional linear regression, but recently has been extended to quantal response models. From the point of view of estimation, an important difference is that, while the random effects approach adds only two parameters, σ_ν^2 and σ_v^2, the fixed effects approach adds N γ_i's and K α_k's. This is computationally burdensome when K or, more likely, N is large. In linear models, the ordinary least squares estimate of the γ_i and α_k is unbiased. In quantal response models estimated by maximum likelihood, there are only asymptotic properties. In both cases, the estimates of γ_i and α_k are consistent only as N and K approach infinity. In practice, K will be small with panel data, making the estimate of the γ_i inconsistent. This is the *incidental parameters* problem (Neyman and Scott, 1948): an increase in N provides no extra information about γ_i, but just raises the number of γ_i. For large-sample properties, any estimate of the fixed effect γ_i is unreliable when K is finite, even if N tends to infinity.

In linear models, the inability to obtain consistent estimates of the γ_i does not affect estimation of the β; fixed and random effects estimators of the β are unbiased and consistent as long as N tends to infinity. In quantal response models, unlike linear models, the maximum likelihood estimators of parameters are not independent of each other (Hsiao, 1986). In fixed effects quantal models with finite K, the inconsistency of γ_i is transmitted to the estimators of the α_k and β. Hence, even if N tends to infinity, the maximum likelihood estimate of the β remains inconsistent. Generalizing Neyman and Scott (1948), E. B. Andersen (1970) showed a way to obtain consistent estimates of structural parameters by maximizing a conditional likelihood function conditioned on a minimum sufficient statistic for the incidental parameters, if one exists that is independent of the structural parameters. Chamberlain (1980) applied this to obtain a computationally convenient and consistent estimate of the β in fixed effects logit models. For fixed effects probit models, however, there does not appear to exist a consistent estimator of the β.

In random effects quantal models, maximum likelihood estimation does provide consistent estimation of the β. However, the estimation is computationally burdensome because of the complex nature of the like-lihood function in this case. For simplicity, we focus on the mixed model (11.92). Even when the ω_{ik} are independently distributed over i and k in (11.92), $E\{u_{ik}u_{il}\} = \sigma_\nu^2 \neq 0$, and the joint log-likelihood of a sample of responses $(y_{11}, \ldots, y_{it}, \ldots, y_{NT})$, where y_{it} is the ith individual's response to the tth discrete-response CV question, can no longer be written as the sum of the marginal log-likelihoods of the y_{it}, as in (11.47). Let $P(y_{it} \mid \nu; X_{it}, \theta)$ denote the probability formula for the ith individual's response to the tth CV question conditional on the random effect ν_i, given the vector of indi-vidual-specific and item-specific attributes, X_{it}, where θ is the vector of parameters not associated with the random effects (i.e. the β and σ_ω^2). Let the density of ν be $g_\nu(\nu; \sigma_\nu^2)$. With this random effects formulation, the log-likelihood function takes the form

$$L(\theta, \sigma_\nu^2 \mid y, X) = \sum_i \ln \int \left[\prod_t P(y_{it} \mid \nu; X_{it}, \theta) \right] g_\nu(\nu; \sigma_\nu^2) d\nu. \qquad (11.93)$$

By contrast, if there is no heterogeneity among individuals (the ω_{ik} are i.i.d. and the individual-specific effects ν_i do not exist), the log-likelihood takes the far simpler form,

$$L(\theta \mid y, X) = \sum_i \sum_t \ln P(y_{it} \mid X_{it}, \theta). \qquad (11.94)$$

Maximizing the random-effects log-likelihood, (11.93), is computationally challenging since, in general, there are integrals in each of the response probabilities $P(y_{it} \mid \nu; X_{it}, \theta)$. The first application to random effects probit was by Heckman and Willis (1975); a faster computational algorithm was developed by Butler and Moffitt (1982). There are also several alternatives to maximum likelihood estimation. Chamberlain (1984) proposes a minimum distance estimator, and Avery *et al.* (1983) describe a related generalized method of moments estimator. The biometrics literature tends to emphasize quasi-likelihood and similar techniques (Longford, 1993).[99]

In both linear and nonlinear models, empirically it can make a substantial difference to the estimates of the β whether one adopts a fixed or random effects formulation. Hence the choice of model is contentious. Mundlak (1978) suggests two criteria. One is the type of inference desired: the effects can always be considered random, but when using the fixed effects model the researcher makes inferences *conditional on the effects in the observed sample.* When the random effects model is used, the researcher makes specific

---

[99] Another possibility, mentioned by Maddala (1986), is simply to ignore the correlation among responses and maximize (11.94) instead of (11.93); this yields estimates of the β that are consistent but inefficient. However, the conventional formula for the variance–covariance matrix of these estimates is incorrect (Robinson, 1982). In a Monte Carlo study, Guilkey and Murphy (1993) find that, despite the misspecification of the error structure, standard probit with a corrected covariance matrix often works relatively well.

assumptions about the distribution of the random effects, and this permits *unconditional* or *marginal* inferences. The other is robustness to specification error. If the distributional assumptions about the error components are correct, the random effects estimator is more efficient. But, if the distributional assumptions are incorrect, the random effects estimator is inconsistent. Because the fixed effects approach does not make any specific distributional assumption about the error components of the model, it is more robust. For example, Mundlak argued that the conventional random effects formulation assumes no correlation between the individual-specific effect, v_i, and the individual-specific covariates, x_{ik}, whereas there is likely to be some correlation in practice. As an alternative, Chamberlain (1980) suggested estimating random effects models with a linear dependence between the x_{it} and v_i. Hsiao (1986) provides details, along with a description of specification tests for the independence of the v_i. In addition, he discusses specification tests for the random effects model (11.93) against the no-correlation formulation (11.94). Lechner (1995) and Hamerle and Ronning (1995) are also useful on these topics.

We have focused so far on fixed versus random effects with respect to the *intercept* of the utility function; the same types of formulation can also be applied to the *slope coefficients*. For example, compared with (11.11), the Box–Cox model (11.10) is a one-way fixed effects slope-coefficient model, since the income coefficient, β, varies with the item (program) being valued—in the set-up of (11.90), where $\lambda = 1$, we write this as

$$u_{ik} = \alpha_k + \sum_r \beta_r x_{ikr} + \sum_s \beta_s x_{is} + \beta_k y_i + \varepsilon_{ik}. \qquad (11.95)$$

The corresponding one-way, random effects formulation is

$$u_{ik} = \alpha_k + \sum_r \beta_r x_{ikr} + \sum_s \beta_s x_{is} + (\beta + v_k)y_i + \omega_{ik}. \qquad (11.96)$$

where $E\{v_k\} = 0, E\{v_k^2\} = \sigma_v^2, E\{v_k v_l\} = 0$ if $k \neq 1$, and $E\{v_k \omega_{il}\} = 0$ for all $i, k,$ and l. This can also be written

$$u_{ik} = \alpha_k + \sum_r \beta_r x_{ikr} + \sum_s \beta_s x_{is} + \beta y_i + \zeta_{ik}, \qquad (11.96')$$

where $\zeta_{ik} \equiv v_k y_i + \omega_{ik}$; because of the dependence on y_i, the error term is now heteroscedastic. Such models, also known as *random coefficient* models, were first introduced by Swamy (1970); Hausman and Wise (1978) give a probit application. A two-way, slope coefficient model is

$$u_{ik} = \alpha_k + \sum_r \beta_r x_{ikr} + \sum_s \beta_s x_{is} + (\beta + v_i + v_k)y_i + \varepsilon_{ik}, \qquad (11.97)$$

where the individual-specific component, v_i, and the programme-specific component, v_k, of the income coefficient are either fixed parameters to be estimated (the fixed effects model) or random variables with some covariance structure to be estimated (the random effects model). Estimation of these models raises essentially the same issues as varying intercept models.

The random effects formulation can be extended to more general error component structures. In presenting (11.91), for example, we assumed that $\sigma_v^2 = E\{u_{ik}u_{jk}\}$ is the same for every pair of programmes and does not vary with k, while $\sigma_\nu^2 = E\{u_{ik}u_{il}\}$ is the same for every pair of programmes and does not vary with i. Random coefficient models such as (11.96) are one way to introduce some heteroscedasticity and relax these restrictions. Another way is to specify directly a more complex covariance matrix for the error components; an example, mentioned in the previous section, is parameterizing the covariance terms in a multivariate normal distribution for contingent ranking as functions of similarity indices. Another extension is to have multiple levels of nesting for the variance components. For example, instead of the one-way individual effects assumed so far, one might identify a hierarchy of groups such that individuals in the same group are more similar than individuals in different groups.[100] The random terms in u_{ik} have both individual and group components. Individual components are all independent. Group components are independent between groups but perfectly correlated within groups. Some groups might be more homogeneous than other groups, which means that the variance of the group components can differ. Such *hierarchical* or *multi-level* models can be rich enough to provide a good fit to complex survey data, while still being parsimonious with the number of parameters. They can be estimated by the EM procedure (Raudenbusch and Bryk, 1986), quasi-likelihood (Longford, 1988), iterated generalized least squares (Goldstein, 1991), or two-stage probit (Borjas and Sueyoshi, 1994). Chapter 12 provides a CV application.

In closing, we note that (11.93) is an example of *compounding*, where heterogeneity among individuals leads to the averaging or integration over a response probability formula. In this case, the compounding is with respect to a variance component, but one can also have compounding with respect to a location parameter; a classic example is the generation of the beta-binomial distribution by compounding a binomial distribution with a beta distribution for the binomial parameter. Another example is *aggregation* of quantal responses. This can occur when there are aggregate rather than individual data on CV responses, or when there are data on individual responses but no observations for one or more variables believed to affect the individual responses. Let X be some such variable; the aim is to estimate the structural coefficients associated with X despite the fact that X is not observed. For this purpose, we assume that the values which X can take

---

[100] In educational statistics, where this originated, one might have information about individual students, class-level information, and school-level information.

follow some density, $f_x(X)$. For example, X could be the respondent's income, which is unobserved in the data, and $f_x(\cdot)$ the income distribution that applies to the sample of respondents. Given the ith observed response, y_i, the probability of this response can be written

$$P(y_i) = \int P(y_i \mid X) f_x(X) dX. \tag{11.98}$$

The functional form of $f_x(\cdot)$ is assumed to be known by the researcher. If its parameters are known (e.g. if it is log-normally distributed with mean and variance known from some external source), one uses the aggregate response probability formula in (11.98) to estimate the parameters of $P(y_i \mid X)$. If the parameters of $f_x(\cdot)$ are not known, they are estimated along with those of $P(y_i \mid X)$ by maximizing the likelihood function based on (11.98).

11.4.2 Double-bounded CV

The double-bounded version of discrete response CV, proposed by Hanemann (1985a) and Carson (1985), follows up on the initial question with a second question, again involving a specific dollar cost to which the respondent can respond with a 'yes' or a 'no'. Let A denote the amount of the first bid. The amount presented in the second bid depends on the response to first bid; if the individual answered 'no' to A, the second bid is some lower amount $A_d < A$, while if she answered 'yes' it is some higher amount $A_u > A$. Thus, there are four possible response sequences: (i) both answers are yes; (ii) both answers are no; (iii) a yes followed by a no; and (iv) a no followed by a yes. Following the logic of (11.6b), for any given underlying WTP distribution $G_c(\cdot)$, the probability of the responses is given by

$$
\begin{aligned}
\Pr\{\text{yes/yes}\} &\equiv P^{yy} = 1 - G_C(A_u) \\
\Pr\{\text{no/no}\} &\equiv P^{nn} = G_C(A_d) \\
\Pr\{\text{yes/no}\} &\equiv P^{yn} = G_C(A_u) - G_C(A) \\
\Pr\{\text{no/yes}\} &\equiv P^{ny} = G_C(A) - G_C(A_d).
\end{aligned}
\tag{11.99}
$$

Any of the WTP distributions in Appendix Tables 2–4 can be used to construct these response probability formulas. Given these, the log-likelihood function for the double-bounded model is

$$\ln L = \sum_{i=1}^{n} \left[I_{yy} \ln P_i^{yy} + I_{yn} \ln P_i^{yn} + I_{ny} \ln P_i^{ny} + I_{nn} \ln P_i^{nn} \right], \tag{11.100}$$

where I_{xz} is an indicator function that equals one when the two responses are xz, and zero otherwise. Estimation is by maximum likelihood or one of the other techniques described in Section 11.3.4.[101]

Using maximum likelihood, Hanemann et al. (1991) compared this double-bounded model with a single-bounded model estimated from the responses to the initial bid, A, using the logit model (11.15). They found that the double-bounded model provided a substantial gain in precision for the variance–covariance matrix of the coefficient estimates, leading to much tighter confidence intervals for the estimate of median WTP. Similar results have been obtained by other researchers who have compared the double- and single-bounded approach. Hanemann et al. (1991) also found that the double-bounded data yielded a lower point estimate of median WTP than the single-bounded data. The same result has been found in many other applications. Both the gain in efficiency and the direction of change in the estimate of median WTP can be explained by a poor selection of the initial bid. When setting their bids, Hanemann et al. had very limited pre-test results and their guess at the point value of median WTP turned out to be far too low. With the hindsight of the field survey results, an optimal design would have used a higher initial bid, A. The double-bounded format corrected for this on the second bid—the follow-up bid A_u came closer to where an optimal design would have placed the bid, and this helped considerably to pin down the estimate of median WTP. In effect, A_u provides insurance against too low a choice of A, and A_d provides insurance against too high a choice of A.

Table 11.4, which parallels Table 11.1 for the single-bounded logit model (11.15), presents calculations of the bias and asymptotic variance of the maximum likelihood estimator for the double-bounded logit model. In the first three examples, the initial bid amount is the median value and the follow-up bid amounts are placed at increasing distances from the median value.[102] As in the single-bounded case, as the bid amounts are placed further away from the middle of the distribution, the biases and variances increase. The fourth example places the initial bid amounts on one side of the median value—at the 62nd, 82nd, and 92nd percentiles of the distribution—with follow-up bid amounts placed $100 on either side of these initial bids. In this case, most of the biases and the asymptotic variance are greater than any of the cases where the initial bid is the median value. But the biases and variance are far less than in the analogous single-bounded model. This is

---

[101] As we noted in the introduction, the likelihood in (11.100) is formally identical to that which arises in the statistical analysis of failure time data with censoring, where the analyst knows upper and lower bounds but not the exact time of failure. Kalbfleisch and Prentice (1980) is a standard reference on such models in biometrics; Lancaster (1990) covers economic applications to unemployment duration, etc.

[102] In general, a one-point design will not identify the two parameters of the model. But with the double-bounded model, two pieces of information are elicited from each respondent, yielding enough information to estimate both parameters.

Table 11.4 Analytical bias and asymptotic variance of WTP: double-bounded logit model

($\alpha = 2.5, \beta = -0.01$, median WTP = $250, number of observations = 250)

Bid design	Bias in α	Bias in β	Bias in median WTP	Asymptotic variance of median WTP
$B = \$250$ (50%) Follow-up $= B \pm \$100$	0.53%	−0.53%	0.00%	128.15
$B = \$250$ (50%) Follow-up $= B \pm \$200$	0.56%	−0.56%	0.00%	135.41
$B = \$250$ (50%) Follow-up $= B+ \$250$ or $B- \$245$	0.66%	−0.66%	0.00%	141.45
$B = \$300, \$400, \$500$ Follow-up $= B \pm \$100$	0.90%	−0.81%	0.09%	217.11

due to the adaptive nature of the double-bounded model. Even though the initial bid design is poor, the follow-up bids provide a second chance to recoup the situation.

With the double-bounded model, experimental design involves the specification of three bid amounts per observation. Although each respondent is offered only two bids, an initial and a follow-up, three bids enter the log-likelihood function because *a priori* it is not known which follow-up bid amount will be offered. Optimal designs for the double-bounded logit and probit models are presented in Table 11.5. In each case, the initial bid amount is the median value, and follow-up bid amounts are symmetrically placed around the median. The results in Table 11.5 have interesting implications for the importance of 'bounding' individuals' WTP values. We can derive the probability of receiving a 'yes' response to the follow-up bid *conditional* on the probability of receiving a 'yes' response to the initial bid. If the initial bid is the median value, then the probability of receiving a 'yes' response to the initial bid is exactly equal to 0.5, as is the probability of receiving a 'no' response. Given the initial response, we can derive the conditional probability for the response to the follow-up bid by dividing the unconditional c.d.f. of the second bid value by 0.5. We obtain the result that the D-optimal bid design for the logit model 'bounds' slightly over 75% of the respondents' WTP values, while that for the C-optimal bid design 'bounds' exactly half. A general rule of thumb might be that it is best to bound between 50% and 75% of observations. Note that this implies that the follow-up bids should not be so high or so low that all observations are bounded.

After the second valuation question, one could follow up with a third or fourth closed-ended valuation question, again using a higher bid amount if the individual responded 'yes' to the previous bid and a lower bid amount if the response was 'no'. The additional questions would give sharper bounds on the individual's WTP. An empirical application of the triple-bounded

Table 11.5 Some optimal designs for double bounded CV data

Design criterion	Criterion description	Double bounded bid design (in percentiles)	
		Logit models	Probit models
D-optimal	Maximize determinant of Fisher Information matrix	$B = 50.0\%$ $B^u = 87.9\%$ $B^d = 12.1\%$	$B = 50.0\%$ $B^u = 91.7\%$ $B^d = 8.3\%$
C-optimal	Minimize variance of median WTP	$B = 50.0\%$ $B^u = 75.0\%$ $B^d = 25.0\%$	$B = 50.0\%$ $B^u = 83.7\%$ $B^d = 16.3\%$

Source: Results from Alberini (1994), Kanninen (1993b), Minkin (1987), Wu (1988).

approach is described in Chapter 15 below. However, in a Monte Carlo simulation analysis, Cooper and Hanemann (1995) found that, compared with the double-bounded approach, adding a third round of closed-ended questions produced a relatively small gain in efficiency. Most of the statistical benefit from the extra information was reaped in going from the single- to the double-bounded format.

However, although there is a gain in efficiency, there can also be some bias in going from a single- to a double-bounded format because there is evidence that some of the responses to the second bid are inconsistent with the responses to the first bid. We have assumed so far that, for a given individual, the *same* utility model and stochastic process generate the answers to both valuation questions. If so, this implies certain relations between the response probabilities for first and second bids which can be used to construct non-parametric tests of consistency among the responses. Suppose, for example, that there are two separate overlapping sets of bids: $\{A = \$10, A_u = \$20, A_d = \$5\}$ and $(A = \$20, A_u = \$40, A_d = \$10)$. The first set starts with $10, and then either goes up to $20 or down to $5; the second starts with $20, and then goes up to $40 or down to $10. Individuals would be assigned one of these bid structures at random. It is a standard result in probability that:

$$\Pr\{\text{'yes' to } \$20\} = \Pr\{\text{'yes' to } \$20 \mid \text{'yes' to } \$10\}\Pr\{\text{'yes' to } \$10\}. \quad (11.101)$$

The LHS of (11.101) can be estimated by taking the respondents who received the second set of bids and calculating the proportion who said yes to the first bid in that set. The RHS of (11.101) can be estimated by taking the respondents who received the first set of bids and multiplying the proportion who said yes to the first bid in that set by the proportion of those respondents who subsequently said yes to the second bid in that set. If the responses to the first and second bids come from the same stochastic generating process, the estimates of the LHS and RHS of (11.101) should be the same, except for sampling variation. An alternative version of this test is to compare two estimates of the probability $\Pr\{\$10 \leqslant \text{WTP} \leqslant \$20\}$. One estimate takes the respondents who received the first bid structure and calculates the proportion of yes/no responses. The other estimate takes those who received the second bid structure and calculates the proportion of no/yes responses. Again, these two numbers should be the same, except for sampling variation. The first test was used by Hanemann (1991), and the second by McFadden and Leonard (1993); in both cases, the test failed. Similar failures of consistency tests have been observed in other applications of double-bounded CV.[103]

How should one deal with the inconsistency? Several approaches are found in the literature. One approach is to disregard the inconsistency and proceed to estimate the model pooling the responses to the first and second bids. While there may be some bias in the coefficient estimates, there also can be a gain in efficiency which offsets this (Alberini, 1995c). A second approach, due originally to Cameron and Quiggin (1994), is to treat the responses to the two bids as though they were valuations of separate items, using one or another of the models described in Section 11.4.1.[104] In Cameron and Quiggin's general model, there are separate WTP distributions for the first and second responses, both based on the linear utility function (11.12), leading to marginal c.d.f.s $G_k(C_k)$, $k = 1$, 2, with marginal means $E\{C_k\} \equiv \mu_k = \alpha_k/\beta_k$ and variances var $\{C_k\} \equiv \sigma_k^2 = 1/\beta_k$. In terms of the underlying utility functions, this is a one-way fixed effects formulation with separate response-specific intercepts, α_k, and slope coefficients, β_k. In addition, there is a non-zero correlation between the first and second responses, represented by a correlation coefficient ρ. Thus, the two WTP distributions are neither identical nor independent. Let $g_{12}(C_1, C_2; \rho)$ be the resulting bivariate WTP density. Instead of (11.99), the double-bounded response probabilities now take a form analogous to (11.73):

$$P^{yy} = \int_A^{C_1^{max}} \int_{A_U}^{C_2^{max}} g_{12}(C_1, C_2; \rho) dC_1 dC_2$$

$$P^{yn} = \int_A^{C_1^{max}} \int_{C_2^{min}}^{A_U} g_{12}(C_1, C_2; \rho) dC_1 dC_2$$

$$P^{ny} = \int_{C_1^{min}}^{A} \int_{A_L}^{C_2^{max}} g_{12}(C_1, C_2; \rho) dC_1 dC_2 \qquad (11.102)$$

$$P^{nn} = \int_{C_1^{min}}^{A} \int_{C_2^{min}}^{A_L} g_{12}(C_1, C_2; \rho) dC_1 dC_2.$$

---

[103] There are also various parametric tests of consistency. For example, one can analyse the two sets of responses separately, and then test whether they come from the same distribution.
[104] This is analogous to the practice in contingent ranking of dealing with inconsistencies in rankings by assuming a separate set of preferences for each ranking.

In their empirical application, Cameron and Quiggin make g_{12} $(C_1, C_2; \rho)$ a bivariate normal, so that (11.102) becomes a correlated, bivariate version of the probit model (11.14).[105]

Cameron and Quiggin also consider formulations that lie somewhere between (11.99) and (11.102). They find empirically that they cannot reject the hypotheses that $\mu_1 = \mu_2$ and $\sigma_1^2 = \sigma_2^2$ (i.e, $\alpha_1 = \alpha_2$ and $\beta_1 = \beta_2$). If it were also the case that $\rho = 1$, then (11.102) would reduce to (11.99), where $G_c(\cdot)$ is the common univariate WTP distribution that generates both responses. With their data, however, Cameron and Quiggin find they *can* reject the hypothesis that $\rho = 1$; it is significantly positive but less than unity.[106] Thus, the two WTP distributions are identical, not independent, but not perfectly correlated either. In terms of the underlying utility functions, this is equivalent to a one-way random-effects formulation for (11.12) with common (fixed) slope coefficient, β, and random intercepts, α, that are correlated draws from a common distribution. Let $G(\cdot, \cdot; \rho)$ be a correlated, bivariate WTP distribution with common marginal c.d.f.s given by $G_c(\cdot)$; in Cameron and Quiggin's empirical application, these are bivariate and univariate normal, respectively. Instead of (11.102), the double-bounded response probabilities now take the form[107]

$$
\begin{aligned}
P^{yy} &= 1 - G_C(A) - G_C(A_u) + G(A, A_u; \rho) \\
P^{yn} &= G_C(A_u) - G(A, A_u; \rho) \\
P^{ny} &= G_C(A) - G(A, A_d; \rho) \\
P^{nn} &= G(A, A_d; \rho).
\end{aligned}
\tag{11.103}
$$

Alberini *et al.* (1994a) develop a two-way random effects version of this model, with individual-specific as well as response-specific effects.

A third approach postulates that the inconsistency arises as some form of response effect, and models this effect explicitly. This can be done in various ways, depending on the type of response effect believed to occur. For example, many CV studies implement the double-bounded approach in a

---

[105] Cameron and Quiggin consider that negative as well as positive preferences are possible, and they model this along the lines illustrated in the lower panel of Fig. 11.3, rather than through a mixture model as in the upper panel of Fig. 11.3. They set $C^{min} = \infty$ and $C^{max} = \infty$, but their WTP distribution needs to be modified by censoring or truncation for the reasons mentioned in Section 11.2.3.

[106] Ward (1995) notes that these hypotheses tests may not be robust if the true WTP distribution is non-normal. Alberini (1995) points out that, since testing for $\rho = 1$ involves a hypothesis at the boundary of the parameter space, the distribution of the test statistic is non-standard and the size of the test statistic is likely to diverge from its nominal level, making the test results of ρ in Cameron and Quiggin unreliable.

[107] Alberini (1995c) conducts a Monte Carlo analysis of the bivariate normal version of (11.103) and the normal version of the double-bounded model (11.99), simulating the error that arises when one model is erroneously fitted to data actually generated by the other. She finds that the double-bounded estimates of mean/median WTP can be surprisingly robust to low values of ρ; even if the double-bounded model is technically misspecified, it is often superior to the bivariate model in terms of mean square error.

manner that makes the second valuation question come as something of a surprise. After having been assured during the presentation of the first bid that the item will cost $\$A$, the respondent is suddenly informed that the cost could instead be $\$A_u$ (or A_d). She may not react to this new information in a neutral manner. If she had said 'yes' to the initial bid, she might see the increased second bid as a crude attempt at bargaining, which she could well resent (Altaf and DeShazo, 1994). Or she might view it as implying a possible cost overrun, which she could similarly resent. In both cases, she might then be inclined to say 'no' to the second bid, not because she doesn't like the item but because she objects to the way in which it is now being offered to her. If so, this would cause a greater preponderance of yes/no responses than would be anticipated on the basis of the 'yes' response to the first question alone. In a similar vein, if she had said 'no' to the initial bid, she might see the reduced second bid as an attempt to pressure her to change her mind, which she could resent, or she might view it as an indication that she is now being offered an inferior and cheaper version of the commodity. If so, this would cause a greater preponderance of no/no responses than would be anticipated on the basis of the 'no' response to the first question alone. Some researchers have suggested a different scenario. Under this scenario, respondents who say 'yes' initially feel called upon to assert and expand their commitment in the face of the 'challenge' implied by the raised follow-up bid; hence there could be a greater preponderance of yes/yes responses than would be anticipated on the basis of the 'yes' response to the first question. Conversely, those who say 'no' initially may feel guilty and decide that they should at least agree to the second bid, causing a greater preponderance of no/yes responses than would be anticipated on the basis of the 'no' response to the first question. In one scenario the second bid creates resentment; in the other, acquiescence.

Both of these scenarios can lead to the Cameron–Quiggin model (11.102), where there are two WTP distributions because the second bid induces a shift in the location parameter of the WTP distribution generating the second response. In terms of the Cameron–Quiggin model, these scenarios explain why μ_2 might be different from μ_1. In the resentment scenario, the second bid causes $\mu_2 < \mu_1$; in the acquiescence scenario, it causes $\mu_2 > \mu_1$. However, they can also be modelled directly as a single WTP distribution combined with a response effect. For the resentment scenario, one extends (11.99) by introducing a background disposition to say 'no' that applies to the second but not the first valuation question. This changes the response probabilities from P^{yy}, P^{yn}, P^{ny}, P^{nn} as given in (11.99) to

$$\begin{aligned}
\bar{P}^{yy} &= (1 - \theta_u)P^{yy} \\
\bar{P}^{yn} &= \theta_u P^y + (1 - \theta_u)P^{yn} \\
\bar{P}^{ny} &= (1 - \theta_d)P^{ny} \\
\bar{P}^{nn} &= \theta_d P^n + (1 - \theta_d)P^{nn},
\end{aligned} \tag{11.104}$$

where θ_u is the background probability of saying 'no' to the second bid given that the respondent said 'yes' initially, θ_d is the background probability of saying 'no' to the second bid given that the respondent said 'no' initially, $P^y = 1 - G_c(A)$ is the probability of saying 'yes' initially, and $P^n = G_c(A)$ is the probability of saying 'no' initially. Under the resentment hypothesis, $\theta_u > 0$ and $\theta_d > 0$.[108] The acquiescence hypothesis is treated similarly by introducing into (11.99) a background disposition to say 'yes', which leads to a modified set of response probabilities analogous to (11.104).

Instead of modelling the second response in terms of resentment or acquiescence, Herriges and Shogren (1996) approach it in terms of anchoring. They postulate that the respondent revises her valuation of the item after the first bid, forming some weighted average of the bid and her original WTP. In linear models like (11.12) they use an arithmetic average, while in the nonlinear model (11.19) they assume a geometric average; for simplicity, we focus here on the linear model. If C_1 is the individual's WTP for the item on receiving the first bid, $G_c(\cdot)$ is the c.d.f. of C_1, A is the first bid, and C_2 is her WTP after the first bid, Herriges and Shogren postulate that

$$C_2 = (1 - \gamma)C_1 + \gamma A \qquad (11.105)$$

for some $\gamma \in [0, 1]$; if $\gamma = 0$, there is no anchoring. Given (11.105), the double-bounded response probability formulas take the following form instead of (11.98):[109]

$$
\begin{aligned}
P^{yy} &= 1 - G_c[(A_u - \gamma A)/(1 - \gamma)] \\
P^{nn} &= G_c[(A_d - \gamma A)/(1 - \gamma)] \\
P^{yn} &= G_c[(A_u - \gamma A)/(1 - \gamma)] - G_c(A) \\
P^{ny} &= G_c(A) - G_c[(A_d - \gamma A)/(1 - \gamma)].
\end{aligned}
\qquad (11.106)
$$

In their empirical application, Herriges and Shogren find no evidence of anchoring in the valuation of an improvement in water quality by local residents, but definite evidence of anchoring for visiting recreationists.

Alternatively, instead of operating on the location parameter, Alberini *et al.* (1994a) suggest that the response effect might shift the dispersion of the WTP distribution. They propose a model where, while $\mu \equiv E\{C_k\}$ is the same for both questions, $\sigma_k^2 \equiv \text{var}\{C_k\}$ varies as a function of the difference between the bid presented to the respondent in the kth question and the central tendency of her WTP for the item. Their formula allows for differences in the strength of this effect among questions,

$$\sigma_k^2 = \exp[\phi + \Psi_k(\mu - A_k)^2], \quad k = 1, 2 \qquad (11.107)$$

---

[108] We leave open the possibility that $\theta_u \neq \theta_d$. Both of these background probabilities could be parameterized as functions of covariates. Kanninen (1995) develops a model similar to (11.104) but with a background probability of saying 'yes/yes'.

[109] These are slightly different from the formulas given by Herriges and Shogren.

where A_k is the bid used in the kth question.[110] Different signs for Ψ_k correspond to different models of cognitive behaviour. If $\Psi_k < 0$, this is model where, the closer the individual is to indifference (i.e., what she has to pay for the item more nearly exhausts what it is worth to her), the less certain she is about how to answer the CV question. If $\Psi_k > 0$, this is a model where the individual is less certain of her response when the bid is more surprising or implausible, in the sense that the cost strikes her as unusually high or unusually low. The model is thus a particular case of the Cameron–Quiggin model (11.102), where $\rho = 1$, $\mu_1 = \mu_2$, and σ_1^2 and σ_2^2 are given by (11.107). When Alberini *et al.* apply this model to three different double-bounded data sets, they find no evidence of heteroscedasticity in two cases but significant evidence in the third case, with Ψ positive and decreasing across questions ($\Psi_1 > \Psi_2 > 0$).

Several conclusions can be drawn from the literature on the double-bounded CV format. While, a variety of response-effect models exist for which there is some empirical support, most analyses apply a particular model to the data at hand rather than pitting many of them against one another. Thus, while it is clear that response effects can occur with the double-bounded format, there is less certainty about their specific form. Moreover, this is something that may vary with the circumstances of the interview. Whether or not the second question connotes bargaining or induces surprise, resentment, or guilt, and whether or not the first question is seen as providing a hint as to how subjects should value the item, could depend on just what is said in the interview and how it is conducted.

For example, it might be possible to eliminate the surprise effect of the second valuation question by arranging for the interviewer to state, well before the first valuation question, that the cost of the item is expected to fall within a range from A_1 to A_h. In the first valuation question, the interviewer selects one end of that range at random and asks whether the subject is willing to pay this amount. Suppose the interviewer selects A_1; if the subject says yes, the interviewer follows up with a second question about paying A_h, but he does *not* follow up with a second question if the subject says no to A_1. Conversely, if the interviewer starts with A_h for the first bid and the subject says no, he follows up with a second question about paying A_1, but does *not* follow up with a second question if the subject says yes to A_h. On average,

---

[110] In this case, some care must be exercised in translating back from the parameters of the WTP distribution to those of the underlying utility function. In cognitive heteroscedasticity models like (11.107), it would be natural to identify *two separate* components of var $\{C\}$: one (denoted $\bar{\sigma}^2$) arises from the variation in preferences implied by the RUM formulation, while the other reflects the respondent's cognitive burden in answering the CV question. In terms of the linear model (11.12), for example, where $\mu = \alpha/\beta$, the variance associated with RUM preferences is $\bar{\sigma}^2 = 1/\beta$. The ϕ in (11.107) is intended to reflect $\bar{\sigma}^2$; the formulation there implies a multiplicative relation between the two components of variance. It might instead be more natural to have an additive formulation: $\sigma_k^2 = \bar{\sigma}^2 + \exp[\Psi_k(\mu - A_k)^2]$.

the interviewer follows up with a second bid only half as often as with the conventional double-bounded format. Cooper and Hanemann (1995) call this the 'one and half bounded format'. Through a simulation analysis, they find that it provides parameter estimates much closer in efficiency to those associated with the double-bounded than the single-bounded format. Thus, it may offer most of the statistical advantages of the double-bounded format without the response effects.

We should emphasize that, in our view, the case for the double-bounded approach is pragmatic rather than one of principle. It is not surprising that asking additional, closed-ended questions provides additional information in the statistical sense. By that token, the most information would be provided by simply asking the open-ended WTP question directly. But, besides the statistical considerations, there are also considerations of cognitive capacity. There is abundant evidence that people do not carry their utility functions or their WTP formulas around in their heads. In our experience, even for market commodities, people cannot readily tell you their maximum WTP as a simple number: they go through a thought process of considering particular amounts and deciding whether or not they would be willing to pay those amounts. Thus, asking people directly for their WTP, even for many market commodities, is asking more than they can say. The closed-ended format comes closer to how they think and what they can answer. The double-bounded approach stays within this constraint while providing more information. Pending further testing of the one-and-a-half bounded format, we would recommend using the double-bounded approach. Even if it produces some bias compared with the single-bounded approach, the experience to date generally suggests that the bias is in a conservative direction and is greatly outweighed by the gain in efficiency in terms of minimizing overall mean squared error.

11.4.3   Extending the response probability model

Most of the response probability models considered so far—including the logistic, normal, log-logistic, lognormal, and Weibull—involve two-parameter probability distributions, with one location parameter and one scale parameter.[111] Adding more location or scale parameters can give greater flexibility, which allows a more sensitive modelling of the data, especially in the tails of the distribution.[112] This is important if the goal is to predict tail probabilities or to measure quantities, such as mean WTP, which are particularly sensitive to them.

---

[111] There are additional coefficients in the model when other covariates are used along with the bid variable, but these all form part of the location and/or shape parameters.

[112] While adding parameters reduces the bias estimates of welfare measures and other quantities of interest, it also increases the variance because of the extra variation associated with the estimates of the additional parameters (Taylor, 1988).

There are several reasons why a more flexible response probability model could be appropriate. First, even at the level of the individual respondent, the WTP distribution could possess a more complex shape than that yielded by conventional, two-parameter models. Second, the researcher may want to draw a distinction between the individual's underlying preferences and the way these are expressed through the survey medium; the additional parameters could be used to model response effects or the individual's uncertainty about her preferences. Third, even if the WTP distribution has a simple shape at the individual level, heterogeneity among respondents resulting from variation in preferences or unmeasured covariates may produce a more complex shape in the aggregate, population-level WTP distribution. Rather than explicitly compounding a two-parameter model as in (11.98), it may be convenient to use a three- or four-parameter distribution to approximate the aggregate response probability model.

The overdispersion model in Section 11.3.4 can be regarded as an instance where one adds a parameter to get a more realistic shape for a WTP distribution. Another example is the model with a spike at zero in (11.33). Besides this, the statistical literature contains a number of multi-parameter distributions which generalize the logistic, including Aranda-Ordaz's (1981) standardized asymmetric distribution[113]

$$F_\eta(\eta) = 1 - (1 + \lambda e^\eta)^{-1/\lambda}, \qquad (11.108)$$

which yields the logistic c.d.f. when $\lambda = 1$ and the extreme value c.d.f. when $\lambda = 0$, and the cubic-logistic of Morgan (1985) with parameters μ, $\gamma > 0$, and $\delta > 0$,

$$F_\eta(\eta) = (1 + \exp[-\gamma(\eta - \mu) - \delta(\eta - \mu)^3])^{-1}. \qquad (11.109)$$

There are also Prentice's (1976) generalization of probit and logit, Stukel's (1988) generalized logistic model, and several other distributions reviewed in El-Saidi *et al.* (1992). The mixing approach to generalizing the logistic is discussed by Follman and Lambert (1989), who apply a non-parametric mixture model with c.d.f.

$$F_\eta(\eta) = \sum_{m=1}^{M} \gamma_m [1 + \exp(-\theta_m - \eta)]^{-1}, \qquad (11.110)$$

where M (the number of atoms in the mixture), the α_m (coefficients unique to each atom), and the γ_m (non-negative weights that sum to unity and constitute the non-parametric c.d.f. of the logistic parameter θ) are all to be estimated from the data. Follman and Lambert show that, in the case of a

---

[113] This was applied to discrete-response CV data by Johansson and Kriström (1988).

single covariate (e.g. the CV bid) that takes k distinct values, there is a restriction that $M \leqslant [(k + 2)^{0.5} - 1]$ for parameter identifiability.[114]

The double-bounded model with a background disposition to 'yes' or 'no', as in (11.104), is an example of a model that introduces an additional parameter in order to represent a response effect in a CV survey. The single-bounded version was introduced by Hanemann (1983b); instead of (11.6b), the response probability is given by[115]

$$\Pr\{\text{response is 'yes'}\} = \theta + (1 - \theta)[1 - G_c(A)], \qquad (11.111)$$

where $\theta \in [0, 1]$ is the background probability of saying 'yes' which could be taken as a constant or made a function of covariates other than the bid, A; this model was derived from the concept of a background mortality rate in biometrics (Hasselblad et al., 1980). Kanninen (1995) notes an alternative interpretation based on an asymmetric version of Copas' (1988) transposition model (11.62): if some proportion θ of the 'no' responses is wrongly recorded as a 'yes', but there is no error in recording the 'yes' responses, this generates the response probability in (11.111).

Another model that uses a parameter to represent response effects is the model of 'thick' indifference curves where a parameter $\delta \geqslant 0$ determines a zone of indifference or ambivalence. The idea that consumers might be insensitive to small differences in utility, thus creating a threshold that must be exceeded in order for them to express a preference for one alternative over another, goes back to Georgescu-Roegen (1936, 1958) and Luce (1956). It was first linked to the concept of a RUM model by Quandt (1956), and was formally incorporated into binary choice models by Deacon and Shapiro (1975) and Krishnan (1977). The first application to discrete-response CV was by Svento (1993).[116] In the single-bounded context, the respondent answers 'yes' only if $v(q^1, y - A, \varepsilon) \geqslant v(q^0, y, \varepsilon) + \delta$; she answers no only if $v(q^1, y - A, \varepsilon) \leqslant v(q^0, y, \varepsilon) - \delta$; otherwise, if $| v(q^1, y - A, \varepsilon) - v(q^0, y, \varepsilon) | \leqslant | \delta |$, she answers 'don't know' or abstains from making a choice. Recasting the indifference zone into monetary units via a parameter Δ, instead of the utility units measured by δ, one obtains a trichotomous choice model where, instead of (11.6b),

$$\Pr\{\text{response is 'yes'}\} = 1 - G_c(A + \Delta) \qquad (11.112a)$$

$$\Pr\{\text{response is 'no'}\} = G_c(A - \Delta) \qquad (11.112b)$$

$$\Pr\{\text{response is 'don't know'}\} = G_c(A + \Delta) - G_c(A - \Delta). \qquad (11.112c)$$

---

[114] If one uses these distributions, it will still be necessary to apply censoring or truncation to ensure that the resulting WTP distribution satisfies the restrictions from economic theory that $0 \leqslant C \leqslant y$.

[115] This should be distinguished from the spike model, (11.33), where the response probability takes the form: $\Pr\{\text{response is 'yes'}\} = \theta - \theta G_c(A)$, where $\theta \equiv 1 - \gamma$.

[116] Opaluch and Segerson (1989) propose that thick indifference curves can explain CV responses without formally modelling it in this way; Mazzotta and Opaluch (1995) model ambivalence as an increase in the variance of the random utility associated with the item being valued.

To estimate the model—and to identify Δ—one needs explicit data on abstentions or 'don't knows'.[117] Svento (1993) used the linear probit and logit models (11.14) and (11.15) in (11.112) and parametrized Δ on attributes of the respondent, finding that it increased slightly with income. Svento and Mäntymaa (1994) tested for separate Δ in (11.112a) and (11.112b) and found that this fitted his data better than the symmetric formulation.[118]

The heteroscedastic model in (11.107) is an example of an approach where one represents response effects in terms of increased dispersion in preferences. In general with this approach, in addition to the random terms ε and η used above to represent variation in preferences among individuals in a population, one adds a new random term v which represents the individual's uncertainty about her own preferences. As in (11.107), the extent of this uncertainty may vary with the circumstances of the CV survey. We now distinguish between C, as defined in (11.5), which is the individual's underlying preference for the item in terms of her true WTP, and $\tilde{C}$, which is how she perceives or expresses her WTP in the survey context. We assume that

$$\tilde{C} \equiv C + v, \tag{11.113a}$$

where v is a random variable with a mean of zero (in the absence of incentives for strategic behaviour) and some c.d.f. $F_v(\cdot)$. It is the c.d.f. of $\tilde{C}$, $\tilde{G}_C(\cdot)$, rather than $G_C(\cdot)$ that governs the responses to the CV survey. Thus, instead of (11.6b), the probability that the respondent answers yes in the survey is

$$\text{Pr}\{\text{response is 'yes'}\} = 1 - \tilde{G}_c(A). \tag{11.113b}$$

Whether or not $F_v(\cdot)$ and $G_c(\cdot)$ can both be recovered depends on the stochastic specification and the form of the data.

Li and Mattsson (1995), who first introduced this model, used the linear probit model (11.14) for C combined with a normal distribution for v having a mean of zero and a variance of σ_v^2. Thus, $\tilde{C} = C + v \equiv (\alpha/\beta) + \omega$ is normally distributed with a mean and median of $E\{\tilde{C}\} = E\{C\} \equiv \mu = \alpha/\beta$ (ignoring the restriction that $0 \leqslant C \leqslant y$), and a variance of $\sigma_{\tilde{C}}^2 \equiv \text{var}\{\tilde{C}\} = \sigma_\omega^2 = \sigma^2 + \sigma_v^2$, where $\sigma^2 = \text{var}\{C\} = 1/\beta^2$. With this specification, σ^2 and σ_v^2 cannot be separately identified from data on the discrete CV responses alone. However, Li and Mattsson had conducted a survey in which, after presenting a closed-

---

[117] While it is always good practice to record a response of 'don't know' when this is spontaneously volunteered by a respondent, there is some question about the necessity of automatically providing an explicit 'don't know' option, as suggested by the NOAA Panel (Arrow et al., 1993). A split-sample experiment by Carson et al. (1995) found that, if one treats 'don't know' as 'no' in analysing CV responses, offering the option does *not* alter the breakdown of yes/no responses or the estimate of WTP.

[118] The trichotomous choice model in (11.112) and the asymmetric model of Svento and Mantymaa can also be viewed as versions of the ordered categorical dependent variable model in (11.89).

ended, single-bounded valuation question, they asked 'How certain were you of your answer to the previous question?' Respondents were asked to record their reply on a scale from 0% to 100%.[119] Li and Mattsson interpreted the answer to the confidence question as information about $F_v(\cdot)$. Suppose the individual said 'yes' to a bid of A and then said 30% in response to the confidence question. The probability of this joint answer can be factored into

$$
\begin{aligned}
&\text{Pr\{says `yes' to } A \text{ and 30\% confident\}} \\
&= \text{Pr\{says 30\% } | \text{ `yes' to } A\}\text{Pr\{says `yes' to } A\},
\end{aligned} \tag{11.114}
$$

where the second probability on the RHS corresponds to (11.113b). To obtain the first term on the RHS, Li and Mattsson assume that, if the subject says she is 30% confident of her response, this implies:

$$
\begin{aligned}
0.3 &= \Pr\{\tilde{C} \geqslant A \mid C\} \\
&= \Pr\{C + v \geqslant A\} \\
&= 1 - F_v(A - \tilde{C}).
\end{aligned} \tag{11.115a}
$$

Hence, the first term on the RHS of (11.114) is given by

$$
\begin{aligned}
\Pr\{\text{says} 30\% \mid \text{`yes' to} A\} &= \Pr\{0.3 = 1 - F_v(A - C)] \mid \text{`yes' to} A\} \\
&= \Pr\{C = A - F_v^{-1}(0.7) \mid \tilde{C} \geqslant A\} \\
&= \Pr\{C = A - F_v^{-1}(0.7) \mid C + v \geqslant A\},
\end{aligned} \tag{11.115b}
$$

where $F_v^{-1}(\cdot)$ is the inverse of $F_v(\cdot)$. Rather than estimating the joint probability on the LHS of (11.114) directly, Li and Mattsson estimate it in two stages. First, they estimate (11.113b) from the CV responses alone, which produces an estimate of (α/β) and $\sigma_{\tilde{c}}^2$. Taking these as given, they estimate (11.115b) from the answers to the confidence question, which produces an estimate of σ_v^2. The estimate of σ^2 is recovered by subtracting the estimate of σ_v^2 from that of $\sigma_{\tilde{c}}^2$. Li and Mattsson find that this provides more efficient coefficient estimates than the conventional approach based on (11.6b)

It would be still more efficient to estimate the LHS of (11.114) in one step directly. When the answer to the confidence question is interpreted as 'exactly 30%', as in (11.115a), one obtains the following direct expression for (11.114):

$$
\text{Pr\{says `yes' to A and 30\% confident\}} = \Pr\{\eta = A - (\alpha/\beta) - F_\nu^{-1}(0.7)\}. \tag{11.115c}
$$

---

[119] Qualitative follow-up questions about how confident one is in one's answer, or how strongly one supports the programme, are not uncommon in CV surveys. For example, Ready et al. (1995) offered subjects six responses in a single-bounded survey: 'definitely yes', 'probably yes', 'maybe yes', 'maybe no', 'probably no', and 'definitely no'. To use Li and Mattsson's approach, one would have to convert the qualitative responses into quantitative probabilities, at least approximately. Instead, Ready et al. treat this as a case of varying intensity of preference and model it on the lines of an ordered categorical dependent variable model.

A more interesting model is obtained when one changes the interpretation or format of the confidence question. Two other formulations are possible. One is that, when the respondent says she is 30% confident, she means '*at least* 30%' in the sense that

$$0.3 \leqslant \Pr\{\tilde{C} \geqslant A | C\} \tag{11.116a}$$
$$= \Pr\{C + v \geqslant A\}.$$

In this case, instead of (11.115c), the joint probability of the responses to the CV question and the confidence question takes the form

$$\Pr\{\text{says 'yes' to } A \text{ and } 30\% \text{ confident}\} =$$
$$\int_{A-\mu-F_v^{-1}(0.7)}^{\eta^{\max}} [1 - F_v(A - \mu - \eta)]g(\eta)d\eta \tag{11.116b}$$

where, for the sake of generality, we write $C = \mu + \eta$, where η is assumed to be independent of v with an upper support of $\eta^{\max}$ and a density $g(\eta)$. The other formulation is that, when the respondent says she is 30% confident, this is taken to imply a particular *probability range*, e.g. from 25% to 35%, so that

$$0.25 \leqslant \Pr\{\tilde{C} \geq A | C\} = \Pr\{C + v \geqslant A\} \leqslant 0.35. \tag{11.117a}$$

The joint probability of the responses to the CV question and the confidence question then becomes

$$\Pr\{\text{says 'yes' to } A \text{ and } 25-35\% \text{ confident}\} =$$
$$\int_{A-\mu-F_v^{-1}(0.75)}^{A-\mu-F_v^{-1}(0.65)} [1 - F_v(A - \mu - \eta)]g(\eta)d\eta. \tag{11.117b}$$

Hanemann *et al.* (1995) and Li *et al* (1995) develop an alternative specification of preference uncertainty which uses (11.113a) but assumes that, conditional on C, the uncertainty term v is *uniformly* distributed over an interval $[C - h, C + h]$ for some parameter $h \geqslant 0$. This creates a probabilistic zone of indifference with width $\Delta = 2h$. It can be shown that, with this stochastic specification, $\tilde{G}_c(\cdot)$ takes the form

$$\tilde{G}_c(x) = (1/2h) \int_{x-h}^{x+h} G_c(x)dx. \tag{11.118}$$

Thus, for example, when $G_c(\cdot)$ is the standard logistic, (11.15), one obtains

$$\tilde{G}_c(x) = (2h\beta)^{-1}\ln\{1 + \exp[\alpha + \beta(x + h)]\}/\{1 + \exp[\alpha + \beta(x - h)]\}. \tag{11.119}$$

This c.d.f. can be regarded as a multi-parameter generalization of the logistic that is an alternative to those in (11.108)–(11.110). Like those, it can be estimated from the CV responses alone, using (11.113b), without requiring a question about confidence in one's answer. Li *et al.* apply a version of (11.118) to Bishop and Heberlein's (1979) data on WTA responses in real and hypothetical markets for goose hunting permits, based on a multiplicative formulation, $\tilde{C} = Ce^v$ rather than the linear formulation in (11.113a) and using the Bishop–Heberlein model utility model, (11.19a), for $G_c(\cdot)$. They find a substantial and interesting difference in the value of h for the two sets of data: h is not significantly different from zero in the real WTA experiment, but it is significantly positive in the hypothetical experiment, and its inclusion brings the estimated welfare measure from the hypothetical experiment much closer to the value of the welfare measure estimated from the real data. This suggests that a key difference between hypothetical and actual markets is that there may be substantially more preference uncertainty in the former.

In this section we have reviewed recent efforts to generalize the response probability distribution so as to provide a more flexible and realistic framework for modelling CV responses. When tested against CV data, each of the models has been found to have some validity in the sense of providing a better fit than the conventional logit and probit models in the earlier literature. This creates quite a strong case for considering a multi-parameter generalization of the conventional models. However, it still remains to be seen *which* is the more appropriate generalization. The next step in CV research is to test these generalized models against one another to get a better of understanding of their similarities and differences and to assess their relative merits.[120]

11.4.4   Non-parametric and semi-parametric models

11.4.4.1   Single-bounded data

We first consider nonparametric and semiparametric estimation for single-bounded CV data, and then address double-bounded data in Section 11.4.4.2. Our starting point is the log-likelihood function (11.48), which we repeat here for convenience

$$\ln L = \sum_{i=1}^{N} y_i \ln P_i + (1 - y_i) \ln (1 - P_i), \qquad (11.120)$$

where $P_i \equiv \Pr\{i^{\text{th}} \text{ observation is a 'yes' }\}$. Focusing for the moment on the bid, A_i, and ignoring all other covariates, following (11.1)–(11.3) and (11.6) we can write

$$\begin{aligned} P_i \equiv H(A_i) &= 1 - G_C(A_i) \\ &= 1 - F_\eta[\Delta \bar{v}(A_i)], \end{aligned} \qquad (11.121)$$

---

[120] Also, bid design for generalized parametric response models is an important area for future research.

where the second line uses the utility difference formulation associated with an additively random utility model, as noted in footnote 11. In a parametric statistical model one adopts a parametric cdf (or survivor function) for $H(\cdot)$ in (11.121). In a parametric RUM model, one adopts a parametric specification for the WTP distribution, $G_C(.)$, or parametric specifications for the indirect utility function, $v(q, y, \varepsilon)$, and the cdf of ε. A fully nonparametric approach estimates $H(A)$—or $G_C(A)$—nonparametrically, without specifying a parametric formula. A semiparametric approach estimates either $F_\eta(\cdot)$ or $\Delta\bar{v}(\cdot)$ in the second line of (11.121)—but not both—nonparametrically. We start with the nonparametric approach and then consider various semiparametric approaches.

With binary response data, nonparametric estimation involves estimation of an unknown function of a variable, $H(A)$, whose value is observed at a discrete set of points A_j, $j = 1, \ldots J$, (we assume these are arrayed from low to high). The function can be estimated only at those points, not at other points which are unobserved. Economic theory restricts $H(A)$ to be monotonically non-increasing in A (see footnote 7). Ayer et al. (1955) developed a nonparametric maximum likelihood estimator for $H(A)$ by treating $P_j = H(A_j)$, $j = 1, \ldots J$, as a set of unknowns to be estimated, subject to the constraints that $P_j \geqslant P_{j+1}$—this is the ultimate extension of the idea of adding extra parameters to better model the observed data. Let $\hat{P}_j$ be the observed sample proportion of respondents who said yes to the jth bid. Ayer et al. proved that, if the $\hat{P}_j$'s form a non-increasing sequence, they are the nonparametric maximum likelihood estimator of $H(A)$. Otherwise, if they are increasing in some region (i.e. $\hat{P}_j < \hat{P}_{j+1}$ for some j), one simply combines the responses for adjacent bids until the revised sequence of sample proportions is monotonically non-increasing. Ayer et al. proved that this 'pool-adjacent-violators' algorithm generates a consistent estimate of the true $H(A)$.[121] This estimator was first applied to single-bounded CV data by Kristrom (1990).

An alternative to the Ayer et al. nonparametric estimator of $H(\cdot)$ is smoothing of the empirical distribution of responses via a kernel function. This was first applied to binary response data in biometrics by Copas (1983), who saw it as being especially useful when there are so few observations at each bid (dose) that one cannot obtain a reliable estimate of the sample proportions of 'yes' and 'no' responses without resorting to some smoothing procedure. Copas describes a method of correcting for the bias due to smoothing, and he presents an estimate of the variance of the estimated response probability. Kernel estimation of dose response models, together

---

[121] Applications of the Ayer et al. estimator are discussed in Barlow et al. (1972). Schmoyer (1984) extends their approach to nonparametric estimation where the unknown WTP distribution is assumed to be unimodal, so that $H(A)$ is sigmoidal as well as non-increasing. Glasbey (1987) extends it to cases where the WTP distribution is assumed to be symmetric and/or bell-shaped.

with confidence intervals for estimated response probabilities, is also considered by Kappenman (1987) and Staniswalis and Cooper (1988). We are not aware of any CV applications as yet.

In the last decade or so, several approaches have been developed for modelling binary data in the semiparametric case where the response probability function $H(\cdot)$ can be decomposed, as in (11.2) or the second line of (11.121), into a cdf, $F_\eta(\cdot)$, which is of unknown form and what is called an *index function*, $T(\cdot)$ or $\Delta v(\cdot)$, which has a known functional form but with unknown coefficients.[122] This formulation allows for other covariates besides the bid. The index function is written $T(Z, \theta)$, where Z is a set of covariates (including A) and θ is a vector of coefficients to be estimated along with $F_\eta(\cdot)$. Some normalization is imposed on θ and it is usually assumed that $T(Z, \theta) = Z\theta$, which would correspond to a linear Box–Cox utility model (11.12') where $Z\theta = \alpha - \beta A$, but nonlinear formulations are also possible.

Coslett's (1983) semiparametric estimator extends the Ayer *et al.* estimator to the case where $H(A) = F_\eta(T(Z, \theta))$ using a two-part maximization of the likelihood function. Given the current estimate of θ, say $\hat{\theta}$, evaluate the index function for each observation. Let $\hat{T}_j$, $j = 1, \ldots, J$ denote the resulting distinct values of the index function, indexed so that they are in increasing order. Estimate $F_\eta(\cdot)$ nonparametrically as a set of constants corresponding to $\hat{P}_j = F_\eta(\hat{T}_j)$, using the pool-adjacent-violators algorithm. Then, concentrate the log-likelihood function and numerically maximize with respect to θ. This is difficult since the concentrated likelihood function varies in discrete steps over θ-space, which precludes conventional maximization techniques based on analytical or numerical derivatives. Instead, following Manski (1975), Coslett takes random sets of orthogonal directions in θ-space, searching for the maximum until a convergence criterion is satisfied. He established that this yields a consistent estimate of θ and $F_\eta(\cdot)$. Li (1996) applied Coslett's estimator to single-bounded CV data and found that, while computer intensive, it was certainly feasible. He compared it to conventional probit, based on (11.14), using Monte Carlo simulation and found that, although probit gave more efficient coefficient estimates when η actually was normally distributed, it produced seriously biased estimates when η was non-normal while the semiparametric estimates remained close to the true values and had a considerably lower mean squared error.

Because the concentrated likelihood in Coslett's approach is not a smooth function of θ, the asymptotic distribution of his estimator is not known; while it is consistent, there is no reason to believe that it is asymptotically normal or efficient. To circumvent this problem, Klein and Spady (1993) replace Coslett's concentrated likelihood function with a nonparametrically estimated function that locally approximates the true likelihood but is a smooth function of θ. They apply Bayes Rule to obtain

---

[122] Horowitz (1993) has an excellent survey of this literature.

$$P_j(\theta) = F_\eta(Z_j\theta) = \Pr\{\text{'yes'}|T_j = Z_j\theta\} =$$
$$\Pr\{T_j = Z_j\theta|\text{'yes'}\} \cdot \Pr\{\text{'yes'}\}/[\Pr\{T_j = Z_j\theta|\text{'yes'}\} \cdot \Pr\{\text{'yes'}\} +$$
$$\Pr\{T_j = Z_j\theta|\text{'no'}\} \cdot \Pr\{\text{'no'}\}]. \tag{11.122}$$

Although $F_\eta(\cdot)$ is unknown, they estimate the RHS of (11.122) by using the sample proportions of 'yes' and 'no' responses as estimates of $\Pr\{\text{'yes'}\}$ and $\Pr\{\text{'no'}\}$, and nonparametric kernel estimates of the conditional densities $\Pr\{T_j = Z_j\theta|\text{'yes'}\}$ and $\Pr\{T_j = Z_j\theta|\text{'no'}\}$, which are smooth functions of θ. Because of this, the RHS of (11.122) can be maximized with respect to θ in a conventional manner. Klein and Spady establish that the resulting estimator of θ is $N^{1/2}$ consistent and asymptotically normal, and attains the asymptotic efficiency bound of Coslett (1987) if η and Z are independent. It has not yet been applied to CV data.

There are several other semiparametric estimators for the case where $F_\eta(\cdot)$ is of unknown form while the index function has a known form, including Han's (1987) maximum rank correlation estimator, the Powell *et al.* (1989) weighted average derivative estimator, Ichimura's (1993) semiparametric least squares estimator, Manski's (1975) maximum score estimator, and Horowitz's (1992) smoothed maximum score estimator. However, these provide estimates of the coefficients θ but not of $F_\eta(\cdot)$, which makes them less useful in a CV context where the interest lies not just in θ but also in welfare measures that depend on $F_\eta(\cdot)$ or its quantiles.

The other major approach to semiparametric estimation of a binary response model reverses this assumption and postulates a known, parametric cdf for $F_\eta(\cdot)$ combined with an unknown form for the index function which is approximated by some flexible form. For example, one might assume that $F_\eta(\cdot)$ is a logistic or normal cdf, while $\Delta\bar{v}(A)$ is a spline function of the bid and other covariates (O'Sullivan, Yandell and Raynor, 1986), a generalized additive function (Hastie and Tibshirani, 1987; Preisler, 1989), or Gallant's (1981) Fourier flexible form. Estimation is by maximum likelihood or, for grouped data, by some form of least squares; in the logistic case, the analog of minimum chi-squared estimates the RHS of (11.15) as a spline, generalized additive function, or Fourier function of A. The logistic-Fourier model has been applied to single-bounded CV data by Chen (1993) and Creel and Loomis (1995).

11.4.4.2   *Double-bounded data*

The log-likelihood function for double-bounded data, (11.99)–(11.100), can be written equivalently in terms of the J distinct values used for the initial bid A and the follow-up bids A_u and A_d, augmented by two 'artificial' bid values of $A_0 \equiv 0$ and $A_{J+1} \equiv \infty$, as

$$\ln L = \sum_{j=1}^{J+1} N_j \ln [G_C(A_j) - G_C(A_{j-1})] \equiv \sum_{j=1}^{J+1} N_j \ln \pi_j, \tag{11.123}$$

where $G_C(\cdot)$ is the WTP distribution function and N_j is the number of respondents for whom $A_{j-1} < C \leqslant A_j$. The aim is to estimate $G_C(\cdot)$ nonparametrically. Define $S_j \equiv G_C(A_j) = \Pr\{\text{says 'no' to } A_j\}$; then $S_j = \sum_{k=1}^{j} \pi_k$. Turnbull (1974, 1976) developed an analog of the Ayer et al. non-parametric estimator for likelihood functions like (11.123), treating the π_j's as a set of unknowns to be estimated, subject to the constraints that $\pi_j \geq 0$ (which makes the S_j's monotone non-decreasing) and $\sum \pi_j = 1$. Turnbull shows that the first order conditions for the likelihood maximization imply the pool-adjacent-violators principle, so that if the observed sample $\hat{S}_j$'s are decreasing in some region one combines adjacent bids until the sequence is non-decreasing.[123] This was first applied to double- bounded CV data by Carson and Steinberg (1990); recent applications include Carson et al. (1992), Carson, Wilks, and Imber (1994), and Huhtala (1994). In principle, the Turnbull estimator can be extended to the semiparametric case where $G_C(A) = F_\eta(T(Z, \theta))$, where Z includes covariates besides A and $T(\cdot)$ has a known parametric form while $F_\eta(\cdot)$ is estimated nonparametrically, in the same way that Coslett (1983) and Klein and Spady (1993) extend the Ayer et al. estimator. This would be computationally challenging, however, and no applications are yet known. The alternative semiparametric formulation where $F_\eta(\cdot)$ is a known cdf and $T(\cdot)$ is estimated nonparametrically as some flexible function of covariates might not be as difficult to implement with double-bounded data.

11.4.4.3 Nonparametric welfare measurement

With nonparametric methods that estimate $H(A)$ by smoothing, and semi-parametric methods that assume a known $F_\eta(\cdot)$ such as the logistic-Fourier model, the estimated response probability distribution is a continuous function to which (11.36) and (11.37) can be applied directly to obtain an estimate of the median WTP, C^*, or any other quantile of the WTP distribution. For the mean, C^+, one must resort to some form of numerical analysis to evaluate the area under the empirical response probability graph based on (11.45) or (11.46).[124] The situation is more complicated when the Ayer et al., Coslett or Klein and Spady estimators are used with single-bounded data, or the Turnbull estimator with double-bounded data. In those cases, the resulting estimate of the response probability function is a step function consisting

---

[123] In (11.123), the observations on WTP are said to be interval censored for $j = 1, \cdots, J$, and left (right) censored for $j = 0 (j = J + 1)$. The case where observations are right censored was treated by Kaplan and Meier (1958), who showed that what is known as the product limit estimate of the P_j's constitutes the nonparametric maximum likelihood estimator of $G_C(\cdot)$. Turnbull extended this to more complex models, including (11.123). Statistical packages for survival analysis generally include the Kaplan–Meier estimator and sometimes the Turnbull estimator.

[124] Staniswalis and Cooper (1988) show how to construct a confidence interval for C^* when $H(A)$ is estimated by smoothing. Otherwise, confidence intervals for these estimates of C^* and C^+ can be obtained by bootstrapping.

of J (or fewer, if there is pooling) distinct estimates, $\hat{P}_1, \cdots, \hat{P}_J$ which are monotonically decreasing and are located at the bid values, $A_1, \cdots, A_J$, where $\hat{P}_j$ is the nonparametric estimate of $H(A_j) = \Pr\{\text{'yes' to } A_j\}$. An example of what the researcher might face is given in Figure 11.5(a), which graphs estimated $\hat{P}_j$'s against A_j's. Unless one of the $\hat{P}_j$'s just happens to take the value 0.5, the estimate of C^* cannot be obtained without some form of interpolation; in Figure 11.5(a), for example, the point estimate of C^* lies somewhere in the interval $[A_4, A_5]$. Thus, C^* no longer has a computational advantage over the C^+, since both require numerical evaluation.

One way to proceed is via linear interpolation, which produces the trapezoidal approximation to the unknown $H(A)$ shown in Figure 11.5(b). The resulting estimate of median WTP, $\hat{C}^*$, is marked on the horizontal axis.[125] We noted earlier that the estimate of C^+ is sensitive to the tails of the WTP distribution. In the nonparametric case, it is heavily influenced by what one assumes about the shape of the WTP distribution to the left of A_1 and to the right of A_J. Suppose one assumes that $P_0 \equiv H(A_0) = 1$, thus ruling out negative preferences. Suppose one also assumes that there is some $C^{\max} \leqslant y$ such that $H(C^{\max}) = 0$. The graph in Figure 11.5(b) applies the linear interpolation between A_0 and A_1 and between A_7 and $C^{\max}$. In biometrics, the estimate of C^+ obtained by integrating the area under the linearly interpolated graph in Figure 11.5(b) is known as the Spearman–Karber estimate of mean WTP, $\hat{\mu}_{SK}$.[126]

An alternative approach to calculating C^+ from the nonparametrically estimated $\hat{P}_j$'s is shown in Figure 11.5(c). This graph differs from that in Figure 11.5(b) in three ways, all of which cause it to produce a more conservative estimate of C^+. First, in the main body of the graph it assumes that, over the interval $[A_j, A_{j+1}], H(A) = \hat{P}_{j+1}, j = 1, \cdots, J - 1$. This is a conservative assumption since, with $H(\cdot)$ monotone nonincreasing, we know that $H(A) \geqslant H(A_{j+1})$ over the interval. Second, in the left tail, it assumes that $H(A) = \hat{P}_1$ for $0 < A \leqslant A_1$, which is conservative for the same reason; in effect, this introduces a spike of $\gamma = \hat{P}_1$ into the estimated WTP distribution at $C = 0$. Third, it censors the WTP distribution from above by imposing a spike at the highest observed bid, A_J. The estimate obtained by integrating the area under the graph in Figure 11.5(c) is known as the Kaplan–Meier–Turnbull estimate of mean WTP, $\hat{\mu}_{KMT}$.[127]

The formulas for these two estimators are

$$\hat{\mu}_{KMT} = \sum_{j=1}^{J} (\hat{P}_j - \hat{P}_{j+1})A_j \equiv \sum_{j=1}^{J} \hat{\pi}_j A_j, \qquad (11.124)$$

[125] This is how Kristrom (1990) estimated C^* when using the Ayer *et al.* estimator with CV data.
[126] In the CV literature, this is used by Kristrom (1990) and Duffield and Patterson (1991).
[127] CV applications include Carson *et al.* (1992), Carson, Wilks and Imber (1994) and Huhtala (1994).

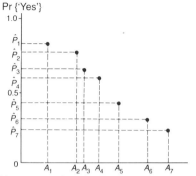

(a) Non-parametric estimate of response distribution

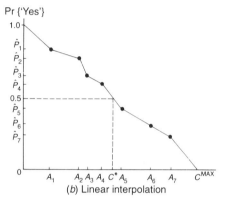

(b) Linear interpolation

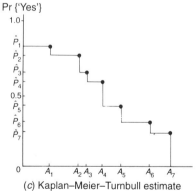

(c) Kaplan–Meier–Turnbull estimate

Fig. 11.5 Welfare measures from a non-parametrically estimated response
distribution
(a) Non-parametric estimate of response distribution, *(b)* Linear interpolation,
(c) Kaplan–Meier–Turnbull estimate

$$\hat{\mu}_{SK} = \hat{\mu}_{KMT} + \left(\frac{1}{2}\right) \sum_{j=1}^{J} (\hat{P}_j - \hat{P}_{j+1})(A_{j+1} - A_j)$$

$$= \sum_{j=1}^{J} (\hat{P}_j - \hat{P}_{j+1})[(A_j + A_{j+1})/2],$$

(11.125)

where $\hat{P}_{J+1} \equiv 0$ and $A_{J+1} \equiv C^{\max}$. The Spearman–Karber estimator $\hat{\mu}_{SK}$ has been shown to be a uniform minimum variance unbiased estimator and a nonparametric maximum likelihood estimator of the discretized mean of the WTP distribution (Miller, 1973; Church and Cobb, 1973). Morgan (1992) gives the formula for the variance of $\hat{\mu}_{SK}$, from which a confidence interval can be constructed. Hamilton et al. (1977) proposed that $\hat{\mu}_{SK}$ could be made more robust by first trimming the data, dropping, say, 5% or 10% of the observations corresponding to the lowest and highest bids. Morgan reviews the results of a number of simulation studies comparing alternative estimators and concludes that a moderately trimmed Spearman–Karber estimator is often a good general-purpose estimator of the mean of a quantal response distribution. In contrast, the Kaplan–Meier–Turnbull measure $\hat{\mu}_{KMT}$ is an estimator of a *lower bound* on the mean of the WTP distribution, C^+, since it is constructed from a lower bound on the graph of $H(A) = [1 - G_C(A)]$. This makes it a conservative estimate if the mean is the chosen welfare measure. Carson et al. (1994) give the formula for the variance of $\hat{\mu}_{KMT}$, from which a confidence interval can be obtained.

Nonparametric or semiparametric estimation of the response probability distribution fundamentally changes the nature of bid design in CV experiments. With parametric response models, the probability distribution is given (assumed by the researcher) and has some small number of parameters which are to be estimated from the data. The bid design takes the distribution into account and makes an initial assumption about the parameter values; in those circumstances, a small number of well-placed design points suffices to provide good estimates of the parameters. Nonparametric or semiparametric response models eliminate the crutch of a predetermined distributional form, resorting instead to a greatly expanded number of parameters to represent the response distribution. Indeed, with the Ayer et al., Coslett, Klein and Spady, or Turnbull estimators, the design points literally determine all that can be known about the response distribution, as Figure 11.5(a) illustrates. Even more than with parametric models, the optimal design depends crucially on what the researcher wants to estimate—the mean, the median, or some other quantile of the WTP distribution.

If the goal is to estimate median WTP and it is possible to vary the bids between experiments, the classic sequential estimator of C^* is the 'up and down' estimator (Dixon and Mood, 1948; Dixon, 1965). In the single-bounded version, one starts with an initial bid, A, obtains some CV responses, computes the proportion of 'yes' responses, $\hat{P}$, and then revises the bid if $\hat{P} \neq 0.5$; the bid is raised by some predetermined amount if $\hat{P} > 0.5$, and lowered if $\hat{P} < 0.5$, and the sequence is repeated until convergence. Modifications designed to make the estimate of C^* more robust or efficient include incorporating an initial delay, corresponding to excluding initial trials (Brownlee et al., 1953), and allowing the step length to decrease as the iterations progress (Cochran and Davis, 1965). There is now an extensive literature on nonparametric sequential estimation of C^*, which is summarized in Morgan (1992).

If sequential estimation is impossible and one is restricted to a single bid vector, Muller and Schmitt (1990) recommend identifying an interval in which C^* is expected to fall and then using as many bid points as possible evenly dispersed over this interval, with only one or a few observations at each bid. McFadden (1994) gives similar advice for estimating C^+—he recommends a relatively large number of closely-spaced bids, spread widely over the interval $[C^{\min}, C^{\max}]$. There certainly is some logic to both recommendations. The fewer the design points, the cruder is the interpolation required to pin down C^*. And, since C^+ depends on the shape of the WTP distribution over its entire length, maximizing the number of bid levels maximizes the number of points at which the WTP distribution is observed. Indeed, this would minimize the bias of estimated mean WTP. But, in our view the argument does not pay enough attention to the *variance* of the estimated response proportions. With a fixed total sample size, when there is an increase in the number of distinct bid levels, J, the number of observations at each bid declines, thereby raising the variance associated with the estimated $\hat{P}_j$. Moreover, the increase in var($\hat{P}_j$) raises the likelihood that some of the observed $\hat{P}_j$'s will violate the monotonicity requirement, thereby causing the pool-adjacent-violators algorithm to shrink the effective number of bid levels and dilute the information associated with the bids that were pooled. These considerations are not adequately addressed in either paper. Just how one should balance the benefits from having many distinct bid points against the benefits from having a reasonable number of observations at each point remains an open question that merits further research.

11.4.4.4 *Concluding observations on nonparametric estimation*

There is currently much interest in nonparametric and semi-parametric approaches to the analysis of discrete-response CV data. Compared to parametric models, these are more robust against possible misspecification of the response probability distribution, and they offer the least restricted characterization of what the data have to say. Whether or not this makes much of a difference in practice depends partly on the goal of the analysis. The experience to date suggests that the estimates of median WTP obtained using nonparametric or semiparametric estimation do not differ greatly from those obtained with a parametric approach; however, the estimates of mean

WTP can differ considerably. Moreover, the lack of structure implied by the nonparametric or semiparametric approach entails some costs as well as some benefits. Since there is no parametric specification of the underlying RUM model, it is not possible to extrapolate from the observed CV responses to the measurement of other items not directly covered in the survey. For example, one cannot derive an estimate of the WTA distribution from the fitted WTP distribution as indicated in footnote 33. The nonparametric and semiparametric estimators are often computationally demanding and, as noted above, some of them make it difficult to include covariates besides the bid. Moreover, in the absence of a parametric structure it may be difficult or impossible to model response effects using the approaches described in Section 11.4.3.

11.4.5   Analysis of non-response bias

There are two general classes of non-response: unit non-response, where survey recipients may simply choose not to respond to the survey at all, and item non-response, where they may choose to not answer certain questions, either out of protest, or because the questions are too difficult, time-consuming, or confusing. Bias occurs when non-responses are not random over the sample population, but instead are correlated with WTP. Although a survey researcher cannot fully account for this bias without collecting responses from the non-respondents, there are techniques available for addressing the component of non-response bias that can be linked to observable socio-demographic or attitudinal characteristics.

11.4.5.1   Unit non-response

Let the total number of survey recipients be n. For each recipient i, let R_i be an indicator which equals one if the recipient responds to the survey and zero if the recipient does not respond. Then, if y_i is the zero/one response to the WTP question, and P_i is the probability of a positive response, we can write the log-likelihood function as follows:

$$\ln L = \sum_{i=1}^{n} R_i[y_i \ln P_i + (1 - y_i)\ln (1 - P_i)], \qquad (11.126)$$

which is simply the sum of the individual log-likelihood functions for units that responded to the survey. The consistency of the maximum likelihood estimators is dependent on the response mechanism which determines $\mathbf{R} = (R_1, \cdots, R_i, \cdots, R_n)$. If $\mathbf{R}$ is randomly and independently distributed across survey recipients, and uncorrelated with factors related to WTP, then unit non-response merely enters as an additional level of sampling in the data collection process. That is, instead of the sample size being n, the number of survey recipients, it is m, the number of survey respondents. The response rate then, affects small-sample properties but does not affect the maximum likelihood consistency and efficiency results. If, however, the probability of responding to the survey varies systematically over the sample population, by demographic characteristics, attitudes, or directly by WTP, then maximization of equation (11.120) will result in inconsistent estimation, owing to the heavier influence of certain groups with high response rates, relative to those with low response rates.

The best solution is to minimize nonresponse in the first place, by designing a data collection process which encourages high participation rates for all groups. This aside, the researcher must rely on what she knows about the characteristics of the population and the sample, and on what she knows or can assume about the response process, in order to infer something about the characteristics of the non-respondents, A key issue is whether, conditional on the observed covariates, members of the sample are missing from the set of respondents at random or not at random (Little and Rubin, 1987). If they are missing at random, there is an unconfounded probability process with $\Pr(R \mid Y) = \Pr(R)$, and $\Pr(R_i = 1 \mid Y) > 0$ for all i and all possible Y, where $Y = (y_1, \ldots, y_i, \ldots, y_n)$. Furthermore, assume that the response probabilities are all equal, positive, and independent, so that the response mechanism is an independent Bernoulli sampling process with the probability of response, $\Phi > 0$. Given the number of survey respondents, m, and the total number of survey recipients, n, we have $\Pr(R_i = 1) = m/n$, or $E(R_i) = m/n$ for all i. Then, taking the expectation of (11.126), we have:

$$E(\ln L) = \left(\frac{m}{n}\right) E \sum_{i=1}^{n} [y_i \ln P_i + (1 - y_i) \ln (1 - P_i)], \qquad (11.127)$$

which shows that maximum likelihood estimation is, on average, unaffected by non-responses drawn from an unconfounded probability responding mechanism. The unit non-responses represent an additional level of sampling which reduces the total sample size, but does not distort the maximum likelihood estimation in any systematic manner.

It is likely, however, that the probability of response is correlated with demographics, and possibly other unobservable factors which are correlated with WTP responses. Taking the expectation of (11.126) in this case does not eliminate the variation in **R** across individuals. Thus, maximum likelihood estimation will be inconsistent unless the weights imposed by **R** are appropriately adjusted with a weighting scheme. We might therefore, assume that the response probabilities are functions of the demographics only, and that within groups stratified by characteristics such as age, education, and income, the responses follow an unconfounded probability responding mechanism, but that between groups the responding mechanisms are not unconfounded. In this case, we can write the likelihood function as:

$$\ln L = \sum_{h=1}^{H} \ln L_h,$$ (11.128)

or

$$\ln L = \sum_{i=1}^{H} \sum_{i=1}^{n_h} R_{hi}[y_i \ln P_i + (1 - y_i) \ln (1 - P_i)]$$ (11.129)

where $h = 1, \ldots, H$ represents all the demographic categories, and n_h represents the sample size of demographic group h. Within a group h, we have $E(R_{hi}) = m_h/n_h$.

If we specify weight adjustments w_h, so that the different groups carry the same weight as they do in the sample population, then we overcome the problem. In particular, we let

$$w_h = \frac{n_h/n}{m_h/m},$$ (11.130)

where m_h/m is the response rate for category h in the sample, and n_h/n is the relative weight of category h in the sample population. The weighted likelihood function is:

$$\ln L^w = \sum_{h=1}^{H} w_h \sum_{i=1}^{n_h} R_{hi}[y_i \ln P_i + (1 - y_i) \ln (1 - P_i)]$$ (11.131)

and the expectation of this likelihood function is given by (11.127). Thus, the stratified weighting scheme can remove the unit non-response distortions in the sample, provided that the stratification fully accounts for the distorted response rates.

11.4.5.2   Item non-response

If there are systematic differences between those who do and do not respond to the WTP question, there will be bias in the estimation of mean or median WTP. The only way to prevent this bias is to collect a complete sample at the start. Short of this, the most common practical remedy for item non-response is imputation. This is where values are imputed for the missing responses using existing information about the respondents and some prediction method based on the responses provided by the other survey respondents.

Imputation is a dangerous art. By substituting predicted values for the missing values, one creates a complete data set, but the data set lacks the variability found in a truly complete data set. The imputed values are typically predicted values based on some model derived from the existing data. But these models will not account for any differences between respondents and non-respondents. The researcher must therefore make assumptions, based on prior information, about the non-respondents' behaviour; either they are assumed to be no different, or they are assumed to be different in some specific, quantifiable way. Either way, it is clear that the assumptions made by the researcher and the resulting predictive model used for imputation will not adequately substitute for the real data. Several alternative procedures have been used that provide a greater amount of variability in imputed responses. One alternative is to use a hot deck procedure, of which there are several varieties,[128] where it is assumed that non-respondents and respondents within a classification group follow the same distribution, and the missing values are imputed by drawing randomly from the existing data within the corresponding classification groups and substituting the drawn responses for the missing values.

Another method, which provides more variability of responses, is the multiple imputation method (see Rubin, 1987). Here, multiple data sets are created using different imputation algorithms, and estimation is performed separately, using each data set. The collection of resulting estimates should be stable in terms of their expected values, but should demonstrate adequate variability for inference purposes.

As indicated, the imputation procedure chosen is based on the instincts of the survey researcher about the behaviour of the non-respondents. The validity of the imputations is not verifiable unless actual responses are eventually obtained from the non-respondents. The researcher must therefore be careful about making assumptions and using point estimates derived from the imputed values based on these assumptions. Alternatively, the researcher must be careful about making inferences using estimates derived without accounting for the missing responses, because these estimates might be systematically biased.

It is impossible to be certain about survey non-response biases. In order to adjust for biases in survey responses, the researcher must make assumptions about what types of bias exist must and believe these biases can be addressed using other information, either theoretical or empirical. If assumptions are correct, then the resulting adjusted estimation is an improvement over the unadjusted estimation. Unfortunately, in the case of non-response, the researcher is unable to verify assumptions. We recommend examining the sensitivity of WTP estimates to the assumptions made about non-respondents. The greater the variation among estimates, the more cautious one must be about drawing inferences based upon any one, or no, imputation scheme.

11.5. CONCLUSIONS

In this survey of the statistical issues in discrete-response CV, we have sought to emphasize three broad themes: the need for thoughtfulness in modelling

---

[128] See Madow (1983, ch. 14) for a review of hot deck procedures.

the stochastic components of the response model; the importance of modelling the entire data generation mechanism, including the elicitation procedure as well as individual preferences; and the importance of experimental design.

There is some tendency in conventional demand analysis to treat the stochastic component as an afterthought when specifying an economic model, and to focus almost exclusively on the deterministic component. The stochastic component is assumed to arise outside the economic model and to have no real significance for the economic interpretation of the statistical results. In RUM models, including those used for discrete-response CV, the situation is different. The stochastic component is an essential part of the economic model; it interacts with the deterministic component and materially affects the model's implications for the prediction of behaviour and the evaluation of welfare. Therefore, both components need to be taken seriously by the researcher. This is illustrated by our analysis in Section 11.2.3 of issues that arise in restricting the distribution of the stochastic components in order to ensure that the indirect utility function is monotone increasing in q. Another example is welfare measurement; with discrete-response CV data one ends up estimating the entire WTP distribution and, as noted in Section 11.2.4, the welfare measures—especially the mean—can be highly sensitive to the specification of the response probability model. Until recently, the CV literature generally used two-parameter probability distributions, with a single location parameter (modelled as a function of covariates) and a single scale parameter. There is growing awareness that this is too restrictive; one often needs multi-parameter probability models that permit more flexibility in the shape of the WTP distribution. There are many possible ways to accomplish this, including inserting a spike at one or both tails of the WTP distribution, adding an overdispersion parameter, making the distribution heteroscedastic, or using models of thick indifference curves or preference uncertainty. One can also use various multi-parameter generalizations of the logistic or related distributions, or switch to a nonparametric approach. The next step in CV research will be comparative analysis, testing the alternative approaches against one another with a view to identifying which might work best in different circumstances.

Another recent development is the growing interest in alternative ways to elicit preferences, including discrete-response CV formats in which individuals can respond with varying degrees of confidence or certainty, and other procedures such as contingent choice, contingent ranking, scaling or other forms of conjoint analysis, and multiattribute utility assessment. These are seen as either alternatives to referendum CV or supplements that can be combined with it in a single interview. We certainly encourage methodological pluralism for the purpose of discovering which approaches work well with different items and different types of people. We have three general observations to offer.

First, it is important to decide whether the goal of the exercise is to value a particular item or to estimate an entire valuation function, since that greatly influences the choice of elicitation procedure. There is a tradeoff since, although estimating an entire valuation function may be more useful, it is also more costly. To value multiple items with the same precision as a single item, either one must increase the number of observations collected, or one must assume that preferences for the items are related to one another in a specific way through a single, underlying hedonic utility model. The hedonic approach makes it possible to value multiple items without more observations, but at the cost of imposing a maintained assumption about preferences which could be inaccurate or unduly restrictive.

Second, when using alternative elicitation formats one should not be surprised that different formats yield different estimates of preferences. In fact one should expect this, because the cognitive demands are not identical. People find choice different than ranking, ranking the top items different than ranking all items, rating different than ranking, matching different than choice, and open-ended CV different than closed-ended CV. Some critics of CV have asserted that one should expect the same results regardless of the elicitation procedure.[129] In our view, this is like asserting that words should have the same meaning regardless of context; it misunderstands the nature of both the organism and the process. At any rate, the evidence in market research as well as environmental valuation overwhelmingly rejects procedural or task invariance.[130] In consequence, the researcher should contemplate modelling the response process itself in combination with the underlying preferences—in effect, the complete data-generating process. This can be done through heteroscedastic models in which the variance of the individual's utility for an item is non-constant, reflecting features of the individual, the item, or the elicitation task; examples are the heteroscedastic models used in choice experiments, (11.82b), rankings, (11.86), and double-bounded CV, (11.107). Other ways to incorporate response effects or cognitive burdens in surveys include the models with background probability of saying 'yes', (11.104) and (11.111), the model of thick indifference curves, (11.112), and the preference uncertainty model, (11.118).

Third, while we favour experimentation, we believe that researchers should resist the temptation of going too far in maximizing the amount of information collected per subject. One reason is cognitive limits. There is no free lunch in collecting information from subjects; wearying them or asking for more precision than they can supply becomes counterproductive. This is

---

[129] 'If people really have this willingness-to-pay, they should shine through. They should shine through these little variations' (Hausman 1993, p. 214).

[130] In addition to cognitive impacts, changing the wording of a question or the survey context may substantively affect the commodity that is being valued. Specifying the item less precisely may signify a wider class of environmental commodities; leaving the timing of commitment more flexible makes the item more economically valuable.

STATISTICAL ANALYSIS OF DISCRETE-RESPONSE CV DATA 409

why we prefer closed- to open-ended CV questions.[131] A second reason is the danger of an inadequately sized sample. Collecting more information from fewer subjects may reduce survey costs, but it is a fragile strategy because, while there is likely to be considerable heterogeneity in preferences between individuals, successive responses from the same subject are unlikely to capture the inter-individual variability. Indeed, successive responses are likely to be correlated because of fatigue or learning, because of anchoring phenomena, or because framing or other factors create individual-specific effects. Consequently, for the purpose of modelling preferences in a population, 100 subjects each valuing twenty items may provide much less information than 1,000 subjects each valuing two items.

In addition to experimentation with alternative elicitation procedures, there is much interest in comparing preferences elicited in surveys with those exhibited in actual (non-experimental) behaviour. In transportation, where much of the research originated, the term *stated preference* is used to describe the elicitation of preferences through surveys or experiments, in contrast to *revealed preference* for the observation of actual behaviour from which preferences are inferred.[132] It is useful to make a distinction between comparisons involving the *same* task performed in different settings, versus comparisons involving *different* tasks that are derived from the same underlying utility function. Examples of the former are comparing referendum CV responses with voting in actual referendum elections, comparing stated preference choices with actual market choices, or comparing self-predictions of demand behaviour with realized demand behaviour.[133] Examples of the latter are comparing CV with realized demand behaviour, or comparing stated preference rankings with actual market choices.

The practice of comparing the results from CV with those from revealed preference goes back to the very first CV study, an open-ended survey of visitors to the Maine woods (Davis 1963); Knetsch and Davis (1966) compared the estimate of WTP with that from a travel cost study and found almost no difference. The first closed-ended CV study, by Bishop and Heberlein (1979), also contained a comparison with a travel cost study,

[131] Also, the open-ended format is significantly less incentive-compatible than the closed-ended format (Hoehn and Randall, 1987; Arrow *et al.*, 1993), and subjects tend to respond to open-ended CV questions by estimating what the item might cost rather than their WTP (Schkade and Payne, 1994).

[132] The use of stated preference in transportation was the subject of special issues of the *Journal of Transport Economics and Policy* Volume XXII, No. 1 (January 1988) and *Transportation* Volume 21, No. 2 (May 1994); its use in market research was the subject of a special issue of the *Journal of Business Research*, Volume 24, No. 2 (March 1992). Morikawa (1989) is a seminal work in transportation; Hensher (1994) provides a summary of the transportation literature.

[133] Constructing a utility model for analysing consumers' assessments of their response to possible price changes—sometimes called *contingent behaviour*—and comparing or combining these with data on their realized demand behaviour is discussed in Dickie, Fisher and Gerking (1987), Hanemann and Chapman (1988), Carson, Hanemann, and Steinberg (1990), Cameron (1992), Chapman *et al.* (1993), Englin and Cameron (1996), and Loomis (1996).

and obtained similar results.[134] However, those were comparisons of reduced-form estimates of WTP; instead, Hanemann (1984a) argued for a structural approach in which one tests for consistency across tasks by reference to a given, underlying utility function that is used to model the responses to each task. In a comparison of CV with travel cost, for example, the CV response is generated by an indirect utility function, as in (11.4) or (11.6a), while the recreation demand function is generated by applying Roy's identity to the indirect utility function:

$$x_i = h^i(p, q, y, s, \epsilon) = -\frac{\partial v(p, q, y, s, \epsilon)/\partial p_i}{\partial v(p, q, y, s, \epsilon)/\partial y}. \qquad (11.132)$$

Consequently, there is a mapping between the ordinary demand functions which underpin revealed preference analysis and the WTP function which underpins stated preference analysis; specifying a particular model for one implies a particular model for the other.[135] This structural approach has now become the standard for comparing or combining preferences elicited through alternative procedures.[136] There is one key limitation: a utility model of the form

$$u = T[v(p, q, y, s, \varepsilon), q] \qquad (11.133)$$

yields the *same* ordinary demand functions for market goods, $h^i(p, q, y, s, \varepsilon)$, as the utility function $v(p, q, y, s, \varepsilon)$ because the ratio of price and income derivatives is the same, while producing *different* WTP functions, $C(p, q, y, s, \varepsilon)$. The revealed preference approach based on integrating an observed system of ordinary demand functions to obtain the underlying utility function is *incapable* of recovering transformations such as $T[\cdot, q]$ in (11.133). Therefore, it omits the portion of WTP which is associated with the second argument of the $T[\cdot, q]$.[137] This must be taken into consideration when comparing results from stated and revealed preference approaches.

However, while adopting a model-based approach, much of the current CV literature comparing stated and revealed preference still pays limited attention to the stochastic specification of the RUM model. Researchers typically assume that the stochastic structure is identical across elicitation

---

[134] This is fairly general finding in the literature. Carson *et al.* (1996) survey over 80 studies containing several hundred comparisons between estimates of WTP based on CV and revealed preference; the results are often fairly close and, overall, the CV estimates are slightly lower.

[135] McConnell (1990) showed how this works, identifying the observable implications of an income-compensation function for ordinary demand functions; see also Whitehead (1995).

[136] Examples include Jakus and Smith (1992), Eom and Smith (1994), Jakus (1994), Chen (1994), and Dickie and Gerking (1996).

[137] McConnell (1983) and Hanemann (1988) equate the unrecovered component with what Krutilla (1967) had called *existence* value, also known as *nonuse* or *passive use* value. The failure to recover $T[., q]$ from observed ordinary demand functions arises from optimization at the margin by consumers, i.e. what Hanemann (1984b) calls their *continuous* choices. If they make discrete or mixed discrete/continuous choices, $T[., q]$ is in principle recoverable from revealed preference data.

tasks and across settings (e.g. hypothetical versus actual markets), and focus exclusively on consistency with respect to the deterministic components of the model. Transportation researchers, by contrast, have allowed for differences in variances when comparing or combining RUM preferences across tasks or settings, along the lines of the heteroscedastic logit model, (11.82b). In discrete choice experiments, they find that the variances typically *do* differ. If the heteroscedasticity is taken into account, the deterministic components of the RUM model often turn out to be consistent across tasks or settings, but not if the heteroscedasticity is ignored.[138] The need to allow for heteroscedasticity could arise because of the cognitive differences mentioned above, differences in task performance (e.g. due to attentiveness or strategic behaviour), differences in perception of the commodity (e.g. there may be a different degree of heterogeneity in perceptions of attributes for hypothetical versus actual choices, depending on how this is controlled in the stated preference exercise), or statistical factors such as differences in the degree of variation among the attributes in stated versus revealed preference. Several studies have found that the revealed preference data sometimes contain more noise and, without rescaling of variances, produce less reliable estimates of model parameters than the stated preference data (Morikawa, 1989; Adamowicz *et al.*, 1994).

While heteroscedastic models have clearly proved their worth, we believe that it may be useful to consider a wider range of models. Examples include models such as (11.104) or (11.111) where the background probability of saying 'yes' varies with the task or setting; the model in (11.112) where the width-of-indifference parameter varies with the context; or a model such as (11.118) where the extent of preference uncertainty varies with the context. For the purpose of comparing or combining stated and revealed preference data, it may pay to use specifications covering all facets of the data generation process that could vary with the task or the setting.

Since stated preference involves data collection in an experimental rather than observational mode, experimental design is an important component of the research process. Experience has shown that careful attention to the statistical design of the CV study, no less than the questionnaire design and sampling plan, can have a large payoff in terms of the quality and reliability of the data collected. But, experience also shows that achieving an effective design requires a clear sense of the goals of the research and the preference structure being modelled. Optimal bid designs are generally sensitive to what the researcher wishes to measure—e.g. mean versus median WTP—and to what he knows (or thinks he knows) about the structure of the response probability model.

---

[138] See the chapter by Adamowicz *et al.*, Swait and Adamowicz (1996), or Louviere (1996), who contends that allowing variances to change has brought about a 'rescaling revolution'.

Current practice in CV research draws on two distinct bodies of design literature. One is the literature on fractional factorial designs (Winer, 1971). This deals with the problem of estimating the effects of several factors on a dependent variable where there may be several possible levels of each factor and the factors can, in principle, vary independently. This creates a large number of potential combinations among the factors. The aim in fractional sampling is to reduce the number of sampling designs by varying several factors simultaneously, instead of experimenting with them one at a time. The typical situation where this arises is the estimation of the models discussed in Section 11.4.1 for valuing multiple items. The problem arises with linear regression as well as with nonlinear response probability models, and is essentially one of dimensionality reduction. Look-up tables can be consulted to find a parsimonious design with certain given properties regarding the interaction effects the researcher wishes to estimate (Green, 1974; Louviere, 1988). The other literature concerns optimal dose design in bioassay, which underpins our discussion of optimal bid design in Section 11.3.5. The context there is estimating the effect of a continuous exogenous variable (the bid) on the discrete CV response, where the response probability is a *nonlinear* function of the bid variable. In consequence, the asymptotic variance–covariance matrix for the parameters of the response probability distribution is itself a function of those parameters. The challenge is to choose design levels for the bid that will minimize the variance (or some related statistic) of the parameter estimates, or the welfare measure constructed from them.

In fact, when one takes a hedonic approach to valuing multiple items, *both* problems tend to arise. On the one hand, CV responses depend on the price associated with each item, which in principle is a continuous variable that must be specified for the purpose of the experiment. On the other hand, preferences for the items depend on their characteristics, which are apt to be sufficiently multi-dimensional as to require some dimensionality reduction. We see combining the two traditions of experimental design in order to facilitate improved estimation of hedonic valuation models as an important area for future CV research.

One of our main themes has been the need to model the entire response process in CV, including the elicitation procedure as well as individual preferences. So far, most of the experimental design research in CV has not adopted this perspective, focusing on the modelling of preferences rather than elicitation procedures, and working off standard, simple response models such as the linear logit model (15), rather than the more complex models discussed in much of this chapter. We see bid design for models of the entire response process as another important area for future CV research.

We end with a word of caution. Good experimental design is rooted not just in statistics but also in survey research. This is because there may always be some limit to what information a researcher is able to convey to subjects, and what she can get them to believe about an item. Those limits constrain what experiments she can design. One usually discovers the limits the hard way, by testing the instrument using various cognitive survey techniques. In this chapter we have focused on what economic theory and statistics have to say about designing discrete-response CV experiments. The third leg on which CV stands is survey research. What makes CV such an interesting subject to study is the practical interplay between economics, statistics, and survey research.

APPENDIX   MAXIMUM LIKELIHOOD ALGORITHMS

In general, optimization algorithms are iterative procedures that begin with a starting value for θ and update the estimate at each iteration using some rule of the form:

$$\theta_{t+1} = \theta_t + \lambda_t \Delta_t, \tag{11A.1}$$

where t represents the iteration number, Δ represents the direction vector and λ represents step size. The various algorithms use different specifications for Δ and λ, and vary in their complexity and convergence properties. When the likelihood function is globally concave, as with the models discussed in this chapter, the Newton–Raphson method is a popular, effective choice. It is based on the linear Taylor series expansion of the first-order condition around θ_0:

$$\frac{\partial L(\theta)}{\partial \theta} = L_\theta = L_\theta^0 + H^0(\theta - \theta_0) = 0, \tag{11A.2}$$

where the superscript 0 indicates that the function is evaluated at $\theta = \theta_0$, L_θ is the first derivative of the log-likelihood function with respect to the parameter vector, θ (also known as the score vector or gradient vector) and H is the Hessian matrix of second derivatives of the log-likelihood function:

$$H = \frac{\partial^2 \ln L(\theta)}{\partial \theta \partial \theta'}. \tag{11A.3}$$

Solving for θ as a function of θ_0 gives

$$\theta = \theta_0 + (H^0)^{-1} L_\theta^0. \tag{11A.4}$$

Letting $\theta_t = \theta_0$ and $\theta_{t+1} = \theta$ gives the Newton–Raphson procedure:

$$\theta_{t+1} = \theta_t + (H^t)^{-1} L_\theta^t. \tag{11A.5}$$

A disadvantage of this procedure is that it uses the second derivative matrix, H, which can be difficult to derive analytically and can easily be the source of errors.[139] It also does not always perform well when the current estimate is very far from the maximum. For the cases of logit and probit, however, the Hessian matrix, H, is positive definite for all values of θ, so the algorithm should always converge.

Other methods are based on (11A.5) but use different expressions for H. The method of scoring, for example, uses the negative of the Fisher information matrix for H:

$$\theta_{t+1} = \theta_t + (-I^t)^{-1} L_\theta^t. \tag{11A.6}$$

The information matrix is the negative of the expected value of the Hessian matrix $(-E(H^{-1}))$ and must be derived analytically. In the case of the logit model, the Hessian is independent of the response vector so that $E(H) = H$, and the method of scoring is equivalent to the Newton–Raphson method.

The Berndt *et al.* (1994) method, uses the outer product of the gradient vector for H:

$$\theta_{t+1} = \theta_t + (L_\theta^t L_{\theta'}^t)^{-1} L_\theta^t. \tag{11A.7}$$

This choice has the advantage of being always positive semi-definite (for any functional form) and less burdensome to derive analytically because it does not involve the second derivative matrix. Furthermore, Berndt *et al.* (1974) have shown that the outer product of the score vector is a consistent estimator for the information matrix.

Another popular algorithm is the Davidon–Fletcher–Powell (DFP) method, which is in the class of quasi-Newton methods. This method starts with an approximation of H (sometimes the identity matrix, sometimes the result of the Berndt *et al.* method), and updates the estimate of H at each iteration using the previous estimate of H and an estimate of the change in the first-derivative vector as a numerical substitute for the second derivative. In a sense, at each iteration, 'information' is added to the estimate of H. The DFP method has excellent convergence properties, but because of its iterative approach to estimating H it cannot approximate the Hessian well when only a few iterations are made. Although this method generally takes more iterations to converge than the Newton–Raphson method, if numerical derivatives are being used, the DFP method can converge more quickly.

---

[139] Numerical derivatives are obtained by taking the difference between a function at two arbitrarily close points. They require twice as many function evaluations as analytical derivatives and can be computationally time-consuming.

Appendix Table 1. Single-bounded discrete response Probability models

(a) Box–Cox model $C = y - \left[y^\lambda - \frac{\alpha}{b} - \frac{\eta}{b} \right]^{1/\lambda}$ $a > 0$ $b > 0$

    (i) η standard normal

$$Pr\{\text{`yes'}\} = \Phi\left(\alpha - by^\lambda + b(y - A)^\lambda \right)$$

    (ii) η standard logistic

$$Pr\{\text{`yes'}\} = \left[1 + e^{by^\lambda - b(y-A)^\lambda - \alpha} \right]^{-1}$$

(b)   Linear model $C = \frac{\alpha + \eta}{\beta}$

    (i) η standard normal (probit model)

$$Pr\{\text{`yes'}\} = \Phi(\alpha - \beta A)$$

    (ii) η standard logistic (logit model)

$$Pr\{\text{`yes'}\} = \left[1 + e^{-\alpha + \beta A} \right]^{-1}$$

    (iii) η standard lognormal

$$Pr\{\text{`yes'}\} = \Phi[-\ln(-\alpha + \beta A)]$$

    (iv) η standard log-logistic

$$Pr\{\text{`yes'}\} = [1 - \alpha + \beta A]^{-1}$$

    (v) η standard Weibull

$$Pr\{\text{`yes'}\} = e^{-(-\alpha + \beta A)^c}   \quad c > 0$$

(c)   Log-model $C = y\left[1 - e^{\frac{(\alpha + \eta)}{\beta}} \right]$

    (i) η standard normal

$$Pr\{\text{`yes'}\} = \Phi\left(\alpha + \beta \ln\left(1 - \frac{A}{y} \right) \right)$$

    (ii) η standard logistic

$$Pr\{\text{`yes'}\} = \left[1 + e^{-\alpha}\left(1 - \frac{A}{y} \right)^{-\beta} \right]^{-1}$$

(d)   Multiplicative model $C = e^{(\alpha + \varepsilon)/\beta}$

    (i) ε standard normal (lognormal probability model)

$$Pr\{\text{`yes'}\} = \Phi(\alpha - \beta \ln A)$$

(ii) ε standard logistic (log-logistic probability model)

$$\Pr\{\text{'yes'}\} = \frac{1}{1 + e^{-\alpha + \beta \ln A}}$$

(iii) ε standard extreme value (Weibull probability model)

$$\Pr\{\text{'yes'}\} = \exp\left[-e^{-\alpha + \beta \ln A}\right]$$

Appendix Table 2.   Canonical response probability models satisfying $C \varepsilon [0, y]$

(a)   Multiplicative model $C = e^{(\alpha + \varepsilon)/\beta}$

    (1) *Truncation at $\varepsilon^{\max}$*

        (i) ε standard normal

$$\Pr\{\text{'yes'}\} = 1 - \frac{\Phi(-\alpha + \beta \ln A)}{\Phi(-\alpha + \beta \ln y)}$$

$$C^+ = y - \frac{1}{\Phi(-\alpha + \beta \ln y)} \int_0^y \Phi(-\alpha + \beta \ln A) dA$$

$$C^* \text{solves: } \Phi(-\alpha + \beta \ln(C^*)) = \frac{1}{2}\Phi(-\alpha + \beta \ln y)$$

        (ii) ε standard logistic

$$\Pr\{\text{'yes'}\} = 1 - \frac{1 + e^{\alpha - \beta \ln y}}{1 + e^{\alpha - \beta \ln A}}$$

$$C^+ = y - (1 + e^\alpha y^{-\beta}) \int_0^y (1 + e^\alpha A^{-\beta})^{-1} dA$$

$$C^* = e^{\frac{\alpha - \ln\left(1 + 2e^\alpha y^{-\beta}\right)}{\beta}}$$

        (iii) ε standard extreme value

$$\Pr\{\text{'yes'}\} = 1 - \frac{\exp\left(-e^{\alpha - \beta \ln A}\right)}{\exp\left(-e^{\alpha - \beta \ln y}\right)}$$

$$C^+ = y - e^{e^\alpha y^{-\beta}} \int_0^y e^{-e^\alpha A^{-\beta}} dA$$

$$C^* = e^{\frac{\alpha - \ln\left(\ln(2) + e^\alpha y^{-\beta}\right)}{\beta}}$$

    (2) *Spike at $\varepsilon^{\max}$*

        (i) ε normal

$$\Pr\{\text{'yes'}\} = \begin{array}{ll} \Phi(\alpha - \beta \ln A) & \text{if } A < y \\ 0 & \text{if } A \geq y \end{array}$$

$$C^+ = \int_0^y \Phi(\alpha - \beta A) dA$$

$$C^* = \min\left(y, e^{\alpha/\beta}\right)$$

(ii) ε logistic

$$\Pr\{\text{‘yes’}\} = \begin{matrix} \left[1 + e^{-\alpha+\beta \ln A}\right]^{-1} & \text{if } A < y \\ 0 & \text{if } A \geqslant y \end{matrix}$$

$$C^+ = \int_0^y \left(1 + e^{-\alpha+\beta \ln A}\right)^{-1} dA$$

$$C^* = \min\left(y, e^{\alpha/\beta}\right)$$

(iii) ε extreme value

$$\Pr\{\text{‘yes’}\} = \begin{matrix} 1 - \exp\left[-e^{\alpha-\beta \ln A}\right] & \text{if } A < y \\ 0 & \text{if } A \geqslant y \end{matrix}$$

$$C^+ = y - \int_0^y \exp\left[-e^{\alpha-\beta \ln A}\right] dA$$

$$C^* = \min\left(y, e^{\alpha/\beta}(\ln 2)^{-1/\beta}\right)$$

(b) **Box–Cox model** $C = y - \left[y^\lambda - \frac{\alpha}{b} - \frac{\eta}{b}\right]^{1/\lambda}$

(1) *Double truncation*
   (i) η beta

$$\Pr\{\text{‘yes’}\} = \int_{by^\lambda - b(y-A)^\lambda - \alpha}^{by^\lambda - \alpha} \left[\frac{(\eta + \alpha)^{\alpha-1}(by^\lambda - \alpha - \eta)^{S-1}}{B(r,s)(by^\lambda)^{r+S-1}}\right] d\eta$$

$$C^+ = \int_0^y \left[\int_{by^\lambda - b(y-A)^\lambda}^{by^\lambda - \alpha} \left[\frac{(\eta + \alpha)^{\alpha-1}(by^\lambda - \alpha - \eta)^{S-1}}{B(r,s)(by^\lambda)^{r+s-1}}\right] d\eta\right] dA$$

$$C^* \text{ solves}: \int_{by^\lambda - b(y-C^*)^\lambda - \alpha}^{by^\lambda - \alpha} \left[\frac{(\eta + \alpha)^{\alpha-1}(by^\lambda - \alpha - \eta)^{S-1}}{B(r,s)(by^\lambda)^{r+S-1}}\right] d\eta = 0.5$$

(ii) η standard normal

$$\Pr\{\text{‘yes’}\} = \frac{\Phi(-\alpha + by^\lambda) - \Phi\left(-\alpha + by^\lambda - b(y-A)^\lambda\right)}{\Phi(-\alpha + by^\lambda) - \Phi(-\alpha)}$$

$$C^+ = \frac{1}{\Phi(-\alpha + by^\lambda) - \Phi(-\alpha)}\left[y\Phi(-\alpha + by^\lambda) - \int_0^y \Phi\left(-\alpha + by^\lambda - b(y-A)^\lambda\right) dA\right]$$

$$C^* \text{ solves}: \Phi\left(-\alpha + by^\lambda - b(y-C^*)^\lambda\right) = \frac{\Phi(-\alpha + by^\lambda) + \Phi(-\alpha)}{2}$$

(iii) η standard logistic

$$\Pr\{`yes'\} = \frac{\left[1 + e^{\alpha - by^\lambda}\right]^{-1} - \left[1 + e^{\alpha - by^\lambda + b(y-A)^\lambda}\right]^{-1}}{\left[1 + e^{\alpha - by^\lambda}\right]^{-1} - \left[1 + e^\alpha\right]^{-1}}$$

$$C^+ = \frac{1}{\left[1 + e^{\alpha - by^\lambda}\right]^{-1} - \left[1 + e^\alpha\right]^{-1}} \cdot$$
$$\left(y\left[1 + e^{\alpha - by^\lambda}\right]^{-1} - \int_0^y \left[1 + e^{\alpha - by^\lambda + b(y-A)^\lambda}\right]^{-1} dA\right)$$

$$C^* = y - \left[y^\lambda - \frac{\alpha}{b} + \frac{1}{b}\ln\left(\frac{2}{\left[1 + e^{\alpha - by^\lambda}\right]^{-1} + \left[1 + e^\alpha\right]^{-1}} - 1\right)\right]^{1/\lambda}$$

(2) Spike at $\eta^{\max}$, truncation at $\eta^{\min}$

(i) η standard normal

$$\Pr\{`yes'\} = \begin{array}{ll} \dfrac{\Phi(\alpha - by^\lambda + b(y-A)^\lambda)}{\Phi(\alpha)} & \text{if } A < y \\[2mm] 0 & \text{if } A \geqslant y \end{array}$$

$$C^+ = \frac{1}{\Phi(\alpha)} \int_0^y \Phi\left(\alpha - by^\lambda + b(y-A)^\lambda\right) da$$

$$C^* \text{ solves: } \Phi\left(\alpha - by^\lambda + b(y-C^*)^\lambda\right) = \frac{1}{2}\Phi(\alpha) \quad \text{if } \Phi(\alpha - by^\lambda) < \frac{1}{2}$$
$$C^* = y, \text{ otherwise}$$

(ii) η standard logistic

$$\Pr\{`yes'\} = \begin{array}{ll} \dfrac{1 + e^{-\alpha}}{1 + e^{-\alpha + by^\lambda - b(y-A)^\lambda}} & \text{if } A < y \\[2mm] 0 & \text{if } A \geqslant y \end{array}$$

$$C^+ = (1 + e^{-\alpha}) \int_0^y \left(1 + e^{-\alpha + by^\lambda - b(y-A)^\lambda}\right)^{-1} dA$$

$$C^* = \min\left(y, y - \left[y^\lambda - \frac{\alpha}{b} - \frac{1}{b}\ln(1 + 2e^{-\alpha})\right]^{1/\lambda}\right)$$

(c) Linear model $C = \frac{\alpha + \eta}{\beta}$

(1) Double truncation
(i) η standard normal

$$\Pr\{`yes'\} = \frac{\Phi(\alpha - \beta A) - \Phi(\alpha - \beta y)}{\Phi(\alpha) - \Phi(\alpha - \beta y)} \quad \text{if } 0 \leqslant A \leqslant y$$

$$C^+ = \frac{1}{\Phi(\alpha) - \Phi(\alpha - \beta y)}\left[\int_0^y \Phi(\alpha - \beta A)dA - y\Phi(\alpha - \beta y)\right]$$

$$C^* \text{ solves: } \Phi(\alpha - \beta C^*) = \frac{1}{2}[\Phi(\alpha) + \Phi(\alpha + \beta y)]$$

(ii) η standard logistic

$$\Pr\{\text{`yes'}\} = \frac{[1 + e^{\alpha - \beta y}]^{-1} - [1 + e^{\alpha - \beta A}]^{-1}}{[1 + e^{\alpha - \beta y}]^{-1} - [1 + e^{\alpha}]^{-1}} \quad \text{if } 0 \leqslant A \leqslant y$$

$$C^+ = \frac{1}{[1 + e^{\alpha - \beta y}]^{-1} - [1 + e^{\alpha}]^{-1}}\left(y[1 + e^{\alpha - \beta y}]^{-1} - \int_0^y [1 + e^{\alpha - \beta A}]^{-1}dA\right)$$

$$C^* = \frac{\alpha}{\beta} - \frac{1}{\beta}\ln\left[\frac{2}{[1 + e^{\alpha - \beta y}]^{-1} + [1 + e^{\alpha}]^{-1}} - 1\right]$$

(2) Spike at $\eta^{\max}$, truncation at $\eta^{\min}$

(i) η standard normal

$$\Pr\{\text{`yes'}\} = \begin{matrix} \frac{\Phi(\alpha - \beta A)}{\Phi(\alpha)} & \text{if } 0 \leqslant A < y \\ 0 & \text{if } A \geqslant y \end{matrix}$$

$$C^+ = \frac{1}{\Phi(\alpha)}\int_0^y \Phi(\alpha - \beta A)da$$

$$C^* \text{ solves: } \Phi(\alpha - \beta C^*) = \frac{1}{2}\Phi(\alpha)$$

(ii) η standard logistic

$$\Pr\{\text{`yes'}\} = \begin{matrix} \frac{1 + e^{-\alpha}}{1 + e^{-\alpha + \beta A}} & \text{if } 0 \leqslant A < y \\ 0 & \text{if } A \geqslant y \end{matrix}$$

$$C^+ = (1 + e^{-\alpha})\int_0^y [1 + e^{-\alpha + \beta A}]^{-1}dA$$

$$C^* = \frac{\alpha}{\beta} + \frac{1}{\beta}\ln(1 + 2e^{-\alpha})$$

(d) Log model $C = y\left[1 - e^{-\left(\frac{\alpha + \eta}{\beta}\right)}\right]$

(1) Truncation at $\eta^{\min}$

(i) η standard normal

$$\Pr\{\text{`yes'}\} = \frac{\Phi\left(\alpha + \beta\ln\left(1 - \frac{A}{y}\right)\right)}{\Phi(\alpha)}$$

$$C^+ = \frac{1}{\Phi(\alpha)} \int_0^y \Phi\left(\alpha + \beta\ln\left(1 - \frac{A}{y}\right)\right) dA$$

$$C^* \text{ solves: } \Phi\left(\alpha + \beta\ln\left(1 - \frac{C^*}{y}\right)\right) = \frac{1}{2}\Phi(\alpha)$$

(ii) η standard logistic

$$\Pr\{\text{'yes'}\} = \frac{1 + e^{-\alpha}}{1 + e^{-\alpha}\left(1 - \frac{A}{y}\right)^{-\beta}}$$

$$C^+ = (1 + e^{-\alpha})\left(\int_0^y \left[1 + e^{-\alpha}\left(1 - \frac{A}{y}\right)^{-\beta}\right]^{-1} dA\right)$$

$$C^* = y\left[1 - (2 + e^{\alpha})^{-1/\beta}\right]$$

Appendix Table 3. Response probability models satisfying $C\varepsilon[0, y]$ with a spike at zero

(1) Mixture models

$\Pr\{\text{'yes'}\} = (1 - \gamma) \cdot \Pr\{\text{'yes'}\}$ where $\Pr\{\text{'yes'}\}$ is any of the formulas in Appendix Table 11.2.

(2) Censored models

   (a) Box–Cox model $C = y - \left[y^\lambda - \frac{\alpha}{b} - \frac{\eta}{b}\right]^{\frac{1}{\lambda}}$

      Truncation at $\eta^{\max}$, spike at $\eta^{\min}$

     (i) η standard normal

$$\Pr\{\text{'yes'}\} = \begin{cases} 1 & \text{if } A = 0 \\ 1 - \dfrac{\Phi\left[-\alpha + by^\lambda - b(y - A)^\lambda\right]}{\Phi(-\alpha + by^\lambda)} & \text{if } 0 < A \leqslant y \end{cases}$$

$$C^+ = y - \frac{1}{\Phi(-\alpha + by^\lambda)}\int_0^y \Phi(-\alpha + by^\lambda - b(y - A)^\lambda) dA$$

$$C^* \text{ solves: } 2\Phi\left(-\alpha + by^\lambda - b(y - C^*)^\lambda\right) = \Phi(-\alpha + by^\lambda)$$
$$\text{if } 2\Phi(-\alpha) < \Phi\left(-\alpha + by^\lambda\right)$$

$C^* = 0$ *otherwise*

     (ii) η standard logistic

$$\Pr\{\text{'yes'}\} = \begin{cases} 1 & \text{if } A = 0 \\ 1 - \dfrac{1 + e^{\alpha - by^\lambda}}{1 + e^{\alpha - by^\lambda + b(y - A)^\lambda}} & \text{if } 0 < A \leqslant y \end{cases}$$

$$C^+ = y - \left[1 + e^{\alpha - by^\lambda}\right] \int_0^y \left[1 + e^{\alpha - by^\lambda + b(y-A)^\lambda}\right]^{-1} dA$$

$$C^* = y - \left(\frac{\ln\left(1 + e^{\alpha - by^\lambda}\right)}{b} - \frac{\alpha}{b} + y^\lambda\right)^{1/\lambda} \quad \text{if } e^{-\alpha} + 2e^{-by^\lambda} < 1$$

$$C^* = 0 \quad \text{otherwise}$$

Spike at η^{max} and η^{min}
(i) η standard normal

$$\Pr\{\text{'yes'}\} = \begin{array}{ll} 1 & \text{if } A = 0 \\ \Phi(\alpha - by^\lambda + b(y-A)^\lambda) & \text{if } 0 < A < y \\ 0 & \text{if } A \geqslant y \end{array}$$

$$C^+ = \int_0^y \Phi(\alpha - by^\lambda + b(y-A)^\lambda) \, da$$

$$C^* = \begin{array}{ll} 0 & \text{if } \Phi(-\alpha) \geqslant 1/2 \\ y & \text{if } \Phi(-\alpha + by^\lambda) \leqslant 1/2 \\ \text{solves: } \Phi(-\alpha + by^\lambda - b(y - C^*)^\lambda) = 1/2 & \text{otherwise} \end{array}$$

(ii) η standard logistic

$$\Pr\{\text{'yes'}\} = \begin{array}{ll} 1 & \text{if } A = 0 \\ \left[1 + e^{-\alpha + by^\lambda - b(y-A)^\lambda}\right]^{-1} & \text{if } 0 < A < y \\ 0 & \text{if } A \geq y \end{array}$$

$$C^+ = \int_0^y \left[1 + e^{-\alpha + by^\lambda - b(y-A)^\lambda}\right]^{-1} dA$$

$$C^* = \begin{array}{ll} 0 & \alpha \leqslant 0 \\ 1 & y^\lambda \leqslant \alpha/\beta \\ y - \left(y^\lambda - \dfrac{\alpha}{b}\right)^{1/\lambda} & \text{otherwise} \end{array}$$

(b) *Linear model* $C = \frac{\alpha + \eta}{\beta}$
Truncation at η^{max}, spike at η^{min}
(i) η standard normal

$$\Pr\{\text{'yes'}\} = \begin{array}{ll} 1 & \text{if } A = 0 \\ 1 - \dfrac{\Phi(-\alpha + \beta A)}{\Phi(-\alpha + \beta y)} & \text{if } 0 < A \leqslant y \end{array}$$

$$C^+ = y - \frac{1}{\Phi(-\alpha + \beta y)} \int_0^y \Phi(-\alpha + \beta A) dA$$

$$C^* \text{ solves}: \Phi(-\alpha + \beta C^*) = \frac{\Phi(-\alpha + \beta y)}{2} \quad \text{if } 2\Phi(-\alpha) < \Phi(-\alpha + \beta y)$$

$$C^* = 0 \quad \text{otherwise}$$

(ii) η standard logistic

$$\Pr\{\text{'yes'}\} = \begin{array}{ll} 1 & \text{if } A = 0 \\ 1 - \dfrac{1 + e^{\alpha - \beta y}}{1 + e^{\alpha - \beta A}} & \text{if } 0 < A \leqslant y \end{array}$$

$$C^+ = y - (1 + e^{\alpha - \beta y}) \int_0^y \left[1 + e^{\alpha - \beta A}\right]^{-1} dA$$

$$C^* = \frac{\alpha - \ln(2e^{\alpha - \beta y} + 1)}{\beta} \quad \text{if } e^{-\alpha} + 2e^{-\beta y} < 1$$

$$C^* = 0 \quad \text{otherwise}$$

Spike at $\eta^{\max}$ and $\eta^{\min}$
  (i) η standard normal

$$\Pr\{\text{'yes'}\} = \begin{array}{ll} 1 & \text{if } A = 0 \\ \Phi(\alpha - \beta A) & \text{if } 0 < A < y \\ 0 & \text{if } A \geqslant y \end{array}$$

$$C^+ = \int_0^y \Phi(\alpha - \beta A) da$$

$$C^* = \begin{array}{ll} 0 & \text{if } \Phi(\alpha) \leqslant 1/2 \\ y & \text{if } \Phi(\alpha - \beta y) \geqslant 1/2 \\ \text{solves}: \Phi(\alpha - \beta C^*) = 1/2 & \text{otherwise} \end{array}$$

(ii) η standard logistic

$$\Pr\{\text{'yes'}\} = \begin{array}{ll} 1 & \text{if } A = 0 \\ \left[1 + e^{-\alpha + \beta A}\right]^{-1} & \text{if } 0 < A < y \\ 0 & \text{if } A \geqslant y \end{array}$$

$$C^+ = \int_0^y \left[1 + e^{-\alpha + \beta A}\right]^{-1} dA$$

$$C^* = \begin{array}{ll} 0 & \text{if } \alpha \leqslant 0 \\ y & \text{if } y \leqslant \alpha/\beta \\ \dfrac{\alpha}{\beta} & \text{otherwise} \end{array}$$

(c) *Log model* $C = y\left[1 - e^{-\left(\frac{\alpha + \eta}{\beta}\right)}\right]$
  Spike at $\eta^{\min}$

(i) η standard normal

$$\Pr\{\text{'yes'}\} = \begin{cases} 1 & \text{if } A = 0 \\ \Phi\left(\alpha + \beta\ln\left(1 - \dfrac{A}{y}\right)\right) & \text{if } 0 < A \leqslant y \end{cases}$$

$$C^{+} = \int_{0}^{y} \Phi\left(\alpha + \beta\ln\left(1 - \frac{A}{y}\right)\right) dA$$

$$C^{*} = \begin{cases} 0 & \text{if } \Phi(\alpha) \leqslant 1/2 \\ \text{solves: } \Phi\left(\alpha + \beta\ln\left(1 - \dfrac{C^{*}}{y}\right)\right) = 1/2 & \text{otherwise} \end{cases}$$

(ii) η standard logistic

$$\Pr\{\text{'yes'}\} = \begin{cases} 1 & \text{if } A = 0 \\ \left[1 + e^{-\alpha}\left(1 - \frac{A}{y}\right)^{-\beta}\right]^{-1} & \text{if } 0 < A \leqslant y \end{cases}$$

$$C^{+} = \int_{0}^{y} \left[1 + e^{-\alpha}\left(1 - \frac{A}{y}\right)^{-\beta}\right]^{-1} dA$$

$$C^{*} = \begin{cases} 0 & \text{if } \alpha \leqslant 0 \\ y\left(1 - e^{-\alpha/\beta}\right) & \text{otherwise} \end{cases}$$

Appendix Table 4.   Response probability models satisfying $C \; \varepsilon [-\alpha, y]$

(1) Mixture models $\Pr\{\text{'yes'}\} = \gamma_1[1 - G_-(A)] + \gamma_2\Pr\{\text{'yes'}\}$ where $\Pr\{\text{'yes'}\}$ is any of the formulas in Appendix Table 11.2 and $G_-(x)$ is a cdf for negative preferences as described in connection with equation (11.34).

(2) Box–Cox model $C = y - \left[y^{\lambda} - \frac{\alpha}{b} - \frac{\eta}{b}\right]^{1/\lambda}$

Truncation at $\eta^{\max}$

(i) η standard normal

$$\Pr\{\text{'yes'}\} = 1 - \frac{\Phi\left[-\alpha + by^{\lambda} - (b - A)^{\lambda}\right]}{\Phi(-\alpha + by^{\lambda})}$$

(ii) η standard logistic

$$\Pr\{\text{'yes'}\} = 1 - \frac{\left[1 + e^{\alpha - by^{\lambda} + b(y - A)^{\lambda}}\right]^{-1}}{\left[1 + e^{\alpha - by^{\lambda}}\right]^{-1}}$$

Spike at $\eta^{\max}$

(i) η standard normal

$$\Pr\{\text{'yes'}\} = \begin{cases} \Phi\left[\alpha - by^{\lambda} + b(y - A)^{\lambda}\right] & \text{if } A < y \\ 0 & \text{if } A \geqslant y \end{cases}$$

(ii) η standard logistic

$$\Pr\{\text{`yes'}\} = \begin{matrix} \left[1 + e^{-\alpha + by^\lambda - b(y-A)^\lambda}\right]^{-1} & \text{if } A < y \\ 0 & \text{if } A \geqslant y \end{matrix}$$

(3) Log model $C = y\left[1 + e^{-\left(\frac{\alpha+\eta}{\beta}\right)}\right]$

(i) η standard normal

$$\Pr\{\text{`yes'}\} = \Phi\left(\alpha + \beta\ln\left(1 - \frac{A}{y}\right)\right)$$

(ii) η standard logistic

$$\Pr\{\text{`yes'}\} = \left[1 + e^{-\alpha}\left(1 - \frac{A}{y}\right)^{-\beta}\right]^{-1}$$

(4) Linear model $C = \frac{\alpha+\eta}{\beta}$

Double truncation at $\eta^{\max} = -\alpha + \beta y$ and $\eta^{\min} = -\alpha - \beta y$

(i) η standard normal

$$\Pr\{\text{`yes'}\} = \frac{\Phi(-\alpha + \beta y) - \Phi(-\alpha + \beta A)}{\Phi(-\alpha + \beta y) - \Phi(-\alpha - \beta y)}$$

(i) η standard logistic

$$\Pr\{\text{`yes'}\} = \frac{\left[1 + e^{\alpha - \beta y}\right]^{-1} - \left[1 + e^{\alpha - \beta A}\right]^{-1}}{\left[1 + e^{\alpha - \beta y}\right]^{-1} - \left[1 + e^{\alpha + \beta y}\right]^{-1}}$$

Double spike at $\eta^{\max} = -\alpha + \beta y$ and $\eta^{\min} = -\alpha - \beta y$

(i) η standard normal

$$\Pr\{\text{`yes'}\} = \begin{matrix} 1 & \text{if } A \leqslant -y \\ \Phi(\alpha - \beta A) & \text{if } -y < A < y \\ 0 & \text{if } A \geqslant y \end{matrix}$$

(ii) η standard logistic

$$\Pr\{\text{`yes'}\} = \begin{matrix} 1 & \text{if } A \leqslant -y \\ \left[1 + e^{-\alpha + \beta A}\right]^{-1} & \text{if } -y < A < y \\ 0 & \text{if } A \geqslant y \end{matrix}$$

Truncation at $\eta^{\max}$, spike at $\eta^{\min}$

(i) η standard normal

$$\Pr\{\text{`yes'}\} = \begin{matrix} 1 & \text{if } A \leqslant -y \\ 1 - \dfrac{\Phi(-\alpha + \beta A)}{\Phi(-\alpha + \beta y)} & \text{if } -y < A \leqslant y \end{matrix}$$

(ii) η standard logistic

$$\Pr\{\text{`yes'}\} = \begin{matrix} 1 & \text{if } A \leqslant -y \\ 1 - \dfrac{1 + e^{\alpha - \beta y}}{1 + e^{\alpha - \beta A}} & \text{if } -y < A \leqslant y \end{matrix}$$

Spike at $\eta^{\max}$, truncation at $\eta^{\min}$

(i) η standard normal

$$\Pr\{`yes'\} = \begin{array}{cc} \dfrac{\Phi(\alpha - \beta A)}{\Phi(\alpha + \beta y)} & \text{if } A < y \\[2mm] 0 & \text{if } A \geqslant y \end{array}$$

(ii) η standard logistic

$$\Pr\{`yes'\} = \begin{array}{cc} \dfrac{1 + e^{-\alpha - \beta y}}{1 + e^{-\alpha + \beta A}} & \text{if } A < y \\[2mm] 0 & \text{if } A \geqslant y \end{array}$$

REFERENCES

Abdelbasit, K. M. and Plackett, R. L. (1983), 'Experimental Design for Binary Data', *Journal of the American Statistical Association*, 78, 90–8.

Adamowicz, W., P. C. Boxall, J. J. Louviere, J. Swait, and M. Williams (1996), 'Stated Preference Methods for Valuing Environmental Amenities', Chapter 13 in this volume.

Adamowicz, W., J. Louviere, and M. Williams (1994), 'Combining Revealed and Stated Preference Methods for Valuing Environmental Amenities', *Journal of Environmental Economics and Management*, 26, 271–92.

Aitchison J. and S. D. Silvey (1957), 'The Generalization of Probit Analysis to the Case of Multiple Responses', *Biometrika*, 44, 131–40.

Alberini, A. (1995a), 'Testing Willingness to Pay Models of Discrete Choice Contingent Valuation Data'. *Land Economics*, 71:1, 83–95.

Alberini, A. (1995b), 'Optimal Designs for Discrete Choice Contingent Valuation Surveys: Single-bound, Double-bound and Bivariate Models', *Journal of Environmental Economics and Management*, 28:3, May, 287–306.

Alberini, A. (1995c), 'Efficiency vs Bias of Willingness-to-Pay Estimates: Bivariate and Interval-Data Models', *Journal of Environmental Economics and Management*, 29, 169–80.

Alberini, A. and R. T. Carson (1993), 'Efficient Threshold Values for Binary Discrete Choice Contingent Valuation Surveys and Economic Experiments', Resources for the Future Discussion Paper, Quality of the Environment Division, Washington, D.C.

Alberini, A., B. Kanninen, and R. Carson (1994), 'Random-Effect Models of Willingness to Pay Using Discrete Response CV Survey Data', Resources for the Future Discussion Paper 94–34, Washington, D.C.

Alberini, A., B. Kanninen, and R. Carson (1994), 'Estimating Willingness to Pay with Discrete Choice Contingent Valuation Data Using Error Component Models', presented at the Allied Social Sciences Associations Annual Meeting, Boston MA, January.

Altaf, Mir Anjum and J. R. DeShazo (1994), 'Bid Elicitation in the Contingent Valuation Method: The Double Referendum Format and Induced Strategic

Behavior', working paper, Harvard University, Arts and Sciences, Urban Planning Committee, March.

Amemiya, T. (1980), 'The n^{-2}-Order Mean Squared Errors of the Maximum Likelihood and the Minimum Logit Chi-Square Estimates', *Annals of Statistics*, 8:3, 488–505.

Amemiya, Takeshi (1985), *Advanced Econometrics*, Harvard University Press, Cambridge.

Anderson, E. B. (1970), 'Asymptotic Properties of Conditional Maximum Likelihood Estimators', *Journal of the Royal Statistical Society, Series B* 32, 283–301.

Anderson J. A. and Richardson (1979), 'Logistic Discrimination and Bias Correction in Maximum Likelihood Estimation', *Technometrics*, 21, 71–8.

Aranda-Ordaz, F. J. (1981), 'On Two Families of Transformation to Additivity for Binary Response Data', *Biometrika*, 68, 357–63.

Arnold, Barry C. (1992), 'Multivariate Logistic Distribution' in *Handbook of the Logistic Distribution*, edited by N. Balakrishnan. New York: Marcel Dekker, Inc.

Arrow, K., R. Solow, P. R. Portney, E. E. Leamer, R. Radner, and H. Schuman (1993), 'Report of the NOAA Panel on Contingent Valuation', *Federal Register*, 58:10, 4601–14.

Ashford, J. R. (1959), 'An Approach to the Analysis of Data for Semiquantal Responses in Biological Response', *Biometrics*, 15, 573–81.

Avery, R. B., L. P. Hansen, and V. J. Hotz (1983), 'Multiperiod Probit Models and Orthogonality Condition Estimation', *International Economic Review*, 24, 21–35.

Ayer, M., B. D. Brunk, G. M. Ewing, and E. Silverman (1955), 'An Empirical Distribution Function for Sampling with Incomplete Information', *Annals of Mathematical Statistics*, 26, 641–7.

Barbera, S. and P. K. Pattanaik (1986), 'Falmagne and the Rationalizability of Stochastic Choices in Terms of Random Orderings', *Econometrica*, 54:3, 707–15.

Barlow, R. E., D. J. Bartholomew, J. M. Bremner, and H. D. Brunk (1972), *Statistical Inference Under Order Restrictions*, New York: John Wiley.

Bateman, Ian J., Ian H. Langford, and Jon Rasbash (1996), 'Elicitation Effects in Contingent Valuation Studies', Chapter 15, this volume.

Beggs, S., S. Cardell, and J. Hausman (1981), 'Assessing the Potential Demand for Electric Cars', *Journal of Econometrics*, 16, 1–19.

Ben-Akiva, M. and S. R. Lerman (1985), *Discrete Choice Analysis: Theory and Applications to Travel Demand*, MIT Press, Cambridge.

Ben-Akiva, M. T. Morikawa, and F. Shiroishi (1992), 'Analysis of the Reliability of Preference Ranking Data', *Journal Business Research*, 24, 149–64.

Berkson, J. (1953), 'A Statistically Precise and Relatively Simple Method of Estimating the Bio-Assay with Quantal Response, Based on the Logistic Function', *Journal of the American Statistical Association*, 48, 565–99.

Berndt, E. R., B. H. Hall, R. E. Hall, and J. A. Hausman (1974), 'Estimation and Inference in Nonlinear Structural Models', *Annals of Economic and Social Measurement*, 3, 653–66.

Bishop, Richard C. and Thomas A. Heberlein (1979), 'Measuring Values of Extra-Market Goods: Are Indirect Measures Biased?' *American Journal of Agricultural Economics*, 61:5, 926–30.

Borjas, George J., and Glenn T. Sueyoshi (1994), 'A Two-Stage Estimator for Probit Models with Structural Group Effects', *Journal of Econometrics*, 64, 165–82.

Boyle, Kevin J., Michael P. Welsh, and Richard C. Bishop (1988), 'Validation of Empirical Measures of Welfare Change: Comment and Extension'. *Land Economics*, 64:1, 94–8.

Brownlee, K. A., J. L. Hodges, and M. Rosenblatt (1953), 'The Up-and-Down Method with Small Samples', *Journal of the American Statistical Association*, 48, 262–77.

Burbidge, John B., Lonnie Magee, and A. Leslie Robb (1988), 'Alternative Transformations to Handle Extreme Values of the Dependent Variable', *Journal of the American Statistical Association*, 83:401 March, Theory and methods, 123–7.

Bulter, J. S. and R. Moffit (1982), 'A Computationally Efficient Quadrature Procedure for the One-Factor Multinomial Probit Model', *Econometrica*, 50, 761–4.

Cameron, Trudy A. (1992), 'Combining Contingent Valuation and Travel Cost Data for the Valuation of Nonmarket Goods', *Land Economics*, 68, August, 302–17.

Cameron, T. A. (1988), 'A New Paradigm for Valuing Non-Market Goods Using Referendum Data: Maximum Likelihood Estimation by Censored Logistic Regression', *Journal of Environmental Economics and Management*, 15, 355–79.

Cameron, T. A. and D. Huppert (1991), 'Referendum Contingent Valuation Estimates: Sensitivity to the Assignment of Offered Values', *Journal of the American Statistical Association*, 86:416, 910–18.

Cameron, Trudy A. and Michelle D. James (1987), 'Efficient Estimation Methods for "Closed-Ended" Contingent Valuation Surveys'. *Review of Economics and Statistics*, 69:2, 269–76.

Cameron, Trudy A. and John Quiggin (1994), 'Estimation Using Contingent Valuation Data from a "Dichotomous Choice with Follow-up" Questionnaire', *Journal of Environmental Economics and Management*, 27:3, 218–34.

Carroll, J. Douglas and Paul E. Green (1995), 'Psychometric Methods in Marketing Research: Part 1, Conjoint Analysis', *Journal of Marketing Research*, 32, November, 385–91.

Carroll, R. J., D. Ruppert and L. A. Stefanski (1995), *Measurement Error in Nonlinear Models*, New York: Chapman and Hall.

Carroll, R. J., C. H. Spiegelman, K. K. G. Lan, K. T. Bailey and R. D. Abbott (1984), 'On Errors-in Variables for Binary Regression Models', *Biometrika*, 71:1, 19–25.

Carson, Richard T. (1985), *Three Essays on Contingent Valuation (Welfare Economics, Non-Market Goods, Water Quality)*, Ph.D. dissertation, Department of Agricultural and Resource Economics, University of California, Berkeley.

Carson Richard T., Nicholas E. Flores, and W. Michael Hanemann (1992), 'On the Nature of Compensable Value in a Natural Resource Damage Assessment'. Presented at the American Economic Association Annual Meeting, New Orleans, January 3, 1992.

Carson, Richard T., Nicholas E. Flores, Kerry M. Martin, and Jennifer L. Wright (1996), 'Contingent Valuation and Revealed Preference Methodologies: Comparing the Estimates for Quasi-public Goods', *Land Economics*, 72, February, 80–99.

Carson, Richard T., W. Michael Hanemann, Raymond J. Kopp, Jon A. Krosnick, Robert C. Mitchell, Stanley Presser, Paul A. Ruud, and V. Kerry Smith, with Michael Conaway and Kerry Martin (1995), 'Referendum Design and Contingent

Valuation: The NOAA Panel's No- Vote Recommendation', Discussion Paper 96–05, Washington, D. C., Resources for the Future, November.

Carson, Richard T., Michael Hanemann, Raymond J. Kopp, Jon A. Krosnick, Robert C. Mitchell, Stanley Presser, Paul A. Ruud, and V. Kerry Smith (1994), *Prospective Interim Lost Use Value Due to DDT and PCB Contamination in the Southern California Bight*, A Report by Natural Resource Damage Assessment, Inc., La Jolla, California, September 30.

Carson, Richard T., Michael Hanemann, and Dan Steinberg (1990), 'A Discrete Choice Contingent Valuation Estimate of the Value of Kenai King Salmon', *Journal of Behavioral Economics*, 19:1, 53–68.

Carson, Richard T., Robert C. Mitchell, W. Michael Hanemann, Raymond J. Kopp, Stanley Presser, and Paul A. Ruud (1992), *A Contingent Valuation Study of Lost Passive Use Values Resulting from the Exxon Valdez Oil Spill*. A report to the Attorney General of the state of Alaska, November 10.

Carson, Richard T. and Dan Steinberg (1990), 'Experimental Design for Discrete Choice Voter Preference Surveys', in *1989 Proceeding of the Survey Methodology Section of the American Statistical Association*. Washington, DC: American Statistical Association.

Carson, Richard T., Leanne Wilks and David Imber (1994), 'Valuing the Preservation of Australia's Kakadu Conservation Zone'. *Oxford Economic Papers*, 46, 727–49.

Chaloner, K. (1986), 'An Approach to Experimental Design for Generalized Models', in *Optimal Design and Analysis of Experiments*, eds. Y. Dodge, V. V. Fedorov, and H. P. Wynn; Elsevier Science Publishers.

Chamberlain, G. (1980), 'Analysis of Covariance with Qualitative Data', *Review of Economic Studies*, 47, 225–238.

Chamberlain, G. (1984), 'Panel data', in Z. Griliches and M. Intriligator, eds., *Handbook of Econometrics*, Amsterdam: North-Holland, 2:22.

Chapman, David, and W. Michael Hanemann (1993), 'Correlated Discrete-Response Contingent Valuation', Department of Agricultural and Resource Economics, Working Paper, University of California. Berkeley, July.

Chapman, David, W. Michael Hanemann, and Barbara Kanninen (1993), 'Non-Market Valuation Using Contingent Behavior: Model Specification and Consistency Tests', Department of Agricultural and Resource Economics, Working Paper, University of California. Berkeley. January.

Chapman, Randall G., and Richard Staelin (1982), 'Exploiting Rank-Ordered Choice Set Data within the Stochastic Utility Model', *Journal of Marketing Research* 19, 288–301.

Chen, Heng Z. (1993), *Semiparametric and Semi-nonparametric Welfare Impact Analyses with Applications to Natural Resource Valuation*, Ph.D dissertation, Ohio State University.

Chen, Yu-Lan (1994), *Valuing Environmental Amenities with Revealed and Stated Preference Information: An Application to Gray Whales in California*, Ph.D. dissertation, Department of Agricultural Economics, University of California, Davis.

Chesher, Andrew, and Margaret Irish (1987), 'Residual Analysis in the Grouped and Censored Normal Linear Model', *Journal of Econometrics*, 34, 33–61.

Church, J. D. and E. B. Cobb (1973), 'On the equivalence of Spearman-Kärber and Maximum Likelihood Estimates of the Mean', *Journal of the American Statistical Association*, 68, 201–2.

Clark, C. (1961), 'The Greatest of a Finite Set of Random Variables', *Operations Research*, 9, 145–62.

Cochran, W. G. and M. Davis (1965), 'The Robbins-Monro Method for Estimating the Median Lethal Dose', *Journal of the Royal Statistical Society*, Ser. B, 27, 28–44.

Collett, D. (1991), *Modelling Binary Data*, London: Chapman and Hall.

Cook, R. Dennis, Stanford Weisberg (1982), *Residual and Influence in Regression*, New York: Chapman and Hall.

Cook, R. Dennis, Stanford Weisberg (1994), *An Introduction to Regression Graphics*, New York: John Wiley and Sons.

Cooper, J. C. (1993), 'Optimal Bid Selection for Dichotomous Choice Contingent Valuation Surveys', *Journal of Environmental Economics and Management*, 24, 25–40.

Cooper, J. C. (1994), 'A Comparison of Approaches to Calculating Confidence Intervals for Benefit Measures from Dichotomous Choice Contingent Valuation Surveys', *Land Economics*, 70:1, 111–22.

Cooper, J., and W. Michael Hanemann (1995), 'Referendum Contingent Valuation: How Many Bounds Are Enough?' USDA Economic Research Service, Food and Consumer Economics Division, working paper, May.

Cooper, J. and J. Loomis (1992), 'Sensitivity of Willingness-to-Pay Estimates to Bid Design in Dichotomous Choice Contingent Valuation Models: Reply', *Land Economics*, 68:2 May, 211–24.

Cooper, J. and J. Loomis (1993), 'Sensitivity of Willingness-to-Pay Estimates to Bid Design in Dichotomous Choice Contingent Valuation Models: Reply', *Land Economics*, 69:2 May, 203–8.

Copas, J. B. (1983), 'Plotting p against x', *Applied Statistics* 32:1, 25–31.

Copas, J. B. (1988), 'Binary Regression Models for Contaminated Data', *Journal of the Royal Statistical Society, B*, 50:2 225–65.

Cosslett, S. R. (1983), 'Distribution-Free Maximum Likelihood Estimator of the Binary Choice Model', *Econometrica* 51:3, 765–82.

Cosslett, Stephen R. (1987), 'Efficiency Bounds for Distribution-Free Estimators of the Binary Choice and the Censored Regression Models', *Econometrica* 55, 559–86.

Cox, C. (1990), 'Fieller's Theorem, The Likelihood and the Delta Method', *Biometrics*, 46, 709–18.

Cox, D. R. (1972), 'The Analysis of Multivariate Binary Data', *Applied Statistics*, 21, 113–20.

Cox, D. R. and D. V. Hinkley (1974), *Theoretical Statistics*, London: Chapman and Hall.

Creel, Michael and John Loomis (1995), 'Semi-Nonparametric Distribution-Free Dichotomous Choice Contingent Valuation', working paper, Department of Agricultural and Resource Economics, Colorado State University, Fort Collins, September.

Davidson, R. and J. G. MacKinnon (1981), 'Several Tests for Model Specification in the Presence of Alternative Hypotheses', *Econometrica*, 49:3, 781–93.

Davidson, R. and J. G. MacKinnon (1984), 'Convenient Specification Tests for Logit and Probit Models', *Journal of Econometrics*, 25, 241–62.

Davis, R. (1963), 'Recreation Planning as an Economic Problem', *Natural Resources Journal*, 3, 239–49.

Deacon, R., and P. Shapiro (1975), 'Private Preference for Collective Goods Revealed Through Voting on Referenda', *American Economic Review*, 65:5, 943–55.

Debreu, G. (1960), 'Review of R.D. Luce Individual Choice Behavior', *American Economic Review*, 50, 186–8.

Desvousges, William H., F. Reed Johnson, Richard W. Dunford, Sara P. Hudson, K. Nicole Wilson, and Kevin J. Boyle (1993), *Measuring Nonuse Damages Using Contingent Valuation: An Experimental Evaluation of Accuracy in Contingent Valuation: A Critical Assessment*, J. A. Hausman, ed., New York: North-Holland, 91–164.

Dickie, M., A. Fisher and S. Gerking (1987), 'Market Transactions and Hypothetical Demand: A Comparative Study', *Journal of the American Statistical Association*, 82, 67–75.

Dickie, Mark and Shelby Gerking (1996), 'Defensive Action and Willingness to Pay for Reduced Health Risk: Inference from Actual and Contingent Behavior', presented at the 1996 AERE Workshop on Combining Stated and Revealed Preference, Tahoe City, June 2–4.

Dixon, W. J., (1965), 'The Up and Down Method in Small Samples', *Journal of the American Statistical Association*, 60, 967–978.

Dixon, W. J. and A. M. Mood (1948), 'A Method for Obtaining and Analyzing Sensitivity Data', *Journal of the American Statistical Association*, 43, March, 109–126.

Duffield, John W. (1993), 'An Economic Analysis of Wolf Recovery in Yellowstone: Park Visitor Attitudes and Values', working paper, Department of Economics, University of Montana, March.

Duffield, J. W. and D. A. Patterson (1991), 'Inference and Optimal Design for a Welfare Measure in Dichotomous Choice Contingent Valuation', *Land Economics*, 67, 225–39.

Efron, Bradley, and Robert J. Tibshirani (1993), *An Introduction to the Bootstrap*, New York: Chapman and Hall.

El-Saidi, Mohammed A., Karan P. Singh, and Effat A. Moussa (1992), 'Symmetric Generalized Logistic Models for Quantal Assay Data: a Review', Proceedings of the American Statistical Association Statistical Computing Section Annual Meeting, 113–18.

Englin, Jeffrey and Trudy Ann Cameron (1996), 'Augmenting Travel Cost Models with Contingent Behavior Data', *Environmental and Resource Economics*, 7, 133–47.

Eom, Young Sook and V. Kerry Smith (1994), 'Calibrated Nonmarket Valuation', working paper, Department of Economics, North Carolina State University.

Fieller, E. C. (1954), 'Some Problems in Interval Estimation', *Journal of the Royal Statistical Society*, Ser. B, 16, 175–85.

Finney, D. J. (1964), *Statistical Methods in Biological Assay* (2nd edition), London: Griffin.

Finney, D. J. (1978), *Statistical Methods in Biological Assays*, New York, NY: Oxford University Press. Fitzmaurice, Garrett M., and Nan M. Laird (1993), 'A Likelihood-Based Method for Analyzing Longitudinal Binary Responses', *Biometrika*, 80, 141–51.

Fitzmaurice, Garrett M. and Nan M. Laird (1993) 'A Likelihood-Based Method for Analyzing Longitudinal Binary Responses', *Biometrika*, 141–51.

Follmann, Dean A. and Diane Lambert (1989), 'Generalizing Logistic Regression by Nonparametric Mixing', *Journal of the American Statistical Association*, 84:405, 295–300.

Freeman III, A. Myrick (1991), 'Factorial Survey Methods and Willingness to Pay for Housing Characteristics: A Comment', *Journal of Environmental Economics and Management* 20, 92–96.

Gallant, A. R. (1981), 'On the Bias in Flexible Functional Forms and an Essentially Unbiased Form', *Journal of Econometrics*, 15, 211–245.

GAUSS 3.0 Applications: Maximum Likelihood (1992), Aptech Systems, Maple Valley, WA.

Georgescu-Roegen, N. (1936), 'The Pure Theory of Consumer Behavior', *Quarterly Journal of Economics*, 570.

Georgescu-Roegen, N. (1958), 'Threshold in Choice and the Theory of Demand', *Econometrica*, 26.

Gill, Philip E., Walter Murray, and Margaret H. Wright (1981), *Practical Optimization*, New York: Academic Press.

Glasbey, C. A. (1987), 'Tolerance-Distribution-Free Analyses of Quantal Dose-Response Data', *Applied Statistics*, 36:3, 251–9.

Goldstein, Harvey (1991), 'Nonlinear Multilevel Models, with an Application to Discrete Response Data', *Biometrika*, 78:1, 45–51.

Gourieroux, C., A. Monfort and A. Trognon (1983), 'Testing Nested or Non-Nested Hypotheses', *Journal of Econometrics*, 21, 83–115.

Gourieroux, C., A. Monfort, E. Renault, and A. Trognon (1984), 'Pseudo Maximum Likelihood Methods: Theory', *Econometrica*, 52:3 May, 681–700.

Green, Paul E. (1974), 'On the Design of Choice Experiments Involving Multifactor Alternatives', *Journal of Consumer Research*, 1, September, 61–8.

Green, Paul E., and V. Srinivasan (1978), 'Conjoint Analysis in Consumer Research: Issues and Outlook', *Journal of Consumer Research*, 5, 103–23.

Green, P. E., and V. Srinivasan (1990), 'Conjoint Analysis in Marketing Research: New Developments and Directions', *Journal of Marketing*, 54:4, 3–19.

Greene, W. H. (1993), *Econometric Analysis*, New York: Macmillan.

Gregory, Robin, Sarah Lichtenstein and Paul Slovic (1993), 'Valuing Environmental Resources: A Constructive Approach'. *Journal of Risk and Uncertainty*, 7:177–97.

Griffiths, W. E., R. Carter Hill and P. J. Pope (1987), 'Small Sample Properties of Probit Model Estimators', *Journal of the American Statistical Association*, 82, 929–37.

Guilkey, D. K. and J. L. Murphy (1993), 'Estimation and Testing in the Random Effects Probit Model', *Journal of Econometrics*, 59, 301–17.

Hajivassiliou, V. (1993), 'Simulation Estimation Methods for Limited Dependent Variable Models', in G. S. Maddala, C. R. Rao and H. D. Vinod, eds., *Handbook of Statistics (Econometrics)*, Vol. 11. Amsterdam: North-Holland, 519–43.

Hajivassiliou, Vassilis A. and Paul A. Ruud (1994), 'Classical Estimation Methods for LDV Models Using Simulation', in R. F. Engle and D. L. McFadden eds. *Handbook of Econometrics*, Vol. 14, Elsevier Science B. V., Chapter 40, 2383–441.

Hamerle, Alfred and Gerd Ronning (1995), 'Panel Analysis for Qualitative Variables', in G. Arminger, C. C. Clogg, and M. E. sobel, eds., *Handbook of Statistical Modeling for the Social and Behavioral Sciences*, New York: Plenum Press, 401–51.

Hamilton, M. A., R. C. Russo, and R. V. Thurston (1977), 'Trimmed Spearman-Karber Method for Estimating Median Lethal Concentrations in Toxicity Bioassay', *Environmental Science and Technology*, 11, 714–19.

Hampel, F. R. (1974), 'The Influence Curve and Its Role in Robust Estimation', *Journal of the American Statistical Association* 62, 1179–86.

Han, Aaron K. (1987), 'Non-Parametric Analysis of a Generalized Regression Model: The Maximum Rank Correlation Estimator', *Journal of Econometrics* 35, 303–16.

Hanemann, W. Michael (1983a), 'Marginal Welfare Measures for Discrete Choice Models', *Economics Letters*, 13, 129–36.

Hanemann, W. Michael (1984b), 'Welfare Evaluations with Simulated and Hypothetical Market data: Bishop and Heberlein Revisited', Department of Agricultural and Resource Economics, Working paper 276, University of California, Berkeley, July.

Hanemann, W. Michael (1984a), 'Welfare Evaluations in Contingent Valuation Experiments with Discrete Responses', *American Journal of Agricultural Economics*, 66, 332–41.

Hanemann, W. Michael (1984b), 'Discrete/Continuous Models of Consumer Demand', *Econometrica* 52, 541–62.

Hanemann, W. Michael (1985a), 'Some Issues in Continuous- and Discrete-Response Contingent Valuation Studies', *Northeastern Journal of Agricultural Economics*, Vol. 14 (April), 5–13.

Hanemann, W. Michael (1985b), 'Welfare Analysis with Discrete Choice Models', Department of Agricultural and Resource Economics, Working Paper, University of California. Berkeley, August.

Hanemann, W. Michael (1988), 'Three Approaches to Defining "Existence" or "Non-Use" Value Under Certainty', Department of Agricultural and Resource Economics, Working paper 691, University of California, Berkeley.

Hanemann, W. Michael (1989), 'Welfare Evaluations in Contingent Valuation Experiments with Discrete Response Data: Reply', *American Journal of Agricultural Economics*, Vol. 71 (November) 1057–61.

Hanemann, W. Michael (1991), 'Reviewer's Comments', in David Imber, Gay Stevenson and Leanne Wilks, *A Contingent Valuation Survey of the Kakadu Conservation Zone*. Canberra, Australia: Resource Assessment Commission, RAC Research Paper No. 3, February, 187–92.

Hanemann, W. Michael (1996), 'Theory Versus Data in the Contingent Valuation Debate', in *The Contingent Valuation of Environmental Resources: Methodological Issues and Research Needs*, edited by David J. Bjornstad and James R. Kahn, Cheltenhan: Edward Elgar Publishing.

Hanemann, W. Michael and David Chapman (1988), 'Beyond Contingent Valuation: Deriving Environmental Benefits from Hypothetical Data', Department of Agricultural and Resource Economics, Working Paper, University of California. Berkeley, October.

Hanemann, W. Michael, Bengt Kriström, and Chuan-Zhong Li (1995), 'Nonmarket Valuation under Preference Uncertainty: Econometric Models and Estimation', paper presented at the Annual Meeting of the European Association of Environmental & Resource Economists, Umea, Sweden, June 17–20.

Hanemann, W. Michael, John B. Loomis and Barbara J. Kanninen (1991), 'Statistical Efficiency of Double-Bounded Dichotomous Choice Contingent Valuation', *American Journal of Agricultural Economics* 73:4, 1255–63.

Hasselblad, Victor, Andrew G. Stead, and John P. Creason (1980), 'Multiple Probit Analysis with a Non-zero Background', *Biometrics*, 36, December, 659–63.

Hastie, Trevor, and Robert Tibshirani (1987), 'Non-Parametric Logistic and Proportional Odds Regression', *Applied Statistics*, 36:2, 260–76.

Hausman, J. A. ed., (1993), *Contingent Valuation: A Critical Assessment*. New York: North-Holland.

Hausman, J. A. and P. A. Ruud (1987), 'Specifying and Testing Econometric Models for Rank-Ordered Data', *Journal of Econometrics* 34, 83–104.

Hausman, J. A. and D. A. Wise (1978), 'Conditional Probit Model for Qualitative Choice: Discrete Decisions Recognizing Interdependence and Heterogeneous Preferences', *Econometrica* 46:2, 403–26.

Heckman, J. (1978), 'Dummy Exogenous Variables in a Simultaneous Equation System', *Econometrica* 46:931–59.

Heckman, J. J. and R. Willis (1975), 'Estimation of a Stochastic Model of Reproduction: An Econometric Approach', in N. Terleckyi ed., *Household Production and Consumption*, New York: National Bureau of Economic Research, 99–138.

Hensher, David A. (1994), 'Stated Preference analysis of Travel Choices: The State of the Practice', *Transportation*, Volume 21, May.

Herriges, J. A. and J. F. Shogren (1996), 'Starting Point Bias in Dichotomous Choice Valuation with Follow-up Questioning', *Journal of Environmental and Management*, 30(1): 112–31.

Hoaglin, David, Frederick Mosteller, John W. Tukey (1983), *Understanding Robust and Exploratory Data Analysis*, New York: John Wiley and Sons, Inc.

Hoehn, John P. (1991), 'Valuing the Multidimensional Impacts of Environmental Policy; Theory and Methods', *American Journal of Agricultural Economics*, 73:2 May, 289–99.

Hoehn, John P., and John B. Loomis (1993), 'Substitution Effects in the Valuation of Multiple Environmental Programs', *Journal of Environmental Economics and Management* 25:1 Part 1, July, 56–75.

Hoehn, John P., and Alan Randall (1987), 'A Satisfactory Benefit Cost Indicator from Contingent Valuation', *Journal of Environmental Economics and Management*, 14, September, 226–47.

Horowitz, J. (1982), 'An Evaluation of the Usefulness of Two Standard Goodness-of-Fit Indicators for Comparing Non-Nested Random Utility Models', *Trans. Research Record*, 874, 19–25.

Horowitz, J. L. (1983), 'Statistical Comparison of Non-Nested Probabilistic Discrete Choice Models', *Transportation Science*, 17:3, 319–50.

Horowitz, J. L. (1992), 'A Smoothed Maximum Score Estimator for the Binary Response Model', *Econometrica*, 60:3 May, 505–31.

Horowitz, J. L. (1993), 'Semiparametric and Nonparametric Estimation of Quantal Response Models', in *Handbook of Statistics, Vol. 11*, G. S. Maddala, C. R. Rao and H. D. Vinod, eds., Elsevier Science Publishers, B. V.

Horowitz, J., Sparmonn, J. and C. Daganzo (1984), 'An Investigation of the Accuracy of the Clark Approximation for the Multinomial Probit Model', *Transportation Science*, 16, 382–401.

Hsiao, C. (1986), *Analysis of Panel Data*, Cambridge: Cambridge University Press.

Huber, P. J. (1981), *Robust Statistics*, New York: John Wiley and Sons.

Huhtala, Anni H. (1994), *Is Environmental Guilt a Driving Force? An Economic Study on Recycling*, Ph.D. dissertation, Department of Agricultural and Resource Economics, University of California, Berkeley, December.

Hurwicz, L. and H. Uzawa (1971), 'On the Integrability of Demand Functions', In J. S. Chipman, L. Hurwicz, M. K. Richter, and H. F. Sonnenschen, eds. *Preferences, Utility and Demand*, New York: Harcourt Brace, 114–48.

Ichimura, Hidehiko (1993), 'Semiparametric Least Squares (SLS) and Weighted SLS Estimation of Single-Index Models', *Journal of Econometrics* 58, 71–120.

Jakus, Paul M. (1994), 'Averting Behavior in the Presence of Public Spillovers: Household Control of Nuisance Pests', *Land Economics*, 70, August, 273–85.

Jakus, Paul M. and V. Kerry Smith (1992), 'Measuring Use and Nonuse Values for Landscape Amenities: A Contingent Behavior Analysis of Gypsy Moth Control', presented at the American Economic Association Annual Meeting, New Orleans, January.

James, B. R. and James, K. L. (1983), 'On the Influence Curve for Quantal Bioassay', *J. Statist. Pl. Inf.*, 8, 331–45.

Jennings, Dennis E. (1986), 'Outlier and Residual Distribution in Logistic Regression,' *Journal of the American Statistical Association*, 81:396 December, 987–990.

Johansson, P. and B. Kriström (1988), 'Asymmetric and Symmetric Discrete Response Models in Contingent Valuation Experiments', Research Papers in Statistics, 7, Dept. of Statistics, University of Umeå.

Johnson, Normal L., and Samuel Kotz (1972), *Distributions in Statistics: Continuous Multivariate Distributions*. New York: John Wiley and Sons, Inc.

Judge G. G., R. C. Hill, W. E. Griffiths, H. Lütkepohl and L. Tsoung-Chao (1988), *Introduction to the Theory and Practice of Econometrics*, Second Edition, New York: John Wiley & Sons.

Kalbfleisch, J. D. and R. L. Prentice (1980), *The Statistical Analysis of Failure Time Data*, New York: John Wiley & Sons.

Kanninen, B. J. (1993a), 'Design of Sequential Experiments for Contingent Valuation Studies', *Journal of Environmental Economics and Management*, 25, S-1–11.

Kanninen, B. J. (1993b), 'Optimal Experimental Design for Double-Bounded Dichotomous Choice Contingent Valuation', *Land Economics*, 69:2, 138–146.

Kanninen, B. J. (1995), 'Bias in Discrete Response Contingent Valuation', *Journal of Environmental Economics and Management*, 28:1 January, 114–25.

Kanninen, B. J. and B. Kriström (1993), 'Sensitivity of Willingness-to-Pay Estimates to Bid Design in Dichotomous Choice Contingent Valuation Models: A Comment', *Land Economics*, 69:2, 199–202.

Kao, C and J. R. Schnell (1987), 'Errors in Variables in the Multinomial Response Model', *Economics Letters*, 25, 249–54.

Kaplan, E. L. and P. Meier (1958), 'Nonparametric Estimation from Incomplete Observations', *Journal of the American Statistical Association*, 53, 457–81.

Kappenman, Russell F. (1987), 'Nonparametric Estimation of Dose-Response Curves with Application to ED50 Estimation', *J. Statist. Comput. Simul.*, 28, 1–13.

Keane, M. (1993), 'Simulation Estimation Methods for Panel Data Limited Dependent Variable Models', in G. C. Maddala, C. R. Rao and H. D. Vinod, eds., *Handbook of Statistics (Econometrics)*, Vol. 11. Amsterdam: North-Holland.

Keeney, Ralph L. and Howard Raiffa (1976), *Decisions with Multiple Objectives: Preferences and Value Tradeoffs*, New York: John Wiley and Sons.

Kent, J. T. (1986), 'The Underlying Structure of Nonnested Hypothesis Tests', *Biometrika*, 73:2, 333–43.

Klein, R. W. and R. H. Spady (1993), 'An Efficient Semiparametric Estimator for Binary Response Models', *Econometrica*, 61:2, 387–421.

Knetch, J. L. and R. K. Davis (1966), 'Comparisons of Methods for Recreation Evaluation', in Kneese A. V., and S. C. Smith, eds., *Water Research*, Baltimore: Resources for the Future Inc., Johns Hopkins Press, 125–42.

Krinsky, I. and A. Robb (1986), 'Approximating the Statistical Properties of Elasticities', *Review of Economics and Statistics*, 68, 715–19.

Krishnan, K. S. (1977), 'Incorporating Thresholds of Indifference in Probabilistic Choice Models', *Management Science*, 23, July, 1224–1233.

Kriström, B. (1990), 'A Non-parametric Approach to the Estimation of Welfare Measures in Discrete Response Valuation Studies', *Land Economics*, 66, 135–39.

Kriström, Bengt, Hans Nyquist and W. Michael Hanemann (1992), 'Dichotomous Choice Contingent Valuation Experiment: A Mixed Distribution Approach', working paper, Department of Economics, University of Umea, Sweden. November.

Krutilla, J. V. (1967), 'Conservation Reconsidered', *American Economic Review*, 57:4, 777–86.

Künsch, Hans R., Leonard A. Stefanski, and Raymond J. Carroll (1989), 'Conditionally Unbiased Bounded-Influence Estimation in General Regression Models, with Applications to Generalized Linear Models', *Journal of the American Statistical Association*, 84:406 June, 460–6.

Lancaster, Tony (1990), *The Econometric Analysis of Transition Data*, Cambridge, MA: Cambridge University Press.

Langford, I. (1994), 'Using a Generalized Linear Mixed Model to Analyze Dichotomous Choice Contingent Valuation Data', *Land Economics*, 70, 507–14.

Langford, Ian H. and Ian J. Bateman, 'Multilevel Modelling and Contingent Valuation', Chapter 12, this volume.

Layton, David Frost (1995), *Specifying and Testing Econometric Models for Stated Preference Surveys*, Ph.D. dissertation, Department of Economics, University of Washington, Seattle, June.

Lechner, Michael (1995), 'Some Specification Tests for Probit Models Estimated on Panel Data', *Journal of Business and Economic Statistics*, 13:4 Oct., 475–88.

Lee, Lung-Fei (1982), 'Specification Error in Multinomial Logit Models: Analysis of the Omitted Variable Bias', *Journal of Econometrics* 20, 197–209.

Lee, Lung-Fei (1983), 'Generalized Econometric Models with Selectivity', *Econometrica* 55:2 March, 507–12.

Lerman, S. R. and C. F. Manski (1981), 'The Use of Simulated Frequencies to Approximate Choice Probabilities', in Manski, C. F. and D. McFadden, eds.,

Structural Analysis of Discrete Data with Econometric Applications, Cambridge, Mass: MIT Press, 305–19.

Li, Chuan-Zhong (1996), 'Semiparametric Estimation of the Binary Choice Model for Contingent Valuation', *Land Economics*, forthcoming, November.

Li, Chuan-Zhong, Karl-Gustaf Löfgren, and W. Michael Hanemann (1995), 'Real versus Hypothetical Willingness to Accept: The Bishop and Heberlein Model Revisited', working paper, Department of Economics, University of Umea, Sweden. September.

Li, Chuan-Zhong and Lief Mattsson (1995), 'Discrete Choice Under Preference Uncertainty: An Improved Structural Model for Contingent Valuation', *Journal of Environmental Economics and Management*, 28:2 March, 256–69.

Liang, Kung-Yee, Scott L. Zeger, and Bahjat Qaqish (1992), 'Multivariate Regression Analyses for Categorical Data', *Journal of the Royal Statistical Society*, Ser. B, 54:1, 3–40.

Little, I. M. D. (1957), *A Critique of Welfare Economics*, New York, NY: Oxford University Press.

Little, Roderick J. A. and Donald B. Rubin (1987), *Statistical Analysis with Missing Data*, New York: Wiley & Sons.

Longford, N. T. (1988), 'A Quasi-likelihood Adaptation for Variance Component Analysis', in *Proc. Sect. Comp. Statist., Am. Statist. Assoc.*, 137–42.

Longford, N. T. (1993), *Random Coefficient Models*, Oxford: Clarendon Press.

Loomis, John B. (1996), 'Panel Estimators Useful for Analyzing Combined Revealed and Stated Preference Dichotomous Choice Data: Application to Visit and Dichotomous Choice CVM Responses for Instream Flow', presented at the 1996 AERE Workshop on Combining Stated and Revealed Preference, Tahoe City, June 2–4.

Loomis, J. B., W. M. Hanemann, and T. C. Wegge (1990), *Environmental Benefits Study of San Joaquin Valley's Fish and Wildlife Resources*. Sacramento, California: Jones & Stokes Associates, Inc. September.

Louviere, Jordan J. (1996), 'Combining Revealed and Stated Preference Data: The Rescaling Revolution', presented at the 1996 AERE Workshop on Combining Stated and Revealed Preference, Tahoe City, June 2–4.

Louviere, Jordan J. (1994), 'Conjoint Analysis', in R. Bagozzi (ed.) *Handbook of Marketing Research*, Oxford: Blackwell Publishers.

Louviere, Jordan J. (1988), *Analyzing Decision Making: Metric Conjoint Analysis*, Newbury Park: Sage Publications.

Luce, R. D. (1956), 'Semiorders and a Theory of Utility Discrimination', *Econometrica*, 24, 178–91.

Luce, R. D. (1959), *Individual Choice Behavior: A Theoretical Analysis*, New York, NY: John Wiley and Sons.

Luce, R. D. and P. Suppes (1965), 'Preference, Utility and Subjective Probability', in R. D. Luce and R. R. Bush and E. Galanter (eds.), *Handbook of Mathematical Psychology*, Vol. 3, New York: John Wiley and Sons, 249–410.

Mackenzie, John (1993), 'A Comparison of Contingent Preference Models', *American Journal of Agricultural Economics*, 75, August, 593–603.

MacKinnon, J. G. (1983), 'Model Specification Tests Against Non-Nested Alternatives', *Econometric Reviews*, 2:1, 85–110.

Maddala, G. S. (1983), *Limited Dependent and Qualitative Variables in Econometrics*, Cambridge: Cambridge University Press.

Maddala, G. S. (1986), 'Limited Dependent Variable Models Using Panel Data', *Journal of Human Resources*, 22, 307–38.

Madow, W. G., I. Olkin and D. Rubin, eds. (1983), *Incomplete Data in Sample Surveys, Volume 2: Theory and Bibliographies*, New York: Academic Press, Inc.

Magat, Wesley A., W. Kip Viscusi, and Joel Huber (1988), 'Paired Comparison and Contingent Valuation Approaches to Morbidity Risk Valuation', *Journal of Environmental Economics and Management*, 15(4), 395–411.

Manski, Charles F. (1975), 'Maximum Score Estimation of the Stochastic Utility Model of Choice', *Journal of Econometrics* 3, 205–28.

Mardia, K. V. (1970), *Families of Bivariate Distributions*, London: Griffin.

Mazzotta, Marisa J. and James J. Opaluch (1995), 'Decision Making When Choices are Complex: A Test of Heiner's Hypothesis', *Land Economics*, 71:4, 500–15.

McConnell, K. E. (1990), 'Models for Referendum Data: The Structure of Discrete Choice Models for Contingent Valuation', *Journal of Environmental Economics and Management*, 18, 19–35.

McConnell, K. E. (1983), 'Existence and Bequest Values' in Rowe, R. and Chestnut, L. eds, *Managing Air Quality and Scenic Resources at National Parks and Wilderness Areas*, Boulder: Westview Press.

McCullagh, P., and J. A. Nelder (1989), *Generalized Linear Models*, 2nd ed., London: Chapman and Hall.

McFadden, D. (1974), 'Conditional Logit Analysis of Qualitative Choice Behavior', in P. Zarembka, ed., *Frontiers in Econometrics*, New York: Academic Press, 105–42.

McFadden, D. (1976), 'Quantal Choice Analysis: A Survey', *Annals of Economic and Social Measurement*, 5, 363–390.

McFadden, D. (1978), 'Modelling the Choice of Residential Location', in A. Karlqvist, ed., *Spatial Interaction Theory and Residential Location*, Amsterdam: North-Holland, 75–96.

McFadden, D. (1987), 'Regression-Based Specification Tests for the Multinomial Logit Model', *Journal of Econometrics*, 34, 63–82.

McFadden, D. (1989), 'A Method of Simulated Moments for the Estimation: Discrete Response Models without Numerical Integration', *Econometrica* 57:5, 995–1026.

McFadden, Daniel (1994), 'Contingent Valuation and Social Choice', *American Journal of Agricultural Economics*, 76, November, 689–708.

McFadden, Daniel, and Gregory Leonard (1993), 'Issues in the Contingent Valuation of Environmental Goods: Methodologies for Data Collection and Analysis', in Hausman, J. A., ed. *Contingent Valuation: A Critical Assessment*. New York: North-Holland, 165–215.

Miller, R. G. (1973), 'Nonparametric Estimators of the Mean Tolerance in Bioassay', *Biometrika*, 60, 535–42.

Miller, R. G. and J. W. Halpern (1980), 'Robust Estimators for Quantal Bioassay', *Biometrika*, 67, 103–10.

Minkin, S. (1987), 'Optimal Design for Binary Data', *Journal of the American Statistical Association*, 82, 1098–103.

Mitchell, Robert Cameron, and Richard T. Carson (1989), *Using Surveys to Value Public Goods: The Contingent Valuation Method*, Washington, D.C.: Resources for the Future.

Mitchell, Robert Cameron, and Richard T. Carson (1981), 'An Experiment in Determining Willingness to Pay for National Water Quality Improvements', Report to the U.S. Environmental Protection Agency, Washington, D.C, June.

Morgan, B. J. T. (1985), 'The Cubic Logistic Model for Quantal Assay Data', *Appl. Statist.* 34:2, 105–13.

Morgan, B. J. T. (1992), *Analysis of Quantal Response Data*, New York: Chapman and Hall.

Morikawa, T. (1989), *Incorporating Stated Preference Data in Travel Demand Analysis*, Ph.D. dissertation, Department of Civil Engineering, Massachusetts Institute of Technology.

Muller, H. G. and T. Schmitt (1990), 'Choice of Number of Doses for Maximum Likelihood Estimation of the ED_{50} for Quantal Dose-Response Data', *Biometrics*, 46:1, 117–30.

Mundlak, Y. (1978), 'On the Pooling of Cross-Section and Time-Series Data', *Econometrica*, 46, 69–86.

Nelder, J. A. and Wedderburn, R. W. M. (1972), 'Generalized Linear Models', *Journal of the Royal Statistical Society*, A, 135, 370–84.

Nelson, Wayne (1982), *Applied Life Data Analysis*, New York: John Wiley & Sons.

Nerlove, M., and J. Press (1973), 'Univariate and Multivariate Log-Linear and Logistic Models', RAND report R-1306–EDA/NIH.

Neyman, J. and E. L. Scott (1948), 'Consistent Estimates Based on Partially Consistent Observations', *Econometrica* 16, 1–32.

Nyquist, H. (1992), 'Optimal Designs of Discrete Response Experiments in Contingent Valuation Studies', *Review of Economics and Statistics*, 74:3, 559–63.

Opaluch, James J., and Kathleen Segerson (1989), 'Rational Roots of "Irrational" Behavior: New Theories of Economic Decision-Making', *Northeastern Journal of Agricultural and Resource Economics* 18 (Oct.), 81–95.

O'Sullivan, F., Yandell, B. and W. Raynor (1986), 'Automatic Smoothing of Regression Functions in Generalized Linear Models', *Journal of the American Statistical Association*, 81, 96–103.

Pakes, A., and D. Pollard (1989), 'Simulation and the Asymptotics of Optimization Estimators', *Econometrica*, 57:5, 1027–57.

Park, T., J. Loomis and M. Creel (1991), 'Confidence Intervals for Evaluating Benefits from Dichotomous Choice Contingent Valuation Studies', *Land Economics*, 67:1, 64–73.

Parzen, Emmanuel (1960), *Modern Probability Theory and its Applications*, New York: John Wiley & Sons.

Pesaran, M. H. and A. S. Deaton (1978), 'Testing Non-Nested Nonlinear Regression Models', *Econometrica*, 46:3, 677–694.

Pierce, Donald A. and Daniel E. Schafer (1986), 'Residuals in Generalized Linear Models', *Journal of the American Statistical Association*, 81:396, December, 977–86.

Poe, Gregory L., Eric K. Severance-Lossin, and Michael P. Welsh (1994), 'Measuring the Difference (X–Y) of Simulated Distributions: A Convolutions Approach', *American Journal of Agricultural Economics*, 76, November, 904–15.

Powell, J. L., James H. Stock, and Thomas M. Stoker (1989), 'Semiparametric Estimation of Index Coefficients', *Econometrica*, 57:6, 1403–30.

Pregibon, D. (1981), 'Logistic Regression Diagnostics', *Annals of Statistics*, 9, 705–24.

Pregibon, D. (1982), 'Resistant Fits for Some Commonly Used Logistic Models with Medical Application', *Biometrics*, 38, 485–98.

Pregibon, Daryl (1988), 'Discussion of the Paper by Copas', contained in 'Binary Regression Models for Contaminated Data, by J. B. Copas', *Journal of Royal Statistical Society*, 50:2, 260–1.

Preisler, H. K. (1989), 'Fitting Dose-Response Data with Non-Zero Background within Generalized Linear and Generalized Additive Models', *Computational Statistics and Data Analysis* 7, 279–90.

Prentice, R. L. (1976), 'A Generalization of the Probit and Logit Methods for Dose Response Curves', *Biometrics* 32, 761–8.

Quandt, R. (1956), 'A Probabilistic Theory of Consumer Behavior', *Quarterly Journal of Economics*, 70:4, 507–36.

Rae, Douglas, A. (1982), 'Benefits of Visual Air Quality in Cincinnati', report to the Electric Power Research Institute by Charles River Associates, Boston.

Rae, Douglas, A. (1983), 'The Value to Visitors of Improving Visibility at Mesa Verde and Great Smoky National Parks', in Robert D. Rowe and Lauraine G. Chestnut, eds., *Managing Air Quality and Scenic Resources at National Parks and Wilderness Areas*, Boulder: Westview Press.

Raudenbush, S. W. and A. S. Bryk (1986), 'A Hierarchical Model for Studying School Effects', *Sociology of Education*, 59, 1–17.

Ready, Richard C. and Dayuan Hu (1995), 'Statistical Approaches to the Fat Tail Problem for Dichotomous Choice Contingent Valuation', *Land Economics*, 71:4, 491–9.

Ready, Richard, John C. Whitehead, and Glenn C. Blomquist (1995), 'Contingent Valuation When Respondents Are Ambivalent', *Journal of Environmental Economics and Management*, 29, 181–96.

Robinson, P. M. (1982), 'On the Asymptotic Properties of Estimators of Models Containing Limited Dependent Variables', *Econometrica* 50, 27–41.

Roe, Brian, Kevin J. Boyle, Mario F. Teisl (1996), 'Using Conjoint Analysis to Derive Estimates of Compensating Variation', *Journal of Environmental Economics and Management*, 31:2, September, 145–59.

Rubin D. (1987), *Multiple Imputation for Nonresponse in Surveys*. New York: John Wiley & Sons, Inc.

Ruud, Paul A. (1983), 'Sufficient Conditions for the Consistency of Maximum Likelihood Estimation Despite Misspecification of Distribution in Multinomial Discrete Choice Models', *Econometrica*, 51:1, January, 225–8.

Santner, Thomas J. and Diane E. Duffy (1989), *The Statistical Analysis of Discrete Data*. New York: Springer-Verlag.

Schkade, David A. and John W. Payne (1994), 'How People Respond to Contingent Valuation Questions: A Verbal Protocol Analysis of Willingness to Pay for Environmental Regulation', *Journal of Environmental Economics and Management*, 26, January, 88–109.

Schmidt, Peter, and Ann Dryden Witte (1989), 'Predicting Criminal Recidivism Using "Split Population" Survival Time Models', *Journal of Econometrics* 40, 141–59.

Schmidt, Peter, and Robert P. Strauss (1975), 'Estimation of Models with Jointly Dependent Qualitative Variables: A Simultaneous Logit Approach', *Econometrica*, 43:4, July, 745–55.

Schmoyer, Richard L. (1984), 'Sigmoidally Constrained Maximum Likelihood Estimation in Quantal Bioassay', *Journal of the American Statistical Association*, 79:386, 448–53.

Staniswalis, Joan G., and Vanessa Cooper (1988), 'Kernel Estimates of Dose Response', *Biometrics* 44, 1103–19.

Stavig, Gordon R., and Jean D. Gibbons (1977), 'Comparing the Mean and Median as Measures of Centrality', *International Statistical Review*, 45, 63–70.

Steinberg, D. and P. Colla (1988), *Survival: A Supplementary Module for SYSTAT*, Evanston, IL, SYSTAT, Inc.

Strand, Jon (1981), 'Valuation of Fresh Water as a Public Good in Norway', Mimeo, Department of Economics, University of Oslo, Norway.

Strauss, D. (1979), 'Some Results on Random Utility Models', *Journal of Mathematical Psychology* 20:1, 35–52.

Stukel, Therese A. (1988), 'Generalized Logistic Models', *Journal of the American Statistical Association* 83:402, 426–31.

Svento, Rauli (1993), 'Some Notes on Trichotomous Choice Discrete Valuation', *Environmental and Resource Economics* 3, 533–43.

Svento, Rauli and Erkki Mäntymaa (1994), 'A Generalized Test for Vagueness in Hypothetical Markets', Annual Meeting of the European Association of Environmental & Resource Economists, June.

Swait, Joffre, and Wiktor Adamowicz (1996), 'The Effect of Choice Complexity on Random Utility Models: An Application to Combined Stated and Revealed Preference Models, or Tough Choices: Contribution or Confusion?' presented at the 1996 AERE Workshop on Combining Stated and Revealed Preference, Tahoe City, June 2–4.

Swamy, P. A. V. B. (1970), 'Efficient Inference in a Random Coefficient Regression Model', *Econometrica* 38, 311–23.

Taylor, Jeremy M. G. (1988), 'The Cost of Generalizing Logistic Regression', *Journal of the American Statistical Association*, Dec., 83:404, 1078–83.

Tsutakawa, R. K. (1972), 'Design of Experiment for Bioassay', *Journal of the American Statistical Association*, 67, 584–90.

Tsutakawa, R. K. (1980), 'Selection of Dose Levels for Estimating a Percentage Point of a Logistic Quantal Response Curve', *Applied Statistics*, 29, 25–33.

Turnbull, B. W. (1974), 'Nonparametric Estimation of a Survivorship Function with Doubly Censored Data', *Journal of the American Statistical Association*, 69:345.

Turnbull, B. W. (1976), 'The Empirical Distribution Function with Arbitrarily Grouped, Censored and Truncated Data', *Journal of the Royal Statistical Society*, 38, 290–95.

von Winterfeldt, Detlof, and Ward Edwards (1986), *Decision Analysis and Behavioral Research*, New York: Cambridge University Press.

Waldman, Donald M. (1983), 'The Information Content of Data in a Random Utility Model', Working Paper, Department of Economics, University of North Carolina, December.

Ward, Michael (1995), *Nonparametric Methods in Economic Analysis*, Ph.D. dissertation, Department of Economics, University of Washington, Seattle.

Wedderburn, R. W. M. (1974), 'Quasilikelihood Functions, Generalized Linear Models and the Gauss-Newton Method', *Biometrika*, 61, 439–47.

Welsh, Michael P. and Richard C. Bishop (1993), 'Multiple Bounded Discrete Choice Models', in W–133 Benefits and Costs Transfer in Natural Resource Planning, Western Regional Research Publication compiled by J. Bergstrom, Dept. of Ag. and Applied Economics, University of Georgia, September.

Werner, Megan. (1994), *Public Choice Issues in Environmental Economics*, Ph.D dissertation, Department of Economics, University of California, San Diego, 1994.

White, Halbert (1994), *Estimation, Inference and Specification Analysis*, Cambridge, Mass: Cambridge University Press.

Whitehead, John C. (1995), 'Willingness to Pay for Quality Improvements: Comparative Statics and Interpretation of Contingent Valuation Results', *Land Economics*, 71, May, 207–15.

Williams, D. A. (1982), 'Extra-binomial variation in Logistic Linear Models', *Applied Statistics*, 31:2, 144–48.

Winer, B. J. (1971), *Statistical Principles in Experimental Design*, New York: John Wiley.

Wu, C. F. J. (1985), 'Efficient Sequential Designs with Binary Data', *Journal of the American Statistical Association*.

——(1988), 'Optimal Design for Percentile Estimation of a Quantal Response Curve', in *Optimal Design and Analysis of Experiments*, eds. Y. Dodge, V. V. Fedorov, and H. P. Wynn; Elsevier Science Publishers.

Wu, Pei-Ing, Stephen Cosslett, and Alan Randall (1922), 'Benefit Evaluation of Complex Environmental Policy from Multiple-Referendum Contingent Valuation Experiments: The Multiple-Response Nested Logit Model', Working Paper, Department of Agricultural Economics, Ohio State University, December.

Yatchew, A. and Z. Griliches (1985), 'Specification Error in Probit Models', *The Review of Economics and Statistics*, 134–39.

Yellot, Jr. J. I. (1977), 'The Relationship between Luce's Choice Axiom, Thurstone's Theory of Comparative Judgement, and the Double Exponential Distribution', *Journal of Mathematical Psychology*, 15, 109–44.

——(1980), 'Generalized Thurstone Models for Ranking: Equivalence and Reversibility', *Journal of Mathematical Psychology*, 22, 48–69.

Zavoina, R., and W. McElvey (1975), 'A Statistical Model for Analysis of Ordinal Level Dependent Variables', *Journal of Mathematical Sociology*, Summer, 103–20.

Zhao, L. P. and R. L. Prentice (1990), 'Correlated Binary Regression Using Quadratic Exponential Model', *Biometrika*, 77, 642–48.

12

Multi-Level Modelling and Contingent Valuation

IAN H. LANGFORD
IAN J. BATEMAN

12.1. INTRODUCTION

Multi-level modelling is a statistical technique designed to analyse data arranged in a natural hierarchy. The technique has proven of great value in analysing social and educational data (Goldstein, 1987; Bryk and Raudenbush, 1992) and is becoming popular in geography and epidemiology (Jones, 1991; Ecob, 1992; Duncan *et al.*, 1993; Langford, 1994*a*, 1995*a*; Langford and Bentham, 1996) as well as health economics (Carr-Hill *et al.*, 1994; Langford, 1995*b*). To take an educational example, it is obvious that data are often hierarchical, with individual children nested within classes, within schools, within local education authorities, and so on. Each stage of this hierarchy may be called a level, with the lowest, most disaggregated level of the data being referred to as level 1 (in this case an individual pupil), the next (classes) as level 2, and so on. In a similar manner, contingent valuation (CV) deals with eliciting information from individual respondents, which may then be aggregated into groups in a number of ways. This chapter will explore, in an introductory manner, the potential advantages of using multi-level modelling in a range of CV survey designs.

Section 12.2 briefly reviews the theoretical basis of the generalized linear model (GLM) most often used to model dichotomous-choice (DC) willingness-to-pay data, namely the logistic regression model. Reasons why this model may not provide an adequate description of the data are discussed in Section 12.3, while Section 12.4 describes the statistical basis of random coefficient models as an extension to GLMs. Random coefficient models allow for the estimation of the random effects present in a model with regard to a set of explanatory variables, as well as giving fixed parameter estimates. Section 12.5 systematically develops an example of a random coefficient model called a multi-level model, using data from a CV survey undertaken on the Norfolk Broads, an internationally important wetland resource in eastern England (Bateman *et al.*, 1995). The implications of using a multi-level model are discussed in Section 12.6, and other applications suggested. A summary of the main conclusions is given in Section 12.7.

12.2. THE CONVENTIONAL APPROACH

The GLM approach to data analysis has a long tradition, and has proved very flexible and useful in modelling a range of quantitative data (McCullagh and Nelder, 1989; Dobson, 1990). The basic GLM may be written as

$$h(y_j) = x_j^T \beta + e_j, \qquad (12.1)$$

where y_j represents the jth element of a vector of responses; x_j^T is the jth row of a design matrix of explanatory or predictor variables associated with a parameter vector β, and e_j is a random-error term. The function h is called the link function, and can be seen as a transformation of the original response variable onto a scale which is linear in the predictor variables.

Considering a model of dichotomous-choice responses, we can model proportions of responses to a number of bid levels $BID_j, j = 1, 2, \cdots, N$ with y_j individuals offering a positive response out of n_j individuals at each bid level. Assuming y_j are independently binomial (n_j, π_j), where π_j is the probability of a positive response to a particular bid level, it is common to model π_j via the logistic transformation, in order to convert the probabilities from a 0-to-1 scale onto a scale that runs continuously from negative to positive infinity, i.e.

$$\ln[\pi_j/(1 - \pi_j)] = z_j = x_j^T \beta + e_j, \qquad (12.2)$$

where z_j is the transformed response variable linear in the predictor variables. Estimation is usually carried out using the principles of quasi-likelihood (Wedderburn, 1974) using an iterative weighted least-squares procedure (McCullagh and Nelder, 1989). The first two moments of the distribution of y_j (the mean and variance) are needed for this procedure, and we can write down these moments from the binomial distribution for modelling proportions as

$$E(y_j) = n_j \pi_j; \, var(y_j) = n_j \pi_j (1 - \pi_j). \qquad (12.3)$$

Hence, we have a model for those individuals who respond 'yes' to each of the j bid levels offered. If only the bid level and an intercept are included in the design matrix, we can write

$$z_j = a + bBID_j + e_j. \qquad (12.4)$$

A common point estimate of willingness-to-pay (WTP) which will be considered here is the median of the fitted distribution of z_j (see Duffield and Patterson, 1991), which can be calculated as $E(\text{WTP}) = -a/b$ from the parameters estimated in equation (12.4).

12.3. PROBLEMS WITH THE CONVENTIONAL MODELLING APPROACH

The model above is a good description of statistical data in many instances. However, the assumptions in the model such as the magnitude and distribution of the error terms may be violated in several ways, leading to inefficient parameter estimates, and incorrect standard errors associated with these parameters. This may in turn lead to incorrect estimates of $E(\text{WTP})$, and inappropriate confidence intervals around $E(\text{WTP})$, as discussed in Section 12.4. Logistic regression models which do not fit the data well are often referred to as possessing extra-binomial variation, i.e. the simple assumption about the variance in Equation (12.3) does not explain all the variability present in the model. Two major potential sources for this extraneous variability are now discussed.

12.3.1   Poorly Specified Models

The source of extra-binomial variation which is of most interest in the modelling process is that which is determined by the independent, explanatory variables included in the model. However, in CV surveys there is often only a small proportion of the extra-binomial variation in a model which can be explained by the known and measured explanatory variables. This problem arises for several reasons, as follows:

1. explanatory variables are often surrogate measures of the factors of real interest;
2. there are often many complex and interrelated factors which lead to an individual's response to a particular bid amount, and only a selection of these can realistically be included within a single model;
3. perhaps most importantly, data are not available on many real factors of interest due to a number of constraints, which may be due to questionnaire design, time and funding for the survey, and interviewing methods and styles. Imperfect knowledge and genuine uncertainty on the part of the respondent may also be seen as a missing-variable problem.

12.3.2   Autocorrelation of the Response Variables

Extra-binomial variation may be present in a model due to the clustering of the response variables, and it is perhaps easiest to think of this effect in terms of the standardized residuals of the model being fitted. If the response variables cluster to a noticeable degree, the residuals will not display their theoretical normal distribution with a single maximum at zero, but may contain other local maxima which will tend to increase their variance and hence the overall chi-squared estimate for the model beyond the expected degrees of freedom value.

In a typical DC CV study, the individual respondents are clustered within the bid amounts offered, and any variation between individuals will not be accounted for if the mean responses of the group of individuals responding to a particular bid amount are used as the dependent variable. This means there may be variation present in the model of mean responses to bid amounts which is not accounted for by the assumption of binomial variance. This leads to the important issue of hierarchy within a statistical model. The model presented in Section 12.2 concerned proportions of individuals responding to a number of bid amounts, but the model was only concerned with these aggregates, not with variables associated with any particular individual, such as their income, age, and so on. Hence, a problem may arise which is sometimes referred to as the 'ecological fallacy', where judgements made on aggregates of people may seriously misrepresent individuals contained within each group. In the GLM of Equation (12.2), there is no way of including individual variability—aggregates of income and so on could be included for each bid amount to look for bias, but we have still lost a potential wealth of information on each individual which is routinely collected in surveys.

One solution would be simply to model individuals rather than bid levels. However, here we may commit the 'atomistic fallacy'. In other words, by solely concentrating on the atomized, individual responses, we may miss some important information associated with bid amounts. It may be that there is variance between bid amounts not associated with individual variability, i.e. there is a general acceptance and/or rejection of certain bid amounts which is due to the size of bid offered, rather than being dependent on any characteristic of the individual. This is, of course, precisely what we are interested in when creating a probability curve for individuals responding 'yes' to different bid levels to calculate $E(\text{WTP})$. However, there is a further, more subtle statistical point. In the conventional GLM, individuals asked to respond to the jth bid amount only support the value of π_j, and have no input to the rest of the model. The model is really a summation of the fits of completely separate components for each bid level. In the multi-level model developed later, we shall see that information for all individuals can support a general bid curve, rather than merely supporting the particular bid amount they are contained within. In other words, each individual contributes information to the overall relationship we are modelling for all bid amounts, not just to the particular bid amount he/she was offered.

12.4. RANDOM COEFFICIENT MODELS

Before explicitly examining multi-level models, it is worth exploring the principles of random coefficient modelling in general, of which multi-level models are a useful subset particularly appropriate for the type of data

collected in CV studies. In order to discuss the importance of random
coefficient models to CV studies, we first need to consider the sort of
response data we are modelling. Most present-day CV studies pose WTP
questions in the form of binary DC referenda, an approach which conforms
to the recommendations of the NOAA Blue-Ribbon Panel (Arrow *et al.*,
1993). In DC studies, as explained above, the binary response data for each
individual are aggregated into proportions of individuals responding to a
pre-selected number of bid amounts. The response variable, usually the logit
of the proportion responding 'yes' to each bid level, is then modelled via a
linear relationship with a set of explanatory variables, such as bid amount
offered, age, sex, use preferences, and so on. However, the model may often
prove to be a poor fit as measured by a goodness-of-fit statistic such as scaled
deviance or chi-squared (Langford, 1994*b*), and in this case we may state
that extra-binomial variation is present in the model after measured explanatory variables have been controlled for.

12.4.1   Random Effects

Apart from the problems discussed so far, it is also true that unexplained
variation may be present in a model due to the effects of important explanatory variables which have not been measured. No matter how comprehensive a survey attempts to be, it is impossible to ask about all the possible
factors which influence an individual's WTP. Williams (1982) proposes that
given these obvious restrictions on data availability, it may be more realistic
to choose to include the effects of a set of unknown covariates in the model
whose distribution and influence can reasonably be suggested. These
unknown covariates are already influencing the outcome of the model via
their influence on the distribution of observations made (Clayton and Kaldor, 1987; Langford, 1994*a*), and so it is reasonable to make some estimate
of the effects of their presence rather than simply ignore them, particularly if
there are strong theoretical grounds for expressing a prior belief about their
influence before modelling begins (Lindley and Smith, 1972). In this case, we
can state that it is impossible to measure all the influences acting upon
individuals when they determine their response to the bid-amount question,
and so 'random effects', as they are often called, are almost certain to be
present in the model. It should be stated at this point that all known
explanatory variables of importance should be included in the model before
the decision to model random effects is taken.

These random effects may cause the residual variance of the fitted model
to be greater than that expected; for example, the residual chi-squared may
be greater than the degrees of freedom present in the model, i.e. its asymptotic expectation (McCullagh and Nelder, 1989). This residual variation is
therefore extra-binomial variation which may thought of as being attributable to unmeasured random effects (Lindley and Smith, 1972; Manly, 1978).

As mentioned previously, these random effects could represent a great number of individual or contextual influences on a respondent's willingness to pay a particular bid level. Williams (1982) suggests modelling these random effects as a set of randomly distributed parameters P_j on $(0,1)$, where

$$E(P_j) = \pi_j; \operatorname{Var}(P_j) = \omega\pi_j(1 - \pi_j), \qquad (12.5)$$

where ω is a single dispersion parameter, and $\omega > 0$ in an overdispersed model. In Bayesian terms, we can say that the results from equation (12.5) are conditional upon the distribution of the P_j. Unconditionally, we can state that the residual variance in the model has been reduced by the presence of ω (sometimes referred to as a hyperparameter), and is now given by

$$\operatorname{Var}(y_j : n_j, P_j) = [n_j\pi_j(1 - \pi_j)]/[1 + \omega(n_j - 1)], \qquad (12.6)$$

where the numerator represents the binomial variance function, and the denominator reflects the effect due to explicitly modelling random effects with ω. We now need a criterion by which we can estimate ω. One solution is to use a goodness-of-fit statistic from the model, such as the residual chi-squared statistic. The purpose of including the dispersion parameter is to account for any residual variance remaining after known and measured explanatory variables have been accounted for. If this has been successfully achieved, then the residual variation now left in the model should equal its asymptotic expectation (McCullagh and Nelder, 1989), i.e. the residual chi-squared statistic should equal its degrees of freedom. In this case, modelling proportions of individuals responding to a set of bid amounts, the degrees of freedom are defined as being the number of unique bid amounts (N) minus the number of parameters included in the model (p). Hence, according to Williams (1982),

$$\chi^2 = (N - p) = \Sigma_j[v_{jj}(y_j - n_j\pi_j)^2]/[n_j\pi_j(1 - \pi_j)], \qquad (12.7)$$

where

$$v_{jj} = [1 + \omega(n_j - 1)]^{-1} \qquad (12.8)$$

are the diagonal elements of an externally defined weights matrix V.

The model with external weights can be fitted iteratively, updating ω from (12.7) and (12.8) until convergence is achieved, or 'best guess' estimates may be made until a value of ω which results in a residual chi-squared close to the degrees of freedom is achieved. The method is described in more detail, with examples, in Langford (1994a). The main result of fitting a random effects model is that confidence intervals for E(WTP) widen to account for the lower confidence that can be placed in a poorly fitting model.

12.4.2   Generalized Linear Mixed Models

Breslow and Clayton (1993) describe a generalized linear mixed model (GLMM) which can include several different hyperparameters associated with random effects in a regression model. If we consider a logistic regression based on the responses of i individuals we can write

$$\ln[\pi_i/(1 - \pi_i)] = z_i = x_i^T \beta + r_i^T \gamma + e_i, \qquad (12.9)$$

where R is now a random design matrix associated with a vector of parameters to be estimated (γ). Hence, we not only have the usual design matrix to model fixed effects, or mean relationships in the regression equation, we have an additional matrix of explanatory variables which can model the residual variance present after fixed effects have been accounted for. In this respect, $x_i^T \beta$ are referred to as 'fixed effects' and $r_i^T \gamma$ as 'random effects' associated with the model. X and R do not have to be the same, as different variables may be included in the fixed and random parts of the model, and R will include a vector of residual-error terms after the model has been fitted. R may also include random effects associated with the j bid levels, as will be shown in Section 12.5. The comparison with (12.1) is that, instead of viewing the residual variation in a model as being an unknown, 'leftover' quantity, it is now being modelled with respect to a set of explanatory variables, and hence (12.9) is a much more powerful and versatile model. Estimation is more complex because of the need to fit fixed and random parameters, and is beyond the scope of this paper. However, full discussions of estimation procedures for linear and non-linear models are given in Goldstein (1991, 1995), Breslow and Clayton (1993), Longford (1993), and Wolfinger (1993), amongst other references.

Multi-level models may be seen as being a subset of GLMMs, where the data are arranged in a natural hierarchy and random effects may occur at each of the different levels of the hierarchy. Goldstein and MacDonald (1988) provide a description of a general multi-level model, which we shall apply to three different situations which may arise in the context of a CV survey.

12.5   MULTI-LEVEL MODELS FOR CONTINGENT VALUATION

In the following sections, a multi-level model is developed for a two-level hierarchy, in which individuals are nested within bid amounts offered. The theory presented previously is given a practical basis, and the model is built in stages to emphasize the key methodological points. The analysis is undertaken using a dedicated multi-level modelling software called MLn, developed by the Multilevel Models Project at the Institute of Education, London. Details of how to obtain this software are given at the end of the chapter.

12.5.1 A Single-Bounded Dichotomous-Choice Survey

One of the main problems in analysing dichotomous-choice data based on responses to a fixed number of bid amounts is that effects may be occurring between individuals, or between bid amounts. Each individual's response may be determined by characteristics such as income, age, knowledge, and usage of the commodity being valued, and these explanatory factors are linked to the binary 'yes/no' response elicited to a particular bid amount. However, DC surveys are usually analysed via the proportions of individuals responding to a set of bid amounts, and in this aggregation process, information at the individual level is lost. Mean income etc. may be modelled at each bid level (Langford and Bateman, 1993), but the situation is really inadequate as the range of incomes of individuals at each bid level is necessarily lost.

12.5.2 Data Structure

In Section 12.4, a random effects model was developed which included, in an uninformed way, the influence of a group of unmeasured explanatory variables. Here, we extend this to include the influence of a group of measured explanatory variables within a hierarchical or multi-level model. The DC survey design is an example of a two-stage hierachy where individual responses (at level 1) are nested within bid amounts (level 2).

For demonstration purposes, data are taken for 1,825 usable responses to a question eliciting willingness to pay an amount in extra taxation over the following year to preserve the Norfolk Broads, an internationally important wetland area, from seawater inundation. Full details of this survey are given in Bateman *et al.* (1995). The 1,825 individual responses (level 1) are nested within 8 bid amounts (level 2) of £1, £5, £10, £20, £50, £100, £200, and £500 with approximately 200 individuals responding to each bid level. The variables included in the analysis are detailed in Table 12.1. The natural logarithms of bid amount and income were used for statistical reasons, as these resulted in a better-fitting model.

Table 12.1 Variables used in the analysis

Variable name	Description
z_{ij}	The response variable, $\ln[\pi_{ij}/(1 - \pi_{ij})]$, where π_{ij} is the probability of a 'yes' response for the ith individual responding to the jth bid amount
$LNBID_j$	The natural logarithm of the jth bid level
$BOAT_{ij}$	Indicates boat ownership on the Norfolk Broads ($0 = \text{no}, 1 = \text{yes}$)
ENV_{ij}	Indicates membership of an environmental group ($0 = \text{no}, 1 = \text{yes}$)
$LNINC_{ij}$	The natural logarithm of an individual's annual income

12.5.3   Fitting a Multi-Level Model

Using the notation of Bryk and Raudenbush (1992), we can write down a fully unconditional ANOVA (i.e. a model without explanatory variables) as

$$\ln[\pi_{ij}/(1 - \pi_{ij})] = z_{ij} = \beta_{oj} + r_{ij}, \qquad (12.10)$$

where z_{ij} is the logit of the response of the ith individual to the jth bid level. β_{oj} is the mean outcome for the jth bid amount, i.e. the proportion of individuals responding 'yes', and r_{ij} is a level-1 (individual) error term, assumed to be distributed on $N(0, \sigma^2)$. This is a level-1 model, as we are dealing with individual responses, but we can also write down a level-2 model for the proportions of individuals responding 'yes' to a particular bid amount as

$$\beta_{oj} = \gamma_{00} + u_{oj}, \qquad (12.11)$$

where γ_{00} represents the grand mean, or the total proportion of 'yes' responses in the entire survey population. The residual u_{oj} is the random effect, or random departure of the proportion of 'yes' responses to the jth bid amount from this grand mean, and is assumed to have zero mean and variance τ_{00}. This model may be written in combined form as

$$z_{ij} = \gamma_{00} + u_{oj} + r_{ij}, \qquad (12.12)$$

where the total variance of the outcome variable is the sum of the random terms in the model, i.e.

$$\text{Var}(z_{ij}) = \text{Var}(u_{oj} + r_{ij}) = \tau_{00} + \sigma^2. \qquad (12.13)$$

Hence, we are partitioning the variance, and ascribing some of it to the difference between individuals (σ^2), and some of it to the difference between responses to different bid amounts (τ_{00}). In MLn, a single column of 1's are inputted to represent the constant, or intercept, in the model and a parameter is estimated for this intercept (CONS). MLn divides the model into fixed effects and random effects as specified in Equation (12.9), and hence the output for this model is as shown in Table 12.2.

In the fixed part of the model, 'CONS' refers to the overall mean, γ_{00}, and therefore represents the logit of the mean number of 'yes' responses in the data set, i.e. $[1 + \exp(0.5959)]^{-1} = 0.645$. The random term CONS/CONS at level 2 is a coefficient representing the mean variance of the u_{0j}, i.e. τ_{00}, whilst the equivalent level-1 term is constrained to be unity to represent binomial variance. Hence, the level-2 term represents extra-binomial variation in the model. The goodness of fit is measured by the scaled deviance (McCullagh and Nelder, 1989). We can remove the constraint of binomial variation and examine whether extra-binomial variation is present in the model by estimating σ^2 as CONS/CONS at level 1, which gives the results in Table 12.3.

Table 12.2

Random effects		
	Level 2	
Parameter	Estimate	St. error
CONS / CONS	1.117	0.5682
	Level 1	
Parameter	Estimate	St. error
CONS / CONS	1	0

Fixed effects		
Parameter	Estimate	St. error
CONS	0.5959	0.3769

Note: scaled deviance = 2,057.9, d.f. = 1,823.

Table 12.3

Random effects		
	Level 2	
Parameter	Estimate	St. error
CONS / CONS	1.122	0.5683
	Level 1	
Parameter	Estimate	St. error
CONS / CONS	0.7445	0.0247

Fixed effects		
Parameter	Estimate	St. error
CONS	0.5958	0.3769

Note: scaled deviance = 1,986.08, d.f. = 1,822.

As can be seen, the model is underdispersed compared to the binomial assumption, i.e. the amount of variance present between individuals is lower than would be expected for a binomial distribution. If the variance was purely binomial, the coefficient for CONS/CONS at level 1 would be 1, as in the previous model where it was constrained, and it is only 0.7445. However, there is still some variation in the model which cannot be explained by the binomial assumption of variation between individuals, and is due to bid-amount level effects. This is the variance estimated by CONS/CONS at level 2 in the random effects part of the model. The next stage is to include explanatory variables in the model. The most obvious reason for variation between proportions of responses to each bid amount is the value of the bid amount. So far, we have not specified the amount (in pounds sterling) of each level-2 unit, only that the units are different by estimating separate β_{oj}. The mean variance of the β_{oj} is that estimated by CONS/CONS at level 2 in the model. We can now include the monetary value of each bid amount as an explanatory variable, and write the following level-1 model:

$$z_{ij} = \beta_{oj} + \beta_{1\bullet}\text{LNBID}_j + r_{ij}. \qquad (12.14)$$

In this case, there can be no random variation of LNBID as it simply attaches monetary values to the units already defined in the structure of the model as being the level-2 units, and hence the variance between these is included in the intercept. Therefore, the level-2 model for $\beta_{1\bullet}$ is trivial, namely:

$$\beta_{1\bullet} = \gamma_{10}. \qquad (12.15)$$

The MLn output for this model is as shown in Table 12.4.

Calculating median willingness to pay (WTP) as $\exp(-\gamma_{00}/\gamma_{10})$ gives a value of £103.15. The exponential is used as we are modelling the natural logarithm of bid level in this case, and the value of $E(\text{WTP})$ has to be transformed back to the original scale. However, other variables may vary randomly at level 1 and level 2. These variables may be dummy variables (BOAT and ENV), or continuous variables such as LNINC (see Table 12.1). Taking LNINC as an example, we can write a level-1 model:

$$z_{ij} = \beta_{oj} + \beta_{1\bullet}\text{ LNBID}_j + \beta_{2j}\text{LNINC}_{ij} + r_{ij}, \qquad (12.16)$$

where the level-2 model for β_{2j} is

$$\beta_{2j} = \gamma_{20} + u_{2j} \qquad (12.17)$$

and γ_{20} represents a fixed parameter estimate with u_{2j} departures from this fixed estimate at level 2. The level-2 variance now contains three terms: τ_{00} (the variance of the u_{oj}), τ_{22} (the variance of the u_{2j}), and also τ_{02}, which represents the covariance between the u_{oj} and the u_{2j}. In simple terms, we have a variance term associated with the intercepts, one with the slopes for

Table 12.4

Random effects		
	Level 2	
Parameter	Estimate	St. error
CONS / CONS	0.144	0.0850
	Level 1	
Parameter	Estimate	St. error
CONS / CONS	0.9711	0.0322
Fixed effects		
Parameter	Estimate	St. error
CONS	2.6440	0.312
LNBID	−0.5703	0.0799

Note: scaled deviance = 1,939.65, d.f. = 1,821.

Table 12.5

Random effects		
	Level 2	
Parameter	Estimate	St. error
CONS / CONS	0.1444	0.0854
LNINC / CONS	0.00	0.00
LNINC / LNINC	0.00	0.00
	Level 1	
Parameter	Estimate	St. error
CONS / CONS	0.9678	0.0321
Fixed effects		
Parameter	Estimate	St. error
CONS	2.009	0.5682
LNBID	−0.5715	0.0789
LNINC	0.0691	0.0518

Note: scaled deviance = 1,934.7, d.f. = 1,819.

LNINC, and another for the variance between the slopes and intercepts. This model provides the MLn output shown in Table 12.5.

The random terms at level 2 including income (τ_{02} and τ_{22}) are both estimated as zero, meaning that there is no estimated variance between the relationship of the response variable and LNINC between bid levels (see Section 12.5.4). These terms can be omitted, and in fact, no significant variance was found at level 2 for any of the explanatory variables. The final model, including all explanatory variables and significant first-order interactions in the fixed part of the model, was as shown in Table 12.6.

Table 12.6

Random effects		
	Level 2	
Parameter	Estimate	St. error
CONS / CONS	0.1482	0.0872
	Level 1	
Parameter	Estimate	St. error
CONS / CONS	0.9692	0.0322
Fixed effects		
Parameter	Estimate	St. error
CONS	1.783	0.6275
LNBID	−0.5814	0.0800
LNINC	0.0730	0.0588
BOAT	1.238	1.223
ENV	0.2562	0.1091
LNINC-BOAT	−0.0711	0.1306

Note: scaled deviance = 1,891.3, d.f. = 1,817.

where LNINC–BOAT represents the interaction between LNINC and BOAT, and significance was judged on reduction in deviance distributed approximately on a chi-squared distribution.

12.5.4   Implications of multi-level modelling

The multi-level model provides a very flexible approach to parameter estimation with CV data. Explanatory variables and their interactions may be fitted in the normal way to the fixed part of the model, and their significance judged on the reduction of scaled deviance achieved by their inclusion (changes in deviance being roughly chi-squared distributed on the appropriate degrees of freedom). Calculating t-values (parameter estimates divided by standard errors) to estimate significance may be misleading for random parameters, as these may not have easily defined distributions, particularly when there are relatively few units making up a particular level, and we only have eight separate bid amounts at level 2 here. The main point to remember is that the variance in the model has been divided between individual effects and effects due to different mean responses to each bid amount offered. The multi-level model is therefore a correct representation of the information gathered in the CV study, as it models the natural hierarchy present in the data.

The division of the model into fixed and random parts leads to greater flexibility, and allows for more conservative estimates of the standard errors of parameters to be made, as the effects at level 2 are empirical Bayes estimates shrunken towards a mean value (Langford, 1994a). However, the desirability of this shrinkage should be evaluated (Bryk and Raudenbush, 1992), and it must be remembered that the variances at level 2 are likely to be underestimated if the number of level-2 units is small. In this example we had only eight bid amounts, and it is most likely that this lack of information accounts for the zero variance estimates for LNINC and other variables at level 2. Therefore, for optimum performance, a multi-level modelling approach needs as many bid levels as possible to improve the variance estimates at level 2 (Langford et al., 1996). Furthermore, because of the hierarchical nature of the model, we no longer require large samples of individuals to be taken at each bid amount. In a conventional weighted least-squares model, the samples of individuals responding to each bid level are considered wholly independent of each other. In the multi-level model, each sample is providing an input into the estimation of population parameters at level 2, with deviations around these for each separate bid amount. Bid amounts which have relatively few individuals will have their estimates shrunken more towards the population mean than bid amounts with relatively many individuals. This Bayesian hierarchical approach therefore requires a sampling strategy which maximizes the number of individual bid amounts rather than the number of individuals responding to each bid amount (Langford et al., 1996).

In summary, the multi-level approach is novel, and requires more thoughtful interpretation than ordinary (or weighted) least-squares equivalents. The software used is rather specialist at present, although multi-level models can be fitted on packages such as GAUSS if the necessary macros are constructed. A conservative approach to survey design is to take a sample with no fewer than about thirty individuals at each bid amount so that conventional modelling is feasible, but to maximize the number of bid amounts within this constraint so that a multi-level model can be fitted as well. Further research is currently being undertaken to collect a data set which is designed specifically for the application of a multi-level model. This should allow for the demonstration of the true power and flexibility of the method compared to conventional approaches, which ignore either individual or group effects in modelling responses to dichotomous-choice surveys.

12.6. OTHER APPLICATIONS

12.6.1 Multiple Bounds

There are several potential extensions beyond the basic two-level model of individuals nested within bid amounts. Two particular possibilities are:

1. The inclusion of a qualitative response of the form 'are you willing to pay anything at all?' which has no monetary amount attached prior to eliciting WTP. Discussion of this issue is given in Bateman *et al.* (1995).
2. The use of multiple bounds, where further questions are posed beyond the first bid amount. Hanemann *et al.* (1991) discuss the estimation of a double-bounded DC format using a multinomial logit model.

In a multi-level model, we can include multiple responses as another level in the model. Hence, we can extend the simple DC data set analysed here to two levels and even three levels, where responses are nested within individuals, who are in turn nested within initial bid amounts. Examples of a triple-bounded model with a qualitative as well as quantitative responses are given in Langford *et al.* (1996) and in Chapter 15. The important point to note is that in the multi-level model we can retain each binary response to each question, whether qualitative or quantitative, and from these simple building blocks construct the model we require, including explanatory variables if appropriate. In fact, any amount of questions may be asked of an individual, so the analysis may be *n*-bounded without any extra sophistication being required in the modelling procedure. Decisions on the structure of the questions asked will then be focused on more substantive issues such as respondent fatigue and so on.

12.6.2 Open-Ended Formats

A further possibility is the analysis of open-ended CV data, where WTP is elicited by allowing respondents to state any amount they wish between zero and infinity. However, this can again be preceded by a qualitative question asking about willingness to pay anything at all as a matter of principle. There are therefore two different responses for each individual, the first a binary response to the qualitative question, the second a continuous response variable which will only have a value if the answer to the qualitative question is 'yes'. A multi-level model may contain mixed responses, and so these two variables can be modelled simultaneously, and the relationship between willingness to pay anything at all and any subsequent stated amount examined in relationship to explanatory variables. Research is currently being undertaken by the authors regarding the application of such a model.

12.7 CONCLUSIONS AND IMPLICATIONS

Multi-level modelling is a relatively new development in statistical analysis, and this chapter has introduced the technique via a relatively simple example, with comments on possible extensions. Whilst full explanation of all aspects of the technique exceeds the scope of the present discussion, there are several important advantages of multi-level over conventional modelling, which may be summarized as:

1. Multi-level modelling is highly flexible, and can account for complex data structures and research designs. Multiple responses are allowed, and there is no need for each individual to answer the same set of questions, or have the same number of responses. Qualitative and quantitative data may be mixed, and responses do not have to have the same distributional form. Binary, binomial, and continuous responses may be included in the same dependent variable.

2. Micro- and macro-level analyses can be undertaken simultaneously. The responses of individuals can be modelled with respect to individual-level variables such as income, and group variables such as initial bid amount offered. The possibilities are virtually limitless. Different social groups could be included as further levels, or geographical location (e.g. which electoral ward each individual lives in) and group variables associated with these levels examined. Hence, the context in which an individual lives can be modelled alongside each individual's personal characteristics.

3. Statistical 'problems' such as autocorrelation of residuals, heteroscedasticity, and variable quantity and quality of information can be modelled explicitly, and cease to be problems, but become avenues of further investigation.

4. Complex models can be built up by the researcher from simple building blocks, such as binary responses. This means that more of the reality of the elicitation format can be preserved, and it is not simply a question of modelling means, i.e. aggregates of responses, or ignoring structures within the data. The specifics of individuals, places, social groups, bidding formats, and so on can be retained, and research designs can be more adventurous as large sample sizes are not necessarily required to support aggregated parameters, such as proportions of individuals responding to a particular bid level. Hence, more useful information can be gathered, and parameter estimation is more efficient. Research is being undertaken by the authors on the application of bootstrapping techniques (Efron and Tibshirani, 1993) to provide confidence intervals around estimated WTP from multi-level models.

Finally, and most importantly, if the contents of this chapter have interested you, the best thing to do is have a go yourself. The models discussed in this chapter were all fitted using the MLn software, available from The Multilevel Models Project, Department of Mathematics, Statistics and Computing, Institute of Education, University of London, 20 Bedford Way, London WC1H OAL, UK.

Multi-level models can be fitted in a wide variety of statistical software packages, but MLn is specifically designed for this type of modelling and therefore extensive macros do not have to be written to account for the multi-level structure in parameter estimation. The authors are currently involved in a number of projects to further test the use of multi-level models in exploring more fully the various substantive and technical issues in contingent valuation, and these results will be published in the literature in due course.

REFERENCES

Arrow, K., Solow, R., Portney, P. R., Leamer, E. E., Radner, R., and Schuman, H. (1993), Report of the NOAA Panel on Contingent Valuation, *Federal Register*, 58: 4602–14.

Bateman, I. J., Langford, I. H., Turner, R. K., Willis, K. G., and Garrod, G. D. (1995), 'Elicitation and Truncation Effects in Contingent Valuation Studies'. *Ecological Economics*, 12: 161–79.

Breslow, N. E., and Clayton, D. G. (1993), 'Approximate Inference in Generalised Linear Mixed Models', *Journal of the American Statistical Association*, 88: 9–25.

Bryk, A. S., and Raudenbush, S. W. (1992), *Hierarchical Linear Models: Applications and Data Analysis Methods*, Sage, London.

Carr-Hill, R. A., Sheldon, T. A., Smith, P., Martin, S., Peacock, S., and Hardman, G. (1994), 'Allocating Resources to Health Authorities: Development of Method for

Small Area Analysis of Use of Inpatient Services', *British Medical Journal*, 309: 1046–9.

Clayton, D., and Kaldor, J. (1987), 'Empirical Bayes Estimates of Age-Standardised Relative Risks for Use in Disease Mapping', *Biometrics*, 43: 671–81.

Dobson, A. J. (1990), *An Introduction to Generalised Linear Models*, Chapman and Hall, London.

Duffield, J. W., and Patterson, D. A. (1991), 'Inference and Optimal Design for a Welfare Measure in Dichotomous Choice Contingent Valuation', *Land Economics*, 67:225–39.

Duncan, C., Jones, K., and Moon, G. (1993), 'Do Places Matter? A Multi-Level Analysis of Regional Variations in Health-Related Behaviour in Britain', *Social Science and Medicine*, 37: 725–33.

Ecob, R. (1992), *A Multilevel Modelling Approach to Examining the Effects of Area of Residence on Fifteen Measures of Health and Functioning*, MRC Medical Sociology Unit Working Paper no. 41, Glasgow.

Efron, B., and Tibshirani, R. J. (1993), *An Introduction to the Bootstrap*, Chapman and Hall, London.

Goldstein, H. (1987), *Multilevel Models in Educational and Social Research*, Charles Griffen, London.

——(1991), 'Nonlinear Multilevel Models, with an Application to Discrete Response Data', *Biometrika*, 78: 45–51.

——(1995), *Multilevel Statistical Models*, Edward Arnold, London.

——and McDonald, R. P. (1988), 'A General Model for the Analysis of Multilevel Data', *Psychometrika*, 53: 455–67.

Hanemann, W. M., Loomis, J., and Kanninen, B. (1991), 'Statistical Efficiency of Double-Bounded Dichotomous Choice Contingent Valuation', *American Journal Agricultural Economics*, 73: 1255–63.

Jones, K. (1991), 'Specifying and Estimating Multi-Level Models for Geographical Research', *Transactions of the Institute of British Geographers New Series*, 16: 148–59.

Langford I. H. (1994a). 'Using Empirical Bayes Estimates in the Geographical Analysis of Disease Risk', *Area*, 26: 142–9.

——(1994b). 'Using a Generalised Linear Mixed Model to Analyse Dichotomous Choice Contingent Valuation Data', *Land Economics*, 70: 507–14.

——(1995a), 'A Log-Linear Multi-Level Model of Childhood Leukaemia Mortality', *Journal of Health and Place*, 1: 113–20.

——(1995b), *Multilevel Modelling In Health Service Resource Allocation: A Review of Current Research, Issues and Future Applications*, Report for the King's Fund Institute, London.

——and Bateman, I. J. (1993), *Welfare Measures for Contingent Valuation Studies: Estimation and Reliability*, CSERGE GEC Working Paper 93–04, University of East Anglia, Norwich.

——and Bentham G. (1996), 'Regional Variations in Mortality Rates in England and Wales: an Analysis Using Multi-level Modelling'. *Social Science and Medicine*, 42.6, 897–908.

——Bateman, I. J., and Langford, H. D. (1996), 'A Multilevel Modelling Approach to Triple-Bounded Dichotomous Choice Contingent Valuation', *Environmental and Resource Economics*, 7.3, 197–211.

Lindley, D. V., and Smith, F. M. (1972), 'Bayes Estimates for the Linear Model (with discussion)', *Journal of the Royal Statistical Society Series* B, 34:1–41.

Longford, N. T. (1993), *Random Coefficient Models*, Oxford University Press.

Manly, B. F. J. (1978), 'Regression Models for Proportions with Extraneous Variance', *Biometrie-Praximetrie*, 18: 1–18.

McCullagh, P., and Nelder, J. A. (1989), *Generalised Linear Models*, Chapman and Hall, London.

Wedderburn, R. W. M. (1974), 'Quasi-Likelihood Functions, Generalized Linear Models, and the Gauss–Newton Method', *Biometrika*, 61: 439–47.

Williams, D. A. (1982), 'Extra-Binomial Variation in Logistic Linear Models', *Applied Statistics*, 31: 144–8.

Wolfinger, R. (1993), 'Laplace's Approximation for Nonlinear Mixed Models', *Biometrika*, 80: 791–5.

13

Stated-Preference Methods for Valuing Environmental Amenities

WIKTOR L. ADAMOWICZ
PETER C. BOXALL
JORDAN J. LOUVIERE
JOFFRE SWAIT
MICHAEL WILLIAMS

13.1 INTRODUCTION

Contingent valuation (CV) has been employed by economists for approximately thirty years to value changes in natural resources and environments. Estimating the value of resource improvements or damages is analogous to the problem in marketing research of estimating the demand for new products or services. There are two basic approaches to this problem which have evolved during the past two decades, although there are minor variations within each (see, for example, Urban and Hauser, 1993). The first approach involves the development of a detailed concept description of the product for which the demand forecast is to be made. This description need not be purely verbal but may require the development of renderings, models, mock-ups, prototypes, multimedia presentations, etc. In any case, the essential element is that the most accurate description possible of one (or at most a very few) potential products is used as the basis for determining the potential demand or share. In the second approach, the product of interest is viewed as one of many possible products which differ in the values or positions they occupy on key product characteristics or features. In this approach, carefully designed arrays of product characteristics are used to develop a number of product concept descriptions to which consumers react. This approach differs in terms of whether the product descriptions are shown 'one at a time', which represents some variant of traditional conjoint analysis (Green et al., 1972; Green and Srinavasan, 1978, 1990; Louviere 1988b, 1994), or presented as sets of competing options, which represents some variant of experimental-choice analysis (Louviere and Woodworth 1983; Louviere 1988a, b, 1994; Batsell and Louviere, 1991; Carson et al., 1994).

The first approach shares many similarities with traditional applications of CV, in which as accurate as possible a description of a resource improvement or damage is formulated, and samples of individuals are asked to respond to that improvement using open- or closed-ended valuation questions. The problem with this approach is that it relies very heavily on the accuracy of a particular description, and any errors in the description discovered after the fact cannot be changed. Thus, in the case of product concepts, if consumers are told the selling price is $5.48, but the actual selling price upon and after introduction is $7.24, there is no way to 'adjust' the forecast to take this into account. Similarly, in the case of a resource damage scenario, if later research indicates that instead of 250 dead ducks, the number was closer to 375, there is no way to take that into account. Similarly, this approach cannot actually value the various and separate components of the description; hence, the value of each duck cannot be determined. Likewise, in marketing research applications, the values of individual product features that make up the product bundle cannot be ascertained.

In contrast, the second approach relies less on the accuracy and completeness of any particular product bundle description, but rather more on the accuracy and completeness of the product characteristics and features used to describe all the bundles. In this approach, a stream pollution 'event' is viewed as one of many possible such events, and the onus is on the researcher to determine as exhaustive a set of variables as possible to describe either stream pollution events in general, or events that fall within a particular mutually exclusive category that includes the event in question. Statistical design techniques are used to sample from the universe of all possible 'events' that are spanned by the variables and the values that the variables can take on in the type(s) of problem of interest. Rather than being questioned about a single event in detail, therefore, consumers are questioned about a sample of events drawn from the universe of possible events of that type. We refer to this latter method as the stated-preference (SP) approach.

While CV methods have attracted environmental and natural resource economists' attention for nearly three decades, SP approaches to eliciting consumer preferences have not. SP methods have remained in the domain of human decision research, marketing, and transportation research, even though support for their use in economic analysis was formalized some time ago (McFadden, 1986). In this paper, the stated-preference approach is outlined, and its use to value environmental amenities described. The advantages of SP techniques, both in relation to CV methods and revealed-preference (RP) techniques, are also discussed.

13.2. THE STATED-PREFERENCE APPROACH

Stated-preference analysis, or the experimental analysis of choice, has its roots in conjoint analysis. Conjoint analysis is a form of analysis used to

represent individual judgements of multi-attribute stimuli (Batsell and Louviere, 1991). Conjoint analysis is a well-known technique and has been
applied in marketing for over twenty years. However, conjoint techniques
have more recently been applied in geography, transportation, and economics (see Louviere, 1991). The particular type of conjoint analysis examined
here is the experimental analysis of choice. This particular approach is
adopted because it parallels the Random Utility Model (RUM) structure
(see McFadden, 1974; Ben-Akiva and Lerman, 1985) that is common in
referendum CV models (Mitchell and Carson, 1989) and in discrete-choice
travel-cost models (Bockstael et al., 1991).

13.2.1   Steps in an SP Experiment

There is a considerable literature that describes the steps to be taken in
designing a CV experiment (Mitchell and Carson, 1989). Similarly, there is
a substantial literature on designing SP experiments (Louviere, 1988a;
Hensher, 1994). A summary of the SP steps is provided here with some
elaboration of the components presented below. These steps are based on
Hensher (1994):

1. Identification of the set of attributes.
2. Selecting the measurement unit for each attribute.
3. Specification of the number and magnitude of attribute levels.
4. Experimental design.
5. Survey instrument design.
6. Model estimation.
7. Use of parameters to simulate choice.

Most of these steps are well known to CV researchers. Tasks 1–3 can be
considered the preparation of the information phase of CV. CV researchers
are concerned with accurate presentation of information in a clear, concise
fashion. Steps 1–3 in SP experiments attempt to describe the choice context in
the form of attributes. This is, in many ways, the most important element of
an SP study. This stage of research typically involves information collection
from secondary sources, focus group research, and pre-testing in order to
identify the attributes of a situation as perceived by the respondent and to
determine the levels of the attributes in a manner that can be understood by
the respondent. In both CV and SP the concern is with presenting the
respondent with information that they can understand and respond to.
Step 4 is unique to SP and is one of the advantages of the approach. It is
discussed in detail below. Step 5 is again comparable with a CV task. Survey
design is important in any stated-preference approach. In SP tasks the fact
that respondents may be asked to consider several choice sets and/or multiple
alternatives within each choice set raises a set of survey design issues that are
different from CV concerns. These are also discussed in more detail below.

In referendum CV models, econometric modelling is necessary and these models are then used to calculate welfare measures. Thus, steps 6 and 7 are common to SP and CV. However, recent advances in the analysis of SP tasks has led to the finding that these data sets can be combined with CV and/or RP data to enrich the data sources. These findings are discussed in Section 13.2.5. Also, since SP employs a RUM formulation, welfare analysis applied to these models in the economics literature can be employed to yield measures of compensating variation from the SP models. This aspect is discussed in Section 13.2.6.

13.2.2. Experimental Designs

One of the fundamental aspects of SP methods is their use of experimental designs to array attributes and levels into choice sets. There is a large literature on this topic and a general consensus that the issues are well-understood (Batsell and Louviere, 1991; Carson *et al.*, 1994). Given a set of attributes and levels, design methods can be used to structure paired comparisons or choice sets with more than two alternatives.

The experimental-choice approach pioneered by Louviere and his associates requires the researcher to design both the 'product' descriptions and the choice sets. These descriptions are designed to satisfy the statistical assumptions and properties of various probabilistic discrete-choice models. Unfortunately, as discussed by Louviere and Woodworth (1983), Batsell and Louviere (1991), and Bunch *et al.* (1992), probabilistic discrete-choice models are non-linear, and research into the construction of designs with desirable statistical efficiency properties for such models has barely begun (see Bunch *et al.*, 1992 for a review of this literature and a discussion of the issues). Thus, the current state of the art in design construction for discrete dependent-variable models is such that there are a large number of construction techniques now known to produce designs that satisfy the properties of the models and permit the identification of a wide range of model forms and utility specifications (see, e.g., Batsell and Louviere, 1991; Bunch *et al.*, 1992; Louviere, 1994). Choosing among any of the candidate designs on the basis of statistical efficiency, however, remains elusive because one must know the true vector of probabilities a priori to optimize any particular design for efficiency, an obvious design impediment.[1] The most recent statement of the state of the art in this area, based on the discussions and conclusions of the Workshop on Experimental Choice Analysis at the Duke Invitational Conference on Consumer Decision Making and Choice Behavior (Carson, *et al.* 1994), concluded that a number of design construction approaches are

[1] It is noteworthy that CV research has focused on optimal statistical bid designs (Cooper, 1993) in order to efficiently estimate this important parameter. SP research, on the other hand, has concentrated on estimating the parameters of various attributes of the choice situation in a relatively (although not optimally) efficient fashion.

probably quite statistically efficient, but that formal proofs of this property are unavailable.

In the research described below, a design construction technique is employed which was first proposed by Louviere and Woodworth (1983) and since applied in many empirical research efforts (e.g., see Adamowicz et al., 1994; Swait et al., 1994). This approach treats the attributes of all competing alternatives (known as 'factors' in the design literature in marketing and statistics) and their associated levels as one large factorial design. The design problem consists of selecting samples of choice sets from the space spanned by the attributes and levels such that various identification properties can be realized. In the present case, the eventual wish is to test for violations of the IIA property of certain probabilistic choice models like the conditional logit model (McFadden, 1974), and to explore more general stochastic choice model forms if necessary. Hence, the choice sets and the descriptions (called 'profiles' in the marketing literature) are designed to permit the estimation of the most general model possible, which in this case is McFadden's (1975) Mother Logit model (see also McFadden et al., 1977).

While the statistical design aspect of SP can be considered an advantage, care must be taken to ensure that the design is capturing the salient elements of the choice process. In cases with many attributes and/or levels, the potential number of combinations is very large. Experimental design can provide a structure that allows the estimation of parameters, however, and this design requires assumptions of zero coefficients on higher-order interactions. For example, most SP research employs main effects plans that preclude the analysis of interaction effects between attributes. This suggests that a well-designed SP study, just like a well-designed CV study, requires a significant amount of pre-test work to identify attributes, levels, and important interactions (Louviere, 1988a).

An important aspect of the design process is that alternatives can be constructed to maintain orthogonality in the attributes. In contrast to revealed-preference (or actual-choice) data, which are often correlated, this property allows the researcher to identify the contribution of each attribute to the choice process. The use of orthogonal experimental designs in SP approaches also allows the SP data to be used as a form of 'external information' to alleviate colinearity in RP models. SP information can be used in a type of mixed estimation process to address this issue. However, in order to be used in such a fashion, the models must be estimated jointly. This aspect of SP models is examined below.

13.2.3.   Survey Design Considerations

An aspect of SP experimental procedures that is different from CV approaches is the determination of the number and size of the choice set.

For example, in Adamowicz *et al.* (1994), respondents were presented with 16 choice sets and were asked to choose 1 of the 3 options available. The experimental design process generated 64 choice sets but this was deemed to be too large a task for any respondent. Thus, the 64 sets were blocked into 4 sets of 16. Clearly, the researcher must consider how many choice sets a respondent can accurately assess and how many alternatives within each choice set can be examined. Referendum CV models essentially provide 1 choice set with 2 alternatives. Research in the marketing literature suggests that a respondent can assess fairly large numbers of choice sets but that providing more than 6 alternatives within each choice set is difficult (Batsell and Louviere, 1991).[2] However, in most environmental analysis cases, the researcher is concerned with the attributes before a change versus after a change. Thus, structuring experiments with 2 or 3 alternatives should represent reality quite well. For example, 2 designed alternatives could be presented along with the *status quo*.

13.2.4.   Model Estimation

In the SP approach the respondent is asked to select the preferred 'object' (described by attributes at various levels) from a choice set. Each alternative (i) in the choice set has an associated utility level represented by

$$U_i = V_i + \epsilon_i. \tag{13.1}$$

This utility is composed of an objective component (V_i) and an error component (e_i). In the economics literature this function is also known as a conditional indirect utility function since it is conditional on the choice of the object (i). Selection of one object (package of attributes) over another implies that the utility (U_i) of that object is greater than the utility of another, say j (U_j). Since overall utility is random one can only analyse the probability of choice of one package over another, or

$$Pr\{i \text{ chosen}\} = Pr\{V_i + \epsilon_i > V_j + \epsilon_j \ \forall j \in C\}, \tag{13.2}$$

where C is the choice set. Specific choices of error distributions lead to methods for the estimation of the parameters of this utility function and to quantitative representations of trade-offs between attributes. An assumption of Type I extreme value distributed errors produces the conditional logit specification of the probability of choice, or

$$Pr\{i\} = \frac{e^{V_i}}{\displaystyle\sum_{j \in C} e^{V_j}} \tag{13.3}$$

---

[2] Providing more than 6 alternatives is possible in cases with few attributes or relatively simple choice situations.

The Random Utility Model described above provides the basis for the experimental-choice process. However, this model is also the basis for the referendum model of CV. Thus, both techniques arise from the same theoretical background. SP, however, typically entails repeated measure responses from the individual while CV does not.[3]

Revealed-preference (RP) models also employ random utility theory. Typically these are models of recreational site choice or some other form of qualitative choice. These models are very popular in measuring economic values of environmental quality change (Bockstael *et al.*, 1991). In this case the objective component of the utility function is composed of measures of attributes of the 'real' alternatives. SP techniques directly parallel these qualitative-choice models, and, moreover, SP approaches avoid measurement error and colinearity effects common in RP methods.

13.2.5.   Joint Estimation of SP, RP, and CV Models

Since SP, RP, and CV models are all Random Utility Models they can be estimated jointly, exploiting the information available in each source. For example, Adamowicz *et al.* (1994) jointly estimate a SP and RP model of recreational site choice. In this case the SP and RP utility models can be specified as

$$U_{RP} = V_{RP} + \epsilon_{RP} \quad \text{and} \tag{13.4}$$
$$U_{SP} = V_{SP} + \epsilon_{SP}, \tag{13.5}$$

where RP indexes the revealed-preference utility function and SP indexes the stated-preference function. Given a similar set of attributes (one set based on the experimental design and the other based on actual conditions) the data can be 'stacked' to estimate a joint model. However, the variances in the two data sets may be different. In multinomial logit models it is common to assume that the scale parameters equal 1.[4] Swait and Louviere (1993) have developed an approach that estimates the relative scale parameter (the ratio of the scale parameters from each data set). This approach also facilitates the testing of the similarity of the models (equality of parameters) conditional on the possibility of different scale effects. In principle, SP, RP, and CV models can all be combined to utilize efficiently the information contained within each data form.

13.2.6.   Welfare Measures

SP models provide estimates of conditional indirect utility function parameters. Therefore, determination of theoretically correct measures of welfare

---
[3] There has been some movement toward a type of repeated measures response in CV via the double-bounded or triple-bounded referendum CV models (e.g. Hanemann *et al.*, 1991).
[4] In multinomial logit models, the scale parameter cannot be identified. Therefore, it is commonly assumed to be unity.

(compensating variation) is possible. Welfare measures arising from multi-nomial logit models are well known (Hanemann, 1984; Bockstael *et al.*, 1991). If one is interested in the value of an improvement at one of several available alternatives (e.g. recreation sites) then the comparison of the expected maximum utility before and after the change becomes the foundation of the welfare analysis.

It is also possible to structure SP welfare analysis along the lines of referendum CV measures. In referendum CV models, the expected value of willingness to pay can be calculated as the area under the distribution of the probability of accepting the bid (Hanemann, 1984). The median welfare measure can be described as the payment level that makes the individual indifferent between the improvement and the *status quo*. Since the SP models are random utility models they can be rearranged to describe the probability of choice of the *status quo* attributes versus the 'improved' attributes.

SP utility function parameters can be used to describe the marginal value of a change in an attribute. As shown by Lareau and Rae (1989) and Mackenzie (1993), in a simple linear model, the ratio of the attribute coefficient to the 'price' coefficient provides a marginal welfare effect. This welfare value, however, is not entirely consistent with the Random Utility Model if the welfare effect being examined is a change in one of several possible alternatives (e.g. quality changes at one of many recreation sites). In such a case information on the probability of choice of that alternative is also required (see Bockstael *et al.*, 1991).

13.2.7. Potential Advantages of SP Methods

Stated-preference methods can reveal the value of attributes as well as the value of more complex changes in several attributes. In terms of eliciting preferences, stated-preference methods, since they are structured as choices, have the same survey design advantages as referendum CV methods. That is, there will likely be fewer refusals and the choice approach is more familiar to the respondent than a 'payment' approach. However, the repeated sampling method employed in SP can alleviate some of the concerns regarding lower informational efficiency that affect the referendum CV model (Carson, 1991). Strategic behaviour should be minimal in SP tasks since the choices are made from descriptions of attributes and it will not be clear which choice will over- or underrepresent a valuation. The phenomenon of 'yea-saying' often arises in CV tasks as the respondents appear to be voting for an environmental 'good cause'. This phenomenon should not arise in SP tasks because the respondents will be choosing from a number of descriptions of situations, rather than a single base case compared to an improved-case situation. Embedding is a significant concern in the CV literature (Kahneman and Knetsch, 1992). SP exercises address embedding directly by having respondents implicitly value components. Alternatively, embedding effects can be tested as part of an SP design.

Stated-preference methods can be used as complements to CV and RP methods or as substitutes. They can be complements in that the information from these approaches can be combined to yield a richer overall result (Swait and Louviere, 1993; Adamowicz et al., 1994; Swait et al., 1994). They can be substitutes since stated-preference methods on their own are representations of individual choice consistent with Random Utility Theory. Furthermore, SP can examine situations (attributes, levels) that do not exist in currently available options. In such cases, RP is limited in scope since it relies on currently available attributes in generating behavioural representations of choice.

13.3.   EXAMPLES OF STATED-PREFERENCE METHODS IN ENVIRONMENTAL VALUATION

While the use of SP techniques in environmental valuation is relatively recent, there have been a few noteworthy examples. Lareau and Rae (1989) studied the value of odour reductions using a type of SP model. They asked individuals to rank alternative combinations of odour contact numbers and increased household costs. Rae (1983) employed SP-type techniques in the analysis of benefits from air quality improvements. Mackenzie (1993) has employed SP-type techniques to examine trade-offs between attributes of recreational hunting experiences. Mackenzie compares a variety of SP methods and illustrates how many of these techniques can be designed to correspond with the Random Utility Model. Opaluch et al. (1993) employed pairwise choices in an SP framework to analyse hazardous waste siting decisions. Viscusi et al. (1991) employed SP-type techniques in analysing health risk trade-offs. Goodman (1989) examines housing attributes in an SP framework (see also Freeman, 1991).

Adamowicz et al. (1994) employed a choice-experiment design to value the impact of a water resource development. This model was constructed to examine recreational site choice. They also examined a revealed-preference model of site choice, and combined the two approaches. Among the interesting findings from this study was the fact that the RP and SP models were not significantly different (once the differences in the scale factors were accounted for).

While there are relatively few examples of stated-preference studies in the environmental valuation field, it is probable that this area of research will increase rapidly. Another example of SP and CV is now presented, based on research in Alberta.

13.4. RECREATIONAL QUALITY IMPROVEMENTS: AN APPLICATION OF STATED-PREFERENCE AND CONTINGENT VALUATION

13.4.1. The Valuation of Recreational Site Quality Improvements

As a test of stated-preference and contingent valuation techniques a research project involving the valuation of recreational hunting quality improvements was undertaken. This particular activity provides an excellent opportunity for the testing of these procedures because: (1) there is a substantial literature on valuing quality changes in recreational activities; (2) the activity is well-defined and the quality attributes are typically well understood by the respondents; (3) the fact that individuals travel to recreation sites provides a realistic payment vehicle; and (4) one can construct a corresponding revealed-preference model of recreational hunting behaviour.

The purpose of the research was to estimate the value of moose habitat improvements in general, rather than the value of a single habitat improvement. However, to the extent that the fundamental variables that influence moose hunters' or other observers' valuations of habitat changes are understood, it should be possible not only to estimate the value of a particular habitat change, but also to value the components of habitat changes in general, regardless of location and extent. To this end, therefore, exploratory research was undertaken with samples of moose hunters in areas likely to be affected by the proposed habitat change(s) to determine how hunters think and talk about (1) moose hunting in general and (2) improvements in habitat as they affect the quality of the moose population that they hunt in particular. From this exploratory research it was possible to determine the kinds of variables, and ranges of values of those variables, that would be likely to influence moose hunters' valuations of habitat changes. These variables could then be related to specific wildlife management actions and measurements that could be taken to improve habitat conditions.

The study specifically focused on changes proposed for a particular Wildlife Management Unit (WMU) in west-central Alberta, Canada. This situation provided an excellent opportunity to compare traditional, event-specific CV valuation with the SP approach. Thus, the problem was conceptualized as one of hunters choosing among alternative WMUs which compete for their time and effort. Not surprisingly, because the research dealt with a real, existing region of WMUs, it was also possible to ascertain where hunters went last and to estimate the value of each WMU, and possibly its characteristics (depending on the statistical properties of the particular sample of WMUs in the region under study), using travel-cost approaches. The SP study was designed to resemble a travel-cost exercise in as many essential details as possible: hence, the SP study was deliberately formulated to resemble the problem faced by hunters as measured in the travel-cost approach.

Hunters face the problem of choosing one WMU in which to hunt on a particular trip from a set of available WMUs. Based on their choices, on associated characteristics of chosen and rejected WMUs, and on measured differences in hunters, a travel-cost model can be estimated using well-established techniques for estimating probabilistic discrete-choice models (McFadden, 1974; Ben-Akiva and Lerman, 1985; Bockstael et al., 1991). In the case of the SP survey, the research problem involves not only the a-priori identification of relevant variables that influence hunter choices and relevant ranges of these variables, but also the development of an appropriate choice experiment that mimics the actual choices faced by the hunters in the real environment. To do this, the study relied heavily on theory and methods described above (Louviere and Woodworth, 1983; Louviere, 1988a,b; Batsell and Louviere, 1991; Carson et al., 1994; Louviere 1994) to design and administer discrete-choice experiments.

The particular design strategy employed in the research involved initially determining a set of decision attributes and levels to represent their variation in the real situation (in this case, the WMUs in our study region). The attributes and levels used in the study were determined from focus group discussions with hunters, and from the authors' knowledge of hunting based on over ten years of research. These attributes are displayed in Table 13.1. The hunters' decision problem was conceptualized as one in which they were offered a choice between pairs of competing WMU descriptions, and then given the option of choosing to hunt in one of the described WMUs or to choose not to go moose hunting at all. The design was based on the attributes and levels described in Table 13.1. The design problem involves selecting a sample of WMU profile pairs from the universe of pairs given by a $(2^2 \times 4^4) \times (2^2 \times 4^4) \times (2 \text{ versions})$ factorial, i.e. treating left- and right-hand pairs as a composite set of attributes and levels. As discussed by Louviere and Woodworth (1983), the necessary and sufficient conditions to estimate the parameters of McFadden's (1975) Mother Logit model can be satisfied by selecting the smallest, orthogonal main effects design from this larger factorial to create the WMU profiles and pairs simultaneously. The smallest orthogonal main effects design consists of 32 pairs, which were blocked into two sets of 16 pairs each using a two-level blocking factor added to the design for that purpose.

This design strategy produced a survey in which samples of hunters in the areas potentially affected by the proposed WMU habitat improvement were shown 16 pairs of WMU profiles and asked what they would most likely do if their choices were restricted to only the left- and right-hand WMUs and the choice of not moose hunting in the region at all (see the Appendix to this chapter for an example of the choice question). Logical reasons why such choice restrictions might occur were suggested, such as floods, wildlife management decisions to close areas to hunting, blocking of access by timber companies, and the like. Such occurrences were realistic and had

Table 13.1   Attributes used in the stated preference experiment

Attribute	Level
Moose populations	Evidence of < 1 moose per day
	Evidence of 1–2 moose per day
	Evidence of 3–4 moose per day
	Evidence of more than 4 moose per day
Hunter congestion	Encounters with no other hunters
	Encounters with other hunters on foot
	Encounters with other hunters on ATVs
	Encounters with other hunters in trucks
Hunter access	No trials, cutlines, or seismic lines
	Old trails, passable with ATV
	Newer trails, passable with 4-wheel-drive vehicle
	Newer trails, passable with 2-wheel-drive vehicle
Forestry activity	Evidence of recent forestry activity
	No evidence of recent forestry activity
Road quality	Mostly paved, some gravel or dirt
	Mostly gravel or dirt, some paved
Distance to site	50 km
	150 km
	250 km
	350 km

occasionally happened in the past; hence, they provide hunters with rational reasons why choices might be restricted. Thus, the data for analysis consisted of the single choice from a trinary set of options observed in each of the 16 sets for each hunter in the sample. As described by Louviere and Woodworth (1983), these choices can be aggregated for analysis if homogeneity of preferences is assumed, or the sample can be categorized into mutually exclusive groups (segments) of hunters with similar tastes and preferences. The latter hypothesis can be tested, and is the subject of ongoing research. Indeed, a key advantage of the design strategy employed is that the design permits tests of violations of the IID error component assumption of stochastic choice models. One such violation is preference heterogeneity, which is currently being investigated. It is worth noting, however, that such investigations are non-trivial undertakings due to the magnitude of the data set(s) involved, and the number of tests required to pin-point the source of the IID violations should they occur (see Louviere 1988a, b, 1994; Batsell and Louviere, 1991; Carson et al., 1994).

As previously mentioned, a major advantage of the experimental-choice approach selected is that it is possible to value separately the attributes (and levels) of WMU profiles. Thus, not only can the value of the particular WMU habitat improvement of immediate interest be estimated, but it is also possible to determine the value of the attributes that comprise it. In this way, valuation can be generalized to any habitat improvement to any WMU that can be described by the attributes and associated levels. Theoretically, therefore, the estimated model(s) can be used to value habitat improvements in any WMU in west-central Alberta without having to repeat the study for each WMU of interest. This latter property of the particular SP approach selected is of great potential significance and value to agencies faced with assessment problems involving multiple sites and/or events of similar types, but lacking budgets and resources to conduct separate studies for each.

Hunters were also asked a CV-type question regarding an improvement in one particular WMU. The CV question was structured as a moose population improvement in WMU 344. This WMU is near the centre of the study area and has a very low moose density. The CV question included a description of the WMU and its moose population level and a description of the population improvement. The quality levels were described using the same terminology as the choice experiment. Moose populations would increase from seeing evidence of one moose per day of hunting to seeing evidence of two moose per day. The payment vehicle was a willingness to incur additional travel costs. This was considered to be a realistic payment vehicle since closing access routes is a common form of policy to lessen pressure on moose populations. Closing access routes requires hunters to travel further to reach another access point. The CV experiment was a referendum model with ranges of additional distance travelled varied using draws from a random uniform distribution (for more details, see McLeod *et al.*, 1993).

13.4.2   Sampling and Data Collection

Samples of hunters were selected from Alberta Fish and Wildlife records. These hunters were mailed a letter indicating that the study was being conducted and that they would be telephoned regarding their participation. The hunters were then telephoned and asked to attend a meeting in their town (alternative dates were provided). Incentives were used to attract the hunters to the meetings. Of the 422 hunters who were telephoned, 312 confirmed that they would attend the sessions. Of these 312, 271 (87 per cent) actually attended the sessions. There were 8 sessions with group sizes ranging from 20 to 55.

Each hunter was asked to complete five survey components: (1) Demographics, (2) Choice Experiment, (3) Record of Moose Hunting Activity (revealed preference), (4) Contingent Valuation, and (5) Perceptions of Moose Hunting Site Quality. Sections 2–5 of the survey were randomized to allow testing of section-ordering bias. Further details of the sampling process and descriptive statistics can be found in McLeod *et al.* (1993).

13.4.3.   Model Results

The CV responses were analysed using standard binary logit techniques (dependent variable = the probability that the individual is willing to accept

Table 13.2   Results of stated preference, referendum CV, and joint estimation

Variable (attribute)	Stated-preference model	Referendum CV	Joint model (stated-preference and CV)
Distance	−0.0056 ∗ ∗	−0.0092 ∗ ∗	−0.0056
	(0.0002)	(0.0023)	(0.0002)
Road quality level 1	0.0185		0.0185
	(0.0260)		(0.0260)
Access level 1	−0.3210 ∗ ∗		−0.3210 ∗ ∗
	(0.0466)		(0.0466)
Access level 2	0.4006**		0.4006**
	(0.0499)		(0.0499)
Access level 3	0.1702**		0.1702**
	(0.0426)		(0.0426)
Congestion level 1	0.6030**		0.6030**
	(0.0442)		(0.0442)
Congestion level 2	0.0687		0.0688
	(0.0484)		(0.0488)
Congestion level 3	−0.2784 ∗ ∗		−0.2786 ∗ ∗
	(0.0464)		(0.0464)
Forestry level 1	−0.0452		−0.0453
	(0.0259)		(0.0259)
Moose population 1	−1.238 ∗ ∗		−1.240 ∗ ∗
	(0.0508)		(0.0494)
Moose population 2	−0.0622	1.188**	−0.0601
	(0.0446)	(0.2750)	(0.0429)
Moose population 3	0.4440**		0.4439**
	(0.0440)		(0.0440)
Relative scale parameter			1.5838**
			(0.4829)
Observations	266	271	537
Log likelihood (max)	−3,418.67	−177.70	−3,596.38
Log likelihood (0)	−4,675.69	−187.84	−4,863.54
ρ^2	0.2688	0.0540	0.2605

** indicates significant at 95% level.
Note: Standard error in parentheses.

the higher travel costs and the improved hunting quality). While analysis that includes demographic characteristics and alternative functional forms has been performed, this paper concentrates on a simple analysis of the CV model with 'bid' as the only independent variable. The results are presented in Table 13.2. The coefficient on bid (additional distance that the hunter is willing to travel) is negative and significant as expected. The median willingness to pay (per trip) for the improvement is $69.93 and the expected value is $85.59.[5] Note that the ρ^2 for the CV model is quite low (0.05).

[5] The calculation of median and mean willingness to pay is based on the measures provided by Hanemann (1984). However, the 'payment' is elicited in additional distance travelled. Therefore, we use $0.27 per kilometre to convert the distance into costs. This same measure of costs per kilometre is used in the stated-preference welfare analysis.

The results of the stated-preference experiment are also provided in Table 13.2. The qualitative attributes are described using effects coding.[6] As expected, distance is negative and significant. Moose population effects codes show rising utility as populations rise. Seeing no other hunters has a positive contribution to utility relative to seeing other hunters on ATVs, which is negative. The ρ^2 for this model is 0.22.

Since the attribute levels for all of the 15 hunting sites (WMUs) are known,[7] the improvement of site 344 can be examined using the expression derived by Hanemann (1984):

$$W = \frac{1}{\mu} \left[\ln \sum_{i \in C} e^{V_{i0}} - \ln \sum_{i \in C} e^{V_{i1}} \right] \qquad (13.6)$$

where W is compensating variation, V_{i0} and V_{i1} represent the utility before and after the change, μ is the marginal utility of income (the coefficient of the travel cost or price attribute), and C is the choice set of the individual (WMUs). As a comparison to the CV model, the value of the improvement of WMU 344 is calculated. Averaged over the individuals in the sample, it is valued at \$3.46 per trip.

13.4.4.   Combining SP and CV Data

The CV question essentially asks the hunter if he/she prefers site 344 as it is currently or if they prefer the site with higher access costs and better moose populations. This comparison can be described in the same framework as the SP model if one considers the CV question as a choice between two sites. The two data sets can be combined by simply defining the CV data as a two-element choice set in which only moose population and distance are different.[8] The results are provided in Table 13.2. Two interesting findings arise. First, the SP and CV data appear to have significantly different scale factors

---

[6] Effects codes are an alternative to dummy variables for qualitative attributes. If an attribute has 4 levels, the first 3 levels are coded as dummy variables (3 columns in the design matrix) and the 4th is coded as -1 for each column. The result is that the coefficient on the 4th level is the negative sum of the coefficients on the 3 other levels. The coefficients can be interpreted directly as the impact of that level of the attribute on utility.

[7] Information on the perceptions of attributes of the sites was also collected, allowing the examination of welfare results from 'objective' versus 'perceived' levels of quality. However, preliminary analysis (McLeod et al., 1993) suggests a reasonable degree of correlation between objective and perceived measures.

[8] The base situation can be represented as utility with current travel distance and current moose populations. The improved situation is represented as utility with current + additional travel distance and improved moose populations. Let moose populations be represented by a dummy variable where $1 =$ improved and $0 =$ base. The two utility functions are: $U_{base} = b_{00} + b_1$ (current distance) $+ b_2 * (0)$ and $U_{Improved} = b_{01} + b_1$ (current distance + additional distance) $+ b_{2*}(1)$. The utility difference expression (improved $-$ base) becomes $d_U = (b_{01} - b_{00} + b_{1*}$ (additional distance) $+ b_{2*}(1)$. The coefficients $(b_{01} - b_{00})$ and b_2 are not uniquely identified. In our empirical example we do not include the intercept terms and thus estimate only the parameter on moose populations.

(significant at a 95 per cent level). Second, the null hypothesis of parameter equality, after adjusting for differences in scale, cannot be rejected. Therefore, the CV and SP responses can be considered as arising from the same preferences. However, the coefficients of the joint model (Table 13.2) are almost exactly the same as those of the SP model. This suggests that the CV model has a high variance and that combining it with the SP data has little impact on the SP coefficients. In other words, the CV model contributes little to the SP estimates. The welfare measures from the joint models can also be determined. However, since the joint and SP model parameters are almost identical, there is little difference in the welfare measures.

13.5. DISCUSSION

The particular case examined here was designed to provide an example of SP techniques and a comparison of environmental valuation techniques. The 'goods' are well-known to the respondents and the quality change should be well understood. The town meeting format was used to aid in information provision and randomization of the task ordering. In general, respondents had no difficulty with the stated-preference questions. There were only a few respondents who did not complete the entire set of replications. The majority of respondents also completed the CV question.

The fact that the CV welfare measure is considerably higher than the SP measure raises questions about the 'correct' estimate. In further research, these results will be compared with RP measures as well as joint model estimates. At this point it is worth noting that the CV welfare measure is remarkably similar to the marginal welfare effect that can be derived using the ratios of coefficients from the SP model.[9] However, as mentioned earlier, this ratio of coefficients approach assumes that the change occurs at all 'sites'. Perhaps the CV measure is capturing the welfare change given that the hunter has already chosen site 344 (i.e. ignoring substitutes). The SP measure employed considers the fact that the hunter can choose one of the substitutes instead of site 344. In any event, these issues will be investigated in future research.

One advantage of the SP approach in this case is that the external validity of the technique can be determined. It is also possible to externally validate the CV model, although this would probably be more difficult. While there have been some positive findings regarding external validity of SP models (Batsell and Louviere, 1991) this is an area in which there will undoubtedly be further research.

---

[9] In discrete-choice models the travel cost term is modeled as (income − travel cost). The marginal utility of income is the parameter on the distance (travel-cost) term. The marginal utility of a quality change can be computed using the change in coefficients from one level to the next. The ratio of these two marginal utilities provides a welfare measure for a quality change.

The findings reported in this study should be considered preliminary in nature. However, given that the data collected include SP, CV, and RP responses and include responses to quality perception questions, there is considerable scope for further testing and refinement of the models. Only the preliminary comparisons, of habitat improvement values estimated from fitting conditional logit models to the choice data collected, have been reported here. SP studies of this type produce very large quantities of data, which can be analysed, adding further complexity and testing for significance, as the research expands.

13.6   CONCLUSIONS

In this paper the stated-preference approach to valuing environmental amenities has been outlined. The flexibility of stated preference and its compatibility with contingent valuation and revealed-preference methods of valuation suggests that it will become a popular method of eliciting environmental preferences. However, in this paper only a basic form of stated-preference model was presented. Recent advances in SP include incorporating uncertainty in the choice models, including dynamic elements (state dependence and serial correlation), incorporating non-choice alternatives, and a variety of experimental design and model validation issues (see Batsell and Louviere, 1991, Hensher, 1994).

Stated-preference models seem to be well suited to addressing questions that have troubled economists for some time. For example, the question of the value of travel time can be addressed using stated preference (e.g. Hensher and Truong, 1989). Stated-preference techniques are likely to be useful for benefit transfer exercises as well. If an activity can be broken down into its attribute components, and if models can be appropriately 'segmented' to account for different types of users, the stated-preference approach may provide a broad enough response surface to allow for accurate benefit transfer calculations.

Stated-preference models have a long history in the marketing and transport literature. They are generally well accepted as methods for eliciting consumer responses to multi-attribute stimuli. These techniques will undoubtedly become more widely used in the valuation of environmental amenities and in the economics literature in general.

EXAMPLE QUESTION FORM: CHOICE OF MOOSE HUNTING SITE

Suppose after examining the descriptions of Site A and Site B below you feel that you would go moose hunting at one of these sites and you prefer Site **B**.

You indicate this choice by checking the box under the Site B column as shown below.

Assuming that the following hunting areas were the ONLY areas available, which one would you choose on your next hunting trip, if either?

Features of Hunting Area	Site A	Site B	
Distance from home to hunting area	50 kilometres	50 kilometres	
Quality of road from home to hunting area	Mostly gravel or dirt, some paved	Mostly paved, some gravel or dirt	
Access within hunting area	Newer trails, cutlines or seismic lines, passable with 2WD vehicle	Newer trails, cutlines or seismic lines, passable with 4WD truck	Neither Site A nor Site B: I will NOT go moose hunting
Encounters with other hunters	No hunters, other than those in my hunting party, are encountered	Other hunters, on ATVs, are encountered	
Forestry activity	Some evidence of recent logging found in the area	No evidence of logging	
Moose population	Evidence of less than one moose per day	Evidence of less than one moose per day	

Check ONE and only one box ☐   ☐   ☐

REFERENCES

Adamowicz, W. L., Louviere, J., and Williams, M. (1994), 'Combining Stated and Revealed Preference Methods for Valuing Environmental Amenities', *Journal of Environmental Economics and Management*, 26: 271–92.

Batsell, R. R., and Louviere, J. J. (1991), 'Experimental Choice Analysis', *Marketing Letters*, 2: 199–214.

Ben-Akiva, M., and Lerman, S. (1985), *Discrete Choice Analysis: Theory and Application to Travel Demand*, MIT Press, Cambridge, Mass.

Bockstael, N. E., McConnell, K. E., and Strand, I. E. (1991), 'Recreation', pp. 227–70 in J. B. Braden and C. D. Kolstad (eds.), *Measuring the Demand for Environmental Quality*. North-Holland, Amsterdam.

Bunch, D. S., Louviere, J. J., and Anderson, D. A. (1992), 'A Comparison of Experimental Design Strategies for Multinomial Logit Models: the Case of Generic Attributes', unpublished working paper, Graduate School of Management, University of California, Davis.

Carson, R. T. (1991), 'Constructed Markets', pp. 121–62 in J. B. Braden and C. D. Kolstad (eds.), *Measuring the Demand for Environmental Quality*, North-Holland, Amsterdam.

—— Louviere, J. J., Anderson, D., Arabie, P., Bunch, D. S., Hensher, D. A., Johnson, R. M., Kuhfeld, W. F., Steinberg, D., Swait, J., Timmermans, H., and Wiley, J. B. (1994), 'Experimental Analysis of Choice', in D. Lehmann (ed.), *Marketing Letters* 5(4) (Special Issue on the Duke Invitational Conference on Consumer Decision Making and Choice Behavior): 351–68.

Cooper, J. C. (1993), 'Optimal Bid Selection for Dichotomous Choice Contingent Valuation Survey', *Journal of Environmental Economics and Management*, 24: 25–40.

Freeman, A. M. (1991), 'Factorial Survey Methods and Willingness to Pay for Housing Characteristics: Comment', *Journal of Environmental Economics and Management*, 20: 92–6.

Goodman, A. C. (1989), 'Identifying Willingness-to-Pay for Heterogeneous Goods with Factorial Survey Methods', *Journal of Environmental Economics and Management*, 16: 58–79.

Green, P. E., and Srinavasan, V. (1978), 'Conjoint Analysis in Marketing Research: Issues and Outlook', *Journal of Consumer Research*, 5: 103–23.

—— and Srinavasan, V. (1990), 'Conjoint Analysis in Marketing Research: New Developments and Directions', *Journal of Marketing*, 54: 3–19.

Carmone, F. J., and Wind, Y. (1972), 'Subjective Evaluation Models and Conjoint Measurement', *Behavioral Science*, 17: 288–99.

Hanemann, W. M. (1984), 'Applied Welfare Analysis with Qualitative Response Models', Working Paper, no. 241, University of California, Berkeley.

—— Loomis, J., and Kanninen, B. (1991), 'Statistical Efficiency of Double-Bounded Dichotomous Choice Contingent Valuation', *American Journal of Agricultural Economics*, 73: 1255–63.

Hensher, D. A. (1991), 'The Use of Discrete Choice Models in the Determination of Community Choices in Public Issue Areas Impacting on Business Decision Making', *Journal of Business Research*, 23: 299–309.

—— (1994), 'Stated Preference Analysis of Travel Choices: the State of Practice', *Transportation*, 21: 107–33.

—— and Truong, T. P. (1989), 'Valuation of Travel Time Savings: a Direct Experimental Approach', *Journal of Transport Economics and Policy*, 9: 237–61.

Kahneman, D., and Knetsch J. L. (1992), 'Valuing Public Goods: the Purchase of Moral Satisfaction', *Journal of Environmental Economics and Management*, 22: 57–70.

Lareau, T. J., and Rae, D. A. (1989), 'Valuing WTP for Diesel Odor Reductions: an Application of Contingent Ranking Technique', *Southern Economic Journal*, 55: 728–42.

Louviere, J. J. (1988a), *Analysing Decision Making: Metric Conjoint Analysis'*, Sage University Papers Series no. 67, Sage, Newbury Park, Calif.

—— (1988b), 'Conjoint Analysis Modeling of Stated Preferences: a Review of Theory, Methods, Recent Developments and External Validity', *Journal of Transport, Economics and Policy*, 10: 93–119.

—— (1991), 'Experimental Choice Analysis: Introduction and Overview', *Journal of Business Research*, 23: 291–7.

—— (1994), 'Conjoint analysis', pp. 223–59 in R. Bagozzi (ed.), *Advanced Methods in Marketing Research*, Blackwell, Oxford.

—— and Woodworth, G. G. (1983), 'Design and Analysis of Simulated Consumer Choice or Allocation Experiments: an Approach Based on Aggregate Data', *Journal of Marketing Research*, 20: 350–67.

Mackenzie, J. (1993), 'A Comparison of Contingent Preference Models', *American Journal of Agricultural Economics*, 75: 593–603.

McFadden, D. (1974), 'Conditional Logit Analysis of Qualitative Choice Behavior', pp. 105–42 in P. Zarembka (ed.), *Frontiers in Econometrics*, Academic Press, New York.

—— (1975), 'On Independence, Structure and Simultaneity in Transportation Demand Analysis', Working Paper no. 7511, Urban Travel Demand Forecasting Project, Institute of Transportation Studies, University of California, Berkeley.

—— (1986), 'The Choice Theory Approach to Market Research', *Marketing Science*, 5: 275–97.

—— Train, K., and Tye, W. B. (1977), 'An Application of Diagnostic Tests for the Independence from Irrelevant Alternatives Property of the Multinomial Logit Model', *Transportation Research Record*, no. 637: 39–46.

McLeod, K., Boxall, P. C., Adamowicz, W. L., Williams, M., and Louviere, J. J. (1993), 'The Incorporation of Non-Timber Goods and Services in Integrated Resource Management. I. An Introduction to the Alberta Moose Hunting Study', *Project Report 93–12*, Department of Rural Economy, University of Alberta, Edmonton.

Mitchell, R. C., and Carson, R. T. (1989), *Using Surveys to Value Public Goods: the Contingent Valuation Method*, Johns Hopkins University Press, Baltimore, for Resources for the Future.

Opaluch, J. J., Swallow, S., Weaver, T., Wessels, C., and Wichlens, D. (1993), 'Evaluating Impacts from Noxious Waste Facilities, including Public Preferences in Current Siting Mechanisms', *Journal of Environmental Economics and Management*, 24: 41–59.

Rae, D. A. (1983), 'The Value to Visitors of Improving Visibility at Mesa Verde and Great Smokey National Parks', pp. 217–34 in R. D. Rowe and L. G. Chestnut (eds.), *Managing Air Quality and Scenic Resources at National Parks and Wilderness Areas*, Westview Press, Boulder, Colo.

Swait, J., and Louviere, J. J. (1993), 'The Role of the Scale Parameter in the Estimation and Comparison of Multinomial Logit Models', *Journal of Marketing Research*, 30: 305–14.

—— —— and Williams M. (1994). 'Sequential Approach to Exploiting the Combined Strength of SP and RP Data: Application to Freight Shipper Choice', in D. Hensher (ed.), *Transportation*, 21 (Special Issue on the Practice of Stated Preference Methods): 135–52.

Urban, G., and Hauser, J. (1993), *Design and Marketing of New Products*, 2nd edn., Prentice-Hall, Englewood Cliffs, NJ.

Viscusi, W. K., Megat, W. A., and Huber, J. (1991), 'Pricing Environmental Health Risks: Survey Assessments of Risk–Risk and Risk–Dollar Trade-offs for Chronic Bronchitis', *Journal of Environmental Economics and Management*, 21: 32–51.

PART III

Case Studies

14

Option and Anticipatory Values of US Wilderness

RICHARD G. WALSH
JOHN R. MCKEAN

14.1. INTRODUCTION

Considerable effort has gone into attempts to model and quantify the option value of US wilderness and to include it in public cost–benefit analysis. The idea originated with Weisbrod (1964), who suggested that option value may exist for non-market use of parks and other environmental amenities. He observed that actual visits may understate value of the giant redwoods in Sequoia National Park because people who anticipate visiting the park at some time in the future but who, in fact, may never visit it, nonetheless would be willing to pay for an option that guarantees the possibility. This seems consistent with people's perceptions of resource services reported in the Alaska state oil spill study (Carson *et al.*, 1992). Although less than 10 per cent of a sample of US households had ever visited Alaska, fully one-third reported *anticipating a future visit* and the variable was highly significant in explaining their total willingness to pay for a ten-year oil spill prevention programme.

Although the concept of an option for the anticipatory-use value of US wilderness appears to be responsive to policy needs for valuation information, economic models of market behaviour generally are based on the assumption that utility derives from goods that are produced and consumed, not from the non-market anticipatory activity associated with knowing that wilderness and other environmental amenities are available for possible use. Options are traded for market goods, such as real estate and securities, because of uncertainty, as to supply, demand, and price of a good, during the option period. Difficulties with the concept of option markets arise when

The study was funded, in part, by the Colorado Agricultural Experiment Station, Western Regional Project W-133. Additional results are summarized in Walsh and McKean (1992). We are grateful for the assistance of K. H. John in the statistical analysis and for the helpful comments of K. T. McConnell and J. B. Loomis. Errors and omissions are, of course, the sole responsibility of the authors.

it is applied to non-market activities. It applies directly to a single good rather than to resource-related activities as the basic object of choice. It is argued here that anticipatory behaviour may be another source of utility and option value.

Recently, the traditional risk premium model stating that option value (*OV*) is the difference between option price (*OP*) and expected consumer surplus (*ES*) has been challenged as lacking in internal consistency and meaning as a separate category explaining the complex reality of total value in the context of non-market valuation of recreation and environmental resources. Some have gone so far as to suggest that the model be abandoned or substantially modified. Smith (1987) has noted that it mixes two perspectives of welfare theory that are fundamentally non-comparable: *OP* as *ex ante* planned-use value (i.e. willingness to pay now for future use given the uncertainty recreation consumers face) and *ES* as *ex post* actual-use value (i.e. after the uncertainty has been resolved). He was among the first to show that the *ex ante* planned expenditure function approach properly treats welfare changes under uncertainty since it allows all benefit concepts to be described in comparable terms, i.e. *ex ante* total value including *ex ante* existence services and *ex ante* uses. The concept of *ex ante* use value appears to adequately address the problem that led to development of the risk premium model of *OV* (Randall, 1991). If this is correct, the traditional risk-based *OV* model would have limited relevance to applied welfare analysis.

Also, Bishop (1986) has shown that the clear division between *ex ante* and *ex post* value 'breaks down in the real world'. Revealed-preference data sets based on travel-cost and hedonic methods appear to include both *ex ante* (advance reservations, added mobility of a 4-wheel drive, etc.) and *ex post* value (adjusting on-site consumption for known conditions), as is true also of market prices for goods and services such as electricity, and factors of production including labour and real estate. If *ex ante* decisions are generally present in consumptive behaviour, *OV* could not be considered a meaningful correction factor for conversion of *ES* data to *OP* estimates; *ES* data would not be *ex post* enough.

Several studies, cited later in this chapter, that have attempted to measure *OV* as a separate category of total value appear to have failed. Freeman (1993) concluded the empirical results thus far are not consistent with the traditional risk premium model that claims *OV* can only be the algebraic difference between *OP* and *ES*, nor with any known economic theory. Also, the size of reported *OV* in relation to on-site recreation-use value (*ES*) has been much larger than expected based on the traditional model of *OV* as a risk premium (Freeman, 1984). This suggests that individual understanding of the consumptive uses of an option may be more comprehensive than the risk premium assumption would suggest.

14.2   AN ALTERNATIVE MODEL

Smith proposed omitting *ES* and provided an alternative definition of *OP* as the 'sum of the payment for access and the payment for use' (1987:287). This introduces the possibility that OP may represent a sequence of two *ex ante* use values: (1) right of access and (2) on-site use, where on-site use is not possible without access right but access right can be the sole basis for *OP* with on-site use absent. The model could be applied to situations where recreation use would be precluded at all prices and a payment for the right of access could be made to relax that constraint. Then, consumption would be possible and travel costs associated with trips would provide the relevant basis for rationing on-site use. This seems plausible since economists have long known that the purchase of any good or service really entails two exchanges: first, for transfer of the property right or ownership and second, for the service of delivery or possession (Coase, 1937). The importance of the institution of property rights that define conditions under which resources are made available may have been overlooked because travel cost or delivery usually represents a larger part of price for recreation activities than for ordinary goods.

Although Smith did not propose access rights as a more general formulation of *OV*, his definition of the purchase of access could represent a fixed payment now for the option to plan possible trips during the payment period. To assume that right of access represents a more comprehensive formulation of *OV* would be a logical extension of his model consistent with common usage and standard dictionary definitions of the term 'option'. Also, it appears to be identical to the original concept proposed by Weisbrod (1964) that many individuals who anticipate possibly visiting Sequoia National Park would be willing to pay for the utility of an option that guarantees their right of access. It is generally consistent with several attempts to measure *OV* in the past that appear either to have asked two distinct *ex ante* WTP questions (1) for *OV* defined as right of access and (2) for *OV* as on-site use (Sanders *et al.*, 1990); or to have asked for *OP* as the sum of (1) and (2), and for (2) separately with *OV* as the difference (Smith and Desvousges, 1986). If *OV* is not simply a risk premium, then where should we look for its source of value? If it is perceived as an individual right to personal freedom of choice, is it a dimension of the institutional structure of society that facilitates indirect and/or direct use benefits? (Driver *et al.*, 1991)

Smith suggests the importance of his proposed alternative model is 'recognition of how the opportunities available to the individual to adjust plans for use, affect option price' (1987: 288). Although this anticipation and planning phase represents the first of five distinct activities in the recreation experience (Clawson and Knetsch, 1966), it has received little attention in economic theory or empirical research. To do so may require 'a fundamental change in what we generally mean by consumption' (Smith, 1990) of ordinary goods because it becomes important to understand how people learn about consumptive opportunities as well as those activities that provide enjoyment without conventional types of on-site use.

If progress is to be made in understanding the non-market value of options in the context of recreation behaviour, then perhaps consideration should be given to the possible advantages of modelling them on the theory of household production (HP) and consumption of non-market commodities or activities (Becker, 1965). This would introduce the resource-related activities of transacting for possible recreation trips in the decision set. The concept of transacting is associated with the early work of Coase (1937). He observed that some important economic phenomena can only be understood when transacting is made an explicit part of the model. This suggests the consumer's activities of gaining better information about potential activities at available sites, searching alternative sellers of necessary goods and services, visualizing themselves participating in activities on-site, negotiating among potential trip participants, preparing necessary equipment and supplies, etc. should be considered.

These and related activities may represent indirect uses of the environmental resource in the household production framework as discussed by Randall and Stoll (1983), Boyle and Bishop (1987), Madariaga and McConnell (1987), and others. Activities are produced and consumed by households combining leisure time and effort, purchased goods and services, environmental quality and other public goods. To maximize utility, they pursue the activities until their marginal benefits equal marginal costs. The process is constrained by a limited discretionary budget, leisure time, and technology (knowledge, skill, and durable capital resources). The proposed model would distinguish the indirect-use value of an option related to considering the real possibility of a trip from any other indirect uses of the resource for existence or bequest services.

Then the empirical problem would become one of exploring the relationship between indirect use of an option and direct use on site. To what extent and under what conditions are they joint, complementary, substitute, or independent consumptive activities? The null hypothesis would be that an option as access right is strongly complementary or a joint product included in estimates of on-site use value and thus indistinguishable as an independent consumptive activity. There are two points that should be made. First, the null hypothesis is consistent with most applied welfare studies that have treated cases as if recreation economic decisions are assumed to be known rather than *ex ante* problems in which individuals make plans and commitments before uncertainty is resolved. Studies have implicitly assumed that different consumers spend the same amount of time considering recreation trips and have the same opportunity cost. Reasonable results could be obtained if indirect use did not vary directly with trip costs.

Second, any role for options in considering possible trips can be left out of empirical analysis if the only source of utility is the market information gathered. For example, the benefits of shopping for goods and services and other activities related to possible trips may be approximately equal to the resulting savings in price times the quantity purchased (Stigler, 1961). The optimum amount of any transacting activity would be where its marginal cost equals the expected marginal reduction in trip expense already measured as increased value of trips. Then the problem reduces to one of correctly measuring the perceived price for trips to a site by different consumers.

One possible alternative hypothesis might state that an option is conceived as own right of access whose value may be complementary to, a substitute for, or independent of direct on-site use, reflecting the enjoyment or utility of indirect use of the resource in considering a possible trip as a non-market household commodity or activity (Becker, 1965, 1991). The rationale is straightforward. In a free society, it is generally believed that individuals cherish their right to choose (Bromley, 1991). Presumably options could provide utility from the use value of time allocated to the process of deciding how or whether to exercise an option as well as from its execution. Individuals behave differently when an option is available than when it is not (Manfredo, 1989, 1992). They enjoy rolling over in their minds and visualizing the consequences of exercising the option. They enjoy discussing the possibility with friends and relatives. Their enjoyment of reading an article or watching a TV programme that features the resource is enhanced when the site is available for use. They enjoy contemplating the consequences of a possible trip to the site compared to other sites in their decision set. This suggests that the approach of Henry (1974) to modelling option value may have been correct in emphasizing the *ex ante* value of information to individual choice, although it omitted the process of learning as a potentially valuable non-market activity.

When the basic conditions for the irrelevance of indirect-use value of options do not hold, because, for example, trip decisions are modelled as *ex ante* and consumers spend different amounts of time considering a trip and have different opportunity costs or utilities of time, what are the implications for estimating on-site use value from trip demand functions? Are coefficients biased and if so, by how much? Similar questions have been raised by McConnell (1992) with respect to excluding the closely related good, on-site time, from trip demand functions. What is the magnitude of complementary and substitution effects on estimates of on-site use value and option price welfare changes? The purpose of this study is to extend the concept of an option as access right, to begin understanding its behavioural consequences, and to demonstrate its possible economic significance. The following section specifies a possible model in an *ex ante* framework of total value based on the planned expenditure function. This is followed by a description of the pilot study and use of the data to test the hypotheses. The results are discussed relative to the structure of demand for non-market consumptive activities, trends in the allocation of leisure time, several conceptual issues, and implications for future research.

14.3. THEORETICAL APPROACH

Within the neo-classical framework of choice, the consumer plans recreation activities for a period of time, typically a week, month, or season. Since individuals make plans before uncertainty is resolved, the theory for applied welfare analysis becomes *ex ante*. To define total value, some economists have recently recommended use of the *planned expenditure function* (Smith, 1987; Randall, 1991),

$$\tilde{e} = \tilde{e}(p_1, p_2, p_3, p_4, \pi, q, EU^0), \tag{14.1}$$

where total expenditure $(\tilde{e})$ is a function of the prices of four environmental services (p), the probabilities associated with environmental quality (q), the probability of policy-independent states of the world (π), and expected utility (EU^0).

Ex ante total value of protecting environmental quality at the current (baseline) level is defined in terms of Hicksian compensating or equivalent welfare measures, as

$$TV = \tilde{e}(p_1^*, p_2^*, p_3^*, p_4^*, \pi^0, q^0, EU^0) - \tilde{e}(p_1^0, p_2^0, p_3^0, p_4^0, \pi^0, q^0, EU^0) \tag{14.2}$$

where total value (TV) is the difference between a baseline level of environmental quality with services available at current prices (p^0) and the choke prices (p^*) where without protection, availability of environmental services is precluded at all prices and a single payment could be made to relax that constraint.

Also, it is possible to estimate the value of each major environmental service in a sequential valuation procedure with total value equal to the sum of environmental services (Randall, 1991).

$$TV = \tilde{e}(p_1^*, p_2^*, p_3^*, p_4^*, \pi^0, q^0, EU^0) - \tilde{e}(p_1^0, p_2^*, p_3^*, p_4^*, \pi^0, q^0, EU^0) \tag{14.3}$$
$$+ \tilde{e}(p_1^0, p_2^*, p_3^*, p_4^*, \pi^0, q^0, EU^0) - \tilde{e}(p_1^0, p_2^0, p_3^*, p_4^*, \pi^0, q^0, EU^0) \tag{14.4}$$
$$+ \tilde{e}(p_1^0, p_2^0, p_3^*, p_4^*, \pi^0, q^0, EU^0) - \tilde{e}(p_1^0, p_2^0, p_3^0, p_4^*, \pi^0, q^0, EU^0) \tag{14.5}$$
$$+ \tilde{e}(p_1^0, p_2^0, p_3^0, p_4^*, \pi^0, q^0, EU^0) - \tilde{e}(p_1^0, p_2^0, p_3^0, p_4^0, \pi^0, q^0, EU^0) \tag{14.6}$$

Note that the value of environmental services depends on their position in the valuation sequence, i.e. they are path-dependent. Assume that the first variable (p_1) is existence value since it is a prerequisite for any kind of use. Individuals could be asked to value protection of the natural ecosystem as a habitat for plants and animals, given that human use is unavailable at any price. The second variable (p_2) could be the added value of an option for possible use. Respondents might be asked to value own right of access under given conditions, bearing in mind the time they spend considering the real possibility of a visit before they no longer enjoy doing so without actually taking a trip. Then, the next variable (p_3) would be the added value of individuals' direct use for on-site activities during trips, if any, assuming independence in consumption with p_4. The final variable (p_4) would be the added value of knowing others, both current and future generations, have a right to enjoy these environmental services.

For purposes of this study, assume a programme is in place to protect the existence of a site as a natural ecosystem (p_1) and the problem is to understand the behavioural basis for OP (as an extension of Smith, 1987) representing the sum of the value of an option for possible access (p_2) and on-site recreation-use value (p_3). One possible approach, following Becker (1991), would be to assume independent household production and consumption of these two desired activities in terms of (1) indirect uses related to a possible trip, and (2) an actual site visit, each of which directly provides utility. Neither can be purchased in the market-place but enjoyment of each activity (Becker's Z) is produced as well as consumed by households with possibly many types of time (T), opportunity costs (P), and environmental inputs (Q). In the simple model,

$$Z = f(T, P, Q). \tag{14.7}$$

By itself, Equation (14.7) does not provide insight into the special interdependent relationship between the two closely related non-market activities. The extent to which they have a complementary or substitute relation would be indicated by the sign and value of the cross-price and quantity variables for the other activity.

For purposes of this paper, assume first that Z can be specified as indirect-use value of an option and the usual independent variables in the activity's function can be extended to include variables that measure the relationship to site visits. The extended model would be similar to the inverse demand function traditionally used to analyse contingent valuation data on willingness to pay which is *ex ante*. Moreover, indirect-use value appears to be consistent with Becker's (1965, 1991) general definition of dependent variable, Z, as individual enjoyment of a non-market activity. Most economists would agree that the consumer surplus of an activity is a reasonable approximation of its enjoyment or utility. Thus, one possible model is

$$\text{WTP} = f(T_t, P_t, Q_t, P_s, V_s, P_x), \tag{14.8}$$

where indirect-use value (WTP), defined as marginal willingness to pay for enjoyment of the indirect use of an option, is a function of: own time (T_t), opportunity costs (P_t), environmental inputs defined as potential recreation sites entering the decision set (Q_t), the price of site visits (P_s), the number of sites visited (V_s), and the cross-price of visiting alternative sites (P_x).

Second, to introduce the effect of pre-trip activities on site visit decisions, assume that Z can be specified as the demand for site visits. This would be analogous to Becker's (1991) specification of dependent variable Z as household demand for number of children. Bockstael and McConnell (1981) observe that the ordinary travel-cost method (*TCM*), with trips dependent, is one type of household production function. The dependent variable could be assumed to represent primarily *ex-ante* planned decision-making similar to predictive models of the regional *TCM* in outdoor recreation research. Then the decision to visit a recreation site is a function of its own price, cross-price of visiting alternative sites, household income, and environmental inputs, plus the price of indirect use and indirect-use time:

$$V_s = f(P_s, P_x, Y, Q_t, P_t, T_t), \qquad (14.9)$$

where Y is household income and other variables are as described above.

Environmental services do not have market prices because they are not purchased, but they do have shadow prices equal to the cost of goods and time spent in household production and consumption. The choke price can be interpreted as the price that raises the marginal cost of household production of an environmental-related activity or commodity (Z) to the point where the quantity demanded of Z falls to zero. Indirect-use value of transacting for the *real possibility* of a trip cannot continue after right of access is denied, or the resource is destroyed (compare to some environmental services which may continue after resource destruction, as the natural history of the dinosaur, discussed in Boyle and Bishop, 1987; Brown and Callaway, 1990). Direct use, if any, is conditional on indirect use of the option being choked off by an increase in its shadow price. Then, the choke price of site visits can be interpreted as the price that raises the marginal costs of household production of a visit to the point where the individual would choose not to visit the site. Also it is reasonable to assume independence in consumption decisions related to use by other individuals (outside the household) currently or by future generations. Thus, it is argued that in this case, indirect-use value of an option and direct on-site use value can be aggregated as option price within an *ex-ante* total value framework.

14.4   RESEARCH METHOD

Indirect-use value of an option is measured using the contingent valuation method (CVM) recommended by US Government guide-lines (US Water Resources Council, 1983; Arrow *et al.*, 1993) as suitable for non-market valuation of on-site recreation use and passive use of resource protection programmes. To apply the method, a sample of the affected population is asked direct questions about their recreation behaviour and values associated with availability of the resource. Respondents were asked to recall the number of occasions during the previous Four-week period in October when they considered (anticipated, planned, or prepared for) possible recreation trips. Then they were asked how much time they spent on the average occasion. The product of these two bits of information equals total time. This was followed by a question on how much it cost in total out-of-pocket expenses during the month. Shadow price is defined as the opportunity cost of time and purchases. From this starting-point, they were asked to estimate the maximum additional amount of money they would pay to increase or reduce their total time by one hour. The valuation questions were as follows:

Some people feel that their time spent anticipating and preparing for possible recreation trips is an inconvenience while others enjoy it. How about you? During the month, did you: (Check *one answer* and place a dollar value in the appropriate blank after reading the guidelines below.)

—— Enjoy it. What is the maximum amount of money you would pay for an *additional hour*?

—— Prefer to reduce it. What is the maximum amount of money you would pay to *reduce* it *one hour*?

GUIDELINES: Please tell me the highest amount you WOULD REALLY PAY in added out-of-pocket expenses. In other words, what's it worth to you? Remember it's your choice. Bear in mind how much you are able to pay, other possible enjoyable activities that may be available to you, and how much you enjoy anticipating possible recreation trips.

The questions were designed to obtain *ex-ante* willingness to pay for a marginal unit of time as the indirect-use value of options, net of purchases, and the opportunity cost of time in forgone wages or benefits of alternative non-market activities. Answers to the first question were recorded as a benefit (with a positive sign) and to the second question as a cost (negative sign). Each value represents one point on a negatively sloped demand curve where change in willingness to pay is in response to a fixed level of use, as in the Seller *et al.* (1985) study of boating in Texas and the Walsh *et al.* (1990*b*) study of the consumptive-use value of travel time in the Rocky Mountains.

Subsequently, respondents were asked to estimate the maximum amount of time they would devote to indirect use of an option, representing the amount that results in optimal total enjoyment or utility from the activity. The contingent behaviour question was the following:

On the average, about how much total time do you spend enjoying the anticipation of a possible trip to a particular recreation site before you no longer enjoy doing so if you do not actually take the trip?

The question was designed to obtain the allocation of time to indirect use of an option independent of any direct on-site use. They also were asked how many sites were considered, and how many actually visited in the study period. They described the most important sites considered, including location, expected activities, and days away from home.

The basic data are from a 1991 survey of undergraduate students in a natural resource economics course at Colorado State University. The questions were self-administered by 37 individuals at a time convenient to themselves. Although the sample necessarily undersampled women (20 per cent), it may generally represent western land-grant college students as a group. Obviously it differs in important ways from the adult population of western states. Few students are employed full-time (about 10 per cent) but nearly half work part-time. They are probably more active in outdoor sports and recreation because of age (22.7) and available leisure time (36.7 days vacation per year), though constrained by lower income ($18,300 per year) and by available free time for weekend trips during autumn semester, with 6–18 hours per week in scheduled classes plus a variable amount of required study time.

The questionnaire was pre-tested and designed for clarity and ease of answering. The legitimate scientific purpose of the study was established by use of the university logo. An introductory statement explained the usefulness of the study and the importance of participation. The survey was introduced as a scientific experiment administered to a representative sample whose answers may affect recreation resource programs. Participants were assured their answers would be confidential and reported as part of sample averages.

The questionnaire was designed to be completed in less than twenty minutes. It included thirty questions to obtain information on willingness to pay and to participate, out-of-pocket and investment costs, reasons why indirect use is valued, importance of various types of indirect use, with similar information on site visits, and socio-economic characteristics of the sample. A copy of the questionnaire is reproduced in Walsh and McKean (1992).

An assessment by Cummings et al. (1986) concluded that several conditions should be met if willingness-to-pay and-to-participate questions are to provide reasonably accurate measures of the value of recreation resources. Respondents should understand the resource to be valued, and have prior experience valuing it and choosing how much to consume under conditions of little uncertainty. There is reason to believe that these conditions are generally present in this study. Respondents were introduced to the concept by the placement of behaviour questions prior to the economic valuation questions. This was designed to help them clarify motivations. Virtually everyone sampled had prior experience considering possible visits to recreation sites.

The value questions were designed to be as realistic and credible as possible. Direct out-of-pocket expense for goods and services was used as the payment vehicle because most people actually pay for inputs to indirect use. Thus, they have experienced additional expense to increase indirect-use time. This payment vehicle would appear to be superior in this case to alternative methods such as payment into a special fund, user fee, or tax. However, seven persons who reported they enjoyed indirect-use activities would not pay additional expenses, two of whom rejected the payment vehicle and were removed from the analysis. Nearly a quarter of the sample (nine) reported that they incurred no indirect-use expenses although they engaged in indirect-use activities. This suggests that in future research, a superior payment vehicle might include the opportunity cost of forgone wages or other non-market activities (Shaw, 1992).

Individuals were asked by open-ended direct questions to write down their maximum willingness to pay and to participate. The open-ended question approach is recommended by the CVM guide-lines for small projects characteristic of most recreation sites studied. Open-ended questions in self-administered surveys may have several advantages. The question can be answered at home and at a time convenient to the respondent. Household members can engage in extensive discussion before giving a value. In the hypothetical situation posited for this study, no individuals could benefit directly from either overstating or understating their true WTP. There is no possibility that an interviewer may influence the answers (yea-saying), or that other bias may be introduced by alternative procedures (discussed in Mitchell and Carson, 1989). The preferred method in recent research has been to ask a dichotomous-choice value question in a referendum format which introduces special problems of its own, especially in statistical analysis (Arrow *et al.*, 1993). Open-ended questions yield values that are usually somewhat more conservative than or not significantly different from dichotomous-choice questions.

Potential indirect uses of an option are defined broadly as resource-related non-market activities of: watching TV, videos, and movies; listening to radio; reading newspaper and magazine articles, maps, etc.; attending talks, slide shows, and training sessions; discussing with other persons; resting and relaxing, quiet reflection, etc.; shopping for trip supplies, clothing, equipment, etc.; making reservations for airline, lodging, car rental, etc.; renting equipment, trying it out, etc.; borrowing equipment, etc. from friends; preparing food, making things, cleaning, repairing, etc. Indirect use of an option while on the job, attending work-related meetings, driving to or from work, during work breaks, and at lunch time, also could be included. It is intended to concentrate on all informational and other activities in considering a possible visit to a recreation site.

Any study of indirect use introduces a unique recall problem since frequency is greater and duration per occasion less than is usually the case for direct site visits. For this sample, indirect use of options typically takes a quarter-hour per occasion and occurs a few times per day. For the study period, the average individual reported 72.4 occasions averaging 16.4 minutes each. In an attempt to minimize recall bias, respondents were asked to report indirect use during the previous Four-week period in October. Autumn in Colorado typically has less outdoor recreation (hunting, sightseeing, etc.) than winter (skiing), spring (boating, fishing, biking, etc.), and summer (camping, hiking, biking, fishing, etc.). Individuals were asked to report indirect use throughout the year by allocating 100 points among the four seasons. On this basis, it would be possible to obtain a rough estimate of total annual indirect use of options from the October results by applying an

Table 14.1 Description of Variables in the Analysis

Name	Mean	Definition of variable
Indirect-use value	3.30	Reported willingness to pay for enjoyment of a marginal unit of indirect use of an option, dollars per hour.
Price of time per hour	6.52	Opportunity cost of time: reported marginal wage rate for those who would work more; average marginal wage rate for those who would not work more (proxy for marginal product of time in the household sector), dollars per hour.
Direct cost of indirect use	24.50	Reported out-of-pocket expenses for transacting goods and services during the study period, dollars.
Travel cost, per trip	26.63	Reported travel cost and onset expenses plus travel time at 30 per cent of opportunity cost, dollars per trip.
Travel cross-price	93.87	Reported distance to the most preferred alternative site, miles.
Investment, indirect use	4.38	Reported total cost of capital equipment and other durables used for transacting recreation trips, hundreds of dollars.
Indirect-use time, per site	3.25	Reported maximum hours of indirect use enjoyed per alternative trip considered.
On-site time	33.90	Total on-site hours reported for the study period.
Sites visited	3.09	Total number of recreation sites visited during the study period.
Alternative sites considered	5.47	Total number of alternative sites considered and not visited during the recreation period.
Options demanded	8.57	Environmental protection of options perceived as access rights to sites entering the individual's decision set during the study period, total sites considered.
Media resource information	3.80	Importance of natural resource depicted in the media relative to the producer or writer (TV, articles, etc.), 5-point scale, 5 = much more important.
Visualizing own use	4.17	Mental activity of visualizing recreation sites, 5-point scale, 5 = very important.
Income	18.27	Reported annual household income before taxes, thousand dollars.
Gender	0.20	Sex of respondent, 1 = female; 0 = male.

expansion factor of 16.12. In future research, it might be preferable to survey in each season.

Table 14.1 defines the dependent and independent variables included in the analysis. Most are standard measures and require no further explanation. For the most part, sites visited during the study period were constrained to those within the region that could be reached by private auto on weekends. Individuals in the sample reported a total of 3.1 sites were visited representing 33.9 hours of on-site time. Most were single-day or overnight visits averaging nearly one 12-hour recreation visitor day (RVD) per trip. Travel cost or price was estimated as about $27 per trip including reported travel and on-site expenses plus round-trip travel time (61 minutes one way) at 30 per cent of the wage rate, which is an estimate of opportunity cost recommended by TCM guidelines (US Water Resources Council, 1983). The proxy for cross-price of sites not visited was reported travel distance to the most preferred alternative (94 miles one way).

Individuals in the sample reported willingness to pay $3.30 for a marginal hour and to participate in a maximum of 3.25 hours of indirect use per option considered. On average, they demanded 8.6 options during the study period, 5.5 or two-thirds of which were alternative sites considered and not visited during the study period. They incurred out-of-pocket expenses of $24.50 during the study period and reported an investment of $438 in capital equipment and other durables. Opportunity cost of time (wage rate) was estimated as $6.52 per hour. Preference for the mental activity of visualizing own use of a site was especially important to them (4.2 on a 5-point scale). They estimated that the resource itself contributed approximately 60 per cent (3.8 on a 5-point scale) of the total site information provided by the media (including TV, articles, etc.) compared to the contribution of the producer, writer, etc.

14.5.   EMPIRICAL ANALYSIS

Table 14.2 illustrates a possible statistical function where the dependent variable to be explained is individual willingness to pay for the enjoyment of participation in a marginal unit of time considering a possible site visit. The empirical equation is specified to include the usual independent variables in an inverse demand function for the indirect use of an option and variables that measure the relationship to site visits as in Equation (14.8). Table 14.3 illustrates another possible function with the dependent variable specified as sites visited during the study period. The explanatory variables include the usual arguments in the TCM model plus interaction variables for indirect use, as in equation (14.9). The explanatory variables are defined in Table 14.1.

Statistical tests of alternative functional forms resulted in selection of the semi-log model with the dependent variable in each equation converted to

Table 14.2 Semi-Log Indirect-Use Value Function for an Option with Recreation Site Visit Variables

Variable	Coefficient[a]
Indirect-use time, per site	−0.7239*
	(−3.11)
Price of time	1.1753*
	(2.47)
Options demanded	0.2289**
	(2.00)
Sites visited	0.3790
	(0.99)
Travel cross-price	0.0764*
	(3.87)
Gender	−8.4387*
	(−3.95)
Constant	−10.9384*
	(−2.94)
Adjusted R^2	0.47
F-value	5.22*
Cases	30

Dependent variable: log (indirect-use value, per hour).
[a] T-test in parentheses: * = 0.01 significance, ** = 0.05 significance.

natural logs and all independent variables in linear form. The R^2 indicates that 47 to 78 per cent of the variation in the dependent variable is explained by the variables included in the functions, which is considered a satisfactory level of explanation for data from a consumer survey. The F-statistic shows the overall equations are significant at the 0.01 level and the t-statistics (in parentheses) show that the regression coefficients for the independent variables are significant at the 0.01 to 0.05 levels (with one exception). Multicorrelation is low to moderate and appears to have little effect on the precision of the estimates.

Thus, while the number of observations, 30, appears to be sufficient for statistical analysis in this case, it represents a minimum sample size for demand analysis. Tests of the assumptions of the model resulted in the removal of seven cases (19 per cent) from the original data set of 37 cases. This is somewhat more than the maximum of 15 per cent removed to obtain a 'solid core' of values as recommended by CVM guidelines (US Water Resources Council, 1983). The data were adjusted to remove outliers and rejections of the payment vehicle. Two cases reported zero indirect-use value, indicating rejection of the payment vehicle, and were removed from the data set as recommended by the guide-lines. A plot of residuals identified outliers, as is typical of small samples, which were removed following standardized procedures.

The inverse demand curve for an option is that part of the regression function presented in Table 14.2 expressing the relationship between WTP

Table 14.3   Semi-Log Demand Function for Recreation
Site Visits With Indirect-Use Variables

Variable	Coefficient[a]
Travel cost, per trip	−0.0275*
	(−3.83)
On-site time	0.0796*
	(3.99)
Travel cross-price	0.0073*
	(3.00)
Income	0.0286**
	(1.97)
Price of time	0.8325*
	(2.63)
Direct cost of indirect use	−0.0541*
	(−3.17)
Indirect-use time, per site	−0.9414*
	(−5.27)
Alternative sites considered	−0.3058*
	(−3.79)
Investment indirect use	−0.1895*
	(−5.02)
Visualizing own use	1.4212**
	(2.39)
Media resource information	−2.3174*
	(−4.24)
Constant	1.0890
	(0.21)
Adjusted R^2	0.78
F-Value	10.55*
Cases	30

Dependent variable: log (sites visited).
[a] T-test in parentheses; * = 0.01 significance; ** = 0.05 significance.

and indirect use. The negative coefficient for indirect-use time is consistent with the theory of diminishing marginal utility reflected in a downward sloping curve. As is typical of most goods and services, a reduction in quantity is associated with an increase in value, and conversely, an increase in quantity leads to a decrease. Consistent with theory, the effect of quantity changes as its level changes; the larger the time variable, the smaller its marginal effect on value. The t-statistic in parentheses below the coefficient indicates that the effect is highly significant at the 0.01 level.

Changes in the other variables shift the curve. This means that the value of each hour of indirect use either becomes more or less than before, depending on whether the curve has shifted to the right or to the left. Consider the effect of the number of options demanded. The positive and significant coefficient indicates that sites within the region are complementary. Apparently, individuals enjoy the greater freedom of choice provided by right of access to additional sites entering the individual decision set, which shifts the curve to

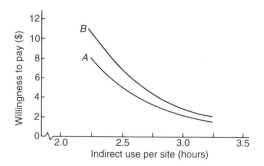

Fig. 14.1   Willingness to pay for the indirect use of an option *(A)* shifts with additional sites considered *(B)*

the right (Figure 14.1). Consistent with theory, value of the activity increases at a decreasing rate with increases in options demanded. The variety or novelty provided by the protection of two or more suitable sites may induce households to invest more time and resources and receive more benefits from the activity, whereas the protection of only one such site may not justify participation.

The direction of influence and strength of other variables are generally consistent with a-priori expectations. The positive time price variable has two interpretations. First, options are normal goods for which an increase in ability to pay would increase willingness to pay. Second, time price also is a measure of the opportunity cost of individual time. This means that as the scarcity value of time rises, individuals would reduce the time allocated to non-market activities, and their reported marginal value of indirect use would rise as individuals equalize the net marginal value of the last hour devoted to each activity at a higher level. Gender indicates that the indirect-use value of options for women is 8.4 per cent less than for men during the autumn and early winter hunting and skiing seasons. The state leads the nation in licence sales for hunting with 12 per cent and skiing with 20 per cent. Fewer women participate in these activities.

Several variables were inserted in trial equations to statistically test the two basic interaction effects of site visit decisions: a quantity effect holding travel cost or price constant, and a price effect holding quantity constant. Travel cost of own site visits would not enter the equation; it was not significantly different from zero at any acceptable level of significance, meaning independence of indirect-use value cannot be rejected in this case. The only statistically significant interaction variable in the final WTP function is travel cross-price; distance to the most preferred alternative site not visited is positive. Apparently, individual enjoyment of indirect use of an option to visit more distant sites rises in anticipation of higher quality and longer stay. This means that as travel costs rise with increased distance, the enjoyment of considering a possible visit substitutes for actually taking a trip to the most preferred alternative site in the decision set.

The quantity variable, sites visited, enters the equation at less than an acceptable level of significance, suggesting we reject the hypothesis that indirect-use value is simply derived from the final demand for site visits as would be the case for ski-lift tickets and other entrance permits (Walsh, 1986: 278). Although the sites-visited variable is not statistically significant in this case, the positive coefficient (0.3) suggests that for a larger sample, site visits may be complementary to indirect-use value, consistent with previous surveys of the general population showing an increase in option value for individuals who report they will, in fact, visit a site (Sanders *et al.*, 1990). Two-thirds of the students reported that enjoyment of considering the possibility of taking a trip that does occur is somewhat more than a trip that does not. And nearly everyone reported that enjoyment of anticipating a site visit increases the nearer the time of actual departure and arrival at the recreation site.

For the site visit demand function presented in Table 14.3, the negative coefficient for travel cost or price is consistent with the theory of diminishing marginal utility reflected in a downward sloping demand curve for sites visited. The semi-log form permits the effect of travel cost to change as its level changes, consistent with economic theory. An on-site time variable is included to account for the effect of fixed length of stay (trail miles control hiking time) on demand for sites visited (McConnell, 1992). Thus, students constrained to spend less time engaged in on-site recreation activities are able to visit fewer sites. The positive cross-price variable shows substitution between sites; increasing the price of visits to alternative sites would increase demand for the sites visited. The positive income variable indicates that demand for site visits is a normal good. Also, the time price variable shows that as the opportunity cost of time increases, demand for site visits rises.

Visiting a recreation site does not appear to be the main vehicle by which information about a site is obtained (compare to McConnell *et al.*, 1990). Indoor recreation activity substitutes for outdoor recreation as a source of information about the resource. Individuals who obtain increasing information about the resource from the media and other indirect uses tend to demand fewer site visits which would enable them to learn about the resource by personal experience. The variable, number of alternative sites considered, shows that individuals who have more options available demand fewer site visits, a substitution effect. Also, increases in indirect use per site substitutes for time devoted to actual site visits.

Complementarity of indirect use to site visits is shown by the positive variable, visualizing own use, as an enjoyable mental activity occurring prior to taking a trip. Also the economic variables, direct cost and investment cost, indicate indirect use is complementary to number of sites visited. The coefficients for both short-run and long-run costs of indirect use are negative, meaning that an increase in the price of indirect use reduces trips, similar to travel cost.

14.6. WELFARE IMPLICATIONS

The primary goal of recreation demand analysis is welfare measurement, usually approximated as the net effect on consumer surplus. There are several alternative procedures to estimate the welfare effect of the indirect use of an option. The simplest and most direct method is the CVM. An approximation of the Hicks compensating measure of the welfare effect of an option can be obtained by simply multiplying the reported average net willingness to pay for an additional hour of indirect use by the reported maximum hours of indirect use enjoyed per option considered (from Table 14.1). On this basis, the value of the indirect use of an option would be at least $12 for an optimal 3.6 hours, with a 95 per cent confidence range of about $7.50 to $16.50. With 2.8 options considered per actual trip taken, the value of options would equal about $33 per site visited, with a 95 per cent confidence interval of $21 to $46.

To estimate the welfare effect of direct and indirect use, the rule for semi-log TCM functions can be applied so that consumer surplus equals the number of trips divided by the coefficient of price. For ordinary demand functions, the rule is equivalent to calculating the amount a perfectly discriminating monopolist could collect. Earlier it was assumed that the price of the recreation experience may have two components, payment for an option as access right and payment of travel cost for on-site use (similar to the two-part tariff discussed by Oi, 1971). The two coefficients are shown in Table 14.3 as direct cost of indirect use and direct cost of travel per site visited, respectively. The price coefficient for indirect use is assumed to shift the vertical price intercept (as would a separate coefficient for travel time) rather than the horizontal site visit intercept. Then the model suggests that the indirect-use value of options could be estimated as $57 (3.1/0.0541) compared to the consumer surplus of direct on-site use, $112 (3.1/0.0275), and the combined price effect suggests that the value of the total recreation experience would be approximately $169 with 3.1 sites visited in the option period. This is equivalent per site visit to an indirect-use value of options of $18, an on-site use value of $36, and an option price of $54.

The rationale for including the expense of a closely related activity such as indirect use as a second price variable in a TCM demand function is as follows. For each of the 3.1 site visits demanded, 2.8 alternative sites are considered. The price of evaluating the 8.6 alternative sites considered during the option period is assumed to be exogenous in this equation on grounds that the package of sites represents an endowment of the region and the necessary expense of recreation decision-making depends on the efficiency of each individual, which is fixed. It would be irrational to consider only site A when sites B and C may represent potentially superior alternatives. Thus, to make an informed choice, each individual would incur a fixed amount of expense. McConnell (1992) discusses alternative TCM procedures when a closely related activity is assumed to be endogenous.

To describe indirect-use value in relation to sites visited in a TCM demand function represents a convenience in this case. Other models may be more efficient. For example, a model with the dependent variable specified as number of options considered during the study period, and independent variables specified as in Equation (14.8), would make demand for options analogous to the traditional TCM trips demand model (Bockstael and McConnell, 1981), and the HP model of demand for children in a household (Becker, 1991). The HP model of demand for options may ultimately provide more efficient and complete estimates of the consumer surplus of indirect use of an option. Preliminary statistical analysis of a larger sample illustrates how the model might be applied. Following Greene (1992), a poisson regression suitable for truncated count data was run with number of options considered dependent:

$$\log Q_t = \underset{(1.39)}{0.43} - \underset{(-6.19)}{0.03} (T_t P_t) + \underset{(3.76)}{0.15} (\log Y) - \underset{(-1.77)}{0.004} (\log P_s)$$

$$+ \underset{(6.33)}{0.35} (\log R) + \underset{(1.72)}{0.05} (\log H) + \underset{(2.96)}{0.12} (\log L), \qquad (14.10)$$

$$\text{Cases} : 69, \qquad R^2 = 0.21$$

where R is reported driving time, H is household size, L is reported leisure time, and other variables are as described in Equation (14.8). Note the $T_t P_t$ price variable is specified as the sum of out-of-pocket expense plus opportunity cost of indirect use (wage rate times hours) per site considered. This alternative, more realistic specification of the price variable may improve the estimate of consumer surplus.

For comparison purposes, a TCM poisson regression also was run with number of sites visited dependent:

$$\log V_s = \underset{(0.15)}{0.075} - \underset{(-3.28)}{0.02} (P_s) + \underset{(4.01)}{0.29} (\log Y) - \underset{(-2.56)}{0.003} (P_t)$$

$$- \underset{(-1.37)}{0.04} (\log P_x) + \underset{(2.97)}{0.14} (\log L) + \underset{(5.13)}{0.38} (\log S), \qquad (14.11)$$

$$\text{Cases} : 71, \qquad R^2 = 0.21$$

where S is on-site time and other variables are as described above and in Equation (14.8). The P_s price variable was specified as the sum of out-of-pocket expenses of a trip plus travel time at 75 per cent of the wage rate for those who worked and $3 per hour for those who reported they did not work. Tests for overdispersion indicate that the *t*-statistics somewhat overstated significance of variables. An expanded sample in the autumn of 1992 added 41 usable cases to the initial 30 in 1991.

The preliminary estimate of consumer surplus based on the poisson HP model of demand for options is substantially higher than the previous estimates. The poisson TCM regression also estimates higher consumer surplus for site visits. Consumer surplus of the indirect-use value of an option is estimated as $33 (1 / 0.03) per site considered compared to direct use of $50 (1 / 0.02) per site visited. Both non-market activities show inelastic price effects. Price of site visits (-0.17) is more inelastic than the price of indirect use (-0.23) of sites considered. The cross-price terms for the other activity in the sites visited and sites considered demand functions are negative, indicating a low complementary relationship.

The earlier procedures for estimating the welfare effect of the indirect use of options suggested a consumer surplus range from $12 to $15 per option considered, compared to consumer surplus of $36 per site visited. Both the CVM model and the insertion of a price variable for indirect use in an ordinary TCM demand curve may be less efficient in capturing the total price effect of indirect use than the HP model with a more complete price variable. However, the expanded sample resulted in a substantial increase in the CVM estimate of consumer surplus, from $12 per site considered to $20, based on willingness to pay $6 for a marginal hour with 71 cases. For the TCM model, the reason indirect-use values are lower appears to be that some students report no direct cost of indirect uses. Thus dollars are not a sufficient measure of price; for these respondents the opportunity cost of time (wage rate forgone times hours) would become the necessary shadow price of participation.

The principle of indirect-use value of an option may have important implications for benefit transfer. On-site use value was estimated as $36 to $50 in this case, comparable to the average consumer surplus of outdoor recreation in the US, estimated as $40 per day (1991 dollars, Walsh *et al.*, 1992), both of which may understate the option price measure of welfare by a substantial amount. If indirect-use value of alternative sites considered is distributed among sites proportionally to the on-site use value, then the recommended option price measure of the recreation experience in this case of ordinary day-to-day activities would be approximately 1.5 to 2.5 times the TCM estimates of on-site use value alone. For purposes of benefit transfer, larger samples of the general population could be interviewed to estimate the ratio and develop an index for important recreation activities and resources. The ratio might vary greatly by geographic location, quality of the resource, and other variables. For rare events such as a large Alaska oil spill, as an example, the indirect-use value of an option may be thousands of times greater than on-site use value for the US population (Randall, 1992).

Typically, the results reported in most of the previous studies of US wilderness and other environmental resources imply that annual indirect-use value of an option may range from $10 to $40 per household for specific resources and sites or 30 to 60 per cent as much as on-site recreation use value. The 14 CVM studies that compare option value and on-site use value include: Greenley *et al.* (1981, 1985); Mitchell and Carson (1981); Walsh *et al.* (1984); Hageman (1985); Sutherland and Walsh (1985); Smith and Desvousges (1986); Walsh (1986); Loomis (1988); Willis (1989); Barrick and Beazley (1990); Clonts and Malone (1990); Sanders *et al.* (1990); Walsh *et al.* (1990*a*); and Gilbert *et al.* (1992). In several of these studies, individuals were asked to report separately the consumer surplus of on-site use and option value, as in Sanders *et al.* (1990):

1. Payment to *actually visit* these rivers for recreation use.
2. In addition to your actual recreation-use value, how much of an 'insurance premium' would you be willing to pay each year to *guarantee your choice* of recreation use of these rivers *in the future*?

These questions are consistent with the Smith (1987) definition of option price as the sum of payment for right of access and payment for on-site use. It would be incorrect to say that in (1) 'use was defined as the right to visit the resource during the present year' (Freeman, 1993). Part (1) is payment for actual on-site use, if any. Part (2) is payment for the right of access each year of the option period. Freeman probably is correct in saying that 'respondents must have something quite different from the traditional risk premium definition of option value in their minds when they make their allocations' to option value (2) above.

There are at least two problems with past approaches to empirical measurement of option value. First, empirical studies that have attempted to combine (1) and (2) in a single option price question may have omitted a significant amount of value as indirect use of alternative sites during the study period. Respondents were told to include the value of actual and possible visits, but not reminded to include possible indirect-use value of the option to visit. Likewise, separate option value measures such as question (2) above did not remind respondents to include possible indirect-use value of the option. As a result, in several cases no option value as right of access is reported unless the site is visited during the study period. The indirect-use value of options for both sites visited and alternative sites not visited could be substantial. Second, some economists have objected to asking individuals to allocate the total value of an environmental asset among two or as many as four categories of direct and indirect use as in Equations (14.3, 4, 5, and 6) on grounds that option value (for oneself), existence value (for itself), and bequest value (for others) can only represent motives defined as tastes that do not directly enter the utility function since economic theory does not explain the formation of tastes (Mitchell and

Carson, 1989; Cummings and Harrison, 1992; Freeman, 1993). However, there is no inherent reason why the allocation of total value to direct and indirect uses and services cannot be modelled, following Becker (1991), as the production and consumption of non-market resource-related physical and mental activities.

The results support a recent US court decision that the benefit estimation procedures of Government agencies be enlarged to include option value. The model presented here possibly could support the US Court of Appeals ruling in the case *State of Ohio* v. *US Department of the Interior* (880 F.2nd 432 (DC Cir. 1989)), which states:

Option and existence values may represent 'passive' use, but they nonetheless reflect utility derived by humans from the resource, and thus *prima facie*, ought to be included in damage assessment.

The ruling could have been challenged on grounds that the traditional model of option value cannot be a separate category of total value, and is correctly excluded from the list of possible total benefit categories in CVM guide-lines (Mitchell and Carson, 1989). More recently, Carson *et al.* (1992, p. 1 note) appear to have recognized that 'passive use values encompass what economists refer to as option values, existence values, and other nonuse values.' Apparently, CVM economists are beginning to consider the possibility that benefit categories can include the indirect-use value of an option modelled as part of total value in an *ex-ante* theory of applied welfare analysis.

Randall (1992) argues that when studying complex phenomena, such as non-market valuation of environmental services and uses, appropriate reliability tests are multifaceted rather than simple (like a litmus test for acidity):

Modern philosophy of science...has moved away from the claim that there are simple and clear-cut tests for valid scientific methods and warrantable scientific knowledge. Current thinking tends more toward tentative judgements based on a preponderance of the evidence...there remains scope for differences of opinion among experts as to exactly what is the best way to do some of the tasks involved. This provides the opportunity for...experiments to map the responsiveness of... values to changes in valuation conditions. The results of such tests, while seldom individually conclusive, do contribute to the larger preponderance of the evidence test.

14.7. LEARNING FROM TIME STUDIES

Economic research on the trade-off between on-site and off-site recreation activities would augment the increasing literature on allocation of time summarized in Juster and Stafford (1991). Few studies, thus far, have considered time allocated to the process of making a decision whether to exercise an option. Cadez and Gartner (1985) reported that 80.2 per cent of

Utah households consider pre-trip planning a major part of the vacation process. Requests for brochures, itinerary and route selections, etc. often take more time than the actual trip. Many people report that they receive as much enjoyment from reading about certain areas and planning their trips around visits to these areas as actual visitation. McInnis and Price (1990) studied the effect of visualizing activities on possible recreation trips during spring break (six or more days) at a large western US university. The before and after study showed that spending additional time imagining what they will do has a positive effect on satisfaction (a 5-point scale) whether or not the actual trip turns out as imagined. This is part of a growing literature on 'imaging' possible leisure activities.

Loewenstein (1987) asked 30 undergraduates at the University of Chicago to specify the most they would pay now to obtain a kiss from the movie star of their choice at designated times. With WTP for immediate direct use set at 1.0, indirect-use value of the option increased the initial value to 1.30 for a delay of 3 hours, compared to 24 hours, 1.59; 3 days, 1.78; 1 year, 1.31; and 10 years, 0.64. Apparently individuals are willing to pay 30 to 78 per cent more for indirect use of the option during a one-year option period. He assumed indirect use in this case was primarily anticipation rather than preparations such as special clothing, haircut, cologne, etc.

Csikszentmihalyi (1990) describes a study of 107 adults who rated satisfaction of individual activities (10-point scale) at random times within 2-hour periods from 8 a.m. to 10 p.m. during a week. The results indicate that individuals tend to optimize enjoyment of subjective experience from non-market consumption activity valued for itself even if nothing else happens as a result. This appears to be the case for indoor and outdoor recreation activities and individuals in all walks of life. He reports optimal enjoyment (or utility) occurs when individuals achieve an equilibrium between the challenge of the opportunity present in any given situation compared to their skill and other endowments (presumably available budget, leisure time, equipment, etc. representing constraints).

Robinson and Godbey (1996) reported that the leisure time of adults in the US increased by 6–7 hours to 40–1 hours per week in the 20-year period from 1965 to 1985. Now fewer men are in the work-force full time and women spend less time on household chores. Most leisure time is used for indoor recreation activities such as watching TV and videos (16 hours per week), eating, reading, visiting with friends and relatives, exercising, etc. Apparently, indoor recreation is increasing relative to recreation outdoors. US surveys find that people take shorter trips and participate in fewer activities, and overall growth is relatively flat. With more leisure time devoted to indoor recreation, there are shifts in demand for information on wildlife and natural resources, reflecting technological advance and changes in income and relative prices of indirect and direct use. Also, preferences have changed for human rights in general, world-wide, with the right of access to a natural or clean environment becoming increasingly important. It should not be surprising if the indirect-use value of an option for possible access to wilderness and other environmental resources would be of increasing importance under these circumstances.

Much more research is needed to understand the relevant economic and non-economic questions concerning the indirect-use value of an option. For example, one important question is to what extent the results depend on the unique preference patterns and income sources of college students compared to a sample of the adult population. Second, do the results adequately reflect the dynamic interaction among members of the household or group considering a possible trip? Some individuals in the party may do the shopping, make the arrangements or hire someone else to do it, etc., while others go along for the ride. Third, would option value be reported for an inventory of sites that were not considered this year? Individuals may pay to protect the possibility of considering them in future years. Or perhaps they were considered in past years and may be reconsidered in future years (Carson *et al.*, 1992). Fourth, would it significantly affect the results to ask respondents their travel cost to each specific site in a regional TCM study rather than rely on the average travel cost for pooled sites visited during the study period? This question also relates to the possibility of identifying site-specific options demanded by a sample of the general population. Fifth, it would be interesting to compare opportunity cost of time measured by the wage rate to a shadow price equal to the marginal product of time in non-market activities. In the household production model, the budget constraint is specified as full income equal to the total value of work and leisure time, estimated as 2–3 times regular income (Becker, 1991: 22). The more comprehensive concept of income may help explain WTP in CVM surveys. Finally, a larger sample could be partitioned to test the effect of asking respondents to report daily, weekly, monthly, or annually; historic behaviour or future intentions; option value defined as a risk premium or indirect uses associated with right of access; total value with or without explicit information on indirect use of an option; etc.

14.8. CONCLUSIONS

This study developed and applied a more comprehensive model of the option price measure of welfare as the sum (1) of payment for indirect use of an option for possible access to US wilderness and other environmental resources and (2) payment for direct on-site use in an *ex-ante* framework of applied welfare analysis. The objective was to extend the concept of an option as access right, to begin understanding its behaviour basis, and to demonstrate its possible economic significance. Data from a pilot study were used to estimate the statistical interaction between the two closely related non-market activities of considering a possible site visit and actual visitation. The émpirical question was 'to what extent and under what circumstances are the activities likely to complement or substitute in consumption?' This is important because the valuation of environmental protection programmes may be affected by the information available on complementary and substitute relationships.

Apparently, there are two contexts in which the indirect use of an option is valued, one when it leads to a decision to visit a site and another when it does not. An option as access right is essential to site visits, as is a minimum of indirect use to plan the trip and prepare to depart. But site visits are not essential to the indirect-use value of options for resource-related activities such as obtaining information from reading, watching TV, and discussing the site with other persons. Since indirect use of an option involves a large number of different activities, its relation to recreation behaviour exhibits both complementary and substitute linkages.

Increasing the number of options (sites) available in the region significantly shifts the demand curve to the right for indirect use per site. Consistent with theory, it increases at a decreasing rate holding sites visited constant, indicating complementarity between sites with respect to indirect use. As a result, future growth in the option price of the recreation experience may result from increases in the value of indirect relative to direct use. This would be the case where a package of intraregional amenities are potential complements in production of indirect-use value of options, outweighing the substitution effects inherent in constrained valuation (Hoehn, 1991).

The values reported here should be considered first approximations subject to improvement with further work. The estimates are sufficient, nonetheless, to demonstrate that the indirect use of options could represent a substantial benefit of programmes to protect and enhance environmental resources. Without information on the WTP for the indirect use of options, insufficient resources may be allocated to US wilderness and other environmental protection programmes.

REFERENCES

Arrow, K., Solow, R., Potney, P. R., Learner, E. E., Radner, R., and Schuman, H. (1993), 'Report of the NOAA Panel on Contingent Valuation', *Federal Register*, 58: 4602–14.

Barrick, K. A., and Beazley, R. I. (1990), 'Magnitude and Distribution of Option Value for the Washakie Wilderness, Northwest Wyoming, USA', *Environmental Management*, 14: 367–80.

Becker, G. S. (1965), 'A Theory of the Allocation of Time', *Economic Journal*, 75: 493–517.

——(1991), *A Treatise on the Family*, 2nd rev. edn., Harvard University Press, Cambridge, Mass.

Bishop, R. C. (1986), 'Resource Valuation under Uncertainty: Theoretical Principles for Empirical Research', in V. Kerry Smith (ed.), *Advances in Applied Micro-Economics*, iv, JAI Press, Greenwich, Conn., p. 133–52.

Bockstael, N. E., and McConnell, K. E. (1981), 'Theory and Estimation of the Household Production Function for Wildlife Recreation', *Journal of Environmental Economics and Management*, 8: 199–214.

Boyle, K. J., and Bishop, R. C. (1987), 'Valuing Wildlife in Benefit–Cost Analysis', *Water Resources Research*, 23: 943–50.

Bromley, D. W. (1991), *Environment and Economy: Property Rights and Public Policy*, Basil Blackwell, Colchester, Vt.

Brown, G. M., and Callaway, J. M. (eds.) (1990), *Methods for Valuing Acidic Deposition and Air Pollution Effects*, State of Science and Technology Report no. 27, National Acid Precipitation Assessment Report, Washington.

Cadez, G., and Gartner, W. C. (1985), 'Utah Study Shows that Planning's a Major Part of a Vacation Process', *Woodall's Campground Management*, 16(10): 10–23.

Carson, R. T., Mitchell, R. C., Hanemann, W. M., Kopp, R. J., Presser, S., and Ruud, P. A. (1992), *A Contingent Valuation Study of Lost Passive Use Values Resulting from the Exxon Valdez Oil Spill*, Report to the State of Alaska by Natural Resources Damage Assessment, Inc., La Jolla, Calif.

Clawson, M., and Knetsch, J. L. (1966), *Economics of Outdoor Recreation*, Johns Hopkins University Press, Baltimore.

Clonts, H. A., and Malone, J. W. (1990), 'Preservation Attitudes and Consumer Surplus in Free-Flowing Rivers', in J. Vining (ed.), *Social Science and Natural Resource Recreation Management*, Westview Press, Boulder, Colo., pp. 301–17.

Coase, R. H. (1937), 'The Nature of the Firm', *Economica*, 4: 386–405.

Csikszentmihalyi, M. (1990), *Flow: the Psychology of Optimal Experience*, Harper and Row, New York.

Cummings, R. G., and Harrison, G. W. (1992), *Identifying and Measuring Nonuse Values for Natural and Environmental Resources: a Critical Review of the State of the Art*, Report to the American Petroleum Institute, Washington.

——Brookshire, D. S., and Schulze, W. D. (1986), *Valuing Environmental Goods: An Assessment of the Contingent Valuation Method*, Rowman and Allenheld, Totowa, NJ.

Driver, B. L., Brown, P. J., and Peterson, G. L. (1991), 'Research on Leisure Benefits: an Introduction to This Volume', in B. L. Driver, P. J. Brown, and G. L. Peterson (eds.), *Benefits of Leisure*, Venture Publishing, State College, P, pp. 3–11.

Freeman, A. M. III (1984), 'The Sign and Size of Option Value', *Land Economics*, 60(1): 1–13.

——(1993), 'Non-Use Values in Natural Resource Damage Assessment', in R. J. Kopp and V. K. Smith (eds.), *Valuing Natural Assets: the Economics of Natural Resource Damage Assessment*, Resources for the Future, Washington, pp. 264–303.

Gilbert, A. A., Glass, R., and More, T. (1992), 'Valuation of Eastern Wilderness: Extramarket Measures of Public Support', in *The Economic Value of Wilderness*, General Technical Report no. SE-78, Southeastern Forest Experimental Station, Forest Service, US Department of Agriculture, Athens, Ga.

Greene, W. H. (1992), *LIMDEP User's Manual and Reference Guide, Version 6.0*, Econometric Software, Inc., Bellport, NY.

Greenley, D. A., Walsh, R. G., and Young, R. A. (1981), 'Option Value: Empirical Evidence from a Case Study of Recreation and Water Quality', *Quarterly Journal of Economics*, 96: 657–73.

——— and—— (1985), 'Option Value: Empirical Evidence from a Case Study of Recreation and Water Quality: Reply', *Quarterly Journal of Economics*, 100: 294–99.

Hageman, R. K. (1985), *Valuing Marine Mammal Populations: Benefit Valuations in a Multi Species Ecosystem*, Administrative Report no. LJ-85-22, National Marine Fisheries Service, Southwest Fisheries Center, La Jolla, Calif.

Henry, C. (1974), 'Option Values in the Economics of Irreplaceable Assets', *Review of Economic Studies* (Symposium on the Economics of Exhaustible Resources), 41: 89–104.

Hoehn, J. P. (1991), 'Valuing the Multidimensional Impacts of Environmental Policy: Theory and Methods', *American Journal of Agricultural Economics*, 73: 289–99.

Juster, F. T., and Stafford, F. P. (1991), 'The Allocation of Time: Empirical Findings, Behavioural Models, and Problems of Measurement', *Journal of Economic Literature*, 29: 471–522.

Loewenstein, G. (1987), 'Anticipation and the Valuation of Delayed Consumption', *Economic Journal*, 97: 666–84.

Loomis, J. B. (1988), 'Broadening the Concept and Measurement of Existence Value', *Northeastern Journal of Agricultural and Resource Economics*, 17(1): 23–9.

Madariaga, B., and McConnell, K. E. (1987), 'Exploring Existence Values', *Water Resources Research*, 23: 936–42.

Manfredo, M. J. (1989), 'An Investigation of the Basis for External Information Search in Recreation and Tourism', *Leisure Science*, 11(1): 29–45.

——(ed.) (1992), *Influencing Human Behaviour*, Sagamore, Champaign, Ill.

McConnell, K. E. (1992), 'Revisiting the Problem of On-Site Time in the Demand for Recreation', *American Journal of Agricultural Economics*, 74: 918–25.

——Strand, I. E., and Bockstael, N. E. (1990), 'Habit Formation and the Demand for Recreation: Issues and a Case Study', in V. K. Smith and A. N. Link (eds.), *Advances in Applied Micro-Economics*, v, JAI Press, Greenwich, Conn., pp 217–35.

MacInnis, D. J., and Price, L. L. (1990), 'An Exploratory Study of the Effects of Imagery Processing and Consumer Experience on Expectations and Satisfaction', *Advances in Consumer Research*, 17(1): 41–7.

Mitchell, R. C., and Carson, R. T. (1981), *An Experiment in Determining Willingness to Pay for National Water Quality Improvements*, draft report to the US Environmental Protection Agency, Washington.

—— and—— (1989), *Using Surveys to Value Public Goods: the Contingent Valuation Method*, Resources for the Future, Washington.

Oi, W. Y. (1971), 'A Disneyland Dilemma: Two-Part Tariffs for a Mickey Mouse Monopoly', *Quarterly Journal of Economics*, 86(1): 77–96.

Randall, A. (1991), 'Total and Nonuse Values', in J. B. Braden and C. D. Kolstad (eds.), *Measuring the Demand for Environmental Quality*, Elsevier Science Publishers, New York, pp. 303–22.

——(1992), 'Discussion of the Status of CVM, Nonuse Values and Cambridge Economics Symposium', memo to European Association of Environmental and Resource Economists, University of Agricultural Sciences, Umeå, Sweden.

——and Stoll, J. R. (1983), 'Existence Value in a Total Valuation Framework', in R. D. Rowe and L. G. Chestnut (eds.), *Managing Air Quality and Scenic Resources at National Parks and Wilderness Areas*, Westview Press, Boulder, Colo., pp. 265–74.

Robinson, J. P. (1981), *How Americans Use Time*, Praeger, New York.

——and Godbey, J. (1996), *Time for Life*, Pennsylvania State University Press, State College, Pa.

Sanders, L. D., Walsh, R. G., and Loomis, J. B. (1990), 'Toward Empirical Estimation of the Total Value of Protecting Rivers', *Water Resources Research*, 26: 1345–57.

Seller, C., Stoll, J. R., and Chavas, J. P. (1985), 'Validation of Empirical Measures of Welfare Change: a Comparison of Nonmarket Techniques', *Land Economics*, 57(:) 156–75.

Shaw, W. D. (1992), 'Searching for the Opportunity Cost of an Individual's Time', *Land Economics*, 69(1): 107–15.

Smith, V. K. (1987), 'Uncertainty, Benefit–Cost Analysis, and the Treatment of Option Value', *Journal of Environmental Economics and Management*, 14: 283–92.

——(1990), 'Can We Measure the Economic Value of Environmental Amenities?' *Southern Economic Journal*, 54: 865–78.

——(1993), 'Nonmarket Valuation of Environmental Resources: an Interpretive Appraisal', *Land Economics*, 69(1): 1–26.

——and Desvousges, W. H. (1986), *Measuring Water Quality Benefits*, Kluwer-Nijhoff, Boston.

Stigler, G. (1961), 'The Economics of Information', *Journal of Political Economy*, 69: 213–25.

Sutherland, R. J., and Walsh, R. G. (1985), 'Effect of Distance on the Preservation Value of Water Quality', *Land Economics*, 61: 281–91.

US Water Resources Council (1983), *Economic and Environmental Principles and Guidelines for Water and Related Land Resources Implementation Studies*, US Government Printing Office, Washington.

Walsh, R. G. (1986), *Recreation Economic Decisions: Comparing Benefits and Costs*, Venture Publishing, State College, Pa.

——and McKean, J. R. (1992), 'Indirect Option Value', in Western Regional Committee W-133, *Benefits and Costs in Natural Resource Planning*, Fifth Interim Report, Oregon State University, Corvallis, Ore.

——Loomis, J. B., and Gillman, R. S. (1984), 'Valuing Option, Existence and Bequest Demands for Wilderness', *Land Economics*, 60(1): 14–29.

——Bjonback, R. D., Aiken, R. A., and Rosenthal, D. H., (1990*a*), 'Estimating the Public Benefits of Protecting Forest Quality', *Journal of Environmental Management*, 30: 1975–89.

——Sanders, L. D., and McKean, J. R. (1990*b*), 'The Consumptive Value of Travel Time on Recreation Trips', *Journal of Travel Research*, 29(1): 17–24.

——Johnson, D. M., and McKean, J. R. (1992), 'Benefit Transfer of Outdoor Recreation Demand Studies, 1968–1988', *Water Resources Research*, 28: 707–13.

Weisbrod, B. A. (1964), 'Collective-Consumption Services of Individualized-Consumption Goods', *Quarterly Journal of Economics*, 78: 471–7.

Willis, K. G. (1989), 'Option Value and Non User Benefits of Wildlife Conservation', *Journal of Rural Studies*, 5: 245–56.

15

Willingness-to-Pay Question Format Effects in Contingent Valuation Studies

IAN J. BATEMAN
IAN H. LANGFORD
JON RASBASH

15.1 INTRODUCTION

The willingness-to-pay (WTP) or willingness-to-accept (WTA) question forms the central focus of any contingent valuation (CV) exercise. It is the point at which the valuation being sought is elicited. However, a review of the literature reveals a variety of methods for asking such questions. In this chapter we present results from a study examining the impact of varying the elicitation method for WTP responses and show that each is open to some criticism. Five approaches are assessed, as follows:

1. Open-ended (OE). Here the respondent is asked 'How much are you willing to pay?' The respondent is therefore free to state any amount.
2. Single-bound dichotomous-choice (1DC). Here respondents face a single question of the form 'Are you willing to pay X?' with the bid level X being varied across the sample.
3. Double-bound dichotomous-choice (2DC). Here those respondents previously asked the 1DC question are asked a supplementary dichotomous question on the basis of their prior response. Those who agreed to pay the 1DC bid face a higher 2DC amount while those refusing to pay the 1DC bid face a lower 2DC amount.
4. Triple-bound dichotomous-choice (3DC). This extends the previous procedure for a further question.

The authors are particularly grateful to Richard Carson and Michael Hanemann for many helpful comments on an earlier draft of this paper. We also wish to thank Guy Garrod, Harvey Goldstein, Colin Green, Hugh Langford, Alistair Munro, V. Kerry Smith, Chris Starmer, Robert Sugden, Sylvia Tunstall, R. Kerry Turner, and Ken Willis for advice and comments on parts of this chapter and to Peter Doktor, Andreas Graham, and all the interviewers for assistance. None of the above bears any responsibility for any errors in this chapter. This research was funded in part by the UK Environment Agency and the UK Economic and Social Research Council (ESRC) (Grant N.S. W119–25–1014 and L320223014).

5. Iterative bidding (IB). Here the bidding game formed by the various dichotomous-choice questions is extended by a supplementary open-ended question asking respondents to state their maximum WTP. Such a procedure is appropriate to all respondents in the DC bidding game irrespective of whether they answer positively·or negatively to individual DC questions.

In the following section we review the literature with respect to these elicitation techniques and consider the various sources of bias which each approach may induce within responses. Section 15.3 describes our study design while Section 15.4 reports results. Here, following Duffield and Patterson (1991) and Langford (1994), we report both median willingness-to-pay measures and estimated bid functions. Particular attention is paid to the DC approaches, which have dominated the recent literature. Discussion of these results is presented in Section 15.5 while Section 15.6 draws conclusions.

15.2. LITERATURE REVIEW

15.2.1.   A Cautionary Note

Before we consider the literature regarding elicitation effects we should first of all mention the more fundamental issue of whether or not the WTP statement made in response to hypothetical CV questions is a good indicator of actual WTP. This is vital as many of the theoretical papers concerning appropriate elicitation techniques start by assuming that any such divergence will be insignificant. However, a number of studies both in the field (Bishop and Heberlein, 1979) and laboratory (Kealy *et al.*, 1988; Neill *et al.*, 1994; Cummings *et al.*, 1995; Loomis *et al.*, 1995) have questioned this assertion. If sustained then such criticisms would define the results reported below as being merely examples of how individuals react to CV surveys with no wider consequence. While some critics would clearly agree with such a conclusion, many would not. Hanemann (1994, 1995) argues that divergence between such measures is a product of WTA formats or laboratory WTP experiments utilizing auction formats, and not a feature of non-auction WTP studies (such as follows). This conclusion is supported by Carson *et al.* (1996), who present results from a meta-analysis suggesting that CV estimates are on average smaller, but highly correlated with revealed preference measures.

The broad thrust of this support is also endorsed by the NOAA panel (Arrow *et al.*, 1993). Given this we prefer merely to flag up such criticisms for the reader to ponder and progress on to the central issue of this chapter—elicitation effects.

15.2.2.   Elicitation Methods: Theoretical Expectations and Potential Biases

The OE approach was first applied by Davis (1963) in one of the very first CV studies. Indeed the method dominates the early literature (see Brookshire *et al.*, 1983). However, critics have identified a number of routes through which the technique may lead to underestimates of true WTP. One cause of such understatement is free-riding, whereby a respondent may 'pretend to have less interest in a given collective activity than he really has' (Samuelson, 1954), thereby gaining a public-funded benefit for which he/she has a higher WTP than the amount stated (Marwell and Ames, 1981; Brubaker, 1982). Alternatively, if respondents feel that costs will be shared on a per-capita basis, then they will not wish to pay more than this amount and will respond by stating the expected cost of the programme if this is below WTP and zero otherwise (Hoehn and Randall, 1987). Furthermore, unfamiliarity with OE questions may lead respondents to adopt risk-averse strategies, placing downward pressure upon stated WTP. In their theoretical analysis, Hoehn and Randall (1987) argue that, in an OE format, the respondents' lack of knowledge regarding aggregate costs and benefits gives no incentive for overstatement, while CV surveys which provide imperfect information and place respondents under time constraints (both factors which are almost inevitable to at least some extent) are likely to result in understatement of true WTP. Finally, the unfamiliarity of respondents to determining, rather than reacting to, valuations seems liable to increase uncertainty and therefore variance in responses.

It is partly in response to this latter issue that DC approaches were introduced (see Bishop and Heberlein, 1979). The take-it-or-leave-it nature of the DC question is similar to that of a market transaction and accordingly much more familiar to respondents than the OE approach (Desvousges *et al.*, 1983). Furthermore, Hoehn and Randall (1987) provide a theoretical framework to show that, given appropriate conditions (respondents believe that if a plurality favours the project then it will proceed; that approval is conditional on a level of individual cost specified in the question; and that they will pay that specified cost), then an individual's optimal strategy is truth-telling within a DC questionnaire.

Given its apparently strong basis in economic theory, it is unsurprising that DC applications have grown so that they now dominate the CV literature. However, psychological arguments have been put forward to suggest that the inherent characteristics of the DC approach may induce bias into responses. Kahneman *et al.* (1982), among others, have argued that respondents faced with an unfamiliar situation (particularly where the good is also not well-described) will interpret the bid level to be indicative of the true value of the good in question (Tversky and Kahneman, 1974; Kahneman and Tversky, 1982; Roberts *et al.*, 1985; Kahneman, 1986; Harris *et al.*, 1989; Hoevenagel, 1992). Here the introduction of a specific bid level raises the probability of the respondent accepting that bid. Kahneman *et al.* see this 'framing' or 'anchoring' effect as arising where a respondent has not previously considered their WTP for a resource (which is likely with regard to public or quasi-public goods) and/or is very unclear in their own mind about their true valuation.[1] In such cases the initial (1DC) bid level may provide the most readily available point of reference onto which the respondent latches.

Such an effect would clearly bring into question the validity of CV responses. However an alternative explanation is provided by Farmer and Randall (1995) and Hanemann (1995), who argue that a strong relationship between the initial DC bid amount and the individual's response is not inconsistent with utility-maximizing behaviour. Here, Hanemann argues, it is more likely that respondents view the DC bid amount as an expression of cost rather than value, such that two very different mechanisms underlie the relationship between bid level and response: (i) a 'powerful social norm that one should never pay more than necessary' (Hanemann, in a letter to authors, 1996) and; (ii) the notion that the bid level conveys information about the quality of the good (ibid).

One practical problem with this 'cost-response' argument may be that if different bid amounts are taken as implying different qualities of provision, then aggregation of this data within a single function may give misleading welfare change estimates for the scenario purportedly under investigation. A separate empirical problem arises from attempts to distinguish the cost-response from anchoring effects as both will result in a positive relationship between bid amount and individual's response. One approach to disentangling this trail of motivations is to engage respondents in post-survey deconstruction of their responses in studies such as the verbal protocol analysis of Schkade and Payne (1993). However, even here, assessment of responses is open to contrasting interpretation, with Hanemann (1995) at variance with Diamond and Hausmann (1993) as to whether Schkade and Payne's findings support or undermine the validity of CV findings. Given this debate we have confined ourselves to purely empirical analysis of the data at hand. In particular we examine whether data from the other elicitation formats support either the cost-response or anchoring arguments and consider whether or not we can infer from such results to the DC question.

The 2DC approach is a relatively recent innovation (Carson *et al.*, 1987; Hanemann *et al.*, 1991) although it is increasing in popularity (e.g. Carson *et al.*, 1994a). The main advantage of such an approach arises from the additional information elicited, which results in an observed gain in statistical efficiency as reflected in reductions in the confidence interval around welfare measures. While improved accuracy of estimation is clearly of interest, we

---

[1] Further potential causes of anchoring effects in DC studies are reviewed in Bateman *et al.* (1995).

identify two ways in which the 2DC approach may still be subject to bias. First, extending Kahneman *et al.*; the initial bid presented in the 1DC question may anchor respondents' perceptions of the value of the good and thereby frame responses to subsequent questions (McFadden and Leonard, 1993). In a test of such an effect Herriges and Shogren (1994) note significant differences between the WTP distributions implied by 1DC and 2DC responses, resulting in substantially different welfare measures. A number of hypotheses have been put forward regarding these effects including respondent weariness, uncertainty, and yea-saying (Hanemann *et al.*, 1991; Kanninen, 1995). However, Herriges and Shogren argue that such an effect is more reminiscent of the starting-point bias identified by Boyle *et al.* (1985) in similar CV bidding games. A second problem may arise from the iterative structure of double-(and multi-)bound bidding games. It may be that, even after controlling for the absolute amount concerned, a positive (or negative) response to the 1DC question influences responses to subsequent questions. So, for example, respondents who in the 1DC question agree to pay some amount £X may then become more likely to reject some higher amount £Y than they otherwise would have been. Carson *et al.* argue that such an effect may arise because those who agree to pay the 1DC sum refuse to pay a higher amount 'because they feel that the government would waste the extra money requested' (1994*b*: 11). However, an alternative explanation is that the individual feels that a bargain has been struck at £X and it is impertinent to then 'raise the price' to £Y. The reverse may apply when a respondent rejects the 1DC sum, as feelings of guilt and social responsibility may then raise the probability of accepting a subsequent lower 2DC bid.[2] However, this now runs contrary to the arguments of Carson *et al.* (1994*b*), who feel that some of those who reject the 1DC sum may see the lower 2DC amount as implying a lower-quality good (or doubt the ability of the Government to provide an original good at that lower price) and so become relatively more likely to reject the 2DC bid. In essence, then, the argument concerns whether or not the 2DC question is perceived by individuals as implying a change in the price of a given constant good (as usually intended by the CV researcher) or as implying a change in the quality of that good.

The 3DC question is a simple extension to the DC bidding game and therefore all the above arguments continue to apply. We would expect a further increase in statistical efficiency. However, any of the starting-point and iteration effects evident in the 2DC responses might also be expected to occur in the 3DC replies.

The IB approach generally pre-dates the DC (see Randall *et al.*, 1974) and has been subject to criticism both because of the starting-point effects attributed to bidding games (Rowe *et al.*, 1980; Boyle *et al.*, 1985) and as a

---

[2] See discussion of civic duty motivations and their implications by Sugden in Chapter 5.

result of potential understatement arising from the open-ended nature of the final question upon which valuations are based (Hoehn and Randall, 1987). Nevertheless we felt that conducting such an experiment may provide further useful information regarding both the interaction of DC- and OE-format questions and our investigation of biases within the DC bidding game.

In order simultaneously to assess the impact of these various elicitation methods it was decided to test all options within a single study, details of which we now present.

15.3 STUDY DESIGN

15.3.1. The Case Study

Scenario credibility is often a major concern in CV studies. Clearly if respondents feel that a public good will continue to be provided irrespective of their response or that the mode of provision presented in the scenario is unrealistic then the CV exercise may be undermined (Rowe and Chestnut, 1983; Mitchell and Carson, 1989). Fortunately, this study was presented with an almost ideal test case: the threat of saline flooding in the Norfolk Broads.

The Norfolk Broads is a unique freshwater wetland area located near to the North Sea in the East Anglia region of England. It consists of a system of small lakes and marshlands interlinked by rivers. The site is of national and international wildlife importance, being a designated Environmentally Sensitive Area and containing twenty-four Sites of Special Scientific Interest including two sites notified under the international RAMSAR convention. The area is also a major focus for recreation and has recently been accorded National Park status. The character of the low-lying landscape of 'Broadland' is dependent on 210 kilometres of reinforced river embankments for protection from saline tidal waters. However, these flood defences are increasingly at risk from failure, both because of their considerable age and, more fundamentally, as a result of settlement and sinkage of the surrounding marshlands. Thus the standard of flood protection afforded by these essentially man-made defences is decreasing over time. If breached, the ensuing saline flooding would fundamentally and enduringly alter the nature of the area both in terms of its habitat capabilities and in respect of the recreational opportunities currently afforded.[3] However, a number of flood-risk alleviation options are available including the strengthening of existing walls and/or the construction of a movable tidal barrier.

The debate surrounding the threat of flooding is long-running and well-known amongst visitors[4] and the local population. We therefore had an ideal

---

[3] Further details in Bateman et al. (1993).

[4] Our survey found that 72% of respondents were on a repeat visit to the area.

CV mix of an informed sample being asked questions about a well-known risk for which a credible solution was available.

15.3.2. Samples Sizes and the Payment Principle Question

The study itself generally conformed to the CV testing protocol laid down subsequently by the NOAA Blue-Ribbon Panel (Arrow *et al.*, 1993).[5] Survey design was extensively pre-tested with any changes to the questionnaire being retested over a total pilot sample of some 433 respondents. One of the many findings of this process was that a tax-based annual payment vehicle appeared optimal when assessed over a range of criteria (details in Bateman *et al.*, 1993).

The finalized questionnaire was applied through on-site interviews with 2,951 visitors at representative sites around Broadland (details in Bateman *et al.*, 1993). After some 35 incomplete questionnaires were discarded this left a usable sample of 2,916 respondents. This sample was divided, with 846 interviewees being administered the OE WTP questionnaire and the remaining 2,070 having the DC WTP version presented to them. However, in both cases, prior to any WTP question, respondents were asked whether or not they were personally willing to agree to the principle of paying anything extra for the defence of the area. This qualitative 'payment principle' question was included to validate zero WTP responses as it was felt that omission of such an explicit option was liable to inhibit such responses. Such an approach also conforms to the conservative design principles emphasized by Arrow *et al.* (1993). Of those respondents (unknowingly) presented with the OE questionnaire, 131 refused the payment principle compared to 240 of those facing the DC and bidding game questionnaire, leaving sample sizes of 715 and 1,830 respectively. Except where indicated, all those refusing the payment principle are treated as having zero WTP in calculating subsequent WTP measures.

15.3.3. Setting the Bid Amounts

Following Boyle and Bishop (1988) it was decided that bid levels for the 1DC WTP question were to be set upon the basis of information gained from OE responses and the latter experiment was started first to facilitate this. Such an approach has been questioned in recent papers (Cooper, 1993; Kanninen, 1995). However, given that we are interested in comparing differences induced by changing elicitation method, such an approach remains optimal for our purposes as, in the absence of elicitation effects, such an approach to 1DC bid vector design should produce results similar to the OE experiment. Furthermore, given that we used the first 427 OE responses for

---

[5] See Bateman *et al.* (1995) for discussion of this aspect of the study.

this purpose, any significant difference in resultant WTP measures is difficult to attribute purely to the choice of 1DC bid levels. Eight initial bid amounts were accordingly specified for the 1DC experiments being distributed on a roughly logarithmic scale.

Respondents facing the DC questionnaire were randomly allocated one of these initial bid amounts, from which the 1DC response was elicited. Such respondents then passed on into the bidding game as previously described. To avoid unnecessary complexity the 2DC amount was set as twice the 1DC amount where the latter had been accepted and at half the 1DC amount where the latter had been refused. This procedure was then repeated to fix the 3DC amount, after which a final open-ended question was asked eliciting what we term the IB response (for comparison, see the approach of Farmer and Randall (1995)). Figure 15.1 illustrates the potential question tree for one particular 1DC amount (here £100).

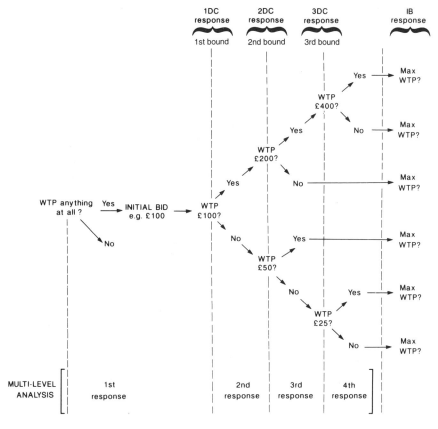

Fig. 15.1 Bidding tree for DC and IB experiments

15.3.4. Analytical Techniques

15.3.4.1. Estimation Methods

Figure 15.1 also raises the issue of estimation. While calculation of WTP measures for OE and IB responses is straightforward, when dealing with DC data such measures are taken from the estimated bid function, linking the probability of either a 'yes' or 'no' response to the bid level asked of the respondent. In this case we model the probability of a 'no' response, i.e. we expect the coefficient on the bid level variable to be positively signed.

The modelling of 1DC responses is often achieved using a logit link function (Bishop and Heberlein, 1979; Loomis, 1988) and, for comparative purposes, such an analysis is reported subsequently (in this and all other analyses a log-logistic model provides the best fit).[6] While such an approach can be extended to double-bounded data (Hanemann *et al.*, 1991), analysis becomes more complex given the variety of pathways which respondents can take through the bidding game. This complexity multiplies when we consider a triple-bounded structure, such that conventional analysis becomes arduous. One alternative to such an approach is provided by multi-level modelling (MLM).

A detailed exposition of MLM techniques as applied to CV data is given in Chapter 12.[7] That chapter analysed responses to the 1DC question posed in the Norfolk Broads survey and was principally concerned with identifying individual-level effects as separate from the bid amount effects commonly focused upon in CV studies. Accordingly the random part of the MLM was divided between that attributable to individuals (at level 1) and that due to bid amounts (at level 2). In this chapter we are principally concerned with separating out effects due to the response structure of multi-bound DC designs from those due to individuals. Consequently, here we consider a two-stage hierarchy[8] with responses nested within individuals by defining the former as level-1 variation and the latter as level-2.[9] Equation (15.1) details the basic multi-level model:

$$\text{LOGIT}_{ki} = a + b\text{LNBID}_{ki} + u_i + e_{ki}, \tag{15.1}$$

where

i = indexes individuals

---

[6] Kerr (1996) discusses many of the various link functions which can be applied to DC CV data and their impact upon welfare measures.

[7] Further details regarding multi-level modelling estimation procedures are given in Bryk and Raudenbush (1992); Longford (1993); Wolfinger (1993); and Goldstein (1995). A detailed exposition of the application of random-effects models to DC CV data is given in Alberini *et al.* (1994).

[8] Langford *et al.* (1996) present a three-level MLM with responses nested within individuals nested within initial bid amounts.

[9] This forms a 'repeated measures' model, i.e. we have repeated WTP measurements for each individual.

k = indexes responses within individuals
LOGIT = $\ln[\pi_k/(1 - \pi_{ki})]$, where π_{ki} is the probability of a negative response[10]
LBID_{ki} = ln[bid amount asked in question k to individual i]
a = the average intercept across all individuals
b = the average slope across all individuals
u_i = random effects between individuals (level 2), $u_i \sim N(0, \sigma_u^2)$
e_{ki} = random effects between responses (level 1), $e_{ki} \sim$ binomial $[0, \sigma_{cki}^2 \pi_{ki}(1 - \pi_{ki})]$

The first two right-hand-side terms of (15.1) are referred to as the 'fixed' part of the model while the remainder is referred to as the 'random' part. We can use Equation (15.1) to move from 1DC to 2DC or 3DC (or more) elicitation designs by specifying successive variance terms e_{ki}. So if we only consider 1DC responses we only need one level-1 variance parameter (which we can label σ_{1x}^2, with '$1x$' denoting that this refers to the first amount presented to an individual). If we include 2DC responses we will need a further two variance parameters, one for responses to questions which are twice the initial amount (σ_{2x}^2) and one for responses to questions posing half the initial bid ($\sigma_{0.5x}^2$). Adding in 3DC responses requires a further two level-1 variance parameters for those being asked either four times or one-quarter the initial bid (σ_{4x}^2 and $\sigma_{0.25x}^2$ respectively). Further bounds can be catered for in a similar manner.

The model in Equation (15.1) regresses the logit of the probability of a negative response on the log of the bid amount. The intercepts of this regression equation are allowed to vary randomly across individuals, while a constant slope is estimated for all individuals. The variance of the intercepts is $\text{Var}(u_i) = \sigma_u^2$. We can extend this model by allowing the slope coefficients to vary randomly across individuals. The variance of the slopes is $\text{Var}(v_i) = \sigma_v^2$. We can also estimate a covariance between the intercepts and slopes, which is $\text{Cov}(u_i, v_i) = \sigma_{uv}$.

One of the main flexibilities of using an MLM approach is that it is not necessary for all individuals to answer all questions. Hence, for example, only individuals who answer the triple-bounded DC questions support the estimates of the variance parameters associated with those questions, but the complete data on all responses from all individuals support the fixed parameter estimates and hence median WTP. Due to this flexibility it is easy to include those who said 'no' to the payment principle question as a qualitative response not linked to a particular bid level. Rather than, as usual, omitting such respondents from the analysis, they can be included by means of a dummy variable within the fixed part of the model and a separate variance parameter (σ_{ANY}^2) within level 1 of the random part.

---

[10] Note that many US papers model positive responses, thus reversing the signs on coefficients reported in subsequent results.

Equation (15.2) details the resulting 'random slopes' model which is obtained from the above extensions:

$$\begin{aligned}\text{LOGIT}_{ki} = a &+ b\text{LNBID}_{ki} + c\text{ANY}_{ki} \\ &+ u_i + v_i\text{LNBID}_{ki} + e_{ki}\text{OTHER}_{ki} + f_{ki}\text{ANY}_{ki}\end{aligned}, \qquad (15.2)$$

where

ANY_{ki} = 1 if individual said 'no' to payment principle question (0 otherwise)

$\text{OTHER}_{ki} = 1 - \text{ANY}_{ki}$

V_i = allows random slopes, $v_i \sim N(O, \sigma_v^2)$

f_{ki} = random effects due to payment principle responses, $f_i \sim N(O, \sigma_{\text{ANY}}^2)$

Other variables as previously discussed.

The above model can be extended to include further explanatory variables (e.g. respondents' income, preference characteristics, etc.) in the fixed part as required.

15.3.4.2. Testing for Cost-Response Anchoring and Starting-Point Effects

Most examinations of elicitation effects have compared WTP measures between OE and DC studies, with the majority reporting DC means exceeding those from OE experiments (Sellar *et al.*, 1985; Walsh *et al.*, 1989; Kriström, 1990, 1993). The approach of Kriström (1993) is interesting as he compares implicit bid acceptance probability curves for the two approaches, noting that, at any bid amount, rates of acceptance for DC questions exceed rates of commitment from OE responses.

In this experiment we compare WTP measures across elicitation methods and contrast DC and OE bid-acceptance probability curves. However, such comparisons do not provide conclusive proof of either cost-response anchoring effects in DC responses for, as we have already noted, there is good reason to expect understatement in OE experiments such that we cannot argue that either is, a priori, unbiased and therefore neither can act as a perfect measuring rod for the other.

By comparison, starting-point effects are relatively easy to identify. For example, a simple test is to examine the probability of accepting common bid amounts presented at differing bounds of a DC bidding game. Certain of the DC bid amounts were chosen specifically for this purpose. For example the amounts £5, £10, and £20 were all chosen as 1DC sums. Each of these have the amount £10 within their bidding tree, either as the 1DC question or as possible 2DC questions. Examination of acceptance probabilities for common bid amounts across differing bidding trees allows us to examine the impact of differing starting-points upon such probabilities. Furthermore, we can examine whether the 'direction of travel' along bidding trees (i.e. previously giving positive or negative answers) has any impact upon responses to specific bid amounts. We can also use the data so collected to infer back along a bidding tree to the 1DC question. However, given that we have evidence suggesting that specific design effects cut in as soon as we move from the 1DC question to successive bounds (see previous discussion of Carson *et al.*, 1994*b*), then this line of enquiry can at best only provide a weak indicator of the motivations underpinning responses to that initial question.

15.4. RESULTS

15.4.1   The OE Experiment

Treating all those who answered 'no' to the payment principle question as having a zero WTP gives median WTP = £30 for the overall OE sample (95% *CI* = £18.29–£46.49).[11] A bid function was investigated both for validation and comparative purposes. A full range of potential explanatory variables was considered. Functional form was a-priori uncertain (although linear forms were theoretically undesirable), but an initial analysis indicated that a high degree of overall explanation was unlikely to be achieved (a characteristic of OE studies). Therefore detailed (e.g. Box-Cox) analysis of functional form was bypassed in favour of using standard forms. The best model was provided by a double log form which is reported in Equation (15.3). This model narrowly outperformed a semi-log (dependent) form which contained the same explanatory variables.

$$\text{LWTP(OE)} = \underset{(0.22)}{0.1934} + \underset{(3.32)}{0.2920\,\text{LINC}} + \underset{(4.15)}{0.2695\,\text{RELAX}} + \underset{(3.93)}{0.2473\,\text{ENV}},$$

$$(15.3)$$

where

LWTP (OE) = Natural log of open-ended WTP response
LINC = Natural log of respondent's income (continuous variable)
RELAX = 1 if respondent often visits area to relax/enjoy scenery (0 otherwise)
ENV = 1 if respondent is a member of an environmental group (0 otherwise)
R^2(adj) = 5.29%; d.f. = 800;[12] figures in brackets are *t*-statistics.

The explanatory variables given in (15.3) are all significant at the 99% level, while no further variables were significant at even the 95% level. The major feature of this 'best model' is its very poor overall degree of explana-

---

[11] Calculated from 299 bootstrap samples (see Efron and Tibshirani, 1993).

[12] Equation (15.3) omits all responses for which information on any explanatory variable was missing (see Bateman *et al.*, 1995).

tory power. While this is exacerbated by inclusion of the payment principle refusals in (15.3), exclusion of these respondents only increased the fit statistic to $R^2(\text{adj}) = 7.1\%$.[13] Such poor fits are typical of OE experiments (although particularly pronounced here). It seems therefore that the standard socio-economic predictors included in (15.3) are unable satisfactorily to explain OE bids.

15.4.2.   The Single-Bound DC Experiment

15.4.2.1.   Conventional Analysis[14]

Conventional analyses of single DC responses, such as that elicited by our 1DC question, are restricted to those who answered that question. We therefore omit payment principle refusals from the following analysis although these are included in our subsequent MLM model.

Both linear and log models were tested using both logit and probit link functions. Log models gave a markedly better fit than linear specifications. The choice between link functions was more difficult as both logit and probit approaches performed similarly well.[15] However, a log-logistic model gave a marginally better fit and as this has been used extensively elsewhere, it was preferred for further analysis. We report $E(\text{WTP}) = e^{-a/b}$, i.e. the median, as this is a more robust estimate than the mean (Duffield and Patterson, 1991; Langford, 1994).

In all cases the most remarkable feature of the estimated models was the very high explanatory power of the bid level in determining WTP response. Equation (15.4) presents the log-logistic model resulting from the single explanatory variable LBID, the natural logarithm of the bid level (£) presented to respondents.

$$\text{LOGIT}(\pi_j) = \begin{array}{cc} -4.932 & + \ 0.9999 \ \text{LBID} \\ (-19.74) & (18.39) \end{array} \tag{15.4}$$

Deviance change $= -594.4$; residual deviance $= 1,325.7$; d.f. $= 1,624$. Figures in brackets are t-values.

As can be seen from equation (15.4), a log-logistic model with the single explanatory variable LBID fits the dichotomous-choice data set extremely well and yields a median WTP estimate of £144 (95% CI $=$ £75–£261).[16]

---

[13] Results of this analysis are given in Bateman *et al.* (1992).

[14] Full details in Bateman *et al.* (1995).

[15] Full details in Bateman *et al.* (1993).

[16] In an ancillary test of this result, individual models were fitted for the data within each bid level ($214 \leqslant n \leqslant 227$ for each level). All of the eight models produced were exceptionally weak. This is inevitable for the lower bid levels, where very few respondents registered refusals, ie. very little variation. However, even the best of these models (for the £50 bid level) only provided a low degree of explanation (a change in deviance of -24.65, with residual deviance being 223.73). These results confirm the key role of the bid level in determining responses.

Further explanatory variable were then added to this model in an attempt to improve the fit.[17] The best log-logistic model is given as Equation (14.5):

$$\text{LOGIT}(\pi_j) = \underset{(-6.23)}{-3.736} + \underset{(18.40)}{1.026}\ \text{LBID} - \underset{(-1.34)}{0.0907}\ \text{LINC} - \underset{(3.35)}{0.5888}\ \text{BOAT}$$

$$- \underset{(-2.58)}{0.3756}\ \text{RELAX} - \underset{(-2.22)}{0.3126}\ \text{ENV}, \tag{15.5}$$

where:

BOAT = 1 if respondent does participate in some boating activity (0 otherwise)

Other variables as previously defined.

Deviance change = 622.9; residual deviance = 1,297.2; d.f. = 1,620.

Figures in brackets are t-values.

The introduction of additional explanatory variables made minimal impact both in terms of the fit of the model (deviance change between (15.4) and (15.5) is just -28.5 with residual deviance of 1,297.2 for the move from 1 to 5 explanatory variables) and in its implications for median WTP, which declines marginally to £140. The relatively low significance of all the non-bid amount variables (LINC is included purely to underline this point) in Equation (14.5) makes them somewhat of an irrelevance with respect to our subsequent analysis of potential anchoring/starting-point effects and these variables are dropped from further consideration.

15.4.2.2.   MLM Analysis

The MLM analysis was conducted using the MLn software[18] developed at the Institute of Education, University of London.[19] If we omit payment principle refusals and non-bid amount explanatory variables and only specify one level of variance (as per the conventional logit model) then we obtain the same estimated model as reported in equation (15.4) and identical WTP measures. However, the flexibility of MLM approaches means that if, for comparative purposes, we continue to omit non-bid amount explanatory variables and payment principle refusals we can now separate out two levels of variance: that at the response level (e_{ki}, with $k = 1$) and that at the individual level (u_i), as described in Equation (15.1). Langford and Bateman (Chapter 12) estimate this model for the probability of a 'yes' response. So as to fit in with the other analyses presented in this chapter we change this to model 'no's' and obtain the model given in (15.6) below:

---

[17] Alternative models are considered in Bateman *et al.* (1993).

[18] So called because it allows the specification of n levels of variance.

[19] See details in Chapter 12.

Fixed Effects

Parameter	Estimate	St. error
a	−2.6440	0.3120
b	0.5703	0.0799

Random Effects

Parameter	Estimate	St. error
	Level 2 (Individuals)	
σ_u^2	0.1440	0.0850
	Level 1 (Responses)	
σ_{1x}^2	0.9711	0.0322

(15.7)

Residual deviance = 1,939.65; d.f. = 1,821.

In comparison to the conventional logit model estimated in (15.4), the separation of variance into response and individual levels facilitated by (15.6) results in both a reduction in the median to £103.15 and a considerable improvement in statistical efficiency (95% CI = £80–£126).[20]

15.4.3. The Double-Bound DC Experiment[21]

The model of 1DC responses given at (15.6) conforms to the simple variance components model described in Equation (15.1). By moving to additionally consider 2DC responses we can allow for the possibility of intercept and slope variance at the individual level as per the random slopes model detailed in Equation (15.2). In line with the latter model we now also demonstrate the flexibility of MLM approaches with respect to the incorporation of the qualitative payment principle information, an extension which, we argue, more accurately reflects the payment intentions of the entire visiting population. This is achieved through assuming that a payment principle refusal implies a refusal of both the 1DC and 2DC bid amounts. This can be modelled by including the parameter c in the fixed part and estimating a separate level-1 variance (σ_{ANY}^2) for this group of individuals. This is joined by the new parameters σ_{2x}^2 and $\sigma_{0.5x}^2$ capturing variance at the second bound of the DC bidding tree. The resulting estimated model is reported in (15.7).

Fixed Effects

Parameter	Estimate	St. error
a	−4.591	0.128
b	1.025	0.033
c	2.917	0.121

---

[20] 95% CI calculated using the delta method (Adelbasit and Plackett, 1983; Duffield and Patterson, 1991).

[21] Further details are given in Langford *et al.* (1996).

Random Effects

Parameter	Estimate	St. error
	Level 2 (Individuals)	
σ_u^2	5.561	0.359
σ_{uv}	−0.753	0.087
σ_v^2	0.174	0.023
	Level 1 (Responses)	
σ_{ANY}^2	0.270	0.040
σ_{1x}^2	0.141	0.011
σ_{2x}^2	2.234	0.089
$\sigma_{0.5x}^2$	1.507	0.104

(15.7)

Residual deviance = 4273.15; d.f. = 5,428.

The fixed part of (15.7) gives estimates for the mean intercept (a) and slope (b) as well as on the dummy for those who refused the payment principle question (c). However, it is in the random part that we begin to see the advantages of adopting an MLM approach.

The simultaneous analysis of both 1DC and 2DC responses (responsible for the large increase in d.f.) through an MLM allows us to see that at level 1 (responses) variance appears to increase as we progress along the DC bidding tree (both in bid-increasing or-decreasing directions). Results at level 2 show very high and significant variance in intercepts (σ_u^2) between individuals. Variance in slopes (σ_v^2) and intercept/slope covariance (σ_{uv}^2) is smaller in absolute terms but still statistically significant.

(15.7) gives Median WTP = £88.15; however, the calculation of a confidence interval for both 2DC and 3DC MLM models is problematic. These require the use of bootstrapping and other resampling schedules (Efron and Tibshirani, 1993); however, a number of issues are yet to be resolved regarding resampling strategies in hierarchical models and these are the subject of ongoing research by the authors.[22]

15.4.4.   The Triple-Bound DC Experiment[23]

The addition of 3DC responses to our data set results in a further increase in d.f. and additional information at level 1 of the random part of our MLM model. Estimation results are reported in (15.8).

Fixed Effects   (15.8)

Parameter	Estimate	St. error
a	−2.172	0.097
b	0.478	0.023
c	0.499	0.075

[22] First results from the analysis are presented in Langford *et al.* (forthcoming).
[23] Further details are given in Langford et al. (1996).

Random Effects

Parameter	Estimate	St. error
	Level 2 (Individuals)	
σ_u^2	7.159	0.236
σ_{uv}	−1.667	0.057
σ_v^2	0.384	0.015
	Level 1 (Responses)	
σ_{ANY}^2	0.000	0.000
σ_{1x}^2	0.494	0.020
σ_{2x}^2	0.909	0.039
$\sigma_{0.5x}^2$	1.010	0.071
σ_{4x}^2	1.014	0.056
$\sigma_{0.25x}^2$	1.183	0.118

Residual deviance = 6,087.60; d.f. = 6,370.

Although (15.8) is slightly underdispersed it does provide a wealth of additional detail relative to the double-bound model. In the fixed part we can see a substantial shift in all parameter estimates relative to (15.7) due to further extra-binomial variation being explained in the random part. However, turning to this we can see that this extra explanation of variance is not due to payment principle refusals ($\sigma_{ANY}^2 = 0.000$) but rather to variance being soaked up by other terms at both level 1 and 2. At level 1 a particularly interesting finding is the increase in response variance as we progress along the bidding tree, whether in an upward (bid-increasing) or downward (bid-decreasing) direction. However, it is at level 2 that the most powerful effect is detected. While the slope variance (σ_v^2) and intercept/slope covariance (σ_{uv}) are significant they remain relatively small compared to the intercept variance (σ_u^2), which is even stronger than in our double-bounded model and highly significant. Finally (15.8) yields a median WTP estimate of £93.70.

15.4.5.   The IB Experiment

As illustrated in Figure 15.1, at the end of the DC bidding game respondents are presented with a final open-ended question asking them to state their maximum WTP. This yielded median WTP = £25 (95% CI = £18.99–£35.15)[24] with the best-fit bid function as reported in Equation (15.9).

$$\text{LWTP(IB)} = \underset{(22.18)}{2.104} + \underset{(19.79)}{0.3733\,\text{LBID}} + \underset{(1.86)}{0.000005\,\text{INC}} + \underset{(3.67)}{0.1758\,\text{BOAT}}$$

$$+ \underset{(4.70)}{0.1720\,\text{ENV}} - \underset{(-2.89)}{0.1222\,\text{FIRST}}, \tag{15.9}$$

[24] As per the OE experiment, this was calculated from 299 bootstrap samples (see Efron and Tibshirani, 1993).

where

LWTP (IB) = natural log of respondent's final WTP statement in the IB game

INC = respondent's household income (continuous variable)

FIRST = 1 if respondent is on his/her first visit to the area (0 otherwise)

Other variables as previously defined.

$R^2 = 21.86\%$; d.f. $= 1,634$. Figures in brackets are t-values.

Signs on the explanatory variables of Equation (15.9) are as expected. The variable INC is included for interest although it is only significant at the 90% confidence level. Interestingly, when tested the variable LINC was found to be significantly weaker. As per our DC models, ignoring the constant, by far the most powerful explanatory variable was the (log) bid level first presented to respondents.

15.5. DISCUSSION: BIAS IN ELICITATION METHODS

Table 15.1 collects together the various estimates of Median WTP and 95% CI's reported above.

Even a cursory glance at Table 15.1 indicates that there are strong elicitation and estimation effects at work here. Considering the latter, comparison of the two single-bound DC models indicates that the superior modelling of variance permitted by the MLM approach results in a considerable improvement in the statistical efficiency of estimates as well as, in this case, a substantial decrease in our estimate of median WTP. The considerable range in median values across Table 15.1 is due in part to the exclusion of non-

Table 15.1 Median WTP for various elicitation and estimation techniques: Norfolk Broads preservation study

Elicitation method	Notes	Median WTP (£ p.a.)	95% CI (£ p.a.)	d.f.
OE	PP refusals included as zeros	30	18–46	800
Single-bound DC	Conventional analysis; PP refusals excluded	144	75–261	1,624
Single-bound DC	MLM analysis; PP refusals excluded	103	80–126	1,821
Double-bound DC	MLM analysis; PP refusals included as zeros	88	*	5,428
Triple-bound DC	MLM analysis; PP refusals included as zeros	94	*	6,370
IB	PP refusals included as zeros	25	19–35	1,634

Notes: PP = payment principle question.
  * = the subject of ongoing research into bootstrapping hierarchical models (see Langford *et al.*, forthcoming).
  MLM analysis divides variance into two levels: (1) response; (2) individual.

payers from our two 1DC analyses necessitated by our desire to compare standard and MLM estimation. Aside from this, the main point to notice is the clear and significant divergence between the two open-ended formats (OE and IB) and the other dichotomous approaches. Within the various DC models, the exclusion of payment principle refusals clearly contributes towards higher estimates for median WTP. Despite this, all the DC medians lie within the reported confidence intervals, indicating that these are not significantly different measures.

Considering the effects of each elicitation method in turn, a priori our main reservation regarding the OE method was the theoretical expectation that this would produce understatements of true WTP. Given our caution-ary note regarding the apparent disparity between hypothetical and actual WTP we cannot with certainty say much regarding this relationship of OE bids to true WTP. However, we do note that such bids are substantially lower than those elicited through other approaches. We cannot therefore refute theoretical expectations regarding understatement and would add that the poor degree of fit given by the OE bid function (15.3) may reflect respondents' unfamiliarity with answering such questions, inducing uncer-tainty which may result in risk-averse strategies, placing further downward pressure upon OE bids.

Comparison of OE with 1DC responses is also interesting. Figure 15.2 presents both 1DC and OE response distributions in the form of survival functions for those willing to pay at least some amount (i.e. excluding, for both formats, all those respondents who refused to pay anything at all). Here the proportion of 1DC respondents giving positive responses at each bid level is compared with the proportion of OE respondents stating WTP

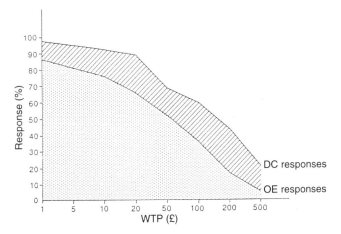

Fig. 15.2   Survival functions for OE and DC responses
Source: Bateman *et al.* (1995)

sums equivalent to or greater than that bid level. In the absence of any elicitation effects these proportions should roughly coincide across the bid vector. However, we can see that the 1DC format apparently generates a response distribution which is shifted upwards compared to that of the OE approach.

Figure 15.2 suggests that it is more likely that a respondent will agree to pay a particular amount X when presented with that amount as a 1DC bid level, then freely state a WTP of X (or greater) in an OE experiment.

Viewed from the perspective of economic theory such a discrepancy can be seen as further evidence of understatement within the OE approach (Hoehn and Randall, 1987). However, we do not have to reject such a theory to also see Figure 15.2 as additionally indicating a potential relation between the DC bid amount and responses, which can be interpreted either as the cost-response effect suggested by economic theory or a psychological anchoring effect. Purely anecdotal support for the latter explanation is provided by the uncertainty observed in OE responses, which lays the ground for Tversky and Kahneman's (1974) 'anchoring heuristic' to operate in the DC experiment as respondents latch onto the bid amount presented to them as a value clue regarding an appropriate WTP sum.

Further evidence for the anchoring hypothesis can also be inferred from the result shown in Equation (15.5) that the bid amount presented to respondents dominates their responses, to the virtual exclusion of other socio-economic and preference factors. However, as before the economic counter-argument can be made here. Under the cost-response view the bid level presented to respondents in a DC experiment is analogous to an asking price for a good and would therefore be expected to be a (quite possibly *the*) dominant predictor of response. While the degree of dominance is somewhat extreme, nevertheless this latter line of argument means that we cannot claim to have found clear proof of anchoring within 1DC responses; rather we cannot rule out its presence.

As outlined previously, we constructed our DC bidding tree with at least one eye open to the possibility of starting-point effects. To test for this we ensured that certain 1DC amounts were selected such that subsequent 2DC and 3DC amounts could be reached from various initial bids. In the absence of starting-point effects, the probability of bid acceptance should be roughly similar at any given amount irrespective of the initial bid or whether it was encountered on the first, second, or third bound. Table 15.2 details cumulative bid-acceptance probabilities (aggregating from highest bid down to lowest) for the eight initial bid amounts and their consequent bidding trees used in the triple-bounded DC experiment (note that, as per Figure 15.2, we are reporting the probability of a yes rather than no response). Figure 15.3 illustrates the relationships detailed in Table 15.2.

Figure 15.3 provides graphic evidence of starting-point bias within the DC bidding game. At any given bid amount the probability of acceptance is

Table 15.2 Cumulative bid-acceptance probabilities for eight DC initial bid amounts and derived triple-bounded DC bid trees (aggregating from highest bid down to lowest)

Bid amount	Initial bid amount							
	£1.00	£5.00	£10.00	£20.00	£50.00	£100.00	£200.00	£500.00
£0.25	1.000							
£0.50	1.000							
£1.00	**1.000**							
£1.25		1.000						
£2.00	0.904							
£2.50		0.995	0.982					
£4.00	0.761							
£5.00		**0.986**	0.968	0.977				
£10.00		0.804	**0.959**	0.968				
£12.50					0.944			
£20.00		0.521	0.635	**0.900**				
£25.00					0.837	0.912		
£40.00			0.324	0.445				
£50.00					**0.704**	0.837	0.923	
£80.00				0.150				
£100.00					0.277	**0.595**	0.755	
£125.00								0.606
£200.00					0.089	0.195	**0.438**	
£250.00								0.473
£400.00						0.056	0.091	
£500.00								**0.212**
£800.00							0.019	
£1,000.00								0.015
£2,000.00								0.000

Note: Responses to initial bid amount (1DC) question shown in bold.

markedly greater for respondents presented with relatively high initial bid amounts than for those presented with relatively low initial bid amounts. For example if we consider a bid amount of £100 we can see that the probability of acceptance rises from $p = 0.28$ where the initial bid amount was £50, to $p = 0.59$ with an initial bid of £100, and to $p = 0.75$ where the initial bid is £200. (15.8) shows this relationship with the initial bid to be clearly statistically significant.

This of itself causes problems for multi-bound DC studies, however: do such results tell us anything about the validity of the 1DC response? As before two interpretations are feasible. Following Carson *et al.* (1994*b*) we can argue that as we move away from the first bound question so either the cost or quantity/quality of the good becomes endogenous to the bidding process. Here individuals see the second bound bid amount as implying some change in these parameters and starting-point effects ensue. Here therefore, bias in the second or third bounds says nothing regarding the validity of the 1DC response. The second, contrary interpretation arises

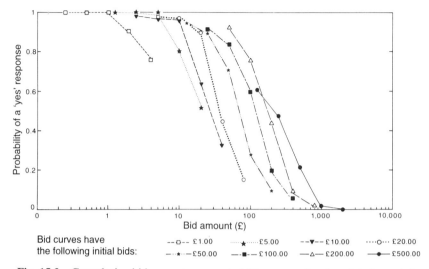

Fig. 15.3 Cumulative bid–acceptance probability curves for the triple-bounded DC experiment.
The initial bid is shown as the central of the five points that constitute each curve.

from the similarity between starting-point and anchoring effects; in both the response is altered by the bid level presented to the respondent. Following this argument, if stated WTP on a second or third bound can be influenced by the amount presented on the first bound then we should expect that first-bound response to have also been influenced by the size of the 1DC amount presented to the respondent. In other words, the presence of starting-point effects gives support to the contention that 1DC responses suffer from anchoring effects.

We shall return to the bidding game shortly but at this point it is appropriate to briefly consider results from our IB experiment. This posed an open-ended WTP question to respondents and so we might expect the understatement incentives attributed to the OE method to be evident here, and indeed we do find that median WTP for the IB approach lies considerably below that for any of the DC experiments. Inspection of the IB bid function (15.9) shows the strongest explanatory variable to be the initial bid amount presented to respondents at the start of their DC bidding tree as the 1DC question. Again this result can be interpreted in accord with either the cost-response or anchoring arguments.

Returning to the DC responses, we were interested to investigate the possibility of unique elicitation effects within the higher 'branches' of the DC bidding tree. In particular we wished to test the hypothesis that a positive (or negative) response at a lower bound might of itself influence the probability of a particular response at subsequent bounds. We envisaged at least two psychological influences which might produce a relationship here, namely 'indignation' and 'guilt'.

Indignation (raising the probability of a negative response) may occur in respondents who agree to an initial 1DC amount and resent then being asked whether they are willing to pay a higher amount in the 2DC question.[25] In effect such respondents may feel that they have struck a bargain with their 1DC response which the interviewer is subsequently trying to alter (to the respondent's detriment) in the 2DC question. Such an effect, if detected, might be expected to continue on into the third bound. Conversely, guilt (lowering the probability of a negative response) might occur in respondents who refuse an initial 1DC bid amount and then feel a heightened sense of social responsibility or simply embarrassment when presented with the lower 2DC bid amount such that they feel inhibited from rejecting that amount.[26] Again such an effect, if detected, might be expected to transfer to the third bound.

Clearly in investigating such effects we need to control for the underlying effect of differing bid amounts at each bound, i.e. those who accept a 1DC bid will always face a higher 2DC bid which will of itself lead to higher rejection rates. Similarly, rejecting the 1DC amount means that a lower 2DC bid is then faced, thereby raising acceptance probabilities.

We tested our indignation hypothesis by creating two new explanatory dummy variables within our data set of all DC responses (1DC, 2DC, and 3DC), although for simplicity payment principle refusals were omitted. As in our previous models, the dependent variable is the logit probability of a negative response. The explanatory variable $Y1$ was given a value of 1 where the respondent was answering a 2DC question having previously answered 'yes' to the 1DC question (and 0 otherwise). Similarly the variable $Y2$ was given a value of 1 where the respondent was answering a 3DC question having previously answered 'yes' to the 2DC question (and 0 otherwise). Note that $Y2$ can only equal 1 where $Y1 = 1$ but that just because $Y1 = 1$ does not mean that $Y2$ *has* to equal 1.[27] The standard positive bid amount/acceptance probability relationship was controlled for by including the variable LBID with our focus variables in the model although, due to their low significance, other predictors were excluded. Running the model against the full set of DC responses gave Equation (15.10):

$$\text{LOGIT}_{ki} = -4.107 + 0.829 \text{ LBID} + 0.9791 \text{ } Y1 + 1.246 \text{ } Y2.$$
$$(28.20) \quad (26.11) \qquad (10.71) \qquad (11.48)$$

$$(15.10)$$

[25] A similar effect would result from the Carson *et al.* (1994*b*) argument reviewed previously.
[26] This runs contrary to the Carson *et al.* (1994*b*) expectation.
[27] Tests showed that collinearity between $Y1$ and $Y2$ was not significant.

Variables as defined in text. Numbers in brackets are t-values.
Residual deviance = 4098.2; d.f. = 4353.

Although (15.10) is slightly underdispersed it yields some very strong predictors which tell an interesting story regarding the hypothesized effects of the DC bidding game. Remembering that we are modelling rejections of DC bids, the positive sign on LBID is as before and expected. The positive and highly significant coefficient on $Y1$ indicates that, irrespective of the bid amount, answering a prior 1DC question positively raises the probability of answering the subsequent 2DC question negatively. Given that the bid amount is controlled for, this is an interesting finding which is in line with our 'indignation' hypothesis. Respondents resent having their initial agreed bid increased. This effect becomes even stronger when we reach the 3DC question, where acceptance of the prior 2DC (and by implication 1DC) question results in an even higher probability of refusal. Notice that our model does not attempt to test our guilt hypothesis. This is because any free-riders in the sample will tend to accumulate in the refusals side of the bidding tree, complicating the modelling of any guilt effect amongst the same sub-samples. This issue is the subject of ongoing research.

As mentioned previously, there are counter-explanations of such results. Carson *et al.* (1994*b*) argue that an individual who accepts a 1DC bid may reject a higher 2DC amount even if they would have accepted it on the first bound, if they feel that the Government would waste the extra money involved. Carson *et al.* also argue that a respondent who rejects a 1DC bid and would have accepted a 2DC sum had it been the one initially presented will have an increased probability of rejection, as the lower 2DC sum will be taken as indicating that a lower-quality good is being offered.

Following our own interpretation of these results, such findings do have considerable implications for multi-bound DC formats. That such effects operate irrespective of the bid amount raises questions concerning the validity and wider applicability of such methods (although in our simple theory of such effects one might argue that indignation and guilt may tend to cancel each other out to some extent). However, as before, we should emphasize that, under the cost-response interpretation, biases in 2DC and 3DC responses do not compromise the validity of the 1DC experiment.

15.6 CONCLUSIONS

We have found evidence of substantial elicitation effects in certain of the formats under investigation. Examining these in turn we find no evidence to refute the theoretical expectation of understatement within OE responses and would add that, in our study, the technique seemed to exacerbate uncertainty within respondents, which may in turn have reinforced under-statement. A similar conclusion can be drawn for the open-ended IB format, which also appears to suffer from the starting-point bias observed in the two upper bounds of the DC bidding tree. These 2DC and 3DC responses also exhibit their own unique bias properties, which we suggest may be indignation (and possibly guilt) effects. While we recognize competing interpretations we feel reasonably confident that for each of these formats we have established (if not quantified) the existence of elicitation effects. The one area of open debate concerns the 1DC response. Here we recognize competing explanations of response effects with very different implications for the validity of such welfare measures.

What then should be done? One simple solution would be to abandon CV as an imperfect tool. We would argue that in many cases this would be unwise.[28] Although there is considerable work still to be done in understanding and improving the technique it remains in many cases the only valuation option available. Also, it is a perhaps sad fact that in the UK (and we suspect elsewhere), the money numeraire is the only fluently spoken language of the decision-maker. Furthermore, we would argue that even where elicitation effects are established they can be viewed as a form of psychological variance around a central economic relationship. Indeed all the WTP measures reported in Table 15.1 lie within 40 per cent of a central value.

Given the above we conclude with the perhaps predictable and certainly well-worn recommendation that more research is needed. In particular the conflicting explanations of how respondents react to the 1DC question need to be addressed in a research design which explicitly tests both the psychological-anchoring and economic cost-response hypotheses.

POSTSCRIPT

As noted early on in this paper, the Norfolk Broads CV study was conducted in answer to a real-world question regarding the funding of flood defences in Broadland. The study fed into a wider cost–benefit analysis which also examined the agricultural, property, and infrastructure damage-avoided benefits of such defences. The benefit–cost ratio of the latter items was calculated at 0.98 (NRA, 1992).

Given our findings the National Rivers Authority chose to use the downwardly biased OE WTP measure in their attempt to argue the case for funding from the UK Treasury (a body renowned for its preference for lower-bound assumptions). Using such a figure as the users' value of

---

[28] For a contrary view see Diamond and Hausman (1994) while for support see Hanemann (1994).

preservation raised the benefit–cost ratio to 1.94. As a consequence the principle of funding flood defences in Broadland has now been accepted and the construction of new defences has recently commenced.

REFERENCES

Adelbasit, K. M. and Plackett, R. L. (1983), 'Experimental Design for Binary Data', *Journal of the American Statistical Association*, 78: 90–8.

Albernini, A., Kanninen, B., and Carson, R. T. (1994), '*Random-Effect Models of Willingness to Pay using Discrete Choice Contingent Valuation Survey Response Data*', Discussion Paper 94–33, Resources for the Future, Washington.

Arrow, K. J., Solow, R., Portney, P. R., Leamer, E. E., Radner, R., and Schuman, E. H. (1993), 'Report of the NOAA panel on contingent valuation', *Federal Register*, 58: 4602–14.

Bateman, I. J., Willis, K. G., Garrod, G. D., Doktor, P., Langford, I. H. and Turner, R. K. (1992), *Recreation and Environmental Preservation Value of the Norfolk Broads: a Contingent Valuation Study*, Report to the National Rivers Authority, Environmental Appraisal Group, University of East Anglia, Norwich.

——Langford, I. H., Willis, K. G., Turner, R. K., and Garrod, G. D. (1993), 'The Impacts of Changing Willingness to Pay Question Format in Contingent Valuation Studies: an Analysis of Open-Ended, Iterative Bidding and Dichotomous Choice Formats', Global Environmental Change Working Paper 93–05, Centre for Social and Economic Research on the Global Environment, University of East Anglia, Norwich, and University College London.

——Langford, I. H., Turner, R. K., Willis, K. G., and Garrod, G. D. (1995), 'Elicitation and Truncation Effects in Contingent Valuation Studies', *Ecological Economics*, 12: 161–79.

Bishop, R. C., and Heberlein, T. A. (1979), 'Measuring Values of Extra-Market Goods: Are Indirect Measures Biased?' *American Journal of Agricultural Economics*, 61: 926–30.

Boyle, K. J., and Bishop, R. C. (1988), 'Welfare Measurement using Contingent Valuation: a Comparison of Techniques', *American Journal of Agricultural Economics*, 70(1): 20–8.

——Bishop, R. C., and Welsh, M. P. (1985), 'Starting Point Bias in Contingent Valuation Bidding Games', *Land Economics*, 61: 188–94.

Brookshire, D. S., Eubanks, L. S., and Randall, A. (1983), 'Estimating Option Price and Existence Values for Wildlife Resources, *Land Economics*', 59: 1–15.

Brubaker, E. (1982), 'Sixty-eight percent Free Revelation and Thirty-two percent Free Ride? Demand Disclosures under Varying Conditions of Exclusion', pp. 151–66 in V. L. Smith, (ed.), *Research in Experimental Economics*, ii, JAI Press, Greenwich, Conn.

Bryk, A. S., and Raudenbush, S. W. (1992), *Hierarchical Linear Models: Applications and Data Analysis Methods*, Sage, London.

Carson, R. T., Hanemann, W. M., and Mitchell, R. C. (1987), 'The Use of Simulated Political Markets to Value Public Goods', unpublished paper, Economics Department, University of California, San Diego.

—— Wilks, L., and Imber, D. (1994a), 'Valuing the Preservation of Australia's Kakadu Conservation Zone', *Oxford Economic Papers*, 46 (Supp.): 727–49.

—— Mitchell, R. C., Hanemann, W. M., Kopp, R. J., Presser, S., and Ruud, P.A. (1994b), *Contingent valuation and lost passive use: damages from the Exxon Valdez*, Discussion Paper 94–18, Resources for the Future, Washington.

—— Flores, N. E., Martin, K. M., and Wright, J. L. (1996), 'Contingent Valuation and Revealed Preference Methodologies: Comparing the Estimates for Quasi-Public Goods, *Land Economics*, 72 (1): 80–99.

Cooper, J. (1993), 'Optimal Bid Selection for Dichotomous Choice Contingent Valuation Surveys', *Journal of Environmental Economics and Management*, 24: 25–40.

Cummings, R., Harrison, G., and Rutstrom, E. E. (1995), 'Homegrown Values and Hypothetical Surveys: Is the Dichotomous Choice Approach Incentive Compatible?' *American Economic Review*, 85(1): 260–6.

Davis, R. K. (1963), *The Value of Outdoor Recreation: an Economic Study on the Maine Woods*, Ph.D. thesis, Harvard University.

Desvousges, W. H., Smith, V. K., and McGivney, M. P. (1983), *A Comparison of Alternative Approaches for Estimating Recreation and Related Benefits of Water Quality Improvements*, Office of Policy Analysis, US Environmental Protection Agency, Washington.

Diamond, P. A., and Hausman, J. (1993), 'On Contingent Valuation Measurement of Nonuse Values', in J. A. Hausman, (ed.), *Contingent Valuation: A Critical Assessment*, North-Holland, New York.

—— and —— (1994), 'Contingent Valuation: Is Some Number Better than no Number?' *Journal of Economic Perspectives*, 8(4): 45–64.

Duffield, J. W., and Patterson, D. A. (1991), 'Inference and Optimal Design for a Welfare Measure in Dichotomous Choice Contingent Valuation', *Land Economics*, 67: 225–39.

Efron, B., and Tibshirani, R. J. (1993), *An Introduction to the Bootstrap*, Chapman and Hall, London.

Farmer, M. C., and Randall, A. (1995), 'Understanding Starting Price Effects in Contingent Valuation Data Sets', paper presented at Sixth Annual Meeting of the European Association of Environmental and Resource Economists, University of Umeå, Sweden, 17–20 June.

Goldstein, H. (1995), *Multilevel Statistical Models*, Edward Arnold, London.

Hanemann, W. M. (1984), 'Welfare Evaluations in Contingent Valuation Experiments with Discrete Responses'. *American Journal of Agricultural Economics*, 66: 332–41.

—— (1994), 'Valuing the Environment through Contingent Valuation', *Journal of Economic Perspectives*, 8(4): 19–43.

—— (1995), 'Contingent Valuation and Economics', in K.G. Willis, and J. T. Corkindale, (eds.), *Environmental Valuation: New Perspectives*, CAB International, Wallingford, Oxon, pp. 79–117.

—— Loomis, J., and Kanninen, B. (1991), 'Statistical Efficiency of Double-Bounded Dichotomous Choice Contingent Valuation', *American Journal of Agricultural Economics*, 73: 1255–63.

Harris, C. C., Driver, B. L., and McLaughlin, M. J. (1989), 'Improving the Contingent Valuation Method: a Psychological Approach', *Journal of Environmental Economics Management*, 17: 213–29.

Herriges, J. A., and Shogren, J. F. (1994), 'Starting Point Bias in Dichotomous Choice Valuation with Follow-up Questioning', mimeo, Department of Economics, Iowa State University, Ames, Iowa.

Hoehn, J. P., and Randall, A. (1987), 'A Satisfactory Benefit–Cost Indicator from Contingent Valuation', *Journal of Environmental Economics and Management*, 14: 226–47.

Hoevenagel, R. (1992), 'An Assessment of Contingent Valuation Surveys', pp. 177–94 in S. Navrud, (ed.), *Pricing the European Environment*, Scandinavian University Press, Oslo.

Kahneman, D. (1986), 'Comments', pp. 185–94 in R. G. Cummings, D. S. Brookshire, and W. D. Schulze (eds.), *Valuing Environmental Goods: a State of the Arts Assessment of the Contingent Method*, Rowman and Allanheld, Totowa, NJ.

—— and Tversky, A. (1982), 'The Psychology of Preferences', *Scientific American* no. 246: 160–73.

—— Slovic, P., and Tversky, A. (1982), *Judgement under Uncertainty: Heuristics and Biases*, Cambridge University Press, New York.

Kanninen, B. J. (1995), 'Bias in Discrete Response Contingent Valuation', *Journal of Environmental Economics and Management*, 28(1): 114–25.

Kealy, J., Dovidio, J., and Rockel, M. (1988), 'Accuracy in Valuation is a Matter of Degree', *Land Economics*, 64: 158–71.

Kerr, G. N. (1996), *Probability Distributions for Dichotomous Choice Contingent valuation*, CSERGE Global Environmental Change Working Paper, Centre for Social and Economic Research on the Global Environment, University of East Anglia and University College London.

Kriström, B. (1990), *Valuing Environmental Benefits using the Contingent Valuation Method: an Economic Analysis*, Umeå Economic Studies no. 219, University of Umeå, Sweden.

—— (1993), 'Comparing Continuous and Discrete Valuation Questions', *Environmental and Resource Economics*, 3: 63–71.

Langford, I. H. (1994), 'Using a Generalized Linear Mixed Model to Analyze Dichotomous Choice Contingent Valuation Data', *Land Economics*, 70: 507–14.

—— Bateman, I. J., and Langford, H. D. (1996), 'A Multilevel Modelling Approach to Triple-bounded Dichotomous Choice Contingent Valuation', *Environmental and Resource Economics*, 7(3): 197–211.

—— Bateman, I. J., Jones, A. P., and Langford, H. D. (forthcoming), *Efficient Estimation of Willingness to Pay in Dichotomous Choice Contingent Valuation Studies*, CSERGE Global Environmental Change Working Paper, Centre for Social and Economic Research on the Global Environment, University of East Anglia and University College London.

Longford, N. T. (1993), *Random Coefficient Models*, Oxford University Press.

Loomis, J. B. (1988), 'Contingent Valuation using Dichotomous Choice Models', *Journal of Leisure Research*, 20: 46–56.

—— Brown, T., Lucero, B., and Peterson, G. (1995), 'Improving Validity Experiments of Contingent Valuation Methods: Results of Efforts to Reduce the Disparity of Hypothetical and Actual WTP', paper presented at the W-133 Regional Research Meeting, March 1995, Monterey, Calif.

Marwell, G. and Ames, R. E. (1981), 'Economists Free Ride; Does Anyone Else?' *Journal of Public Economics*, 15: 295–310.

McFadden, D., and Leonard, G. K. (1993), 'Issues in the Contingent Valuation of Environmental Goods: Methodologies for Data Collection and Analysis', in J. A. Hausman (ed.), *Contingent Valuation: A Critical Assessment*, North-Holland, New York.

Mitchell, R. C., and Carson, R. T. (1989), *Using Surveys to Value Public Goods: the Contingent Valuation Method*, Resources for the Future, Washington.

Neill, H., Cummings, R., Ganderton, P., Harrison, G., and McGuckin, T. (1994), 'Hypothetical Surveys and Real Economic Commitments', *Land Economics*, 70: 145–54.

NRA (National Rivers Authority) (1992), *A Flood Alleviation Strategy for Broadland*, Final Report, Annex Four: *Cost–Benefit Studies*, NRA (Anglian Region), Peterborough.

Randall, A., Ives, B. C., and Eastman, C. (1974), 'Bidding Games for Valuation of Aesthetic Environmental Improvements', *Journal of Environmental Economics and Management*, 1: 132–49.

Roberts, K. J., Thompson, M. E., and Pawlyk, P. W. (1985), 'Contingent Valuation of Recreational Diving at Petroleum Rigs, Gulf of Mexico', *Transactions of the American Fisheries Society*, 114: 155–65.

Rowe, R. D., and Chestnut, L. G. (1983), 'Valuing Environmental Commodities: Revisited', *Land Economics*, 59: 404–10.

——d'Arge, R. C., and Brookshire, D. S. (1980), 'An Experiment on the Economic Value of Visibility', *Journal of Environmental Economics and Management*, 7: 1–19.

Samuelson, P. (1954), 'The Pure Theory of Public Expenditure', *Review of Economics and Statistics*, 36: 387–89.

Schkade, D. A., and Payne, J. W. (1993), 'Where Do the Numbers Come From? How People Respond to Contingent Valuation Questions', in J. A. Hausman, (ed.), *Contingent Valuation: A Critical Assessment*, North-Holland, New York, pp. 271–303.

Sellar, C., Chavas, J-P., and Stoll, J. R. (1986), 'Specification of the Logit Model: the Case of Valuation of Nonmarket Goods', *Journal of Environmental Economics and Management*, 13: 382–90.

Tversky, A., and Kahneman, D. (1974), 'Judgements under Uncertainty: Heuristics and Biases', *Science*, no. 185: 1124–31.

Walsh, R. G., Johnson, D. M., and McKean, J. R. (1989), 'Issues in Nonmarket Valuation and Policy Application: a Retrospective Glance', *Western Journal of Agricultural Economics*, 14: 178–88.

Wolfinger, R. (1993), 'Laplace's Approximation for Nonlinear Mixed Models', *Biometrika*, 80: 701–95.

16

Household Demand for Improved Sanitation Services: A Case Study of Calamba, the Philippines

DONALD T. LAURIA
DALE WHITTINGTON
KYEONGAE CHOE
CYNTHIA TURINGAN
VIRGINIA ABIAD

16.1. INTRODUCTION

The urban population of the Philippines is about 16 million, and it is growing at a rate of about 5 per cent per year. If this growth rate continues, the urban population will double in less than 15 years. The Philippines currently has about 40 cities with populations greater than 100,000.

The sanitation situation in these cities is generally bleak. Urban environments are dirty, large quantities of household waste water are discharged into roadside ditches and drains, and local streams are highly polluted. About 12 million urban residents outside Metro Manila are reported to have 'sanitation facilities'. About 8 million of them are served by private latrines that discharge into holding tanks and/or surface drains or water bodies; piped sewerage is found in only three cities in the Philippines outside Metro Manila, and only in parts of them. The other 4 million urban residents have either inadequate or no facilities.

The consequences of the unsanitary conditions in Philippine cities are substantial. The quality of groundwater and other sources of domestic water supply is reported to be in steady decline. Pollution of lakes and rivers has adversely affected commercial fishing, many residents are concerned about eating contaminated fish, crop irrigation with polluted water poses a health risk, and tourism is affected.

The resources of the Government to remedy the unsanitary conditions in the cities of the Philippines are severely constrained. Government units lack

The findings, interpretations, and conclusions reported in this chapter are those of the authors. They should not be attributed to the World Bank, its Board of Directors, or any of its member countries.

the financial resources to heavily subsidize solutions to these problems. The beneficiaries themselves must pay a larger portion of the cost if improved sanitation services are to be provided. If beneficiaries are to pay more than in the past, they must be consulted and drawn into the planning process in a meaningful way. Because the beneficiaries are not wealthy, they must be given a range of options from which to choose. Depending on the option selected, beneficiaries may also play a larger role in the operation and management of any new sanitation facilities once they are constructed.

Based on this philosophy, the World Bank, with funding from Japan, executed a project that included the following components: (1) preparation of a national urban sanitation strategy plan, (2) formulation of an action plan for implementing the strategy, and (3) formulation of a local strategic sanitation plan for each of five cities that were selected by the Government as representative of urban conditions in the Philippines. This paper describes part of the research that was conducted for Calamba, one of the five cities selected as part of this World Bank project.

The research effort in Calamba had two main objectives. First, it sought to obtain accurate, reliable information on household demand for improved sanitation services in Calamba. In other words, information was required that would predict how different groups of households would respond if they were actually offered the opportunity to purchase an improved sanitation service at a specified price. Second, an understanding was required of the existing household sanitation situation in Calamba and the reasons why households did or did not want improved sanitation services. This required examining households' perceptions of their existing sanitation services and their priorities for environmental improvements. Thus the study sought to understand how households viewed sanitation problems within the context of overall environmental problems in Calamba.

To accomplish these objectives, one of the largest and most complicated contingent valuation surveys to date in a developing country was designed and conducted. The contingent valuation questionnaire was designed in the field in collaboration with a team of Filipino professionals and a large group of local enumerators using a variety of participatory approaches. The results of the survey indicate that, although most households have already installed water-sealed toilets for their exclusive use, they are only willing to pay a small amount per month for a connection to a sewer system (less than 1 per cent of household income).

The next section of this chapter describes the study area. Section 16.3 discusses household water supply and sanitation conditions in Calamba. Section 16.4 describes the research design, and Section 16.5 presents the results. The final section summarizes the findings and conclusions.

16.2. DESCRIPTION OF THE STUDY AREA

Calamba is located in the province of Luzon, about 60 km south of Manila; it has a population of about 175,000. The city has a 20-km-long east–west axis and is partially bounded on the east by Laguna de Bay, a large inland lake that sustains commercial fishing. The average north–south dimension of Calamba is about 7 km. Los Banos, a popular tourist area with hot and cold springs, is located about 20 km from Calamba; buses, trains, and the national highway pass through Calamba *en route* to Los Banos.

Calamba covers an area of about 14,500 hectares (ha); it has 54 political subdivisions called *barangays*. Although the average population density of Calamba is only 12 persons per ha, the *barangay* population densities range from 1 per ha to about 250 per ha. Seven contiguous *barangays* with densities from about 125 to 250 per ha constitute the built-up commercial centre of the city, which is called *Poblacion*. This centre is in the eastern part of the city, about 3 km from Laguna de Bay. Densities decline with distance from *Poblacion*. The terrain of the city is generally flat, and the climate is tropical.

Large tracts in the municipality are devoted to agribusiness and industry. The principal crops under cultivation are sugar cane and rice. In addition, some *barangays* have forests and fish ponds. Parts of Calamba thus have the appearance of being urbanized, while other parts seem quite rural. Calamba officially designates *Poblacion* plus one other *barangay* as urbanized; the population of this area is about 44,000 (25 per cent of the total).

During the Marcos Administration, a presidential decree forbade development of new industry in the proximity of Metro Manila. As a result, Calamba and similar municipalities within one hour's driving distance from Manila have experienced rapid industrial growth and substantial in-migration. Peak growth in Calamba occurred in the late 1970s, when the annual rate was about 4.5 per cent. In 1990 the annual population growth rate was estimated at 3.6 per cent, which is 1.3 percentage points higher than the national average. By the year 2000, the population of Calamba is predicted to be about 250,000.

Two rivers plus smaller tributaries pass through Calamba and discharge into Laguna de Bay. In addition, the municipality has an extensive system of irrigation canals. Both the natural rivers and the canals serve as drainage ditches for the city and are heavily polluted. *Poblacion* and some of the low-lying *barangays* near the lake are regularly flooded. Calamba has about 100 industrial facilities. Many of these are located in an industrial park, but others are scattered throughout the municipality. The vast majority of industrial wastewater is discharged without treatment into rivers, ditches, and streams, and water pollution levels in the Calamba area are high.

Calamba is an active tourist centre for Filipinos. Main attractions are the hot and cold springs. The municipality has about 80 licensed tourist establishments, 30 of which include 'pool' or 'springs' in their titles; 20 more say they are 'resorts', and the remainder are 'rest houses' and 'restaurants'.

16.3 HOUSEHOLD WATER SUPPLY AND SANITATION IN CALAMBA

The Calamba Water District (CWD) operates a piped distribution system that has about 7,600 connections, all with meters. The piped system is served by two groundwater sources, both with pumps, plus a ground-level reservoir. Only 40 per cent of the water produced is sold; the remaining 60 per cent is unaccounted for. About 90 per cent of the connections are domestic consumers. The number of households served by the CWD is about 20 per cent of the total population of Calamba (35,000 persons). Average consumption is about 190 litres per day per household, which amounts to about 40 litres per capita per day.

Calamba has 51 subdivisions inhabited mostly by middle- and high-income families. Most of these have their own separate piped-water system. Many dwellings in Calamba have private wells; some have two wells, one with an electric pump and the other with a hand pump for back-up. Some dwellings have two wells plus a connection to the CWD piped system. By law, each *barangay* is required to have at least one public tap. In areas not served by the CWD, households typically use shallow wells with hand pumps.

In aggregate, about 31 per cent of the households in Calamba use a private connection as their primary water source, 48 per cent use a private well, 10 per cent obtain their water from neighbours, and 10 per cent use public hand pumps. The households with private connections are concentrated in the high-density urban areas. On the other hand, none of the respondents in the medium-density areas without agriculture had water connections; here, public hand pumps were much more widely used than elsewhere. Private wells are most common in medium-density areas with agriculture.

The majority of households in Calamba (86 per cent) have already installed either flush or pour-flush toilets for the exclusive use of their household members and were quite satisfied with the service these facilities provided. These private facilities were installed by private contractors or by the household members themselves, without government assistance. As would be expected, flush toilets were more common in the high-density areas, where more households had private water connections. The private sector has thus already largely solved its households' waste-disposal problems. These private facilities empty into either lined or unlined septic tanks, which commonly overflow into either drains or ditches that run through town, eventually to empty into Laguna de Bay. Very few private toilets are connected to proper septic fields. Thus, while the existing sanitation system of flush and pour-flush toilets solves the immediate needs of households by removing their toilet wastes from their living space, it creates neighbourhood health problems and water pollution in Laguna de Bay.

Households without either pour-flush or flush toilets in their house for the exclusive use of their members use a combination of other types of facilities. Only 1 per cent have no facilities (i.e. use 'wrap and throw'). Among households without pour-flush or flush toilets for the exclusive use of their household members, 70 per cent use water-sealed toilets (often shared with neighbours). Others use 'overhung toilets', which are structures built over water bodies—either streams, ditches, or the lake—from which wastes simply drop into the water below. Less than 1 per cent of the households reported using public latrines as their primary sanitation facility. Some use the toilets of neighbours; others use a few public toilets in town.

In summary, a water supply is available in the house or yard of almost everyone in Calamba, and excreta and wastewater are being effectively and safely removed from most households' immediate living space. The sanitation problems that remain involve the removal of wastewater from neighbourhoods and the treatment of these wastes before disposal into surface-water bodies.

16.4. STUDY DESIGN

The study design for this contingent valuation survey can be best considered in two parts: (1) the contents of the survey questionnaires and (2) the overall experimental design. The two parts are described in turn. Survey implementation and sampling procedures are described in Appendix 1.

16.4.1. Contents of the Survey Questionnaires

Many different household questionnaires were administered in Calamba, but all of them contained some common questions. Each questionnaire included six basic parts. The first section included questions about the household's and respondent's demographic characteristics, such as the number of children and adults in the household. The second and third sections focused on the household's existing water and sanitation situation and its level of satisfaction with these services. The fourth section sought information about the respondent's knowledge and level of concern about specific water pollution problems in Calamba and their priorities for environmental improvements of various types. The fifth section asked questions about the household's willingness to pay for improvements in sanitation services if they were offered at different prices. Finally, the sixth section included questions about the socio-economic characteristics and housing conditions of the household.

16.4.2. Experimental Design

Most research attention was focused on the majority of households that owned their houses and already had flush or pour-flush toilets for their exclusive use, because these households were in a position to make a decision on whether or not to connect to a sewer line in their neighbourhood if one were installed. This was not a realistic proposition for renters and households without a pour-flush or flush toilet already in their home. Households that already had flush or pour-flush toilets for their exclusive use received what was termed a 'long questionnaire'.

Renters and households without pour-flush or flush toilets for their exclusive use were also surveyed; they received what was termed a 'short questionnaire'. At first glance, one might imagine that these households should be asked about their demand for a lower level of service, such as on-site sanitation or public latrines. However, as noted, on-site sanitation services in the form of pour-flush and flush toilets are already widely available in Calamba, having been provided efficiently and effectively by the private sector. People that already have these kinds of facilities are quite satisfied with them, and there is thus little justification for public sector involvement in the development of alternative on-site technologies (such as ventilated pit latrines) or for public subsidies of pour-flush toilets.

Based on focus group discussions and pre-tests, it was felt there was little demand for an extension of the public latrine system in Calamba. Households seemed much more interested in having their own pour-flush toilet than in investing in additional public latrines. The short questionnaire—for households currently without pour-flush or flush toilets—sought to confirm this initial perception and to determine whether this group of households had plans to install pour-flush or flush toilets in their homes in the near future.

The experimental design can be most easily conceptualized by considering the overall stratified random sample of 1,500 households in Calamba (the sampling methodology is described in Appendix 1). As illustrated in Figure 16.1, the original sample of 1,500 households was split between two groups. First, households with a pour-flush or flush toilet for their exclusive use were targeted to receive one of thirty different versions of the long questionnaire. Households without pour-flush or flush toilets for their exclusive use were targeted to be interviewed using the short questionnaire. As shown in Figure 16.1, 171 of these short questionnaires were actually completed during the course of the fieldwork.

16.4.3. Time-to-Think Experiment

Interviews were successfully completed with 1,104 households targeted to receive the long questionnaire. These 1,104 households were split into two

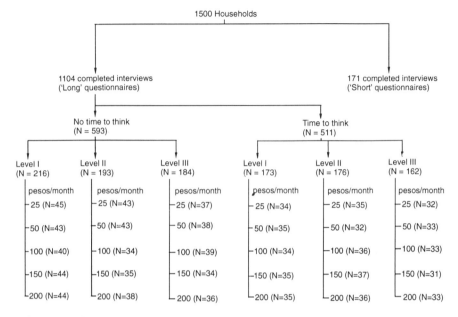

Fig. 16.1   Study design (Calamba)

different groups. For the first group, consisting of 593 households, an in-person interview was conducted with a respondent from each household. Either heads of households or their spouses were interviewed. For this first group of households, the enumerator completed the entire interview during one sitting. An interview took an average of about 45 minutes.

For the second group, consisting of 511 households, the in-person interview took place over the course of two or three days. On the first day, the enumerator asked the respondent questions from the first four parts of the questionnaire (i.e., demographic characteristics of the household, existing water services, existing sanitation services, and environmental attitudes and perceptions). The enumerator then read the respondent a description of one of three different levels of improved sanitation service (described in Table 16.1) and asked him or her to think about how much the household would be willing to pay per month for this level of service. A brochure with this same information was left with the respondent for his or her household to study and reflect upon. On the second or third day, the enumerator returned to the household, located the same respondent, and completed the rest of the questionnaire.

The purpose of this 'time-to-think' experiment was to see if respondents' answers to the willingness-to-pay questions would change after they had had

Table 16.1   Levels of sanitation service offered to respondents

---

Service Level I: Sewer system only—no waste water treatment plant

   Implication: Neighbourhood environmental and public health conditions in Calamba would improve, but the quality of water in the lake would get worse.

Service Level II: Sewer system plus waste water treatment plant

   Implication: Neighbourhood environmental and public health conditions would improve in Calamba, and the quality of water in the lake would not get worse (it would not improve much either).

Service Level III: Sewer system plus waste water treatment plant in Calamba and a regional plan that would ensure that other communities around the lake also treated their waste water discharges.

   Implication: Neighbourhood environmental and public health conditions in Calamba would improve, and the quality of water in the lake would improve.

---

a chance to think more carefully about the improved sanitation service (see Whittington *et al.* (1992) for further details). It may be that respondents' initial answer to a willingness-to-pay question is not carefully considered and that people need time to reflect upon their budget and competing needs before deciding whether or not to assume a significant financial commitment to pay for improved sanitation service. In industrialized countries, people often take time to think carefully about a major purchase such as a car or major appliance and evaluate the advantages and disadvantages of different alternatives. For example, consumer-advocacy groups and publications urge buyers not to get caught up in high-pressure sales tactics designed to make them decide *immediately* to purchase an item. From this perspective, giving people time to think about their answers should result in more reasoned, serious responses to willingness-to-pay questions.

16.4.4.   Variations in Levels of Improved Sanitation Service

Figure 16.1 also shows the next variation in the survey design. Each respondent that received the long questionnaire (both those given time to think and those that were not) was first offered one of three different levels of improved sanitation service (Table 16.1). One-third of the respondents were offered the lowest level of service (Service Level I): the opportunity to connect their pour-flush or flush toilet system to a sewer line that would run through their neighbourhood and would then discharge wastewater untreated into Laguna de Bay. Respondents were shown diagrams of a sewer system in a neighbourhood. They were told that the wastewater from their toilet, kitchen, and bath could be discharged into this sewer pipe, and that if they decided to connect, their household would have to pay a monthly fee to the water district, just like a water bill. They were also told that there would be no initial connection fee or any replumbing costs for connecting to the sewer line (these charges would be paid by the water authority). This group of respondents was told that the benefits of connecting to the sewer line would include improved neighbourhood health conditions, but that because there would be no wastewater treatment plant, the quality of Laguna de Bay near Calamba would probably get worse.

The second third of the respondents receiving the long questionnaire were also asked about their willingness to pay for connection to a sewer line in their neighbourhood, but in this case the wastewater collected by the sewer system would be treated at a wastewater treatment plant before being discharged into Laguna de Bay. This was termed the next higher level of sanitation service (Service Level II) and it was hypothesized that households would be willing to pay more for Service Level II than for Service Level I. In addition to the diagrams of a sewer line, respondents were shown large colour photographs of a type of secondary wastewater treatment plant in operation about thirty kilometres from Calamba. In this case respondents were told that they would receive neighbourhood health benefits if they connected to a sewer system, and that the water quality of the lake would stay about the same. The water quality of the lake would not improve significantly, because there was no assurance that other communities and industries around the Laguna de Bay would clean up their wastewater.

The third group of respondents was offered an even higher level of service (Service Level III). Not only were they given the opportunity to connect to a sewer line with an associated wastewater treatment plant, but they were told that there would be a regional water quality management plan that would ensure that other communities around Laguna de Bay would also clean up their wastewater discharges. The respondents would benefit from improved neighbourhood environmental conditions and also improved water quality in the lake.

It is important to emphasize that no respondent answered the willingness-to-pay questions for Service Level I and then subsequently answered the same questions for Service Levels II and III. Only one of the three service levels was offered to respondents in each of the three independently drawn random subsamples. If we had asked each respondent willingness-to-pay questions about Service Level I and then asked about Service Levels II and III, the answer he or she gave to Service Level I could affect the answers given to Service Levels II and III. Our research design precluded this possibility.

One reason why the survey was designed to offer respondents these three different levels of improved sanitation service was to gain insight into why people were willing to pay for improved sanitation service, in other words, to determine the characteristics of the service that they most desired. Many observers have speculated that improved regional environmental quality is not a high-priority concern to poor households in developing countries. They would thus expect that households in Calamba would mainly want improved neighbourhood environmental conditions, not improved water quality in Laguna de Bay. The answer to this question has important implications for the design and financing of a new sanitation system for Calamba. Obviously it would be cheaper to design a new sewage collection network for Calamba without a wastewater treatment plant, but this would cause water quality problems for neighbouring communities.

Following down the chain of split-samples (as shown in Figure 16.1), the following six groups of households received the long questionnaire:

1. households who were asked about Service Level I and given no time to think ($n = 216$);
2. households who were asked about Service Level II and given no time to think ($n = 193$);
3. households who were asked about Service Level III and given no time to think ($n = 184$);
4. households who were asked about Service Level I and given time to think ($n = 173$);
5. households who were asked about Service Level II and given time to think ($n = 176$);
6. households who were asked about Service Level III and given time to think ($n = 162$).

As described below, each of these split-samples was further subdivided into five groups depending on the precise willingness-to-pay questions respondents received (i.e. the first monthly fee offered the respondent).

16.4.5.   Elicitation Procedure (Willingness-to-Pay Questions)

A referendum approach with follow-up was used to elicit respondents' willingness to pay for the different service levels. After the enumerator read the respondent a description of the sanitation service level that had been randomly assigned to the household, the enumerator asked the respondent to suppose that it was possible to connect his or her house to a sewer line. The respondent was told that if his or her household decided to connect, they would have to pay a monthly fee just like a water bill. The enumerator then asked:

If the monthly fee to be connected to the sewer line was [25, 50, 100, 150, or 200] pesos, would you want to connect to the sewer line, or would you prefer not to connect?

Which of the five monthly fees (i.e., 25, 50, 100, 150, or 200 pesos[1]) a particular respondent received was randomly assigned. Each of the five monthly fees was assigned to approximately one-fifth of the respondents.

---

[1] At the time of our survey 25 pesos = US$1.

In this way there was no possibility that a respondent's answer to the first price offered was influenced by the answer given to any other price.

The purpose of this referendum approach was to ensure that an incentive-compatible procedure was used to obtain information on how households in Calamba would respond to different monthly fees without having to rely on a single respondent's answers to a series of questions about whether or not his household would connect at different prices. Individual respondents were not asked sequentially whether their households would want to connect at all five of these prices.

After the respondent answered this first question as to whether or not to connect to the sewer line at the first price offered, the enumerator asked one or more follow-up questions. For example, suppose a respondent was initially asked about a monthly fee of 50 pesos and he indicated that his household would connect at this price. The respondent was then asked to suppose that the costs of installing the sewer line had been underestimated and that the final cost to his household was actually 200 pesos per month. He was then asked whether his household would connect at this new price. If he said 'no', the price was then changed to 100 pesos per month. If the respondent had answered 'no' to the initial price of 50 pesos, he would be asked to suppose that the costs had been overestimated and that the final cost to his household was actually 25 pesos. If he answered 'no' to this second price of 25 pesos, he would be asked, 'What is the most your household would be willing to pay per month to connect your toilet to the sewer line?'

This elicitation method results in two sets of information regarding households' willingness to pay for the sanitation service level offered. The first set is the respondents' 'yes/no' answers to the initial price offered. These data cannot be influenced by the subsequent sequencing of questioning. The second set is the *final* amount that each respondent indicated he or she would be willing to pay to connect. These amounts potentially provide a more precise estimate of an individual's willingness to pay but may be influenced by the sequence of questions asked.

The study design for the long questionnaire thus results in 30 distinct subsamples (2 treatments for time/no time $\times$3 service levels $\times$ 5 monthly fees). Table 16.2 presents the number of interviews completed in Calamba for each of the 30 'cells'. As shown, more than 30 questionnaires were completed for every cell in the study design. Thirty-five per cent of the long questionnaire respondents were asked about Service Level I, 33 per cent about Service Level II, and 31 per cent about Service Level III. The portion of the sample respondents receiving each of the five monthly fees varied between 19 and 21 per cent. Because the implementation of the fieldwork was considerably more complicated for the respondents given time to think than for respondents given no time to think, fewer time-to-think interviews were successfully completed (511 vs. 593). Overall, the study design was successfully implemented in the field in the sense that the random

Table 16.2 Number of questionnaires completed in Calamba for households with flush or pour-flush toilets (by different versions of the survey instrument)

Price of sanitation service indicated to respondent (pesos/month)[a]	Type of improved sanitation service offered the respondent			
	Sewerage only	Sewerage and treatment	Sewerage, treatment, and regional plan	Total
Respondent given no time to think				
25	45	43	37	125
50	43	43	38	124
100	40	34	39	113
150	44	35	34	113
200	44	38	36	118
Respondent given time to think (1–2 days)				
25	34	35	32	101
50	35	32	33	100
100	34	36	33	103
150	35	37	31	103
200	35	38	33	104
Total no. of interviews	389	369	346	1,104

[a] 25 pesos = US $1.

assignment of respondents to the thirty cells resulted in the completed interviews being well distributed across these cells.

16.5. RESULTS OF THE ANALYSIS

Results are presented based on both sets of information regarding households' willingness to pay: (1) the answers to the first monthly fee offered in the referendum format, and (2) the final answers given to the follow-up questions. However, a socio-economic and housing profile of the sample respondents is first presented. This is followed by some simple summary results on willingness to pay for the three levels of improved sanitation service. The results of a series of multivariate analyses of the determinants of the willingness-to-pay responses are then outlined. Finally, information collected on respondents' environmental attitudes and perceptions is summarized.

16.5.1. Socio-Economic and Housing Profile of Sample Respondents

Table 16.3 summarizes the socio-economic characteristics of the sample respondents who received either long or short questionnaires. The information for the respondents receiving the long questionnaire is broken down according to where the respondent lived. The average household size of

Table 16.3 Socio-Economic profile of sample respondents

	Households with pour-flush or flush toilets (long ques.)				Other types of households (short ques.)	Total
	High-density	Medium-density with agriculture	Medium-density w/o agriculture	Subtotal		
Household size (number of persons)	5.7	5.7	5.6	5.7	5.2	5.6
Number of children living in household	2.6	2.6	2.7	2.6	2.7	2.6
Households headed by women (%)	14.9	17.2	13.2	15.9	11.1	15.0
Education of head of household (number of years)	10.1	9.2	9.8	9.5	8.8	9.4
Education of spouse of head of household (number of years)	10.1	8.7	9.4	9.1	8.5	9.0
Household income (pesos/month)	6,600	6,300	6,900	6,500	4,200	6,200
Household expenditures (pesos/week)	1,070	920	880	930	650	900
Electricity bill (pesos/month)	380	270	320	300	156	281
Water bill (pesos/month)	170	118	—	140	—	140

sample respondents is 5.6 persons. Female-headed households constituted 15 per cent of the total sample.

Education levels in Calamba are relatively high. The average head of household in our sample had 9.5 years of education. This was only slightly lower for households without water-sealed toilets than for those with such facilities (9.5 years vs. 8.8 years). Education levels were slightly higher in the high-density urban areas than in the medium-density agricultural areas (10.1 years vs. 9.2 years). The education levels of the spouse of the head of household were generally comparable to those of the head of household.

Average reported household income levels in Calamba were on the order of 6,200 pesos per month (US$3,000 per year). Incomes of households without water-sealed toilets for their exclusive use were substantially lower than for households with such facilities (4,200 pesos per month vs. 6,500 pesos per month). The reported household expenditure data show the same pattern.

Average household electricity bills in Calamba are quite high: 281 pesos per month (US$11). Electricity bills of households without water-sealed toilets for their exclusive use were again substantially lower than for households with such facilities (156 pesos per month vs. 300 pesos per month). The average household water bill was about 140 pesos per month (US$6).

Table 16.4 summarizes the housing conditions of the sample respondents. The majority of households live in single-family buildings (86 per cent). Very

Table 16.4   Housing conditions of sample respondents

	Households with pour-flush or flush toilets (long ques.)				Other types of households (short ques.)	Total
	High-density	Medium-density with agriculture	Medium-density w/o agriculture	Subtotal		
Households living in single-family buildings (%)	80.1	89.3	88.4	87.6	76.6	86.0
Households living in buildings with 1 or 2 other families (%)	17.1	9.2	9.7	10.6	15.8	10.0
Households living in buildings with 3 or more other families (%)	2.8	1.5	1.9	1.8	7.6	4.0
Subtotal	100.0	100.0	100.0	100.0	100.0	100.0
Households living in subdivisions (%)	24.4	15.2	59.1	27.4	12.9	24.0
Households living in flood zones (%)	23.3	24.0	15.4	21.8	43.5	32.0
Households living in high-crime areas (%)	9.0	13.2	2.3	9.8	13.9	10.0
Age of housing (years)	16.9	16.1	10.4	15	13.1	14.8
Housing construction Concrete (%)	90.7	85.3	93.7	88.2	60.0	84.0
Wood/light material (%)	9.3	14.7	6.3	11.8	40.0	16.0
Floor area used by household (m³)	80	69	67	71	38	67
Lot area (m³)	169	194	198	191	98	183
Value of house (1000 pesos)	238	141	210	175	28	158
Value of lot (1000 pesos)	389	299	258	299	152	286
Value of lot and house (1000 pesos)	575	435	507	478	132	442
No. of households interviewed	182	654	268	1,104	171	1,275

few households live in buildings with three or more households (4 per cent). Almost a quarter of the sample respondents live in self-identified 'subdivisions'. About a third of the households live in areas at risk of flooding. Only 10 per cent perceived that they lived in a 'high-crime' area.

Most housing in Calamba is relatively new; the average age of respondents' dwelling units is 15 years. Most housing is built with concrete block. However, households without a water-sealed toilet for their exclusive use are much more likely to live in houses constructed with wood or other light material. Housing prices in Calamba are quite high. The average reported value of a respondent's house and lot was 442,000 pesos (approximately US$18,000).

16.5.2. Willingness to Pay (WTP) for Improved Services: Summary Results from Households with Water-Sealed Toilets for their Exclusive Use (Long Questionnaire)

Table 16.5 presents the percentage of respondents who agreed to connect to the sewer line at the first price offered for different service levels and different monthly fees (the respondents who were given time to think and those that were not are lumped together in the results presented in this table). Several aspects of these results are noteworthy. First, for all three service levels, respondents' answers on whether or not to connect to a sewer line are sensitive to the monthly fee charged: as the price goes up, the percentage of respondents who agree to connect decreases. This result is true for every service level at every price. This suggests that respondents were listening to the description of services provided to them in the interview and responding differently depending on what information was conveyed.

Second, it appears that respondents clearly preferred Service Level II to Service Level I, and Service Level III to Service Level I. This is as anticipated: at a given price, a higher percentage of respondents would be expected to agree to connect at higher service levels. For example, at a price of 50 pesos per month, 39 per cent of the respondents who were offered Service

Table 16.5   Per cent of respondents who gave positive response to referendum question (by referendum amount)[a]

Referendum amount (pesos/month)[b]	Percent of respondents agreeing to referendum amount for		
	Sewerage only (Level I)	Sewerage and treatment (Level II)	Sewerage, treatment, and regional plan (Level III)
25	57	71	71
50	39	57	62
100	35	27	29
150	9	21	14
200	8	11	6

[a] For households with pour-flush or flush toilets which are exclusively for household use.
[b] 25 pesos = US $1.

Level I wished to connect to the sewer line, while 57 per cent of the respondents who were offered Service Level II wished to connect (and 62 per cent who were offered Service Level III). However, it does not seem that respondents preferred Service Level III to Service Level II as hypothesized. The percentages of respondents who agreed to connect at a given price are roughly the same for Service Level II and Service Level III. In fact, in two of the five cases (150 and 200 pesos), a higher percentage of respondents agreed to connect for Service Level II than for Service Level III, although the difference is not statistically significant.

Third, at the lowest price offered (25 pesos per month), a rather high percentage of households indicated that they did not want to connect to the sewer line. This was true for all levels of service. For Service Level I, 43 per cent of the respondents did not want to connect at a monthly fee of 25 pesos. Even for Service Levels II and III, 29 per cent of the respondents did not want to connect.

Fourth, at the highest price offered (200 pesos per month), very few respondents agreed to connect to the sewer line. This was again true for all three levels of service. Some critics of the contingent valuation method have suggested that many respondents will say 'yes' to any hypothetical proposition or scenario offered to them, and will agree to pay unrealistically high amounts. The results here do not support this conjecture. It is of course possible that a few respondents who agreed to pay 200 pesos per month may have been engaged in such 'yea-saying', but there is little doubt that a further increase in the monthly fee would have resulted in even fewer respondents agreeing to connect to the sewer line. Although these four findings are only based on a simple tabulation of the responses to the first referendum question, they are all supported by more sophisticated multivariate analyses of the data described below.

Table 16.6 summarizes by land-use type and socio-economic characteristics the results of the second set of willingness-to-pay information (i.e. the point estimates of WTP from the answers to the final WTP question) for Service Level II (sewer connection and treatment) for households with water-sealed toilets for their exclusive use. The overall mean WTP for the sample households was 55 pesos per month (about US$2).

Table 16.6 shows that respondents with low education levels (< 7 years) were willing to pay less for improved sanitation service than were respondents with more education ($\geqslant 7$ years). Table 16.6 presents three different measures of the economic well-being of sample households: (1) the value of their respondent's house and lot; (2) weekly household expenditures; and (3) reported household income. For all three measures, household willingness to pay increases as economic status increases. For example, there is a marked, positive relationship between willingness to pay and household income. The average willingness to pay of households with incomes less than 3,000 pesos per month was 35 pesos per month; for households with incomes greater

Table 16.6 Average household willingness to pay (pesos/month) for piped sewerage and treatment (Service Level II), by socio-Economic characteristics[a]

Socio-economic characteristic	High-density	Medium-density with agriculture	Medium-density w/o agriculture	Entire sample
Education of respondent (years)				
0–6	19	39	55	41
7–12	61	57	65	60
> 12	73	70	58	60
Value of house and lot (1000 pesos)				
≤ 150	51	39	64	46
151–300	100	49	55	54
301–450	31	48	62	53
> 450	80	79	61	73
Household expenses (pesos/week)				
≤ 500	20	33	45	34
501–750	62	52	55	54
751–1000	65	49	67	55
> 1000	70	75	67	72
Household income (pesos/month)				
≤ 3,000	23	35	50	35
3,001–6,000	45	49	51	49
6,001–9,000	57	54	61	56
> 9,000	93	86	75	84
Overall mean	55	53	60	55

[a] For households with pour-flush toilets for their exclusive use.

than 9,000 pesos per month, the average willingness to pay was 84 pesos per month.

Table 16.7 presents the mean willingness to pay of respondents given time to think and those given no time to think by land-use type and service level. (As for Table 16.6, these averages are based on the point estimates of WTP from the answers to the final WTP question.) These data reveal a consistent pattern: respondents who were given time to think about their willingness to pay consistently bid less than those who were given no time to think. This result generally holds for the three land-use types and for the three levels of service. This finding is consistent with the results of similar time-to-think experiments elsewhere (see Whittington *et al.*, 1992). We consider the lower bids given by respondents who were given time to think to be better indicators of households' preferences for improved sanitation services.

As noted, many respondents receiving the long questionnaire were not willing to pay anything for Service Levels I, II, or III. Table 16.8 shows the percentages of respondents in each land-use type and for each service level that bid zero. For the entire sample, 37 per cent of the respondents receiving Service Level I, 18 per cent of the respondents receiving Service Level II, and 20 per cent of the respondents receiving Service Level III bid zero. For

Table 16.7   Relationship between willingness to pay (pesos/month) and time to think, by land-use type and service level[a]

Average willingness to pay for: Questionnaire version	Land-use type			
	High-density	Medium-density with agriculture	Medium-density w/o agriculture	Total
Sewerage only (Level I)				
No time to think	73	37	31	42
Time to think	57	24	25	29
Average	66	31	28	36
Sewerage and treatment plant (Level II)				
No time to think	67	51	67	57
Time to think	40	55	53	53
Average	55	53	60	55
Sewerage, treatment, and regional plan (Level III)				
No time to think	67	62	59	62
Time to think	56	41	36	43
Average	61	52	48	53

[a] For households with pour-flush or flush toilets for their exclusive use.

Table 16.8   Zero willingness to pay by land use and service level[a]

Stratum	Sewer only (Level I)		Sewer and treatment (Level II)		Sewer, treatment, and regional plan (Level III)	
	No. of households	(%)	No. of households	(%)	No. of households	(%)
High-density	67	100	51	100	64	100
WTP = 0	11	16	12	24	13	20
WTP > 0	56	84	39	76	51	80
Medium-density with agriculture	228	100	225	100	200	100
WTP = 0	81	36	38	17	40	20
WTP > 0	147	64	187	83	160	80
Medium-density without agriculture	94	100	92	100	82	100
WTP = 0	52	55	18	20	16	20
WTP > 0	42	45	74	80	66	80
Entire sample	389	100	368	100	346	100
WTP = 0	144	37	68	18	69	20
WTP > 0	245	63	300	82	277	80

[a] For households with pour-flush or flush toilets for their exclusive use.

Service Levels II and III, there does not appear to be much variation in the proportion of zero bids by where the respondents lived. For Service Level I, only 16 per cent of the respondents in the high-density areas bid zero, while 55 per cent of those in the medium-density areas without agriculture bid zero.

Table 16.9   Effect of time to think on unwillingness to pay[a]

Stratum	Respondents unwilling to pay for								
	Sewer only (Level I)			Sewer and treatment plant (Level II)			Sewer, treatment plant and regional plan (Level III)		
	No. of HH	No. of HH WTP zero	% of HH WTP zero	No. of HH	No. of HH WTP zero	% of HH WTP zero	No. of HH	No. of HH WTP zero	% of HH WTP zero
High-density	67	11	16	51	12	24	64	13	20
No time to think	39	3	8	28	3	11	34	7	23
Time to think	28	8	29	23	9	39	30	6	18
Medium-density with agriculture	228	81	36	225	38	17	200	40	20
No time to think	124	38	31	115	17	15	112	16	14
Time to think	104	43	41	110	21	19	88	24	27
Medium-density without agriculture	94	52	55	92	18	20	82	16	20
No time to think	53	30	57	49	11	22	42	6	14
Time to think	41	22	54	43	7	16	40	10	25
Entire sample	389	144	37	368	68	18	346	69	20
No time to think	216	71	33	192	31	16	184	29	15
Time to think	173	73	42	176	37	21	162	40	25

[a] For households with pour-flush or flush toilets for their exclusive use.

Table 16.9 shows the effect of time to think on the prevalence of zero bids by land-use type and service level. The number of observations with zero bids in the various cells is very small, so one must be careful in drawing conclusions about the statistical significance of the results. However, in general a higher per cent of the respondents gave zero bids after having had time to think. For example, for Service Level I, 33 per cent of the respondents with no time to think gave zero bids, compared with 42 per cent of the respondents with time to think.

Respondents who bid zero were asked why they were not willing to pay anything for an improved service level. The majority said that they were satisfied with their existing situation. Only one-quarter of the respondents who bid zero indicated that they could not afford the improved sanitation service.

16.5.3.   Willingness to Pay for Improved Services: Results of Multivariate Analyses

In order better to understand the determinants of the households' willingness-to-pay responses and to see whether these determinants are consistent with economic demand theory, a series of multivariate analyses were performed with the data obtained from the long questionnaires. Various independent variables were used to attempt to explain the variation in different measures of household's willingness to pay for the three levels of improved sanitation service.

Two sets of information on households' willingness to pay were used as the dependent variable in these analyses. First, the final monthly fee accepted by the respondent (i.e. the answer to the last question of the bidding game) was treated as a point estimate of the household's willingness to pay. Second, the respondent's answer to the first 'yes/no' question asked was treated as a discrete-choice response. Ordinary least-squares models were used to explain the variation in the first set of willingness-to-pay responses. In addition, Tobit models were also used to explain the variation in the respondents' answers to the last question of the bidding game, but in this case, the dependent variable was restricted to non-negative values. Logit models were used to model the differences in the 'yes/no' responses to the first referendum question.

Five principal types of independent variables were used in the models. First, some variables described the respondent's characteristics (e.g., gender, years of education). Second, additional variables described the characteristics of the respondent's household (e.g., income, housing conditions). Third, a few variables described the characteristics of the specific questionnaire the respondent received (e.g., starting value of the bidding game, whether the respondent was given time to think, the service level initially offered the respondent). Fourth, other variables described the water and sanitation situation of the respondent's household (e.g., whether the household had a private water connection, if the household's wastewater went to a septic tank, what type of septic tank was used). A fifth set of independent variables concerned the respondent's knowledge and attitudes about environmental and sanitation issues (e.g., whether the respondent knew what a sewer system and/or treatment plant were, beliefs about the water quality trends in Laguna de Bay, concern over contaminated fish, degree of satisfaction with existing sanitation system). Table 16.10 lists both the dependent and independent variables used in the multivariate analyses and their means and standard deviations.

Table 16.11 presents the results of six multivariate models of the determinants of the WTP responses: two each for the ordinary least-squares, Tobit, and Logit models. The first model associated with each technique (termed the 'full model') includes a complete list of independent variables. The second model (termed the 'reduced model') includes a restricted set of independent variables. Seven of the independent variables are statistically significant determinants of household willingness to pay in all six of the multivariate models. These results are discussed before turning to the interpretation of some of the other independent variables.

Table 16.10   Description of selected variables used in the analysis

Variable name	Mean (S.D.)	Description	Expected sign in regression models
Dependent variables			
FINAL BID	53.37 (48.15)	maximum monthly amount household would pay for specified services (pesos): the amount was taken from the last yes to the bidding questions (for OLS & TOBIT models)	
REFERENDUM BID	0.34	'yes' and 'no' responses taken from the first bidding questions: 0 = respondent is not willing to pay bid amount for specified service; 1 = respondent is willing to pay bid amount for specified service (for LOGIT model)	
Independent variables			
TTT	0.46 (0.50)	1 = respondent was given time to think; 0 = no time to think	−
START	104.54 (64.40)	starting point of bidding game taken as continuous values; 25, 50, 100, 150 and 200 pesos	+
TTTSTART	48.98 (68.41)	dummy for testing the combined effects of time to think and START (TTT * START)	−
PRICESTRT	104.54 (64.40)	prices randomly assigned for referendum question; 25, 50, 100, 150 and 200 pesos	−
TTTPRICE	48.98 (68.41)	dummy for testing the combind effects of time to think and START (TTT * PRICESTRT)	?
TYPE3	0.31 (0.46)	1 = service level 3 (sewer, treatment plant, & regional plan) was offered; 0 otherwise	+
TYPE1	0.35 (0.48)	1 = service level 1 (sewer only) was offered; 0 otherwise	−
FEMALE	0.61 (0.49)	1 = gender of respondent is female; 0 otherwise	?
EDUCATION	9.31 (3.43)	years of education for respondent	+
WATER CONNECT	0.32 (0.47)	1 = the major source of drinking water is from NAWASA connection; 0 otherwise	?
DISCHARGE TANK	0.16 (0.37)	1 = wastewater from kitchen or bath goes to septic tank; 0 otherwise	−
INCOMPLETE TANK	0.64 (0.48)	1 = septic tank does not have either concrete wall or floor; 0 otherwise	+
SATISFY	0.41 (0.49)	1 = respondent is very satisfied with existing sanitation system; 0 otherwise	−

Table 16.10   *(contd.)*

Variable name	Mean (S.D.)	Description	Expected sign in regression models
FISH QUALITY	0.57 (0.50)	1 = respondent believes water quality of lake over last 20 years has become worse (or much worse) and is also very concerned about contaminated fish; 0 otherwise	+
KNOW SEWER	0.10 (0.30)	1 = respondent is somewhat (or very) familiar with sewer system; 0 otherwise	+
KNOW TREAT PLANT	0.13 (0.34)	1 = if respondent is somewhat (or very) familiar with treatment plant; 0 otherwise	+
INCOME	6.52 (3.98)	total monthly income for all wage earners of a household (1,000 pesos/ month)	+
FLOOD	0.22 (0.41)	1 = house is located in flood zone; 0 otherwise	+
SUBDIVISION	0.26 (0.44)	1 = house is located in subdivision; 0 otherwise	?
HI DENSITY	0.17 (0.37)	1 = respondent lives in high-density (Poblacion) area; 0 otherwise	+
MED DENSITY	0.59 (0.49)	1 = respondent lives in an area that has agricultural activity; 0 otherwise	−
INTERVIEW QUALITY	0.32 (0.47)	1 = enumerator assessed the interviewee made effort to answer WTP questions truthfully and also thinks the interview quality was good; 0 otherwise	+

First, household income has a statistically significant but small effect on household willingness to pay: households with larger incomes are willing to pay more for improved sanitation service than households with lower incomes. This is true for all types of models and specifications. The results suggest that if monthly household income increases by 1,000 pesos per month, the household's willingness to pay will increase by about 2–3 pesos per month (0.2–0.3 per cent of the increase in income).

Second, households living in high-density areas bid substantially more for improved sanitation services than households living elsewhere. After controlling for other factors, households in high-density areas were willing to pay about 30 to 35 pesos per month more than households in medium-density areas without agriculture. Households in medium-density areas with agriculture were willing to pay about 10–13 pesos per month more than households in medium-density areas without agriculture. These results suggests that at a given monthly fee, a higher percentage of households would connect to a sewer line in the high-density areas and that greater cost recovery can be achieved there than elsewhere in Calamba.

Third, households clearly understood the difference between Service Level I and the two higher levels of service (II and III), and were willing to pay significantly *less* for Service Level I than for the other two. Respondents were willing to pay 18–25 pesos per month less for Service Level I than for Service Level II. This result lends substantial credibility to the reliability of the WTP responses. Respondents appear to have been listening to the explanation of the service level provided by the enumerator, and their WTP responses were different depending on the service level offered.

There was, however, no statistically significant difference between respondents' willingness to pay for Service Levels II and III. Given respondents' ability to distinguish between Service Levels I and II, it appears that respondents are actually not interested in participating in a regional water quality management plan for the lake. This could be because they were acting strategically, hoping that residents of Calamba could 'free-ride' if other communities would undertake such a plan. It seems more plausible, however, that residents of Calamba simply did not have much faith that the Government could successfully implement a regional plan and did not wish to get entangled in a possibly complicated, time-consuming regional solution that might involve cross-subsidizing other communities. Also, it is possible that, given their knowledge of the hydrology of the lake, residents of Calamba did not find it plausible that they would benefit much from co-operative water quality management efforts.

Fourth, the first price offered the respondent is statistically significant in all six models. However, its interpretation is different in the Logit model than in the OLS and Tobit models. In the Logit model the starting price is used to explain the probability that a respondent accepted (i.e., answered 'yes' to the scenario and first price offered). Here economic theory and common sense would suggest that the higher the price, the less likely a respondent would be to answer 'yes', other things equal. The negative and statistically significant effect of this 'price variable' in the Logit model is thus as hypothesized and lends credence to the plausibility of the WTP responses. In the OLS and Tobit models the starting price variable (START) indicates whether the respondent's final WTP bid (the dependent variable) was influenced by the first price the respondent was offered. Here the statistically significant effect indicated a 'starting-point bias'.

Fifth, for the OLS and Tobit models the data from the time-to-think experiment were used to construct a variable interacting between the first price offered and whether or not the respondent had time to think. This variable is statistically significant and has a negative effect in all of the models. If the respondent was given no time to think, this interaction variable (TTTSTART) takes a value of zero. The coefficient for this interaction variable is negative, which indicates that giving respondents time to think reduces willingness to pay. The net effect of giving respondents time to think and the starting-point bias is obtained by adding the coefficients of the two variables (START and TTTSTART) together. The results in Table 16.11 indicate that the effect of giving respondents time to think largely cancels out the starting-point bias.

For the Logit model the negative coefficient of the interaction variable (TTTPRICE) indicates that giving respondents time to think reduces the probability that a respondent will say 'yes' (i.e. agree to the first price offered). It is also statistically significant in both the full and reduced model.

Sixth, a dummy variable (FISH QUALITY) was used to see if those respondents who (1) believed that the lake had got much worse over the last twenty years *and* (2) were very concerned about eating contaminated fish would be willing to pay more for improved sanitation than would other households. This was indeed the case: the effect is statistically significant and large in all of the models. Respondents that held these beliefs were willing to pay about 14–17 pesos per month more for improved sanitation services.

Seventh, the enumerator was asked to make a subjective judgement as to the quality of the interview and whether the respondent appeared to make an effort to tell the truth. Enumerators rated approximately one-third of the interviews to be of 'high quality'. The results in Table 16.11 indicate that respondents participating in interviews judged to be high-quality by the enumerator bid substantially more than respondents in the other interviews (22 to 28 pesos per month more).

Other independent variables were statistically significant in some of the models, but not others. For example, the number of the respondent's years of education had a positive and statistically significant effect on willingness to pay in both of the OLS models and both of the Tobit models, but not in the Logit models. The magnitude of the effect was not, however, large: an additional year of education added about 1 peso per month to the respondent's monthly willingness to pay.

Overall, these multivariate results are in accord with economic theory and prior expectations, and are robust with respect to estimation technique and model specification. The overall explanatory power of the models is not high; for example, the adjusted R^2 value for the OLS models is 0.15. However, the large number of statistically significant independent variables and the robustness of the results indicate that the willingness-to-pay responses are not random but rather are systematically related to respondents' and households' characteristics and the treatments introduced in the experimental design.

16.5.4. Households' Environmental Priorities, Attitudes, and Perceptions

Average household willingness to pay for improved sanitation services is low in Calamba, and many households apparently are not willing to pay

Table 16.11. Multivariate models of the determinants of households' willingness-to-pay responses

Variables	OLS		Tobit		Logit	
	full model	reduced model	full model	reduced model	full model	reduced model
Dependent variables:	FINAL BID	FINAL BID	FINAL BID	FINAL BID	REFERENDUM BID	REFERENDUM BID
Independent variables						
INTERCEPT	7.229	5.980	−0.157	0.345	−0.059	−0.053
	(0.857)	(0.828)	(−0.016)	(0.041)	(−0.253)	(−0.332)
START	0.096	0.095	0.091	0.088	—	—
	(3.518)*	(3.503)*	(2.859)**	(2.790)*	—	—
TTSTART	−0.082	−0.082	−0.101	−0.100	—	—
	(−3.165)*	(−3.151)*	(−3.310)*	(−3.294)*	—	—
PRICESTRT	—	—	—	—	−0.011	−0.011
					(−13.043)*	(−13.039)*
TTTPRICE	—	—	—	—	−0.002	−0.002
					(−2.121)**	(−2.103)**
TYPE3	−3.607	−3.211	−4.925	−5.227	−0.042	−0.034
	(−0.925)	(−0.828)	(−1.092)	(−1.158)	(−0.374)	(−0.303)
TYPE1	−18.066	−17.921	−24.661	−24.961	−0.303	−0.286
	(−4.674)*	(−4.652)*	(−5.442)*	(−5.503)*	(−2.740)*	(−2.619)*
FEMALE	1.428	—	1.372	—	−0.057	—
	(0.426)		(0.352)		(−0.589)	
EDUCATION	1.113	0.984	1.371	1.245	0.020	—
	(2.233)**	(2.009)**	(2.352)*	(2.163)**	(1.405)	
WATER CONNECT	−12.538	−12.378	−13.218	−12.329	−0.123	—
	(−3.002)*	(−2.999)*	(−2.720)*	(−2.572)*	(−1.032)	
DISCHARGE TANK	−5.698	—	−9.179	−9.788	−0.032	—
	(−1.291)		(−1.766)***	(−1.891)***	(−0.255)	
INCOMPLETE TANK	−1.882	—	−3.615	—	−0.119	—
	(−0.550)		(−0.905)		(−1.224)	

	(1)	(2)	(3)	(4)	(5)	(6)
SATISFY	-4.805 (-1.287)	—	-7.174 (-1.646)***	-6.014 (-1.435)	-0.162 (-1.524)	—
FISH QUALITY	13.670 (4.029)*	13.404 (4.001)*	16.539 (4.184)*	16.720 (4.266)*	0.209 (2.159)**	0.169 (1.806)***
KNOW SEWER	-2.979 (-0.417)	—	-7.529 (-0.903)	—	-0.259 (-1.282)	—
KNOW TREATPLANT	-1.530 (-0.243)	—	0.157 (0.021)	—	0.139 (0.780)	—
INCOME	2.402 (5.807)*	2.295 (5.626)*	2.519 (5.247)*	2.408 (5.061)*	0.073 (5.607)*	0.073 (5.760)*
FLOOD	7.767 (1.910)***	7.189 (1.786)***	7.747 (1.637)	—	0.469 (0.418)	—
SUBDIVISION	0.027 (0.007)	—	-0.494 (-0.105)	—	0.027 (0.237)	—
HI DENSITY	29.941 (4.815)*	30.306 (4.994)*	35.589 (4.917)*	35.147 (4.908)*	0.387 (2.203)**	0.329 (2.276)**
MED DENSITY	10.019 (2.222)**	10.224 (2.466)*	13.003 (2.473)*	13.461 (2.704)*	0.192 (1.484)	0.191 (1.719)***
INTERVIEW QUALITY	24.094 (6.396)*	22.093 (6.237)*	27.974 (6.384)*	28.274 (6.492)*	0.521 (4.808)*	0.473 (4.716)*
log (L)	—	—	-4,463.1	-4,465.6	-507.32	-511.77
X^2	—	—	—	—	348.68	339.79
Pseudo R^2	—	—	—	—	0.256	0.249
R^2	0.164	0.160	—	—	—	—
Adjusted R^2	0.147	0.149	—	—	—	—
F value	9.679	14.959	—	—	—	—
N	955	955	955	955	1,058	1,058
% correct predicted	—	—	—	—	76.8%	74.9%

Note: The numbers in parentheses below the estimated coefficients are the ratio of these coefficients to the estimates of their asymptotic standard errors.   * indicates null hypothesis of $b = 0$ is rejected at 1% of significance level.   ** indicates null hypothesis of $b = 0$ is rejected at 5% of significance level.   *** indicates null hypothesis of $b = 0$ is rejected at 10 % of significance level.

anything for a sewer connection. There are several possible reasons why households may not be able or willing to pay for such improved sanitation service. For example, household income could be too low: there may simply be other more pressing personal priorities for people to spend their money on. Alternatively, households that have already invested in private toilet facilities may feel that they have largely solved their sanitation problems and may not perceive the need for sewage collection and treatment. In the household survey, a series of questions was designed to better understand these preferences.

Respondents who had water-sealed toilets for their exclusive use were asked how satisfied they were with their existing sanitation system. A summary of their answers is presented in Table 16.12. Only 2 per cent of the sample respondents receiving the long questionnaire reported that they were not satisfied with their existing toilet and septic-tank system. This suggests that improving their sanitation system is not uppermost in the minds of most respondents.

In order to see how environmental concerns compared to other social priorities, respondents were given a list of eight social problems and asked to indicate their first and second priorities (i.e. the ones they wanted solved the most). As indicated in Table 16.13, the overwhelming top priority was 'unemployment'. The next two 'medium-level' priorities were 'water

Table 16.12   Households' satisfaction with existing sanitation system

Households reported being:	% from long questionnaire	% from short questionnaire	Total (%)
Very satisfied	42	27	40
Somewhat satisfied	56	53	56
Not satisfied	2	20	4
Total	100	100	100

Table 16.13   Social priorities in Calamba

Respondent's social concerns	Vote for first priority (% of respondents)	Vote for second priority (% of respondents)	Total[a] (% of respondents)
Unemployment	69	12	40
Malnutrition	1	3	2
Air pollution	2	5	4
Crime	4	13	8
Water pollution in lakes and rivers	12	23	17
Public education	1	6	4
Traffic congestion	1	7	4
Drug addiction	10	31	21

[a] Votes for either the 1st or 2nd priorities.

Table 16.14   Environmental priorities in Calamba

Respondents' environmental concerns	Vote for first priority (% of respondents)	Vote for second priority (% of respondents)	Total[a] (% of respondents)
Air pollution	6	6	6
Drinking water contamination	6	6	6
Solid waste	45	13	29
Household excreta and wastewater disposal	9	13	11
Food contamination	2	5	4
Water pollution in lakes and rivers	17	21	19
Hazardous waste	15	33	24
Noise pollution	1	3	2

[a] Votes for either the 1st or 2nd priorities.

pollution in lakes and rivers' and 'drug addiction'. The environmental problem of 'water pollution' thus appears to be perceived as important, even if it is the first priority of only 12 per cent of the respondents.

Respondents were asked a similar type of question regarding their environmental priorities. Table 16.14 shows the first and second priorities indicated by respondents from a list of eight environmental problems. Respondents' top environmental priority in Calamba was 'solid waste'. However, the problem of 'water pollution in lakes and rivers' received the second largest number of 'first-place votes', and 'household excreta and wastewater removal' received 9 per cent. Together, 'water pollution in lakes and rivers' and 'household excreta and wastewater removal' received 30 per cent of the total votes (either first or second priority). This was interpreted to mean that sanitation and water pollution are a 'medium-level' concern in Calamba: clearly more important than air or noise pollution, or food contamination, but not as important as solid-waste problems.

To explore in more depth the reasons for respondents' concerns about 'water pollution in lakes and rivers', a series of questions was asked about their use of Laguna de Bay. Almost everyone in Calamba is affected either directly or indirectly by changes in the water quality of the lake. Twenty-eight per cent of respondents said that they go swimming or bathing in the lake. Almost all respondents reported that they eat fish from the lake. However, 60 per cent said that they were 'very concerned' about the possibility of eating contaminated fish. Only 43 respondents reported that they do not eat fish from the lake, and over 70 per cent of these said that they did not eat fish from the lake *because* of fear of contamination.

Not only do people use the lake, but they perceive its water quality to have got 'much worse' over the last twenty years (Table 16.15). Ninety-nine per cent of respondents felt the lake was 'somewhat worse' or 'much worse' for swimming and bathing. Seventy-eight per cent reported that the type and size of fish caught was 'somewhat worse' or 'much worse'.

Table 16.15 Respondents' perception of the changes of environmental quality in Laguna de Bay in the last twenty years

Perception of changes	Types of environmental concern (% of respondents)			
	No. of fisherman	Type and size of fish caught	Water quality of the lake	Suitability of the lake for swimming and bathing
Much better	21	2	0	0
About the same	25	21	1	1
Somewhat worse	43	61	32	42
Much worse	11	17	67	57

There thus seems to be a clear sense among residents of Calamba that something important has been lost in terms of their quality of life as the water quality of Laguna de Bay has deteriorated. However, respondents do not appear to perceive (perhaps correctly!) that their household bears much responsibility for the problem of poor disposal of human wastes and household wastewater. As shown in Table 16.16, the majority of respondents, irrespective of the zone in which they live and of their income group, report that their household contributes *less* to this problem than other households. This perception probably contributes to a sense of reduced responsibility for this problem and thus reduced willingness to pay for community-wide solutions such as sewage collection and treatment.

Table 16.16 Attitude towards the problem caused by inadequate sanitation system

	Respondent thinks his/her household contributes to the problem of poor disposal of human wastes and household water (% of households)		
	Less than other households	About the same as other households	More than other households
By stratum			
High density	75	21	4
Med. density with ag.	69	28	3
Med. density without ag.	75	21	4
Total	71	25	4
By household income (pesos/month)			
≤3,000	64	33	3
3,000–6,000	67	27	6
6,001–9,000	79	19	2
> 9,000	80	19	1
Total	71	25	4

16.6. SUMMARY AND CONCLUSIONS

The situation in Calamba is unlike that reported in any of the existing literature on household willingness to pay for improved sanitation services in developing countries. In Calamba, the transition to private sanitary toilets in houses is almost complete. Ninety-seven per cent of the sample respondents in the study already used water-sealed toilets. Eighty-seven per cent of the population had water-sealed toilets for the exclusive use of their household's members. This represents a substantial investment in *private* sanitation infrastructure, almost all of which was made without public sector involvement or participation. There is thus little need to devote substantial resources to promote on-site sanitation technologies such as ventilated pit latrines, or to build additional public latrines. The problem in Calamba has moved beyond the level of the individual household: community-wide solutions are now needed for the collection of household wastewater to remove it from roadside ditches in neighbourhoods and for treatment to improve surface-water quality.

This posed a dilemma: the results of this study show that households' willingness to pay is quite low. In fact, many households indicated that they were not willing to pay anything for the three levels of improved sanitation service offered. For example, 21 per cent of the sample respondents who were given time to think offered zero bids for Service Level II (sewerage and treatment); 42 per cent offered zero bids for Service Level I (sewerage only). Depending on where households lived and their socio-economic circumstances, of those households with a positive willingness to pay, most offered

Table 16.17 Comparison of mean willingness-to-pay values for improved sanitation, Calamba (pesos/month)

Mean WTP bids by level of service		
Sewer collection (Level I)	Sewer collection with treatment plant (Level II)	Sewer, treatment, and regional plan (Level III)
1. *Final bids taken as continuous variable*		
36	55	53
($n = 374$; S.D. $= 49$)	($n = 354$; S.D. $= 53$)	($n = 330$; S.D. $= 54$)
2. *Estimates from Logit models*[a]		
(*a*) Using the sample values from the respondents		
45	67	67
($n = 374$; S.D. $= 34$)	($n = 354$; S.D. $= 35$)	($n = 330$; S.D. $= 35$)
(*b*) Using the average characteristics of sample[b]		
41	65	63

[a] All estimates are based on coefficients from the reduced Logit model in Table 16.11.

[b] For each level of service, the following average characteristics for households in Poblacion were used: household income = 6,500 pesos per month; FISH QUALITY = 0; INTERVIEW QUALITY = 0.

bids of less than 100 pesos per month (US$4). The average WTP amount for most categories of households for a sewer connection and a treatment plant were on the order of 50 pesos per month (US$2), less than 1 per cent of monthly income for most households.

Average willingness to pay for this level of service showed little variation based on how the averages were calculated, i.e., whether directly from household responses to the last 'yes/no' contingent valuation question or from the fitted Logit model, as shown in Table 16.17. Variation was similar for each of the other two levels of service depending on calculation method. However, average willingness to pay for Service Levels II and III was significantly higher than for Level I.

A useful way to represent the analysis result is to use a cumulative distribution function, with percentage of households willing to pay for improved sanitation on the ordinate and the monthly fee for improved service on the abscissa. Figure 16.2 is based on the reduced Logit model described in Table 16.11. This graph shows the probability of households in *Poblacion* connecting to the three different levels of improved sanitation service at alternative monthly fees.

Consider, for example, a fee of 50 pesos per month (US$2). Figure 16.2 shows that at this amount, probably 70 per cent of the households in *Poblacion* would connect to either Service Level I or III (sewer only or sewer, treatment plant, and regional plan) if they were offered, and about 80 per cent of the households would connect to Service Level II if it were offered. Note that at a fee of 200 pesos per month or above (US$8), which is more likely to represent the cost of improved sanitation in Calamba, probably less than 10 per cent of the households in *Poblacion* would connect to any of the three levels of improved sanitation if they were offered. Note further that even if the fee were zero, only 85–90 per cent of the households would connect to improved sanitation if available. This is because of the relatively high numbers of households that gave zero bids, as shown in Table 16.8.

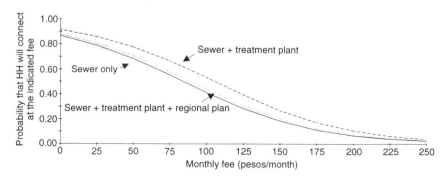

Fig. 16.2   Probability of households in Poblacion connecting to improved sanitation at different fees

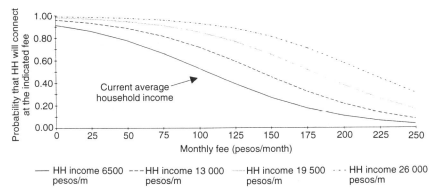

Fig. 16.3 Probability of accepting the price offered for sewers and treatment (Level II service) as household income increases: high density areas

Using the Logit model, predictions were made of the probabilities of households in *Poblacion* that would adopt Service Level II (sewers and treatment plant) as household income increases, holding other conditions constant. For example, at a monthly fee of, say, 100 pesos, only about 50 per cent of the households in the built-up parts of Calamba (with present average income of 6,500 pesos per month) would opt for the improved system. However, if income were to double (13,000 pesos per month), about 70 per cent would want the improved system, and if it were to quadruple (26,000 pesos per month), more than 90 per cent would connect (see Fig. 16.3).

Households in the high-density urban areas in Calamba are willing to pay about 30 pesos per month more than households in medium-density areas without agriculture (and about 20 pesos per month more than households in medium-density areas with agriculture). Also, households concerned about deteriorating water quality conditions in the lake and contamination of fish were willing to pay about 15 pesos per month more than other households.

The analysis of the determinants of the willingness-to-pay data suggests that these results are quite robust, and that their general magnitude can be accepted with considerable confidence. Especially compelling is the fact that the percentage of respondents agreeing to pay for improved sanitation service declined as the price increased (recall that these results were obtained from independent split-samples of respondents). This was true for *each* of the three sanitation levels offered *and* for each initial starting price.

Moreover, very few respondents accepted any of the three levels of improved sanitation service at an initial price of 200 pesos per month (US$8). This suggests that the results are not likely to be biased by respondents agreeing to pay prices they cannot really afford in order to please the enumerator or for other reasons.

In most industrialized countries, cities built their sewer system first and then later, when they could afford it, they built treatment plants. This staged approach improved public health conditions in the cities because it removed the human waste from town, but rivers and lakes were often badly polluted by the discharge of untreated wastewater. Despite their generally low willingness to pay, residents of Calamba do not seem ready to take this increment approach. Household willingness to pay just for Service Level I is on the order of 18–25 pesos per month lower than for Service Level II, and a higher proportion of households was not willing to pay anything for this level of service – particularly after they had time to think about it!

A sewage collection project without treatment is thus likely to be both unpopular and financially unattractive, since full costs would not be covered by the amounts households indicated they were willing to pay. The dilemma is that substantial numbers of people in Calamba want a community-wide solution to wastewater collection *only if* it does not exacerbate water pollution problems in Laguna de Bay, but in aggregate they are not yet ready to pay very much to have such a sanitation improvement implemented.

The analysis of households' environmental attitudes and perceptions shed some light on respondents' low willingness to pay for improved sanitation. The majority of respondents were aware that the water quality in Laguna de Bay has been deteriorating, and many people were concerned about the contamination of fish. Some respondents even reported that they no longer ate fish from the lake for fear of contamination. Despite this awareness of the problem, many households in Calamba had environmental concerns of higher priority. In particular, solid-waste collection and disposal is perceived by many people to be a more significant problem than the improper disposal of human excreta and wastewater or water pollution in lakes and rivers. A casual stroll through many of the neighbourhoods in Calamba would convince most individuals that this is a quite reasonable position. Particularly in medium-density areas with agriculture, there are large numbers of animals living in neighbourhoods, and the collection of human wastewater is unlikely to make much of a difference in terms of neighbourhood sanitation conditions. If the people of Calamba were given a grant for urban environmental improvements, survey results suggest that most would prefer that the municipality tackle the solid-waste problem before the collection and treatment of household wastewater.

While the study of attitudes and priorities sheds light on Calamba residents' low willingness to pay for piped sewerage, it is important not to lose sight of the fact that households' income is also a key determinant. Although not as high a priority as solid waste, sewerage is still a medium-level need of Calamba. However, incomes simply are not high enough to make full-cost recovery possible. Moreover, other conditions, such as the household level of education, will also have to improve before Calamba is ready for sewerage.

Given the financial constraints facing the national Government of the Philippines and the fact that there are more pressing sanitation problems in other cities in the Philippines, there is little justification for providing large subsidies to construct a sewer collection system and a treatment plant in Calamba at this time. The people of Calamba should, of course, be given the option of proceeding with such a sanitation improvement if they are willing to pay for it. However, based on the results of this study, it is unlikely that the people of Calamba would choose this option if they were required to pay anything close to the full costs. Moreover, if subsidies are to be provided to Calamba to address environmental problems, it appears that priority should probably be given to solid-waste collection and disposal, because this seems to be people's highest priority (and it will undoubtedly be less expensive in capital cost than providing sewerage and treatment). However, if the subsidy would not cover the full cost of the system, a contingent valuation study similar to that reported herein should probably be made to determine the amounts households are willing to pay for solid-waste collection and disposal.

This does not mean that the residents of Calamba will never have piped sewerage and treatment. Rather, it is a question of timing. The appropriate question to ask is *when* investment in sewerage and treatment should occur. In our opinion, the answer is 'probably not yet'. However, income and education levels are rising in Calamba, and concerns over the environment are growing. It thus seems likely that demand for improved sanitation services will also increase over time. The residents of Calamba will be the best judges of when to make an investment in a sewerage collection system.

REFERENCE

Whittington, D., Smith, V.K., Okorafor, A., Okore, A., Liu, J.L. and McPhail, A. (1992) Giving respondents time to think in contingent valuation studies: a developing country application, *Journal of Environmental Economics and Management*, **22**: 205–225.

APPENDIX 1: FIELDWORK PROCEDURES AND SURVEY IMPLEMENTATION

Enumerators

The enumerators were all recruited from Calamba. At the request of the study team, the mayor's office assembled a group of about sixty candidates, about half of whom worked for the city's Tax Mapping Office. The other half worked for the local National Statistics Office (NSO), which conducts about four household surveys per year in Calamba. All the candidates were experienced in conducting household surveys, and all but a few had earned a bachelor's degree. The enumerators received training in four different areas: (1) the technologies of improved sanitation, (2) the mechanics of question-naire completion, (3) the contingent valuation method for eliciting willing-ness-to-pay responses, and (4) quality control. The enumerators were also instructed in how to answer questions that might be raised by households unfamiliar with the proposed technologies.

Questionnaire Development

The household questionnaires were developed over a three-week period of pre-testing and discussions with the team of enumerators and additional focus groups. The questionnaire development process was thus participatory in character, involving both the enumeration team and the principal invest-igators in daily discussions of both qualitative and quantitative information obtained through the pre-tests and the enumerators' knowledge of local conditions and attitudes. The principal investigators and enumerators went to the field to informally hold focus groups and interview individual households to learn the following: (1) what sanitation facilities were in use? (2) were they working? (3) were users satisfied? (4) were improved facilities needed? and (5) would households pay for them if provided? A large *bar-angay* near *Poblacion* was selected for developing the questionnaire, which continued to be used for the next few weeks. A second pre-test *barangay* was also selected.

Sampling

Because of the improbability of improving sanitation throughout the entire municipality due to sparse populations and long distances from *Poblacion*, the first task in sampling was to decide the boundaries of the target popula-tion. After reviewing land-use maps, and *barangay* population and density data, and holding meetings with local officials, it was decided to eliminate all *barangays* with densities less than 10 households per hectare from the target population. This resulted in a study area with 28 contiguous *baran-gays* in the eastern part of the city, near Laguna de Bay. These *barangays*, about 50 per cent of the total number, contained about 60 per cent of the total population.

A two-stage stratified sampling procedure was used in order to ensure that the predominant characteristics of Calamba were adequately represented in the household survey. A list of *barangays* with medium and high densities served as the frame for sampling at the first stage. The National Statistics Office in Calamba has a list of households in each *barangay*, which was updated in the 1990 census. In addition, the captains of each *barangay* maintain current lists of households. These lists of households constituted the sampling frame for the second stage.

Barangays were divided into more or less homogeneous subpopulations (strata) according to the predominant land-use characteristics of Calamba: high-density urban areas (*Poblacion*), non-urban areas with agricultural activities, and non-urban areas without agricultural activities. In order to reflect the heterogeneous characteristics of the population, 11 *barangays* were selected out of the total of 28 (approximately 40 per cent) in the first stage of sampling. The 11 *barangays* were then allocated proportionally to each stratum and were drawn independently using simple random sampling within each stratum.

Having selected 11 *barangays* in the first stage of sampling, the next task was to select the households in each sample *barangay* to be interviewed. A simple rule of thumb, that at least 30 observations are needed to reliably address each treatment in an experimental design, was used to determine required household sample size. The design for Calamba included 30 treatments (3 levels of service × 2 questionnaire versions based on time to think × 5 different starting-points for the bidding games). Hence, by this criterion, 900 households that exclusively use water-sealed latrines were needed for the WTP questionnaires. Estimates were not available of the proportion of households in Calamba that own and exclusively use such latrines. However, the NSO had estimates from census data of the proportion of households in *barangays* that have access to such latrines; the average was about 60 per cent. Hence, to obtain 900 owners and exclusive users of water-sealed toilets assuming a 100-per cent response rate, the required sample size was 1,500.

The total number of households had to be allocated among the 11 *barangays*. If the proportion of households with water-sealed toilets in each sample *barangay* based on NSO data were the same (say, 60 per cent), then the 1,500 sample households could be allocated using the proportion of total households in each *barangay* as a basis. For example, if, say, 200 sample households had to be allocated between 2 *barangays*, *X* with 250 households and *Y* with 750 households, then the number of sample households that should be drawn from *X* is 50 and the number from *Y* is 150. In our case, the proportion is not exactly 60 per cent in each of the 11 *barangays*. In fact, of the 1,483 sample households, 1,104 were found to own and have exclusive use of water-sealed toilets, and 171 were found not to have water-sealed toilets for their exclusive use. Thus, 1,275 of the total sample households were interviewed (86 per cent), and the remaining 14 per cent (208 households) were not interviewed, mostly because the households could not be found or, if found, were empty.[2] The numbers of households interviewed are

[2] This is a *very* high response rate; it is rarely achieved in even the highest-quality academic surveys carried out in industrialized countries.

shown in Table 16.2. The numbers of interviews completed in different land-use areas are presented in Table 16.4.

Survey Management and Quality Control

Once the household survey was under way, the enumerators were sent out each morning with specific assignments of the households they were to contact. Around 5 p.m. they returned to the office. During the day, while they were in the field, the office staff made copies of questionnaires, collated them, and kept a stock of new forms for use by the enumerators when they returned. Also, during the day, when enumerators were in the field, completed questionnaires from the previous day were reviewed by two persons who were under the supervision of one of the study team. The reviewers made notes on each form of the matters to be discussed with the enumerators when they returned in the late afternoon.

When the enumerators returned to the office in the afternoon, they were given new forms for the following day's work, and they met with the 'checkers' to review the forms from the previous day. In addition, enumerators logged in their current forms and were given their household assignments for the next day. Forms were developed to keep track of the scheduling and progress of each enumerator. In addition, two large charts were kept on the wall to show the progress of each enumerator and the progress in interviewing the sample households in each *barangay*.

One of the most important steps in the daily routine was giving each enumerator his/her assignment for the next day. Before starting the household survey, the enumerators were sent into the field to meet with *barangay* captains to find the location of the households on the sample list. To the smaller *barangays*, the enumerators went alone or in groups of two, but to the larger *barangays*, six to nine enumerators were frequently sent. They made sketch maps of each *barangay* showing the locations of all the houses in the sample, block by block. Copies of the lists of households and maps were given to all the enumerators working in each of the *barangays*.

Handling the questionnaires in which respondents were given time to think was a challenging problem. So as not to bias results, the households *not* given time to think in a *barangay* had to be interviewed first, and the interviews had to be completed quickly so that these households did not have time to discuss the interview with neighbours who were also not given time to think. In large *barangays*, this usually meant that several enumerators had to work in the area so as to finish the work within one day. Having to make return visits if respondents were not at home always proved difficult. Once the no-time-to-think questionnaires were completed, the households that were given time to think were interviewed. In smaller *barangays*, it was frequently possible to finish the no-time-to-think questionnaires and start the time-to-think interviews the same day.

APPENDIX 2: EXAMPLE OF A SCENARIO DESCRIPTION AND VALUATION QUESTIONS (FOR SERVICE LEVEL II, NO TIME TO THINK)

Scenario Description

Most cities in industrialized (high-income) countries use the same kind of sanitation system to remove human wastes from the city and to protect the public health of their people. This kind of sanitation system has two parts: a sewer system and a wastewater treatment plant. I'd like to take a few minutes and explain these two parts of a sanitation system to you.

A sewer system is a network of pipes underground that is used to carry human wastes and wastewater, as well as wastewater from commercial establishments and small industries, away from a neighbourhood such as this *barangay* and out of town. The sewer pipes are usually placed underground along streets and lanes. The attached figure illustrates how a system of sewer pipes would work.

If a household's toilet or septic tank is connected to the sewer pipe, the wastewater from the house would flow into the pipe. Kitchen water and wastewater from bathing and the laundry could also be discharged to the sewer. Both pour-flush toilets with septic tanks and flush toilets emptying into holding tanks could be connected to a sewer pipe. However, no animal wastes or garbage could be put into the sewer. If a house connected to a sewer pipe, the wastewater from the house would flow into the sewer pipe. In this case the household would not have to empty its septic tank, or build a new septic tank when the old one is full. Because human excreta would be collected and carried away, there would be less chance of contamination of ground water. The quality of water people obtain from wells might thus improve.

Wastewater from large industries would not be put into this sewer system. Most large industries would have to treat their wastewater separately. Also, it is important to understand that a sewer system would not carry away drainage water from rains or eliminate flooding problems.

How familiar were you with a sewer system before I came here and described it to you?

Very familiar   ——
Somewhat familiar   ——
Not at all familiar   ——

The second part of a sanitation system is a wastewater treatment plant. The sewer pipes in town would join together and carry the wastewater to the 'wastewater treatment plant', where it would be cleaned. There are different ways of treating the wastewater collected in the sewer pipes. One kind of treatment plant would look like a factory with a pond next to it and would purify the water. The water from the treatment plant could then be discharged safely into the lake or river.

In most industrialized countries, cities built their sewer system first and then later, when they could afford it, they built the treatment plant. This staged approach improved public health conditions in the cities because it removed the human waste from town. However, the rivers and lakes were often badly polluted by the discharge of untreated wastewater from the cities.

If a sewer system with a treatment plant were built here, the citizens of Calamba would obtain three kinds of benefits:

1. The public health and environmental conditions in Calamba would be improved because human excreta, kitchen water, and bath water would not be spread so easily around your neighbourhood and other parts of town.
2. Commercial wastewater and wastewater from some small industries could be discharged to the sewer and treated at the treatment plant. This would reduce some of the harmful environmental effects of commercial and industrial water pollution.
3. The quality of water people obtain from wells might improve because there would be less chance of contamination of groundwater.

As you may know, the water in Laguna de Bay is considered by many people to be quite polluted. Improving the quality of the water in Laguna de Bay will require many kinds of actions, such as industrial wastewater treatment and better control of fertilizers and pesticides by farmers to prevent them from running into the rivers and the lake. Household wastewater is not the major source of pollution of the lake. In fact, installing a sewer system without a treatment plant could increase the pollution in the lake somewhat because it would collect all the wastewater and discharge it in one place. If a sewer system was installed with a treatment plant for Calamba, the water quality of the lake would probably not get worse. However, this action alone would not improve the water quality in the lake much either. All industries and communities around the lake would have to work together and all would have to install wastewater treatment plants in order to substantially reduce the pollution in the lake.

How familiar were you with a wastewater treatment plant before I came here and described it to you?

Very familiar   ——
Somewhat familiar ——
Not at all familiar ——

Do you have any questions about the wastewater treatment plant or pollution in the lake that you would like to ask me?

Valuation Questions

I now want to ask you some questions about how much you would be willing to pay to connect your house to a new sewer system and treatment plant in Calamba. It is important to us that you think carefully about this and try to give realistic answers. Please do not just agree to pay if you cannot afford it or if you feel you have other, more important things to spend your money on. It will hurt our study if you agree to pay more than you are really willing to and then later change your mind.

Suppose that this sewer system was installed throughout Calamba, and a sewer pipe ran near your house.

I want you to assume that it was decided that the project would have both parts of a sanitation system:

1. underground sewer pipes, and
2. a wastewater treatment plant for Calamba.

In other words, the wastewater would be collected from your neighbour-hood in a system of underground pipes, and then it would be treated before it was discharged into the lake or into a river.

Suppose that it was possible to connect your house to this sewer line so that the wastewater from your house (including the waste from the toilet, bath, and kitchen) would be discharged into this sewer pipe. If your household decided to connect to the sewer line then you would have to pay a monthly fee to the water district, just like a water bill. For example, for those households with a NAWASA connection, this monthly fee would be included on their water bill. If you missed a payment one month, then the following month you would have to make two payments. Let's assume that the water or sanitation authority would not charge a fee to connect your house to the sewer pipe and that the costs of replumbing your existing toilet to connect to the sewer line could be paid over time on your monthly bill.

a. If the monthly fee to be connected to the sewer line was 50 pesos, would you want to connect to the sewer line, or would you prefer not to be connected?

      YES—Connect to sewer line   *(go to qu. b)*
      NO—Not connect   *(go to qu. d)*

b. Suppose that the engineers designing the project confronted some unexpected technical problems, and that instead of 50 pesos the monthly fee was 200 pesos. In this case would you want to connect to the sewer line, or would you prefer not to connect?

      YES—Connect to sewer line   *(finished; go to qu. 3)*
      NO—Not connect   *(go to qu. c)*

c. Suppose that instead of 200 pesos the monthly fee was 100 pesos. In this case would you want to connect to the sewer line, or would you prefer not to connect?

YES—Connect to sewer line   (*finished; go to qu. 3*)
NO—Not connect   (*go to qu. f*)

d. Suppose that instead of 50 pesos the monthly fee was 25 pesos. In this case would you want to connect to the sewer line, or would you prefer not to connect?

YES—Connect to sewer line   (*finished; go to qu. 3*)
NO—Not connect   (*go to qu. e*)

e. Suppose that instead of 25 pesos the monthly fee was 15 pesos. In this case would you want to connect to the sewer line, or would you prefer not to connect?

YES—Connect to sewer line   (*finished; go to qu. 3*)
NO—Not connect   (*go to qu. f*)

f. What is the most you would be willing to pay per month to be connected to the sewer line?

Maximum amount——pesos per month

(*zero bids; follow-up question*)

1. Did the respondent indicate that he/she would not be willing to pay anything (i.e. gave a zero amount for willingness to pay)?

YES—Gave zero amount   (*go to qu. 2*)
NO—Gave a positive amount   (*go to qu. 3*)

2. There are several reasons why someone might not be willing to pay anything to connect to a sewer line. Could you please explain the reasons why you are not willing to pay?

Don't have any money; cannot afford   ——
Satisfied with the existing situation   ——
Government's responsibility   ——
Industries' responsibility   ——
Replumbing cost is too high   ——
Other (specify)   ————

3. *[Enumerator: check to see the highest amount the respondent indicated he/she was willing to pay per month—Max. willingness-to-pay——pesos / month]*

You indicated that your household would be willing to pay [*Max. WTP amount*] per month to have your house connected to a sewer line. On which of the following items do you think your household would reduce its expenditures in order to be able to afford to pay this amount?

Food   ——
Transport   ——
Entertainment   ——
Clothing   ——
Medicine   ——
Less savings   ——
Other (specify) ————

4. Do you think it is realistic that you could reduce your expenditure(s) on these items by this amount [*Max. WTP*] every month in order to pay for a connection to a sewer line?

    YES—End

    NO—Go to ques. 5

5. What do you think is a more realistic amount that you could actually afford every month for a connection to a sewer pipe?

    Revised amount——pesos / month

PART IV

Institutional Frameworks

17

Contingent Valuation Methodology and the EU Institutional Framework

FRANÇOIS BONNIEUX
PIERRE RAINELLI

17.1. INTRODUCTION

Throughout the European Union (EU) the past two decades have seen public concern regarding environmental issues rise in line with awareness of increasing pollution levels, loss of natural habitat and other natural resources, and the effects of environmental degradation upon human health and well-being. These concerns have already been translated into specific legislative action, a trend which seems likely to continue and expand over the foreseeable future.

When questioned regarding their concern about protecting the environment and fighting pollution, 85 per cent of a recent European sample thought that this was an immediate and urgent problem (CCE, 1992). However, the market mechanism does not recognize the total value of natural goods and services. Benefits such as landscape amenity or those provided by wilderness areas are public goods not amenable to market pricing. Here public intervention is needed to protect such ecosystems. However, the true value of an ecosystem is often only recognized once some of its functions are lost or damaged, for example after an accident such as an oil spill. An estimation of the total economic value of such assets while still intact would clearly be of great help in ensuring its conservation and sustainable utilization. Therefore it would be relevant to obtain reliable and valid information on the general public willingness to pay for such goods.

A number of non-marketed values can be quantified in monetary terms. The experience gained in Europe during the last decade shows that contingent valuation (CV) is a promising technique which could potentially help public decision-making. A number of empirical studies conducted in various contexts show that the approach is well-accepted by the general public. During the 1980s CV studies were conducted in the UK, Norway, and

Special thanks are due to Ian Bateman for many useful suggestions and his invaluable guidance regarding the English language.

Sweden, while the 1990s have seen the first studies in France and Denmark. It seems that people are generally sufficiently aware of environmental challenges, and have enough information and training to participate in contingent valuation scenarios. However, integration of non-marketed values within environmental policy will require a significant improvement in the reliability and validity of such estimates. It will also require new legal provisions regarding the obligation to monetize the benefits and costs of public policies as fully as possible. It is in this respect that the EU could prove instrumental in promoting a symbiotic relationship between decision-makers and those economists whose ultimate objective is to improve the economic efficiency of environmental policy.

This chapter consists of three parts. The first gives an overview of the legal foundation of EU environmental policy and discusses the way in which European thinking is likely to shape future policy. The second part focuses on the European experience of CV. Here a number of studies, conducted in EU member states and Scandinavian countries, are reviewed. The final section addresses the future. Here we attempt to identify those factors likely to influence the integration of CV within public decision-making.

17.2.   THE EVOLUTION OF EU ENVIRONMENTAL POLICY

European policies stem from the Treaty of Rome and its subsequent amendments, the Single European Act and the Treaty on European Union. Environmental policies arising from this legislation is considered in Section 17.2.1 below. Current environmental policy is based on the first two treaties, since the Treaty on European Union, which was adopted on 11 December 1991 in Maastricht, only came into force on 1 November 1993. While these major treaties define the guiding principles of EU thinking, environmental policy has also been expressed through various regulations and directives passed since the late 1960s. The most significative of such legislation is discussed in Section 17.2.2, which illustrates how the principles behind these texts emerged. In order to give a more complete picture we also consider here certain environmental 'action programmes', long and comprehensive documents in which the Commission states its intentions for the coming years. Such documents are very useful in understanding the evolution of European environmental thinking.

For at least two decades there has been increasing pressure on governments to deal with a variety of issues such as noise, wildlife and countryside, waste, and air and water pollution. EU environmental policy has, to a considerable extent, arisen as a response to public concern regarding these issues. Policy initially consisted of a series of specific and separate environmental obligations upon member states. However, the late 1980s saw a shift in approach towards the integration of environmental concerns within wider sectoral policies. Such integration presents a new challenge for policy-makers, a challenge which to date has only been addressed to any significant degree within changes to the Common Agricultural Policy. However, a consistent set of basic principles has now been widely accepted by national governments. These should come to play an increasing role in the design of future EU environmental policy. Such issues are considered in Section 17.2.3.

17.2.1. The Legal Framework

The Treaty of Rome (1957) gives no clear legal basis for EU action relating to the environment. In the early days of the EU (or European Community, to use its name at that time), environmental policy was often a by-product of the collective desire to remove trade distortions (Mors, 1994). Article 30 of the Treaty of Rome, which guarantees the free movement of goods and services, provided the foundation for several Directives. For example, there is a series of Directives dealing with air pollution emissions from vehicles which regulates the characteristics of the vehicle. The parent Directive (70/220) was introduced primarily to prevent the member states from creating barriers to trade by setting more stringent standards than those specified. This point could also be illustrated with a series of Directives, originating from Directive 70/157, which regulate noise emissions from four-wheeled vehicles. While initially designed to stimulate free trade this directive came to have a second purpose: namely to reduce noise limits for environmental reasons. Further environmental measures were introduced under Articles 100 and 235 of the Treaty of Rome: the former provides the basis for harmonizing laws which directly affect the establishment or functioning of the common market; the latter allows the EU to take appropriate action to attain objectives not expressly provided for by Treaty powers. Some environmental legislation, such as Directive 79/409 on the conservation of wild birds, are founded on these provisions of the Treaty although they do not have a clear environmental significance.

The Single European Act amending the Treaty of Rome came into effect on 1 July 1987, thus providing the first explicit legal basis for EU environmental policy. Under the Act, EU policy is mandated to consider the environmental dimension and give high priority to environmental protection (Article 100A). Provisions in Article 130R are of particular relevance, stating the following objectives within its opening paragraph:

to preserve, protect and improve the quality of the environment;
to contribute towards protecting human health;
to ensure a prudent and rational utilisation of natural resources.

Further general policy guide-lines are given in paragraph 2 of the same Article, as follows:

Action by the Community relating to the environment shall be based on the principles that preventive action should be taken; that environmental damage should as a
priority be rectified at source, and that the polluter should pay. Environmental
protection requirements shall be a component of the Community's other policies.

The general philosophy is thus to reconcile free trade with a high level of
environmental protection in order to achieve sustainable development. The
Treaty on European Union both emphasized the need to implement an EU-
wide environmental policy (Article 3k) and introduced the precautionary
principle (amended Article 130R) as a basic guide-line for future European
policy. This switch from preventative to precautionary action can be seen as
a basic acceptance that irreversible impacts should be limited. There is an
implicit acknowledgement of the concept of quasi-option value.

17.2.2.   The Emergence of a Policy

The environmental provisions of the Single European Act and their amendments in the Treaty on European Union can be considered as resulting from
a process that began in the early 1960s. In spite of the lack of a clear legal
basis, an environmental doctrine progressively emerged through Community
legislation and jurisprudence. The first Directive concerned with the environment was enacted in 1967 (67/548). It set out a procedure for classifying
dangerous substances according to the degree of hazard and the nature of
the risks entailed as well as provisions for packaging and labelling, the
purpose being to protect individuals, particularly in the work place. Only a
limited number of items of such legislation were passed until 1972.

The decision to set up a formal environmental policy was taken at the
Paris Summit of October 1972. This directed the Commission to establish
the First Action Programme on the Environment (1973). Since then, every
few years, the Commission has drafted an Action Programme on the environment, outlining its intentions for legislation and other activities in the
years ahead. The first two Programmes (1973–6 and 1977–81) focused on the
curative approach to reducing pollution and to improving natural and urban
environments. They also highlighted the role of education in promoting
awareness of environmental problems, especially those concerning the depletion of natural resources. The Third Action Programme (1982–6) signalled a
major shift of emphasis towards the preventive approach, while the Fourth
Action Programme (1987–92) considered the implications of those amendments to the Treaty of Rome discussed above. This Programme also presented certain wider reflections concerning future pollution control policy in
which the intention to use the majority voting mechanism of Article 100A to
implement policy was made clear. The Fifth Programme, adopted on 15
December 1992, looks toward the achievement of an ecologically sustainable
development and focuses attention upon the international dimension of
environmental problems. There is also a shift of emphasis towards sector-

oriented policies rather than specific action plans. Agriculture, industry, energy, transport, and tourism were selected as sectors 'where a Community approach is the most efficient level at which to tackle the problems those sectors cause or face' (CEU, 1992).

The Action Programmes cannot strictly be regarded as constituting Community policy but they do provide a general framework for future legislation since they reflect agreement on broad ideas in environmental policy. Consequently, in practice, these Programmes have been the driving force for the formulation and adoption of environmental legislation. The volume of such legislation grew throughout the 1970s and 1980s, much of it concerned with specific regulations regarding air and water pollution, noise, waste management, and chemicals. To date, despite the efforts of the Third Action Programme, comparatively little has been achieved regarding policy integration.

Turning to consider specific, implemented policy as opposed to general programme initiatives, relevant early measures appear primarily motivated by the desire to remove trade distortions rather than by environmental concerns. This only changed towards the end of the 1970s (EU, 1990), a point which can be illustrated by consideration of the development of the (currently) seventeen directives concerning the testing, classification, packaging, and labelling of new chemical substances. While the parent Directive (67/548) says little regarding the environment, the sixth amendment (79/831) introduced a new classification of substances 'harmful to the environment' and associated tests required prior to marketing. This move arose in part from the First Action Programme, which charged the Commission 'to investigate the measures still required to harmonize and strengthen control by public authorities over chemicals before they are marketed'. However, Haigh (1990) stresses the fact that EU initiatives such as the Action Programmes were far from the only impetus behind subsequent EU policy. National legislation both within and without the EU, and pressure from other transnational bodies (notably the OECD), also had an effect. Examples here include recommendations regarding the environmental impact of chemicals from both the OECD (November 1974) and the French Government (June 1975), both of whom made recommendations regarding assessment of the environmental impact of chemicals, which can be seen to have influenced subsequent EU policy. Similarly while initial EU legislation regarding air pollution can be seen as being mainly concerned with free trade (Directive 80/779), following pressure from the German Government (provoked by widespread acidification damage to their forests), a subsequent Directive (84/360) directly addressed the impacts of industrial emissions.

A further route for EU policy formulation has been through emergency response to disasters. Directive 82/501, regarding the prevention of major accidental impacts upon the environment, arose as a direct response to the disastrous release of dioxins from an industrial plant at Seveso in 1976. Subsequent revisions have been proposed by the Commission and the

European Parliament following later accidents at Bhopal and the Sandoz plant in Basle.

Despite these various informal influences upon EU environmental policy, it is clear that the Action Programmes have given an impetus to legislation. The First Action Programme resulted in a comprehensive set of Directives (80/778) covering the quality of water intended for human consumption, bathing, shellfish growth, or fish life. However, the standards arising from such Directives are themselves often the subject of lengthy negotiation and heated debate. For example the above water quality Directive considers three types of standard: the guide level, the maximum admissible concentration, and the minimum required concentration. Because of conflicting cost and health standards, it has been very difficult to agree on values for these standards. Whereas The Netherlands pushed for very stringent sodium, chloride concentration, and electrical conductivity limits, effectively restricting the activities of upper Rhine countries, which were polluting the river from potash mines, the latter nations raised strong objections to such standards.

The legislation dealing with waste management is helpful in illustrating the emergence of the principle of subsidiarity within environmental policy. Until the early 1970s waste disposal was regarded as a local or regional problem in member states. However, such an approach raised problems regarding the appropriate level of responsibility for forwarding EU policy. Directive 75/442 placed a general duty on member states to undertake those measures necessary to ensure that waste is disposed of without endangering human health and without harming the environment. This Directive presented both a general framework for waste management policy (a combination of the polluter-pays principle and an encouragement of recycling) and, through introducing the concept of a 'competent authority', defined the administrative level upon which such policy is enacted. In any given subsidiarity zone the competent authority became responsible for the planning, organization, authorization, and supervision of waste management disposal operations. The specific problems posed by toxic and dangerous waste streams are addressed in Directive 78/319, while Directive 84/631 considers the international dimensions of transfrontier shipment of toxic waste.

Directive 79/409 on the conservation of wild birds illustrates the extension of Community action to new areas of environmental concern. It stemmed from the public disquiet in northern Europe at the annual slaughter of migratory birds, common in southern Europe and northern Africa. Questions regarding this issue were initially raised in the European Parliament as early as 1971 and such concerns were reflected in the First Action Programme. This proposed a study of the potential for harmonizing national regulations regarding the protection of animal species and migratory birds in particular. The resulting Directive placed a general responsibility on member states to maintain the population of all 'species of naturally occurring birds in the wild state in the European territory'. It covers general rules of protection, limits the number of species which can be hunted and the methods of hunting, and regulates the trade in wild birds. Particular attention was paid to habitat protection and the protection of wetlands.

The interconnection between environmental and agricultural policy was made explicit in the First Action Programme of 1973. At the time, it was affirmed that the Commission would increase 'its campaign in the future for the protection of the natural environment and particularly within the framework of the agricultural policy'. A first response to the need to integrate environmental concerns within agricultural policy is provided by Directive 75/268 and its subsequent amendments (76/400, 80/666, 82/786) regarding farming in mountains, hills, and certain less-favoured areas. The Directive aims to promote, via financial incentives, 'the continuation of farming thereby maintaining a minimum population level or conserving the countryside' in such areas. Such legislation only indirectly addresses environmental objectives. A more direct approach was provided by Regulation 797/85 on improving the efficiency of agricultural structures. Under Article 19, member states are permitted to introduce their own national agricultural assistance schemes to support appropriate farming practices in 'environmentally sensitive areas'. These ESAs, promoted primarily by the UK, represented a new concept in EU environmental thinking. Defined as being areas 'of recognized importance from an ecological and landscape point of view', farmers within ESAs are offered standard payments for 'conserving the natural habitat' by adopting farming practices compatible with environmental preservation. The operation of Article 19 could involve trade distortions incompatible with Articles 92 to 94 of the Treaty of Rome. Therefore, and in order to avoid any tortuous implementation of this scheme, the Commission is required to produce an annual report in order to assist the Council in evaluating this measure. Regulation 2328/91 has since amended Regulation 797/85 but the philosophy of the latter remains in force under Articles 21 to 24 of the amendment.

17.2.3.   Future Policy

Current EU environmental policy has arisen from an evolutionary process. Three major influences can be identified: internal pressures; legislation in non-EU countries; and major transnational environmental impacts such as specific accidents or more general global environmental change (GEU). Internal pressures such as those contained within the Action Programmes have already been discussed in some detail. The First Environmental Action Programme, initiated at the Paris Summit of 1972, can be seen as a landmark ushering in the environmental era of the EU. The impact of non-EU pressures can most clearly be seen in the similarity between EU legislation dealing with air and water quality and chemical use and relevant laws in the USA such as: the Clean Air Act; the Clean Water Act; the Safe Drinking Water Act; the Federal Insecticide, Fungicide and Rodenticide Act; and the Toxic Substances Control Act. Finally, the effect of accidents, such as the Amoco Cadiz oil spill or the Chernobyl disaster, and GEUs, such as ozone depletion and global warming, can also be seen to have influenced the adoption of specific legislation. It seems most likely that all three of these major influences upon historical policy will continue to exert pressure upon the formulation of legislation in the future. However, it does seem that future policy will also become increasingly influenced by fundamental ideas of environmental economics such as the polluter-pays principle (PPP).

A more stringent enforcement of the PPP will require an improved understanding of both the benefits and the costs of pollution control. Consequently the Commission supports a number of research and education programmes. These include Regulation 1872/84 regarding action by the Community relating to the environment. Community finance was made available for environmental protection in three fields: 'clean technologies'; measuring the quality of the environment; and habitats for endangered species. The initial scheme, known as Actions Communautaires pour l'Environnement (ACE), formally ended in 1991 but has been continued by Actions Communautaires pour la Conservation de la Nature (ACNAT), which focuses on seriously threatened habitats and biotopes of endangered species.

Decision 85/338 created an environmental information system, Coordination des Informations sur l'Environnement' (CORINE), initially operating for the period 1984–90. Decision 90/150 extends the CORINE work programme for a further four to six years and brings it under the auspices of the European Environment Agency, which in turn was established by Regulation 1210/90 to provide the EU and member states with 'objective, reliable, and comparable information at the European level' although it is not intended to be an enforcement agency.

The direction of future policy is also indicated by the contents of the most recent (Fifth) Action Programme, which emphasizes the need to integrate legislation and develop environmental research and education. This philosophy has already been translated into legislative action within the programme Financial Instrument for the Environment (LIFE). It provides the funding base for a variety of ongoing projects including: ACE; ACNAT; Mediterranean Special Programme of Action (MEDSPA); the North Sea Special Programme of Action (NORSPA); and a range of research and extension pilot programmes addressing objectives both within and without the EU.

Another likely influence of environmental economics upon future legislation is the expected move away from emission standards and towards the use of an economic incentives approach to emissions control, with particular emphasis upon the use of emissions charges and marketable permits. This change may encounter resistance from existing polluters as it has been argued that standards permit higher profits and tend to exclude competitors (Buchanan and Tullock, 1975). Furthermore a review of present legislation shows that the use of standards is well-established. However, recent EU thinking highlights the efficiency gains thought likely to be achieved through market mechanisms (EU, 1990). Such pronouncements are our best indicators of likely future legislation.

The principle of subsidiarity is also likely to influence environmental policy. Article 130R (paragraph 4) of the Single European Act makes clear that environmental problems should be devolved to the lowest appropriate level of political decision-making, being handled at the national level except where transnational interests are involved.

Fair application of the subsidiarity principle requires uniform adoption of European legislation in order to avoid trade barriers. Based upon US experience, Folmer and Howe (1991) argue that common legislation is required to induce member states to undertake active environmental policy and avoid a gap in environmental quality between the rich and the less prosperous member states. The drive for such legislation may well provide a feature of future environmental policy.

A final principle which is liable to influence the development of EU policy is that of prevention rather than cure of pollution. Evidence of such an influence can already be seen in Directives such as 85/337 regarding 'the assessment of the effects of certain public and private projects on the environment'. This requires that certain planned developments be subject to environmental impact appraisals to establish that 'no unreasonable harm' is caused to the environment. It seems highly likely that similar precautionary legislation will constitute a significant element of EU environmental policy in the future.

17.3. CV AND PUBLIC DECISION-MAKING

To date, techniques for the monetary valuation of environmental damage and benefits have been more extensively developed and applied in the United States than in Europe. In part, this reflects the difference in public concern for the consequences of changes in the quality and quantity of available natural resources and the effects of pollution on human health. However, a number of other factors further limit the use of monetary environmental benefit valuation methods (particularly CV) in Europe. For Barde and Pearce (1991), three categories of obstacle exist: ethical/philosophical; political; and methodological/technical. Our opinion is that the main obstacle is the first one, because methodological problems are overestimated and political obstacles are linked to the fact that valuation techniques are largely unknown by policy-makers, or are rejected for philosophical and ethical reasons.

In many European societies there is considerable resistance to the idea of estimating monetary values for human health or safety, landscape, or national heritage. The willingness-to-pay criterion is rejected both by conservationists and also by the school of 'institutionalist' economics (Kapp, 1970). The former group question the philosophy and practice of economic valuation, while the latter claim that the principle of maximizing expected utility is too reductionist and inadequate for quantifying such goods. Such critics also point to the lack of consensus amongst neo-classical economists regarding the accuracy and comprehensiveness of CV benefit estimates as further supporting their reservations.

Nevertheless there is a growing body of CV literature in EU member states, and also in Scandinavian countries, showing people's willingness to pay for environmental goods. This literature reflects both the changes which have occurred in recent years in the environment debate and the fact that the protection of the environment has moved to the forefront of the political agenda. As a consequence there is a greater use of environmental benefit assessment techniques for decision problems, alternative actions, or regulatory measures.

17.3.1. General Framework

According to Kuik *et al.* (1992), the use of benefit estimates in decision-making can be examined through a matrix combining purposes and decision levels. Monetary evaluations may serve up to four basic purposes:

1. Valuing amenity losses or gains stimulates public debate and creates public awareness of that specific case or asset. A monetary benefit assessment constitutes a readily understandable indicator of concern even if its accuracy is debatable.
2. Assessments influence particular decisions by allowing comparison of the actual benefits and costs of a given course of action.
3. Valuation aids identification of optimal alternatives when there is a choice among competing options.
4. Valuations support and justify the actions of a Government agency in the field of the environment and provide policy-making guidance.

Concerning the decision level, three broad categories can be distinguished: policy, regulations, and projects.

1. Policy: a distinction may be drawn between environmental policy, focused on the environment itself, and decisions in other policy areas which may impose positive or negative side-effects on the environment.
2. Regulations: at this level, the need for accurate and reliable benefit estimates depends on the institutional context. If a complete and comprehensive assessment of benefits is required, controversial techniques such as CV will need to be used. More cursory analyses may focus

Table 17.1   Level and purposes of benefit estimates

Purpose level	Stimulate awareness	Influence decisions	Identify decisions	Evaluate and justify
Policy	yes	possible	unlikely	unlikely
Regulations	yes	likely	possible	possible
Projects	no	yes	likely	likely

Source: Kuik *et al.* (1992).

upon use values alone to the exclusion of non-use values. In such a case CV may possibly still be used although less controversial techniques may be preferred.

3. Projects: the environmental benefit or disbenefit assessment of a project may originate from governmental or legal decisions such as any mandatory requirement for environmental impact assessment (EIA) concerning large or specific projects.

Table 17.1 represents the possible objectives of benefit assessments for each decision level. Roughly it shows that, at the policy level, valuing environmental goods with sophisticated measurement techniques is useful only in creating public awareness, with perhaps some possibility of influencing decisions. At the regulation level, the valuation of environmental goods stimulates awareness, is likely to influence decisions, and may also be helpful in identifying the best decisions, as well as in the evaluation and justification of a programme. At the project level, benefit estimates are unlikely to raise general public awareness, but do offer a good basis for analysing various alternatives and for taking into account the claims of the social groups involved in specific actions.

Studying Table 17.1 we can see that the 'identify decisions' and 'evaluate and justify' columns can be merged into a single vector relating to the trade-off of alternative options for environmental action.

17.3.2.   European Countries' Experience of CV

A number of CV studies have been carried out in Europe since the early 1980s, and there has been an accompanying trend towards CV papers in the economic literature. The research effort has been especially noticeable in the UK and Scandinavia with a more recent dissemination across the various European countries. The book edited by Navrud (1992) gives an excellent review.[1] However, since its preparation new members have joined the CV club. Most studies have been conducted by universities and research institutes through which considerable expertise has been amassed. Some, may be

---

[1] Notable omissions from this book are various Italian studies (see Merlo and Della Puppa, 1993) and a Spanish CV (Riera, 1992).

the majority, of these studies have been funded or commissioned by public bodies in charge of environmental policy or public development projects. However, the impact of such findings within the public decision-making process is less clear.

It is a difficult task to identify the real factors which influence public decision-making and delineation of the influence of CV in this process is particularly complex. Where guide-lines stipulate the use of cost–benefit analyses (CBAs) or EIAs, explicit application of CV is rarely mentioned.[2] It may be that the increasing use of the method in European countries has influenced policy-makers, but it is also likely that the limited expertise in environmental economics of those in charge of environmental policy is a factor limiting the further expansion of CV. This point is mentioned by Markandya *et al.* (1991) in the context of the UK and is probably the major reason why the French Minister of the Environment has been so reluctant to sponsor valuation studies. However, this position may be set to improve. Römer and Pommerehne (1992) report that one of the consequences of the monetary valuation studies of air quality improvement in Berlin conducted by Ewer and Schulz during the 1980s has been Schulz's promotion to the Federal Environmental Agency, where he is now responsible for 'economic environmental questions'. Under his direction, the agency and the Secretary of the Environment recently launched a major project entitled 'Benefits of Environmental Protection–Cost of Environmental Pollution'.

Although the European use of valuation techniques for securing monetary measures of environmental benefits began in the UK during the late 1960s and early 1970s, The Netherlands was the first EU country to use CV. A 1973 study asked individuals for their desired level of compensation for accepting aircraft noise, while a year later a separate study assessed the monetary damage due to air pollution (reported in Hoevenagel *et al.*, 1992). Such policy level monetary evaluations were used to create awareness of the fact that environmental action not only costs money, but can also yield economic benefits. However, with the exception of the estimation of damage due to an accident in a nuclear plant, no monetary estimates of environmental benefits have yet been made for the evaluation of regulations or projects in The Netherlands (Kuik *et al.*, 1992). Instead the acceptance of environmental valuation within the decision-making process has remained limited. Dutch studies have not been used to trade off costs and benefits but rather to justify Government actions and to stimulate public awareness.

In the UK major CBA work was first undertaken by the Roskill Commission (Roskill, 1971) in finding a site for the third London airport. This study attempted an innovative incorporation of certain environmental impacts

---

[2] The UK Department of the Environment's project appraisal guide-lines do discuss the use of CV (DoE, 1992).

such as an analysis of noise nuisance using a simplified hedonic house-pricing and CV approach (Dasgupta and Pearce, 1972). The possibility of valuing national heritage impacts was also considered although this was omitted from the final report. The approach taken, particularly with regard to noise evaluation, was much criticized (Adams, 1992), setting the trend for continued hostility by environmentalists to CBA. However, the use of economic analysis in decision-making has consistently grown so that CBA now dominates UK Government appraisals of projects and (increasingly) policies. The market-oriented emphasis of the Conservative Government, which has been in power since 1979, has been instrumental in an increasing acceptance both in legislative and wider social circles of economic and particularly willingness-to-pay measures and a concern for efficiency in the application of environmental policy (Turner et al., 1992). Monetary valuation of environmental preferences entered into official Treasury and Scottish Office guide-lines in 1991 (HM Treasury, 1991). These guide-lines do not reject the possibility of measuring option or existence values, but an emphasis upon pragmatism prevails and valuation techniques have been applied mainly to use values, where they seem appropriate and not too controversial (Turner et al., 1992). Explicit use of CV has also influenced policy choice by the Forestry Commission (re forest recreation), the National Rivers Authority (re flood alleviation) and the Ministry of Agriculture (re environmentally sensitive areas). In addition the CV values of avoided fatal and non-fatal accidents obtained by Jones-Lee et al. (1985) are taken into account in the choice of transport projects where accident reductions are involved.

Germany is one of the few European countries which have made a more systematic use of CV for the promotion and acceptance of environmental policy, particularly in the field of air pollution and its effects on forest development, housing, and human health, and in the area of water quality. Here benefit estimates are used for the promotion and acceptance of policy in a broad sense, allowing a 'softer approach' which includes the use of more controversial methods such as CV. This more positive attitude can be traced to a federal regulation, passed in 1969, stipulating that economic efficiency studies be performed for all major public projects (chapter 7 of Bunders Haushaltsordnung, Kuik et al., 1992). The German approach is essentially CBA, with all items assessed using actual, adjusted, or simulated market prices. In principle environmental effects are treated in a similar manner. However, in practice, only certain sectors, such as transport, are subject to this rigorous, extended CBA approach. Schulz and Schulz (1991) emphasize several political and administrative barriers mitigating against a wider use of CBA. Decision-making aids strictly geared to economic values do not necessarily provide the information demanded by politicians. For these authors, the politicians' rationality primarily considers the political rather than the economic consequences of a project so that they feel uncomfortable with purely economic analyses. Moreover, decisions in the environmental arena are seen as the result of a compromise between both social and natural scientists. However, many of the latter seem unwilling to accept economic, let alone environmental economic, thinking.

In Italy, the market mechanism prevails and economic planning has for some time been used to define objectives in a reasonably consistent way. Since the early 1960s major public bodies such as the Mezzogiorno Development Agency (Panella, 1991) and the Fondo Investimenti Occupazioni have used CBA to guide their investment programmes. However, the methodology used did not generally take into consideration environmental benefit estimates. Nevertheless, several commissions and public bodies responsible for the management of public agricultural and forest properties have now used monetary estimates of the recreational benefits provided to the general public by areas under their control. Such studies have been used for at least two main purposes (Merlo and Della Puppa, 1993): (1) valuation of the benefits enjoyed by the public, and (2) quantification of compensation to farmers. Both travel-cost (TC) and CV methods have been used, with CV now beginning to gain acceptance in public decision-making at least at the regional level. As an example, in the Veneto region, compensation paid to mountain farmers is set in accordance with CV estimates of the benefits enjoyed by tourists and visitors.

To some extent the situation in Norway is more similar to the somewhat *ad hoc* approach of the UK. Although not enshrined in legislation, governmental CBA guide-lines recommend a consideration of 'unpriced' effects (Navrud, 1991) and the pollution inspectorate has led the way in putting these recommendations into practice. The Locally Adapted Regulatory Impact Analysis (Navrud and Strand, 1992) provides a CBA framework for assessing potential measures to reduce emissions of pollutants to specified local levels. Benefit values for different measures are assessed according to a set of weights provided by CV analyses. Such an approach derives from various suggestions for the development of an environment index in which public opinion polls provide an element in weighting various environmental issues (Hope and Parker, 1990).

During the 1980s a number of CV studies were conducted in Sweden (Johansson and Kristöm, 1992). These dealt with a variety of issues such as land-use conflicts and air and water quality. However, very few of these studies have had a noticeable impact on decision-making. An interesting exception is the social cost–benefit analysis of the Vaalaa Valley, in which CV and travel-cost methods were combined. Upon completion of the study the area was designated as a National Nature Reserve, a decision which appears to have been partly influenced by this study.

Compared to the above, other European countries have less experience of CV. In France, for example, the first CV study was undertaken in 1990 (Bonnieux *et al.*, 1992). This study, conducted in co-operation with various angling societies, was aimed at evaluating *ex ante* the potential benefit of public investments aimed at improving angling facilities. A second study, commissioned by the national electrical utility, examined an alternative management strategy for a large reservoir in which a constant level of water was maintained, thereby improving ecosystem quality and recreational use, but at the cost of eliminating protection from spring floods.

Despite the apparent lack of environmental valuation studies, France has an established tradition of CBA. Furthermore, for some years planning permission applications for oil refineries, non-nuclear power stations, steelworks, integrated chemical installations, special roads, long-distance railways, large aerodromes, various types of waste disposal, and intensive rearing installations have had to be accompanied by environmental assessments. The requirement for such assessment can be traced back to the 1917 Act on Hazardous Establishments. This legislation was brought up to date by the Classified Installations for Environmental Protection Act (1976) and a recent Ordinance (1992) concerning the protection of neighbourhood amenities, health, security, agriculture, natural resources, and the environment, and conservation of cultural sites and monuments. Activities covered by this legislation are classified by size into either a 'reporting' or 'permission' regime. A reporting establishment must adhere to the rules laid down by the Préfet, who is in turn under the Government's authority.[3] The permission regime is more stringent, requiring a public inquiry into the possible impact of the project on the environment. The keystone of the permission regime is the EIA which the applicant has to provide. This gives details on the source, nature, and magnitude of any disamenities liable to result from the installation concerned. Disamenities include noise, use and discharge of water, the protection of underground waters, and waste disposal. In France therefore there are two categories of installation and an EIA is only mandatory for those projects whose effects on the environment are likely to be significant.

Table 17.2 presents a brief summary of how CV benefit estimates have been used at various decision-making levels across different EU member states.

We can draw two conclusions from Table 17.2:

1. There is a complete absence of any cases within the regulation/trade-off cell. This illustrates the limited diffusion of CV in most of Western Europe due to the ethical and philosophical obstacles reviewed earlier.
2. Germany and to a lesser extent The Netherlands appear often. These two countries most closely approach the US situation *vis-à-vis* the use of CV in the decision-making process.

---

[3] The Préfet is the highest-ranking Government official at the *départment level*, the second-highest level of French regional government.

Table 17.2 CV and decision-making processes in EU member states

Purpose level	Awareness	Influence decisions	Trade off alternatives
Policy	Germany The Netherlands	Germany	n/a
Regulation	n/a	n/c	n/c
Projects	n/a	Germany The Netherlands United Kingdom Italy France	Germany The Netherlands United Kingdom Italy France

Note: n/a = not applicable; n/c = no cases.

17.3.3. Experience at the EU Level

It was only in 1983, with the Third Action Programme, that the principle that economic policy should reconcile economic development with environmental protection began to emerge. The necessity of taking environmental considerations into account when formulating other sectoral policies was also affirmed at this time. However, the major landmark in EU environmental legislation is undoubtedly the Single European Act (SEA) of 1987, whose objectives included: (1) the development of economic and social cohesion; (2) improvements in the health and safety of workers; (3) strengthening of science and technology; (4) monetary and economic co-operation; (5) protection of the environment. More precisely, the SEA requires that the environmental dimension be an integral part of Community policies and that Commission proposals give high priority to environmental protection.

What evidence then is there of CV influencing policy, regulation, or projects at the EU level? Considering the policy level first, it appears possible that estimates of the likely environmental benefits from implementing legislation are needed to stimulate public awareness and support for policy development. For example, in one case the Commission justified its action using the results of a study which calculated that benefits of between 81 and 230 million Ecu could be made by reducing salinity levels in the Netherlands section of the Rhine (EU, 1990). The report indicates that a large proportion of this would be through an increase in willingness to pay for recreational benefits. In this case, benefit estimates are used both for public awareness purposes and to justify the decision.

Concerning regulatory measures, the Commission recently commissioned the preparation of guide-lines for assessment of the potential benefits of environmental measures (Kuik *et al.*, 1992). This study analysed the current state of knowledge and practice, drawing on two representative examples showing the preparation of regulatory measures:

1. the decision process leading to the issuing of the Community Directive on large combustion plants;

2. the evaluation of environmental effects used in the formulation of acid-rain and photochemical-oxidant control policies.

This report concluded that, in the preparation of the Directive on large combustion plants, one major element of the decision was the importance of damage reduction using different emission strategies. Furthermore, in the second example, the aim was to provide policy-makers with the information necessary to decide on an emission control strategy in the face of uncertainty. Both examples imply a cost–benefit comparison of the various control and non-control strategies. In both cases the decision analysis made a comparison of the costs and benefits in quantitative terms, but no actual monetary assessments of the benefits were made. Moreover the report also states that, when interviewed, at least one official expressed scepticism regarding the use of monetary assessment approaches for the preparation of regulations (Kuik et al., 1992).

We therefore have little evidence of CV studies directly influencing regulations and only circumstantial indications of an effect upon wider policy. However, there is more support for the suggestion that CV may in the future (if not necessarily yet) have an impact upon individual projects. A recent study supported by the Commission showed how the MEDSPA selected 35 projects from 227 proposals. The evaluation of the environmental effects of the projects was made rather intuitively due to lack of time, and MEDSPA officials expressed the opinion that a monetary evaluation of the environmental benefits of projects would have been helpful (Kuik et al., 1992).

Clearly then there is a potential role for CV within EU project appraisal. However, as the environmental impact assessment Directive (85/337) illustrates, present EU legislation does not directly encourage the use of CV. This Directive states that projects having a significant impact on the environment must give information about effects on humans, flora and fauna, soil, water, air, climate, material assets, and cultural heritage. However, there is no requirement for monetary evaluation of these impacts. This approach (which is similar to French national policy) has a serious drawback in that many projects which are minor in scale do not fall within the requirements of an EIA although their cumulative impact may be significant. In our opinion the use of purely qualitative assessments is a major limitation of current EIAs since the applicant has only to demonstrate that the project complies with basic building regulations and emission standards. This concentration upon the cost side alone to the exclusion of monetary benefits is one of the major flaws in current, EIA-dominated, decision-making.

17.4. THE POTENTIAL USE OF CV

This final section is divided into two subsections, the first of which considers the likely consequences of the creation of the European Environmental

Agency (EEA). Within this discussion the United States experience is used to demonstrate the need for CV studies in connection with the assessment of regulations and with the development of project appraisal techniques. The second subsection is concerned with reform of the Common Agricultural Policy and in particular with integration of the environmental dimension. It is shown that CV studies might be useful in calculating future direct payments to agricultural producers.

17.4.1. The European Environment Agency (EEA)

Regulation 1210/90 set up the EEA as a new European statutory body to be sited in Copenhagen. Once operational, the task of the EEA 'will be to provide objective and comparative data on the state of the environment in Member States, thereby providing a sound scientific basis for newly drafted Commission directives and enhanced authority for those trying to enforce existing ones' (EU, 1990). It is therefore relevant to compare the EEA with the United States Environmental Protection Agency (EPA) although a major difference between the two is that, unlike the powerful EPA, the EEA will neither have a policy role nor be an enforcement agency. Nevertheless, it is valuable to have an overview of the evolution of the EPA in order to gain an insight into the possible future role of the EEA.

In the EU the use of methods for the monetary evaluation of environmental preferences, particularly CV, has lagged behind that of the USA. This lag is mainly due to differences in the institutional context and the legal system. The American system differs widely from the European system and is a powerful instrument, which has encouraged methodological development and empirical application of CV. The US National Environmental Policy Act (NEPA) of 1969, which promoted EIA and the creation of both the Council of Environmental Quality and (in 1970) the EPA, has favoured the legitimization and proliferation of environmental valuation. The EPA employs more than 16,000 people and its primary functions are to (1) interpret, (2) implement, and (3) enforce, for the executive branches of Government, the environmental laws passed by Congress. Nevertheless this does not mean that environmental standards are set on the basis of a judicious balancing of costs and benefits at the margin. The cost–benefit approach is not the rule; indeed Burtraw and Portney (1993) argue that 'rather than permitting EPA officials to take costs into account when establishing the national ambient air quality standards, Congress instead appears to have forbidden such an approach.' Despite this limitation, the EPA and other agencies gave strong impetus to academic research during the 1970s. By the late 1970s certain valuation tools had become codified in the Water Resource Council's Principles and Standards for Planning Water and Related Land Resources. In connection with outdoor recreation, both the TC and the CV methods were recognized as being legitimate means for measuring costs and benefits. Such developments coincided with a progressive acceptance of non-use value and the relevance of CV for its assessment. Apart from universities and agencies, the diffusion of environmental evaluation methods has come from Executive Order 12291 (1981) and from the Comprehensive Environmental Response, Compensation and Liability Act (CERCLA) of 1980 (Hanemann, 1992). The former explicitly required all agencies to prepare a Regulatory Impact Analysis before undertaking any major regulatory act, which in turn led the EPA to invest in development of CV. CERCLA contained provisions establishing a liability on the potentially responsible parties to pay damages for injuries to natural resources resulting from the spill or release of hazardous substances. Nowadays, after multiple litigations, the courts have recognized the applicability of CV to the estimation of non-use values; see *Idaho* v. *Southern Refrigerated* (Loomis and Anderson, 1992).

If US experience is any guide, it can be expected that the application of the Treaty of European Union will increase use of both CBA and environmental valuation methods at the regulatory level. A major purpose of the Treaty is to improve the economic efficiency of EU legislation. In theory, this is achieved by selecting options maximizing net social benefit. For the EEA, this may require the use of economic valuation methods in order to price environmental goods. If so, the EEA may follow the US EPA in becoming an important agency for funding such research.

Finally, it may be that the very shortcomings of the current EIA Directive (outlined above), highlighted by environmental pressure groups and the European Parliament itself, may provide a further impetus for change in the way that public goods are assessed within the decision-making process. It would be ironic, yet not infeasible, if pressure groups (themselves often opposed to monetization) caused the EEA to respond by increasing the use of such an approach.

17.4.2. CAP Reform and Agri-environmental Measures

Over the last three decades the Common Agricultural Policy (CAP) has been based on output-related support. This policy provided sufficient food for a growing population and raised producer confidence, encouraging further investment in the sector. However, the rapid technological change this induced created major supply surpluses involving heavy public spending.

The traditional producer price support approach to agricultural subsidy has persistently distorted relative prices. This has given economic incentives not only to overproduce, but also to the overuse and degradation of natural resources such as soil (compaction and erosion problems) and water (decline in water quality and reduction in the capacity of aquifers), as well as over-intensification in the use of fertilizers and chemical pesticides. The increasing tendency towards highly specialized agricultural monocultures has caused important losses in species abundance and diversity and a decrease in landscape amenity and heritage. The conservation of valued ecosystems is unlikely to succeed if its economic value is not greater than the alternative land use. However, as noted by Pearce (1992), 'conservation has to compete not with the "true" rate of return to the alternative land use but with a distorted rate of return, inflated by protectionist policies.'

With this background plus the anti-interventionist pressures imposed by the Uruguay round of GATT negotiations, CAP reform is taking place. Briefly, this reform amounts to a reduction of the intra-EU prices of the major crops, milk, beef, and sheep meat. However, rather than use direct income subsidies, the EU compensates producers for this in a complex way. In essence two new principles are being introduced:

1. fixed payments per hectare, or per animal, rather than per unit of output produced;
2. for larger farms with a considerable area planted with cereals and oilseeds, a 15 per cent fallow set-aside scheme is enforced, for which compensation is based upon the value of forgone output up to a specified limit.

This system of direct payments leads to a partial decoupling of income support from price guarantees or product-specific compensations. The objective is to produce a less distorted system, eliminating the need to subsidize the disposal of surpluses. However, as indicated by Burrell (1992), this approach raises a new problem regarding the determination and justification of the level of direct payments to be applied.

The social justification of direct payment levels depends upon the extent to which income distribution can be allowed for. From this point of view market price support is a particularly inefficient instrument because of the large share of assistance which goes to non-priority farmers. Direct payments are potentially more effective in targeting assistance towards those producers who are considered 'disadvantaged' by size or region. However, the environmental justification for direct payments comes from the role of agriculture in providing positive externalities. Here it is often economically small farms which appear best to promote the conservation of the environment and rural communities. In particular such farms are often associated with enhanced landscape amenity.

Figure 17.1 highlights the need for valuation of such landscape amenity. It displays the current situation in a specific area, say an ESA, in which agriculture provides both positive and negative externalities: for low levels of intensification positive externalities dominate, while for high levels of intensification negative externalities dominate (Bonnieux et al., 1992).

The level of intensification is given on the horizontal axis and is measured by a simple indicator Q which is the output per hectare. The price is given on the vertical axis. Agricultural supply is given by the marginal private cost

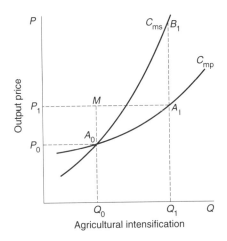

Fig. 17.1 Agricultural intensification and externalities

curve C_{mp}. The second curve, C_{ms}, depicts marginal social cost, i.e. marginal private cost plus the marginal externalities of the agricultural sector. Point A_0 is the intersection of the two curves: on the left C_{ms} is under C_{mp} and on the right it is above. So if Q is smaller than Q_0 agriculture generates positive externalities which are equal to the area between C_{mp} and C_{ms}. For levels of output above Q_0 negative impacts progressively dominate the positive externalities.

The price support involved in the Common Agricultural Policy results in a price P_1 greater than P_0. This policy leads to equilibrium point A_1 with output level Q_1, where the negative impact on the environment is given by area $A_0 A_1 B_1$. In this case the slopes of the curves are such that a marginal decrease in output results in a larger reduction in negative externalities than producer surplus, leading to an improvement in net social benefits. Furthermore such gains can be used to fully compensate farmers for their income loss. This remains the case for all output levels in excess of A_0 since, if we start at level A_1, we can see that area $A_0 A_1 B_1$ is greater than area $A_0 A_1 M$.

Given the inherently non-market nature of many environmental goods, price subsidies are clearly inappropriate instruments for encouraging farmers to produce landscape amenity benefits. The EU has responded to this problem via an *ad-hoc* array of voluntary incentive schemes which attempt to induce rather than force farmers to adapt their farming methods so as to protect and enhance the environment. This philosophy underlies Article 19 of Regulation 797/85 and its further amendments, i.e. Articles 21 to 24 of Regulation 2328/91. The farmers' role as guardians of the countryside is firmly acknowledged. Direct payments are justified because farmers accept constraints on their profit-maximizing activity, resulting in a reduced level of negative externality. These schemes can be interpreted as a redefinition of property rights, the payment being the price paid by the public authorities for purchasing or renting such rights (Crabtree, 1992; Whitby, 1989).

Direct payments are currently based on profit forgone, i.e. the area A_0A_1M plus some premium to induce farmers to participate in the scheme. There is no precise link with the provision of benefits, i.e. area $A_0A_1B_1$. One major difficulty in implementing these policy schemes is that of valuing the benefits produced. A future demand for such valuation studies is therefore expected.

An alternative to considering the environmental effects of farming is to treat the environmental output itself as a direct product from farm resources. Here emphasis is then placed on the bundle of private and public goods produced by farmers. As farmers receive a price for producing commodities, there is a rationale for direct payments. For example, if the output price decreased from P_1 to P_0 farmers would receive a payment equal to the area between C_{mp} and C_{ms} with Q varying from Q_1 to Q_0. Here, payment schemes are not implemented in order to compensate farmers but in order to pay for the provision of public benefits. It is obvious that the implementation of such schemes would require an evaluation of these public benefits.

Initially, implementation of such direct payment schemes was restricted to environmentally sensitive areas. However, the scope for their application has greatly increased following recent CAP reforms recognizing that farmers have a countryside management function that justifies support. Regulation 2078/92 (on agricultural production methods compatible with the requirements of environmental protection and the maintenance of the countryside) extends direct payment schemes beyond ESAs. Here subsidies are explicitly linked to both profit forgone and the value of public benefits:

the measures must compensate farmers for any income losses caused by reductions in output and/or increases in costs and for the part they play in improving the environment. (Regulation 2078/92)

The environmental role of agriculture is taking an ever more prominent place in the development of the CAP. The encouragement of environmentally friendly farming has two main objectives: (1) to remove the negative externalities of agriculture, and (2) to promote the positive protection and enhancement of the environment and countryside. Alongside the study of mechanisms for delivering agri-environmental policy, there is a clear need to extend information regarding the value of such legislation. By valuing environmental benefits it is possible to provide a firm economic basis on which the amount and direction of EU and national expenditure in this field can be soundly based.

Agriculture can and, in certain areas, does provide a wide range of non-market benefits. However, documentation of these areas, let alone measurement of benefits, remains rudimentary in many EU countries. Clearly any such analysis involves considerable research resources; nevertheless some progress is evident.

Table 17.3 (Bonnieux and Rainelli, 1992) refers to an area of wetlands located in the Cotentin peninsula (the north-west of France) which has been designated under Article 19 of Regulation 757/85 as being an environmentally sensitive area. This means that the wildlife, landscape, and historical interest of the countryside depend upon the maintenance of specific farming practices. Table 17.3 categorizes benefits into various value types, illustrating the wide diversity and nature of values delivered by such a complex natural asset.

While Table 17.3 shows the complexity of environmental goods, we can see that these benefits arise from two principal sources: biological diversity

Table 17.3 The provision of benefits by agriculture in the Cotentin wetlands (France)

Value categories	Benefit sources	Policy measures	Valuation techniques
Use value	rural character	labelling quality products	market pricing
use value: recreational value	wildlife: waterfowl, birds, fish	countryside protection: hedge replanting, maintenance of drainage channels and ditches	market pricing (licences for fishing, hunting) TCM CVM
Use value: aesthetic value	landscape quality: variety in shape and colour, cultural heritage	management prescriptions and good agricultural practices	market pricing (eco-tourism) TCM CVM HPM
Indirect-use value	flood control groundwater recharge	maintenance and good agricultural practices	averting costs damage cost avoided market pricing (drinking water) CVM
Ecological value	life support	biodiversity protection and enhancement	CVM
Use value: off-site (indirect)	assimilative capacity	waste recycling compost using surface impoundment	alternative substitute costs CVM
Existence value	wildlife of specific interest (internationally protected sites under the RAMSAR convention)	habitat protection	CVM

Notes: HPM: Hedonic pricing method
TCM: Travel-cost method
CVM: Contingent valuation method

and landscape. Traditional extensive farming methods tend to be harmonious with or even enhance these factors. However, modern intensive agricultural practices are often at odds with the natural environment and synonymous with biodiversity loss, both in terms of the quantity and range of species and in terms of landscape degradation via the loss of terraces, hedges, trees, and traditional buildings and an increase in monoculture systems. While, as Table 17.3 illustrates, a number of techniques exist for the estimation of the use-value benefits of traditional agriculture, only CV has the theoretical capability of addressing non-use as well as use values. Partly as a consequence of this ability, a number of CV studies have now been undertaken regarding agricultural externalities.

In Sweden, where the emphasis is put on the positive role played by agriculture in the maintenance of an open landscape in areas dominated by forests, CV has been used to estimate the non-market value of agricultural landscapes. A study conducted by Drake (1992) of such landscape goods revealed a mean annual WTP of 78 Ecu per person, or 140 Ecu per ha, per year. WTP per ha varied both by region and according to land use from 123 Ecu for main crops to 237 Ecu for grazing land and 299 Ecu for wooded pasture (ibid.). Such values could potentially be used as guide-lines for direct payments.

In Britain, where the impact of agricultural policy on the countryside receives great attention, CV techniques have been used to value the benefits which residents and visitors might derive from alternative landscapes. In a case study of the Yorkshire Dales National Park, Willis and Garrod (1991) present respondents with a choice of eight possible landscape scenarios. Here both resident and visitor groups favoured retention of the present landscape, expressing a mean WTP of approximately £24 per household per annum. In a similar study, Bateman (unpub. diss., 1996) analyses a proposed conversion of agricultural land into recreational woodland, comparing potential visitors' WTP with farmers' willingness to accept compensation (WTA) for such a scheme. Here visitors' aggregate WTP significantly exceeded that necessary to compensate farmers, indicating that such studies could provide useful information both to national policy decision-making and to local CBA project appraisal.

In the case of biodiversity, a significant number of CV studies of endangered or rare species and highly valued ecosystems exist. As noted by both Pearce (1992) and Bateman et al. (1994), the results from these studies are interesting because of their broad consistency. Habitat appears to be more highly valued than species, a result which appears logical given that habitat is the main determinant in species conservation. For specific habitats or ecosystems, CV provides the only approach theoretically capable of estimating the amount of compensation society should be willing to pay to farmers for protecting these areas. One study of relevance here is an analysis of three UK Sites of Special Scientific Interest conducted by Willis (1990). This recorded an annual WTP of approximately £1.00 per person (1986 prices) although the considerable variance of WTP responses meant that this implied a per-hectare value ranging from £440 to £2,290 per annum.

In conclusion, CV may well provide the only feasible means of implementing the new CAP at the local level. This is especially true where the existence value of environmental goods such as landscape and biodiversity are important. Nevertheless, even if we side-step concerns regarding refinement of the method itself, there is a clear need for a much greater and more systematic use of CV if we are to amass the databank needed to assess the public's WTP and farmers' WTA for provision of a wider range of environmental goods.

17.5. CONCLUSION

Concern regarding environmental issues has increased dramatically since the creation of the EU in 1957. There was no environmental provision in the original treaty signed in Rome and it was only with the Single European Act in 1986 that separate environmental legislation was introduced. The role of environmental considerations within policy-making was only recently strengthened with the full ratification of the Treaty of European Union on 1 January 1994.

Such environmental legislation results from a process originated in the First Environmental Action Programme in 1973. A consistent set of basic principles emerged through the ensuing five Environmental Programmes. Future developments are likely to be led by four further principles, namely: the polluter-pays principle; the precaution principle; the subsidiarity principle; and sustainable development. Such ideas reflect an ongoing shift in approach towards the integration of environmental concerns within wider sectoral policies.

Cost-effectiveness pressures upon the Commission mean that environmental goals will have to be achieved with the lowest possible costs for the economy. Currently environmental policy-making is still dominated by lawyers, engineers, and natural scientists rather than environmental economists. However, a major stated aim of the Treaty of European Union is to improve the economic efficiency of EU legislation and consequently the role of environmental economists is expected to increase in the near future, with an expanding demand for environmental valuation at policy, regulation, and project level.

To date there has been a noticeable absence of guidance regarding the use of valuation techniques within EU decision-making. However, it may be that the very shortcomings of the current EIA Directive will cause a swing towards CBA (and thereby monetary) appraisal of decisions. The forthcoming establishment of the EEA may well enhance such a process, resulting in a considerable expansion of what has, to date in the EU, been a minor approach to the appraisal of decisions at the policy, regulation, and project level.

REFERENCES

Adams, J. (1992), 'Horse and Rabbit Stew in Valuing the Environment', in A. Coker and C. Richards (eds.), *Economic Approaches to Environmental Evaluation*, John Wiley, Chichester, pp. 65–76.

Barde, J. Ph., and Pearce, D. W. (eds.) (1991), *Valuing the Environment: Six Case Studies*, Earthscan, London.

Bateman, I. J. (1996), *A Comparison of Forest Recreation, Timber and Carbon Fixing Values with Agriculture in Wales: a GIS/CBA Approach*, Ph.D. thesis, Nottingham University.

——Willis, K. G., and Garrod, G. D. (1994), 'Consistency between Contingent Valuation Estimates: a Comparison of Two Studies of UK National Parks', *Regional Studies*, 28: 457–74.

Bonnieux, F., and Rainelli, P. (1992), 'Paiements directs et préservation de l'environnement: application au cas des zones humides de Basse-Normandie', Proceedings of the 30th EAAE Seminar, *Direct Payments in Agricultural and Regional Policies*, Château d'Oex, Switzerland, pp. 199–216.

——Desaigues, B., and Vermersch, D. (1992), 'France', in Navrud (1992), pp. 43–64.

Buchanan, J., and Tullock, G. (1975), 'Polluter's Profits and Political Response: Direct Controls versus Taxes', *American Economic Review*, 65: 139–47.

Burrell, A. (1992), 'The Role of Direct Income Support in Agricultural Policy Reform', Proceedings of the 30th EAAE Seminar, *Direct Payments in Agricultural and Regional Policies*, Château d'Oex, Switzerland, pp. 50–64.

Burtraw, D., and Portney, P. R. 'Environmental Policy in the United States', in D. Helm (ed.), *Economic Policy towards the Environment*, Blackwell, Oxford, pp. 289–326.

CCE (1992), *Eurobaromètre 37*, CCE, Brussels.

CEU (1992), *Towards Sustainability: a European Community Programme of Policy and Action in relation to the Environment and Sustainable Development*, ii, CEU, Brussels.

Crabtree, J. R. (1992) 'Effectiveness of Standard Payments for Environmental Protection and Enhancement', Proceedings of the 30th EAAE Seminar, *Direct Payments in Agricultural and Regional Policies*. Château d'Oex, Switzerland, pp. 144–56.

Dasgupta, A. K., and Pearce, W. D. (1972), *Cost–Benefit Analysis: Theory and Practice*, Macmillan, London.

DoE (Department of the Environment) (1992), *Project Appraisal and the Environment*, London, HMSO.

Drake, L. (1992), 'The Non-Market Value of the Swedish Agricultural Landscape', *European Review of Agricultural Economics*, 19: 351–64.

EU (1990), *Environmental Policy in the European Community*, 4th edn., DG Information, Communication, Culture, Publication Division, EU, Brussels.

Folmer, H. and Howe, C. W. (1991), 'Environmental Problems and Policy in the Single European Market', *Environmental and Resources Economics*, 1: 7–41.

Haigh, N. (1990), *EEU Environmental Policy and Britain*, 2nd rev. edn., Longman, London.

Hanemann, M. W. (1992), 'Preface', in Navrud (1992), pp. 9–35.

HM Treasury (1991), *Economic Appraisal in Central Government: a Technical Guide for Government Departments*, HMSO, London.

Hoevenagel, R. (1990), 'The Validity of the Contingent Valuation Method: Some Aspects on the Basis of Three Dutch Studies', Proceedings of the conference Environmental Cooperation and Policy in the Single European Market, Venice.

——Kuik, O., and Oosterhuis, F. (1992), 'The Netherlands', in Navrud (1992), pp. 100–7.

Hope, C., and Parker, J. (1990), *Environmental Information for All: the Need for a Monthly Index*, Management Studies, Research Paper no. 5/90, Cambridge University.

Johansson, P. O., and Kriström, B. (1992), 'Sweden', in Navrud (1992), pp. 136–49.

Jones-Lee, M. K., Hammerton, M., and Philips, P. R. (1985), 'The Value of Safety: Results of a National Sample Survey', *Economic Journal*, 95: 49–72.

Kapp, K. (1970), 'General Issues and Methodological Problems', *Social Science Information*, 4: 15–32.

Kuik, O. J., Oosterhuis, F. H., Jansen, H. M. A., Holm, K., and Ewers, H. J. (1992), *Assessment of Benefits of Environmental Measures*, Graham and Trotman, London.

Loomis, J., and Anderson, P. (1992), 'Idaho *v*. Southern Refrigerated', in K. H. Ward and J. W. Duffield (eds.), *Natural Resources Damages: Law and Economics*, John Wiley, Chichester, pp. 389–414.

Markandya, A., Pearce, D., and Turner. R. K. (1991), 'The United Kingdom', in Barde and Pearce (1991), pp. 203–35.

Merlo, M., and Della Puppa, F. (1993), *Forestry and Farming Public Benefits Valuation in Italy: a Review of Applications*, Dipartimento Territorio e sistemi Agro-Forestali, University of Padova.

Mors, M. (1994), 'Applying Environmental Economics in the European Union', paper presented at the Fifth Annual Meeting of the Association of Environmental and Resource Economists, Dublin.

Navrud, S. (1991), 'Norway', in Barde and Pearce (1991), pp. 141–202.

——(ed.) (1992), *Pricing the European Environment*, Scandinavian University Press, Oslo.

——and Strand, J. (1992), 'Norway', in Navrud (1992), pp. 108–35.

Panella, G. (1991), 'Italy', in Barde and Pearce (1991), pp. 64–105.

Pearce, D. (1992). *Economic Values and the Natural World*, CSERGE, London.

Riera, P. (1992), *The Improvement of Standard Cost–Benefit Analysis through its Combination with the Contingent Valuation Method: a Case Study*, Department of Applied Economics, Autonomous University of Barcelona.

Römer, A. U., and Pommerehne W. N. (1992), 'Germany and Switzerland', in Navrud (1992), pp. 65–83.

Roskill, E. W. R. (1971), *Commission on the Third London Airport*, HMSO, London.

Schulz, W., and Schulz, E. (1991), 'Germany', in Barde and Pearce (1991), pp. 9–63.

Somsen, H. (1993), 'Legal Basis of Environmental Law', *European Environmental Law Review*, 2: 124–9.

Turner, R. K., Bateman, I. J., and Pearce, D. W. (1992), 'United Kingdom', in Navrud (1992), pp. 150–76.

Whitby, M. (1989), 'Environmental Application of Article 19 of EU Directive 797/85 in the UK', in A. Dubgaard and A. Nielsen (eds.), *Economic Aspects of Environmental Regulation in Agriculture*, Wissenschaftsverlag Vauk, Kiel.

Willis, K. G. (1990), 'Valuing Non-Market Wildlife Commodities: an Evaluation and Comparison of Benefits and Costs', *Applied Economics*, 22: 13–30.

——and Garrod, G. (1991), *Landscape Values: a Contingent Valuation Approach and Case Study of the Yorkshire Dales National Park*, ESRC Countryside Change Initiative. Working Paper 21, University of Newcastle upon Tyne.

18

Contingent Valuation Methodology and the US Institutional Framework

JOHN B. LOOMIS

18.1. INTRODUCTION

Contingent valuation (CV) has been used officially and unofficially by Federal and State agencies in the United States for about two decades, although its use has accelerated since the early 1980s. This chapter traces the accelerating and broadening use of CV in the United States during the last two decades. In addition, it comments on some recent developments in what has become a controversial application of CV to valuing existence values in natural resource damage assessments.

18.2. FEDERAL GOVERNMENT USE OF CV

18.2.1. CV's Initial Emergence as a Recreation Valuation Technique

From its birth in 1963 in Robert Davis's dissertation at Harvard University (and its subsequent publication in Davis, 1963) to its return in the early 1970s (Brown and Hammack, 1972; Randall et al., 1974) CV was seen originally as a technique to value recreational use of natural resources. In one sense, CV has found relatively rapid endorsement as an acceptable technique in the Federal Government. This may be partly attributable to the thorough and influential report by Dwyer et al. in 1977, recommending the Federal Government use CV in cost–benefit analysis of Federal water projects. In part this rapid adoption was also due to the strategic position that Robert Davis occupied in the Office of Policy Analysis in the Department of Interior. He and other economists at the Department of Interior were able to incorporate Randall's draft of acceptable CV procedures into the 1979 US Water Resources Council cost–benefit regulations for water-

I would like to thank Michael Hay, US Fish and Wildlife Service, for his information on the use of CV by the US Fish and Wildlife Service, and Richard Walsh for additional examples of the use of CV in the US Forest Service. Robert K. Davis provided valuable insights on the early adoption of CV by the United States Government. Finally, Ian Bateman's and Ken Willis's comments helped to improve the organization and focus of this chapter. As always, what follows is the sole responsibility of the author.

related Federal agencies such as the US Army Corps of Engineers and the US Bureau of Reclamation. These regulations recommended CV (along with the travel-cost method) as the preferred technique for quantifying recreation benefits (Davis, letter to the author, 1992). With moral support from the US Department of Interior (again due to Robert Davis's position), joint Department of Interior and US Army Corps of Engineers training sessions were held throughout the early 1980s to train agency economists in techniques such as travel-cost and contingent valuation methods.

The US Army Corps of Engineers (COE) was one of the first agencies to begin to apply CV. The COE used a two-prong strategy: (1) issuing a handbook for performing CV studies to field offices as part of its cost–benefit manual series (Moser and Dunning, 1986); (2) implementing a series of applications of CV to different types of COE projects. The first of these was for valuing the construction of small boat marinas after the US Office of Management and Budget had disallowed its old approach as not being consistent with the definition of benefits as willingness to pay (Hodgson, 1986). In 1986 the Houston District of the COE conducted a CV survey to estimate the value of urban recreation as part of a flood control planning study (Hansen *et al.*, 1990). A Sacramento District COE study (Mannesto, unpub. diss., 1989) applied CV to value water-based recreation at the Sacramento Delta for the agency's cost–benefit analysis.

The US Bureau of Reclamation, while slower in starting to use CV, has used CV on two of its more politically important resource conflicts: the Glen Canyon Hydropower–Grand Canyon National Park study and the San Joaquin Valley Agricultural Drainage programme. The Glen Canyon study merits significant discussion as this was the Bureau's first major and perhaps most influential CV study. The focus of the study was on how recreational fishing and white-water boating in Glen Canyon National Recreation Area and Grand Canyon National Park were affected by upstream hydropower releases. Historically, the hydropower releases had emphasized peaking power production, with concomitant rapid and severe downstream river fluctuations. The Bureau hired a team of economists and sociologists to perform the study, since in-house expertise was inadequate. The carefully crafted CV study by Richard Bishop and colleagues (see Boyle *et al.*, 1987) showed a statistically significant relationship between fishing and rafting benefits and flow. Optimum steady releases during the summer recreation season resulted in a gain of several million dollars of recreation benefits over the current peaking power operation. In conjunction with the environmental studies on beach erosion and effects on fish and wildlife, the Bureau has instituted more constant baseflows during the main recreation season while it prepares an Environmental Impact Statement on permanently changing the flows away from an emphasis on peaking power. While both the biology and the economics have played a role, given the influence of the Western Area Power Authority, who market the power, having dollar values acceptable to such groups as the Bureau and the National Park Service is an important defence of more optimum flows.

18.2.2.   US Forest Service Use of Contingent Valuation

The US Forest Service Rocky Mountain Forest and Range Experiment Station has performed or funded several CV studies since the early 1980s. One large effort involved CV and travel-cost method (TCM) valuation of fishing and hunting in Idaho (Donnelly *et al.*, 1985; Sorg *et al.*, 1985; Sorg and Nelson, 1986). More recent studies related to the value of instream flow in Montana (Duffield and Butkay, 1989).

In terms of direct policy use, the Forest Service has relied upon dollar values generated by CV (and the TCM) to arrive at their unit day values (called Resource Planning Act or RPA values) for recreation in National Forests. These values are used to calculate the benefits of alternative five-year strategic plans for the entire National Forest System as well as when performing cost–benefit analysis of individual Forest Plans. For both the 1985 and 1990 Resource Planning Act Program, the Forest Service's initial values for fishing, hunting, forest recreation, and wilderness were derived from a mix of CV and TCM studies (Loomis and Sorg, 1982; USFS, 1984: F-10; Walsh *et al.*, 1988; USFS, 1990: B16–24).

Agencies such as the Forest Service also apply CV-derived values available from the literature in their Environmental Impact Statements (EIS). For example, the Forest Service in Colorado included CV-derived values of recreation-use, option, existence, and bequest values derived by Walsh *et al.* (1981) in the Oh-Be-Joyful Wilderness Study Draft EIS (USFS, 1981: E7). Field offices of the US Forest Service have also commissioned and used CV studies to improve the management of a wide range of National Forest resources. For example, the Forest Service funded Walsh and Olienyk (1981) to perform a CV study on the benefits of controlling pine beetles in National Forests in Colorado. The Forest Service funded and used a study by Walsh and Gilliam (1982) to reduce the number of visitors to Indian Peaks Wilderness Area closer to a CV-defined social carrying capacity (Walsh, letter to the author, 1992).

18.2.3.   Use by Other Federal Agencies

The US Fish and Wildlife Service uses CV as part of its National Survey of Fishing, Hunting and Wildlife Associated Recreation. In 1980, 1985, and 1990 CV questions have been asked to value fishing, hunting, and, in 1985, non-consumptive wildlife use. The agency has published and distributed its CV analysis of these data in a series of reports (Brown and Hay, 1987; Hay, 1988*a*, *b*).

The National Park Service (NPS) has commissioned or participated in several CV studies. CV has been used by the NPS for valuing the improvement of air quality related visibility at several National Parks (Rowe and Chestnut, 1983). One of the first NPS applications of CV was to the benefits of reducing congestion in Yosemite National Park (Walsh, 1980). More recently NPS commissioned a CV study on the economic benefits of the wolf reintroduction program in Yellowstone National Park (Duffield, 1991).

Bergstrom *et al.* (1990) performed a study on the recreation value of maintaining more water for recreation in Federal reservoirs managed by the Tennessee Valley Authority. They used the CV approach to value recreation with different reservoir levels. Bergstrom reported, at the annual Agricultural Experiment Station regional research meeting on non-market valuation in 1990, that his study results were one of the factors influencing the Tennessee Valley Authority to change the reservoir water management to hold more water for recreation as compared to hydropower.

18.2.4.   Administrative and Other Uses of CV

One of the earliest administrative law cases where CV values appeared to have a significant influence on the outcome is a hydroelectric proposal for the Kootenai Falls area in Montana. The CV-derived values, for willingness to accept compensation for the proposed hydroelectric dam, indicated that the benefits of preservation exceeded the benefits of the dam. To quote Duffield (1992: 314), the economist who performed the CV study measuring willingness-to-accept values and who presented them before the administrative law judge,

the judge's decision turned on the aesthetic and recreation values. This is an interesting case in that not only was contingent valuation the primary valuation method but, additionally, a compensation-demanded measure was apparently accepted as plausible. The utility appealed the judge's decision to the full Federal Energy Regulatory Commission (FERC), which upheld the rejection of the application. Our understanding is that this is one of only two or three cases where FERC has not approved an application for a major hydroelectric project.

18.2.5.   Recent Additional Uses of CV

Much of the increase in the use of CV has been tied to the increasing use of Cost–Benefit Analysis (CBA) by Federal agencies. One of the major expansions of the use of CBA and hence CV in the US was when the Reagan Administration issued Executive Order 12291 requiring a CBA on major regulations (see Smith, 1984).

With the passage of this law the US Environmental Protection Agency's effort, both inside and via funding outside, toward CV was given new urgency. Some of the most influential studies on water quality included Walsh *et al.* (1978), Mitchell and Carson (1981, 1984), and Desvousges *et al.* (1983). These studies were influential for a number of reasons. First and foremost was the inclusion of benefits to the general populace, who might not even use the resource in a recreational manner. These option (Weisbrod, 1964) and existence values (Krutilla, 1967) represented an important broadening of the beneficiaries. It also established that CV was capable of measuring these important values, something that other methodologies could not. These studies were also influential in terms of CV methodology. The development of the payment card approach and visual aids such as the water quality ladder represented significant advances in the application of CV.

But even beyond these demonstration studies was the need to apply CV to specific proposed environmental regulations. There were many environmental regulations related to water quality, air quality standards for scenic visibility, occupational health and safety, etc. in which CV was the valuation method of choice. For example, the Environmental Protection Agency contracted the Research Triangle Institute (Naughton and Desvousges, 1986; Desvousges *et al.*, 1992) to estimate the benefits of proposed EPA regulations for reducing pollutant loadings from pulp and paper mills on twelve rivers. Calculation of per-household water quality benefits were based on two CV studies and one TCM study (Desvousges *et al.*, 1992: 681).

EPA has also employed CV to quantify the value of health risks associated with water treatment by-products (THM) and Giardia (Mitchell and Carson, 1986). The THM study employed in-person interviews of households in the State of Illinois. A sample of households were asked their willingness to pay (WTP) to reduce the risk of cancer from THMs. The risk of cancer was portrayed using a ladder which displayed risks from smoking, different types of work, accidents, etc. This gave some perspective on the risk from THMs to individuals.

18.2.6. CV's Use in Valuing Environmental Externalities from Power Generation

When the Federal Government began investigating the economic benefits forgone from acid rain (formally called acid deposition), CV was one of the methodologies studied. As one of the conclusions of the review of the literature the authors recommended CV be used for valuing the effects of acid deposition 'precursors' on visibility (Callaway and Plummer, 1990).

Both the Environmental Protection Agency and the utility operating the Navajo Power Plant that was reducing air quality over Grand Canyon National Park used CV analyses to evaluate the efficiency of pollution control strategies at the plant.

According to Palmer and Krupnick (1991), 28 States in the US either require or are considering requiring public utilities operating in their States to include the environmental costs of alternative power sources in their utility planning process. It is very likely that CV will be used to measure some of these environmental costs.

Bonneville Power Administration (BPA) is a Federal agency which is responsible for the management of hydropower and other electrical resources in the Pacific Northwest. BPA is in the study design phase of a research project called 'The Environmental Costs of Electricity Production Using the Contingent Valuation Methodology' (BPA, 1992). The agency is having a consulting firm in Oregon propose the appropriate CVM format for

Contingent Valuation Method surveys of ratepayers in the Bonneville Power Administration service area. Evaluations will focus on the willingness to pay to avoid environmental externalities resulting from energy produced by electrical generation technologies.

In part, BPA's interest stems from requirements in the Northwest Power Planning and Conservation Act to consider the environmental costs in its economic analyses of power supply decisions. BPA proposes to use the CV-derived values to adjust prices/costs of different power supplies to better reflect the full cost of the power supply options.

18.3. INDIVIDUAL STATES' USE OF CVM

Much like the management of resident fish and wildlife, the allocation of water rights is a power vested with the respective States rather than the Federal Government in the United States. One contentious water allocation issue that has pitted environmentalists against municipal water diversions in Los Angeles relates to Mono Lake in the eastern Sierra Nevada mountains near Yosemite National Park. The City of Los Angeles's diversion of streams that would normally flow into Mono Lake resulted in the lake dropping about forty feet over the last forty years. This had serious adverse consequences on the birds using Mono Lake. After several lower court rulings, the California Supreme Court ruled that the State must balance its authority to grant water rights with its responsibility under the Public Trust Doctrine to protect the environment of Mono Lake.

To provide information on what was a reasonable balance between Los Angeles's purchase of more expensive replacement water and the value of the Mono Lake environment, a CV study of the total economic value (recreation-use, option, existence, and bequest values) of preserving Mono Lake (Loomis, 1987) was performed. This relatively small-scale study demonstrated the utility of CV for quantifying the public-trust values of the lake, and that the benefits of preservation appeared greatly to outweigh the costs. This study was partly responsible for the State of California Water Resources Control Board requiring the CV technique be used by Los Angeles's consultant to develop information on recreation use and existence values in the Environmental Impact Report being prepared on the revision of City of Los Angeles water rights from Mono Lake. The resulting values were included in the Environmental Impact Report and were part of the information used to decide how much to reduce the City of Los Angeles's water rights to protect Mono Lake. Several hundred thousand dollars is being spent on the CV studies in this case.

One of the interim measures to protect Mono Lake that has been initiated by the State of California, while the Environmental Impact Report is being prepared, is a Mono Lake water trust fund. The State has allocated $60 million to allow the City of Los Angeles to buy replacement water from California farmers to replace water they were previously obtaining from Mono Lake. Now the establishment of this trust fund occurred after the Mono Lake CV survey results were published. The Mono Lake CV had a trust-fund and a water-bill payment vehicle, where the money would be used to buy replacement water. The conclusion from the report was that it was economically efficient to buy replacement water for the City of Los Angeles (Loomis, 1987). Now one cannot claim the survey results were the primary reason that the State of California allocated $60 million to a trust fund to buy replacement water, but such an action is certainly consistent with the results and recommendations of the study.

The expansion in use of CBA and hence CV has not been limited to Federal agencies. Several State fish and game agencies have hired or contracted with economists to evaluate natural resource issues. Several of these economists have employed CV as one of their valuation techniques. States like Montana have been at the forefront in the use of TCM and CV. In 1985 the State appropriated nearly $300,000 for a series of hunting and fishing economic studies in which CV played a prominent role (Duffield and Allen, 1988; Loomis et al., 1988). The economist hired by Montana Fish, Wildlife and Parks frequently applies CV to value fish-and wildlife-related recreation (Brooks, 1990, 1991). The State of Montana also requires an economic analysis of habitat acquisitions. In one such economic analysis of the acquisition of private ranch land for elk winter range outside Yellowstone National Park, Duffield (1989) used dichotomous-choice CV. His survey asked visitors if they would contribute to a trust fund for purchase of elk winter range to maintain elk populations. The results of this study, along with estimates of local economic impacts from elk hunting, indicated that the acquisition would result in net social benefits to Montana. Montana went ahead and purchased the property.

The State of Rhode Island is using a 'paired comparison' approach to CV (formulated by Swallow et al., 1992) as part of their siting process for a landfill

(ibid. 291). The Metropolitan Water District of Southern California has
employed CV to value water supply reliability (Carson and Mitchell, 1987).

18.4. THE ATTAINMENT OF REBUTTABLE PRESUMPTION OF CV IN NATURAL RESOURCE DAMAGE ASSESSMENT

When the US Congress passed the Comprehensive Environmental
Response, Compensation and Liability Act of 1980 (CERCLA) there were
provisions for compensation of public resource values both temporarily and
permanently lost as a result of toxic waste sites and hazardous material
spills. The Federal and State Governments are viewed as 'Trustees' that
manage the publicly owned wildlife and fisheries on behalf of the citizens.
In the United States most fish and wildlife that do not migrate across
international boundaries are the property of the State in which they reside.
As such, States often restrict themselves to measuring damages to the
citizens of their State. However, this cannot often be strictly adhered to in
practice as recreationists often visit from other States to hunt and fish. The
benefits that these non-resident users receive are (rightly) counted when a
State performs a damage assessment. In addition, if Federal lands are
involved, Federal interests dictate that losses to all United States users be
counted, regardless of the State of origin. To the extent there are international visitors to these areas, they would no doubt be included in the damage
assessment as well. The monies received by the State and Federal Governments from the polluter must be used for either restoration of the damaged
habitat or acquisition/protection of similar habitats. The damages are
defined as response and restoration costs plus any (either permanent or
temporary) lost use and non-use values. A variety of measurement methods
are given 'rebuttable presumption' in the regulations, including TCM and
CV. What rebuttable presumption means is that the Federal Government
finds these methods are reliable and the best available techniques for quantifying natural resource damages. As such, damage estimates derived from
application of these methods are given the presumption of acceptability
before the court. If the industry feels these damage estimates are too large,
they may only attack the particular application of the method in the case at
hand, not the method in general.

The regulations also required two types of approaches for calculating the
lost benefits (DOI, 1986). The first was called Level A, which was a compu-
terized model reflecting average unit losses from a spill. The economic values
that went into the Level-A computer model (EA, 1986) relied on CV studies
to value recreation use of beaches. The regulations also allowed for the
calculation of existence-value-type benefits, but only when there were no
on-site use values. Of course, this directly implied the use of CV, as CV is the
only way in which existence values can be measured.

18.4.1. US Court of Appeals Supports Use of CVM

The issuance of the regulations brought appeals by many parties. Industry groups challenged the use of CV to establish damage assessments. They claimed CV resulted in merely speculative values. The District Court of Appeals ruled that the Department of Interior (DOI) had carefully considered the strengths and weaknesses of CV and even eliminated the use of CV to measure willingness-to-accept values. The US Court of Appeals 'find DOI's promulgation of Contingent Valuation methodology reasonable and consistent with congressional intent, and therefore worthy of deference' (US Court of Appeals, 1989). The court went on to dismiss industry's challenge to rebuttable presumption for CV and the use of CV for measuring option and existence values. In 1991 DOI issued proposed regulations that retained CV as a technique still having rebuttable presumption and one that can be used to measure existence values (DOI, 1991).

While the legal details of the CERCLA regulations were being debated, several actual damage assessments were being performed. One of the earliest and most scrutinized cases involved the release of hazardous substances from the Eagle Mine in Colorado. In performing its damage assessment the State of Colorado performed two CV surveys. One survey was of Eagle County residents near the mine, the other a survey of 6,000 Colorado households. The results of these analyses are discussed in Kopp and Smith (1989).

In the case of an oil spill soiling coasts in both the State of Washington and Vancouver Island in British Columbia (Canada), Rowe *et al.* (1992) used CV to quantify total economic values. Rowe *et al.* performed a series of CV studies to arrive at a range of estimates of WTP to avoid oil spills similar to the spill that actually occurred. The CV values were developed for both the United States and the British Columbia Ministry of the Environment.

In an oil spill in the Martinez Straits, located between San Francisco Bay and the Sacramento Delta, a CV survey was proposed by the State of California's economist and agreed to by Shell Oil's economists, and was led by William Desvousges and Richard Dunford of Research Triangle Institute (Hanemann, 1992: 568–70). However, a timely out-of-court settlement of the damages amounting to $11.5 million dollars (for 432,000 gallons of crude oil) alleviated the need for the study. As part of the settlement with Shell Oil Company, the State of California allocated $645,000 of its settlement money to developing a CV survey and benefit estimates of protecting coastal beaches in California (ibid. 570). It is quite clear that the California Office of Attorney General and the California Department of Fish and Game strongly support the use of CV when developing their natural resource damage assessments. This CV survey will be aimed at estimating both use and existence benefits associated with protecting recreational beaches and coastal wetlands.

18.4.2.   The Exxon Valdez Oil Spill and the Use of CV

The use of CV received much notoriety when both the State of Alaska's natural resource damage economists and the Federal Government's natural resource damage economists used CV for valuing the loss in total economic value stemming from the large oil spill in Prince William Sound in Alaska. In many respects, the largest single part of either the State or the Federal Government's damage assessment would have likely been the existence value. Reports in newspapers put the CV estimates of the existence value damages at between $3 billion and $15 billion. No doubt reports of these estimates provided added incentive for Exxon to settle out of court for about $1 billion.

18.5.   THE FUTURE OF CV

While industry had been thwarted by the Federal Appeals Court in their attempt to rule out use of CV in general and especially for measuring non-use values, they tried a new route in the spring of 1992. Exxon-funded CV studies conducted as background research for the Prince William Sound oil spill damage assessment were presented in Washington, DC (CE, 1992). None of these studies were specific to the Exxon oil spill, but rather most of them attempted to investigate the sensitivity of WTP estimates for existence value to various design features. Others attempted to obtain greater understanding as to what respondents were thinking of when answering WTP questions. While most of these studies simply demonstrated that poorly designed CV studies would yield unreliable results, they and the economists that prepared them were successful in pressuring the National Oceanic and Atmospheric Administration (NOAA) to reconsider the use of CV for measuring the existence values of natural resources under the Oil Pollution Act. NOAA appointed a Blue-Ribbon Panel, co-chaired by two Nobel Prize economists, Kenneth Arrow and Robert Solow. This panel received dozens of opinions and studies on why CV should or should not be used for measuring lost non-use values associated with oil spills.

In January 1993 the Panel concluded that carefully designed and implemented CV studies convey useful information for judicial and administrative decisions involving non-use or existence values. They further determined that such information is as reliable as marketing analyses of new products and damage assessments normally allowed in court proceedings. The Panel presented several guide-lines on the design of CV studies for valuing non-use damages to natural resources. For example, to make CV as reliable as possible the referendum approach should be used rather than open-ended WTP questions, and in-person (or telephone) interviews should be used rather than mail surveys. (See (Arrow *et al.*, 1993) for more details.)

With this acceptance of CV for measuring non-use values and the suggested procedures, we will no doubt see the continuation of CV applications to natural resources with both use and non-use/existence values. The procedures of Arrow *et al.* raise the standards to which CV studies undertaken for policy and damage assessment must meet. As such, fewer but more carefully designed and conducted studies may be performed. At the same time, the suggestions of Arrow *et al.* provide many testable hypotheses and require much refinement before routine implementation. In this sense the research agenda for CV has now been spelled out in more detail than at perhaps any other time. Due to the higher cost of attaining the standards, the rate of progress will depend very heavily on whether agencies upgrade their funding to match the standards required by Arrow *et al.*

REFERENCES

Arrow, K., Solow, R., Portney, P., Leamer, E., Radner, R., and Schuman, H. (1993), *Report of the NOAA Panel on Contingent Valuation*, National Oceanic and Atmospheric Administration, Washington.

Bergstrom, J., Cordell, K., and Klinko, D., (1990), 'Recreational Benefits of Reservoir Water Level Management', pp. 1–24 in J. Hoehn (ed.), *Benefits and Costs in Natural Resources Planning*, Third Interim Report, Department of Agricultural Economics, Michigan State University, East Lansing, Mich.

Bonneville Power Administration (BPA) (1992). *Statement of Work: Contingent Valuation Methodology Study*, Portland, Ore., 8 May.

Boyle, K., Welsh, M., Bishop, R., and Baumgartner, R. (1987), 'Analyzing the Effects of Glen Canyon Dam Releases on Colorado River Recreation Using Scenarios of Unexperienced Flow Conditions', pp. 111–30 in J. Loomis (comp.), *Benefits and Costs in Natural Resources Planning*, Interim Report no. 1, Division of Environmental Studies, University of California, Davis, Calif.

Brooks, R. (1990), *A Contingent Valuation of Lake and Reservoir Fishing*, Montana Department of Fish, Wildlife and Parks, Bozeman, Mont.

——(1991), *Warm Water Fishing in Montana: A Contingent Valuation Assessment of Angler Attitudes and Economic Benefits of Selected Waters Statewide*, Montana Department of Fish, Wildlife and Parks, Bozeman, Mont.

Brown, G., and Hammack, J. (1972), 'A Preliminary Investigation of Migratory Waterfowl', pp. 171–204 in J. Krutilla (ed.), *Natural Environments: Studies in Theoretical and Applied Analysis*, Resources for the Future, Washington.

——and Hay, M. (1987), 'Net Economic Values for Deer and Waterfowl Hunting and Trout Fishing: 1980', Working Paper 23, Division of Policy and Directives Management, US Fish and Wildlife Service. Washington.

Callaway, J., and Plummer, M. (1990), 'Summary and Conclusions', pp. 197–20 in G. Brown and J. Callaway (eds.), *Methods for Valuing Acidic Deposition and Air Pollution Effects*, NAPAP Report 27, National Acid Precipitation Assessment Program. Washington.

Cambridge Economics, Inc. (CE) (1992). *Contingent Valuation: A Critical Assessment*, Cambridge. Economics Inc., Cambridge, Mass.

Carson, R. T., and Mitchell, R. C. (1987), *Economic Value of Reliable Water Supplies for Residential Water Users in the State Water Project Service Area*, Report prepared for the Metropolitan Water District of Southern California, Los Angeles.

Davis, R. K. (1963), 'Recreation Planning as an Economic Problem', *Natural Resources Journal*, 3: 239–49.

Desvousges, W., Smith, K., and McGivney, M. (1983), *A Comparison of Alternative Approaches for Estimating Recreation and Related Benefits of Water Quality Improvements*, EPA Report 230–05–83–001, US Environmental Protection Agency, Washington.

—— M., Naughton, and G. Parsons, (1992), 'Benefit Transfer: Conceptual Problems in Estimating Water Quality Benefits Using Existing Studies', *Water Resources Research*, 28: 675–83.

DOI (1986), 'Natural Resource Damage Assessments: Final Rule', *Federal Register*, 51: 27674–753, 1 August.

—— (1991), 'Natural Resource Damage Assessment: Notice of Proposed Rulemaking', *Federal Register*, 56: 19752–773, 29 April.

Donnelly, D., Loomis, J., Sorg, C., and Nelson, L. (1985), 'The Net Economic Value of Recreational Steelhead Fishing in Idaho', *Resource Bulletin RM-9*, Rocky Mountain Forest and Range Experiment Station, US Forest Service, Fort Collins, Colo.

Duffield, J. (1989), *Nelson Property Acquisition: Social and Economic Impact Assessment*, Report for Montana Department of Fish, Wildlife and Parks, Helena, Mont.

—— (1991), 'Existence and Nonconsumptive Values for Wildlife: Application to Wolf Recovery in Yellowstone National Park', pp. 2–39 in C. Kling (comp.), *Benefits and Costs in Natural Resources Planning*, 4th Interim Report, Department of Agricultural Economics, University of California, Davis, Calif.

—— (1992), 'Contingent Valuation: Issues and Applications', pp. 311–50 in K. Ward and J. Duffield (eds.), *Natural Resource Damages: Law and Economics*, John Wiley, New York.

—— and Butkay, S. (1989), *Economic Value of Recreation and Preservation Benefits of Instream Flow*, Report to the Rocky Mountain Station, US Forest Service, Fort Collins, Colo.

—— and Stewart, A. (1988). *Angler Preference Study: Final Economics Report*, Montana Department of Fish, Wildlife and Parks, Helena, Montana.

Dwyer, J., Kelly, J., and Bowes, M. (1977), *Improved Procedures for Valuation of the Contribution of Recreation to National Economic Development*, Water Resources Center Report, University of Illinois, Urbana.

Economic Analysis Inc. (EA) (1986), *Measuring Damages to Coastal and Marine Natural Resources: Concepts and Data Relevant for CERCLA Type A Damage Assessments*, Economic Analysis Inc., Wakefield, RI.

Hanemann, M. (1992), 'Natural Resource Damages for Oil Spills in California', pp. 555–80 in K. Ward and J. Duffield (eds.), *Natural Resource Damages: Law and Economics*, John Wiley, New York.

Hansen, W., Mills, A., Stoll, J., Freeman, R., and Hankamer, C. (1990), *A Case Study Application of the Contingent Valuation Method for Estimating Urban*

Recreation Use and Benefits, IWR Report no. 90-R-11, Institute for Water Resources, US Army Corps of Engineers, Fort Belvoir, Va.

Hay, M. (1988*a*), *Net Economic Recreation Values for Deer, Elk and Waterfowl Hunting and Bass Fishing: 1985*, Report 85-1, Division of Policy Directives and Management, US Fish and Wildlife Service, Washington.

——(1988*b*), *Net Economic Values of Nonconsumptive Wildlife Related Recreation*, Report 85-2, Division of Policy Directives and Management, US Fish and Wildlife Service, Washington.

Hodgson, R. (1986), *An Example of a Mailed Contingent Valuation Survey Method in a Marina Feasibility Study*, Instruction Report R-86-1, Waterways Experiment Station, US Army Corps of Engineers, Vicksburg, Miss.

Kopp, R., and Smith, V. K. (1989), 'Benefit Estimation Goes to Court: the Case of Natural Resource Damage Estimates', *Journal of Policy Analysis and Management*, 8: 593–612.

Krutilla, J. V. (1967), 'Conservation Reconsidered', *American Economic Review*, 57: 777–86.

Loomis, J. (1987), *An Economic Evaluation of Public Trust Resources of Mono Lake*, Institute of Ecology Report #30, Division of Environmental Studies, University of California, Davis, Calif.

—— and Sorg, C. (1982), *A Critical Summary of Empirical Estimates of the Values of Wildlife, Wilderness and General Recreation Related to National Forest Regions.* Rocky Mountain Forest and Range Experiment Station, US Forest Service, Fort Collins, Colo.

—— Cooper, J., and Stewart, A. (1988), *The Montana Elk Hunting Experience: a Contingent Valuation Assessment*, Montana Department of Fish, Wildlife and Parks, Bozeman, Mont.

Mannesto, G. (1989), *Comparative Evaluation of Respondent Behavior in Mail and In-Person Contingent Valuation Method Surveys*, Ph.D. dissertation, Graduate Group in Ecology, University of California, Davis, Calif.

Mitchell, R. C., and Carson, R. T. (1981), *An Experiment in Determining the Willingness-to-Pay for National Water Quality Improvements*, Report to the US Environmental Protection Agency, Washington.

—— and —— (1984), *A Contingent Valuation Estimate of National Freshwater Benefits.* Technical Report to the US Environmental Protection Agency, Washington.

—— and —— (1986), *Valuing Drinking Water Risk Reductions Using the Contingent Valuation Method: a Methodological Study of Risks from THM and Giardia*, Report to the US Environmental Protection Agency, Washington.

Moser, D., and Dunning, M. (1986), *National Economic Development Procedures Manual-Recreation*, ii, *A Guide for Using the Contingent Value Methodology in Recreation Studies*, IWR Report 86-R-5, Institute for Water Resources, US Army Corps of Engineers, Fort Belvoir, Va.

Naughton, M., and Desvousges, W. (1986), *Water Quality Benefits of Additional Pollution Control in the Pulp and Paper Industry*, Final Report to the US Environmental Protection Agency, Research Triangle Institute, Research Triangle Park, NC.

Pahmer, K., and Krupnick, A. (1991), 'Environment Costing and Electric Utilities' Planning and Investment', *Resources*, 105, Resources for the Future, Washington.

Randall, A., Ives, B., and Eastman, C. (1974), Bidding Games for Valuation of Aesthetic Environmental Improvements. *Journal of Environmental Economics and Management* 1, 132–149.

Rowe, R., and Chestnut, L. (1983), *Managing Air Quality and Scenic Resources at National Parks and Wilderness Areas*. Westview Press, Boulder, CO.

—— Shaw, D., and Schulze, W. (1992), 'Nestucca Oil Spill', pp. 527–44 in J. Ward and J. Duffield. (eds.), *Natural Resource Damages: Law and Economics*, John Wiley, New York.

Smith, V. K. (1984), *Environmental Policy Under Reagan's Executive Order: the Role of Benefit–Cost Analysis*, University of North Carolina Press, Chapel Hill, NC.

Sorg, C., and Nelson, L. (1986), *Net Economic Value of Elk Hunting in Idaho*, Resource Bulletin RM-12, Rocky Mountain Forest and Range Experiment Station, US Forest Service, Fort Collins, Colo.

—— Loomis, J., Donnelly, D., Peterson, G., and Nelson, L. (1985), *The Net Economic Value of Cold and Warm Water Fishing in Idaho*, Resource Bulletin RM-11, Rocky Mountain Forest and Range Experiment Station, US Forest Service, Fort Collins, Colo.

Swallow, S., Opaluch, J., and Weaver, T. (1992), 'Siting Noxious Facilities: an Approach that Integrates Technical, Economic and Political Considerations', *Land Economics*, 68: 283–301.

US Court of Appeals (for District of Columbia) (1989), *State of Ohio v. US Department of Interior, Case no. 86–1529*, 14 July.

US Forest Service (USFS) (1981), *Oh-Be-Joyful Wilderness Study Draft Environmental Impact Statement*, Region 2, Grand Mesa Uncompahgre and Gunnison National Forests, Delta, Colo.

—— (1984), *1985–2030 Resources Planning Act Program*, Draft Environmental Impact Statement, US Forest Service, Washington.

—— (1990), 'The Forest Service Program for Forest and Rangeland Resources: a Long Term Strategic Plan: Recommended 1990 RPA Program', US Forest Service, Washington.

US Water Resources Council (1979), 'Procedures for Evaluation of National Economic Development (NED) Benefits and Costs in Water Resources Planning. Final Rule. *Federal Register* 44(242): 72892–72976.

Walsh, R. (1980), *An Economic Evaluation of the General Management Plan for Yosemite National Park*, Water Resources Research Institute, Colorado State University, Fort Collins, Colo.

—— and Gilliam, L. (1982), 'Benefits of Wilderness Expansion with Excess Demand for Indian Peaks', *Western Journal of Agricultural Economics*, 7: 1–12.

—— and Olienyk, J. (1981), *Recreation Demand Effects of Mountain Pine Beetle Damage to the Quality of Forest Resources in the Colorado Front Range*, Colorado State University, Fort Collins, Colo.

—— Greenley, D., Young, R., McKean, J., and Prato, A. (1978), *Option Values, Preservation Values and Recreational Benefits of Improved Water Quality*, EPA Report 600/5-78-001. US Environmental Protection Agency, Office of Research and Development, Research Triangle Park, NC.

—— Johnson, D., and McKean, J. (1988), *Review of Outdoor Recreation Demand Studies with Nonmarket Benefit Estimates, 1968–1988*, Technical Report no. 54,

Colorado Water Resources Institute, Colorado State University, Fort Collins, Colo.

——Gillman, R., and Loomis, J. (1981), *Wilderness Resource Economics: Recreation Use and Preservation Values*, Colorado State University, Fort Collins, Colo.

Weisbrod, B.A. (1964), 'Collective-Consumption Services of Individual-Consumption Goods', *Quarterly Journal of Economics*, 78: 471–7.

INDEX OF AUTHORS

INDEX OF SUBJECTS